Asia Bible Commentary Series

# PSALMS 73–150

Asia Bible Commentary Series

# PSALMS 73–150

Federico G. Villanueva

General Editor
**Andrew B. Spurgeon**

Old Testament Consulting Editors
**Yohanna Katanacho, Joseph Shao, Havilah Dharamraj, Koowon Kim**

New Testament Consulting Editors
**Steve Chang, Brian Wintle**

© 2022 Federico G. Villanueva

Published 2022 by Langham Global Library
*An imprint of Langham Publishing*
www.langhampublishing.org

Langham Publishing and its imprints are a ministry of Langham Partnership

Langham Partnership
PO Box 296, Carlisle, Cumbria, CA3 9WZ, UK
www.langham.org

Published in partnership with Asia Theological Association
ATA
QCC PO Box 1454–1154, Manila, Philippines
www.ataasia.com

ISBNs:
978-1-83973-264-5 Print
978-1-83973-655-1 ePub
978-1-83973-656-8 Mobi
978-1-83973-657-5 PDF

Federico G. Villanueva has asserted his right under the Copyright, Designs and Patents Act, 1988 to be identified as the Author of this work.

All rights reserved. No part of this publication may be reproduced, stored in a retrieval system or transmitted, in any form or by any means, electronic, mechanical, photocopying, recording or otherwise, without the prior written permission of the publisher or the Copyright Licensing Agency.

Requests to reuse content from Langham Publishing are processed through PLSclear. Please visit www.plsclear.com to complete your request.

All Scripture quotations, unless otherwise indicated, are taken from the Holy Bible, New International Version®, NIV®. Copyright ©1973, 1978, 1984, 2011 by Biblica, Inc.™ Used by permission of Zondervan.

Scripture quotations marked ESV are from The Holy Bible, English Standard Version® (ESV®), copyright © 2001 by Crossway, a publishing ministry of Good News Publishers. Used by permission. All rights reserved.

Scripture quotations marked NRSV are from the New Revised Standard Version Bible, copyright © 1989 National Council of the Churches of Christ in the United States of America. Used by permission. All rights reserved.

Scripture quotations marked NEB are taken from the New English Bible, copyright © Cambridge University Press and Oxford University Press 1961, 1970. All rights reserved.

**British Library Cataloguing-in-Publication Data**
A catalogue record for this book is available from the British Library
ISBN: 978-1-83973-264-5

Cover & Book Design: projectluz.com

Langham Partnership actively supports theological dialogue and an author's right to publish but does not necessarily endorse the views and opinions set forth here or in works referenced within this publication, nor can we guarantee technical and grammatical correctness. Langham Partnership does not accept any responsibility or liability to persons or property as a consequence of the reading, use or interpretation of its published content.

To my father, the late Bishop Butch Villanueva,
who instilled in me early on a love for the Bible

# CONTENTS

## Commentary

*Author's Preface* ................................................................... ix
*Series Preface* ..................................................................... xi
*List of Abbreviations* ........................................................ xiii
Introduction ........................................................................... 1
Commentary on Psalms 73–150 ............................................ 8
Selected Bibliography ......................................................... 415

## Topics

The Challenge of Lament to Asian Christians ............................ 18
A Word for Lament in Filipino ................................................... 35
Remembrance of God's Faithfulness and *Utang na Loob*
   (Debt of Gratitude) ............................................................... 44
Psalm 109 and the Filipino Concept of *Pagsusumbong* ........... 198
God's Deliverance as *Kaginhawaan* (Well-being) .................... 249
Jose Rizal's Critique of Filipinos' Practice of Worship ............. 252
The Filipino Word for "Mercy" and Psalm 123 ......................... 288
Broadening Our *Sakop* (Scope of Our Reach) .......................... 307
Psalm 133 and the Concept of *Kapwa* (Fellow Human Beings) ............ 329
How Can We Praise a God Who Gives the Lands of Others to
   One Nation? ....................................................................... 338
God and gods in the Filipino Context ....................................... 342

# AUTHOR'S PREFACE

I finished writing the major portion of this commentary during the almost two-year pandemic due to the Coronavirus. Prior to this, my time at the Nagel Institute at Calvin University in Grand Rapids, Michigan provided the foundation for the writing and research that followed. I am grateful to the team at Nagel Institute, especially to Donna Romanowski, the program director, for hosting me from September to early December 2019 as a research scholar. The "Prophet's chamber" became a home for me during those months. Only two months after returning to my home country, the Philippines, the pandemic struck. In a way, the three months at Nagel prepared me for the isolation and lockdown that followed, though admittedly, no one can really prepare for that.

What made this season of lockdown bearable for me was the companionship and support of my wife, Rosemarie. While I was in Michigan, she transformed the small room downstairs into an office. I used to have only a table of my own, which I moved from room to room whenever the need arose. Now, I am finally able to settle down in one place. I cannot thank Rosemarie enough for all the love and sacrifices she has made so that I could finish writing this commentary on top of my other responsibilities, especially with Langham Partnership.

I thank Pieter Kwant and Luke Lewis for being supportive of my writing activities, particularly the writing of this commentary. I also thank the rest of the team at Langham Literature for their continuing commitment to give voice to majority world scholars. I also would like to thank Riad Kassis for his encouragement to continue my writing, even as I provided pastoral care to our current Langham scholars. My regular online prayer fellowship and calls with the current Langham Asian scholars have been an ongoing source of learning and encouragement, especially during the past two years.

I thank Dr. Theresa Lua, the General Secretary of the Asia Theological Association (ATA), along with the whole publications team of ATA, for their continuing partnership with Langham Literature in the Asia Bible Commentary Series. I thank Andrew Spurgeon for his leadership as general editor of the series during a most challenging time. During times like this, we need committed team members who will help maintain consistency. I thank Bubbles Lactaoen for her consistency and her excellent job in making sure the manuscript would meet the standard. I am also blessed to have an excellent English editor in Karen Hollenbeck Wuest. A special thanks to Dr.

Kelvin Friebel for taking the time to read the manuscript very carefully. I have benefited much from his comments and suggestions.

During the second year of the pandemic, my father was struck by critical COVID-19 and was taken away from us. The night he died, I was awakened from my sleep, sobbing. During that entire week, I would go to my office, stare at my books, and just weep. During my formative years, my dad's preaching became an inspiration to me. I would imitate his preaching from the previous Sunday by delivering his sermons to my classmates at elementary school. I would memorize one Bible verse per day and came to the point when, even before my dad could utter a verse, I already knew it.

I dedicate this commentary to the memory of my father, Bishop Federico H. Villanueva.

# SERIES PREFACE

What's unique about the Asia Bible Commentary Series? It is a commentary series written especially for Asian Christians, which incorporates and addresses Asian concerns, cultures, and practices. As Asian scholars – either by nationality, passion, or calling – the authors identify with the biblical text, understand it culturally, and apply its principles in Asian contexts to strengthen the churches in Asia. Missiologists tell us that Christianity has shifted from being a Western majority religion to a South, South-Eastern, and Eastern majority religion and that the church is growing at an unprecedented rate in these regions. This series meets the need for evangelical commentaries written specifically for an Asian audience.

This is not to say that Asian churches and Asian Christians don't want to partner with Western Christians and churches or that they spurn Western influences. A house divided cannot stand. The books in this series complement the existing Western commentaries by taking into consideration the cultural nuances familiar to the Eastern world so that the Eastern readership is not inundated with Western clichés and illustrations that they are unable to relate to and which may not be applicable to them.

The mission of this series is "to produce resources that are biblical, pastoral, contextual, missional, and prophetic for pastors, Christian leaders, cross-cultural workers, and students in Asia." While using approved exegetical principles, the writers strive to be culturally relevant, offer practical applications, and provide clear explanations of the texts so that readers can grow in understanding and maturity in Christ, and so that Christian leaders can guide their congregations into maturity. May we be found faithful to this endeavor and may God be glorified!

*Andrew B. Spurgeon*
*General Editor*

# LIST OF ABBREVIATIONS

## BOOKS OF THE BIBLE

### Old Testament
Gen, Exod, Lev, Num, Deut, Josh, Judg, Ruth, 1–2 Sam, 1–2 Kgs, 1–2 Chr, Ezra, Neh, Esth, Job, Ps/Pss, Prov, Eccl, Song, Isa, Jer, Lam, Ezek, Dan, Hos, Joel, Amos, Obad, Jonah, Mic, Nah, Hab, Zeph, Hag, Zech, Mal

### New Testament
Matt, Mark, Luke, John, Acts, Rom, 1–2 Cor, Gal, Eph, Phil, Col, 1–2 Thess, 1–2 Tim, Titus, Phlm, Heb, Jas, 1–2 Pet, 1–2–3 John, Jude, Rev

## BIBLE TEXTS AND VERSIONS

### Divisions of the canon
| | |
|---|---|
| NT | New Testament |
| OT | Old Testament |

### Ancient texts and versions
| | |
|---|---|
| LXX | Septuagint |
| MT | Masoretic Text |

### Modern versions
| | |
|---|---|
| ESV | English Standard Version |
| NASB | New American Standard Bible |
| NEB | New English Bible |
| NIV | New International Version |
| NRSV | New Revised Standard Version |
| RSV | Revised Standard Version |

### Journals, reference works, and series
| | |
|---|---|
| AB | Anchor Bible |
| ABC | Africa Bible Commentary |
| *ABD* | *Anchor Bible Dictionary* |

| | |
|---|---|
| BBR | *Bulletin for Biblical Research* |
| Bib | *Biblica* |
| CBQ | *Catholic Biblical Quarterly* |
| DCH | *Dictionary of Classical Hebrew* |
| HALOT | *The Hebrew and Aramaic Lexicon of the Old Testament* |
| HBT | *Horizons in Biblical Theology* |
| Int | *Interpretation* |
| JBL | *Journal of Biblical Literature* |
| JETS | *Journal of the Evangelical Theological Society* |
| JPS | The Jewish Publication Society Tanakh |
| JSOT | *Journal for the Study of the Old Testament* |
| JSOTSup | Journal for the Study of the Old Testament Supplement Series |
| JTS | The Journal of Theological Studies |
| NIB | The New Interpreter's Bible |
| NIDOTTE | *New International Dictionary of Old Testament Theology and Exegesis* |
| OTE | *Old Testament Essays* |
| RB | *Revue Biblique* |
| SJOT | *Scandinavian Journal of the Old Testament* |
| TDOT | *Theological Dictionary of the Old Testament* |
| TynBul | *Tyndale Bulletin* |
| VT | *Vetus Testamentum* |
| VTSup | *Vetus Testamentum* Supplements |
| ZAW | *Zeitschrift für die alttestamentliche Wissenschaft* |

# INTRODUCTION

*"The Holy Father regrets the fact that so many commentaries have applied themselves almost exclusively to matters belonging to 'the historical, philological and other auxiliary sciences.'"* – Thomas Merton[1]

This volume is a continuation of the commentary on Psalms 1–72 under the Asia Bible Commentary Series.[2] As indicated in the description of this series, this is a "pastoral and contextual commentary." Unlike most Western commentaries, which put the application at the end or after the exegesis, this commentary places the application at the beginning. Each chapter begins with a summary of the message of the psalm, along with discussions about the psalm's canonical context and genre. This is followed by a detailed commentary that integrates exegesis and application without separating application from meaning.[3] The two are held together, for as Gadamer argues, "all reading involves application, so that a person reading a text is himself part of the meaning he apprehends."[4]

## WHY EMPHASIZE THE APPLICATION?

The emphasis on application is necessary for two reasons. First, for most of its history, modern biblical interpretation of the Psalms has focused mainly on "what the text meant." Scholars have been preoccupied with the "first world" in what has come to be known as the "three worlds of the text." This first world is the "world *behind* the text," which concerns the meaning of the text within its ancient historical context. In the latter part of the twentieth century, a more adequate attention began to be given to the "second world" – or the "world *within* the text." The rise of canonical approaches to the Psalms as well as the focus on the poetry of the Psalms demonstrate this shift. But concern with the "third world" – "the world *in front of* the text – has been lagging behind. This "third world" represents the reader or the community of readers, and the effects, meaning, and relevance of the text to them. Without neglecting

---

1. Thomas Merton, *Bread in the Wilderness* (New York: New Directions, 1953), 34.
2. Federico G. Villanueva, *Psalms 1–72: A Pastoral and Contextual Commentary* (Carlisle, UK: Langham Global Library, 2016).
3. This is a reflection of an Asian way of reading, which is more holistic. See Federico G. Villanueva, "The Challenge of Asian Biblical Interpretation Today," *Journal of Asian Evangelical Theology* 18, no. 1 (2014): 12–14.
4. Hans-Georg Gadamer, *Truth and Method* (New York: Seabury Press, 1975), 340.

the other two worlds, the present commentary provides more attention to the "third world."

The "third world" of the text connects to the needs of the church.[5] This highlights the second reason for this commentary's emphasis on application. Because of the strong influence of secularism in the Western world, most commentaries on the Psalms were written as though God is unrelated to the writer of the commentary and to commentary readers. In some commentaries, God is referred to simply as "the deity." Kyung Lee comments that one of the reasons for the failure of Western Christianity is that it "could not provide any meaningful answers to people's spiritual searches."[6] She warns that a similar future awaits Asian Christianity "if we cannot breathe in new life and hope through our interpretation of the Bible."[7]

We are aware of the major shift in world Christianity from a dominant Western church to a more majority world church.[8] There are now more Christians outside the Western world than before, which has implications for how we do biblical interpretation.[9] Those in the majority world ought to be interpreting the Bible for their own Christian communities. However, most – if not all – commentaries on the Psalms were written by Western biblical scholars, who focus on the "first world" of the text. Moreover, the little application within these commentaries is directed to Western readers, which leaves those in the Asian church with almost nothing in the way of application.

This presents a particular problem among Asian Christians. For Chinese Christians, Yieh argues that "the relevance of scripture to the life of the reader is always treated with urgency."[10] This is true also in my own Filipino context, where 72 percent of our population believe that the Bible is the "actual word of God."[11] The Bible is quoted by ordinary citizens as well as by senators. Even the president quotes from the Bible, and his supporters use it to defend his

---

5. When I say, "church," I refer to communities who consider themselves followers of Jesus Christ. This includes not only Protestants but also Catholics and others who may not see themselves belonging to these two but count themselves Christians.
6. Kyung Sook Lee, "Wandering in the Wilderness: Asian Biblical Studies" (Society of Asian Biblical Studies Annual Conference, Seoul, South Korea, 2016).
7. Lee, "Wandering in the Wilderness: Asian Biblical Studies," 35.
8. Sebastian C. H. Kim and Kirsteen Kim, *Christianity as a World Religion* (London: Continuum, 2008), 223.
9. Villanueva, "The Challenge of Asian Biblical Interpretation Today," 5–6.
10. John Y. H. Yieh, "Chinese Biblical Interpretation: History and Issues," in *Ways of Being, Ways of Reading: Asian American Biblical Interpretation*, ed. Mary F. Foskett and Jeffrey K. Kuan (Saint Louis: Chalice, 2006), 30.
11. Ricardo G. Abad, "Religion in the Philippines," *Philippine Studies* 49, no. 3 (2001): 345.

# Introduction

"war on drugs."[12] As a Filipino biblical scholar, I see it as part of my calling to communicate the full message of the Psalms, which includes what it teaches us about how to respond to acts of injustice (see comments below to Psalms 82 and 97).

## READING THE PSALMS IN THE TIME OF THE PANDEMIC

The need for application is not confined to the church. As I write, the whole global community is struggling due to the coronavirus pandemic. We may describe what we are going through today as a "collective trauma." According to the *Comprehensive Textbook of Psychiatry*, "helplessness" and "loss of control" are common symptoms for psychological trauma.[13] Who has not felt helpless? Who has not felt out of control? Herman cites "being taken by surprise, trapped, or exposed to the point of exhaustion" as some of the "identifiable experiences related to trauma."[14] We were all "taken by surprise" in 2020. Many of us feel "trapped." Our life has been disrupted – and the disruption is not temporary, so it is taking a toll on us.

During this uncertain time, our world needs the book of Psalms, for it captures what we are going through together. The Psalter was put together after Israel's experience of exile. Although some of the individual psalms can be read within their earlier history or setting, the experience of the exile shaped the whole character of the book. Thus in this commentary, I will interpret the psalms from the perspective of the exile, which is one of the most traumatic events.[15]

Like the book of Lamentations, the Psalms may be read as a response to the people's experience. This explains why there are more laments than praise in the Psalter. The most significant contribution of the book of Psalms is its message about lament.

---

12. The Bible is used even by pastors and Christian leaders to defend the "War on drugs." See Jayeel Cornelio and Erron Medina, "Christianity and Duterte's War on Drugs in the Philippines," *Politics, Religion & Ideology* 20, no. 2 (2019): 151–169.
13. Quoted in Judith Herman, *Trauma and Recovery: The Aftermath of Violence – from Domestic Abuse to Political Terror* (New York: Basic Books, 1992), 33.
14. Herman, *Trauma and Recovery*, 34.
15. Samuel E. Balentine, "Legislating Divine Trauma," in *Bible Through the Lens of Trauma*, ed. Elizabeth Boase and Christopher G. Frechette, Semeia Studies (Atlanta: SBL Press, 2016), 163.

# Psalms 73–150

## A COMMUNITY OF LAMENT

Books I and II of the Psalter highlight the importance of the individual lament. Most of the individual laments are found in Books I and II. In the first volume,[16] I included discussions on lament (pp. 57–58), depression and the lament Psalms (pp. 88–89), and communal lament and the church today (pp. 232–233).

This commentary focuses on Books III, IV, and V which consists of the following psalms:

| | |
|---|---|
| Book III | Psalms 73–89 |
| Book IV | Psalms 90–106 |
| Book V | Psalms 107–150 |

In Book III, we notice a shift from individual lament to communal lament. Of the eleven communal laments in the whole Psalter, eight are found in the second half of the Psalter, with six in Book III and two in Book V:[17]

| | |
|---|---|
| Book III | Psalms 74, 79, 80, 83, 85, 89 |
| Book V | Psalms 126, 137 |

The opening two psalms in Book III mark the shift from individual to more communal lament. Book III opens with an individual lament (Psalm 73), followed by a communal lament (Psalm 74). A brief look at the transition from Book II to Book III highlights the importance of this shift. Book II ended with a psalm emphasizing the justice of God, a prayer that God will "endow the king with your justice" (72:1). The psalm begins with an inclusio of the key terms: "justice" and "righteousness" (vv. 1–2):

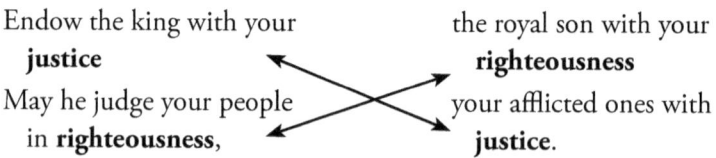

The hope is that the king "will deliver the needy who cry out, the afflicted who have no one to help" (v. 12). Psalm 72 ends with a vision that sees "all nations will be blessed through him [the king]" (v. 17). But when we turn

---

16. Villanueva, *Psalms 1–72*.
17. The rest are found in Books I (Psalms 12, 14) and II (Psalms 44, 60).

# Introduction

to Psalm 73, we hear the lament of one who sees things differently from the vision presented in Psalm 72: the wicked prosper (73:3) while those who are trying their best to live godly lives are afflicted (vv. 12–14).

The psalmist testifies that he has almost lost his faith. But one thing he does that helps him is to enter the sanctuary of God (73:17). Although we are not told what he does there, the close link between Psalms 73 and the following communal lament in Psalm 74 provides some clue. As the individual in Psalm 73 complains about the incongruity of the situation around him, so the community in Psalm 74 complains to God about the severity of their suffering. The implication is that the individual does not lament alone; he laments together with the community (see comments in Psalm 74 below for the connections between these two psalms).

If we are going to survive this pandemic or any tragic event we encounter, we will need a community of lament to accompany us through our continuing suffering. Shelly Rambo describes trauma as "a suffering that remains."[18]

## LINGERING LAMENT

The shape of Books III–V reflects this experience of continuing suffering. Book III ends with the tragic lament over the failure of God's covenant with David. Scholars consider Book IV as the "center" of the Psalter because here we find the "answer" to the problem posed at the end of Book III. According to Wilson, "Pss. 90–106 function as the editorial 'center' of the 'answer' to the problem posed in Ps. 89 as to the apparent failure of the Davidic covenant with which Books One-Three are primarily concerned."[19] Ortlund writes: "The fourth book of the Psalter . . . wastes no time in answering this tragedy."[20] But if Book IV is the "answer" to the "problem," then the answer is a feeble one that is lacking finality. For the very first psalm in Book IV (Psalm 90) remains very much a lament. The community feels exhausted and complain that they have only experienced suffering (or in Filipino: *panay na lang hirap*). There are certainly fewer laments and more psalms of confidence and hymns in Book IV,

---

18. Shelly Rambo and Stephanie N. Arel, eds., *Post-Traumatic Public Theology* (Germany: Springer International Publishing, 2016), 3.
19. Gerald Henry Wilson, *The Editing of the Hebrew Psalter* (Chico: Scholars Press, 1985), 215. Compare Raymond C. Van Leeuwen simply takes for granted that Book IV is the "theological heart of the Psalter." Van Leeuwen, "Why Do the Trees of the Forest Sing a New Song? (Psalms 96 and 98)," *The Covenant Quarterly* 62, no. 3 (2004): 28.
20. Eric Ortlund, "An Intertextual Reading of the Theophany of Psalm 97," *SJOT* 20, no. 2 (2006): 89.

but lament lingers. In Psalm 94:3, the characteristic cry of the lament – "how long?" – is heard two times. In Psalm 102, we hear an afflicted person pour out a lament (see superscription).

Lament lingers till the end of the Psalter. In Book V, we find two communal laments – Psalms 126 and 137. In the former, the people continue to pray, "restore our fortunes" (126:4), even after they have already declared and rejoiced over their restoration (vv. 1–3). This psalm is similar to the communal lament in Psalm 85 (Book III).

The canonical arrangement of Psalm 137 is the opposite of Psalm 8. Zenger considers Psalm 8 the "theological center of the composition of Psalms 3–14."[21] Whereas Psalm 8 is surrounded by laments, Psalm 137 is surrounded by praise. It is preceded by two hymns (135–136) and followed by an individual declaration of Thanksgiving (138). The refrain, "His love endures forever," is repeated twenty-six times in Psalm 136. In between the praises and thanksgiving, a lament which insists, "How can we sing the songs of the LORD while in a foreign land?" (137:4), survives the waves of praise. Firth describes this placement in a particularly striking way: "under the sparkling river of praise is a dark undercurrent of pain, which surfaces in Psalm 137."[22]

The continuing presence of individual laments towards the very end of the Psalter (Psalms 140–143) reflects the continuing nature of suffering. Herman's insights about trauma apply here: "Resolution of the trauma is never final; recovery is never complete . . . Issues that were sufficiently resolved at one stage of recovery may be reawakened as the survivor reaches new milestones in her development."[23] Restoration and healing are not one-time events, but long processes. Thus, we need persistence and faith.

## PERSISTENCE IN FAITH

One of the reasons why the Israelites in the OT were able to cope with their many tragic experiences was because they knew how to lament. And in their laments, they did not shrink from expressing their views to God. They reason with him, argue against him, and yet they never give up on God. Lament is not a sign of weak faith, but on the contrary, is a sign of bold faith. The

---

21. Erich Zenger, "Was wird anders bei kanonischer Psalmenauslegung," in *Gott, Eine Offenbarung* (Würzburg: Echter, 1991), 405 (translation mine).
22. Gillian C. Firth, "The Re-Presentation of David in Psalms 140–143" (Ph.D. thesis, Melbourne, Ridley College, 2016), 2.
23. Herman, *Trauma and Recovery*, 211.

# Introduction

reason we don't lament is because we are weak. As one of the characters in the novel *Noli Me Tangere*, written by the Filipino national hero Jose Rizal says, "*Hindi dumaraing ang bayan sapagkat walang tinig. Hindi kumikilos sapagkat nanghihina.*" (The people do not lament because they don't have a voice. They do not act because they feel weak.)[24]

A community persists in God because they have already encountered God. Lament is founded on praise, for in the latter, the people express their experience of God. They cry out for justice because they believe that God is a God of justice (see Pss 94:3; 97:2). Based on their own experience, they have come to know God as one who hears the cry of the oppressed, the hungry, the prisoner. Book V opens with a portrayal of some of the most difficult experiences of the people: how in their distress, they cried out to God, and how God responded to them, hearing their cry and delivering them (Psalm 107). What attracts the people most about God is the fact that even though he is High and lifted up, he stoops down to reach those who are bowed down. He "raises the poor from the dust and lifts the needy from the ash heap" (113:7). The final Hallelujahs (Psalms 146–150) praise the Lord because he is a God who "upholds the cause of the oppressed and gives food to the hungry," a God who "watches over the foreigner and sustains the fatherless and the widow" (Ps 146:7, 9).

As you read through this commentary, may you encounter the God who is spoken to and spoken of in the Psalter. May you feel the presence of the "community of lament" in its pages, encouraging you as you struggle through your journey. Isn't the "community of lament" also part of the "cloud of witnesses" mentioned by the author of Hebrews? Finally, may you persist in your faith, knowing you are not alone.

---

24. José Rizal, *Noli Me Tangere*, trans. Virgilio S. Almario (Quezon City: Adarna House, 1999), 162–163.

# PSALM 73

Mowinckel is on the right track when he comments that the psalmist feels "resentment"[1] in Psalm 73, yet he does not specify to whom this feeling is directed. Also, "resentment" seems to be a step further than what the psalmist is feeling. His feet have "almost slipped" (v. 2), but he has not given up. Perhaps it's not resentment that he feels, but what we call *tampo* in Filipino.

*Tampo* is a feeling of hurt that comes from a failure on the part of a loved one to fulfill what is expected. *Tampo* can be understood only within the context of intimate relationships. One does not feel *tampo* with someone who is not a close friend, loved one, or relative.[2] In Psalm 73, the psalmist feels *tampo* with God as he sees the prosperity of the wicked in contrast to his own suffering. The fact that he is struggling with *tampo* indicates that he is close to God, but he has to sort out his feelings of hurt. *Tampo*, if it is not dealt with, can lead to resentment, which can turn into bitterness and hatred.[3] Some have completely drifted away from God for failing to deal with their feelings of hurt with God.

Psalm 73 models a way of dealing with feelings of hurt with God. First, it affirms the experience of *tampo*, teaching that it is alright to have hurt feelings with God. Understood from the concept of *tampo*, having feelings of hurt with God is an indication of intimacy. Only those who are close to God can be hurt deeply. At the same time, *tampo* provides an opportunity for further intimacy. But for this to occur, the feelings of hurt have to be confronted. This is what the psalmist does in Psalm 73. Interestingly, he does not immediately

---

1. Sigmund Mowinckel, *The Psalms in Israel's Worship*, trans. Dafydd Rhys Ap-Thomas, vol. 2 (Grand Rapids: Eerdmans, 2004), 36.
2. Melba Padilla Maggay, *Pahiwatig: Kagawiang Pangkomunikasyon ng Filipino* (Quezon City: Ateneo de Manila University Press, 2002), 138. For further discussion, see "Lament as *Pagtatampo sa Diyos*" in Federico G. Villanueva, *Psalms 1–72*, 137–138.
3. Filipino psychologists Enriquez and Alfonso explain that when *tampo* is ignored, it turns to bitterness and then to anger. "*Tampo* is different from anger because the one who has *tampo* does not mean he/she is already angry. But *tampo*, when it is not given attention or appropriate answer, could become worse . . . and lead to ill feelings . . . ill feelings which if ignored can turn to bitterness. Bitterness, which in the end could become anger." ("*Ang tampo ay iba sa galit sapagkat ang taong nagtatampo ay hindi nangangahulugang galit na nga. Ngunit ang tampong hindi rin binibigyang-pansin o sapat na katugunan ay maaaring tumindi . . . na maaaring mauwi sa sama ng loob . . . ang sama ng loob na hindi pinapansin ay nauuwi sa hinanakit. Hinanakit, na sa bandang huli ay maaaring maging galit.*"). Virgilio G. Enriquez and Amelia B. Alfonso, "Ang Pananaw sa Buhay at Weltanschauung na Mahihiwatigan sa Sikolohiya ng Wikang Tagalog," in *Mga Babasahin Sa Sikolinggwistikang Filipino*, ed. Lilia F. Antonio, Anatalia G. Ramos, and Albano-Aura Abiera (Quezon City, Philippines: C & E Publishing, 2011), 83.

come to God. Like Filipinos, who express their *tampo* indirectly,[4] the psalmist expresses his feelings of hurt to others first. Verses 1–16 are directed more to his own audience.[5] Then, after dealing with his *tampo* indirectly, the psalmist goes directly to God by entering "into the sanctuary of God" (v. 17). Psalm 73 highlights the importance of being open to the one who causes us pain. Asians tend not to be frank about what we really feel, unlike our Western counterparts. But we also have a saying in Filipino, "Those who are honest about what they really feel bring the relationship to closer intimacy."[6]

The emphasis on the importance of being honest to God about what one truly feels sets the tone for the communal laments that fill Book III. Of the sixteen psalms in Book III, ten are communal laments or contain elements of lament (Psalms 74, 77, 79–80, 82–83, 85–86, 88–89). Psalm 73 does not begin with, "Why?," which is the characteristic cry of a lament psalm, as we see in the opening of Psalm 74 (for the canonical context of Psalm 73, see comments in Psalm 74 below). Nevertheless, Psalm 73 can also be considered a lament. Though the belief in divine retribution that is reflected in Psalm 73 points to the wisdom tradition, the implicit complaint (vv. 1–16) and the sudden change of mood in the latter part of the psalm (vv. 17–28) bring the psalm closer to a lament. The absence of an opening invocation to God may be explained by the indirect nature of the lament in the opening verses. Viewed from the concept of *tampo*, the lack of an invocation directed to God reinforces the complaint. The fact that the psalmist does not feel he is able to address God directly signifies his feelings of hurt toward God. It is only after he resolves to *go* to God that a change becomes possible.

Structurally, Psalm 73 may be divided into three parts, using the Hebrew word *akh* (surely), which occurs three times:

> "*Surely* [*akh*] God is good to Israel" (v. 1).
> "*Surely* [*akh*] in vain I have kept my heart pure" (v. 13),
> "*Surely* [*akh*] you place them on slippery ground" (v. 18).

---

4. Maggay notes that Filipinos express their *tampo* indirectly through *pagdadabog* (stamping one's feet), *pagmamaktol* (murmuring). Maggay, *Pahiwatig*, 138–139.
5. It is not specified exactly to whom, but from the psalm, it seems to be addressed to his own community.
6. "*Ang nagsasabi ng tapat, nagsasama ng maluwat.*"

# Psalms 73–150

## 73:1–17 "GOD IS GOOD, ALL THE TIME"?

In Christian gatherings in the Philippines, it is common to hear the declaration, "God is good. All the time." The emcee will say to the congregation, "God is good!" And everyone will shout in response, "All the time!" The composer of Psalm 73 would have no problem joining in to this call and response. In fact, he says, "Surely God is good!" (v.1). In Hebrew, the word "good" is emphatic. Literally, verse 1 reads, "Surely, *good* to Israel is God." But first, the psalmist would add a qualification: the object of God's goodness is not everyone, but only "those who are pure in heart" (v. 1b). As Martin Buber says, it is the condition of one's "heart that determines" God's goodness.[7] His point is similar to Romans 8:28, which says that God works in all things "for the good of *those who love him*" (emphasis mine).

But even with this qualification, the psalmist would still find a problem, for from his own experience, it is not those "who are pure in heart" who experience "prosperity," but the wicked (v. 3). The word "prosperity" in verse 3 is the Hebrew word "shalom," which reflects a life characterized by "completeness, soundness, welfare, peace."[8] *Shalom* is for those whose heart is determined to follow God. In the Aaronic blessing, *shalom* is the final word: "The Lord bless you and keep you . . . and give you peace [*shalom*]" (Num 6:24–26). In Psalm 73:3, however, *shalom* has become the property of the wicked. Literally, verse 3b reads, "the *shalom of* the wicked." As the psalmist looks around him, he admits that he is tempted to be envious of the wicked, for he sees them bearing the very mark of a life of blessedness and calm. They look healthy and without the struggles of normal people (v. 4). It's as if they are exempted from the common ills that beset other humans (v. 5).

Whereas the wicked are not "plagued" (*naga'*) "by human ills" (v. 5), the psalmist is "afflicted" (*naga'*) "all day long" (v. 14). The repetition of this Hebrew word *naga'* (to afflict) in verses 5 and 14 emphasizes the contrast. The psalmist feels as if he is always being punished. "All day long" is an expression that could mean "all the time." For the psalmist, the declaration, "God is good, all the time," is not true for him, but it is true for the wicked. Not only are

---

7. Martin Buber, "The Heart Determines: Psalm 73," in *Theodicy in the World of the Bible*, ed. James L. Crenshaw (Philadelphia: Fortress Press, 1983), 109.
8. *BDB*, 2022.

the wicked shielded from the troubles of life, but they are also successful in whatever their hearts set out to do.[9]

So what happens when the wicked experience *shalom*, when they are able to accomplish all that they set out to do? First, they become more arrogant and shameless (v. 6). They no longer hide their "violence" (v. 6b) and "oppression" (v. 8). They wear their pride like a "necklace" and "clothe themselves with violence" (v. 6). This means that they "display" these things "openly, unashamedly, as though they [are] virtues and not defects."[10]

Second, they are no longer afraid of God. Verse 8b literally reads, "from on high they speak oppression." The phrase "from on high" could mean "with arrogance." Or, since verse 9 says, "Their mouths lay claim to heaven," speaking "from on high" could mean speaking from the place that is devoted only to God. They think so highly of themselves that they speak like God (compare Ps 12:4). Later, in verse 11, they insult God, saying, "Does the Most High know anything?" (73:11b).[11]

A third consequence when the wicked continue to remain unchecked is that people are drawn to them (v. 10). Verse 10 has a lot of textual problems, but it cannot be relegated to a gloss because it forms an important turn in the psalm. It begins with the word, "therefore" (*laken*), which parallels verse 6, providing an additional explanation.[12] The NIV translates verse 10 as follows: "Therefore their people turn to them and drink up waters in abundance." Who are the "people" being referred to here? God's people or the wicked? Grammatically, the former is more likely. The wicked are referred to in the plural in the preceding and following verses, while the people of God are referred to in the singular – "his people" (see v. 10, ESV). The LXX has "my people." History also supports this reading. We sometimes wonder how theologians, intelligent people, and church leaders can support people such as Hitler. This is true even today, for in our Filipino context, President Rodrigo Duterte has explicitly likened himself to Hitler. Bonhoeffer explains that "the upsurge of power makes such an overwhelming impression that men are deprived of their

---

9. Takamitsu Muraoka translates the LXX of verse 7b as follows: "they set about (realising) their heart's inclination." Takamitsu Muraoka, *A Greek-English Lexicon of the Septuagint* (Louvain: Peeters, 2009), 150.
10. Robert Galveston Bratcher and William D. Reyburn, *A Translator's Handbook on the Book of Psalms*. Helps for Translators (New York: United Bible Society, 1991), 635.
11. This reminded me of Philippine President Rodrigo Duterte, who called God, "stupid." See https://www.rappler.com/nation/duterte-stupid-god-common-sense; accessed on August 2, 2021.
12. In Hebrew, the word *laken* (therefore) occurs twice (vv. 6 and 10) marking a transition to some sort of an explanation as to the consequence of the success of the wicked.

independent judgment, and – more or less unconsciously – give up trying to assess the new state of affairs for themselves."[13] Verse 10b describes the "waters" of "abundance" from which the people drink. Zenger proposes the verb "to lap greedily," commenting that "what goes forth from the arrogant is greedily received by their followers."[14]

The fourth consequence is personal. The psalmist himself begins to wonder whether it is still worth maintaining a pure heart. "Surely," he says, "in vain I have kept my heart pure" (v. 13). The word "surely" corresponds to the beginning of the psalm ("*Surely*, God is good," v. 1). Ironically, the psalmist is no longer sure. The more he tries to understand this injustice, the more disturbed he becomes (v. 16). He is on the brink of drinking from the same "fountain" of the wicked (v. 10). It is tempting to believe what the wicked are saying – which is that God does not know (v. 11) and therefore that God does not care.

Two things prevent the psalmist from totally slipping. First, he remembers his community. Thinking about the consequences of his action to God's people, he says, "If I had spoken out like that, I would have betrayed your children" (v. 15). What is the psalmist referring to when he says, "like that"? Is he referring to the wicked's manner of speaking (v. 11) or to his own way of thinking (vv. 13–14). Both are possible, though the latter is closer. The psalmist is concerned about the effect of verbalizing his honest thoughts to his community. While God may be able to take our laments, our community may not be prepared for them.

For the first time since verse 1, the psalmist addresses God directly: "I would have betrayed *your* children" (v. 15b, emphasis mine). Before this, God is only referred to in the third person (vv. 1–14). The word "spoken out" (*safar*) is repeated at the end of the psalm to declare the deeds of God (v. 28). Those who experience the works of God are expected to declare the good things that God has done. As far as the psalmist is concerned, however, he cannot think of anything to declare – at least not yet. He could have spoken like the wicked, forever doubting God in his heart, but then the thought of causing a stumbling block to God's precious children hinder him from taking this path.

So the psalmist resolves to take the path that leads to God. When he can no longer understand what is happening around him, he goes into "the

---

13. Dietrich Bonhoeffer, *Letters and Papers from Prison*, ed. Eberhard Bethge (London: The Folio Society, 1971), 8.
14. Frank-Lothar Hossfeld and Erich Zenger, *Psalms 2: A Commentary on Psalms 51–100*, ed. Klaus Baltzer, trans. Linda M. Maloney (Minneapolis: Fortress Press, 2005), 223.

sanctuary of God" (v. 17).[15] This is the second thing that keeps the psalmist from losing his faith, which stems from his decision to continue in his walk with God, even though things no longer make sense. The psalmist does not have to wait for God to do something. Normally, in the cultural concept of *tampo*, the one who is hurt waits for the other person to make the initial move towards mending the relationship. But in verse 17, the psalmist goes to the "sanctuary of God." The "sanctuary" is the place where God is. By going there, the psalmist conveys his desire to meet with God. His action highlights human agency, a feature that will appear again in Book III (e.g. Psalm 77).

The psalmist's coming to God (v. 17) marks the turning point in the psalm. Though his external situation remains the same (see v. 20 below), his perspective has changed. If earlier he "saw the prosperity of the wicked" (v. 3b), now he understands "their final destiny" (v. 17b). There is a difference between seeing things through one's eyes and seeing things from God's perspective. Verse 16b literally reads, "it is wearisome *in my eyes*." Similarly, Lot looked and saw the richness of the land, but he failed to see beyond it (Gen 13:10–11). The psalmist, however, begins to see things from God's perspective when he enters "the sanctuary of God" (v. 17).

The text does not say what the psalmist says to God when he goes into the sanctuary or what transpires there. We could say that his indirect expressions of *tampo* paved the way towards more open and direct communication with God. Having expressed his ill feelings indirectly (vv. 1–16), the psalmist is now free to pour out his heart to God. A consideration of Psalm 74 (see discussion below) suggests that the psalmist expresses his own lament to God.

## 73:18–28 "IT IS GOOD TO BE NEAR GOD"

After coming to the place where God is, the psalmist gains a new perspective of the situation of the wicked. He now understands that they are on "slippery ground" (v. 18). The psalmist knows what it means to walk on slippery ground. Earlier, he testified that he almost slipped (v. 2). He thought that the wicked were the ones on firm ground; they even "set" (*shyt*) their lips against heaven (v. 9). But now, God sets (*shyt*) them on slippery ground (v. 18). Whereas earlier the wicked speak "from on high" (v. 8), now they are "cast down to ruin" (v. 18). Verse 19 begins with the word "how!" (*'eyk*), which is used in dirge: "How suddenly are they destroyed" (compare 2 Sam 1:25). Wicked people

---

15. *Where* we go when life is hard is crucial. Psalm 73 opens the invitation to go to God.

in power may feel invincible, but they are likened to a dream, which vanishes when one awakes (v. 20a). They are gone "when you arise, Lord" (v. 20).

Verse 20 indicates that the situation confronting the psalmist has not yet changed, for the Lord has yet to "arise." The statements in the preceding verses were made through the eyes of faith. In the next verses, the psalmist reveals what sustains him even though his situation remains unchanged. Verses 21–22 come after the transformation in verse 17, but they look back to the psalmist's earlier experience (vv. 1–16), before he came to God, providing glimpses of what he does in the sanctuary.

The psalmist confesses that he came to a point when his "soul was embittered" and "was pricked in heart" (v. 21, ESV). The feelings of hurt (*tampo*) were turning to bitterness, the pain was becoming deeper. Verse 21b can be translated, "I had a deep pain in my heart."[16] Like the speaker in Psalm 22, who considers himself as "a worm and not a man" (22:6), the psalmist says, "I was a brute beast before you" (73:22b). The words "before you" are important. Though the psalmist may feel and act like a "brute beast," he can still go to the presence of the Lord just as he is. He does not need to be alright to be acceptable to God. He knows he will be accepted. So with a persistence comparable to his coming to God in verse 17, the psalmist declares, "I am always with you" (v. 23a). Even when there is so much pain in his heart, even when his soul is embittered, the psalmist says, I continue to come to you.

This psalm exemplifies a beautiful balance between human striving and divine accompanying. After the psalmist declares, "I am always with you" (v. 23a), he says, "you hold me by my right hand" (v. 23b). In Filipino, the word for "you hold" is *inaalalayan*, which depicts an image of someone struggling to walk and then someone coming to assist. The help is not given to someone who is not trying. This is important, for there is a tendency for us to think that everything is up to God. But here, the psalmist is trying, though he continues to struggle. And as he tries, God comes alongside and assists him. It is as we continue, even when we're struggling and falling, that we experience the guiding hand of God: "You guide me with your counsel" (v. 24a). The psalmist experiences even more: "afterward you will take me into glory" (v. 24b). This could mean that the psalmist is delivered from whatever he is facing. Others think this speaks of being taken to heaven. The language is mystical and the text is not specific, but what is important is that "*you* will take me." Wherever that may be, here or in the next life, the important realization is that "I am

---

16. Bratcher and Reyburn, *A Translator's Handbook on the Book of Psalms*, 642.

with you" and "you are with me" (compare Phil 1:21). The psalmist does not long for anything on earth or in heaven but God (v. 25). Even when "My flesh and my heart may fail," the psalmist is confident that God will be "the strength of my heart and my portion forever" (v. 26).

Verse 27 is a summary statement comparable to verse 12. Both employ the Hebrew word *hinneh* (behold) (see ESV). In verse 12, the psalmist describes how successful the wicked people are, whereas in verse 27, he says that the wicked will perish, and he also describes them as "unfaithful" and "those who are far from you." The wicked may be wealthy and healthy, but if they are far from God, it's all in vain. The word "good" is repeated at the very end (v. 28), echoing the very beginning where "good" is first mentioned. Earlier, the psalmist declares, "Surely God is good to Israel" (v. 1). Now, he confesses, "But as for me, it is good to be near God" (v. 28). The meaning of the word "good" has not changed. Rather, the *direction* has changed. The first looks from God to humans: God is good. The last looks from humans to God: because of the psalmist's own journey, which includes all of his struggles and encounters with God, he has come to realize that what is "good" is "to be near God" (v. 28). Intimacy in the relationship is key, but to develop intimacy, one has to be honest. Lament is one way of being honest.

# PSALM 74

Psalm 74 begins rather abruptly with, "Why?" Most English versions begin with the invocation, "O God," but in Hebrew, the word "why?" is the first word. Gerstenberger feels that this is a "hasty opening that ignores etiquette."[1] However, Psalm 74 opens this way because it is not meant to be read alone, but is intended to be a companion to Psalm 73. As McCann observes, there are close links between Psalms 73 and 74: the superscription for both Psalms are by Asaph; both refer to the "sanctuary" (73:17 and 74:7); both refer to violence (73:6; 74:20); both talk about the "right hand" (73:23; 74:11); both refer to "ruins" (73:18; 74:3). McCann argues that these connections "suggest that Psalms 73 and 74 should be heard together."[2]

Psalms 73 and 74 perform a function similar to Psalms 1 and 2 in Book I. Like Psalm 1, Psalm 73 also contains elements of the wisdom tradition, specifically the idea of divine retribution. The former takes for granted that the wicked will perish (1:4–6) while the righteous will flourish (1:3, 6b). This perspective is in the background of Psalm 73. Both Psalms 1 and 73 are also followed by a psalm that begins with the question, "why?"[3] This question disturbs the rather settled convictions in the previous psalms:

"*Why* do the nations conspire?" (2:1)
"*Why*, O God, have you rejected us forever?"
(74:1, translation mine)

There are also similarities between Books II and III. Book II begins with an individual lament (Psalms 42–43), which is followed by a communal lament (Psalm 44). Likewise, Book III begins with Psalm 73, which has elements of an individual lament (see above), and is followed by Psalm 74, which is a communal lament. The similarities between Psalms 73–74 and the opening psalms in Books I and II further affirm the connections between Psalms 73 and 74. These two form a pair, and when read together, we cannot see Psalm 74 as a psalm that "ignores etiquette," because the way has already been prepared through Psalm 73.

Psalm 73 highlights the importance of confronting one's feelings of hurt with God (see above discussion). Rather than ignoring these feelings, the

---

1. Erhard S. Gerstenberger, *Psalms Part 2 and Lamentations* (Grand Rapids: Eerdmans, 2001), 78.
2. J. Clinton McCann, "Psalms," in *NIB*, vol. 4 (Nashville: Abingdon Press, 1996), 972.
3. Compare Villanueva, *Psalms 1–72*, 29.

psalmist processes them by expressing them to his audience and then going to God's sanctuary (73:17). By doing so, the psalmist "offers a model for the whole people in confronting the prosperity of the wicked."[4] Just as the psalmist goes to God's sanctuary to deal with his pain (Psalm 73), the people can go to God to pour out their hearts to him (Psalm 74). Though the psalmist does not explicitly ask God "why?" in Psalm 73, the lament is already implied in the prayer. As Yohanna Katanacho's rendering of Psalm 73:1 puts it, "O Lord! If you are good then *why* don't you remove oppression?"[5] The "why?" in Psalm 74 confirms the lament in Psalm 73. Just as the psalmist goes to God's sanctuary to pour out his lament in Psalm 73, the people in Psalm 74 gather together "in a sanctuary or in the temple in Jerusalem to cry out to God about a situation of grave danger."[6]

In the aftermath of a disaster, a common reaction among Asians is to explain what happened as a punishment of God. For example, when Mayon volcano erupted in 1897, the survivors saw it as "the punishment of God to us," which has to be "accepted because we probably disobeyed you."[7] The Israelites also saw the destruction of Jerusalem and the experience of exile as a punishment of God, but this did not prevent them from asking God, "why?" Conspicuously, there is no mention of sin or repentance in Psalm 74. Instead of confessing their sins, the people lament, asking God, "why?" and "how long?" (v. 10). They reason with and protest against God.

Psalm 74 contains an important message for the community of faith today. As Gunkel reminds us, the people of God in the OT are not always obliged to "sing praises and give thanks; there is also a time to grieve and lament. Alongside the happy festivals of rejoicing in the community stand the days of lamentation. When crop failure, pestilence, and danger from the enemy afflicted the people, such a day of lamentation was observed."[8] So it is with us. We can also express our questions to God in the face of tragic events.

---

4. McCann, "Psalms," 972.
5. Yohanna Katanacho, *Praying through the Psalms* (Carlisle: Langham Creative Projects, 2018), 145, emphasis mine.
6. Nancy deClaisse-Walford, "Psalm 44: O God, Why Do You Hide Your Face?," in *My Words Are Lovely: Studies in the Rhetoric of the Psalms*, ed. Robert L. Foster and David M. Howard (New York: T & T Clark, 2008), 745.
7. Greg Bankoff, *Cultures of Disaster: Society and Natural Hazard in the Philippines* (London and New York: RoutledgeCurson, 2003), 176. Compare Bernard Adeney-Risakotta, "Is There a Meaning in Natural Disasters? Constructions of Culture, Religion, and Science," *Exchange*, January 1, 2009.
8. Hermann Gunkel, *The Psalms: A Form-Critical Introduction* (Philadelphia: Fortress Press, 1967), 13.

Structurally, the psalm consists mainly of lament:

lament (vv. 1–11),
hymn (vv. 12–17),
lament (vv. 18–23).

The pattern – complaint followed by petition – is repeated twice:[9]

Complaint: "Why?" (v. 1) / Petition: "remember" (v. 2);
Complaint: "Why?" (v. 11) / Petition: "remember" (v. 18).

### 74:1–11 "WHY, O GOD?"

As noted above, the question "why?" is the first word in Psalm 74: "Why, O God?" While translations placing the invocation before the interrogative ("O God, why?") may be liturgically justifiable (see ESV), this weakens the emphasis on the question, "why?" The "why?" is important because, as noted above, it connects Psalm 74 with Psalm 73 and also links it with the opening psalms in Book I (Psalms 1–2, see above). The "why?" is also the characteristic cry of the lament, occurring twice in Psalm 74 (vv. 1, 11) to form an inclusio in the first section.

> ### THE CHALLENGE OF LAMENT TO ASIAN CHRISTIANS
>
> Asians—and Filipinos in particular—do not usually question the ways of God. We simply accept the will of heaven or God. Traditionally, we show respect to the elderly and do not question their authority. So how much more should we respect God's authority? Our colonial experience reinforced this. Most countries in Asia have gone through the painful experience of colonization. The Philippines was under the Spaniards for more than three hundred years. Just when we thought we were free, the Americans came, and then later, the Japanese had their turn. Having been under colonial rule for so long, it has become harder for us to ask, "why?" Our sense of self has been brought low.

---

9. The second pattern above is separated by the mythic hymn in verses 12–17. Some argue that the hymn was a later insertion (see below).

> It's easier to simply accept and submit. Unfortunately, the Christian tradition we inherited from the West, which has tended to limit or control our expressions of lament,[1] further stifled the question, "why?"
>
> Without giving up the traditional view of respect for the elderly, prayers of lament empower the people of God to voice their complaints to God. Psalm 74 reveals that the question, "why?" is not a sign of weak faith or immaturity. On the contrary, it is a mark of bold faith and maturity. This type of prayer is not for the novice. Only those who are intimate with God can pray in this manner.[2]
>
> ---
> 1. Kathleen D. Billman and Daniel L. Migliore, *Rachel's Cry: Prayer of Lament and Rebirth of Hope* (Cleveland: United Church Press, 1999), 46–66.
> 2. Belden C. Lane, "Hutzpa K'Lapei Shamaya: A Christian Response to the Jewish Tradition of Arguing with God," *Journal of Ecumenical Studies* 23 (September 1986): 567–587.

In the OT, the great prophets such as Jeremiah and Moses ask God, "why?" For example, when God is about to destroy the Israelites because of their idolatry, Moses prays: "*why* should your anger burn against your people . . .? *Why* should the Egyptians say, 'It was with evil intent that he brought them out, to kill them in the mountains and to wipe them off the face of the earth'?" (Exod 32:11–12). Moses asks God "why?" twice, and then he pleads with God to "*remember* your servants Abraham, Isaac and Israel" (v. 13). Psalm 74 follows Moses's pattern of prayer in Exodus 32, as shown in the following diagram:

| Comparison Between Moses's Prayer in Exodus 32 and Psalm 74 | | |
|---|---|---|
| Prayer | Exodus 32 | Psalm 74 |
| "Why?" | "*Why* should your anger burn against your people . . .?" (v. 11). "*Why* should the Egyptians say . . .?" (v. 12). | "*Why*, O God?" (v. 1). "*Why* do you hold back your hand?" (v. 11, ESV). |
| "Remember" | "*Remember* your servants Abraham, Isaac and Israel" (v. 13). | "*Remember* your congregation" (v. 1, ESV). "*Remember* this, O LORD, how the enemy scoffs" (v. 18, ESV). |

But there are two key differences. First, the prayer in Psalm 74 is not the prayer of a great prophet like Moses, but is presented as a prayer of the people. Though the prayer was most likely composed by someone associated with the Temple (a Levite or a scribe), it is intended as a prayer of the people in view of the communal nature of the suffering as well as the use of the plural personal pronoun "our" in verse 9. Second, whereas Moses pleaded with God to "remember Abraham, Isaac, and Israel" (Exod 32:13), the people in Psalm 74 ask God to "remember your *congregation*" (v. 1, ESV). Here, the people of God have been elevated to a status comparable to the patriarchs of old. The people of God, as a congregation gathered in the presence of God, can stand before God just as Moses and the great prophets of old did. They, too, can ask God, "why?" Jesus's similar cry on the cross, "My God, my God, *why* have you forsaken me?" (Matt 27:46), affirms lament as an expression of God's people.

The question "why?" is not only a sign of intimacy, for it is also an indication of great need. Though Filipinos do not normally ask God "why?" we learn to utter the complaint when we experience extreme suffering. As Lane observes, "One can never speak forcefully to God from a position of security. Some levels of spirituality are grasped only when balancing on the edge of the abyss."[10]

The lament in Psalm 74 arises from those who are "balancing on the edge" of such an abyss. From the ruins of the destroyed temple, the people cry to God, "Turn your steps toward these everlasting *ruins*" (v. 3, emphasis mine). The Hebrew text literally reads, "lift up your steps." Though the LXX tries to smoothen the reading by changing "steps" to "hand," the Hebrew reading should be retained. The people are asking God to arise and turn his *steps* toward the ruined temple. Just as the psalmist goes to the sanctuary of God in Psalm 73 (v. 17), so the people ask God to visit the sanctuary and see "*all* that the enemy have destroyed" (74:3b, my translation).

The destruction of the Temple is one of the most traumatic events for the people of God. To experience recovery, they have to go through the process of mourning. As Judith Herman explains, "Only through mourning *everything* that she has lost can the patient discover her indestructible inner life."[11] In Psalm 74, the people tell God what it was like when their enemies came "in the place where you met with us" (v. 4), roaring like animals (v. 4), wielding axes as

---

10. Lane, "Hutzpa K'Lapei Shamaya: A Christian Response to the Jewish Tradition of Arguing with God," 579.
11. Judith Herman, *Trauma and Recovery*, 188, emphasis mine.

if "in a forest of trees" (v. 5),[12] smashing up the carved work "with hatchet and hammers" (v. 6), and burning the very "dwelling place of Your name" (v. 7).

The people of God will never forget how the enemies burned "all the meeting places of God in the land" (v. 8, ESV). The phrase, "meeting places," comes from the Hebrew *moʿed*, which means "appointed time," but here it is used to refer to the sanctuary. The very place where they used to meet with God and with one another, the place of worship and fellowship, is now all in ruins. In verse 9, the poet refers to the communal experience of the tragic event for the first time, saying, "*we* do not see *our* signs" (v. 9a, ESV). The "signs" are the cultural/religious symbols that are closely associated with the people's identity (e.g. flag, religion). The enemies knew that the demolition of the people's cultural symbols would be far more enduring than the physical devastations. With the disappearance of the "signs," the community becomes like a ship without an anchor. Even the prophets are nowhere to be found, and so there is no one to tell the people how long their suffering will last (v. 9b).

The ruins are described in verse 3 as "forever," and so the people cry out, "How long?" (v. 10). Though they hear the roaring of the enemies (v. 4), the silence of God is deafening. For the second time in the psalm, the people ask God, "Why?" – "Why do you hold back your hand, your right hand?" (v. 11). This cry is similar to the lament in Psalm 10, "Why, O LORD, do you stand far away? Why do you hide yourself in times of trouble?" (v. 1, ESV). In both psalms, the people are protesting God's inaction. The "hand" in Psalm 74 (v. 11) symbolizes God's saving power, but God's hands remain folded, kept under his bosom. A more literal translation of verse 11b reads, "Why is your right hand hidden on your bosom?" (my translation).[13]

## 74:12–17 "BUT GOD IS MY KING FROM LONG AGO"

Despite the bitter complaint expressed in the questions, "how long?" (v. 10) and "why?" (v. 11), the psalmist insists, "But God is my King from long ago" (v. 12).[14] The radical transition represents persistent faith, a trust that never

---

12. Verse 5 is problematic. Literally, it reads: "it is known as one who comes upwards, in a forest/thicket of trees axes." The BHS notes propose *gadah* instead of *yadaʿ*. Kirkpatrick's attempt to preserve the MT reading could help here: "They seem as men that lift up axes in a thicket of trees." A. F. Kirkpatrick, *The Book of Psalms* (Cambridge: University Press, 1895), 444.
13. Here I follow the BHS suggestion which takes the verb "to hide" (*kala*) instead of "to complete" (*kalah*). For the "bosom" I follow the *Qere* reading rather than the *Ketiv* ("statue").
14. Greene views verses 12–17 as not originally part of Psalm 74. He argues that verse 18 follows verse 11 more naturally. The pattern, "why" followed by the petition "remember" is similar to

lets go of God. Just as the psalmist in Psalm 22 cries, "why have you forsaken me?" but nonetheless refers to God as "*my* God," so the psalmist in Psalm 74 calls God "*my* King" (v. 12) even after asking, "why?" (v. 11). The use of the possessive pronoun "my" points to the people's history with God. They go back "from long ago," even before the Temple came to be.

Drawing from the surrounding cultural resources of their ancient West Asian background, the psalmist recalls God's victory over the sea (v. 13). Consideration of this background is important in understanding this section. The Hebrew word for sea is *Yam*. In Canaanite mythology, a conflict occurred between Yam (sea) and Baal. Baal defeated Yam, after which he was proclaimed king. Yam is also equivalent to "Leviathan," the seven-headed dragon in Canaanite mythology. Yet in the biblical account, the psalmist applies these ancient myths to his own experience and to God. The psalmist describes God not simply as "king," but as "*my* king." It is *not* Baal or Marduk who defeated the sea monsters, but God: "It is *you* who split open the sea by your power" (v. 13a, emphasis mine); it is "*you* who broke the heads of the monster in the waters" (v. 13b, emphasis mine) and who "crushed the heads of Leviathan" (v. 14). The powerful seven-headed mythological dragon is no match for Yahweh.[15]

In the Babylonian myth called *Enuma elish*, Marduk's victory over the sea goddess Tiamat is associated with creation. Marduk divided the body of Tiamat from which he created the waterways and organized the heavenly bodies. Similarly, in verse 15, God crushes and smashes the heads of the dragon, an act that is followed by the manipulation of bodies of water,[16] which could be a reference to creation. The explicit reference to creation in verses 16–17 supports this connection to creation. In verses 16–17, the psalmist goes back to the very beginning, referring to creation itself with the establishing of the heavenly lights (v. 16), the setting up of "the boundaries of the earth," and the "forming" of summer and winter (v. 17). The word "forming" (*yatsar*) is the same word used in Genesis 2:7 to refer to the creation of man.

---

verses 1–2. As verse 1 contains the question "why?" followed by the petition "remember" in verse 2, so the "why?" in verse 11 should be followed by the "remember" in verse 18. Greene describes the insertion of verses 12–17 as "violent," reflecting the destruction of the temple. Nathaniel E. Greene, "Creation, Destruction, and a Psalmist's Plea: Rethinking the Poetic Structure of Psalm 74," *JBL* 136, no. 1 (2017): see esp. 100.

15. John Day, *God's Conflict with the Dragon and the Sea* (Cambridge University Press, 1985), 4.

16. Debra Scoggins Ballentine, "Revising a Myth: The Targum of Psalm 74 and the Exodus Tradition," in *"The One Who Sows Bountifully": Essays in Honor of Stanley K. Stowers* (Providence: Brown Judaic Studies, 2013), 109–110.

Another important detail from the ancient West Asian background is the link between kingship and temple building. After Baal and Marduk were proclaimed king, a temple was erected in their honor.[17] The proclamation of God as "my King" brings the temple to the fore, recalling God's victory in primordial times, which brings hope to the people in the midst of their situation. But verses 12–17 do not "resolve" the contradiction.[18] The jarring juxtaposition between the hymnic declaration and the present situation paints a question mark about God's ability to maintain control over his creation, underscoring the tension between God's past victory and the people's present reality.[19]

### 74:18–23 "ARISE, O GOD!"

In spite of this tension, the psalmist persists in his faith, affirming that "God's defeat of the monster and creation of the world, are not locked away in the vanished past. They are still available. That power, that energy, that unassailable mastery is still needed. It can be reactivated yet."[20] The following series of ten petitions within these six verses illustrate the psalmist's continuing trust in God's power:[21]

1. "Remember this, O Lord, how the enemy scoffs" (v. 18).
2. "Do not deliver the soul of your dove to the wild beasts" (v. 19).
3. "Do not forget the life of your poor forever" (v. 19).
4. "Have regard for the covenant" (v. 20).
5. "Let not the downtrodden turn back in shame (v. 21).
6. "Let the poor and needy praise your name" (v. 21).
7. "Arise, O God" (v. 22).
8. "Defend your cause" (v. 22).
9. "Remember how the foolish scoff at you all the day" (v. 22).
10. "Do not forget the clamor of your foes" (v. 23).

The related petitions, "remember" and "do not forget," envelop this last section of the psalm (vv. 18–19 and 22–23). The imperative verb, "remember," is a petition for God to do something about the continuing scoffing

---

17. Day, *God's Conflict with the Dragon and the Sea*, 24.
18. Contra Frank-Lothar Hossfeld and Erich Zenger, *Psalms 2*, 248.
19. Jon Douglas Levenson, *Creation and the Persistence of Evil: The Jewish Drama of Divine Omnipotence* (Princeton: Princeton University Press, 1994), 23.
20. Levenson, *Creation and the Persistence of Evil*, 74.
21. Compare the series of petitions in Lamentations 5. See Federico Villanueva, *Lamentations: A Pastoral and Contextual Commentary* (Carlisle, UK: Langham Global Library, 2016), 103.

of the enemy, which is a serious concern (vv. 18, 22). To allow the scoffing to continue means bad news for the poor, whose life is described as "your dove," which is an image of vulnerability and powerlessness (v. 19). Earlier, the psalmist recalls how God "gave" (*natan*) the Leviathan "as food for the creatures of the wilderness" (v. 14, ESV). Now, the psalmist pleads for God not to "deliver [*natan*] the soul of your dove to the wild beasts" (v. 19). Unlike the Leviathan, doves are defenseless, and so the psalmist prays for God not to forget the life of the poor (v. 19).

The psalmist maintains that what happens to the poor is a direct concern of God, part of God's "covenant"[22] (v. 20). Saint Augustine believes that the work of God is justice. God should not allow the downtrodden (*dak*) to be put to shame, so that the "poor and needy" may praise his name (v. 21). The poor have nowhere else to go to but God (compare 10:14), and so God should "arise," for the fight for their welfare is "your cause" (v. 22).

---

22. The MT simply has "covenant," but the LXX has the second personal suffix–"your" (your covenant). The parallel idea in verse 22 supports the presence of the suffix.

# PSALM 75

In times of disaster or catastrophe, it is important for a faith community to be given space to lament, mourn, and pour out their hearts before the Lord. This is what the people did in Psalm 74. Out of the ruins of the Temple, their cries went up to God. But for a community to continue in the face of ongoing disaster, the people also need God's assurance. In Psalm 75, the people receive a word of assurance from God, who tells them that even "when the earth and all its people quake, it is I who hold its pillars firm" (v. 3). God's word assures the people that he is near to them, even in the midst of tragedy. For this assurance, they offer thanksgiving to God (v. 1).

From a canonical point of view, we can consider the destruction of the Temple in Psalm 74 as the situation out of which Psalm 75 may be read.[1] As Tournay observes, "It all sounds as if Psalm 75 was the response to the anguished appeals of the preceding Psalm 74."[2] One of the key phrases in Psalm 74, "your name," occurs three times (Ps 74:7, 18, and 21). This same phrase also occurs at the beginning of Psalm 75 when the people declare, "your Name is near" (v. 1a). In Psalm 74, the divine name is trampled upon in the very place where the people meet with God (v. 8), which is called the "appointed place" (Heb. *mo'ed*). In Psalm 75:2, the word *mo'ed* occurs again, but here God is declaring that at the appointed time, he will judge with equity.

Admittedly, there is no explicit deliverance in Psalm 75, only "the closeness of the divine name" (v. 1a), but that is still a reason to be thankful. At the end of Psalm 73, the psalmist declares that being near to God is what really matters: "But as for me, it is good to be near God" (v. 28). For those who are going through uncertainties, the assurance of the divine presence is enough to sustain them, and so the people are thankful.

Structurally, Psalm 75 may be outlined as follows:

thanksgiving (v. 1–3),
divine speech (vv. 4–8),
thanksgiving (vv. 9–10).

---

1. For a recent analysis of the canonical shape of Psalms 73–78, see Stephen J. Smith, "The Shape and Message of Psalms 73–78," *CBQ* 83, no. 1 (2021): 18–37. Smith argues that Psalm 75–76 affirms the view expressed in the second half of Psalm 73.
2. Raymond J. Tournay, *Seeing and Hearing God with the Psalms: The Prophetic Liturgy of the Second Temple in Jerusalem* (Sheffield: Sheffield Academic Press, 1991), 183.

The divine speech begins as part of the thanksgiving (v. 2), forming the central part of the psalm. The people are grateful to the Lord because he has spoken, giving a word of promise on the issue of justice. After the declaration of the divine word, the psalm ends with a vow of praise.

## 75:1–3 THANKSGIVING

The psalm begins with a two-fold thanksgiving: "we give thanks to you, O God, we give thanks." The pattern is similar to Psalm 57:1:

"Have mercy on me,     my God,    have mercy on me" (57:1).

"We give thanks to you,    O God,    we give thanks"    (75:1, ESV).

The two-fold repetition of the plea for mercy in Psalm 57 reflects the psalmist's sense of urgency and intensity. Similarly, we can say with Calvin that the two-fold repetition of thanksgiving in Psalm 75 signifies a "strong affection" and an "ardent zeal in singing the praises of God."[3] Verse 1 begins with the people's expression of thanksgiving (v. 1a) and ends with their declaring or telling of God's "wonderful deeds" (v. 1b).[4]

Usually, a thanksgiving is followed by a reason for the thanksgiving, and here, the reason given is "for your Name is near."[5] Unlike other thanksgiving psalms, Psalm 75 contains no clear account of deliverance. The canonical context points to a present situation that is full of ruins. The people ask God, "why?" and "how long?" (74:1, 10). There is no indication in Psalm 75 that their situation has changed, but as they pour out their heart in lament (Psalm 74), they realize God's nearness. The word "near" recalls the end of Psalm 73, where the psalmist declares that "for me it is good to be near God" (73:28). Though the sanctuary, the "place of your name" (74:7), has been destroyed, God's name remains.

---

3. John Calvin, *Calvin's Commentaries (Complete)*, trans. John King, Accordance electronic ed. (Edinburgh: Calvin Translation Society, 1847), paragraph 14927.
4. The Hebrew of verse 1 has third person plural–"They recount your wondrous deeds" (see ESV). It is possible that the original Hebrew has the first person plural for the verb "recount"–we recount–but that the following word which begins with a *nun* may have caused the confusion, resulting in the third person plural reading. The LXX supports a first person plural reading of the verb, though it reads the MT's "near" as a verb–call: "We call upon your name."
5. Though the conjunction "for" (*ki*) is not used here, this is implied in the context. Compare Targum's translation: "for the Shekinah of your name is near," 147.

# Psalm 75

"Name" here refers to the attributes of God, what defines him.[6] The significance of the "name" goes back to Moses's encounter with God in the book of Exodus. When Moses asks God what "name" will he give the people when they ask him for it (Exod 3:13), God answers, "I am who, I am" (v. 14), which can also be translated, "I am who I will be" and "I will be who I am." It is a way of saying, "As I was with my people in the past, so I am now with you." In view of the Israelite's slavery in Egypt, such a statement assures Moses that he is not alone. God is with him.

Just as God spoke to Moses, so now God speaks to the people. There is a shift in verse 2 from first person plural to first person singular. The NIV supplies the words, "You say," at the beginning of verse 2 to indicate a change in speaker. The people are grateful to God because God is near, which they know because he has said that at the "appointed time," he will "judge with equity" (v. 2). This links God's nearness directly with justice, a question that is behind the laments of the psalmist in Psalm 73 (see below for further links between Psalms 73 and 75). The people in Psalm 74 are also crying out for justice on behalf of the "oppressed, the poor and needy" (74:21). This suggests that we can know that God is near when there is justice.

Yet this justice remains a future reality: "the earth and all its people quake" (75:3). In Psalm 82, we learn that when the poor and needy are oppressed and treated unjustly, "all the foundations of the earth are shaken" (v. 5). In Psalm 75, God does not deny the quaking of the earth, nor does he say that he will stop the quaking, but he promises, "It is I who hold its pillars firm" (v. 3b).[7] The pronoun "I" here is emphatic and occurs earlier in verse 2: "It is I who judge with equity." When the disciples are confronted by a great windstorm and their boat is about to break, Jesus gets up and commands the raging sea, saying, "Be still," and the sea stops (Mark 4:39). In Psalm 75, God does not calm the quaking of the earth, but he holds the pillars, strengthening and sustaining them so that the earth and its inhabitants can withstand the quaking.

---

6. J. G. McConville, *Deuteronomy* (Nottingham, England; Downers Grove: Apollos InterVarsity Press, 2002), 230.
7. The Hebrew word for "hold" (*tkn*) is similar to the word "established" used in Psalm 99:4, which declares: "you have established equity." The "piel of *tqn* are similar in meaning, as is *kûn* in the basic sense of 'be firm'" (*TDOT*, 15:663).

## 75:4–8 DIVINE SPEECH

The previous verses speak of divine justice, with God declaring, "it is I who judge with equity" (v. 2). Verse 4 provides a hint that the quaking of the earth is related to injustice, as God warns the "arrogant" to "boast no more." The words "arrogant" and "boast" come from the same Hebrew verb, *halal*. The word is also used earlier in Psalm 73, where the psalmist confesses his struggles with his faith because of the injustice that he sees all around him: "For I envied the arrogant [*halal*]" (v. 3). He asks how the wicked and arrogant are prosperous and successful while the righteous are suffering. Though no explicit response is given to the psalmist in Psalm 73, Psalm 75 offers a response, for God tells the wicked not to "lift up your horn on high" (v. 5, ESV).

The word "horn" is mentioned four times in Psalm 75 (vv. 4, 5, and twice in v. 10) and is a "symbol for power, majesty, dignity."[8] Each person has her/his own "horn" (dignity), but only the Lord lifts up an individual's horn. As Hannah declares, "my horn is exalted in the LORD" (1 Sam 2:1). God alone "exalts" (Ps 75:7), or as Psalm 113 puts it, only God "raises the poor from the dust and lifts the needy from the ash heap" (Ps 113:7–9). This act of *exalting* does not come "from the east, nor from the west, nor from the desert" (Ps 75:6). In Hebrew, the last word in this verse comes from the verb, "to lift up" (*harim*), which is the same form for the word "mountains" (*harim*). Inhabiting a very high place (such as a mountain) does not make one high, for God alone "puts down one and exalts another" (Ps 75:7). Note that in the shift from verse 6 to verse 7, there is a transition from God as the speaker to someone speaking *about* God in the third person to affirm God's divine promise (vv. 7–8).

Psalm 75 parallels the story of Hannah in 1 Samuel 2, but the psalm is focused on bringing down, and the divine speech is directed to the arrogant. The emphasis is on the "God who judges," for God will make sure that the wicked and arrogant will be judged for their deeds (literally, "drain and drink" the wine "down to its very dregs," Ps 75:8).

## 75:9–10 THANKSGIVING

In verse 9, the speaker changes from the Lord (vv. 2–6) to the psalmist, who vows that he "will declare this forever" and will "sing praise to the God of Jacob." In verse 9, the antecedent for "this" is not explicit. The Hebrew says, "I will declare forever." Based on the preceding context (vv. 5–7), "this" refers

---

8. Marvin E. Tate, *Psalms 51–100* (Dallas: Word Books, 1990), 259–260.

to God's earlier promise to execute his equitable justice (see v. 2 above). God will "cut off the horns of all the wicked, but the horns of the righteous will be lifted up" (v. 10). Notice the repetition of the word "all" from verse 8. God's judgment is thorough: "*all* the wicked of the earth" will drink from the cup of God's judgment (v. 8) and "*all*" the "horns of the wicked" will be "cut off" (v. 10).

# PSALM 76

One of the most striking things about Psalm 76 is the way it presents God as one who is awesome and great, feared by princes and kings (see v. 12), and yet this same God reaches down from heaven to deliver and save the poor (v. 9). The word "poor" comes from the Hebrew *anawim*, which can mean "humble," "lowly," but here it refers to the "poor and weak," those who are "oppressed by rich and powerful."[1] The emphasis on the judgment of the arrogant and the similarities with Hannah's prayer in the previous psalm (75:4–8) support this view.

Jesus later quotes a passage from Isaiah that focuses on the poor: "The Spirit of the Lord is on me, because he has anointed me to proclaim good news to the *poor*" (Luke 4:18, emphasis mine, quoting Isa 61:1). By reciting this passage, Jesus announces his mission to the poor, bringing the message of Psalm 76 to a deeper level. Psalm 76:8–9 begins with the word "heaven" and ends with the word "earth." In Jesus, God has come down from heaven to the earth in order to reach the poor.

Psalm 76 shows affinities with the Zion psalms (see Psalms 46 and 48), which celebrate Mount Zion as the place where God dwells, emphasizing that it is impregnable and secure.[2] However, Psalm 76 does not emphasize the impregnability of Zion as a place, but rather focuses on "the resident of Zion."[3]

The canonical shape of the psalms provides a hint about the reason for this shift in emphasis. Psalm 76 comes after the communal lament in Psalm 74, which mourns the destruction of the Temple, the very place where God's name and glory resides. This could suggest the reason for the softening of the confidence found in the other Zion psalms. It is interesting to note that Psalm 46 comes after an earlier communal lament in Psalm 44. This canonical arrangement suggests that a possible purpose or function of the Zion psalms is to make the following bold assertion amidst the chaos of the destruction of the Temple: the same God who is known in Zion (Psalms 46, 48) remains the God who delivers the *anawim*, the poor, the afflicted (Psalm 76).

The psalm may be outlined as follows:

---

1. *BDB*, 776.
2. For a list of the similarities between these psalms, see Hossfeld and Zenger, *Psalms 2*, 261.
3. James Luther Mays, *Psalms* (Louisville: John Knox Press, 1994), 250.

# Psalm 76

God's presence in Zion (vv. 1–3),
The awesome Warrior God (vv. 4–8)[4]
    God is to be feared (vv. 6–7),
    "You are to be feared" (v. 8),
The Righteous Judge who cares for the poor (vv. 7–10),
Exhortation (vv. 11–12).

## 76:1–3 GOD IS *IN* ZION

The repetition of the preposition "in" within these verses emphasizes God's presence and concreteness in the experience of the people:

"God is known *in* Judah" (v. 1a),
"His name is great *in* Israel" (v. 1b),
"His tent is *in* Salem" (v. 2a),
"His dwelling place *in* Zion" (v. 2b).

One does not experience God in the abstract – "up there," as it were. Rather, one encounters God right here, *in* a particular place or context. The phrase, "God is known" (v. 1), is a way of saying, "we have experienced him!" Where? In Zion.

What have they known about God in Zion? "There," the psalmist says, God "broke" the weapons of war and war itself. The NIV translates the Hebrew word *milhamah* as "weapons of war" (v. 3), but *milhama* usually means "war" and should be maintained here. Verse 3 is talking about breaking the weapons of war (arrows, shields, and sword) and also breaking war itself. The two are separate, though related. As Waldman points out, "In Biblical passages the two themes of breaking weapons and the ending of war, with God as ruler of the world, are combined."[5]

In every war, it's the poor who suffer the most, since they are the most vulnerable. As Pleins observes, "War is an obstacle to a full realization of both God's peace and God's justice for the poor."[6] Thus the ending of war, first of all, benefits the poor.

---

4. There is a shift from third person to second person address in verse 4.
5. Nahum M. Waldman, "The Breaking of the Bow," in *The Jewish Quarterly Review* 69 no. 2 (1978): 84.
6. David J. Pleins, *The Psalms: Songs of Tragedy, Hope, and Justice* (Maryknoll, NY: Orbis Books, 1993), 121.

## 76:4–10 THE AWESOME WARRIOR GOD

This section shifts from third person ("God is known in Judah," v. 1) to second person direct address to God ("You are radiant with light," v. 4). The second person perspective continues through verse 8 ("you pronounced judgment"), then shifts back to the third person in verse 9 ("When God arose"). In verse 10, the perspective returns to address God ("the wrath of man shall praise You").

These shifting perspectives serve as structural markers, since verses 4 and 8 are both followed by accounts of God's awesome power. Verses 5–6 portray how helpless powerful men are before the awesome power of God, recalling God's victory over the ancient Egyptians.[7] In response to the manifestation of God's power, the psalmist declares, "It is you alone who are to be feared" (v. 7). This is a much-needed warning to arrogant and wicked people who continue to strike terror among God's people, especially the weak.

In verse 7, the psalmist transports us to the heavens, where God pronounces judgment: "From heaven you pronounce judgment" (v. 8). This anticipates Psalm 82, which depicts God taking his stand in the council of the gods in order to judge, and also indicates the close link between heaven and earth. What is done in heaven has an effect on earth. In Psalm 76, "the land feared and was quiet" (v. 8b).

The silence signifies that we are in the climax of the psalm, the memory of when God rose up to save the poor (v. 9). The powerful human warriors are no match for God, who is described as radiant with light (v. 4) and one to be feared (v. 7), but God's concern is for the weak and afflicted, his power for the powerless, his presence for the abandoned.[8]

## 76:11–12 EXHORTATION

In the last section of the psalm, the psalmist uses the second person perspective to address his audience with an exhortation. This pattern is similar to the thanksgiving psalms, where the psalmist recounts what God has done and then

---

7. The word "rebuke" (v. 6), according to Ollenburger, "is used frequently in the Jerusalem cult tradition to indicate Yahweh's conquest of chaos in creation." Ben C. Ollenburger, *Zion the City of the Great King: A Theological Symbol of the Jerusalem Cult* (Sheffield: Sheffield Academic Press, 1987), 73.

8. The text of verse 10 is problematic. Emerton's proposal based on his reconstruction is "Surely thou dost crush the wrath of man: Thou dost restrain the remnant of wrath." John A. Emerton, "Neglected Solution of a Problem in Psalm 76:11," *VT* 24, no. 2 (1974): 145. Compare Hossfeld and Zenger, *Psalms 2*, 259: "Indeed, burning human wrath will/must praise you. The remnant of wrath will/must celebrate you."

## Psalm 76

turns to his audience. This reflects the communal aspect of our experience of God. When we experience God's awesome power, we want to share it with others. This is part of the idea of the exhortation, but the primary focus is on the people's response to God's awesome power. They are to bring their vows, which they promised to bring to the Lord once God answered their petitions. Note that there is no mention of the temple, and even the "neighboring lands" are invited to bring their gifts to "the One to be feared" (v. 11).

With the ascription, "the One to be feared," we remember God's actions over his enemies. He destroys the "spirit of rulers" (v. 12a), and kings are afraid of him (v. 12b). These references add a political flavor to the psalm. Because God's action extends from heaven to earth, everyone witnesses it. As Hossfeld and Zenger describe it, "The heavenly scenery of this proclamation of judgment also enables it to be heard by everyone everywhere – by the poor *and* by their oppressors, by the victims *and* the perpetrators!"[9]

---

9. Hossfeld and Zenger, *Psalms 2*, 270.

# PSALM 77

In the aftermath of Typhoon Yolanda (international name: Haiyan), newspapers printed a photo of a woman standing in front of the ruins of a chapel after the typhoon devastated the city of Tacloban. Alone and soaked in the rain, the woman's face is turned towards the place where the altar had stood. This image captures the persistent faith of Psalm 77. Within the context of the destruction of the Temple (Psalm 74)[1] and the aftermath of exile, Psalm 77 testifies to the unwavering faith of the people. Despite the continuing absence of divine intervention, the psalmist persists in his faith and declares that he will "remember the deeds of the Lord" (v. 11), even as he laments the absence of God's remembrance of his own people. This faith is similar to the faith of Daniel's three friends, after Nebuchadnezzar threatens to throw them into the fire, and they reply that even if God does not save them, they will not bow down to the god of the Babylonians. Even without God's response, the psalmist declares that he will "remember" the things God has done (v. 11), which is a way of saying, "I trust in God."

The first half of this prayer is a lament (vv. 1–10), and the second half is a hymnic recollection of God's previous acts (vv. 11–20). There is no clear transition from the lament to the hymn, and there is no divine response – only the persistence of the psalmist to "remember" (v. 11). One possible purpose of recollecting God's previous acts of deliverance is to petition God to repeat his saving action in the present situation. In this way, the lament continues through the hymnic portion of the psalm, but the juxtaposition of lament and hymn creates tension. The word "remember" is repeated in verses 3 and 6 in the first section and in verse 11 in the second section, which contrasts the human response with the divine response. While the psalmist "remembers" God's faithfulness, one wonders if God will remember his promises. Katanacho's rendering of Psalm 77 captures this aspect of the lament: "Will you forget us while we remember you?"[2]

At the beginning of Psalm 74, the psalmist pleads with God to "remember" his people (v. 2), and then later asks God to "remember" what his enemies did (v. 18). Psalm 74 does not end with a divine response, but rather pleas

---

1. On a discussion of the canonical link between Psalms 73–78, see Smith, "The Shape and Message of Psalms 73–78."
2. Katanacho, *Praying through the Psalms*, 153.

that God will "not ignore" what the people's enemies are doing (v. 23). Read in this context, Psalm 77 picks up where Psalm 74 ends:

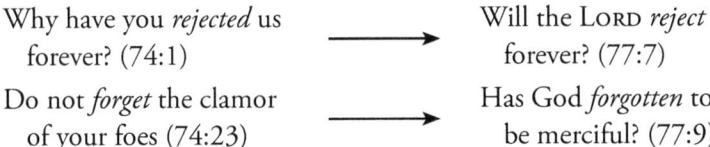

| Why have you *rejected* us forever? (74:1) | → | Will the LORD *reject* forever? (77:7) |
| Do not *forget* the clamor of your foes (74:23) | → | Has God *forgotten* to be merciful? (77:9) |

The psalmist's feeling of rejection and abandonment by God is even more painful in the lament of Psalm 77, but through the declaration, "I will remember" (v. 11), the emphasis falls on the psalmist's faithful and resolute response.

## 77:1–10 LAMENT: "MY SOUL REFUSES TO BE COMFORTED"

Psalm 77 begins with the words, "I cry aloud to God" (v. 1, ESV). The verb "cry aloud" comes from the Hebrew word *tsaʿaq*, which is used in desperate contexts of bitter lament, as when Esau learns that his brother Jacob has deceived him (Gen 27:34), or when the Israelites find themselves caught between the raging armies of Pharaoh and the sea (Exod 17:4).

---

### A WORD FOR LAMENT IN FILIPINO

In Filipino, the word for lament means "a loud cry" (*panaghoy*),[1] and the name of the biblical book, Lamentations, is *"Mga Panaghoy."* The word *"panaghoy"* comes from the word *"taghoy,"* which means "a loud cry." This fits in with the Hebrew in verse 1, where the phrase, "my voice to God," is repeated twice.

---

1. Other Filipino words for lament are *daing* and *panambitan*.

---

Verse 1 literally reads, "My voice to God, I cry aloud, my voice to God," with the verb "to cry aloud" (*tsaʿaq*) forming an ellipsis. Thus the translation, "I cry aloud to God . . . I cry out to God." The repetition indicates the intensity of the psalmist's intention to cry loud enough so that God will hear him (Ps 77:1b).

Yet the emphasis in Psalm 77 is not on God's response, but human determination.[3] Verse 2 consists of three lines. The first line narrates how the psalmist sought the Lord in his time of distress: "When I was in distress, I sought the LORD." Elsewhere, this statement is used to describe how God intervened, where the words "and he answered me" come after the distressed cry (see Pss 34:4; 120:1). But here, there is no answer from above. Instead of the hand of God reaching down to the psalmist, the second line depicts the outstretched hand of the psalmist beseeching God: "I stretched out untiring hands." The lifted hand is a posture of prayer (Ps 28:2), but this hand is "stretched out." The Hebrew word for this verb (*nagar*) usually means "to pour out," so some commentators think the verse is talking about tears being poured out of the psalmist. But the text is clearly referring to the "hand." This may suggest the ancient form of wailing, where the hand moves up and down to express intense suffering. The description "untiring" hands in this second line expresses determination. The third line in verse 2 reiterates the persistence of the psalmist, who insists, "my soul refuses to be comforted" (v. 2c). This language throughout this verse reflects contexts of lament and mourning (see Lamentations).

Verse 3 begins with the psalmist saying, "I remember God," but instead of experiencing relief, the psalmist "groaned" and his "spirit grew faint" (v. 3). His remembrance of God does not bring comfort, but makes him so troubled that he cannot speak (v. 4). Why does his remembrance fail to bring comfort? As he recalls the "former days, the years of long" (v. 5), he realizes how God showed his power among his people, but this is no longer true in his time. Verse 10b is better translated, "the changing of the right hand of the Most High," as the "right hand" is the symbol of God's power. But the psalmist no longer sees any manifestations of God's power, and so he grieves. Verse 10a is better translated, "my grief is this."[4] He has a *tampo* (hurt feelings) with God (see Psalm 73 for a discussion of the Filipino concept of *tampo*).

Whereas the author of Psalm 73 goes to the Temple to process his grief, the psalmist here remembers his "song in the night" (v. 6). The word "night" is mentioned in verse 2 (it is night when the psalmist stretches out untiring hands), but in verse 6, the "song in the night" is a song of lament.

---

3. Though verses 13–20 refer to the mighty works of God, they are the result of the psalmist's remembering. There is no indication in the text that God answers the psalmist's lament. The initiative is all by the psalmist.
4. Tate, *Psalms 51–100*, 270.

Verses 7–9 reflect the content of this song of lament. Each verse begins with the interrogative particle *ha*, which indicates a question in Hebrew:

[*ha*] "Will the Lord reject forever?
   Will he never show his favor again?" (v. 7).
[*ha*] "Has his unfailing love vanished forever?
   Has his promise failed for all time?" (v. 8).
[*ha*] "Has God forgotten to be merciful?
   Has he in anger withheld his compassion?" (v. 9).

This pattern of three-fold questions also occurs in Psalm 88:10–12:

[*ha*] "Do you show your wonders to the dead?
   Do their spirits rise up and praise you?" (v. 10).
[*ha*] "Is your love declared in the grave,
   your faithfulness in Destruction?" (v. 11).
[*ha*] "Are your wonders known in the place of darkness,
   or your righteous deeds in the land of oblivion?" (v. 12).

The lament intensifies as it moves from one question to the next, with the third being the most distressing. These three verses in Psalm 77 express the depth of the psalmist's agony and act as a sort of bookend for the lament in Psalm 74 by repeating the keywords "reject" (*zanakh*) (74:1; 77:7) and "forget" (*shakach*) (74:23; 77:9).

## 77:11–20 "I WILL CONTINUE TO REMEMBER EVEN IF GOD DOES NOT"

The keyword, "remember," from verse 3 ("I remember God," ESV) and verse 6 ("I remember my song in the night," my translation) is repeated twice in verse 11:

"I will remember the deeds of the Lord. . . I will remember
   your miracles."

In both the earlier accounts, the result of the psalmist's remembering is not positive. The psalmist groans and becomes restless (vv. 3–4), and his song in the night (v. 6) is a dark lament comparable to Psalm 88. Verse 9 expresses a dramatically bitter lament, "Has God forgotten to be merciful?" (compare Lam 2:2). Daffern notes that it is rare, or at least unexpected, for God to forget: "while sinful humans may be expected on occasion to forget or fail to remember, for God – the primary agent of memory – to forget is truly striking and indeed lamentable."[5]

At this point in the psalm, it would have been encouraging if God had said, "I will remember." But the psalmist's bitter laments remain unanswered, and yet the psalmist persists in his faith. Even if God does not remember, the psalmist insists, "I will remember the deeds of the LORD" (v. 11). For the first time in the psalm, the psalmist uses the covenant name, "Yahweh," which is followed by a direct address: "I will remember *your* miracles of long ago" (v. 11, emphasis mine). Throughout the first half of the psalm, God is referred to in the third person, but here the psalmist speaks directly to God: "Your ways are holy" (v. 13). Although the psalmist says, "I will remember," it is as if he is trying to remind God of his faithful actions to his people:

- "You are the God who performs miracles; *you* display *your* power among the peoples" (v. 14).
- "With *your* mighty arm *you* redeemed *your* people . . ." (v. 15).

The background for verses 16–18 is the ancient story of the conflict in the Egyptian sea, where God led his people into freedom from slavery. In Psalm 77, the sea is depicted as a monster that is defeated by the deity (see comments in Ps 74:12–17), and Yahweh is presented as a mighty warrior from whom the powerful forces of the sea flee. Even the "very depths were convulsed" (v. 16). The psalmist employs the ancient tradition of the conflict at sea to remember what God did in the exodus by leading his people "like a flock by the hand of Moses and Aaron" (v. 20).

---

5. Megan I. J. Daffern, "The Semantic Field of 'Remembering' in the Psalms," *JSOT* 41, no. 1 (2016): 96.

# PSALM 78

We have a saying in Filipino: "Those who do not know how to look back will not reach their destination."[1] Psalm 78 "looks back" (vv. 12–72), but like the other "historical" psalms, it does not review the past for its own sake. Rather, as Gärtner says, "The historical psalms are concerned with interpreted history for the immediate situation of the petitioners."[2] The Filipino word for history – *kasaysayan* – comes from the word *saysay* (sense, meaning, relevance). History (*kasaysayan*), according to Salazar, has *kahulugan* (meaning), *katuturan* (sense), and *kabuluhan* (relevance).[3] We look back in order to make sense of the present and so we can learn from the past.

Looking back is an important part of teaching. The first part of Psalm 78 (vv. 1–11), emphasizes teaching and belongs to the "wisdom" genre. Though there is no accurate scholarly definition of the "wisdom" genre, its main purpose "is to help the next generation gain insight and understanding."[4] The original historical setting for Psalm 77 has been debated. Some place the psalm in the monarchical period while others locate it during the Persian period. Though we do not know the exact time period when the psalm was composed, we do know that it was collected along with the other psalms during the exilic/post-exilic period. This is a valid horizon from which to interpret the psalm, where the situation is one of crisis and suffering.

What can the people learn from their own history to interpret their present reality? In Psalm 78, the speaker is presented as a wisdom teacher, who emphasizes the importance of remembering. The people need to remember what God has done in the past so that they will "put their trust in God and . . . not forget his deeds" (v. 7). Psalm 77 provides a model for what it means to "remember," for the psalmist determines to remember God's past wonders even when such miracles are absent in the present.[5] To "remember," is to believe, and so one's heart has to be firmly established in God (see v. 8 and

---

1. *Ang hindi marunong tumanaw sa pinanggalingan hindi makararating sa paroroonan.*
2. Judith Gärtner, "The Historical Psalms: A Study of Psalms 78; 105; 106; 135, and 136 as Key Hermeneutical Texts in the Psalter," *Hebrew Bible and Ancient Israel* 4, no. 4 (2015): 374.
3. Zeus Salazar, "Ang Pantayong Pananaw sa Agham Panlipunan," in *Pantayong Pananaw: Ugat at Kabuluhan*, ed. Atoy Navarro, Mary Jane Rodriguez, and Vicente Villan (Diliman, Lungsod Quezon [Manila]: Palimbang ng Lahi, 2000), 71.
4. Rebecca Whitten Poe Hays, "Trauma, Remembrance, and Healing: The Meeting of Wisdom and History in Psalm 78," *JSOT* 41, no. 2 (2016): 185.
5. The link between the two psalms is supported by the similarities of the beginning and end of both psalms (see comments on vv. 1 and 72 below).

v. 37 below). The psalmist's forefathers, however, "did not remember [God's] power" (literally, "his hand," v. 42). Thankfully, as the following outline shows, the story does not end with the people's failure to remember, but with God's compassion (vv. 38–39, 65–72):

> Introduction (vv. 1–11)
> Wilderness (vv. 12–39)
>   God's miraculous acts (vv. 12–16)
>   People's rebellion (vv. 17–20)
>   God's anger and judgment (vv. 21–31)
>   People's sin (vv. 32–37)
>   God's compassion (vv. 38–39)
> Egypt to Canaan (vv. 40–64)
>   People's rebellion (vv. 40–42)
>   God's miraculous acts (vv. 43–55)
>     In Egypt (vv. 43–51)
>     To Canaan (vv. 52–55)
>   People's sin (vv. 56–58)
>   God's anger and judgment (vv. 59–64)
> God's compassion and divine actions (vv. 65–72)

## 78:1–11 INTRODUCTION: "GIVE EAR THAT YOU WILL NOT FORGET"

Psalm 78 begins with a call for the people to "hear": "Give ear, O my people" (78:1, ESV). To "give ear" also means to do something, to act. The verb "give ear" (*'azan*) also occurs at the beginning of Psalm 77, where the psalmist says that he has cried out to God so that God will hear (*'azan*) him. Prayer is an expression of one's dependence on God, but "prayer without action is dead." We tend to overemphasize dependence on God to the point of minimizing or totally disregarding our human responsibility. But as a Filipino saying puts it, "With God belongs mercy, but action belongs to humans" (*Nasa Diyos ang awa, nasa tao ang gawa*).

Armed with a sense of responsibility, the speaker declares to his audience all the "things we have heard and known, things our ancestors have told us" (v. 3). The tone is similar to the opening of the Apostle John's letter: "That which . . . we have heard, which we have seen with our own eyes, . . . we proclaim to you . . ." (1 John 1:1–3). The psalmist insists that "we will not hide them from their descendants," but "will tell the next generation" (78:4). The verbal form of the verb "to tell" (*safar*) indicates continuing action.[6]

The people are to declare three things (v. 4): first, the praiseworthy deeds of the Lord; second, his power; third, his wonders. In short, they are to remember all the things that God has done for them out of his pure grace. Right after mentioning the wonderful things that God has done, the psalmist introduces the covenant (v. 5). Because the covenant is introduced in the context of God's gracious acts, keeping the commands in the Law is understood as the appropriate response to God's gracious initiatives. Thus the psalmist emphasizes both the Law and what God has done. The juxtaposition of "his deeds" with "his commands" in verse 7 makes this clear: "Then they would put their trust in God and would not forget *his deeds* but would keep *his commands*" (emphasis mine).

The word "forget" and its related word, "remember," both function as key terms in this psalm. They should continue to declare to the people what God has done so that they and subsequent generations will "not forget" (v. 7). The people must continually "remember" what God has done so that they will not be like their forefathers, who did not keep God's commands (v. 10) and who "forgot what he had done" (v. 11). The psalmist refers to that generation as a generation "whose hearts were not loyal to God" (v. 8). The words "not loyal" come from the Hebrew word *kun*, which means "not established" or "not steadfast." Alongside the word "heart," it means "to be firmly resolved."[7] The wicked people, however, are *not* established, but are like chaff, which the wind drives away (Psalm 1). Sadly, this was also characteristic of God's people in Psalm 78 – and it continues to be true of some of God's people today.

## 78:12–20 GOD'S GRACIOUS ACTS AND THE PEOPLE'S REBELLION

In the previous section, the psalmist mentions the "wonders" that God "has done" (v. 4). In this section, he summarizes these acts in a general way:

- the crossing of the Red Sea (v. 13),
- the pillar of cloud by day and fire by night (v. 14),
- water from the rock (vv. 15–16).

---

6. *Safar* (to tell) is a participle in Hebrew.
7. *HALOT*, 2:465.

God performed all these wonders "in the sight of their ancestors" (v. 12). The word "in the sight of" (*neged*) is the first Hebrew word in verse 12 and is deliberately placed to highlight how God has done all these miracles right before the eyes of their fathers. Their fathers have seen these things with their very own eyes.

And yet, the people still "continued to sin . . . rebelling in the wilderness against the Most High" (v. 17). Witnessing miracles is not a guarantee that one will change or place one's trust in God. Even in the NT, many people saw the miracles that Jesus did, but Jesus himself did "not entrust himself to them . . . for he knew what was in each person" (John 2:23–25). Despite all the miracles that God has done "in the sight of" the Israelites, they continue to doubt God's power. Even more troubling, they want to use God's power to meet their own desires. Because their hearts are "not established" (v. 8), they continue to yearn for their own satisfaction and demand "the food they craved" (v. 18).[8]

What a person asks, especially in times of need, shows a lot about one's heart. In the desert, one is happy as long as there is enough food to last the journey. But here the people are asking for a feast in the middle of the desert. In this place of scarcity, they are craving luxury. Earlier, the psalmist recounts how God "gave them water as abundant as the seas" (v. 15). Now, they are asking God to do the same with the food. "Can God really spread a table in the wilderness?" they grumble (v. 19). "Can he supply meat for his people?" (v. 20).

## 78:21–31 GOD'S ANGER AND DIVINE JUDGMENT

So God opens the "doors of heaven" and rains down manna (vv. 23–24), which the psalmist describes as the "bread of angels." God also rains down meat from heaven by setting loose the east wind and causing the south wind to blow by "his power" (v. 26). The description "by his power" recalls the great miracle of the exodus (Exod 15:13). The people can never say that all of these miracles are mere coincidences, for God ensures that the birds are all right there, "inside their camp" (literally, "in the midst of their camp," v. 28; compare v. 12).

But even though God miraculously provides for the people's cravings, the careful reader knows that something is amiss. The whole account of the miracle of provision is told from the perspective of divine judgment, with God's "anger" bookending the section (vv. 21, 31). In verse 21, God's "wrath

---

8. The Hebrew word *nephesh* can be translated here as "for themselves." but it "may also refer to desire, emotions, and appetite." Tate, *Psalms 51–100*, 282.

[*'af*] rose against Israel." Then verses 23–30 recount God's miracle of raining down manna and meat from heaven. And yet again, "God's anger [*'af*] rose against them" in verse 31.

The people are still satisfying their cravings when God's anger burns against them, and so God "put to death the sturdiest among them" (v. 31). The word "sturdiest" comes from a word that also means "fat" (*mishman*). The image of a fat person reminds us of some of the *prayle* (priest) during the Spanish colonization of the Philippines. While many Filipinos were dying of hunger, the *prayles* were fat and well-fed. God is angry that the people are craving more than they need while others can't even afford to have a little. As Saint Teresa puts it, "Live simply so that others can simply live."⁹

## 78:32–39 MERCY IN SPITE OF SINFULNESS

This section continues the theme of divine judgment and the people's sinfulness, though divine mercy breaks through. "In spite of all this" (God's miraculous provision and judgment), the psalmist states, "they kept on sinning" (v. 32; compare v. 17), and so God made their days end in futility (v. 33). The word "futility" comes from the Hebrew word *hebel*, which is translated as "vanity." Even with all the abundance and satisfaction, there is no meaning, sense, or value.

In verse 35, the psalmist acknowledges that the people "remembered" God, but only after experiencing death (v. 34). They only remember God because they need him, much like an emergency prescription we keep in our medicine cabinet. They confess belief in God, but only with their lips; their hearts remain unestablished. Literally, verse 37 reads, "their heart was not established with him" (compare v. 8).

Then rather surprisingly, mercy rains down from heaven like manna: "Yet he was merciful" (v. 38). God forgives their sins and restrains his anger. Earlier, the people remember God as "their Rock" (v. 35), which suggests stability, firmness, and permanence. But when God remembers his people in verse 39, he remembers that they are "but flesh." Unlike "rock," "flesh" speaks of impermanence, frailty, and weakness.

---

9. See https://www.goodreads.com/quotes/4391-live-simply-so-others-may-simply-live; accessed February 16, 2022.

## 78:40–58 "NO DEBT OF GRATITUDE"

Ironically, though humans are mere flesh, they are able to inflict pain on God and cause God to grieve. For the psalmist cries out, "How often they rebelled against him in the wilderness and grieved him in the wasteland!" (v. 40; compare v. 58). The verb translated as "grieved" comes from the Hebrew word *'atsab*, which means "to hurt someone's feelings"[10] or "to cause pain."[11] One would think that humans, as mere "flesh," would realize their limitations and see their need of God. On the contrary, they rebel against God and fail to "remember his power" (v. 42), which causes God much pain. Thus the need for the people to recollect their history so that they will *remember* what God has done.

### REMEMBRANCE OF GOD'S FAITHFULNESS AND *UTANG NA LOOB* (DEBT OF GRATITUDE)

Remembrance is an important discipline, because remembering God's faithfulness is connected to believing and trusting in God himself. When we remember, we look back to our "debt of gratitude," which we call *utang na loob* in Filipino. *Utang na loob* results when someone who is in deep trouble experiences an act of kindness from another person. When we consider an act to be *utang na loob*, we are forever indebted to the other person, and we will never forget their act of kindness in times of need. *Utang na loob* is highly valued in Philippine society, and so a failure to remember would make one *walang utang na loob* (no debt of gratitude), which is one of the worst possible character traits.

The psalmist recalls the many "debts of gratitude" that Israel should have remembered of their God. Foremost are the "signs and wonders" he performed in Egypt (vv. 43–51). Psalm 78 only cites seven of the ten plagues: 1) turning the rivers into blood (v. 44), 2) the swarm of flies (v. 45), 3) frogs (v. 45), 4) grasshoppers (v. 46), 5) locusts (v. 46), 6) hail and lightning (v. 47), and 7) the killing of the firstborn (v. 51). Though this list differs in arrangement when compared with the account in Exodus 7–12 (compare Psalm 105), the purpose of recounting the miracles is not to give a complete, orderly, comprehensive list, but to remind the people about how God manifested his power

---

10. *HALOT*, 2:864.
11. *BDB*, 780.

> for their sake and how he unleashed his wrath against the Egyptians in the process of bringing them out of Egypt. This portrayal contrasts sharply with how God deals with Israel in verses 52–55, where God is a good shepherd, who leads his flock (v. 52) and guides them to safety even while their enemies are being swallowed by the sea (v. 53). By his "right hand" (v. 54; compare 77:10), God brings them to the "border of the holy land" and then drives out nations in the land, just as he promised, so that they could settle there (v. 55).

This whole section (vv. 40–55) recalls how God graciously and powerfully acted for his people by leading them out of Egypt, through the desert, and into the Promised Land. Though it behooves the people to remember these acts as their debt of gratitude, they do not remember what God has done for them (v. 42). Ungratefulness slips easily to rebellion, and so it should be no surprise that in verse 56, the people "rebelled against the Most High." The Filipino word *pandaraya* (treachery) captures the meaning[12] of the people's sin in the desert. The psalmist says that they "acted treacherously like their fathers" (v. 57). Having failed to fulfill their debt of gratitude (*walang utang na loob*), they go to other gods and begin worshiping idols in the "high places" (v. 58).

## 78:59–64 JUDGMENT STARTS IN THE HOUSEHOLD OF GOD

In the previous section, the people's ungratefulness brings pain to God (v. 40b). Yet their continuing rebellion and sin angers God so much so that he becomes "furious" (v. 59). First, God pours out his anger by abandoning Shiloh (v. 60), which is the place where the people met with God prior to building the Temple and where the priest, Eli, and later Samuel ministered (1 Sam 1:9; 3:1). Shiloh is supposed to be the place where God is present, and so this act of abandonment is a grave judgment. Moreover, the fact that Shiloh, the place of worship, became the center of the judgment reminds us that it is the sober responsibility of God's people to declare the works of God and to pass on the faith to the next generation. This reminder echoes the introduction of Psalm 78. If the people rebel or turn against God, the first to be judged are those who are responsible for the household of God (compare 1 Pet 4:17).

---

12. José M. De Mesa and De La Salle University Publishing House, *A Theological Reader* (2016), 354–362.

God's judgment is tragic. The ark is sent into captivity, young men and women are killed (v. 63), priests are put to death, and their widows cannot weep (v. 64). In ancient Israel, the act of weeping and lamenting over the death of a loved one was an important part of the religious custom and also provided a way for people to process grief. The inability to weep is a sign of hopelessness, as we see in Lamentations 2:10, where the "elders . . . sit on the ground in silence" and "young women . . . bowed their heads to the ground." The poet had to exhort them to "Arise, cry out in the night" (Lam 2:20).

## 78:65–72 DIVINE ANGER AND A NEW BEGINNING

In the previous section, God becomes very angry with his people and rejects them (v. 59). The verb "rejected" is modified by the adverb "very" or "utter" (from the Hebrew word *me'od*). Together, the phrase can be translated, "he utterly rejected them." Yet even though the text says that God "rejected Israel completely," he has not given up on them. The psalmist describes God as a man who has suddenly awakened from his sleep or who is overcome with wine (v. 65), and then the Lord rises up and strikes his enemies (v. 66).

In the desert, God actively led and guided his people, and here again, God initiates on behalf of his people. Having defeated their enemy (v. 66), he now sets to fix his "household," which is represented by the "tents of Joseph" and the "tribe of Ephraim" (v. 67), which represent the northern tribes. But God does not totally reject his people, for in their place he "chose the tribe of Judah" (v. 68). In place of the rejected sanctuary in Shiloh, God "built his sanctuary" (v. 69) on Mount Zion. After choosing the place of worship, "which He loved" (v. 68), the psalm mentions that God "chose David," who is described as "His servant," and how he "took him from the sheep pens, from tending the sheep . . . to be shepherd of his people" (vv. 70–71). When Jesus calls his disciples, he uses a similar pattern, saying that he has taken them from being fishermen to becoming "fishers of men" (Matt 4:19).

Psalm 77 ends with a recollection about how God led his people through Moses (v. 20). This psalm ends with God now leading his people through his servant, David, who will be a shepherd for his people. God has not given up on his people, but continues to lead them through his servants. Though this psalm remembers God's miraculous actions on behalf of his people, it also emphasizes human agency and responsibility. Our world today needs leaders who can guide people with "integrity of heart" and "skillful hands" (v. 72)!

# PSALM 79

Psalm 79 is written within the context of the exile, which was the most traumatic event for the people of Israel.[1] In order to deal with trauma, one has to go back to the past. As Herman explains, "Like traumatized people, we need to understand the past in order to reclaim the present and the future."[2] Psalm 78 exhorts us to remember the past to help us understand our present circumstances. Having done that, we still need to process our grief. According to Herman, recovery after trauma involves three steps:[3] first, establishing safety; second, reconstructing the trauma story (remembering and mourning); third, restoring the connection between survivors and their community.

Psalm 79 is concerned with the second step: remembering and mourning. Psalm 79 is a communal lament (see also Psalms 44, 74, 89), where the people come to God to pour out their heart (v. 3), reason with God (v. 5), plead for mercy (vv. 8–9), reason with God again (v. 10), and ask for justice (vv. 6–7, 11–12).

Psalm 79 may be outlined as follows:

Invocation (v. 1),
Complaint (vv. 1–5),
Petitions (vv. 6–12),
Declaration of trust (v. 13).

## 79:1–5 INVOCATION AND COMPLAINT

The images in Psalm 79 are traumatic: Jerusalem city is reduced to rubble (v. 1), dead bodies are left outside for the birds and wild animals to feed on (v. 2), and blood has been poured out like water (v. 3). Herman notes that in the midst of extreme suffering and trauma, "people spontaneously seek their first source of comfort and protection. Wounded soldiers and raped women cry for their mothers, or for God."[4] In Psalm 79, the people go to God. The very first word in Psalm 79 is "God." In the midst of their continuing trauma, the people have someone to go to – God. A study shows that the number one coping mechanism among Filipinos in times of disaster is prayer and

---
1. Samuel E. Balentine, "Legislating Divine Trauma," 163.
2. Herman, *Trauma and Recovery*, 2.
3. Herman, *Trauma and Recovery*, 155.
4. Herman, *Trauma and Recovery*, 52.

spirituality.⁵ Karl Gaspar observes that in the aftermath of Typhoon Yolanda, the people come to God with their lamentations.⁶

Like the disciples of Jesus, who cried out to him because the waters were coming into their boat (Matt 8:25), so the people lament, "O God, the nations have invaded your inheritance" (v. 1). God drove out the nations and allotted their lands as an inheritance to Israel (78:54–55), but now the nations have returned to take back their land. Three words from Psalm 78 reoccur in Psalm 79:1: "nations" (*goyim*, 78:55), "inheritance" (*nahalah*, 78:55), and "invaded" (*bo'*, 78:54).

The people emphasize that their land is "your inheritance," where "your" is emphatic: "*your* inheritance" (v. 1), "*your* holy temple" (v. 1), "*your* servants" (v. 2), and *your* faithful (v. 2, ESV). The destruction and devastation are a very serious matter, because the nations have defiled God's temple. They have poured out the blood of God's precious people all around Jerusalem, which recalls the blood of the animal sacrifices being poured out around the altar. For the psalmist, the death of God's servant is costly (116:15). Even more painfully, they have been put to shame because the bodies of the dead have been left outside to be eaten by birds and wild animals. As Lemos observes, "Shame is above all visual and public."⁷ Thus the people lament, "We are objects of contempt to our neighbors" (v. 4).

This experience of shame leads to a bitter cry of lament: "How long, Lord?" (v. 5). As the blood of the servants of God has been poured out, so the people pour out their hearts to God, just as Lamentations 2:19 instructs: "pour out your heart like water in the presence of the Lord." The people become honest to God about what they really feel and think. They cannot understand how God can allow his people to suffer in this way because they are God's inheritance. They also feel that God's punishment has gone on for too long. Thus they ask, "how long?"

---

5. Lourdes Ladrido-Ignacio, "Basic Framework: Transformation of Victims of Disasters to Survivors," in *Ginhawa: Well-Being in the Aftermath of Disasters*, ed. Lourdes Ladrido-Ignacio (Philippine Psychiatrists Association and World Association for Psychosocial Rehabilitation, 2011), 47.
6. Karl M. Gaspar, *Desperately Seeking God's Saving Action: Yolanda Survivors' Hope Beyond Heartbreaking Lamentations* (Quezon City, Philippines: Institute of Spirituality in Asia, 2014), xix.
7. T. M. Lemos, "Shame and Mutilation of Enemies in the Hebrew Bible," *JBL* 125, no. 2 (2006): 228, quoting David D. Gilmore.

# Psalm 79

## 79:6–13 PETITIONS

Having expressed their lament, the people ask God to pour out his wrath on "the nations that do not acknowledge you" (v. 6). The word "poured out" (*shapak*) comes from the same word used in verse 3 (referring to the blood of the people being poured out). The people demand justice, because their enemies have "devoured Jacob" (v. 7). The verb "devoured" is an appropriate description for the trauma described in verses 1–4.

In verse 8, the people acknowledge that their forefathers have sinned terribly, but then they quickly appeal to God's mercy in light of their desperate situation: "may your mercy come quickly to meet us, for we are in desperate need" (v. 8). Though they remember the "sins of the past generations" (literally, "former sins," v. 8), and they refer to "*our* sins" (v. 9), they also know that throughout their history, God's mercy persists in spite of their sinfulness (see 78:38–39).

However, they make their appeal not only on the basis of God's mercy and their dire situation, but also for God himself – his own glory, his very name. There is a progression from "for the glory of your name" to "for your name's sake" (v. 9). God's name represents his very nature, and so, according to the argument of the people, the shame is not only of the people, but also God himself, his own glory. Their continuing situation has implications for God, for "Why should the nations say, 'Where is their God?'" (v. 10). Their appeal to God is similar to what Moses did when confronted with the threat of God's destruction of the Israelites. He argued, "Why should the Egyptians say, 'It was with evil intent that he brought them out, to kill them . . . and to wipe them off the face of the earth'?" (Exod 32:12).

Because God's own glory is at stake, the people ask God for vengeance twice (vv. 10, 12). In verse 10, they ask God to "avenge the outpoured blood of your servants" (v. 10b). The "outpoured blood" recalls verse 4. Then they ask God's vengeance to be done "before our eyes" (v. 10b). Just as they have experienced shame before their enemies, they want their enemies to experience shame before them. Moreover, they ask God to "pay back into the laps of our neighbors seven times the contempt they have hurled at you, Lord" (v. 12).

How are we to understand this prayer for vengeance? (For more discussion about this topic, see the comments in Psalms 83 and 137 below.) First, to understand such prayer, one has to bear in mind that the people who did this to the Israelites did not know God (v. 6), were ruthless (v. 7), and were extremely violent (vv. 2–3). Second, the prayer for vengeance arises from the context of groaning, pain, and death. In between the two demands for vengeance, the psalm mentions the "groans of the prisoners" and those "condemned to die" (v. 11). Third, the prayer for vengeance is part of the process of pouring out one's heart to God. While the people are honest enough to articulate these thoughts in the presence of God, this does not mean that they represent the ultimate perspective of the people. Moreover, God does not answer such prayers for vengeance just because people pray them. Fourth, the Babylonian exile is certainly a crisis. A crucial element in a crisis is one's identity, which "can threaten the very sense of group identity itself."[8] Psalm 79 is one of the attempts by the people to maintain their identity by making sure that they keep their identity as the people of God alive. Because of the people's covenant relationship with God, they have to keep asserting their identity with God ("we your people, the sheep of your pasture," v. 13), empowering themselves, and voicing their thoughts, concerns, and ideas to God.

For Christians, the most challenging aspect of this prayer for vengeance is the praise at the end: "we . . . will praise you forever" (v. 13). How can we praise God for destroying or defeating other people?

---

8. Daniel L. Smith, *The Religion of the Landless: The Social Context of the Babylonian Exile* (Bloomington: Meyer-Stone Books, 1989), 52.

# PSALM 80

Some people attribute national disasters, such as the devastation caused by typhoons, to the sins of the people (see commentary on Psalm 74 above). When Typhoon Yolanda destroyed Tacloban, one of the prayers of the survivors was *patawarin mo kami* (forgive us).[1] While Scripture – and the psalms in particular – teach us about the consequences of sin (see Psalm 78), it also gives us space to express and lament our experiences of pain and suffering. Some of the words we utter may contradict Scripture or the teaching and theology we have received, yet God invites us to pour out our hearts honestly before him. The honest pouring out of the heart to God in words of lament which we see in Psalm 80 provides a corrective to an overemphasis on sin in response to disaster.

Though Psalm 80 was written in response to a national disaster, there is no explicit admission of sin or repentance on the part of the people. While the refrain, "restore us," is repeated three times, the emphasis is not on repentance or spiritual restoration, but rather deliverance from the enemies who have ravaged the people's land. In Psalm 80, the community questions God's actions as if Psalm 78 does not exist. One of the main points of argument advanced in Psalm 78 is that the people's sinfulness and rebellion has caused them to suffer from their enemies. Psalm 80 mentions that God "transplanted a vine from Egypt" (v. 8), referring to Israel. The use of the imagery of Israel as God's vine (80:8) recalls Isaiah 5, which expresses God's disappointment over his vine. For instead of bearing good fruit, Israel only produced "bad fruit" (Isa 5:2). So God declared judgment against his vine (Isa 5:5–6). But instead of simply accepting the actions of God, the people in Psalm 80 ask God "why?" Why would God plant a vineyard, cause it to grow, and then break down "its walls" (v. 12)? If Isaiah 5 expresses God's disappointment over Israel, Psalm 80 articulates the people's feelings of *tampo* (hurt feelings; see commentary on Psalms 73) or *sama ng loob*" (ill feelings) about God's action.

Instead of censuring this reproach of God, Psalm 80 creates space for it, teaching us that asking for forgiveness is not the only acceptable response to God when we face calamities, for God invites us to speak our minds and be honest about our true feelings. Psalm 80 is a communal lament, and like many laments, it does not stop with complaining, but asks God for restoration. The

---

1. Gaspar, *Desperately Seeking God's Saving Action*, 109.

refrain, "Restore us, O God," is repeated three times (vv. 3, 7, 19). The word "restore" also occurs in verse 14. This verse may have also formed a refrain, but it has been shortened to serve a purpose (see commentary on this verse below). Psalm 80 may be outlined as follows:

> Invocation and petition (vv. 1–3),
> Complaint: "How long?" (vv. 4–7),
> Complaint: "Why?" (vv. 8–13),
> Petitions (vv. 14–19).

## 80:1–3 INVOCATION AND PETITION

The invocation (v. 1) is unusually elaborate, with three ascriptions to God: "Shepherd of Israel," "you who lead Joseph," and "You who sit enthroned." The invocation in Psalm 79 simply says, "O God" (79:1; compare 83:1). In Hebrew, the three ascriptions in Psalm 80 are in participial form, conveying God's continuing action as "one who shepherds," "one who leads," and "one who sits enthroned." The first two ascriptions echo previous psalms. Regarding the first, Psalm 28 mentions David as the one who "shepherded" God's people (v. 72). Psalm 79 ends with an assertion of the people's identity as the sheep of God's own pasture (v. 13). Picking up on this theme, Psalm 80 appeals to the "Shepherd of Israel," God himself. The direct appeal to the "Shepherd of Israel" signals the severity of the people's situation, for "the sheep" of God's "pasture" do not want Moses, Aaron, or David, but God himself (79:13). The second ascription ("You who lead Joseph") is parallel to the first and echoes Psalm 77, which cites God as the one who "led your people . . . by the hand of Moses and Aaron" (v. 20).

However, the third ascription ("you who sit enthroned") belongs to a different sphere. While the first two ascriptions communicate God's nearness (or in theological terms, God's immanence), the third communicates God's transcendence. The NIV translates this ascription, "You who sit enthroned between the cherubim" (v. 1). In Hebrew, this verse consists of two words, "one who sits" and "cherubim," and so the NIV supplies the word "between." Cherubim are associated with the ark of the covenant, which is believed to be the earthly throne of Yahweh.[2] The cherubim serve as the throne guardians, which explains the translation in the NIV ("between the cherubim"). However,

---

2. John Walton, Mark W. Chavalas, and Victor Harold Matthews, *IVP Bible Background Commentary: Old Testament* (Leicester: Inter-Varsity, 2000), 542.

as Eichler demonstrates on grammatical and contextual grounds, the construction, "one who sits," when it is followed by an absolute noun, connotes the sense of "inhabitant of . . ." or "one who dwells in . . ." Thus the ascription should be translated, "one who dwells among the cherubim."[3] Cherubim are also associated with heavenly creatures, and so refer to God's transcendence, his distant realm in the heavens. The repetition of "God of hosts [*tseba'ot*]" (vv. 4, 7, 14, ESV) and the appeal to God to "look down from heaven" (v. 14) support this emphasis on transcendence in the third ascription. God is the people's shepherd, who leads them, but he is also the one who dwells in heaven. This understanding is also reflected in the Lord's Prayer, where God is addressed as "Our Father" who dwells "in heaven" (Matt 6:9).

But the situation in Psalm 80 focuses more on God's distance. The people are down on earth; God is far above the people in the heavens. The very first petition, "Shine forth," reflects the darkness that is enveloping the land because God is so far away. God seems to be sleeping, and so the people cry out, "Awaken your might; come and save us!" (v. 2).

In verse 3, the phrase, "restore us," appears, which will be repeated two more times in the psalm (see vv. 7, 19). A parallel line follows this phrase, asking God to "make your face shine on us" (see also vv. 14, 19). Earlier, the people ask God to "shine forth," and they make a similar request here. This petition is also used in the Aaronic blessing (Num 6:24–26), where the priest declares God's blessing upon the people. The use of this petition in Psalm 80, paired with the request for restoration, points to a very dark situation, where the light and life of the community are about to be extinguished.[4] Unless God does something to rekindle, restore, and breathe new life into the people, the flickering light will die.

## 80:4–7 COMPLAINT: "HOW LONG?"

Suffering, even if it is painful, is bearable when one knows it will end one day. But if the suffering goes on and on, seemingly without end, then it becomes more and more unbearable. This seems to be the people's experience in this psalm, as right after the refrain, they cry out, "How long, LORD God Almighty, will your anger smolder against the prayers of your people?" (v. 4). They know God is angry, because he continues to "smolder against" their prayers. Though they continue to cry out to God, God does not answer. Their experience is

---

3. Raanan Eichler, "The Meaning of הַכְּרֻבִים יֹשֵׁב," *ZAW* 126, no. 3 (2014): 358–371.
4. In Filipino, *aandap-andap na ang ilaw*.

similar to the people's experience in Lamentations: "You have covered yourself with a cloud so that no prayer can get through" (3:44).

The people are in an extremely difficult situation, which is made even worse by the fact that God has deliberately caused them to suffer: "You have fed them with the bread of tears" (v. 5). The language is similar to Psalm 42: "My tears have been my food . . . while people say to me all day long, 'Where is your God?'" (v. 3). "Bread of tears" (80:5) could be interpreted literally as the loss of appetite caused by suffering. On a more fundamental level, it could refer to the loss of the will to live, the loss of life itself. The people blame God for making them eat the "bread of tears" (v. 5), and, as in Psalm 42:3, their enemies taunt them (v. 6).

With the light of their life ebbing away, they plead to God for a second time, "Restore us, God of hosts" (v. 7, ESV). The refrain takes on its more complete form here, with the addition of the title, "Almighty" (or "God of hosts," ESV), whereas verse 3 simply says, "Restore us, O God."

### 80:8–14 COMPLAINT: "WHY?"

In this section, the community recalls their history by employing a parable that is similar to Ezekiel 17:1–10 (see also Ezek 19:10–14). They liken themselves to a vine in order to drive home their central complaint to God, saying, "you transplanted" this vine from Egypt and then "drove out nations and planted it" (v. 8). This verse recalls Psalm 78:55 (where God also "drove out nations" from the land so that they could settle there), but their recollection of God's action is not followed by an account of the people's rebellion. Instead, they linger on the metaphor of the vine, talking about how the vine "took root and filled the land" (v. 9). In verse 8, God was actively involved ("you transplanted . . ."), but in verses 9b–11, the subject shifts to the vine, whose achievement is remarkable. Its shade covers the mountains, even the mighty cedars (v. 10), and its reach is extensive – "as far as the Sea . . . [and] the River" (v. 11).

So "why?" the people ask, "have you broken down its walls [hedges]?" (v. 12). This lament is difficult to comprehend when read in the light of Psalm 78 and the historical recounting of Israel. Surely, the people know the answer to this question. To understand this lament, it is important to remember the people's long experience of exile. The people are not denying the role of their sin in God's abandonment, but they are complaining about the duration of their suffering. They have been praying to God, offering their prayers of repentance, and pleading for a long time, but God does not seem to be listening. If God is not listening, he must be angry with their prayers.

Meanwhile, their enemies continue to taunt them. The description "all who pass by" (v. 12) recalls Lamentations 1:12 ("Is it nothing to all you who pass this way?"). The people are in a vulnerable situation, without protection, and they are filled with shame. In verse 13, the psalmist employs an image of a wild boar from the forest coming in and devouring whatever it finds. If the people are going to be restored, they know that there has to be a "change" in God. This leads to the third refrain, where there is a slight change from the first two:

> Refrain 1: "Restore us, O God" (v. 3);
> Refrain 2: "Restore us, O God of hosts" (v. 7, ESV);
> Refrain 3: "Return, O God of hosts" (v. 14, my own translation).

The NIV translates verse 14 as "Return to us," but the words "to us" are not present in Hebrew. The people have been "turning" to God, but unless God "returns" to them, they have no hope. As noted above, God seems so far above them in the heavens, dwelling among the cherubim, and so they plead with him to "Look down from heaven and see!" (v. 14). The Jerusalem Bible translates this verse, "Please, Yahweh Sabaoth, relent! Look down from heaven, look at this vine, visit it" (v. 14).

## 80:15–19 PETITIONS

Verse 15a continues the petition from verse 14, where the community pleads with God to "visit" the vine. The first word in verse 15 could be understood either as a noun ("stock" or "root") or a verb ("establish"),[5] but the sense of the verse is similar in both cases, either "the root your right hand has planted" or "establish that which your right hand has planted." The important detail in this verse is the phrase, "right hand," which is used in the book of Exodus to refer to God's saving power in Egypt (Exod 16:6). The phrase is also used in the Psalms to speak of God bringing the people to the border of the holy land (78:54). This verse recalls the parable of the vine in verses 8–11, reminding God of the great effort he has already exerted for this vine. Rather than abandoning it, which does not make sense (see question "why?" in v. 12), God

---

5. The LXX reflects the latter reading while the MT the former.

needs to strengthen it.⁶ One can sense the boldness with which the people argue their point with God.

God needs to visit the vine that his right hand planted because it is in terrible condition and has been cut down and burned with fire (v. 16a). It is not clear whether verse 16b is a continuation of the people's terrible situation or a petition for God to punish the enemies who devastated the vine. The subject of the verb "perish" is ambiguous, as it could either be the Israelites who perish or their enemies, in which case the verb should be translated, "let them perish." The latter is more likely, since the phrase, "at your rebuke," is used to refer to the enemies (see Pss 18:15; 78:6). Also, the series of petitions surrounding verse 16 suggests that this petition is directed against the people's enemies (see vv. 14, 17–19).

In verse 17, the focus turns to the "man of your right hand" (ESV). Elsewhere, God's "right hand" is used in connection to the king (see Pss 18:35; 20:6).⁷ Though there is no explicit reference to the king in Psalm 80, the imagery of the vine is used elsewhere to refer to specific kings as representatives of the nation (see Ezekiel 17 and 19). Since the fate of the people is tied to their king, then praying for the king ensures the welfare of the people. If God answers their prayer, they will no longer "turn away from you" (v. 18; compare Isa 63:17). Ultimately, they are dependent on the Lord, for they will only be able to continue if God revives them (80:18). Thus, the psalm ends with the familiar refrain, seeking God's restoration so "that we may be saved" (v. 19).

---

6. The second half of verse 15 refers to "the son you have raised up for yourself." But this is problematic, for it does not make sense with the first half of the verse. It reoccurs later as part of verse 17. Here, I follow the suggestion [BHS notes] that verse 15b should be deleted here, for it forms part of verse 17 later. See Alexander Rofé, "The Text-Criticism of Psalm 80–Revisited," *VT* 61, no. 2 (2011): 298–309.
7. Hossfeld and Zenger, *Psalms 2*, 316.

# PSALM 81

Psalm 81 resembles a modern-day worship service, as it begins with a call to worship (vv. 1–5a) and is followed by a sermon or homily (vv. 5b–16). The former suggests a time of singing and celebration, but unlike modern worship services, which tends to have a one-sided emphasis on celebration,[1] Psalm 81 moves from celebration to lament. The first part of the psalm pertains to the celebration of the Feast of Tabernacles, "the most joyous festival" for the people of Israel.[2] Also known as the Feast of Booths, this feast was held after the harvest (Deut 16:13; Lev 23:39) and is therefore a time of rejoicing and celebration. In the second portion of the psalm, both the speaker and mood shift, for right in the midst of the celebration, God himself delivers a sermon and pours out his heart in a lament (see v. 13 below). This prophetic sermon on divine judgment contrasts sharply with the celebratory mood of the call to worship, creating an anti-climax and an element of tragedy.

In Psalm 80, the people pour out their lament to God (see comments to 80:9–13), but here in Psalm 81, God pours out his lament to the people. In the sermon portion of the psalm, God is presented as the speaker. This may be a prophetic oracle, where God is speaking through his prophet. This is similar to modern-day preaching in churches when the preacher is expected to speak God's word to the people. The Apostle Peter exhorts those who are entrusted with the gift of preaching to speak "as one who speaks the very words of God" (1 Pet 4:11).

Some scholars see Psalm 81 as God's answer to the people's lament in Psalm 80. For example, Cole argues that "Psalm 81 serves principally as a divine answer to the questions of 79–80, just as 78 answered the complaints of 77."[3] Yet it should also be noted that God's response takes the form of a prophetic lament, and so Psalm 81 looks forward to God's further lament in Psalm 82.

Psalm 81 can be divided into two main sections:

The call to celebrate a festival (vv. 1–5a),
The Divine speech (vv. 5b–16).

---

1. The worship style of some evangelical churches in Asia is influenced by the upbeat type of worship music from the west. In most of these gatherings, the emphasis is on rejoicing and victorious Christian living. Those who design these worship gatherings make sure that the theme and mood are consistent throughout. The sermon should also be positive. The worship service must end on a high note, on celebration.
2. John E. Hartley, *Leviticus* (Dallas: Word Books, 1992), 387.
3. Robert Luther Cole, *The Shape and Message of Book III (Psalms 73–89)*, JSOTSup (Sheffield: Sheffield Academic Press, 2000), 98.

## 81:1–5 A CALL TO WORSHIP AND CELEBRATION

The opening verses of Psalm 81 resemble a hymn of praise: "Sing for joy to God our strength; shout aloud to the God of Jacob!" (v. 1). This call to worship is similar to Psalm 98:1: "Sing to the LORD a new song, for he has done marvelous things." The "marvelous thing" that God has done is implied in the ascription, "God our strength." Because God has done great things for his people, they will respond with singing and praise.

This time of celebration and praise is accompanied by music. Verses 2–3 mention playing several instruments, including the tambourine, harp, lyre, and ram's horn (*shofar*). The blowing of the ram's horn accompanies the "joyous celebration of the festival."[4] Psalm 150, the final hymn of the Psalter, cites many other instruments that accompany music that is offered in praise to God (see Ps 150:3–5).

The festival here is the Feast of the Tabernacles, one of the three great festivals of the Israelites, along with the New Year and the Day of Atonement.[5] In the Feast of the Tabernacles, the people remember what God has done for them (v. 5). God has made a "decree for Israel" (v. 4) and a "statute for Joseph" (v. 5) for its commemoration. As noted above, the Festival of the Tabernacles is "most joyous" and should be marked by "rejoicing" in the presence of the Lord (see Lev 23:40; Deut 16:14).[6] The second part of the psalm, however, contrasts sharply with the joyful mood of the call to celebration and praise.

## 81:5B "I HEAR A LANGUAGE I HAD NOT KNOWN"

In verse 5b, the speaker turns from addressing the congregation to speaking about something that he has heard. Literally, verse 5b reads, "I hear a language I had not known" (ESV). The word translated "language" comes from the Hebrew word *sapah*, which literally means "lip" and by extension can also mean "language."[7] The sense of the sentence is clear enough, but what does it mean in the context of the psalm? How does it relate to the preceding mood of celebration and the following mood of lament?

---

4. Kirkpatrick, *The Book of Psalms*, 490.
5. Walton, Chavalas, and Matthews write: "The only pilgrimage feast that potentially spans the New Moon and Full Moon is the Feast of Tabernacles." Walton, Chavalas, and Matthews, *IVP Bible Background Commentary: Old Testament*, 542–543.
6. Mitchel Modine, *Numbers: A Pastoral and Contextual Commentary* (Carlisle, U.K.: Langham Global Library, 2018), 158.
7. *BDB*, 974; *HALOT*, 3:1348.

Some scholars try to connect the statement in verse 5b with its preceding context (v. 5a), which mentions "Egypt." From this interpretation, the "language I had not known" could refer to the Israelites' experience among the Egyptians, whose language they did not know. Here, the speaker is identifying with the people's experience.[8] One problem with this view, however, is that it would leave verse 5 with no transition into the divine speech in the next section (vv. 6–16).

An alternative reading connects the statement in verse 5b as an introduction to the divine speech that follows. This is reflected in the NIV, which translates this verse, "I heard an unknown voice say."[9] This statement signifies that the speaker, presumably a prophet, has received a message from God. But why does he describe the message as something "I had not known"?[10] Perhaps it's because the message is so unexpected. The prophet is about to declare something to the people that is completely contrary to their expectations. The psalm started with praise, rejoicing, and singing, but the message from God is one of judgment and lament. Admittedly, it is not easy to know the precise meaning of verse 5b, but this verse introduces an important word, "hear," which is mentioned five times in Psalm 81 (vv. 5, 8 [2x], 11, and 13). The poet "heard," but will the people "hear"?

## 81:6–16 GOD'S LAMENT

The divine speech begins by recounting what God has done for the people. God recalls the hardship which the people experienced in Egypt. The words "burden" and "basket" (v. 6) are metaphors for the tasks the Israelites were forced to do as slaves.[11] The book of Exodus tells us how the people of Israel "groaned in their slavery and cried out" (Exod 2:23). In Psalm 81, God tells the people that when they called out in their distress, "I rescued you" (v. 7a). It should be noted that in both Exodus 2 and Psalm 81, the text does not say that the people "cried out *to God*." The text simply says, "they cried out." This is a testimony that God hears every cry, whether it is directed to him or

---

8. See Tate, for this and other views. Tate, *Psalms 51–100*, 319–320.
9. Notice the colon after the word "say."
10. Kirkpatrick explains that this is the prophet's way of identifying with Israel during the time of the Exodus, when Israel had just started to hear and learn God's message. Kirkpatrick, *The Book of Psalms*, 491. For Keil and Delitzsch, it is "unknown" because it is the "language of a known, but still also unknown God." Carl Friedrich Keil and Franz Delitzsch, *Keil and Delitzsch Commentary on the Old Testament*, trans. Francis Bolton, vol. 5 (Grand Rapids: Eerdmans, 1989), 396.
11. Bratcher and Reyburn, *A Translator's Handbook on the Book of Psalms*, 722.

not. Even though the people may not have directly called out to God, God says, "I answered you" (v. 7b). The word "answer" implies that God "heard" their cries (Exod 2:24), and then answered "out of a thundercloud" (literally, "secret place of thunder"). This metaphor is often assumed to refer to the Sinai experience, but the immediate context supports a connection with God's mighty acts in Egypt.[12]

Though God "answered" the people, they did not listen to him when it was God's turn to call upon them. God called out, "Hear me, my people" (v. 8), but "my people would not listen to me" (v. 11). Verse 9 recalls the first commandment, "You shall not worship any god other than me," as people become like the one they worship. Because God is holy, his people ought to be holy. Because God is just, his people should execute justice. This command flows out of God's gracious love for his people. Verse 10, "I am the LORD your God, who brought you up out of Egypt," functions as the motivation for the command given in verse 9.[13]

Yet the people did not listen to God, and so God gave them over to the stubbornness of their heart (v. 12). This language is echoed in Romans 1:24–25: "God gave them over in the lusts of their hearts." The Bible makes it clear that humans are unable to live alone, because without help and guidance from God, they will falter and fall. The psalmist declares that they are but flesh (Ps 78:39), and so they need God to guide them, deliver them, and feed them (81:10c). Leaving them "to follow their own devices" brings about disaster (v. 12).

God does not intend disaster for his people, nor does he enjoy punishing them. Rather, God laments even as he judges his people. Verse 13 begins with the Hebrew word, *lu*, which means, "If only," or "O that!" This is the same word used when Abraham laments because Ishmael cannot be the son he has been waiting for: "*Oh that [lu] Ishmael might live before you!*" (Gen 17:18, ESV). This word is also used in Job's lament: "*Oh that [lu] my vexation were weighed, and all my calamity laid in the balances!*" (Job 6:2, ESV). In Psalm 81, God laments: "Oh [*lu*], that my people would listen to me!" (Ps 81:13, ESV). The Gospel of Luke says that as Jesus drew near the city of Jerusalem, "he wept over it" and lamented, "Would that you, even you, had known on this day the things that make for peace! But now they are hidden from your eyes" (Luke 19:41–42).

---

12. Tate, *Psalms 51–100*, 323.
13. In the LXX, verse 10 begins with the preposition "for."

## Psalm 81

In spite of all that God has done for his people – listening to them, delivering them, and offering them satisfaction and abundance – they still rebelled against him. The overall movement from celebration to lament in this psalm captures the tragic consequence of the people's disobedience. This causes God to lament, and yet he still promises that if they obey his voice, they "would be fed with the finest of wheat; with honey from the rock I would satisfy you" (Ps 81:16).

# PSALM 82

Psalm 82 declares that the God who dwells among the cherubim (80:1) hears the cry of the oppressed and cares about the welfare of the least and most vulnerable. If whatever makes us angry indicates what is really important to us, then justice is of utmost importance to God, for in Psalm 82, God is angry at injustice, and he laments that other gods show "partiality to the wicked" (v. 2).

Psalm 82 has been categorized as a prophetic hymn, prophetic liturgy, prophetic tribunal, and prophetic social critique,[1] but the overall tone and movement of the psalm is a lament.[2] In the previous psalms, the people pour out their laments to God (see Psalms 74, 76, 79), but in Psalm 82, God continues the lament he started in Psalm 81 (see Ps 81:13 above). Yet in Psalm 82, his lament is directed against the "gods" instead of his people. Unfortunately, scholars have been hampered by the debate on the identity of the "gods" in their interpretation of this psalm. As Adu-Gyamfi notes, "The focus has mostly been in determining what אֱלֹהִים [*elohim*] means in verses 1b and 6a. Thus the controversy overlooks the reason for God's judgment on the 'gods.'"[3] But this controversy may not be an issue for Asians, who are familiar with a polytheistic background (see further discussion below).

The lament in Psalm 82 may be outlined as follows:

> Setting: divine council (v. 1),
> God's lament against the "gods" (vv. 2–3),
> God's command, or petition (vv. 4–5),
> God's complaint (v. 6),
> God's divine decree, or the "certainty of a hearing" (vv. 6–7),
> Petition by the psalmist (v. 8).

This lament is unique in that it is set in the heavenly realms (v. 1). In Psalm 82 God is both the lamenter and the judge who responds to his own lament. Instead of humans, it is God himself who laments. The complaint, "how long?" recorded in verse 2 is usually uttered by humans, as we can see, for example in the lament of the people in Psalm 74:10 – "How long will

---

1. Tate, *Psalms 51–100*, 332.
2. Compare Daniel O. McClellan who argues that Psalm 82 is a "complaint." Daniel O. McClellan, "The Gods-Complaint: Psalm 82 as a Psalm of Complaint," *JBL* 137, no. 4 (2018): 833–851.
3. Yaw Adu-Gyamfi, "Psalm 82 and Injustice: Implications for African Church Leaders," *Ogbomoso Journal of Theology* 19, no. 1 (2014): 15. Compare Simon B. Parker, "The Beginning of the Reign of God: Psalm 82 as Myth and Liturgy," *RB* 102, no. 4 (October 1995): 553.

the enemy mock you, God?" But here, it is God himself who cries out, "how long?" (80:2). The words, "defend," "uphold," "rescue," and "deliver" (vv. 3–4) are analogous to the petitions in the lament (see for example the petitions in Ps 74:18–23 following the complaint in verse 10). But since it is God who is uttering the words in Psalm 82, the petitions are transformed into commands. That is the difference in the heavenly realm, unlike in the earthly realm where humans can only lament and plea. The last verse of the psalm shifts focus to the earth, as the psalmist cries out for justice, asking that God's justice in the divine council will also be done on earth (v. 8). The overall movement of this psalm is reflected in the Lord's Prayer, which asks for God's will to "be done, on earth as it is in heaven" (Matt 6:10).[4]

Psalm 82 shows us the heart of God. Our Lord Jesus became angry with the religious leaders of his day for their injustice (Matt 23:23). In his Sermon on the Mount, he commanded his disciples to become like "your heavenly Father" (Matt 5:48). Those who wish to follow Jesus should walk as he did (1 John 2:6). If God became angry with "gods" for their oppression of the poor, and if Jesus called the religious leaders a "brood of vipers" and uttered "woes" against them, shouldn't Christians become angry at injustice? Loving one's enemy does not mean tolerating what is wrong. Love, if it is to be "genuine," must "hate what is evil" (Rom 12:9).[5]

## 82:1 GOD IN THE ASSEMBLY OF THE GODS

Verse 1 is densely populated by the gods. Out of the seven words in Hebrew, the word "God" is repeated three times: twice as *'elohim* (God/gods) and once as *'el*, which is another word for god/God. The first word in verse 1 is "God" (*'elohim*) and refers to the same God to whom the psalmist cries out at the end of the psalm: Yahweh, the covenant God of the Israelites. According to verse 1, God "presides in the great assembly." The word "preside" comes from the Hebrew word *nitsab*, which means "to stand" or "to take up a position." Here, the word is used in the latter "behavioral" sense.[6] Or even better, God

---
4. Federico G. Villanueva, "The Lord's Prayer and Psalm 82," in *Ama Namin: The Lord's Prayer in Philippine Life and Spirituality*, ed. Timoteo D. Gener and Jason Tan, forthcoming.
5. Miranda's remarks are spot on: "frankly I do not see how there can be an authentic compassion for the oppressed without there being at the same time indignation against the oppressor." José Porfirio Miranda, *Marx and the Bible* (Maryknoll, NY: Orbis; SCM Press, 1974), 74.
6. Peter Machinist, "How Gods Die and Otherwise: A Problem of Cosmic Restructuring," in *Reconsidering the Concept of Revolutionary Monotheism*, ed. Beate Pongratz-Leisten (Winona Lake, Indiana: Eisenbrauns, 2011), 200.

"takes a stand" against the "great assembly." When it comes to issues of justice, there is no neutral ground; one has to take a stand.

The phrase "great assembly" literally means, "the assembly of *El*." *El* or *Elyon* is associated with the Canaanite deity, but this title is also applied to Yahweh, who is considered *El Elyon*, the Most High God (see v. 6). The background behind the phrase, "assembly of *El*," is ancient West Asia, where the world is populated by many gods, not one. Asians in general would be familiar with many gods. India, for example, has millions of gods. Filipinos believe that the world or universe is inhabited not only by humans, but by super-humans, spirits, and gods.[7] The Tagalogs believe that there are many gods, and the highest God is *Bathala,* who "presided over the lesser divinities who cared for the needs of the people and guarded the general welfare of the reverent families."[8] This picture of *Bathala* is similar to the divine council mentioned in Psalm 82:1. While the concept of many gods may be disturbing to those who have been brought up in a Western Christian background, the OT preserves the tradition of there being a multiplicity of gods.[9] Psalm 82 depicts a world where the heavenly and earthly realm intertwine.

### 82:2–4 GOD LAMENTS AGAINST THE GODS

In this divine council, God "takes a stand" with the other gods in order to defend the poor, lamenting, "How long will you defend the unjust?" (v. 2a). The question, "how long?" often occurs in human laments to indicate that a situation has been going on for a long time. In verse 2, the implication is that the gods have been practicing injustice, showing "partiality to the wicked" (v. 2b) for a long time now, and God hates partiality in favor of the wicked. The Apostle James hurls one of his strongest rebukes against communities who show favoritism to the rich but reject the poor (Jas 2:1–13). The sign of true religion, James says, is "to look after orphans and widows in their distress . . ." (1:27).

Verses 3–4 outline the job description of a just god:

> Defend the weak and the fatherless;
> Uphold the cause of the poor and the oppressed.
> Rescue the weak and the needy;
> Deliver them from the hand of the wicked.

---

7. Gaspar, *Desperately Seeking God's Saving Action*, 83–89.
8. F. Landa Jocano, "Notes on Philippine Divinities," *Asian Studies* 6, no. 2 (1968): 170.
9. Patrick D. Miller, "Cosmology and World Order in the Old Testament: The Divine Council as Cosmic-Political Symbol," *HBT* 9, no. 2 (1987): 54–55.

These two verses make six references to poor/suffering people: "weak" (*dal*) (2x), "fatherless" (*yatom*), "poor" (*'ani*), "oppressed" (*rosh*), "needy" (*'ebyon*) (compare Psalms 9–10).[10]

Psalm 82 makes it clear that God's priorities are not for the rich or powerful, but for those who are deprived of justice. At the center of Psalm 82 is concern for what we now call "social justice." In the OT, this concern is often expressed through the words "justice and righteousness."[11] These words are used in Psalm 82 in their verbal forms, "give justice" (*shapat*) and "maintain the right" (*tsdq*) (v. 3, ESV), suggesting that these actions are to be expected from the entire "assembly" of gods.

## 82:5 GOD COMPLAINS AGAINST THE GODS

Yet the "gods" failed in their job description. Because they failed to execute justice, "all the foundations of the earth are shaken" (v. 5c). Notice the word "all." When the weak, orphans, and poor are oppressed, the world is shaken to its core. According to verse 5, the gods do not "know" anything, nor do they "understand" anything, for "they walk in darkness." The Hebrew is not explicit about the subject of these verbs, but there are at least two possibilities: the wicked or the "gods." The former occurs at the end of verse 4, but the later judgment (in v. 6) is directed against the "gods." Moreover, God's earlier lament (v. 2), which is directed against the "gods," supports the view that the subject of the verb in verse 5 is the "gods." We can also combine the two, as the wicked are the instruments of the "gods" and so work together. Yet God's judgment is delivered against the "gods," but not the wicked. Thus the psalmist has to ask God to "rise up" and "judge the earth" at the end (v. 8).

## 82:6–7 GOD JUDGES THE "GODS"

In verses 6–7, God indicts the gods who failed to execute justice. He declares, "you are gods" and the "sons of the Most High." Then God condemns them to mortality – like humans, they will now die. This is the cost of injustice. It does not matter if you are the president of the country, the richest person in the world, or even a "god." If you trample on the poor, God will throw you down.

---

10. Federico G. Villanueva, "'Break the Arm of the Wicked!' Understanding the Imprecations in Psalm 9/10," in *Scripture and Service: Essays in Honor of Joseph Too Shao*, 171–172.
11. Moshe Weinfeld, "'Justice and Righteousness' Mshpt Wtsdqh the Expression and Its Meaning," in *Justice and Righteousness: Biblical Themes and Their Influence* (Sheffield: JSOT Press, 1992), 228–246.

## 82:8 "LET YOUR WILL BE DONE ON EARTH AS IT IS IN HEAVEN"

In the last verse of the psalm, there is a shift from heaven to earth as the psalmist asks God to do what he has already done in the heavenly realm on earth. The petition to "judge the earth" indicates that the same situation of injustice is taking place on earth. This ending reflects a sense of tension and contradiction. God has already judged the gods, so why does God need to judge the earth? What is true in the heavens should also be true on earth, since God is the God of heaven and earth. But the reality for the psalmist is that God's rule, while true in heaven, has yet to be realized on earth.[12]

The word "arise" in verse 8 also occurs in Psalm 12:5, where God himself declares, "I will now arise" because "the poor are plundered and the needy groan." In Psalm 82:8, the petition is similar. Since God has already arisen against the "gods," he should now arise on earth because all the nations are his.

---

12. Knierim Rolf, "Cosmos and History in Israel's Theology," *HBT* 3 (1981): 79.

# PSALM 83

> Make them like tumbleweed, my God, like chaff
>   before the wind.
> As fire consumes the forest or a flame sets the mountains
>   ablaze, so pursue them with your tempest and terrify them
>   with your storm.
> Cover their faces with shame, Lord, so that they will seek your
>   name. – Psalm 83:13–16

This prayer is an example of an "imprecatory" prayer. Read on its own, it could appear as a very harsh nationalistic prayer of one nation against others. The imprecations in verses 13–17 are brutal and cruel. To understand this psalm, we need to read it closely in light of its canonical context and interpret it with our own cultural resources.

As a Filipino, one cultural resource I find helpful in understanding imprecatory prayers is our concept of *pagsusumbong*,[1] an indigenous concept that is difficult to capture in English. *Pagsusumbong* literally means "reporting," but this does not capture three key elements in the word: 1) a strong bully, 2) a weak victim (usually a child), and 3) someone to whom the victim goes in order to make the *pagsusumbong*.

In the communal lament in Psalm 83, we see these three elements of *pagsusumbong* at play. First, the community is confronted with enemies who are much more powerful. A total of ten nations have banded together (vv. 6–8) with the aim of wiping out the memory of Israel (v. 4). Second, the community goes to God to report what their enemies are saying (vv. 4, 12) and doing (vv. 5–8) and to ask God to do something about it (vv. 9–17), implying how weak they are. Third, that is why they go to God because they view him as more powerful and also because they know and trust him. They know his power through their own previous experience of God's deliverance (vv. 9–11). Their intimacy with God is reflected in the way the psalmist addresses him as "my God" (v. 13).

It is important to bear in mind that the imprecatory prayers are arising from extreme experiences of oppression and injustice. To understand Psalm 83, we need to consider its canonical context. The previous psalm (Psalm 82)

---

1. For more discussion, see Villanueva, *Psalms 1–72*, 274–276.

highlights the injustice and oppression of the poor and the vulnerable. The central theme of Psalm 82 is the justice of God. The psalmist depicts a scene in the council of the gods, where Yahweh is presented as a God who hates injustice and oppression and judges even the gods. The psalmist prays that God's justice "in the heavens" may also be true on earth.

Thus Psalms 82 and 83 are closely linked. The opening verse of Psalm 83 employs the two words used to refer to God in the opening verse of Psalm 82 – *'elohim* and *'el* (see v. 1). In Hebrew, Psalms 82:1 and 83:1 contain words that sound alike: *yishpot* ("he renders judgment") and *tishqot* ("be still," ESV), respectively. Psalm 83 ends with a declaration of Yahweh as the Most High (*'elyon*), recalling Psalm 82:6, where the same title occurs.

Psalm 83 may be outlined as follows:

Petition (v. 1),
"Reporting" to God (*Pagsusumbong*) (vv. 2–4),
Imprecatory prayers (vv. 13–17),
Closing petition (v. 18).

## 83:1–8 PETITION WITH MOTIVATIONS

Though Psalm 82 ends with a cry for God to "rise up" (v. 8), Psalm 83 reflects a situation where God has not yet arisen. God is inactive, and so the psalmist prays, "do not remain silent" (83:1). Indeed, God is not only silent, but he is also not listening: "do not turn a deaf ear" (v. 1). Nor does God seem to care about what is happening: "do not stand aloof" (v. 1).[2] The triple use of the negative particle signals panic and despair in the psalmist. This image is similar to the disciples, who cry out to Jesus as the waves break into their boat: "Teacher, don't you care if we drown?" (Mark 4:38).

The psalmist and his community cry out to God not to be silent, because the enemies are in an uproar: "See how your enemies growl" (Ps 83:2). The situation is similar to Psalm 2, where "the nations conspire" (2:1). Similarly, the enemies "rear their heads" (83:2; compare 2:2). According to Hossfeld and Zenger, to lift up one's head signifies "a decision to fight and an assurance of victory (compare Judg 8:28; Pss 27:6; 110:7)."[3]

---

[2]. The verb translated "stand aloof" (*shaqat*) is used elsewhere to "describe a state of peace and rest from war" (Josh 11:22; Judg 3:11, 30). It speaks of "being tranquil or having rest," *NIDOTTE* 4:234.
[3]. Hossfeld and Zenger, *Psalms 2*, 341.

# Psalm 83

The psalmist presents this situation as God's responsibility, for the enemies are "*your* enemies," and the foes "hate *you*" (v. 2, emphasis mine). Moreover, because the community is "your people," any action against it is also against God himself (v. 3). Verse 5 also describes the enemy alliance as "against you."

This situation is similar to the early church in Acts 9, when Saul (later Paul) encounters Jesus in a vision while he is on his way to Damascus to persecute Christians. Struck by a blinding light, Saul falls to the ground and hears a voice (whom he later learns is Jesus) saying, "Saul, Saul, why do you persecute me?" (9:4). Earlier in Acts, when the church is being persecuted, they gather and pray, quoting Psalm 2 (see Acts 4:23–30), which bears resemblance to Psalm 83.[4] Though the situation in Acts was much simpler than the injustice of Psalm 83, the persecuted believers tell God (*pagsusumbong*) to "consider their threats" (Acts 4:29).

In Psalm 83, the people tell God (*pagsusumbong*) what the enemies are saying: "Come . . . let us destroy them as a nation" (v. 4). They want Israel to be wiped out, its memory forgotten forever. The verb "saying" in verse 4 (in reference to the enemies) is repeated again in verse 12. This verb makes a subtle contrast with the silence of God. While the enemies are growling and speaking, God remains silent (v. 1).

But the people do not give up. After telling God what the enemies are saying, they report (*pagsusumbong*) what the enemies are doing: "they plot together" (v. 5). Ten nations, including the powerful Assyria, have formed an alliance (vv. 6–8).[5] It is nearly impossible to identify a specific historical event that corresponds to Psalm 83:5–8, and so it is better to read these verses symbolically. Judah has fought and struggled against all ten nations in the past, and so they are "emblematic for the world of nations experienced and feared by Israel throughout its history."[6] The lumping together of these nations creates unimaginable terror, from which there is no escape. Only God's intervention can help them.

---

4. Psalm 2:2 (NASB) reads: "The kings of the earth take their stand and the rulers take counsel together against the Lord and against his annointed." Acts 4:26 (NASB) reads: "The kings of the earth took their stand, and the rulers were gathered together against the Lord and against his Christ."
5. For background on each of these ten nations, see Walter C. Kaiser, Jr., "The People of Psalm 83," *Bibliotheca Sacra* 174, no. 695 (July 2017): 259–266.
6. Hossfeld and Zenger, *Psalms 2*, 342.

## 83:9–18 IMPRECATORY PRAYERS

Drawing from the cultural concept of *pagsusumbong* (see above), the enemies are presented as powerful bullies. The people are no match for them, and so they have nowhere else to go but God. In verses 9–12, the people ask God to come against these enemies, just as he did in the past against the Midianites, who are described as "thick as locusts" and whose camels could no more be counted than the "sand on the seashore" (Judg 7:12). Yet God miraculously delivered Gideon and his army of three hundred against the overwhelming army of the Midianites. Similarly, God delivered Deborah and Barak from King Jabin, whose commander, Sisera, "had nine hundred chariots fitted with iron" (Judg 4:3), which he used to cruelly oppress Israel for twenty years.

By recalling these events, Psalm 83 not only shows the strength of their enemies and God's history of powerful intervention, it also provides important background regarding the suffering and oppression of the Israelites. In light of this background, we can see that the imprecatory prayers in verses 13–17 (quoted at the beginning of this chapter) arise from the Israelites' position of powerlessness and vulnerability. In Psalm 83, the Israelites are like "the weak and the fatherless," "the poor and the oppressed" in the previous psalm (82:3). Yet like the petition at the end of Psalm 82, the prayers in Psalm 83:13–17 express the people's hope that their just God will act on their behalf in accordance to his righteousness. These prayers are not concerned with one nation's glory and power over another. Rather, the purpose of these petitions is twofold. The first purpose is "that they will seek your name" (v. 16b). One of the tendencies of humans is that when they become powerful they begin to think, speak, and act like God (see comments to Ps 73:9 above). Thus, the second purpose is that they may know "that you alone are the Most High over all the earth" (v. 18). This is similar to the imprecatory prayer in Psalm 10, asking God to "break the arm of the wicked" (v. 15) "so that mere earthly mortals will never again strike terror" (v. 18).

# PSALM 84

As I write this commentary, we are in the midst of a lockdown due to the pandemic caused by the coronavirus. For the first time, all churches, mosques, and places of worship are closed down, and this is now the sixth consecutive Sunday that we have not been able to go to church. When something has been taken away from us, we often come to appreciate its value all the more.

Psalm 84 is one of the so-called Zion hymns, written when the Temple was still in existence. It begins with an exclamation, "How lovely is your dwelling place" (v. 1). These words would have been perfect during the time of the monarchy, when the Temple still existed. This psalm was eventually incorporated into what we now know as the Psalter during the time of the exile. How would those who were in exile sing the words of this psalm? How could they even utter the word "lovely" when the sanctuary had been burned to the ground and "the dwelling place" had been defiled (74:7)?

In its canonical context, Psalm 84, which is attributed to "the sons of Korah," follows the Asaph collection (Psalms 73–83). A number of these psalms lament the destruction of the dwelling place of God. Reading Psalm 84 in its canonical context thus creates a sense of disjuncture, a stark contrast with the previous psalms in the Asaph collection, particularly Psalms 74 and 79. At the same time, one can appreciate the contradiction and the absence of the Temple, as it is often when something is taken away that we learn to appreciate its value.[1] From the context of exile, separation, and the pain of isolation, we realize the importance of the Temple, which is associated with the presence of God. To go there is to "see" God (Ps 42:2b; compare Ps 84:7).

Our sense of longing for God is often deepened when we experience a sense of God's absence. When the signs of his presence are nowhere to be found, the inner eyes of faith are sharpened as we strain to see beyond the present moment. The community may be far from the Temple, or the Temple may have been destroyed, but the longing for God's presence remains alive. Our focus shifts to the journey towards the sanctuary (Ps 84:5–7).

Structurally, Psalm 84 can be divided as follows:

Praise for God's dwelling place (vv. 1–3),
Declaration: identifying the blessed ones (vv. 4–7),

---

[1]. For example, when somebody dies, that's when the good things about the person are talked about.

Petition with motivation (vv. 8–11),
Refrain: "Blessed is the one who trusts in you" (v. 12).

## 84:1–3 PRAISE FOR GOD'S DWELLING

The psalm begins with a hymn praising God's dwelling place: "How lovely is your dwelling place" (v. 1). What makes this place "lovely"? First, it is the place where one encounters the "living God" (v. 2). The phrase "courts of the LORD" (v. 2a) parallels the subsequent description of "the living God" (v. 2b). In Psalm 42 (another Korah psalm), the psalmist remembers when he went into the "house of God" (v. 4), where he experienced "seeing the face of God" (v. 2, translation mine). Remembering, the psalmist longs for those occasions! In Psalm 84, the psalmist feels the same longing for God: "My soul yearns, even faints" (v. 2). The verb "faints" (*kalah*) in verse 2 is used in lament psalms as well (see Ps 31:11; 69:4; 71:9; 73:26). The yearning for "the courts of the LORD" and the longing that makes one's soul faint is similar to Psalm 42, where the psalmist likens his longing for the "living God" (v. 2) with that of a thirsty deer who is desperately looking for water (v. 1). This description of the "living God" appears again in Psalm 84:2. In a context of exile and death, we *long* for the "*living* God."

Second, the dwelling place of God is "lovely" because "even the sparrow has found a home, and the swallow a nest for herself" (v. 3). The word "even" (*gam*) implies an analogy from the least to the greatest, where "even" (*gam*) the smallest and the seemingly insignificant can find a place in God's house. The verse begins with the mention of the birds and ends with "my King and my God," a comprehensive sweep that houses "even" the smallest and most vulnerable in the dwelling place of the "LORD Almighty, my King, and my God." During the time of Jesus, sparrows "were one of the cheapest items sold for poor people's food in the marketplace, the cheapest of all birds."[2]

It is very interesting that of all the details the psalmist could mention about God's dwelling, he mentions the birds. This could be because the birds reflect his own view of himself.[3] Later in verse 10, he is prepared to be a "doorkeeper," if only he can be near God. But the image of the bird dwelling comfortably near the sanctuary also expresses the psalmist's deepest longing, for this is where he wants to be. He observes how the swallow makes "a nest

---

2. Craig S. Keener, *The IVP Bible Background Commentary: New Testament*, 2nd ed (Downers Grove, IL: IVP Academic, 2014), 74.
3. One of our Filipino laments, *Bayan ko* (my "nation"), compare our people with a bird.

for herself, where she may have her young" (v. 3) in the most important part of the temple – "near your altar" (v. 3).[4] Thus the psalmist declares, "My soul yearns, even faints" to be in that place! (v. 2).

## 84:4–7A DECLARATION: WHO THE BLESSED ONES ARE

Thus in verse 4, the psalmist says that all "those who dwell in your house" are "blessed." This list includes the Levites, priests, and temple servants, whom the psalmist imagines must be always praising God, so they are blessed indeed! But what about those who live outside the temple? This question is particularly relevant during this time, when the pandemic has made going to church impossible.

Interestingly, though the psalmist declares the blessedness of those who dwell in the temple, the psalm focuses on those who do *not* live in it. In verse 5, the psalmist talks about the blessedness of "those whose strength is in you" (v. 5a) and "whose hearts are set on pilgrimage" (v. 5b). We tend to imagine or wish that we would already be at our destination, or that we would already attain our longings. However, the psalmist does not speak of the destination as blessed, but the journey, the pilgrimage. In Hebrew, verse 5b reads literally as "highways are in their heart," where the "highways" are those leading to Zion. While Kraus thinks that the MT does not make sense,[5] such a view lacks imagination. Having the highways in one's mind or heart expresses the longing to be where God is, and even the longing for this journey invigorates one's faith and provides the strength needed for the journey itself. In this psalm, the destination and journey are enmeshed, the former providing the inspiration for the latter.

Verse 6 refers to passing through the "Valley of Baka." The NIV seems to interpret "Baka" as a literal place, but the noun *baka* refers to a balsam tree/shrub.[6] Interestingly, both the LXX and Targum and other Hebrew manuscripts have "*bekeh*" (weeping). This suggests that the journey towards Zion is filled with tears (compare Ps 42:3). Yet those whose heart is set on following God can transform their valley of tears into a "place of springs" (v. 6). Along the way, they experience showers of blessings as they "go from strength to strength" (v. 7a).

---

4. For the translation of *'et* as "beside" or "near," see Tate, *Psalms 51–100*, 353.
5. Hans-Joachim Kraus, *Psalms 60–150: A Commentary* (Minneapolis: Fortress Press, 1993), 166.
6. Bratcher and Reyburn, *A Translator's Handbook on the Book of Psalms*, 740.

## 84:7B–11 PETITION WITH MOTIVATION

Verse 7b finally identifies the destination: "till each appears before God in Zion." But what might seem to be the high point of the journey is eclipsed by the prayer that follows: "Hear my prayer . . . listen to me . . ." (v. 8). Though the psalmist is looking toward the destination, it is clear that he has not yet arrived. Thus the petition is rather anticlimactic, similar to the movement from the vow of thanksgiving to the prayer for help in Psalm 27, which also speaks of the longing to dwell in the house of the Lord: "One thing I ask from the LORD . . . that I may dwell in the house of the LORD all the days of my life" (v. 4). At the end of Psalm 27:6, the psalmist offers a vow of thanksgiving, which characteristically signals a movement from lament to praise, but his vow is immediately followed by a petition: "Hear my voice" (v. 7). We encounter a similarly abrupt and incongruent transition from verse 7b to verse 8 in Psalm 84.

The psalmist asks God specifically to "look on our shield" (v. 9a), which could refer to the king (in which case the psalm could be pre-exilic). But "shield" could also be a reference to the high priest, and because the word "anointed" (v. 9b) could be used to refer either to the king or the high priest, the text is not clear. Regardless, the prayer is clearly directed toward the leader, rather than the psalmist's own personal intention. This verse confirms the importance of human leadership. Any nation rises or falls according to their leadership.

In Hebrew, Psalm 84:10 begins with the particle "for," which literally reads, "For a day in your courts . . ." (ESV). The particle "for" connects verse 10 with the preceding petition for God to "look on our shield" and "the face of Your anointed," providing the motivation for this request.[7] The psalmist is arguing that God should answer his prayer because his longing is for the courts of the Lord. If the "highways" to Zion are in the hearts of God's people (v. 5), then their ever-present longing is to go wherever the Lord is dwelling. This resolve reflects what Mary Jerome Obiorah describes as "a resolution to walk in his ways. This physical motion towards the temple will in v. 12 [v. 11] become another sapiential metaphor for blameless life."[8] In verse 10, the psalmist declares that "one day in your courts" is better than a thousand elsewhere. He has resolved to give up a life of prosperity and chosen a life of

---

7. Thijs Booij, "Psalm Lxxxiv, a Prayer of the Anointed," *VT* 44, no. 4 (October 1994): 435.
8. Mary Jerome Obiorah, *"How Lovely Is Your Dwelling Place": The Desire for God's House in Psalm 84* (St. Ottilien: Eos, 2004), 147.

difficulty if this means living in God's house. Even if he suffers, he would rather be a "doorkeeper" (or someone who is outside the temple, like a beggar) than be in the "tents of the wicked" (v. 10).

The particle "for" appears again in verse 11, serving as another motivation for the psalmist's petition. The psalmist is confident that God will be a "sun and a shield," bestowing favor and honor and not withholding anything good to "those whose walk is blameless" (v. 11). In this verse, the moral qualifications for those who will be allowed to ascend the mountain of the Lord become clear (see Psalms 15 and 24).

## 84:12 REFRAIN

The final verse for Psalm 84 returns to the "blessed" refrain, which highlights the psalmist's resolve to remain loyal to his commitment, even when he is far away from the Temple, or the presence of God. Rather than identifying the one who lives *inside* the Temple as blessed, the psalmist concludes by saying that the one "who trusts in you" is blessed (v. 12). This reminds us of the words of Jesus to Thomas: "Because you have seen me, you have believed; blessed are those who have not seen and yet have believed" (John 20:29).

# PSALM 85

In Psalm 85, we see that restoration is not a one-time event, but an ongoing process. The first stanza (vv. 1–3) intimates that the people have already been restored, for the psalmist declares: "You, LORD, showed favor . . . you restored . . . You forgave . . . You set aside all your wrath and turned from your fierce anger." And yet, in the very next verse, he asks God to "restore us again" (v. 4) and then laments in verse 5: "Will you be angry with us forever?" Mays locates this psalm "in the postexilic period when the community could look back on their amazing deliverance as a real 'restoration of fortune' and yet had to live with such failure, frustration, and conflict that they cried out for salvation, the situation assumed by the restoration prophets."[1]

The experience of exile is traumatic and is a "suffering that remains."[2] The question is not how or when the community can be healed completely or restored perfectly, but how it can cope with the continuing suffering. Psalm 85 shows us how the community tries to cope with the "suffering that remains." An important part of this process is its ability to live in the tension between restoration and the ongoing absence of restoration. This is reflected in the tension between verses 1–3 (which depict a restored situation) and verses 4–7 (which reflect the absence of restoration). The juxtaposition between these verses reflects the community's suffering and continuing sense of contradiction. At the same time, the articulation of the tension paves the way for the reception of the divine word which follows. The psalmist is able to hear God's word for the community in verses 8–13 only after he pours out his heart to God.

The genre of Psalm 85 is not straightforward. Some tend to minimize the tension between the positive declarations in the first stanza (vv. 1–3) with the lament in the second stanza (vv. 4–7). Tate, for example, argues that the element of complaint is present, but it is "not expressed directly."[3] Zenger calls the psalm a "prophetic liturgy," which contains "a prayerful assurance of Yhwh's mighty promises of salvation."[4] His emphasis on "assurance" mutes the element of complaint. But the complaint is explicit in verse 5: "Will you be angry with us forever?" This complaint stands in direct contradiction to the

---

1. Mays, *Psalms*, 276. Compare Craig C. Broyles who also sees the postexilic as the context for the psalm. Craig C. Broyles, *The Conflict of Faith and Experience in the Psalms: A Form-Critical and Theological Study* (Sheffield: Sheffield Academic Press, 1989), 166.
2. Shelly Rambo and Stephanie N. Arel, *Post-Traumatic Public Theology* (2016), 3.
3. Tate, *Psalms 51–100*, 367.
4. Hossfeld and Zenger, *Psalms 2*, 363.

declaration in verse 3: "You set aside all your wrath and turned from your fierce anger." Note the word "all" and the repetition of the word "anger" (vv. 5, 3). The juxtaposition of the declaration about God's restoration and forgiveness (vv. 1–3) with the lament (vv. 4–7) emphasizes the tension between the past and the present reality. The community does not dismiss or lessen the tension but confronts it while also yearning for the fulfillment of God's complete restoration. The community conveys the same resilience that the psalmist demonstrates in Psalm 77 (see comments above).

The most fitting category for this psalm is a communal lament. In the previous psalm, the psalmist expresses his yearning for the house of the Lord. Here, Coetzee observes that the "poet puts into words the yearning of the returned exiles for final and complete restoration."[5]

The psalm is divided into three main parts:

Restoration (vv. 1–3),
Petition and lament (vv. 4–7),
Yearning for restoration (vv. 8–13).

## 85:1–3 RESTORATION: "YOU RESTORED THE FORTUNES OF JACOB"

The psalm begins with a direct address to God: "You, Lord, showed favor to your land" (v. 1b). The statement is general, but the next line makes it more specific and links it to the people's restoration from captivity. Verse 1b literally reads: "You have turned, O Lord, the captivity of Jacob." This is another way of saying, "You have brought back Jacob from captivity."[6] One of the prerequisites for restoration is the people's return to God. The text does not explicitly say that the people repented, but this is implied by the mention of the people's "iniquity" (v. 2a) and "all their sins" (v. 2b).[7] The iniquity/sin of the people was the reason for God's "wrath" and his "fierce anger" (v. 3). But now God has "set aside" his wrath and "turned" from his anger (v. 3). The emphasis in these opening verses is on the divine action of forgiveness and restoration rather than the people's return to God, which is not mentioned. God is the subject of all the verbs in verses 1–3:

---

5. Johan H. Coetzee, "Psalm 85: Yearning for the Restoration of the Whole Body," *OTE* 22, no. 3 (2009): 555.
6. Compare *DCH*, 8:228.
7. It is interesting that though the psalmist addresses God directly, he refers not to "our sins" but to "*their* sins."

"You . . . showed favor" (v. 1),
"you restored" (v. 1),
"You forgave" (v. 2a),
"[you] covered all their sins" (v. 2b),
"You set aside all your wrath" (v. 3),
"[you] turned from your fierce anger" (v. 3).

## 85:4–7 PETITION AND LAMENT

After the declarations in verses 1–3, we might expect a thanksgiving or praise,[8] but the psalm suddenly turns to lament. The element of complaint forms the central structure of this section (compare Ps 77:8–9):

*Petition:* "Restore us again" (v. 4).
   *Complaint:* "Will you be angry with us forever?" (v. 5).
   *Complaint:* "Will you not revive us again?" (v. 6).
*Petition:* "Show us your unfailing love" (v. 7).

Repeating the verb "turned" (*shub*) from verse 3b, the psalmist asks God on behalf of the community to "Restore [*shub*] us again." If they were already restored, why are they asking God to restore them again? This reveals the reality of restoration, which is that it is not a one-time event, but a process. The lament in verse 5 stands in stark contrast to verses 2–3. If God has already forgiven their sins and turned from his wrath, then why is the psalmist asking God, "Will you be angry with us forever?" (v. 5). The complaint is similar to Psalm 77:7. God may have restored them in the past, but they are not experiencing its reality in their present situation. This is confirmed by the next lament in verse 6: "Will you not revive us again?" The people continue to long for God's "unfailing love" (v. 7).

## 85:8–13 YEARNING FOR RESTORATION

The shift to first person singular in verse 8 marks the transition to the next section, when the psalmist says that he will "listen to what God the LORD says" (v. 8). In Hebrew, the word "God" (*'el*) and "LORD" (*Yahweh*) are separated. The NIV combines the two. But *Yahweh* is in the nominative and can serve as the subject of the next verb, so verse 8 could read, "I will hear what

---

8. From a form-critical point of view, we might expect this, but while form criticism has been helpful in providing a more general orientation to the psalms, it has failed to see the unique elements in the psalms.

God will say; Surely, the LORD will speak peace." This statement is similar to Habakkuk 2:1, where the prophet says, "I will look to see what he will say to me." Having uttered a lament in the previous stanza, the prophet now makes himself available to listen to God. After we express our laments to God, it is important for us to silence ourselves so we can hear what God has to say. Or, in the case of Habakkuk, to "see" what God will say. The pouring out of lament clears the way for our hearts to receive God's word or guidance. God told Habakkuk to wait.

Though God does not speak directly to the psalmist in Psalm 85 (as the message is not introduced with the prophetic words, "Thus says the LORD"), the verses that follow may be understood as God's message being expressed to the people through the psalmist. In Psalm 77, the psalmist persists in his faith, declaring that he will "remember," despite the absence of God's answer. Here, we see a similar expression of endurance and faith, which highlights the important role of human agency. Out of the psalmist's own conviction and faith, he declares that God will speak "peace" (v. 8). The word "peace" comes from the Hebrew word *shalom*. *Shalom* does not simply mean "peace of mind," but refers more comprehensively to soundness of body, mind, and spirit resulting from a restored relationship with God.[9]

The psalmist is confident that God will speak *shalom*, but the experience of *shalom* is conditional. Sometimes, in our desire to please others, we easily give them our peace. "God bless" has become a familiar expression uttered casually, and *shalom* also means God's blessing. In Psalm 85, the psalmist says that *shalom* is not given to everyone, but to "his people, his faithful servants" (v. 8). This idea is also reflected in the Apostle Paul's words to the Romans: "All things work together for good *for those who* love God, *who* are called according to his purpose" (Rom 8:28, NRSV, emphasis mine). There is both divine and human responsibility: God restores, and his people respond in faithfulness. The last part of Psalm 85:8 provides a warning: "but let them not turn to folly." This further underlines the conditional emphasis of God's *shalom*. Verse 9 provides an additional description of the recipients of God's *shalom*. For "those who fear him [God]," the psalmist declares, "salvation is near." Moreover, when people fear God, his "glory" will "dwell in the land."[10]

---

9. *BDB*, 1023.
10. The infinitive construct in verse 9b has the notion of "consecration." Paul Joüon and T. Muraoka, *A Grammar of Biblical Hebrew* (2008), 405. Verse 9b shows the result of having people who fear God–"his glory will dwell in our land."

Verse 10 personifies the common attributes of God: "Love and faithfulness meet together; righteousness and peace kiss each other."[11] These attributes are absent when the Lord does not dwell in the land. There is a dynamic interaction between these attributes that assumes a long period of separation, full of longing and yearning.[12] There is a meeting together "after a time of separation from the land which has not seen justice and peace, truth and steadfast love at all."[13] Verse 11b, "righteousness looks down from heaven," is an answer to Psalm 80:15, which asks God to "return" and "look from heaven and see." This view from heaven is balanced by the view from the earth: "Faithfulness springs forth from the earth" (v. 11a). These two perspectives betray the condition for restoration (see v. 8 above). "Righteousness looks down from heaven" (v. 11b) and "our land will yield its harvest" (v. 12) when there is "faithfulness" on earth (v. 11a).

But the journey has just started. The psalm ends on the road: "Righteousness goes before him" (v. 13a). In Hebrew, the subject of the verb in verse 13b is not clear. It could be referring to Yahweh, where "Justice before Him goes, that He set His footsteps on the way."[14] Or the subject could be "righteousness," where righteousness "prepares the way for his steps." The ambiguity reflects the unity of Yahweh and the divine attributes, for righteousness and justice are the foundations of his throne (Ps 97:2). The psalm ends with the vision that one day, this will be a reality on earth.

---

11. See Isaiah 59:14, where there is a beautiful personification of righteousness and justice.
12. Sigrid Eder, "Do Justice and Peace Really Kiss Each Other? Personifications in the Psalter and an Exemplary Analysis of Ps 85:11," *VT* 67, no. 3 (2017): 387–402.
13. Eder, "Do Justice and Peace Really Kiss Each Other? Personifications in the Psalter and an Exemplary Analysis of Ps 85:11," 399.
14. Robert Alter, *The Book of Psalms: A Translation with Commentary* (New York: W.W. Norton, 2007), 302.

# PSALM 86

Psalm 86 is the only psalm attributed to David in Book III. This is also the first time that a psalm attributed to David appears since Psalm 72, which concludes by saying, "The prayers of David, the son of Jesse, are ended" (72:20, ESV).[1] Most of the psalms in Book I (Psalms 1–41) and Book II (Psalms 42–72) are attributed to David, and many of these are individual laments, which tend to move from lament to praise. Psalm 86, on the other hand, is a communal lament that moves from praise (vv. 8–10) and a vow of thanksgiving (vv. 12–13) to lament (vv. 14–16). A similar movement occurs in Psalm 27 (see vv. 6–7; compare Psalms 9–10).[2]

Psalm 86 begins with two sets of petitions that include motivations about why God should answer the psalmist (vv. 1–5 and 6–13). The second set of petitions concludes with a vow of thanksgiving (v. 12). While the prayer could have ended with the vow of thanksgiving, it turns instead into another lament as the psalmist turns to God reporting to him (making *sumbong* [report]) what the "arrogant foes" are doing (v. 14). Thus rather than following the traditional pattern of a lament, where the complaint (e.g. "Why?") is followed by a petition and then turns toward praise, Psalm 86 begins with a petition, then turns to praise, and then issues a complaint.

This raises a question about the composition of the psalm. An author can create a sense of expectation in a reader by employing the familiar conventions of a genre.[3] But if a poet deviates from the traditional conventions, the reader needs to pay attention. In Psalm 86, the turn to lament after the vow of thanksgiving creates a sense of the tragic, which accurately reflects the overall mood of Book III, as it contains the most communal laments in the Psalter. The most prominent communal lament in Book III is Psalm 89, which also moves from thanksgiving to complaint (see discussion on Psalm 89 below). Moreover, as we saw previously, Psalm 85 also follows this unexpected movement from praise for God's restoration (vv. 1–3) to petition and lament (vv. 4–7). J. A. Loader demonstrates the interplay between lament and praise in this series of psalms by showing how the two Korahite psalms on either side

---

1. This gives us a glimpse of the rather complicated nature of the history of the composition of the Psalter. See Klaus Seybold, *Introducing the Psalms* (Edinburgh; New York: T & T Clark, 1990), 14–23.
2. For a discussion on the meaning or significance of the return to lament in Psalm 27, see Villanueva, *Psalms 1–72*, 158–162.
3. Mark R. Sneed, "Is the 'wisdom Tradition' a Tradition?," *CBQ* 73, no. 1 (2011): 55.

of Psalm 86 trace the movement from praise to lament.[4] What he failed to observe is the movement from praise to lament within Psalm 86 itself. I have reflected this in the following:

Psalm 84 (praise) – Psalm 85 (lament)
*Psalm 86 (praise – lament)*
Psalm 87 (praise) – Psalm 88 (lament)

This emphasis on the tragic reflects the reality of life in both the exilic and postexilic period. Thus the overall structure of Psalm 86 expresses the experience of God's people in times of hardship. Along with hymns and prayers of thanksgiving, there are also pleas for mercy and complaints. Yet the people of God never give up, because they continue to believe that God will be their help and comforter.

Structurally, Psalm 86 yields to the following division:

Petition with motivations (vv. 1–5),
Petition, hymn, and vow of thanksgiving (vv. 6–13),
Return to lament (vv. 14–17).

## 86:1–5 PETITION WITH MOTIVATIONS

Psalm 86 begins with the psalmist begging God to answer him because he is "poor and needy" (v. 1). In Hebrew, the sound *"i"* dominates this verse, as "answer me" is *'aneyni*, "poor" is *'ani*, and "I" is *'anoki*. This assonance underlines the connection between the petition and its motivation. The motivation for God to answer the psalmist because he is "poor and needy" is common in the lament psalms (see 70:5; 109:22). This not only reflects the situation of the psalmist, but also the perception of God's character as one who hears the cry of those who are suffering (see Ps 9:9; Exod 2:23–24).

The word "poor" includes material poverty, but does not apply to all poor. The poor are those "who through the experience of being brought low allow themselves to bend inwardly."[5] Jesus refers to them as "poor in spirit" (Matt 5:3). The "poor in spirit" are those who may not have been originally poor, but because of their loyalty to God suffered "oppression and material

---

4. J. A. Loader, "Levels of Contextual Synergy in the Korah Psalms: The Example of Psalm 86," *OTE* 23, no. 3 (2010): 674.
5. David J. Pleins, *The Social Visions of the Hebrew Bible: A Theological Introduction* (Louisville, KY: Westminster John Knox, 2001), 421.

disadvantage."[6] They find themselves in trouble. Thus the petition, "Guard my life," which in Hebrew means "don't let me die."[7] The psalmist also describes himself as "faithful" (v. 2), a word that appears previously in Psalm 85 to refer to God's "faithful servants" (v. 8). The word "faithful" comes from the Hebrew *hasid*, which means "pious" or "godly." The psalmist further describes himself as one "who trusts in you" (86:2).

In verse 3, the psalmist refers to himself as one in need of mercy through the petition, "have mercy on me, LORD." This petition is followed by a motivation: "for I call to you *all day long*" (v. 3b, emphasis mine). This is the OT counterpart of the NT exhortation to "pray without ceasing" (1 Thess 5:17). The next verse gives us some clue about the specific nature of the psalmist's petition: "Bring joy to your servant" (v. 4). Poverty, oppression, and suffering can rob us of joy and send us into a downward spiral. When our hope is prostrate on the ground, we need to "lift up" our "soul" (v. 4, ESV). The NIV translates this phrase as "for I put my trust in you." In Filipino, the word *taghoy* (lament) is a loud cry arising out of extreme suffering, which is connected to the word for lament (*panaghoy*). But you cannot cry out a *taghoy* if you are prostrate with your face on the ground. You have to lift up your head, which is a sign of hope.

## 86:6–13 PETITION, HYMN, AND VOW OF THANKSGIVING

Only those who believe that the Lord is "forgiving and good, abounding in love" (v. 5; compare 85:2–3) can continue to cry out to him. Verse 6 employs another plea: "Hear my prayer, LORD." This cry is similar to the cry in verse 1: "Hear me, LORD" (v. 1). The repetition of this prayer for God to hear reinforces the phrase, "all day long" (v. 3), which signifies the persistence of the psalmist. In our modern world, we have gotten used to getting everything in one go, and so repetition is alien to us. But prayer is a process, and we can learn patience and persistence, in particular, from prayers of lament. In Psalm 86, after the psalmist asks God to hear his prayer, he pleads for God to "listen to my cry for mercy" (v. 6). In verse seven, he recalls the times when he was in distress and then declares, "you answer me." Because God is faithful to answer him, he does not give up.

---

6. R. T. France, *The Gospel According to Matthew: An Introduction and Commentary* (Nottingham, England; Downers Grove: Inter-Varsity Press; Intervarsity Press, 2008), 114.
7. Bratcher and Reyburn, *A Translator's Handbook on the Book of Psalms*, 752.

Verses 8–10 resemble a hymn, turning suddenly from petition to praise. The text does not indicate if the prayer has been answered, but the focus changes from the psalmist to God, from "Hear *me*" (vv. 1, 6, emphasis mine) to "there is none like *you*" (v. 8, emphasis mine). The reference to the "gods" in "among the gods" recalls Psalm 82, where God takes his position in the assembly of the gods (see Psalms 82 comments above). Psalm 82 is also linked to Psalm 83, which ends with a declaration "that you alone are the Most High over all the earth" (v. 18). We also find a similar affirmation in Psalm 86: "you alone are God" (v. 10). In this hymn of praise, the psalmist's scope widens from himself to "all the nations" coming in worship to the Lord (v. 9). This shift in perspective often occurs when we pour out our hearts to God.

The experience of worship and awe in verses 8–10 leads the psalmist to articulate his longing to align his life with God's "way" (v. 11) and his heart to "fear" God's name (v. 11b). Thus the psalmist prays: "Teach me your way, O Lord, that I may walk in your truth" (v. 11a). "Truth" here does not refer to general or cognitive knowledge, but to God's knowledge: "*your* truth" (v. 11a, emphasis mine). In Psalm 85, "truth" is personified along with "righteousness" and other attributes associated with God (see 85:10–13). The verb "walk" (*halak*) in Psalm 86:11 (ESV) reflects the dynamic experience of truth, and this word also occurs at the end of the previous psalm: "Righteousness goes [*halak*] before him and prepares the way for his steps" (85:13). In my discussion above, I argue that the subject of the verb "prepare" is ambiguous, but one possible subject is another personified attribute, such as truth. If this is correct, then "truth" is associated with the "way," or road, upon which the Lord wants his people to walk. The psalmist asks God to show him this way so that he might walk in God's truth.

Verses 12–13 contain the vow of thanksgiving, where the psalmist makes a promise: "I will praise you" (v. 12). He makes this vow because of God's great love and because God has "delivered me from the depths" (v. 13). Normally, a vow of thanksgiving marks the end of a lament psalm, but here the psalm unexpectedly turns to a lament, beginning with a complaint (v. 14) and then turning to another petition (vv. 16–17).

### 86:14–17 RETURN TO LAMENT

The psalm could have ended with the psalmist's vow of thanksgiving in verse 13, as laments usually move from lament to praise or thanksgiving (see Psalm 13). But as mentioned above, psalms occasionally return to a lament after making a vow of thanksgiving. The preceding sections contain the three core elements of a lament: the petition, the motivation, and the vow of thanksgiving. Here in the final section, the complaint occurs for the first time as the psalmist complains of "arrogant foes attacking me" (86:14). The word "arrogant" comes from the Hebrew word *zid*, which also means "insolent," "presumptuous," "godless."[8] The psalmist describes the *zid* as those who are "trying to kill me" (v. 14). They would not do this if they knew God, but because "they have no regard for you" (v. 14b), they go about doing violence. Thankfully, in contrast to these tyrants, the psalmist says that "you, Lord, are a compassionate and gracious God" (v. 15; see Exod 34:6). Because of God's compassion and grace, the psalmist trusts that he can come to God, plead for him to "turn to me" (v. 16), and ask for a "sign of your goodness" (v. 16). The psalmist does not specify the sign, but trusts that it will demonstrate the nature of God as One "who gives help and consolation to people who are troubled."[9]

---

8. Tate, *Psalms 51–100*, 376.
9. Hossfeld and Zenger, *Psalms 2*, 376.

# PSALM 87

Psalm 87 is a hymn about Zion and has close links with Psalms 46 and 48. All these Zion hymns extol the beauty and greatness of Zion as a place of worship and express confidence about its security and safety. Because Yahweh dwells within Zion, the people who live there will never be moved. Among the Zion hymns, however, Psalm 87 gives a "more fundamental and comprehensive" picture: "here the nations, among whom are Israel's and YHWH's former enemies [sic] . . . display only enthusiasm and great joy on account of Zion, the city of their origins, from which they still receive all life and good."[1] In Psalm 87, the nations do not go towards Zion, but rather come from Zion. They are born there. In other psalms, the psalmist complains about those who do not know God, but here pagan countries, such as Egypt and Babylon, are counted as "among those who know me" (v. 4).

This extraordinary vision parallels Isaiah 2:1–5; 11:1–10.[2] Kirkpatrick thinks that the purpose of Psalm 87 is to encourage the returned exiles, who could see the frustrating gap between the promises of the prophets and their present situation.[3] But if that is the case, how do we account for its present position in Book III, particularly its neighboring psalms? Psalm 87 is enveloped by two individual laments: Psalms 86 and 88. The latter is one of the darkest psalms, as it ends without any resolution. The tension between the promised restoration and present reality is even worse in the movement from Psalm 87 to 88. As Zenger recognizes, "This tension is deliberately sustained by the psalm composition 84–85 and 87–88, not least by its 'mythicization' of the promises and of YHWH's history with Israel and with all the nations in the dialectic correspondence of primeval time and end time."[4]

Thus even though Psalm 87 depicts Zion in its most fundamental glory, the shift into Psalm 88 warns readers about the danger of placing their trust or hope in a particular place. Jeremiah rebukes those who put their confidence in the Temple but remain wicked in their ways (Jeremiah 7). Even Jesus "refused to endorse the triumphant Zion ideology which viewed the nations as Israel's

---

1. Thijs Booij, "Some Observations on Psalm 87," *VT* 37, no. 1 (1987): 24.
2. Hossfeld and Zenger, *Psalms 2*, 387.
3. Kirkpatrick, *The Book of Psalms*, 519.
4. Hossfeld and Zenger, *Psalms 2*, 397.

servants."⁵ In contrast to the end of Psalm 87, Jesus does not sing and dance as he approaches Jerusalem, but rather weeps and laments (Luke 19:41–44).

## 87:1–2 THE LORD LOVES ZION

Verse 1 is a one-liner that lacks the usual parallel line. Some scholars presume that the first part of the verse has been lost, but there is no evidence for that. As it stands, verses 1–2 serve as the introduction for the psalm. The first word in Hebrew literally reads, "his foundation," which is a way of saying, "he has founded." Isaiah sets this out more clearly: "The LORD has founded Zion" (14:32, ESV). Though the word "city" does not occur until verse 3, we can assume that the Lord has founded Zion, the city of God. This opening statement reminds the postexilic people that they are on solid ground because the Lord himself has founded Zion. Though they may be in exile, God himself founded this city "on the holy mountain" (v. 1). In Hebrew, the form is plural ("mountains"), a reference that could literally refer to "the hills on which Jerusalem is built" or could be more literary, employing the plural of intensification to mean "on *the* holy mountain."⁶

Moreover, the Lord not only founded Zion, but he also "loves" it (v. 2). Among the Zion psalms, this is the only place where God is said to "love" Zion. The word "love" (*ahab*) involves emotional feeling, as does the Filipino word *pag-ibig*.⁷ Compared to "all the other dwellings of Jacob," the Lord is said to love Zion more (v. 2). Specifically, the Lord loves "the gates of Zion." The "gates" could be a synecdoche, a literary device wherein the whole is referred to in terms of one of its parts. Gates have significance in ancient times, as community decisions are made within them. The gates are also where the pilgrims enter the city as they go to the Temple. Furthermore, the gates have moral connotations, as it is no small matter to enter the hill of the Lord. Psalms 15 and 24 expound on the qualities expected or required from those who will be allowed to enter the gates and ascend the hill of the Lord.

---

5. Seán Freyne, *Jesus, A Jewish Galilean: A New Reading of the Jesus Story* (London: T & T Clark International, 2004), 135.
6. Tate, *Psalms 51–100*, 391.
7. *TDOT*, 1:103.

## 87:3–5 "GLORIOUS THINGS ARE SAID OF YOU"

Love not only involves emotional feelings, but also acts of kindness or goodness towards the beloved. The "glorious things" (v. 3) refer to the good and kind things that God has done for Zion. When the glory of God dwells among his people, there is deliverance (Ps 85:9). Moreover, the Zion psalms speak of God dwelling "within her" (46:3; compare 48:3), and therefore she is guaranteed to have victory over her enemies. Thus "glorious things are said of you" (v. 3). In Filipino culture and most Asian cultures, we care deeply about what others say about us. We will do everything to avoid being shamed and will try our best to ensure that others will say good things about us.

In verse 4, the perspective shifts to first person direct address, with God speaking to his people. (Verse 3 uses second person and verses 1–2 use third person.) In one of the most extraordinary statements in the Bible, God says that Egypt (Rahab is a nickname for Egypt) and Babylon are among those "who know me" (v. 4, ESV). In the communal lament in Psalm 79, the people ask God to "pour out your wrath on the nations that do not know you" (v. 6, ESV), which would certainly include Egypt and Babylon. Yet in Psalm 87, God says that Egypt and Babylon, along with Philistia, Tyre, and Ethiopa, were all "born in Zion" (v. 4). Kirkpatrick observes that "By this divine edict, each of them is invested with the full rights and privileges of citizenship as though they had been born in Zion."[8]

Moreover, verse 5 says that people will not only be saying glorious things about Zion, but they will also say, "This one and that one were born in her" (v. 5a). In Isaiah, Zion was the mother of the Israelites (Isa 54:1–10; 66:7–14), but here Zion is depicted as "the mother of the nations."[9] This shift is only possible because the Lord himself "will establish her" (v. 5b). The verb "establish" connects back to the word "founded" at the beginning of the psalm (v. 1).

## 87:6–7 ZION AS THE SOURCE OF WELL-BEING

In verse 6, the psalm transports us to the heavenly realm, where God is pictured as writing the list of people born in Zion in a registry. In other Zion psalms, the nations go up to Zion to worship God, but in Psalm 87, they are already in Zion, making music and singing, "All my fountains are in you" (v. 7). This conveys that "all life, well-being and joy flow to me from you, Zion."[10]

---

8. Kirkpatrick, *The Book of Psalms*, 521.
9. Hossfeld and Zenger, *Psalms 2*, 385.
10. Booij, "Some Observations on Psalm 87," 22.

# PSALM 88

Psalm 88 may be described as a "pure lament."[1] Unlike the typical individual lament psalm, which contains a vow of thanksgiving or a sudden change of mood towards some form of resolution, Psalm 88 is a lament from beginning to end. In Hebrew, the very last word of the psalm is "darkness" (v. 18).

Psalm 88 reminds us that not every experience has a happy ending. As such, it serves as a much-needed companion for those who do not experience healing or restoration, reminding them that they are not alone, for others have walked the dark valley before them. The capacity of the psalmist to remain in the utter darkness and to keep praying into the complete silence of God reveal the persistence of the human spirit in relation to the divine.

The sudden transition from the "glorious things" of Zion (v. 3) and its ever-flowing "fountains of joy" (v. 7) in Psalm 87 to the enveloping darkness of Psalm 88 highlights the sense of the tragic. Whereas Psalm 87 ends with all the nations singing and dancing together, celebrating Zion as the mother of all nations (v. 7), the superscription for Psalm 88 suddenly announces a "song" of petition to be "saved from death." In Hebrew, the verb "sing" in 87:7 shares a root with the noun "song" in the superscription for Psalm 88. This tragic shift from nations rejoicing to an individual suffering alone in the darkness prepares us for another great reversal, which we will encounter again in the abrupt turn from thanksgiving to lament in Psalm 89.

Although the psalm is dark, it is not without hope, for even though its last word is "darkness" (v. 18), its very first word is "Yahweh" (v. 1). We can cling to hope because we are not alone: there is someone to cry out to in the darkness. The darkness is not empty, but rather gives us space to cry, complain, lament. The hope in Psalm 88 is in the act of lament itself. The lament *is* a sign of hope. Psalm 88 is structured around crying out or calling out to God:

"Lord . . . day and night I *cry* out to you" (v. 1);
"I *call* to you, Lord, every day" (v. 9);
"But I *cry* out to you for help, Lord" (v. 13, emphasis mine).

Notice also that the divine name "Yahweh" (translated as Lord), occurs in each of these three verses as well as verse 14 ("Why, Lord, do you reject me?"). The psalm is comprised of a series of calls out to God, and this act of

---

1. Villanueva, *Psalms 1–72*, 325–326. Psalm 70 is another example of a "pure lament."

crying is a sign of hope. The overall structure demonstrates that as long as there is lament, there is hope.

## 88:1–9A "LORD . . . DAY AND NIGHT I CRY OUT TO YOU"

For many scholars, Psalm 88 is "the saddest Psalm in the whole Psalter."[2] Goulder thinks this description is an error, since the psalmist declares that the LORD is "the God of my salvation" from the start (v. 1).[3] However, this positive affirmation in verse 1 is too short to match the length of the subsequent lament, which runs from verse 1a until the end of the psalm. The weight of the lament is simply too heavy to be carried by a single strand of praise. While Goulder argues that an answer comes in the praise portion of the opening sections of Psalm 89,[4] that psalm also moves to lament, which makes the psalmist's situation even more tragic! (This movement is similar to Psalms 9–10, as discussed in the commentary on Psalm 89 below.)

Yet the opening verses of Psalm 88 do reveal the persistence of the psalmist. In the midst of God's silence, the psalmist's prayer continues to "come before you," even as he asks God to "turn your ear to my cry" (v. 2b). The word "cry" at the end of verse 2 comes from the Hebrew word *rinnah*, which refers to a "cry of lament, wailing."[5] Note that this "cry of lament" is referred to as a "prayer" in verse 2a. Psalm 88 is full of complaints, crying, and even blaming God (see vv. 6–8 below), but lest we forget, these are considered to be prayers as well.

As in other lament psalms, the petition (vv. 1–2) is followed by the psalmist's motivation or reason for praying. The psalmist is "overwhelmed with troubles" (v. 3a), and the life he describes in verses 3–5 seems to be taking a downward spiral. In verse 3, he says his "life draws near to Sheol" (ESV).[6] The NEB renders it as my woes "have brought me to the threshold of Sheol." In verse 4a, other people consider him as "among those who go down to the pit." (Notice the *downward* movement to the pit.) In verse 4b, he describes himself as "a man who has no strength" (ESV), but there is an implicit contradiction because the Hebrew word for "man" here, *geber*, "indicates a strong, vigorous

---

2. Kirkpatrick, *The Book of Psalms*, 523. Compare Beat Weber, "'JHWH, Gott Meiner Rettung!': Beobachtungen und Erwägungen zur Struktur von Psalm Lxxxviii," *VT* 58, no. 4–5 (2008): 595.
3. Michael A. Goulder, *The Psalms of the Sons of Korah* (Sheffield: JSOT Press, 1982), 203.
4. Goulder, *The Psalms of the Sons of Korah*, 203.
5. *HALOT*, 3:1247.
6. The verb *nagaʿ* with the preposition *le* means "to approach." *BDB*, 619.

man."[7] The implication is that he is supposed to be strong, and yet he "has no strength." In verse 5a, he sees himself as one "set apart among the dead" (ESV). The phrase "set apart" here comes from the Hebrew word *hofshi*, which means "freed." In Isaiah 58:6, the word *hofshi* is used to speak of the oppressed being set free, but what is the use of being "free" if you are already dead? Finally, in verse 5b, he likens himself to those who "lie down in the grave." Surely, this is the lowest point one can get!

Yet precisely at this lowest point, as the psalmist is imagining himself lying down in the grave, we observe a change of direction upwards, for the psalmist explicitly begins to address God again. Even in the darkest depths, the psalmist is not alone, for he can cry out to God. In verse 5c, the psalmist describes the dead as those "whom *you* remember no more, who are cut off from your care" (emphasis mine), and then in verse 6a, he accuses God of putting "me to the lowest pit." The poet employs an ellipsis in the next line, by not repeating the subject "you" (v. 6a) to draw attention on the nature of this place where God put him: "in the darkest depths" (v. 6b). The word "darkness" is a key theme in this psalm, which ends with that word. What makes the pit experience even more difficult is its social-relational consequence: "You have taken from me my closest friends" (v. 8). Thus his eyes "are dim with grief" (v. 9).

Why did God put him in the depths? The answer is implied in verse 7: "Your wrath." The word "wrath" is linked to the sinfulness of God's people (see Ps 106:23; compare 78:38). Those who are under God's wrath due to their sin feel the heaviness of God's hand. In 88:7, the psalmist describes God's wrath as that which "lies heavily on me" (see also Pss 32:4; 38:4).

### 88:9B–12 "I CALL TO YOU, LORD, EVERY DAY"

In other psalms, we find the psalmist confessing his sins to God (Pss 32:5; 38:4), but in Psalm 88, there is no admission of guilt or repentance. Instead, the psalmist continuously calls out or cries out to God. In verse 9b, the psalmist says, "I call to you, LORD, every day," recalling the "day and night" in verse 1. This time, however, the psalmist adds a movement: "I spread out my hands to you" (v. 9c). This action is similar to the psalmist's turning to God in verse 5b, for stretching out one's hands is also an upward movement, a sign of persistence. When we reach the bottom of a pit, we tend to stay prostrated, with our face downward, no longer wanting to get up, wishing we could stay

---

7. Tate, *Psalms 51–100*, 396.

there forever. But the psalmist is not giving up. He continues to address God by asking him a series of interrogative questions.

In these questions (vv. 10–12), the psalmist hurls his bitter laments at God. The repetition of the interrogative particle *ha* also appears in Psalm 77:7–9 (compare Ps 85:6–7, where the interrogative is used twice). The first question pertains to whether God will still perform his wonders to the dead (v. 10). The word "dead" recalls verses 3–5, which depict his journey downwards to the grave. One notices a similar "downward" movement in the grammatical construction of the next two verses. In verse 10, an active verb, "perform," is used to describe God's active working of wonders. But in the next two verses, the psalmist shifts to passive verbs: "*Is* your love declared in the grave?" (v. 11) and "*Are* your wonders known in the place of darkness . . .?" (v. 12, emphasis mine).[8] Earlier, the divine attributes of love (*hesed*) and righteousness (*tsedeq*) are portrayed as dynamically active in the life of God's people (85:10–13), but that description is only true in the land of the living. While Goulder argues that the questions in verses 11–12 presuppose that the psalmist's faithfulness and steadfast love are "valid,"[9] the attributes of God are actually being questioned rather than affirmed. Thus the answer to all these rhetorical questions is "no," which places the psalmist in the "darkest depths," where there is no more hope.

## 88:13-18 "I CRY TO YOU FOR HELP"

But remarkably, this admission of hopelessness leads the psalmist to persist even more. For the third time, the psalmist cries out to God: "But I cry to you for help, Lord" (v. 13; see also vv. 1b, 9b). The adversative "but" is crucial. Despite the psalmist's awareness of the negation of God's divine attributes, he continues to cry out to him. In verse 13b, the psalmist says, "in the morning my prayer comes before you." In laments, "morning" signifies the dawning of hope, the turning of mourning into dancing (Ps 30:5b), but here, the morning carries no light. The remaining five verses of the psalm remain as dark as ever. In verse 14, the psalmist utters the characteristic cry of the lament, "why" (along with, "how long?"). Right before this cry, the psalmist refers to his words as "my prayer" (v. 13). As noted above, in lament, honest questions are considered to be prayers. In an agonizing cry, the psalmist asks God, "why do you reject me and hide your face from me?" (v. 14).

---

8. The verbs "declared" and "known" are in the *pual* and *nifal* form, respectively.
9. Michael A. Goulder, *The Psalms of the Sons of Korah*, 203.

Verse 15 hints at the chronic nature of his malady or difficulty as something that has afflicted him "from my youth" (v. 15).[10] The words "close to death" appears to have been translated in the LXX as "tired, weary." If this represents the original reading, then the psalmist's experience is similar to chronic depression, but the psalm is open to different types of suffering. In the OT, however, sickness is often interpreted as a sign of God's wrath. The person is suffering because he has sinned against God. Verse 16 refers again to God's wrath (see v. 7), but the psalmist does not mention his sin or offer any admission of guilt. Rather, his emphasis is on the destructive effect of God's wrath. The psalmist compares it to a "flood" that completely engulfs him (v. 17). Most painfully, God has "caused my beloved and my friend to shun me" (v. 18a, ESV). No human being can bear such loneliness and utter dejection. The psalm ends with the words, "darkness is my closest friend" (v. 18). In Hebrew, this sentence consists of two words: "my companions or my friends" and "dark place." The Hebrew word *machshakh* (literally, "dark place") is parallel to Sheol. In light of the use of the word "darkness" (*makhshakkim*) in verse 6, we may also translate the word in verse 18 as "darkness." The verbless Hebrew construction could be translated literally as "my friends are darkness." Or following Alter's rendering, "My friends – utter darkness."[11]

That Psalm 88 ends with "utter darkness" is important. It shows that there is a place in the presence of God for those whose life and experience end in tragedy. This is a much-needed corrective to the one-sided emphasis on victory which characterize much of modern Christianity.

---

10. I can identify very well with the psalmist, as I have been diagnosed with dysthymia, a chronic type of depression. Federico G. Villanueva, *Lord, I'm Depressed: The Lament Psalms and Depression* (Manila, Philippines: OMF Literature, 2020).
11. Alter, *The Book of Psalms*, 310.

# PSALM 89

The psalm's opening words, "I will sing of the Lord's great love forever" (Ps 89:1), echo the famous line from Lamentations: "Because of the Lord's great love we are not consumed . . . They are new every morning; great is your faithfulness" (Lam 3:22–23). Interestingly, Lamentations 3:22–23 is preceded by an individual lament (vv. 1–21) that is comparable to Psalm 88. Berlin notes that Psalm 88 and Lamentations 3 "share not only the same general picture but also a number of the same phrases."[1] In Lamentations 3, the speaker identifies himself as "the *man* who has seen affliction" (3:1). The word "man" comes from the Hebrew word *geber* ("strong man"), which is the same word used in Psalm 88:4b, "I am the *man* who has no strength" (ESV). The word "darkness" also occurs twice in both passages (Ps 88:6, 18; Lam 3:2, 6).[2]

Berlin does not mention, however, the similarity between Lamentations 3 and Psalm 89. Both Lamentations 3 and Psalm 89 move from hymnic declaration to lament. Individual laments usually end on a note of confidence or praise, but the declaration of God's faithfulness in Lamentations 3:22–23 turns to a communal lament in verses 42–66. Similarly, there is a sudden change of mood in Psalm 89 from the initial hymn of praise (vv. 1–37) to a communal lament (vv. 38–52).

Previous scholarship has viewed this psalm as a composite rather than a unity. One influential position understands the development of the psalm into three phases: "the older hymnic tradition (vv. 2–3, 6–19) was integrated into a late-exilic community song of lament (vv. 4–5, 20–46), expanded by two strophes (vv. 47–49, 50–52)."[3] While we no longer have access to the history of the psalm's composition, one important question to consider is why a composer would put a hymn before the lament. This raises another question about the function of the structure of Psalm 89.

The structure of Psalm 89 is similar to Psalms 9–10 and Psalm 44, where the overall movement from a hymn of praise or thanksgiving to a lament depicts a sense of tragedy. This type of structure is often employed to convey

---

[1]. Adele Berlin, *Lamentations: A Commentary* (Louisville, KY: Westminster John Knox Press, 2002), 89.
[2]. Federico G. Villanueva, *The "Uncertainty of a Hearing": A Study of the Sudden Change of Mood in the Psalms of Lament*, VTSup (Leiden: Brill, 2008), 224–225.
[3]. Hossfeld and Zenger, *Psalms 2*, 402.

tragic experiences, such as defeat in a war (Psalm 44), injustice to the poor (Psalm 10), and the failure of the Davidic king (Psalm 89).[4]

Needless to say, present-day communities also go through catastrophic occurrences and heart-rending incidents. Psalm 89 teaches us about the importance of creating space to express our anguish, articulate our grief, and pour out our misery. Unfortunately, many contemporary Christian groups fail to nurture this as a consequence of an overemphasis on positivity and victory. Psalm 89 reminds us that it is alright to admit defeat. But we cannot stop there, for Psalm 89 also endorses active engagement with God. The faith community may need to argue with God, just as Moses did. Citing God's promises to David, the people complain about God's failure to keep his promises. In spite of their complaints, they cling to God, pleading for God to "remember" his servant (v. 50).

## 89:1–4 LET ME SING OF THE LORD'S GREAT LOVE

The opening verse of Psalm 89 is similar to Lamentations 3:22–23. In Hebrew, the first two words are exactly the same: "the steadfast love of the LORD" (Ps 89:1; Lam 3:22; ESV).[5] The word "faithfulness" also occurs in both passages (Ps 89:1; Lam 3:23). Most relevantly, both move from a declaration of God's steadfast love to lament. This shift reflects the reverse movement of the typical form-critical understanding of lament, which describes a lament as moving from lament to praise (see commentary on v. 38 below). In Lamentations 3, it takes 19 verses for the hymn of praise to turn to lament (see Lam 3:42b). In Psalm 89, it takes 35 verses before the hymn of praise turns to lament. But even at the beginning of Psalm 89, there is a hint of the tragic movement that is to come at the end.

Verse 2 begins with an emphatic, "Indeed" (*ki*). The NIV does not translate the Hebrew word *ki*, beginning instead with the word, "I": "I will declare . . ." (v. 2). The ESV translates the word *ki* as "for": "For I said . . ." (v. 2). However, the translation "indeed" is better, because it builds from the previous verse. After the psalmist declares that he will sing of God's steadfast love in verse 1, he reiterates this again in verse 2: "Indeed I said, steadfast love is built up

---
4. See Federico G. Villanueva, "From Thanksgiving to Lament: The Shape of Psalm 120," *VT* 70, no. 3 (2020): 479–497.
5. The Hebrew of both verses simply has two words–*khasde yhwh*.

forever" (my translation).⁶ The psalmist is declaring from the very beginning that he has already declared God's steadfast love, which is confirmed in verse 2 by God himself: "you have established your faithfulness in heaven itself." Thus verse 2 contains both the psalmist's affirmation and Yahweh's confirmation. The subsequent verses will build on these two foundational declarations.

There is a close link between these opening two verses and the divine speech that begins in verse 3. The word "forever," which is used earlier to speak of the steadfast love of the Lord (v. 2), is applied in verse 4 to God's covenant with David: "I will establish your line forever." The word "establish" in verse 4 is the same verb that is used in verse 2b ("you have established your faithfulness"). Finally, the word "built up" (*banah*), which is first used in verse 2a (ESV), occurs again in verse 4, where God promises that he will "build" David's throne forever.

## 89:5–8 LET HEAVENS SING OF THE LORD'S FAITHFULNESS

Verse 5 also parallels verse 1. Just as the psalmist will sing of the "LORD's great love" (v. 1), "the heavens praise your wonders, LORD" (v. 5). The "heavens" not only represent the sky, but also the heavenly beings. The next three verses of the psalm convey the typical ancient worldview, which sees the known world as inhabited by spiritual and divine beings. This is similar to the Filipino worldview.⁷ When the psalmist asks the rhetorical question, "who in the skies above can compare with the LORD?" (v. 6a), he has in mind the plurality of gods, which we also encounter in Psalm 82. Psalm 89 mentions "heavenly beings" (v. 6b) and the "council of the holy ones" (v. 7). Psalm 89 also recalls Psalm 82:1, which speaks of God as presiding "in the divine council" (ESV). Among the gods, the psalmist declares, there is none like the Lord, who is "greatly feared" and "more awesome than all who surround him" (v. 7). Verse 8 asks the same rhetorical question, "Who is like you, LORD?" This second question is followed by a similar affirmation, but instead of being surrounded by a divine council (v. 7), God is surrounded by "your faithfulness" (v. 8b). The shift to the subject of who or what surrounds God is deliberate. What distinguishes God from the other gods and heavenly beings is his character, particularly his

---

6. The LXX has a second person translation–"You said." But this is probably an attempt to smoothen the reading since the following verse begins with a second person verb as well. I go for the more difficult reading preserved in the MT.
7. William Henry Scott, *Barangay: Sixteenth-Century Philippine Culture and Society* (Quezon City: Ateneo de Manila University Press, 1999), 77–86.

faithfulness. The word "faithfulness" is repeated seven times in Psalm 89 (vv. 1, 2, 5, 8, 24, 33, 49), a repetition that is intentional rather than coincidental.[8]

## 89:9–18 THE VICTORIOUS KING WHOSE THRONE IS FOUNDED ON RIGHTEOUSNESS AND JUSTICE

This emphasis on God's character also forms the climax of the next section (vv. 9–14). These verses have to be understood within their ancient West Asian background (see comments in Ps 74:12–17 above). Within this background, the conflict at sea and within creation are closely linked. The deity had to defeat the sea monster before he could create the universe. In Psalm 89, God rules over "the surging sea" (v. 9) and crushes "Rahab," the sea monster (v. 10). Thus the psalmist can claim that the heavens and the earth belong to God (v. 12). God is the creator of both the "north and the south," including "Tabor and Hermon" (v. 13), which are "the mountains of the gods" (42:7).[9]

Verses 13 and 14 are the psalmist's responses to God's power over the forces of chaos and his subsequent acts of creation. Verse 13 praises God's "strong arm," which refers to his power. But what makes God different from the other gods is his character: "Righteousness and justice are the foundation of your throne" (v. 14). This statement, along with the emphasis on justice in Psalm 82, further demonstrates the link between these two psalms. The phrase in Psalm 89:14b, "love and faithfulness go before you," is similar to the language in Psalm 85:10 and 13, which personify the divine attributes.

As the psalmist reflects on the people's fortune to know this great God, he responds with gratitude: "Blessed are the people who know the festal shout" (Ps 89:15, ESV). The "festal shout" refers to "joyful shouting in worship."[10] It is not clear to which specific occasion or festival the "festal shout" refers, but God's people are gathered together in his presence, worshiping him, and they are blessed because they have a God who is not only powerful but also faithful. They are also full of rejoicing (v. 16), because God is the one who gives them strength and victory (v. 17). The "horn" in the second part of this verse is also symbolic of strength or victory. Their victory is closely linked with their king, who is described as "our shield" (v. 18; compare 47:9).

---

8. Tate, *Psalms 51–100*, 420.
9. Hossfeld and Zenger, *Psalms 2*, 409.
10. *DCH*, 677.

## 89:19–37 THE LORD'S EVERLASTING COVENANT WITH DAVID

The reference to "our king" (v. 18) at the end of the previous section transitions into this section, which focuses on the divine promises made to the Davidic king. The "vision" (v. 19a) refers to the vision Nathan describes to David in 2 Samuel 7:17. In Psalm 89, that vision not only pertains to Nathan or David, but also to the people of Israel, which is indicated by the words, "your faithful people" (v. 19). Then God speaks in verse 19b, describing how he bestowed his "strength on a warrior." The word "strength" comes from the Hebrew word *'ezer*, which means "help." Other scholars propose the word *nezer* (crown) to fit with the verb "bestowed" (literally, "set") and in anticipation of verse 40 (see discussion of v. 40 below). Tate argues that the word "boy" (from the Ugaritic *gzr*) is more appropriate in view of the parallelism in verse 20.[11] Yet the context for the following verses highlights how God chose (v. 20), empowered (v. 21), and promised victory through David (vv. 22–24), which supports the Hebrew reading, "help." Because of God's "help," the anointed one will have victory over his enemies. God also promises that through his name, "his horn will be exalted" (v. 24). From a mere shepherd boy, God "found" him and "anointed" him to be king (v. 20). This boy will call God "my Father" (v. 26). God also promised that he would extend his rule, setting "his hand over the sea, his right hand over the rivers" (v. 25). The language is reminiscent of Psalm 80, which speaks of Israel's growth as a powerful nation, likening Israel to a vine whose "branches reached as far as the Sea, its shoots as far as the River" (v. 11). If we follow the movement of Psalm 80, however, we notice that the lament portion of this psalm follows immediately after verse 11. The connection with Psalm 80 might be deliberate, as the psalmist has been trying to build his case through the psalm, and in 89:27, he comes to the highest glory of the Davidic king, whom God says will be the "most exalted of the kings of the earth."

Psalm 89:28–29 echoes back to verses 3–4, returning our focus to the covenant God made with David. God himself promises that he will keep his "steadfast love" with David forever (v. 28; compare v. 4). Moreover, he promises that David's line will continue "as the heavens endure" (v. 29; compare v. 4). Alluding to 2 Samuel 7:14–16, God promises that even when David's sons fail to obey God's commandments, they will be disciplined, but God will never take his steadfast love from them (v. 33a), nor will he betray his "faithfulness" (v. 33b, compare v. 24). In verse 34, the covenant is mentioned for the third time (compare vv. 3, 28), where God promises that he will not

---

11. Tate, *Psalms 51–100*, 410.

violate his "covenant." He has "sworn by my holiness" that he will not lie to David (v. 35) and that his line will be forever (v. 36). There has been debate about the identity of the "witness in the sky" (v. 37), which could refer to God himself, the one who dwells in the skies (v. 6), who is also a faithful witness (Jer 42:5).[12]

## 89:38–52 LAMENT AGAINST GOD AND DOXOLOGY

In this section, there is a sharp turn from the hymn of praise to lament – from God's glorious promises to David to the shameful defeat of the Davidic line. The very first phrase is strongly adversative, "but you" (v. 38). Normally, in psalms of lament, the adversative "but" marks a transition into praise or a vow of thanksgiving (see Ps 13:5–6). But because Psalm 89 begins with praise, the adversative, "but," turns the other direction towards lament. At this point, the psalm also takes on a strong, accusatory tone. "But *you*" recalls the earlier promises God made regarding the vision concerning the election of David ("Once *you* spoke," v. 19). In that vision, God promises that he will strengthen, uphold, protect, and give victory to his servant against his enemies (vv. 21–23) and that his "steadfast love" (*hesed*) will be with him (v. 24). This promise of God's "steadfast love" echoes the very beginning of the psalm. Following the LXX, verse 2 says, "For *you* said, steadfast love will be built forever." The Lord later confirms this promise in verse 28, saying, "My steadfast love I will keep for him forever" (ESV) and then promises to uphold it when David's sons "violate my decrees" (v. 31). The word "violate" is repeated again in verse 34, reiterating the divine promise that "I will not violate my covenant." And yet in verse 38, the psalmist accuses God, saying, "*you* have rejected . . . your anointed one." God has "defiled his crown in the dust" (v. 39), where the word "defiled" shares a root with "violate" in verses 31 and 34, indicating a deliberate attempt to contrast the divine promises with the psalmist's present situation. Though God has promised to give victory to his servant, God has actually "exalted the right hand of his foes" (v. 42). What the psalmist dreads in Psalm 13:4 has transpired: "you have made all his enemies rejoice" (89:42).

The fate of the people is intertwined with that of the fate of their king, so when the king's crown is "defiled," both the king's honor and the people's honor are violated. Verses 40–41 express the people's vulnerability and brokenness. The psalmist complains that God has "broken through his walls" (v. 40) and

---

12. Hossfeld and Zenger, *Psalms 2*, 411.

that "All who pass by have plundered him" (v. 41), recalling the lament in Psalm 80:12–13. As a result, the king and his people have become "the scorn of his neighbors" (89:41).

This note on shame forms the core of the lament, which occurs three times in this section: first, at the end of the initial complaint concerning the failure of the divine covenant to David (vv. 38–41); second, at the end of the next complaint, concerning the failure of the promises of victory to David (vv. 42–45); third, at the end of the psalm (vv. 50–51), where the word "mocked" (*charaf*) occurs once in its nominal form (v. 50) and twice as a verb (v. 51). The word "shame" (v. 45) is followed by the characteristic cry of a lament, "how long?" (v. 46), which further emphasizes the centrality of shame in this lament. In the communal lament in Psalm 79, the people also ask, "How long, LORD?" (v. 5), after complaining that "the nations have invaded your inheritance" (v. 1). The metaphorical language in their lament is very similar:

"How long will your jealousy burn like fire?" (79:5b);
"How long will your wrath burn like fire?" (89:46).

Psalm 89 is also similar to the lament in Psalm 74, as both contain the lament, "how long?" followed by the petition, "remember":

| "How long . . . ?" (74:10) | ⟶ | "Remember how the enemy has mocked you" (74:18); |
| "How long LORD?" (89:46) | ⟶ | "Remember how fleeting is my life" (89:47–48). |

Yet the petition in Psalm 89 is focused on the self and pertains to the experience of the individual, whereas the more communal petition in Psalm 74 is focused on the enemy's actions.

This personal petition in Psalm 89 implies a complaint against God about the transitory nature of human existence. Within Book III, the petition alludes to the historical narration in Psalm 78 about how God "remembered" that humans "were but flesh, a passing breeze that does not return" (v. 39), and therefore extends mercy to his people (v. 38). In Psalm 89:47, the psalmist appeals to the same mercy. The people's present situation has brought home the reality of the fleeting nature of human existence. Literally, verse 47 reads, "I, what is the duration of life?"[13] The experience of shame resulting from defeat has affected the psychological and emotional condition of the psalmist.

---

13. *DCH*, 227.

## Psalm 89

Like the speaker in Psalm 88, who feels that he is a man (*geber*) who has no strength (88:4b), the speaker in Psalm 89 laments, "What man [*geber*] can live and not see death?" (89:48). The words "death" and "Sheol" or "grave" in 89:48 echo the psalmist's sentiments in Psalm 88, where he says he feels like one among the dead (88:3, 5). These two psalms may have been placed side by side to emphasize the parallels between the *geber* in Psalm 88 and Psalm 89. The king in Psalm 89, who is to be a warrior, has become like the man in Psalm 88 – without strength. But like the *geber* in Psalm 88, the speaker in Psalm 89 is also not giving up. He continues to call on God: "Where is your former great love?" (89:49). Lament here is a sign of hope. The psalmist continues to come to God in spite of his situation, pleading until the end for God to "remember."

The petition to "remember" (89:50) reflects the feeling of being forgotten, near the grave, and also contrasts with the psalmist's declaration at the beginning of the psalm that he will sing of the Lord's steadfast love (v. 1). Like the psalmist in Psalm 77, the psalmist in Psalm 89 has remembered God's covenant, but God has forgotten. Nevertheless, the psalmist persists in crying out to God about what his enemies have done to him (vv. 50–51). The psalmist may feel as if he is near the grave, but at least he is not there alone. Because he has someone to cry out to, the benediction at the end of Psalm 89 (and Book III) is not inappropriate or contradictory. Rather, this benediction remains a fitting ending for a "book" that continues to hope in God amidst the darkness.

# PSALM 90

Psalm 90 reflects what we sometimes say in Filipino in the midst of prolonged suffering: "It's been all suffering, with no relief" (*Panay na lang hirap, walang ginhawa*). Some scholars argue that Psalm 90 is the beginning of an answer to the lament in Psalm 89,[1] but if so, it is certainly not the answer one would expect. Rather than a shout of victory or restoration, Psalm 90 is a communal lament, a continuation of the latter part of Psalm 89 (vv. 38–51). In Psalm 90, the people complain, "All our days pass away under your wrath; we finish our years with a moan" (v. 9). If there is one thing the people want, it's *ginhawa*, which means "relief," "comfort," or "good feeling" (*mabuting pakiramdam*).[2] In verse 14, the people beg God to "satisfy us in the morning with your unfailing love." When you are tired, you gasp for breath (*hinahabol ang hininga*), and *ginhawa* ("relief") is close to the word for "breath" (*hininga*).[3] Having suffered for a long time, the people need to find a place where they can rest and breathe.

Psalm 90 is the first psalm in Book IV (Psalms 90–106), which follows the tragic conclusion of Book III (Psalms 73–89). The Temple has been destroyed and now lies in ruins (Psalm 74). The Davidic kingship has failed (Psalm 89). Where will the people go? In the beginning of Book III, the psalmist goes to the sanctuary when he is about to give up his faith (73:17). In Psalm 90, the people do the same when they declare, "LORD, *you* have been our dwelling place throughout all generations" (v. 1, emphasis mine). The community is saying that long before the Temple was built – even before the Davidic kingship was conceived – God was already there. The word "dwelling" (*ma'on*) is used earlier to refer to the sanctuary of God (76:2). Psalm 73 also highlights the importance of the sanctuary as the place where the presence of God dwells. In Psalm 90, however, God *himself* becomes the sanctuary, their dwelling place (*ma'on*). In Filipino, the word for "home" is *tahanan*. One of the blessings of

---

1. Psalm 89 is a tragic lament over the downfall of the Davidic kingship (see comments above).
2. Zeus Salazar, "Ang Kamalayan at Kaluluwa: Isang Paglilinaw ng Ilang Konsepto sa Kinagisnang Sikolohiya," in *Ulat ng pambansang kumperensya sa sikolohiyang Pilipino*, ed. L. F. Antonio, E. S. Reyes, and N. R. Almonte (Quezon City, Philippines: Pambansang Samahan sa Sikolohiyang Pilipino, 1976), 131.
3. Salazar writes, "*Ang ginhawa ang siyang batayan ng kaayusang pandamdamin at pandama ng tao. Ang ginhawa ang siyang nagbibigay ng 'gaan sa buhay' at ng kabaligtaran nito.*" Salazar, "*Ang Kamalayan at Kaluluwa*," 140.

the people of God is that they always have a place to go because their dwelling, their *tahanan*, is God.

This psalm is usually divided into two parts:

the community pours out their heart to God (vv. 1–12);
the community asks God for *ginhawa* ("relief, comfort") (vv. 13–17).

## 90:1–12 THE COMMUNITY POURS OUT THEIR HEART TO GOD

The superscription for Psalm 90 begins, "A prayer of Moses the man of God." When all hope seems to have perished, with the temple in ruins and the Davidic kingdom diminished, where will the people go? What will they do? Psalm 90 tells us that they go to God, and they pray a prayer attributed to Moses, "the man of God."

Moses was remembered as "the man of God" because he had such an intimate relationship with God, and so when Moses asked God to reveal his glory, God honored Moses's request (see Exod 33:21–34:7). Moses was particularly special to the people of God because he was with the Israelites in the desert. In Psalm 90, the people find themselves journeying through a desert experience, and so they turn to Moses to accompany them and guide them through their difficulties.

In verse 1, "Lord, you have been our dwelling place throughout all generations," the Hebrew word used for "dwelling place" (*ma'on*) is not the usual word for "home." *Ma'on* has the "basic meaning of 'den' of wild animals. . . . The description is of a lonely, desolate, and fearful place, far from civilization and inhabited only by wild beasts."[4] It depicts difficult accessibility, a place where people go to escape. The word is also associated with "refuge," which is the translation found in the LXX. In Psalm 76:2, the same word is used to speak of God's dwelling (compare Ps 26:8). In Psalm 84, the psalmist expresses his deep admiration for God's Temple and his longing to "dwell" there, but Psalm 90 is the only place where the psalmist says that God himself is "our dwelling" (v. 1). In Psalm 74, the people lament the destruction of the Temple, but in Psalm 90, the people identify God himself as their dwelling place, to whom they go to find refuge. God is their place of escape from life's troubles, a home away from home. Both Psalm 90:1 and Psalm 89:1 use the phrase,

---

4. *NIDOTTE* 2:1015.

"through all generations," or literally, "generations and generations." In Psalm 89:1, the people say they will make God's steadfast love known through all generations; in Psalm 90:1, the people declare that God has been their home through all generations.

Psalm 90:2 pushes back the time of God's faithful presence even further, to the time preceding creation, "before the mountains were born" (v. 2a). This verse echoes Genesis 1, offering a theological reflection on creation. In Genesis 1, God speaks the word and everything comes into being (except the creation of human beings, which comes in Genesis 2), but in Psalm 90, the act of creating causes God pain, which is not present in the Genesis account. The verb, "you brought forth," is used to describe the labor pains of a woman giving birth (Deut 32:18).[5] Though God is "from everlasting to everlasting" (90:2b), he is so intimately connected to his creation that he shares the people's pain and is with them in their suffering.

All humans have a beginning and an end, and so they can never be described as existing "from everlasting to everlasting." If God says, "Return to dust, you mortals" (v. 3b), then they're gone. The psalmist draws a contrast between God's everlasting nature (v. 2) and human mortality (vv. 3–5). The latter verses form an inclusio, with an emphasis on the divine conception of time:

"You turn people back to dust" (v. 3);
   "For a thousand years in your sight are but as
      yesterday . . ." (v. 4, ESV);[6]
"You sweep people away in the sleep of death" (v. 5).

Verses 3 and 5 highlight divine action and its effect on human existence, which is temporary and vulnerable. From the divine perspective, however, time is limitless. God has all the time in the world, while people have very limited days. Human existence is likened to the grass: "In the morning it springs up new, but by evening it is dry and withered" (v. 6).

Verses 7 and 9 explain that human life is short because of God's anger (v. 7) and wrath (v. 9). In Hebrew, both these verses begin with the preposition "for" (*ki*). Verse 8 focuses on human sin as the reason for divine anger and wrath. In the first part of verse 8, the psalmist says to God, "You have set our iniquities before you." In the second part of verse 8, the psalmist emphasizes

---

5. *HALOT*, 310.
6. Some commentators propose that verse 4 should be moved after verse 2, since it continues the line of thought expressed there. But as the present structure shows, verse 4 fits better in its present position, since it forms the middle part of the inclusio here.

that even "our secret sins" are exposed "in the light of your presence" (compare Ps 19:12–13). Because of God's anger for the people's sins, their days and years are numbered (v. 10). The link between sin and limited life span can be traced from Genesis 6, where God decides to limit the years of human existence due to sin. In Genesis, God sets the limit to one hundred and twenty years (6:3). Psalm 90 puts the number even lower – at seventy years or eighty, if someone is strong (v. 10). Then the psalmist laments that even "the best" of those years are "but trouble and sorrow" (v. 10).

In response to this sobering realization, the psalmist cries out, "Who knows the power of your anger?" (v. 11, my translation). The NIV translates this rhetorical question in Hebrew as a statement, missing the force of the text. Verse 11 repeats the words "anger" and "wrath" (from vv. 7 and 9) to express the severity of God's fury and to solicit fear, reverence, and awe from the people. Moreover, the psalmist asks God to "teach us to number our days" (v. 12), so that the people will begin to perceive the meaning of their life from a divine perspective and seek God's wisdom to make each day worth living.

## 90:13–17 THE COMMUNITY ASKS GOD FOR RELIEF (*GINHAWA*)

The last section looks back to the first part of the psalm, employing the same verb ("return") in verse 13 that is used in verse 3. In verse 3, God speaks to the "children of men" and says, "return." In verse 13, the people ask God to "return" (ESV; compare 80:14). The word "return" comes from the Hebrew word *shub*, which also means "repent" or "relent." The NIV uses "relent." The familiar lament, "how long?" (v. 13a), expresses the agony of the people who have been in the "desert" for a long time and are asking God to change his dealings with them. In the second part of verse 13, they ask God to change his "mind." This is the meaning of the Hebrew verb *nikam*, which is translated as "have compassion" in the NIV. But the meaning "change one's mind" fits more with the preceding context as well as a related text in Exodus 32:12, which is the only other instance where the combination of the verbs "to return" (*shub*) and "to change one's mind" (*nikam*) are used. In Exodus 32, God is very angry because of the sin of the people and wants to destroy them, but Moses intervenes and asks God to "turn" (*shub*) from his fierce anger and "relent" (*nikam*). In response to this prayer, God "relented (*nikam*) and did not bring on his people the disaster he had threatened" (v. 14). In Psalm 90, the people are hoping that God will do the same for them.

The petition in verse 14 looks back to verses 5–6: "Satisfy us in the morning with your unfailing love." The phrase, "in the morning," occurs twice in verses 5–6 to describe human existence under divine wrath because of human sin. This time around, they want to experience joy and gladness of heart rather than trouble and toil (v. 14; compare v. 10). They ask God to "Make us glad as many days as you have afflicted us, for as many years as we have seen trouble" (v. 14). The repetition of the words, "days and years," in this verse emphasizes a connection with the first part of the psalm (v. 9). The psalmist is asking God to reverse the earlier lament of the people. Canonically, Psalm 90 also attempts to "reverse" the tragic turn to lament in Psalm 89 by praying that the people's lament will instead be turned to joy. Whereas Psalm 89 starts with thanksgiving and ends with lament (see comments in Psalm 89), Psalm 90 begins with lament and concludes with prayers for God to bless his people.

In the last two verses of the psalm, the psalmist asks God to reveal to the people the "deeds" of the Lord (v. 16) and to "establish the work of our hands" (v. 17). This last petition is repeated twice, underlining its importance. If the previous psalm declares the uprooting of the Davidic throne, thereby nullifying the "work" of their ancestors, here the people plead with God to establish the "work" of their hands.

# PSALM 91

In Asia and Africa, Psalm 91 has been used as a kind of magic charm, similar to what we call *anting-anting* in Filipino. Verses from this psalm have been found "on amulets and inscribed on buildings,"[1] and legend has it that some Christians "used the prayer to survive epidemics that killed thousands."[2] In the midst of the pandemic caused by the coronavirus, many Christians quote Psalm 91 to claim protection for themselves.[3] Why not? Psalm 91 contains some of the most amazing promises of protection. Angels are commanded to "guard you in all your ways" (v. 11).

But while we need to apply God's word to our life, we need to be careful that we do not distort it. Satan himself quoted from Psalm 91 (vv. 11–12) when he tempted Jesus (Matt 4:5–7; Luke 4:10–11). Yet Jesus turned down Satan's offer, because seeking protection was not his highest goal. Similarly, Daniel's friends chose not to be protected from the fire if it meant denying their faith (Dan 3:16–18). The promises in Psalm 91 are not automatic, but are for those who trust God to be their shelter (Ps 91:1) and who love God (v. 14). But even if we trust and love God, we will not always be protected. As Hebrews 11 reminds us, some people place their trust in God and yet do not receive the fulfillment of God's promises (see vv. 35–37).

Thus it is important to interpret Psalm 91 within its canonical context. Psalm 91 is connected with Psalm 90,[4] as both psalms use the uncommon word *ma'on* for "dwelling" (90:1; 91:9). Just as Psalm 90 begins with an emphasis on God as "our *dwelling* place" (90:1), Psalm 91 begins with a description of someone "who *dwells* in the shelter of the Most High." In this light, Psalm 91 can be read as an answer to the psalmist's prayer in Psalm 90. In Psalm 90, the people ask God to "satisfy us" (v. 14) and to let "your deeds be shown to your servants" (v. 16). In Psalm 91, God promises that he will "satisfy" those who trust in him and "show" them his salvation (v. 16). Read in the context of the exile, Psalm 91 provides words of assurance to those who trust in the Lord.

While Gerstenberger thinks that this psalm could have been part of an individual complaint,[5] he does not develop this idea. I would like to propose instead that Psalm 90 is a lament for which Psalm 91 is the faithful response.

---

1. Philip Jenkins, "The Travels of Psalm 91," *The Christian Century* 135, no. 2 (2018): 36.
2. Philip Jenkins, "The Travels of Psalm 91," 36.
3. One of the most common verses that I saw quoted on social media was Psalm 91.
4. Kirkpatrick rightly sees Psalms 90–92 as forming a group. Kirkpatrick, *The Book of Psalms*, 553.
5. Erhard S. Gerstenberger, *Psalms Part 2 and Lamentations*, 166.

Psalm 91 may be divided into two main parts (vv. 2–13 and vv. 14–16), with verse 1 serving as an introductory statement to establish the main theme of the psalm. Within the first section (vv. 2–13), there are two speakers:

1. A speaker describing his personal relationship with God, using the first person ("I"/"my," vv. 2, 9a);
2. A speaker talking about God ("He"/"His") to another person, using the second person ("you," vv. 3–8, 9b–13).

The second section (vv. 14–16) introduces a third speaker:

3. God addressing the psalmist/others, using the first person ("me"/"I"/"my," vv. 14–16).

## 91:1–13 DWELLING IN THE SHELTER OF THE MOST HIGH

The first verse of Psalm 91, "Whoever *dwells* in the shelter of the Most High," alludes to the first verse in Psalm 90, "LORD, you have been our *dwelling* place" (emphasis mine). The word "shelter" (91:1) comes from the Hebrew word *seter*, which also means "hiding place" (see also Ps 32:7).[6] The background for this verse is a situation of danger. The words "refuge" and "fortress" in verse 2 connote places with difficult access and thus further support this background. To "dwell" in the "shelter of the Most High" is to put one's trust in God, to "hide" in the Lord and make him "my refuge and my fortress" (v. 2). By shifting to the first person in verse 2, the psalmist applies the declaration in verse 1 to himself. Trusting in God is a personal decision that has to be firm and stable. This sense of stability is reflected in the verb "dwell" (v. 1), which signifies permanence.

In the parallel line for verse 1, the poet employs a more temporal verb:

"Whoever *dwells* in the shelter of the Most High" (v. 1a)
"will *rest* in the shadow of the Almighty" (v. 1b).

The word "rest" (v. 1b) comes from a Hebrew verb (*lin*), which means "to lodge for the night." This appears to suggest a regression from a more permanent status ("dwell") to a temporary one ("lodge").[7] However, this will not be a problem when we take into consideration the ancient custom of

---

6. *HALOT*, 2:772.
7. Robert Alter notes that there is a development from one line to the next in a parallelism. So why do we have a regression here? Robert Alter, *The Art of Biblical Poetry* (New York: Basic Books, 1985), 13.

hospitality in ancient Israel,[8] coupled with the meaning of "dwell" in verse 1a. As discussed above, to dwell in the shelter of the Most High means to place one's trust in God, which requires stability and permanence. The word "rest," on the other hand, is appropriate in situations when a resident of a place welcomes travelers, "who find themselves in hostile environments."[9] Part of the responsibility of the resident is to "nourish and protect" the traveler.[10] The use of the word "rest" in verse 1b highlights the blessing of protection from the resident rather than the temporary nature of the stay.

In verse 3, the speaker shifts from first person to the third person, perhaps as a way to share with others what he experiences personally in verse 2. Having experienced God's welcome and protection, he addresses his own community to encourage them that God will also welcome and protect them in the midst of danger. The situation in verse 3 shares the same hostility and danger that is the background for verses 1–2. The psalmist mentions a hidden snare (v. 3), "terror" (v. 5a) and "pestilence" (v. 6a) lurking in the cover of the night, as well as dangers during the day (v. 5b) and even broad day light (v. 6b has "midday"). The images from the avian world in verses 3–4 highlight the vulnerable condition of the potential victim, who is like a helpless bird in the hands of a fowler.[11] Yet the psalmist says to the one who puts his trust in the Lord: "God will cover you with his feathers, and under his wings you will find refuge" (v. 4), so that "you will not fear the terror by night . . . or . . . by day" (vv. 5–6).

In verses 7–8, the psalmist switches to battlefield imagery to address a completely defenseless individual (the pronoun "your" in v. 7 is singular). Surrounded by "a thousand" and even "ten thousand," there is no way "you" can win, but "it shall not come near you" (v. 7). This image recalls Israel being chased by the Egyptians. Before them is the sea, behind them are the chariots of Egypt, and yet God demonstrates that he is able to deliver them by destroying their enemies right before their eyes. Psalm 91 makes the same promise: "You will only observe with your own eyes . . . the punishment of the wicked" (v. 8).

There is a very brief return to the first person in verse 9a, which literally reads in Hebrew, "For you, O Lord, are my refuge" (v. 9a, my own

---

8. Andrew E. Arterbury, *Entertaining Angels: Early Christian Hospitality in Its Mediterranean Setting* (Sheffield, England: Sheffield Phoenix Press, 2005), 2.
9. John Koenig, "Hospitality," in *ABD*, ed. David Noel Freedman (New York: Doubleday, 1992), 299.
10. John Koenig, "Hospitality," 299.
11. See figures 110–118 in Othmar Keel, *The Symbolism of the Biblical World: Ancient Near Eastern Iconography and the Book of Psalms* (New York: Seabury Press, 1978), 90–93.

translation).¹² The implication is that the listener/audience in the previous verses has made the same commitment as the psalmist by making the Most High his "dwelling" (v. 9b). Consequently, verses 10–12 outline several more promises. First, no harm or disaster will "come near your tent" (v. 10). The word "disaster" comes from the Hebrew word *ra'ah*, which also means "plague" (see Exod 11:1). This echoes the Exodus narrative, where the plagues that afflicted the Egyptians did not come "against any of the people of Israel" (Exod 11:7, ESV). Verses 11–12 allude to God's promise in Exodus to send an angel before his people to guard them along the way (Exod 23:20; compare Ps 91:11). In Hebrew, the word for angel (*mal'akh*) means "messenger" or "presence," and in the biblical narrative, angels are seen as representatives or manifestations of God.¹³ God will not only shield the vulnerable individual who trusts in him, but he will also send his angels to carry him so that he will not fall (v. 12). The last verse in this section about the defenseless victim trampling on the lion and cobra (v. 13) echoes the language in Mark 16:18, where Jesus says that those who pick up serpents or drink poisons in his name will not be harmed.

### 91:14–16 DIVINE ORACLE

The parallel between the last verse in the previous section (v. 13) and Jesus's language in the Gospel of Mark (16:18) could further explain why this psalm has been used as a magic incantation. But Psalm 91 is not a magic charm or a *talisman*, for it presumes a relationship of trust in the Lord (v. 1). Moreover, we learn from verse 14 that the recipient of the promises set forth in the preceding verses is one who "loves" God. As the divine word declares, "Because he loves me, I will rescue him" (v. 14). The word "love" comes from the Hebrew word *chashaq*, which means "to be very attached to."¹⁴ The same word is used to speak of God's love for Israel (Deut 7:7; 10:15). The person who loves God is further described as one "who knows my name" (Ps 91:14b, ESV). The verb "to know" here indicates intimacy, and God only promises to answer prayer (v. 15) and grant long life (v. 16) to those who know him in this way. However, these promises are not "automatic," for as Hebrews 11 reminds us, not all the faithful were delivered (see vv. 35–38).

---

12. The NIV is one attempt to make sense of the rather confusing use of first person in 9a and second person in 9b. It translates the Hebrew *ki* as conditional ("if"), but I think it is more causal.
13. John I. Durham, *Exodus* (Grand Rapids: Zondervan, 1987), 335.
14. This is the sense of the verb with the preposition *be* (*HALOT*, 362).

# PSALM 92

Psalm 92 is the only psalm that has a day assigned to it in the Psalter.[1] The superscription says that it is "a song for the Sabbath day." According to Jewish tradition, the Levites sang a psalm for each day of the week: Psalm 24 (Sunday), Psalm 48 (Monday), Psalm 81 (Wednesday), Psalm 82 (Thursday), Psalm 93 (Friday), and Psalm 92 (Sabbath).[2] The note on the Sabbath provides an important hermeneutical lens through which the psalm can be understood.

One of the problems confronting godly people is the prosperity of the wicked. We saw the author of Psalm 73 struggling with this (see comments in Psalm 73). The more he tried to understand the situation, the more troubled he became, and it was only when he "entered the sanctuary of God" that he "understood their final destiny" (v. 17). Though not as serious as Psalm 73, the problem of the wicked is also present in Psalm 92 (see v. 7). The emphasis on the Sabbath in the superscription to Psalm 92 reflects the psalmist's experience when he entered the sanctuary in Psalm 73. On Sabbath, we cease striving and focus on God's work (see 92:5) rather than our own. Taking the time to stop and reflect in worship and rest is crucial in our journey. As South African Rabbi Louis Rabinowitz comments on Psalm 92 concerning the person of faith: "It is only when the Sabbath comes, and he is relieved of material cares, when he makes of the day a day of recreation that in the serenity and tranquil peace of that blessed day he can give himself over to meditation and contemplation. It is then that he can sing of the greatness of God . . . He can attune himself to the spirit of God . . . [and] face the future with confidence and trust."[3]

Canonically, Psalm 92 is closely related to the preceding psalms, as the comments below will demonstrate. Psalm 92 is a thanksgiving psalm, with elements of wisdom poetry (vv. 6–7, 9; 12–15) and a hymn of praise (vv. 5, 8). The opening verse makes it clear that Psalm 92 is a thanksgiving: "It is good to give thanks to the Lord" (v. 1, ESV). Verses 10–11 offer a testimony of what God has done. Though there is no explicit account of the psalmist's suffering or how God has helped him, the connection with Psalm 90 suggests that Psalm 92 is an answer to the prayer in Psalm 90. Psalm 92 is set in the

---

1. J. Clinton McCann, "Psalms," 1050.
2. Herbert Danby, *The Mishnah: Translated from the Hebrew with Introduction and Brief Explanatory Notes* (London: Oxford University Press, 1967), 589.
3. Quoted in Annette M. Boeckler, "The Liturgical Understanding of Psalms in Judaism: Demonstrated with Samples from Psalms 90–106, with a Special Focus on Psalm 92, *Mizmor Shir LeYom HaShabbat*," *European Judaism* 48, no. 2 (2015): 80.

first person singular (an individual), with possibly the king or representative of the community as the speaker.

## 92:1–5 "IT IS GOOD TO PRAISE THE LORD"

Thanksgiving is a response to what God has done. Such a response reflects a deep sense of gratitude, as expressed in the opening verse: "It is good to praise the LORD" (92:1). This is similar to the thanksgiving in Psalm 116: "I love the LORD, he heard my cry for mercy" (v. 1). The phrase, "he heard my cry" (116:1), provides another important element in the thanksgiving psalm, which is to recount an individual's experience of suffering and how the Lord answered his prayers when he cried for mercy. In Psalm 90, the people prayed, "satisfy us in the morning with your unfailing love [*hesed*]" (v. 14). In answer to this prayer, Psalm 92 declares God's "love [*hesed*] in the morning" (v. 2). In Psalm 90, the people complained that their years had been full of "trouble and sorrow" (v. 10), and so they pleaded with God to make them "glad" (v. 15) and let his "deeds be shown" to them (v. 16). God's response to this prayer is reflected in the psalmist's affirmation, "for you make me glad by your deeds, LORD" (92:4).

When we receive an answer to prayer or experience God meeting us in the midst of our trouble, we grow in our understanding of God – his works and his ways. Thus, after the psalmist expresses his thanksgiving for what God has done, he proclaims a hymnic declaration: "How great are your works, LORD, how profound your thoughts!" (v. 5; compare 116:5). Note his emphasis is on God's works. In Psalm 90, the people prayed that God would "establish the work of our hands" (v. 17), a petition that is repeated twice. But in Psalm 92, the psalmist does not mention human works, but praises all God's works. This does not suggest that our works are worthless, but recognizes that unless God works in and through us, our human work will be in vain (compare Psalm 127). Our works should be founded on the works of God.

## 92:6–9 SEEING THE WORLD THROUGH THE EYES OF FAITH

It is easy to lose heart when we look at the world around us, and so we need to focus on what God is doing in the world. We need a vision of reality from God's perspective. As Psalm 90 observes, God's "thoughts are very deep" (92:5b, ESV), and even the people of God can be like the "stupid man" and the "fool," unable to "understand this" (v. 6, ESV). The word "this" in verse 6 refers to the following verse, which is about the flourishing of the wicked (v. 7).

The psalmist in Psalm 73 also struggled with the prosperity of the wicked in contrast to his own troubled existence, despite all his efforts towards godliness. According to Psalm 73, when the psalmist "entered the sanctuary of God," he "understood [the] final destiny" of the wicked (v. 17). Thus his encounter with God changed his perspective about the reality of evil in the world. The liturgical background for Psalm 92 places it within the same sphere as Psalm 73. Viewed from a human perspective, the situation in the world is hopeless, but from the perspective of heaven, the psalmist declares, "you, Lord, are forever exalted" (92:8). From this perspective, the psalmist is confident that even though "all evildoers flourish, they will be destroyed forever" (v. 7; see also v. 9). Verses 7–9 form a chiastic structure, with the word "evildoers" repeated in verses 7 and 9 as bookends for the exaltation of the Lord:

"though evildoers flourish, they will be destroyed forever" (v. 7);
  "But you, Lord, are forever exalted" (v. 8);
"all evildoers will be scattered" (v. 9).

## 92:10–15 "YOU HAVE EXALTED MY HORN"

In the next verses, the psalmist deliberately contrasts the wicked (vv. 7–9) with the righteous (vv. 12–15). The righteous person, who is "blessed," resembles the description in Psalm 1, with its imagery of "a tree planted by streams of water," ever flourishing because its "leaf does not wither" (1:3). The verb "planted" is repeated in Psalm 92, but here the righteous person is "planted in the house of the Lord" (v. 13). In Psalm 84, the psalmist longs to be in the house of the Lord and would be content just to be a mere gatekeeper in the Temple so that he could be near it. Here, the psalmist is "planted" in it! Like the blessed person in Psalm 1, those who are righteous in Psalm 92 are flourishing. Even in old age, the righteous "will stay fresh and green" (v. 14). One of the fears of old people is that they will no longer have any way to contribute or any relevance for their existence. Thus the psalmist prays, "Even when I am old and gray, do not forsake me, my God" (71:18). This prayer is answered in Psalm 92, for even in old age, the righteous will proclaim that "he is my Rock" (v. 15).

The psalmist's assurance is rooted in his own experience of God. In between the verses contrasting the wicked and the righteous, the psalmist recounts his testimony (vv. 10–11) according to the following structure:

Description of the wicked (vv. 7–9),
  The experience of the psalmist (vv. 10–11),
Description of the righteous (vv. 12–15).

The psalmist testifies that the Lord who is "exalted" in verse 8 has "exalted my horn" (v. 10). A "horn" is a symbol of power and strength, and so the psalmist is saying that God has lifted him up by making him strong. The pouring out of oil in the second part of verse 10 may refer to an anointing ceremony, though it is not clear from the text (v. 10b). But verse 11 makes clear that he has been given victory over his enemies. He proclaims, "My eyes have seen the defeat of my adversaries" (92:11a), and he adds that his own "ears have heard the rout of my wicked foes" (v. 11b). Thus God's promise in Psalm 91 that "you will only observe with your eyes and see the punishment of the wicked" (v. 8) is fulfilled in Psalm 92.

# PSALM 93

Psalm 93 belongs to the broader category of so-called "Yahweh kingship hymns."[1] Other psalms in this category include Psalms 47 and 95–99. Because of the position of Psalm 93, some scholars think that it was "anomalously placed"[2] and should have come before Psalm 95. But as the analysis of the canonical context of Psalm 94 demonstrates (see comments in Psalm 94 below), I argue that Psalm 93 has been deliberately placed in its present position.

In its original setting, Psalm 93 may have been an "enthronement psalm." In Hebrew, the phrase, "the Lord reigns," is *Yahweh malakh*, which can also be translated as, "Yahweh has become king." According to Mowinckel, such a psalm "is meant as the song of praise which is to meet Yahweh on his 'epiphany,' his appearance as the new, victorious king."[3] Thus, the title *Yahweh malakh* should be understood as a reference to a one-time event, not a continuing reality. Mowinckel argues that this declaration is the same as "Absalom has become king" in 2 Samuel (15:10).[4]

But while the phrase *Yahweh malakh* may have originally been used in enthronement settings, its present context refers to Yahweh's continuing and eternal rule. As the psalmist declares in 93:2, "Your throne was established long ago." This echoes Psalm 90:2, which affirms that "from everlasting to everlasting you are God." By declaring that "the Lord reigns" in his own time, the psalmist is acknowledging the continuing rule of Yahweh. In the postexilic context, proclaiming that "the Lord reigns" boldly challenges "the political and religious superpower."[5]

The situation is similar for Asian Christians who belong to predominantly non-Christian countries, where declaring that Jesus is Lord is a matter of life and death. The Philippines is an exception because it is predominantly Christian, but that does not mean that proclaiming the reign of God here is easy. In a Christian context, the challenge is to live out the claims of God's rule as we engage our daily life. As Christians, we have to declare through our lives that our ultimate loyalty and allegiance is not to our earthly leaders, but to God. This requires living out the prophetic calling of the church today. Like the prophets of old, the church should not be afraid to criticize the earthly king.

---

1. Gerstenberger, *Psalms Part 2 and Lamentations*, 173.
2. Tate, *Psalms 51–100*, 475.
3. Sigmund Mowinckel, *The Psalms in Israel's Worship*, 106.
4. Sigmund Mowinckel, *The Psalms in Israel's Worship*, 107.
5. Gerstenberger, *Psalms Part 2 and Lamentations*, 176.

The situation during the postexilic period was tricky, as there was a tendency to equate the king with the deity, which made discernment necessary. As Duling explains, "Though Israel adapted Near Eastern ideas of 'divine kingship' for the earthly king, God and the king were not identical; the god/king of the world was also the god/king over the people of Israel, and therefore superior to any earthly 'divine king.' Correspondingly, there was also tension between these two kingdoms."[6]

Psalm 93 consists of three sections, with the first and third emphasizing the kingship of the Lord:

Declaration of the Lord's kingship (vv. 1–2),
Petition and affirmation (vv. 3–4),
Declaration of the Lord's faithfulness (v. 5).

### 93:1–2 "THE LORD REIGNS"

The opening declaration, "The Lord reigns" (93:1), should be understood within the context of Psalm 89, which laments the tragic failure of the Davidic kingship. The people were hoping that the line of David would continue, as God had promised. Yet as Psalm 89 portrays, David's rule met a tragic end. Through this, however, the people realized that their true hope was in the Lord, who reigns forever, for his throne "was established long ago," and he is "from all eternity" (93:2; compare 90:2).

After this declaration of the Lord's kingship, the psalmist describes the garments of the Lord who reigns. In the OT, it is uncommon to describe God's garments,[7] but verse 1 emphasizes that "the Lord is robed" through the following structure:

"he is robed in majesty" (v. 1a);
"The Lord is robed" (v. 1b);
"[he is] armed with strength"[8] (v. 1b).

Gerstenberger finds it "very impressive" that God is robed twice, first "in majesty" and then "with strength."[9] "Majesty" comes from the Hebrew

---

6. Dennis C. Duling, "Kingdom of God/Kingdom of Heaven," in *ABD*, ed. David Noel Freedman, vol. 4 (New York: Doubleday, 1992), 50.
7. *TDOT*, 7:463.
8. This follows the ESV translation. Unfortunately, the NIV translates the first line ("He is robed with majesty") twice, but in Hebrew, the word "majesty" (*ge'uth*) is mentioned only once, thereby missing the emphasis on the fact that the Lord is "robed."
9. Gerstenberger, *Psalms Part 2 and Lamentations*, 174.

word *geʾuth*, which is also used in Psalm 89 to proclaim that God rules "over the surging [*geʾuth*] sea" (v. 9). In ancient mythology, the sea represented the forces of chaos at war with the deity. Thus the image of God ruling over the sea depicts control and victory. By describing God as robed "in majesty," the psalmist declares that God is in control (93:1). Because God is king, the people have a sense of security: "the world is established, firm and secure" (93:1c). This does not mean that there will no longer be any problems or troubles. In the next verses, the rivers "lift up" and the "mighty" breakers of the sea pound (vv. 3–4). Though conflict is not explicit, there is ambiguity in this depiction of the rivers and sea.

### 93:3–4 "THE SEAS HAVE LIFTED UP, LORD"

As noted above, the word "majesty" from verse 1 comes from a word that is associated with the forces of chaos represented by the sea and rivers. Throughout the psalms, the sea and rivers can be presented as a threat or enemy (e.g. Pss 18:4; 42:8) or as entities praising God (Pss 96:11; 98:7).[10]

In Psalm 93, however, it is not clear if the rivers are rising up in hostility against God or if they are praising him. The emphasis on God as king in verse 1 points to praise, but the dynamic presentation of the rivers and sea as well as the context of Psalm 94 (see discussion below) both suggest hostility. The psalmist calls on the Lord and reports to him, as if crying out for help because the seas are lifting up: "The seas have lifted up, LORD" (v. 3). The Filipino cultural concept of *pagsusumbong* (literally, "reporting," see Psalm 83 above) captures this very well. The word "lift up" is repeated three times in verse 3, each time with a different object and growing intensity. After calling on the Lord to pay attention to the lifting of the sea, the psalmist focuses on the noise: "the seas have lifted up their voice" (v. 3). The third occurrence of the verb emphasizes the power of the sea, creating a sense of anxiety: "the seas have lifted up their pounding waves" (v. 3). As Gillmayr-Bucher observes, "First, the rising evokes a visual image, then this action becomes audible and finally, the rivers' power might give rise to anxiety."[11] The NIV translates the verb "lift up" in the perfect tense ("have lifted"), but in Hebrew, the third occurrence of the verb is in the imperfect tense, which the RSV and ESV both translate as

---

10. Susanne Gillmayr-Bucher, "'The Rivers Have Lifted up Their Voice': Imagining the Mighty Waters in Psalm 93," *OTE* 32, no. 2 (2019): 381–383.
11. Gillmayr-Bucher, "'The Rivers Have Lifted up Their Voice': Imagining the Mighty Waters in Psalm 93," 390.

"lift up." This distinction is important, for the use of the imperfect in "the third line looks ahead, thus pointing out, that the rivers might rise (again) with threatening intentions."[12]

In verse 4, even though the rivers and seas may present a threat, the psalmist trusts that God is "mightier than the thunder of the great waters." The word "thunder" repeats the same word as "voice" from verse 3, declaring that though the seas may threaten and attack, the Lord is in control. Thus the Lord is described as one who is "on high" and "mighty" (v. 4).

## 93:5 "YOUR STATUTES STAND FIRM"

The psalm ends with an emphasis on God's stability, just as the end of verse 1 concludes that "the world is established, firm and secure." The word established (*kun*) is repeated four times in Psalm 89 (vv. 2, 4, 21, 37). Psalm 93:4 explains that the world is established because "your decrees are very trustworthy" (ESV). Notice the addition of the word "very," which highlights the stability of God's decrees. Kselman argues that Psalms 89, 93, and 132 all speak about God's covenant with the Davidic throne: "The eternal covenant offered by Yahweh to David and his successors in Pss 89:29 and 132:12 is also the covenant spoken of in Ps 93:5."[13] Kselman understands "your decrees" in 93:5 as the covenant named in 89:28 and 132:12. If God's rule is firmly established, there is a continuing hope that the Lord has not broken his covenant with David. However, this hope also introduces an element of the tragic, as Psalm 93 is followed by Psalm 94, which follows a similar movement to Psalm 89, where the psalmist's affirmation of God's covenant (93:5; compare with the hymn of praise in 89:1–37) is followed by lament (see Ps 94:3; compare with the communal lament in 89:38–52).

---

12. Gillmayr-Bucher, "'The Rivers Have Lifted up Their Voice': Imagining the Mighty Waters in Psalm 93," 390.
13. John S. Kselman, "Sinai and Zion in Psalm 93," in *David and Zion: Biblical Studies in Honor of J. J. M. Roberts* (Winona Lake: Eisenbrauns, 2004), 75.

# PSALM 94

As discussed previously, lament is an expression of faith that perseveres with hope in the midst of a world marked by cruelty and oppression. Those who lament need to continue to trust in God's justice, even as they express their questions and cry out about their experiences of contradiction and abandonment. This is the message of Psalm 94, which is placed in between the so-called "Yahweh kingship hymns" (Psalm 93 and Psalms 95–99). Though some scholars think that Psalm 93 has been "anomalously placed"[1] and should have come before Psalm 95, I believe that Psalm 94 was purposely situated in its present position. The surrounding psalms celebrate the reign of the Lord, proclaiming God's rule over all. By inserting Psalm 94 into this collection of hymns, the community is reminded that God's kingship does not mean that everything is already settled. Because we live in an ongoing tension between God's promises and our present reality, it is very important to continue creating spaces for lament.

The declaration of divine kingship in Psalm 93 should be interpreted in light of the continuing oppression of the poor in Psalm 94. In fact, these two psalms share several connections. First, the verb, "lift up" (*nasa'*), which is repeated three times in Psalm 93:3 (see discussion above), appears again in Psalm 94:2. As discussed previously, images of the rivers and seas were used in ancient times to represent the forces of chaos. In Psalm 93, the people cry out to God because "the seas have lifted up" (v. 3). This dynamic presentation of the seas lifting up and making noise in Psalm 93 becomes the attack of the wicked in Psalm 94:2–4. Second, the "pounding waves" in Psalm 93 (v. 3) become the crushing of God's people in Psalm 94: "They crush your people, Lord" (v. 5). The words "pounding" (*dakah*) and "crushing" (*daka'*) come "from the same root – *dk'*, crush or humble and appear to be poetic variants."[2] Third, the people plead with God, who is described as "robed in majesty" in Psalm 93 (v. 1), to "pay back to the proud what they deserve" in Psalm 94 (v. 2). Here, the words, "majesty" (*ge'ut*) and "proud" (*ge'eh*), come from the same root word (*g'h*), which literally means "to be high."[3]

The first and last sections of Psalm 94 resemble a communal lament (vv. 1–7 and 20–23). The middle section consists of a wisdom-like exhortation

---

1. Tate, *Psalms 51–100*, 475.
2. *TDOT*, 1:943.
3. *TDOT*, 2:346–347.

(vv. 8–15) followed by a testimony supporting the exhortation (vv. 16–19). The combination of lament and wisdom literature is similar to Lamentations 3, which also combines wisdom poetry (vv. 25–42) and communal lament (vv. 43–66). As we will see below, there is a contradiction between the communal lament and the exhortation.

## 94:1–7 COMMUNAL LAMENT

Verse 1 begins with a theological statement: "The LORD is a God who avenges." Unlike some modern theology, however, this statement serves as the foundation for prayer, for the second half of verse 1 repeats the theological statement and then turns it into prayer: "O God who avenges, shine forth" (v. 1b).[4] The petition, "shine forth," is a prayer for a theophany, a figurative way of asking God to appear and intervene in history.

There is a sense of urgency in the corresponding petition in verse 2: "Rise up." This verb recalls the threefold description of the forces of chaos represented by the sea in Psalm 93:3 ("lift up"). Unless God rises up and does something to respond to the threats of the wicked, his people will be in great trouble. The wicked are killing the most vulnerable – the widow, foreigner, and fatherless (v. 6). These groups are the most vulnerable because they have no means of defending themselves in a court of law. Foreigners are looked upon highly in the Philippines because most of them come from more affluent countries, but this was not the case during the time of the OT.[5] Because the vulnerable ones are being killed, the psalmist asks God, the "Judge of the Earth," to "pay back to the proud what they deserve" (v. 2). The NT affirms that we should not take vengeance into our own hands, but leave it to God (Rom 12:19).

Yet sometimes, divine justice takes so long. Like the psalmist, many of us also cry out to God, "How long, LORD, will the wicked, how long will the wicked be jubilant?" (Ps 94:3). Even here in Book IV of the Psalter, which is full of praise and confidence in God as the king and ruler of all, this question, "how long?" is repeated twice (v. 3). Psalm 90 only asks "how long?" once (see v. 13). Some scholars say that Book IV provides the answer to the tragic lament at the end of Book III (Psalm 89). But if this is true, the answer is not that we will no longer lament. Lament persists even in hymns of praise! In fact, the people in Psalm 94 are grappling with the same issues found at the

---

4. The translation "shine forth" follows the suggestion that the verb is a Hifil imperative. The form in the MT is caused by haplography. For the same petition, see Psalm 80:2.
5. J. G. McConville, *Deuteronomy*, 201.

beginning of Book III, particularly Psalms 73 and 74. In Psalm 73, the psalmist confesses, "I envied the arrogant" (v. 3), whose "pride is their necklace" (v. 6), and so they are no longer afraid of God himself. In Psalm 94, the wicked are also arrogant and "full of boasting" (v. 4). The people of God complain that the wicked say, "The LORD does not see, the God of Jacob takes no notice" (v. 7). Similarly, the people in Psalm 73 complain that the wicked mock them, saying, "How would God know? Does the Most High know anything?" (v. 11). There are additional connections with Psalm 73 in Psalm 94:17–18 (see discussion below).

When wicked people are allowed to continue unpunished, they become boastful (see comments in Psalm 73 above), and so the people ask God to intervene, to "shine forth" and "rise up" (94:1–2). They argue that God should act because those who are being killed (v. 6) are "your people," "your inheritance" (v. 5). This line of reasoning is similar to Psalm 74:2, where the people appeal to their own identity as the people of God: "Remember . . . the people of your inheritance."

### 94:8–15 EXHORTATION

In this section, there is a transition from prayer to a wisdom-like exhortation. But who is being addressed here – the wicked, or those who are lamenting (vv. 1–7)? Verse 9b, "Does he who formed the eye not see?," suggests the former, as it appears to be a direct answer to the statement of the wicked that "The LORD does not see" (v. 7). On the other hand, the description, "you senseless ones" and "you fools," recalls Psalm 92, where these descriptions refer to the people in the community who seem to be losing hope that the wicked will be punished. The psalmist is lamenting that the "senseless people" in the community are "fools" because they do not understand that "though the wicked spring up like grass . . . they will be destroyed forever" (92:6–7). Earlier in Psalm 94, the psalmist complains to God, "how long?" (v. 3). Here, he complains to the people, "when will you become wise?" (v. 8).

Thus the immediate context as well as the immediate canonical context both suggest that the speakers in the communal lament (94:1–7) are the audience for this exhortation (94:8–15). Though there is an implied contradiction in the flow of the text from the lament to the exhortation, we also find this in Lamentations 3 (see discussion above). On the one hand, the people lament (Lam 3:43–50); on the other hand, they are discouraged from complaining (Lam 3:26, 28, 39). Similarly, the people complain in Psalm 94 (v. 3), but they are also rebuked (vv. 8–11) and instructed (vv. 12–15). Verse 12 identifies anyone whom the Lord disciplines as "blessed." The word discipline here also means "instruct" and is related to learning from "your law" (v. 12b). This is similar to Psalm 1, which speaks of the blessedness of the person who meditates on God's law (Torah). Like the person in Psalm 1, who "delights in the law of the Lord" (v. 2), the person who receives instruction from the Lord will experience "rest from days of trouble" (v. 13a). When the time comes, "a pit" will be "dug for the wicked" (v. 13b).

Verses 14–15 are words of assurance that the Lord will not "abandon" (v. 14) those who are lamenting in verses 1–7. The words "his people" and "his inheritance" (v. 14) recall 94:5, where the people tell God what the evildoers are doing to "your people" and "your inheritance." Verse 15 assures the people that justice "will again be founded on righteousness."

## 94:16–23 CONTINUING LAMENT

In verse 16, the perspective suddenly shifts when a first-person voice speaks: "Who will rise up for me against the wicked?" This raises questions about who is speaking, who is being addressed, and the purpose of this speech. This could be the same speaker who is exhorting the group of lamenters in verses 8–15, but now the speaker is sharing his own experience in the form of a testimony. This is similar to the first part of Lamentations 3, where the man who has gone through affliction shares his own experience (vv. 1–20). In Psalm 94, the speaker testifies that he, too, was troubled by the wicked and felt helpless. Like the writer of Psalm 73, he admits that his foot almost slipped (94:18; compare 73:2). Had it not been for the Lord's help (v. 17) and consolation (v. 19), he would have "dwelt in the silence of death" (v. 17b). Yet because of his own experience, he is confident that there will be justice (see v. 23).

Thus the speaker's rebuke and instruction does not silence the communal voice of lament, for Psalm 94 starts with the affirmation that God is a God of vengeance and justice (vv. 1–2), and the last verse confirms this view: "He will repay them for their sins" (v. 23). Before this final conclusion, however, the psalm creates space for the voice of lament as the people cry out, "how long?" (v. 3), and then complain to God about the actions of the wicked against the vulnerable (vv. 4–7). Just before the psalm closes, the people respond to the speaker's personal experience by continuing their communal lament, asking God, "Can a corrupt throne be allied with you – a throne that brings on misery by its decrees?" (v. 20), because the wicked "band together . . . and condemn the innocent to death" (v. 21). Again, the psalmist turns to his own experience to validate the people's lament and then point them confidently towards hope in God as a strong refuge in times of difficulty[6] and the promise of his eventual judgment of the wicked.

---

6. See discussion of "refuge" in Psalms 90:1 and 91:2.

# PSALM 95

Psalm 95 begins with a beautiful call to worship. This psalm, along with Psalm 100, is a favorite among modern worship leaders. Psalm 95 also contains one of the most profound theologies in the Psalter, declaring God as "the great King above all gods" (v. 3) and "the Lord our Maker" (v. 6). Yet immediately following this extended call to worship (vv. 1–7b), God issues a rebuke and a word of judgment against his people (vv. 7c–11).

The transition between these two parts of the psalm is unexpected and anticlimactic. Savran describes the change as "one of the most brusque shifts of mood in the entire Psalter."[1] I think the juxtaposition is deliberate to create a mood shift within the readers. Psalm 95 is meant to be a rebuke against those who think that if they go to church every Sunday, utter the right prayers, and fulfill religious functions, then it does not matter how they live their lives. Some commentators (e.g. Kirkpatrick) view the second part of the psalm as a warning. While that aspect is present, it is better to see it as a rebuke, which is supported by the interaction between the two parts.[2] Psalm 95 reminds us that failing to hear what God is saying to us now ("today") makes all our religious rituals empty and worthless before the Lord. To declare God as "King" has implications about issues of justice, because the foundation of God's throne is "righteousness and justice" (Ps 97:2; see also Psalm 82). The call to "come" and "bow down to worship" also has ethical dimensions (see Psalms 15 and 24).

Psalm 95 arose out of "actual worship in the Temple"[3] and can be divided into two main parts: a hymn (vv. 1–7b) and a sermon-like prophetic speech (vv. 7c–11). This resembles the general structure of modern Protestant worship, which usually begins with singing and is followed by the preaching. The second part of the psalm contains a prophetic speech or oracle. Mowinckel notes that prophets "were closely connected with the temples" in ancient times.[4] Gunkel

---

1. George W. Savran, "The Contrasting Voices of Psalm 95," *RB* 110, no. 1 (2003): 18.
2. Savran demonstrates point by point the contrasting views of the two parts. Savran, "The Contrasting Voices of Psalm 95," 18–32.
3. Gwynne Henton Davies writes: "On the whole commentators have gradually come to relate the parts of the Psalm more clearly to the scene of worship — the Temple." Gwynne Henton Davies, "Psalm 95," *ZAW* 85, no. 2 (1973): 187. He adds: "The Psalm is concerned with the entry and the preparation of the people for worship." Davies, "Psalm 95," 195.
4. Mowinckel, *The Psalms in Israel's Worship*, 2:55–56.

designates Psalm 95, along with Psalms 50, 75, and 81, as "prophetic psalms."[5] A number of psalms indicate the presence of a cultic prophet, who announces a word from the Lord (e.g. Psalm 60). The prophetic word could be positive (an oracle of salvation) or issue a judgment.[6] Psalm 95 belongs to the latter category and shares similarities with Psalms 50 and 81 in its combination of a summons to worship and a divine judgment.[7]

## 95:1–7B CALL TO WORSHIP

Psalm 95 consists of two calls to worship (vv. 1–2 and v. 6). Verse 1 is similar to the call to worship in Psalm 81:1, as the verbs "sing for joy" and "shout aloud" occur in both. In Psalm 95, the speaker includes himself in the call – "Come, *let us* sing for joy" (95:1) – rather than simply inviting the congregation to "Sing for joy" (81:1). The worship leader calls on the congregation to come to the Lord (95:1a), who is described in the second line as "the Rock of our salvation" (1b). This image of God as a "Rock" conveys that God is their refuge (see Deut 32:4; Isa 30:29; Ps 18:2, 31, 46).[8]

In verse 2, the speaker progresses from calling the congregation to "sing" to the Lord to inviting them to come into his "presence." In Hebrew, the verb "come" (*qadam*) literally means "to be in front of." The invitation is to come before the presence of the Lord with songs of "thanksgiving" and "with music and song" (v. 2). The word "thanksgiving" comes from the Hebrew word *todah*, which can either mean a thanksgiving sacrifice or a song of praise. The latter is the meaning of the word here. These opening verses are full of joyous celebration.

Verses 3–5 outline the reasons or motivations for the call to worship, focusing on God as the "great God" (v. 3a) because he is "the great King above all gods" (v. 3b). The reference to Yahweh as the "king" alludes to the Canaanite mythology about the deity's victory over the forces of chaos represented by the sea.[9] This is supported by the word "sea" in verse 5, but Yahweh is not only the victorious king, for he is also the creator God. As Tate observes, "The sphere of his power extends throughout all creation, from the depths of the

---

[5]. Stephen Breck Reid, "Psalm 50: Prophetic Speech and God's Performative Utterances," in *Prophets and Paradigms: Essays in Honor of Gene M. Tucker*, ed. Stephen Breck Reid (Sheffield, England: Sheffield Academic Press, 1996), 221.
[6]. Claus Westermann, "Introduction," in *Prophetic oracles of salvation in the Old Testament.* (T & T Clark, 1991), 11–18.
[7]. Peter C. Craigie, *Psalms 1–50*, 364–367.
[8]. Tournay and Crowley, *Seeing and Hearing God with the Psalms: The Prophetic Liturgy of the Second Temple in Jerusalem*, 175–176.
[9]. Compare John Day, *God's Conflict with the Dragon and the Sea*, 23–24.

earth, where the powers of death reside, to the peaks of the mountains, where deities have their assemblies."[10] Thus the psalmist refers to him as "the great King above all gods" (v. 3b). This language recalls Psalm 82, which presents Yahweh in the assembly of the gods.

Building on the preceding verses, the psalmist calls on the congregation to "bow down" in worship "before the LORD our Maker" (v. 6, ESV). The people are to worship him because "he is our God and we are the people of his pasture" (v. 7ab). The language in these verses focuses on who God is and the people's covenantal relationship with God. God initiated the covenant through his miraculous acts of deliverance for his people, and in response, the people pledged loyalty to him. But as history demonstrates, the people of Israel have not been faithful to God – or, more specifically, their forefathers have not been obedient (see Psalm 78). The second part of the psalm describes their disobedience.

To declare God as the "great king" and to have God as "our God" has ethical implications. Those who go up the hill of the Lord should live a life in accordance with the moral standards of the Lord. In Psalm 15, for example, the worshiper should be "one whose walk is blameless" (v. 2) and "who lends money to the poor without interest" (v. 5). Both personal and social aspects are included.

In Jeremiah 7, the prophet stands at the gate of the Temple and rebukes the people for failing to live up to these standards. While claiming "the Temple of the LORD," the people continue to oppress the poor, and so the prophet rebukes them. We may envisage a similar scenario in Psalm 95, which is reflected in the juxtaposition between the call to worship and the warning from God. In Psalm 24, the requirements of those who ascend the hill of the Lord is surrounded by a declaration about who God is – the creator God to whom the earth and everything in it belongs (Ps 24:1; compare Ps 95:5) and the "King of glory" (vv. 7, 10; compare Ps 95:3).

## 95:7C–11 REBUKE

The opening statement, "Today, if you hear his voice" (v. 7c, ESV), highlights the importance of obedience. Following the tradition of the MT, most English versions connect verse 7c with the preceding verses. But verse 7c fits more logically with the subsequent verses. As Smyth argues, "Hearing and Hardening are so compellingly heads and tails of the same coin that the gravitational pull

---

10. Tate, *Psalms 51–100*, 501.

between them has been for many authoritative translators irresistible."[11] To hear is to obey, which underlines the need for discernment. The word "today" in verse 7c refers to what God is saying to his people in their own time and context. The writer of Hebrews applies the words of Psalm 95:7–8 to Christian believers during his own time (see Heb 3:7–4:13). Since this instruction is also part of God's word, Christians today can still learn from the writer of Hebrews.

Although God has already spoken in his word through Jesus Christ, believers still need to rely on the Holy Spirit to guide them "into all truth" (John 16:13). Every generation has to hear what the Spirit is saying in their own time. Listening and obeying are closely connected. The failure to listen to God eventually leads to the hardening of the heart. Thus God warns his people that what happened to their ancestors can also happen to them. In 95:8, God recalls the event in Meribah and Massah (see Exod 17:1–7; Num 20:1–13), where the "Israelites quarreled and . . . tested the LORD saying, 'Is the LORD among us or not?'" (Exod 17:7). This event is representative of how the people dealt with God during the forty years they were in the desert. God does not judge them because of this one event, but this episode is cited as a clear example of the people's tendency to close their heart to God and to stop seeing God's acts of mercy in their midst. For in spite of all God's miracles, the people continued to test God (Ps 95:9).

This verse reminds us that witnessing a miracle does not automatically lead to genuine faith (see John 2:23–25). The Israelites witnessed God's miraculous signs and acts for forty years, and yet they remained a people "whose hearts go astray" (Ps 95:10). The word "therefore" in verse 11 connects the people's failure to know God's ways (v. 10) with his judgment. Savran observes that the psalm's presentation of divine judgment differs from the account in Numbers 14. The judgment in Numbers came right away (in less than two years), but in Psalm 95, God's judgment comes after forty years. This "presents a picture of YHWH's patience wearing thin for the full 40 years until he finally passes sentence on them."[12] In Filipino, we say, *kapag puno na ang salop* ("when the measure is full"). In other words, patience has a limit.[13]

---

11. The quotation in Hebrews 3:7 and 15 reflects this reading. Damian Barry Smyth, "Psalm 95: The 'today' Clause," *The Downside Review* 128, no. 453 (2010): 292.
12. Savran, "The Contrasting Voices of Psalm 95," 25.
13. The combination of the hymn and the rebuke in Psalm 95 instructs us about the unity of worship and the ethical life. Having the right words to say in worship and being able to articulate right theology are useless apart from a life of obedience. The "great King above all gods" is a God of justice (Psalm 82), and those who worship him must live their lives in ways that promote justice and righteousness.

# PSALM 96

Those who fight for justice know how easy it is to feel discouraged. Justice can be torturously slow. As we say in Filipino, justice is "just *tiis*" ("just be patient," where *tiis* is the word for patience). Many cases of crime remain unresolved. Many victims from the Martial Law imposed during the time of former president Ferdinand Marcos are still waiting for justice.

Justice is a central theme in Psalm 96, which was incorporated into the Psalter during the postexilic period, when the Israelites were still living under foreign power and subjected to ongoing abuse and oppression. Though the psalm may have been written earlier, it is full of celebration and praise because of the people's hope that the Lord will one day "judge the peoples with equity" (v. 10) and come to "judge the earth" (v. 13). Revelation 19 speaks of the "King of Kings" (v. 16) who will judge "with justice" (v. 11), and this vision of the coming king keeps our hope alive in the midst of oppression and injustice.

Psalm 96 is one of the so-called "Yahweh kingship hymns," along with Psalms 93, 95, 97–100. The focus of these hymns is God – his glory, power, and beauty. As discussed previously, Psalm 95 ends with a very sober note (v. 11) about the people's failure. But the movement from Psalm 95 to Psalm 96 reminds us not to focus on our failure, but to shift our focus to God, who is able to do so much more than we could ever imagine.

The structure of Psalm 96 alternates between a call to worship and the motivations or reasons for worship:

>Call to worship (vv. 1–3):
>>"Sing to the Lord" (v. 1),
>>"Sing to the Lord" (v. 2),
>>"Declare his glory" (v. 3).
>
>Motivation: "for great is the Lord . . ." (vv. 4–6).
>Call to worship (vv. 7–9):
>>"Ascribe to the Lord" (v. 7),
>>"Ascribe to the Lord" (v. 8),
>>"Worship the Lord" (v. 9).
>
>Motivation: "The Lord reigns" (v. 10).
>>Call to worship (vv. 11–13a):
>>>"Rejoice" (v. 11),
>>>"Exult" (v. 12a, ESV),

"Sing" (v. 12b).
Motivation: "for he comes, he comes to judge the earth . . ." (vv. 13b–c).

The first two calls to worship (vv. 1–3 and 7–9) closely resemble each other. The poet employs the same verb for the first two verses, "sing" (3x in vv. 1–2) and "ascribe" (3x in vv. 7–8), and then uses a different verb for the third verse, "declare" (v. 3) and "worship" (v. 9). The third call to worship (vv. 11–13a) differs from the first two in that it is a response to the preceding motivation (v. 10), which contains the key declaration, "The LORD reigns." The third line then highlights the theme of justice, which forms the final note of psalm: the whole creation should rejoice because the king is coming to "judge the earth" (v. 13).

## 96:1–6 SING A NEW SONG TO THE LORD

The summons to sing a "new song" to the Lord appears six times in the Psalms (Pss 33:3; 40:3; 96:1; 98:1; 144:9; 149:1).[1] What does "new song" mean? To answer this question, we must first answer the question, *"why* is there a new song?" There is a "new song" because God has acted on behalf of his people. In Psalm 96, the "new song" refers to God's salvation: "proclaim his salvation day after day" (v. 2). This not only refers to God's past acts of salvation, for "day by day" (v. 2) implies a continuing experience of God's salvific acts.[2] Like God's steadfast love and compassion, God's salvation is "new every morning" (Lam 3:23). Salvation is "not a matter of individual souls," but about God coming "to make right everything that is wrong . . . to make the crooked straight."[3] Thus God's salvation is not only for the past or present, but also the future[4] (see vv. 10, 13 below).

Psalm 96 is both eschatological and global, casting a vision for "all the earth" (v. 1; compare v. 9b), "the nations" (v. 3; compare v. 7), and "all peoples" (v. 3; compare v. 10). This all-encompassing language is remarkable in light of the psalm's postexilic context, as the people most likely had to gather in "closed worship services,"[5] similar to some of our persecuted brothers and

---

1. Richard Duane Patterson, "Singing the New Song: An Examination of Psalms 33, 96, 98, and 149," *Bibliotheca Sacra* 164, no. 656 (2007): 416.
2. See Villanueva, *Psalms 1–72*, 186.
3. Van Leeuwen, "Why Do the Trees of the Forest Sing a New Song? (Psalms 96 and 98)," 29.
4. McCann, "Psalms," 1065.
5. Gerstenberger, *Psalms Part 2 and Lamentations*, 187.

sisters in other parts of Asia. Though their setting may be small and confined, their faith in a "great" God (v. 4a) who is "above all gods" (v. 4b) allows them to see far beyond their place and situation.

The people's experience of exile has exposed them to the "gods of the nations" (v. 5), and although they have been defeated by these other nations, they declare that God is "to be feared above all gods" (v. 4b). The verb "to be feared" is "synonymous with reverence, worship, and obedience to God's command."[6] While Psalm 96 acknowledges the presence of other gods (see also Psalm 82), they are described as worthless[7] "idols" (v. 5)[8] because they are unable to do anything, whereas the God of Israel "made the heavens" (v. 5). [9]

In the previous psalm, God warned the people in the midst of their worship not to be like their forefathers, who did not obey his word (95:7c–11). In Psalm 96, the poet incorporates the "fear" of God (which implies obedience to God's command) into the act of worship. Verse 6 serves as a transition into the next section by shifting the focus to the "sanctuary."

## 96:7–10 WORSHIP THE LORD

As noted above, the first two verses of the second call to worship begin with the same verb: "Ascribe" (vv. 7–8; compare vv. 1–2). The word "worship" is derived from the Old English word, *weorthscipe* (from worth + -ship).[10] From this origin, we can infer the following about worship. First, worship may be understood as ascribing to God his "worth." Earlier, in verse 4, God is described as "most worthy of praise." In verse 6, the psalmist proclaims that "strength and glory are in his sanctuary," which leads the psalmist to call on the people to "ascribe to the LORD glory and strength" (v. 7). Second, worship involves giving. As soon as the psalmist tells the people to come to the courts of the Lord (v. 7), he also instructs them to "bring an offering" (v. 8). One does not come to the Temple empty-handed. The word "offering" here comes from the Hebrew word *minchah*, which means "gift/present." The context points to a gift that is related to worship, which means an offering for the Temple. Third, worship includes the sense of awe. We cannot come before God without the

---

6. *TDOT*, 6:298.
7. The word "idols" here literally means "worthless." *DCH*, 1:291.
8. *DCH*, 1:291.
9. *TDOT*, 6:298.
10. *Collins English Dictionary: Complete and Unabridged* (Glasgow: HarperCollins, 2005).

feeling of awe. In verse 9, holiness and "trembling in awe" are parallel.[11] God is not only above all gods; he is also not like other gods – he is holy.

One thing that separates God from other gods is that he becomes angry about injustice (see Psalm 82), as his reign is founded on justice and righteousness (see Ps 97:2). Because he reigns with justice and righteousness, the world "is firmly established, it will not be moved" (96:10b). Moreover, his judgment is characterized by equity (v. 10c). This is very important for our modern world, which tends to be "selective" about justice. If you are powerful, you can make sure you receive justice. If you are poor, justice is almost impossible. And so the declaration in verse 10c is an expression of hope: "he will judge the peoples with equity." Though God's judgment is in the future, it gives the people enough hope to ignite rejoicing and jubilation.

## 96:11–13 "HE WILL JUDGE THE WORLD IN RIGHTEOUSNESS"

In this final call to worship, the audience changes from the "peoples" of the earth (v. 7) to all of creation – the heavens, earth, and sea (v. 11), the fields and the trees of the forest (v. 12). The poet's exhortation also changes from singing and declaring to rejoicing and jubilation. As with mourning and weeping, celebration marks the height and the depths of companionship. We can only truly celebrate and mourn with those who are closest to us, those who know and share our experiences.

Given the postexilic context of the psalm, the psalmist might be calling on the rest of creation to rejoice in God's coming justice because he doesn't know if all the peoples and nations will choose to join in the celebration. But the psalmist could also be inviting the created world to rejoice because creation has been the victim of human injustice. The earth was "cursed" because of human sin (Gen 3), and it has been groaning and suffering ever since (Rom 8:22). As "the prophets point out, human injustice, whether Israelite or foreign, causes all of creation to suffer and threatens to return it to a state of primeval chaos (Hos 4:3; Jer 4:23–26)."[12] Thus creation will be the first to celebrate and rejoice in the coming of God's justice. This explains the psalmist's emphasis on the Lord's *coming* as a judge: "for he *comes*, he *comes* to judge the earth" (Ps 96:13, emphasis mine). One can sense creation's eager longing as it waits and yearns for God's justice. For when the Lord finally comes, "he will

---
11. *TDOT*, 4:347.
12. J. J. M. Roberts, "The Enthronement of Yhwh and David: The Abiding Theological Significance of the Kingship Language of the Psalms," *CBQ* 64, no. 4 (2002): 681.

judge the world in righteousness and the people in his faithfulness" (v. 13). The word "world" here refers to the rest of creation, apart from humans – the "peoples" mentioned in the last line.[13] Because God's judgment includes the nonhuman world, creation will finally be "set free" from its slavery to human sin (Rom 8:21). The psalm ends with hope that God's justice will *come* to all creation and all peoples.

---

13. "The meaning of the term 'the whole earth' oscillates in Psalm 96 between those who dwell on earth and the extrahuman universe, depending on the immediate context." Tate, *Psalms 51–100*, 465.

# PSALM 97

As with the previous two psalms, Psalm 97 celebrates the kingship of Yahweh, (see Psalms 93, 95–96, 98–99), picking up where Psalm 96 ends. Psalm 96 ends with the Lord coming to judge the world in righteousness and the peoples in faithfulness (v. 13). Psalm 97:1 announces that the "Lord reigns" (v. 1), and then there is a vision of Yahweh, the king, coming in the form of a theophany (see vv. 2–5). The word "theophany" comes from two Greek words – *theos* (God) and *phainein* (to appear) – and means "the self-disclosure of God.[1] Though the actual coming of the Lord is yet to be realized, this vision of the reign of God is meant to bring encouragement to the whole world and all people in the midst of their chaos and despair. One day, justice will come (v. 8), and the wicked will be put to shame (v. 7). Thus the psalmist calls the earth to rejoice and be glad (v. 1).

But the coming of the king of justice entails an ethical response from those who worship him. Those who love the Lord are commanded to "hate evil" (v. 10) and to work with God (compare 1 Cor 3:9) by building a society of righteousness and justice. We cannot pray, "let your kingdom come," if we do not actively participate with God in longing and laboring for his reign to be realized on earth as it is in heaven. But if we are going to sustain such a task, we need to have a vision of the coming king, who continues to rule, even in our world today.

Psalm 97 can be divided into two main sections:

> Theophany of Yahweh, the King (vv. 1–6),
> The outcome of the coming King (vv. 7–12).

## 97:1–6 THEOPHANY OF YAHWEH, THE KING

Psalm 97 begins with the declaration, "The Lord reigns" (see also Pss 93:1; 99:1), which is followed by a call for the earth to "be glad" and the "distant shores" to "rejoice" (97:1). There is a similar exhortation in Psalm 96, where the psalmist also calls on creation to "rejoice" and "be glad" (96:11) because the king is coming to "judge the peoples with equity" (96:10). The same emphasis on justice can be found in Psalm 97, where the creation is called to rejoice and be glad because the throne of the king who reigns is founded on

---

1. *ADB*, VI: 505.

"righteousness and justice" (97:2). Conversely, the absence of justice makes the foundations of the earth totter (see Ps 82:5).

The phrase "righteousness and justice" refers primarily to "actions on behalf of the poor and the oppressed."[2] While personal righteousness and ethics are important, actions that are righteous and just should ultimately lead towards the care of the marginalized. Unfortunately, the Christian life today is overly personalized, and "worship" is often only understood in terms of a spiritual or corporate gathering. One Christian posted on social media, "So long as they don't prohibit church worship, I will not protest." Even when so many innocent people are being killed, and there is violence and impunity in society, this Christian says she will not be involved. But how can we worship the Great King, whose throne is founded on "righteousness and justice," if we don't care about issues of social justice?[3]

Psalm 97 announces that the Lord reigns, and then the psalmist describes the coming of Yahweh as king, using the language of theophany (vv. 2–5). The appearance of Yahweh is often described using images from nature. In the OT, the thunderstorm is the "most common natural form of divine appearance."[4] Psalm 97 employs this common image in its use of "clouds" (v. 2), "fire" (v. 3), and "lightning" (v. 4). God comes as a warrior in a thunderstorm, with lightning bolts in his hands. In this section, the image of the thunderstorm represents the "malevolent" dimensions of its power (destruction by the lightning).[5] The fire (v. 3), which is derived from lightning, burns up everything in its path; the mountains that are melting like wax (v. 5) represent the defeat of the enemy. Thus the people and the whole created order declare his "righteousness" and "glory" (v. 6). In this verse, righteousness refers to "God's beneficent and saving order."[6] As we will see in the next section, the image of the thunderstorm can also represent "beneficent" dimensions of power, for the thick, dark clouds also bring rain that causes the "seed" that is sown for the righteous (v. 11) to spring forth.

---

2. Moshe Weinfeld, "'Justice and Righteousness' *Mshpt Wtsdqh* the Expression and Its Meaning," 235–236. Compare Walter J. Houston, *Contending for Justice: Ideologies and Theologies of Social Justice in the Old Testament* (London: Continuum, 2009), 61.
3. For further discussion, see Federico G. Villanueva, "Worship and Justice," in *Faith and Bayan: Evangelical Christian Engagement in the Philippine Context* (Carlisle, UK: Langham Global Library, forthcoming).
4. *ADB*, VI: 508–509.
5. *ADB*, VI: 509.
6. *TDOT*, 12:251.

# Psalm 97

## 97:7–12 THE OUTCOME OF THE COMING OF THE KING

God's theophany shames "all who worship images" (v. 7a). The experience of shame is a central theme in many Asian cultures. In the Philippines, we will do anything to avoid defeat because we do not want to be put to shame (*mapahiya*). God will also shame those who "boast in idols" (v. 7b). The word "idols" here is a derogatory term, equivalent to the word "worthless" (see also Ps 96:5). Through the prophet Jeremiah, the Lord warns anyone who boasts to boast of this, "that they have the understanding to know me, that I am the Lord, who exercises kindness, justice and righteousness on earth" (Jer 9:24). The psalmist also calls on these other gods to "worship him" (v. 7c). In Psalm 82, God becomes angry against the other gods because of their oppressive and unjust practices (see vv. 2–3). We become what or who we worship. Those who worship these gods will be put to shame because, like the gods they worship, they have become unjust.

God is worthy of our worship not only because he is powerful and victorious, but because he is also a God of justice. There is celebration and rejoicing in Psalm 97 "because of your judgments, Lord" (v. 8). The sudden change to a second person address in "*your* judgments" emphasizes the psalmist's deep appreciation for "the Most High" God (v. 9a), who is "exalted far above all gods" (v. 9b). Declaring God to be above all gods has ethical implications for human beings (see comments in Psalm 95), and so this exaltation of Yahweh is followed by a call for "those who love the Lord" to "hate evil" (v. 10).[7] To worship God is to boast of God, but to boast of God, we have to know him and his ways. He hates evil, and so those who worship him should do the same.

The second part of verse 10 promises those who live according to God's holiness that God will guard and deliver them. Unlike the psalmist's call to creation (compare 96:1, 11–12; 97:1), only "those who are righteous" are called to rejoice and praise God's name at the end of Psalm 97 (v. 12), for "light is sown for the righteous" (v. 11, ESV). Most ancient versions read "shine" instead of "sown," but this unusual metaphor makes sense within the postexilic experience of God's people.[8] As Ortlund observes, reading this psalm within this context enables us to appreciate the tension expressed in the defeat of the enemy, on the one hand (v. 3), and the final promise of deliverance (v. 10),

---

7. The BHS suggests reading the verb "love" as singular, with Yahweh as the subject. But this requires changing the imperative plural of the verb "to hate" into a plural participle. The problem with this is that both the MT and the LXX supports reading the verb as an imperative.
8. Hossfeld and Zenger, *Psalms 2*, 498.

on the other.[9] In this way, Psalm 97 depicts the life of faith. We continue to struggle to see the fruit of our labor, for many times the light of the kingdom of God is like a small seed. But the good news is that this light has already been "sown," and one day, as we learn from the parable of the mustard seed, it will grow and become "the largest of all garden plants, with such big branches that the birds can perch in its shade" (Mark 4:31–32).

---

9. Ortlund, "An Intertextual Reading of the Theophany of Psalm 97," 276.

# PSALM 98

Psalm 98 is another hymn celebrating the kingship of Yahweh (see Psalms 47, 93, 95–97, and 99). It begins by recalling what God has done in the past (vv. 1–3) as a way of strengthening the people's hope in Yahweh as King. Though the Davidic kingship may have ended in tragedy, not everything is lost. The memory of God's faithfulness to Israel continues to serve as an inspiration to believe in the God who fulfills his promises.

Verse 6 identifies God as "the Lord, the King!" When read within the postexilic context, this declaration is a "risky undertaking in the political environment of the day. Challenging the power of imperial deities had to be considered a subversive act by the authorities."[1] Yet the community makes this bold declaration both to preserve their sense of identity as a people and also to nurture hope amidst the difficult conditions of exile. Living in exile in a foreign land often involves injustice and oppression, because any outsider or minority is more vulnerable. The concluding words of Psalm 98:9b bring hope both to all peoples and the whole creation, for "He will judge the world in righteousness and the peoples with equity."

This emphasis on the king who comes to judge the world is very close to Psalm 96 (see vv. 10 and 13). Indeed, the two psalms form a parallel. But Psalm 97 is also important, as it emphasizes that the divine king's rule is founded on "righteousness and justice" (97:2), an emphasis that reappears in the concluding line of Psalm 98 (quoted above).

Like a typical hymn, Psalm 98 contains a call to worship and the motivations or reasons for praise. There are two calls to worship in Psalm 98, a brief one in verse 1a and an extended one in verses 4–9. Each call to worship is followed by the motivations for worship:

> Call to worship (v. 1a)
> Motivations (vv. 1b–3)
> Call to worship (vv. 4–6a, 7–9a)
> Motivations (vv. 6b, 9b, 9c)

---

1. Gerstenberger, *Psalms Part 2 and Lamentations*, 190.

## 98:1–3 "SING TO THE LORD A NEW SONG"

The psalm begins with a summons of praise: "Sing to the Lord a new song" (v. 1). As discussed in the comments for Psalm 96:1, there is a call for "a new song" because God has done something great for his people. After this exhortation, the psalmist immediately highlights the motivation for praising God: "for he has done marvelous things" (v. 1a; compare 96:1). God's acts are described as "marvelous," because they manifest his saving power, which is represented by his "right hand" and "holy arm" (v. 1b).

The psalm also recalls God's specific act of salvation to the Israelites: "he remembered his love and his faithfulness to Israel" (v. 3a). Scholars debate whether the psalm is recalling the Exodus event or the return from exile here.[2] While both are possibilities, the present form of the psalm does not specify one historical event. Because the psalm is not specific, it is more accessible to the present community of believers.[3]

As Asian Christians, we can also recall how God has acted in our own communities and countries. As a Filipino, I can say that God acted "marvelously" during the so-called EDSA 1 People Power Revolution. After twenty years of dictatorship under President Ferdinand Marcos, we can say with the psalmist that "we have escaped like a bird from the fowler's snare" (Ps 124:7). Though certainly not perfect, the unique thing about this revolution was that it was peaceful, and those at the forefront were Christians, nuns, priests, and ordinary Filipinos, praying in the midst of tanks and military. That 1986 revolution has become known around the world, and the context for Psalm 98 is similar. The declaration about what God has done for Israel is surrounded by an emphasis that this was "revealed to the nations" and reaches to the "ends of the earth":

> A "The Lord has made his salvation known . . . to the nations" (v. 2a).
> > B "He has remembered his love and his faithfulness to Israel" (v. 3a).
> A "All the ends of the earth have seen the salvation of our God" (v. 3b).

---

2. Tremper Longman III, "Psalm 98: A Divine Warrior Victory Song," *JETS* 27, no. 3 (1984): 269.
3. Longman, "Psalm 98: A Divine Warrior Victory Song," 272.

# Psalm 98

## 98:4–9 REJOICE, FOR THE KING IS COMING TO JUDGE WITH EQUITY

In the second call to worship, the scope of praise broadens as the psalmist calls on "all the earth" to "shout for joy to the Lord" (v. 4). The "jubilant song" and the playing of instruments (v. 5) both allude to the welcome given to a returning king after a victorious battle.[4] But the psalm is applicable to other similar situations, for the king celebrated in Psalm 98 is not a human king, but "the Lord, the King" (v. 6b). This declaration is an implied motivation for praise, because the throne of "the Lord, the King" (v. 6b) is founded on "righteousness and justice" (97:2). God is angry at injustice and even rebukes other gods for their unjust acts (see Ps 82:1–3). God has made the fight for the weak and vulnerable his own, and so the people can appeal to it as part of God's "covenant" (74:20). Because God has "remembered" his steadfast love in the past (98:3), the people can be assured that he will do the same in the present.

This second call to worship (vv. 4–9) pertains to the present time. Inspired by God's faithful action in the past, the psalmist looks at his present situation with hope and rejoicing because Yahweh is king. Whereas there is an explicit motivation for praise in the first call to worship ("for he has done marvelous things," v. 1a), the implicit motivation for rejoicing in the second call to worship is that they have Yahweh as their king.

However, there is a second, more explicit motivation for the second call to worship at the end of the psalm, where the psalmist calls the creation and all who dwell in it to praise the Lord because he is coming "to judge the earth . . . in righteousness and the peoples with equity" (v. 9). This psalm is set within the postexilic period, when the people's situation is far from ideal. Suffering and subjugation under foreign powers continue, and so the people cry, "how long?" as they lament to God. But their laments are not hopeless, because the king "comes to judge the earth" (v. 9). The use of the future form of the verb "to judge" in the last line of verse 9 points to an event that has not yet happened: "He will judge the world." Although we may find it difficult to see the reality of this statement amidst our present circumstances, let us not lose the vision of the Lord, the King, who will come to "judge the world in righteousness and the peoples with equity" (v. 9; compare 96:13).

As I write this, I see inequality, around me. Justice is selective. Those who are in power are not penalized, even if they violate the law, but the poor are penalized and put into jail. Imagine when the "Lord, the King" comes (v. 6b).

---

4. Longman, "Psalm 98: A Divine Warrior Victory Song," 270.

Surely his coming will be met with great rejoicing – not just by the peoples of the earth, but by the whole creation. "Let the sea resound, and everything in it" (v. 7). Even the rivers will "clap their hands" and the mountains will "sing together for joy" (v. 8). For creation itself has been groaning since the beginning (Rom 8:19–22) because of human abuse, greed, and unjust acts. But when Yahweh the king comes, he will bring justice – not only to humans, but also to all of creation. What a marvelous day that will be!

# PSALM 99

Psalm 99 is a hymn praising Yahweh, the King, and is closely related to Psalms 47, 93, 95–98. One of the main themes in these psalms is the relationship between divine kingship and justice. The king's throne is founded on justice (97:2), and he is coming to judge the world (see 96:13; 98:9). But each of these psalms also has its own unique contribution. Psalm 99, in particular, shows that the response to the coming judge is not only one of rejoicing (as found in 95:1–2; 96:11–12; 98:4–8), but also one of trembling (99:1). Moreover, this is the only Yahweh kingship psalm that says, "the King . . . loves justice" (99:4).

Another unique characteristic of Psalm 99 is its links to Isaiah 6, which is known for the Trisagion – the threefold repetition of the word "holy." In Psalm 99, Yahweh is declared as "holy" three times (vv. 3, 5, 9). In the vision of Isaiah, he saw the Lord "high and lifted up" (Isa 6:1). The word "high" (*rum*) is also used in Psalm 99 to describe Yahweh as "exalted" (*rum*) over all the nations" (v. 2). The context for Isaiah 6 is the end of the reign of a human king, on whose backdrop Isaiah saw the vision of Yahweh seated on his throne (Isa 6:1). The Lord is surrounded by heavenly beings (seraphim) in the same way that God is described in Psalm 99 as dwelling among "the cherubim" (v. 1). The passage in Isaiah 6, therefore, provides an important guide for interpreting Psalm 99.

Psalm 99 may be structured according to the reoccurrence of the chorus, "he is holy," which falls at the end of each section (v. 3, 5, 9):

> The King who dwells among the cherubim (vv. 1–3),
> The King who loves justice (vv. 4–5),
> Response to the King (vv. 6–9).

## 99:1–3 THE KING WHO DWELLS AMONG THE CHERUBIM

The psalm starts with the declaration, "The LORD reigns" (v. 1), which is similar to Psalm 97:1 (see also Ps 93:1). In Psalm 97, the earth is enjoined to "be glad," while Psalm 99 calls upon the nations to "tremble" (v. 1). The word "tremble" comes from the Hebrew word *ragaz*, which means "to tremble with emotion from terror."[1] In the LXX, it is translated as "to be angry" (*orgizo*). Literally, "let the peoples be angry," which implies that "they have cause to be

---
1. *HALOT*, 3:1183.

angry."[2] This supports the negative response reflected in the Hebrew *ragaz* ("to tremble . . . from terror"). Psalm 99 reminds us that the kingship of Yahweh is not all about rejoicing, for the element of terror is also present. Not all will rejoice when the Judge comes; some will be angry; others will tremble in terror. God is described in verse 3 as "awesome," which in Hebrew literally reads, "terrible." God comes not only to forgive but also to punish (see v. 8b below).

The description, "he sits enthroned between the cherubim" (v. 1b), is better translated as, "he who dwells among the cherubim" (see comments on Ps 80:1 above). The word cherubim (plural of cherub) refer to heavenly beings. Isaiah 6, which has links with this psalm, also mentions heavenly beings (seraphim). Yahweh dwells in the heavens among all these heavenly beings and a multitude of others. Thus he is described as the "LORD of hosts" (84:12).

But even though Yahweh is high and lifted up, he has chosen to reveal his power to the people of Israel. The psalmist declares, "Great is the LORD *in Zion*" (v. 2a, my emphasis). God manifests his power "in Zion," the mountain where the Temple was built. From this place, the Lord "is exalted over all the nations" (v. 2b).[3] The nations are exhorted in verse 3 to "praise your great and awesome name." As noted above, the word "awesome" in Hebrew literally means "terrible." Thus God is worthy of the utmost respect: "He is holy" (v. 3b). This is the first of three occurrences of the word "holy" in Psalm 99, which is similar to the Trisagion in Isaiah 6 (as noted above). The word "holy" refers to God's transcendence and also has moral connotations. God is above everyone: he dwells among the cherubim (v. 1) and is "over all the nations" (v. 2). Another important aspect of God's holiness is his judicial power as king,[4] which is supported by the emphasis on justice in the next verse.

## 99:4–5 THE KING WHO LOVES JUSTICE

The beginning of verse 4 is problematic in terms of translation. Literally, it reads, "the might of the king." Some scholars read this together with the verb from verse 3, "let them praise." In verse 3, the object of the praise is "your name." In verse 4, the object of the praise is "the might of the king." However, the occurrence of the chorus, "he is holy," at the end of verse 3 indicates a

---

2. John R. Kohlenberger III, ed., *The Comparative Psalter: Hebrew-Greek-English* (Oxford: Oxford University Press, 2007), 175.
3. The MT has "peoples/nations" while the LXX has "gods" (compare 95:3). But the context of verse 1 which mentions "peoples/nations" supports the MT reading.
4. Hossfeld and Zenger, *Psalms 2*, 488.

division between these verses. It is better, then, to read the phrase, "the might of the king," with the following phrase, "he loves justice" (v. 4a). But how do we make sense of the relationship between these two phrases?

Kirkpatrick takes "the might of the king" as the subject of the verb "to love": "the king's strength also loveth judgment."[5] But "strength" or "might" as the subject of the verb "love" does not seem right. The NIV takes the king as the subject of the verb and transforms the phrase, "the might of the king," into a sentence: "The king is mighty, he loves justice." This is a good attempt to make sense of the phrase, "the might of the king," but it fails to preserve the emphasis conveyed in the word "might." In the Hebrew text of verse 4, the word "might" is the very first word, which serves a purpose. In Psalm 98, the psalmist highlights God's power and strength: "his right hand and his holy arm have worked salvation for him" (Ps 98:1). In this verse, the adjective "holy" (compare Ps 99:3b) links God's action to God's holiness, which is connected to his justice in Psalm 99. Both God's "right hand" and his "arm" refer to God's power. The same emphasis is present in Psalm 99:4, but in this verse, God's power becomes an expression of his deep-seated desire, his love for justice. As the ESV translation puts it, "The king in his might loves justice."

Not only is his throne founded on righteousness and justice (97:2), but he also loves justice! And the manner in which he loves justice is demonstrated in the way he acts "mightily." One cannot love apart from action, and verse 4 also tells us that God expresses his love for justice in the way that he has "established equity" and "done what is just and right." It takes might to "establish" and "do what is right." In his might, this king loves justice, and we are called to "worship at his footstool" (v. 5). "Footstool" here refers to the ark of the covenant, which represents the earthly throne of God.[6] Verse 5 concludes with the second occurrence of chorus, "he is holy" (compare v. 3).

## 99:6–9 RESPONSE TO THE KING

The third and last occurrence of the word "holy" comes in the final verse of Psalm 99 (v. 9). Because of the presence of the Trisagion (thrice holy), some scholars connect Psalm 99 with the call narrative of the prophet Isaiah (Isaiah 6). In that call, Isaiah receives a vision of the great King, surrounded

---

5. Kirkpatrick, *The Book of Psalms*, 585.
6. John H. Walton, Victor H. Matthews and Mark W. Chavalas, *IVP Bible Background Commentary: Old Testament* (Leicester: Inter-Varsity, 2000), 542.

by heavenly beings. After receiving this vision, the prophet hears a question, "Whom shall I send?" And in response, he responds, "Here am I. Send me!" (Isa 6:8).

Similarly, in Psalm 99, the declaration of Yahweh as the king (v. 1) – who is "exalted over all the nations" (v. 2) and who loves justice in his might (v. 4) – calls for a response. At the end of the previous section, the people are called upon to worship God (v. 5). This section recounts examples of people who responded to God's call: Moses, Aaron, and Samuel (v. 6). Each, in his own way, has a story about how God called him. Aaron was appointed by God to be Moses's spokesman. Moses encountered God in the burning bush. And Samuel heard God's call as a child. The description, "among his priests" (v. 6), is not limited to Moses and Aaron, for Samuel also functioned as a priest when he made an offering on the altar (1 Sam 7). Similarly, the description, "among those who called on his name" (v. 6), does not only apply to Samuel, for Moses also called on God's name. Rather, these descriptions express how all three "priests" responded to God's call in their life.

Moreover, when Moses, Aaron, and Samuel called on the Lord, the psalm says that "he answered them" (v. 6b). Interceding on behalf of God's people is one of the main functions of a priest, and yet God does not always answer the prayers of his people. In Isaiah 59, the prophet tells the people that God's arm "is not too short to save" (v. 1). And then he says, "but your iniquities have separated you from your God" (v. 2). In Jeremiah 7, God commands the prophet, "do not pray for this people . . . for I will not listen to you" (v. 16), because the people were worshiping in the Temple while continuing to oppress the poor. Worship requires obedience, and God will only hear his people when they pray if they keep his "statutes and decrees" (Ps 99:7). The structure of verses 6b–8a shows the connection between our obedience and God's answer:

> A "he answered them" (v. 6b),
> >  B "they kept his statutes" (v. 7),
> A "you answered them" (v. 8a).

The theology in verse 8b supports this: God is a forgiving God, but also an "avenger of their wrongdoings" (ESV). Some scholars tend to diminish the element of punishment. For instance, Whitley repoints the Hebrew verb "to punish" to mean "to cleanse," so that it reads, "and he cleanseth them from their evil deeds."[7] He explains that the idea of punishing does not fit with the

---

7. Charles Francis Whitley, "Psalm 99:8," *ZAW* 85, no. 2 (1973): 230.

emphasis on forgiveness in the first part, especially since the audience remains the same (the Israelites, who kept the statutes). But the description at the beginning of the psalm ("the nations tremble," v. 1), along with the description of God as "terrible" (v. 3), both make way for the reading of God as one who punishes his people. The story of Moses interceding on behalf of the Israelites during their sojourn in the wilderness (Num 14:11–25) demonstrates that even though God forgives (vv. 18a, 19), he also punishes (v. 12, 18b). Moreover the history of the people's sinfulness recounted in Psalm 78 further supports this view. The emphasis throughout Psalm 99 is that God is holy, and "the core of YHWH's holiness . . . is his personal, loving care that does not exclude, but rather includes the seriousness of judgment."[8]

---

8. Hossfeld and Zenger, *Psalms 2*, 491.

# PSALM 100

In Psalm 99, God is referred to as "holy" three times, recalling the Trisagion in Isaiah 6. Because God is holy, he is transcendent, high and lifted up, and "awesome" (v. 3). Though he dwells among the cherubim (v. 1), he chose to reveal himself to humanity through the Israelites "in Zion" (v. 2) and "in Jacob" (v. 4). He is also a God who "loves justice" (v. 4). Thus Psalm 100 can declare, he is "good" (v. 5). God is holy, and he is also good.

Though a very short psalm, Psalm 100 has captured the hearts of worshipers throughout the ages. Kirkpatrick notes, "From ancient times it has been used in the daily service of the Synagogue . . . . It was used in the early morning of Lauds, and at the revision of the Prayer Book in 1552 it was added as an alternative for the *Benedictus*." It came to be "universally known and loved as the 'Old Hundredth.'"[1] Even in many churches in the Philippines, Psalm 100 is a favorite among worship leaders, in part because of its brevity and its common liturgical language (100:1 is exactly the same as 98:4; compare 100:3 with 95:6–7). Moreover, its central theological themes climax with the statement that "the LORD is good" (v. 5).[2]

Psalm 100 is a classic example of a hymn, which usually begins with a call to worship, followed by motivations for praise, and ends with a final summons to praise. In Psalm 100, four out of five verses are a summons to worship (vv. 1–4). The final verse is the reason/motivation for praise, which forms the climax of the psalm.

## 100:1–3 WHAT DOES IT MEAN TO WORSHIP THE LORD?

The superscription in Psalm 100 contains the words, "For giving grateful praise." This is the translation for the Hebrew word, *letodah*, which literally means, "to/for thanksgiving." The word *todah* can mean at least three things:[3]

1. confession,
2. thanksgiving offering/sacrifice,
3. thanksgiving.

---

1. Kirkpatrick, *The Book of Psalms*, 558.
2. For the parallels between Psalms 100 and 95, see Savran, "The Contrasting Voices of Psalm 95," 21.
3. Gérard Nissim Amzallag, "The Meaning of *Todah* in the Title of Psalm 100," *ZAW* 126, no. 4 (2014): 535–545. Amzallag adds a fourth possible meaning–antiphonal reading.

Confession is derived from the basic meaning of the verb *yahah*, from which the word *todah* is derived.[4] The thanksgiving offering/sacrifice refers to one of the sacrifices offered in the Temple. Modern Christians are more familiar with the third meaning, "thanksgiving," which refers to a verbal offering of thanksgiving offered to God. It is not necessary to limit the interpretation of *todah* to one of these meanings, as a combination of all three is present here. These three meanings are all important when interpreting the psalm.

Psalm 100 contains a series of calls to worship. The first begins with a summon for "all the earth" to "shout for joy to the Lord" (v. 1), which is exactly the same as Psalm 98:4. In Psalm 98, the phrase, "all the earth," refers not only to humans but also to the whole of created order, including the sea, the rivers, and the mountains (vv. 7–8). In Psalm 96:12, fields and forests rejoice and sing for joy. While the context of Psalm 100 does not mention the natural creation, this should not prevent us from interpreting the phrase, "all the earth," in the same way as Psalms 96 and 98, for the whole of creation is capable of worshiping God. What makes Psalm 100 unique is that it applies to all of creation ideas that are commonly reserved for human agents, such as serving (v. 2) and knowing (v. 3). But what does it mean for all of creation to "serve" and "know" God?

Verse 2 begins with the command to "serve the Lord" (ESV). The word "worship" (v. 2) comes from the Hebrew word *'abad*, which also means "to serve." But as Mays points out, the verb *'abad* is "surprisingly infrequent in the Psalter for a 'cultic' term, and used always in relation to a royal figure (human or divine)."[5] The meaning of "serve" here has political connotations. Within the context of the preceding Yahweh-kingship psalms, serving the Lord "is conduct which excludes slavery to human government or subjection to the power of the 'gods.'"[6] Unfortunately, we have seen Christians becoming slaves of human governments or leaders. During the time of Hitler, some of the brightest theologians, pastors, and philosophers bowed down in allegiance to this evil leader.[7] In my country, some Christians continue to support and even praise President Rodrigo Duterte, even after he compared himself to Hitler.[8]

---

4. *HALOT*, 2:389.
5. James Luther Mays, "Worship, World, and Power: An Interpretation of Psalm 100," *Int* 23, no. 3 (1969): 321.
6. Mays, "Worship, World, and Power: An Interpretation of Psalm 100," 322.
7. Robert P. Ericksen, *Theologians under Hitler: Gerhard Kittel, Paul Althaus and Emanuel Hirsch*, 2010.
8. Duterte said, "Hitler massacred three million Jews . . . there's three million drug addicts. There are. I'd be happy to slaughter them," https://www.nytimes.com/2016/10/01/world/asia/

His so-called "war on drugs" has led to the killing of thousands of Filipinos, mostly poor. Many Filipino Christians use Romans 13:1 to support his rule: "Let everyone be subject to the governing authorities, for there is no authority except that which God has established." Yet they are interpreting this text in isolation from the rest of Scripture. It is important to consider other passages, such as Psalm 100, when interpreting Romans 13,[9] for Psalm 100 puts service to human leaders in proper perspective (v. 2). Or, as we are reminded in Acts 5:29, "we must obey God rather than human beings"!

The command to "serve the LORD" (v. 2, ESV) should be understood in relation to the second command to "Know that the LORD is God" (v. 3). The verb "know" is used here to mean "acknowledge." When we acknowledge or confess that Yahweh is God, we can serve him "with gladness" and approach him "with joyful songs" (v. 2). In previous psalms, we learn that "the LORD, the king" (98:6) is coming to judge the world (96:13; 98:9). His coming will be met by two contrasting responses: rejoicing (96:11–13; 98:7–9) or trembling (99:1), depending on whether one acknowledges Yahweh as God, or not. Rejoicing entails obedience to his commands (99:7), and trembling suggests disobedience or the failure to listen to what God is saying (95:7–11).

To confess Yahweh as God is to acknowledge that "it is he who made us" (100:3b). This acknowledgment is either followed by, "and we are his," or, "and not we ourselves."[10] Although most Western scholars tend to argue for one correct reading, I affirm with Delitzsch that "both readings accord with the context, and it is clear that they are both in harmony with Scripture."[11] Delitzsch prefers, "we are his," but, "and not we ourselves," is a powerful affirmation of the acknowledgment that Yahweh is God. The opposite acknowledgment would be to say that we are our own masters. As the wicked say in Psalm 12, "With our tongue we will prevail, our lips are with us; who is master over us?" (v. 4, ESV). Thus to acknowledge Yahweh as God declares that we are not the "captain of our soul." The reading, "we are his," fits with the succeeding context of Psalm 100:3: "we are his people, the sheep of his pasture." The creator God is our Shepherd, and in the New Testament, believers are told by Jesus that he is their Good Shepherd, and so he knows them and they know

---

philippines-rodrigo-duterte-hitler-drugs.html; accessed on June 18, 2021.

9. For those who may say that Psalm 100 is from the OT and thus not as important as Romans 13, it is important to remember that Jesus himself quoted from the Psalms (e.g. Matt 27:46).

10. The former is the *Keri* while the latter is the *Kethib*. The latter is supported by the LXX, Syriac, and Vulgate, though the former is supported by the context of Psalm 95:7.

11. Keil and Delitzsch, *Keil and Delitzch Commentary on the Old Testament*, 5:105–106.

him (John 10:11, 14–15), and they recognize his voice (John 10:4). Later, he likens himself to the vine, his disciples to the branches, and his Father to the gardener who takes care of the vine (John 15:1, 5).

## 100:4–5 WHY WORSHIP THE LORD

After the loaded theological implications of the preceding verses, the psalmist invites those who "serve" the Lord and acknowledge him as "God" to "Enter his gates" (v. 4). This reminds us that there are requirements for entering into God's holy place (see Psalms 15 and 24). It is not about having the right words to say or the "correct" theology (see comments in Psalm 95). Rather, just as serving God is to be accompanied by "gladness" and "joyful songs" (v. 2), worshipers are to enter God's courts "with thanksgiving" and "praise" (v. 4). In other words, the worshiper does not come empty-handed. In light of the threefold meaning of the word thanksgiving (see above), this means coming with a humble and repentant heart, an offering, and a heart full of gratitude to God.

Verse 5 proclaims the motivation for coming into the sanctuary to worship: because "the Lord is good." At the beginning of Book III, the psalmist doubts if God is really good (Ps 73:1–2). As a concluding word to the Yahweh-kingship psalms (Psalms 93, 95–99), the psalmist affirms in Psalm 100 that God is good. Despite the people's situation, which is far from ideal, the psalmist declares that God is good because one day God will come to make things right again. The present situation does not represent the whole story about God and his dealings with the world and his people, for his "love endures forever" and "his faithfulness through all generations" (v. 5).

# PSALM 101

Psalm 101 may be read as a continuation of Psalm 100. Whereas Psalm 100 invites worshipers to "enter into his gates" that they may worship the Lord (v. 4), Psalm 101 shows us a picture of how a worshiper ought to conduct his life once he goes out of the house of the Lord, thereby teaching worshipers to apply the virtues from God's house within one's own house.[1] The word "house" is often used to refer to God's Temple (Pss 93:5; 135:2; compare 122:9), but here the word "house" is used to refer to a home. This psalm is attributed to David and is the first Davidic psalm in Book IV. The speaker in Psalm 101 vows to "conduct the affairs of my house" (v. 2) in the same way that he conducts them in the Temple. Those who go to the Temple are those "whose walk is blameless" (see Ps 15:1–2). The words "walk" (*halak*) and "blameless" (*tamim*) (Ps 15:2) are also used in Psalm 101:2: "I will ponder the way that is blameless [*tamim*] . . . . I will walk [*halak*] with integrity of heart" (ESV). But in Psalm 101, the blameless walk is extended to the home.

Worship should extend beyond the Temple precincts and not only penetrate our home, but also the wider society. Psalm 101 begins with singing of "justice" (v. 1). But how can we sing of justice if we don't even care about injustices in our own society, or if there is no love and justice in our homes? Psalm 101 is a challenging psalm to read and sing, because we cannot simply recite its words unless we are prepared to live out its commitments.

The psalm may have originally been written as a charter of a king at the time of his enthronement,[2] as verse 6 seems to portray someone who can afford to have servants. But the psalm has also been applied in other settings. During the postexilic era, the psalm may have been used to promote the ethics of Yahweh by encouraging the faithful to "dissociate themselves from certain groups and certain types of conduct and associate themselves with like-minded people."[3] Thus Psalm 101 is not limited to the king but is applicable to every believer. The close links with Psalm 1 and the book of Proverbs affirm this.[4]

---

1. Phil J. Botha, "Psalm 101: A Supplication for the Restoration of Society in the Late Post-Exilic Age," *Hervormde Teologiese Studies* 72, no. 4 (2016): 1–8.
2. Mowinckel, *The Psalms in Israel's Worship*, 2:65.
3. Botha, "Psalm 101: A Supplication for the Restoration of Society in the Late Post-Exilic Age," 7.
4. Botha, "Psalm 101: A Supplication for the Restoration of Society in the Late Post-Exilic Age," 5–6.

# Psalm 101

Psalm 101 contains elements of both a hymn (v. 1) and a lament (v. 2), but it is predominantly a wisdom psalm. Specifically, Psalm 101 is closely linked to Proverbs 11:20 and 17:20. In the Hebrew Bible, "the concept of a 'false,' or 'twisted,' or 'devious' heart" is found only in these three passages.[5] In the book of Psalms, Psalm 101 is similar to Psalm 1. Both contrast the way of the righteous with the way of the wicked, characterizing the righteous by what he does *not* do. The word "not" is repeated three times in Psalm 1: "Blessed is the one who does *not* walk in the counsel of the wicked, and does *not* stand in the way of sinners, and does *not* sit in the company of mockers" (v. 1, my translation). The NIV and other modern versions do not repeat "not" to avoid redundancy, but in doing so, they miss an important emphasis in the text. After identifying what the righteous person does *not* do, Psalm 1 identifies what he or she *does*: meditates on the law of the Lord (v. 3). Psalm 101 also describes the things that the righteous person will *not* do. The word "not" is repeated six times in Psalm 101 (vv. 3a, 3b, 4b, 5b, 7a, and 7b) to emphasize the importance of choosing the right company. Our friends can either help or hinder us as we walk the road towards godliness. To maintain a blameless heart, we have to choose our associates carefully.

The psalm may be outlined as follows:

Worship and justice (vv. 1–2),
Hating evil (vv. 3–8).

## 101:1–2 WORSHIP AND JUSTICE

While it is common to sing of God's "steadfast love" (v. 1, ESV) it is more "unusual"[6] to sing of God's justice. But the connection between worship and justice is affirmed elsewhere in Scripture (see Isaiah 58; Jer 7:1–11). In Psalm 101, singing of God's "justice" parallels singing praise to the Lord. Worship flows out of our knowledge of God, and God himself declared, "I am the LORD, who exercises kindness, justice and righteousness on earth" (Jer 9:24). But how can we praise God and sing of "justice" if we are not angry at injustice, as God is (see Psalm 82)? How can we worship the king whose throne is founded on "righteousness and justice" (Ps 97:2) if we don't promote justice in the way we live?

---

5. Botha, "Psalm 101: A Supplication for the Restoration of Society in the Late Post-Exilic Age," 5.
6. Erich Zenger and Frank-Lothar Hossfeld, *Psalms 3: A Commentary on Psalms 101–150*, ed. Klaus Baltzer, trans. Linda M. Maloney (Minneapolis: Fortress Press, 2011), 14.

But justice is not only God's concern. In Psalm 101:1, the words "justice" and "steadfast love" do not have the usual third person suffix connecting them to God ("*his* steadfast love," "*his* justice"). Instead, the psalmist is singing of "justice" and "steadfast love." While the preceding psalms suggest that these words refer to God's attributes (see Pss 98:3; 100:5), the context of Psalm 101 suggests that they refer to the practice of human justice (compare Mic 6:8, which clearly states that justice is every human's responsibility). Right after singing of justice in verse 1, the psalmist proposes what he will do: "I will be careful to lead a blameless life" (v. 2a). The words, "I will be careful," come from the verb *sakhal*, which means "to understand." This is the same verb used in Jeremiah 9:24, which speaks of the "understanding" to know God. Together with the preposition *be* ("in"), the verb means, "closely attend to." To know God in a way that leads to singing of justice requires concentration, focus, and resolve. Thus the psalmist resolves to "lead a blameless life" (Ps 101:2a), which not only means being righteous inside God's house, but also in one's own house: "I will conduct the affairs of my house with a blameless heart" (v. 2b). Earlier, the word "house" was used to refer to the Temple (93:5), but here it refers to the house of the speaker (or the palace if he is a king).

Verse 2 is about the general orientation of the psalmist's life. Specifically, it pertains to what the individual speaker will do. The theme is similar to Psalm 1, describing the life of the blessed or righteous person. Whereas Psalm 1 begins by emphasizing what the blessed person does *not* do and then describes what he or she *does*, Psalm 101 reverses the pattern, beginning with what the righteous person commits to do (v. 2) and then describing what he or she will *not* do (vv. 3–5).

Before these statements about the psalmist's commitment to orient his life to the overall direction of righteousness (vv. 3–5), there is a question that has puzzled many scholars: "when will you come to me?" (v. 2). Some argue that this is a lament, but others posit that it cannot be a lament due to the preceding hymn of praise (v. 1). Yet a hymn can certainly move into lament (see Psalm 89).[7] While the question, "when will you come to me?" may not be a fully developed lament, it suggests an implied complaint about an unfulfilled longing for God's visitation through a dream or vision. The psalmist is longing for an affirmation that his life is pleasing to God. In the NT, Jesus

---

7. I have dealt with this question more extensively. See Federico G. Villanueva, *The "Uncertainty of a Hearing,"* 101–131.

receives the best affirmation that any human being can receive when the voice from heaven says, "This is my son in whom I am well-pleased" (Matt 3:17).

## 101:3–8 HATING EVIL

For the psalmist in Psalm 101, however, such an affirmation does not come. Nevertheless, he continues to commit himself to doing what pleases God. Like Daniel's friends, he sets his heart not to "look with approval on anything that is vile" (v. 3). Through a close analysis of the overall structure of the psalm, Botha sees that "Psalm 101 is about choices of association and disassociation in one's personal life and in the public sphere."[8] The psalmist is aware that "bad company corrupts good character" (1 Cor 15:33). Thus he resolves to "hate what faithless people do" (Ps 101:3b) and "have nothing to do with what is evil" (v. 4). We normally hear that we should hate what is wrong but love the sinner, but after the psalmist distances himself from the wicked person's actions, he says that he will "destroy" the slanderer (v. 5a) and will "not tolerate" the boastful (v. 5b). The Apostle Paul reminds us that love involves *hating* what is evil as much as loving what is good (Rom 12:9).

People who love the Lord will hate whomever the Lord hates (see also Ps 139:19–22) and so will avoid their company (see Ps 1:1–2). The psalmist says that those "with a perverse heart shall be far from me" (Ps 101:4, ESV), but his "eyes will be on the faithful in the land" (v. 6). In the words of Psalm 15, the one who will be allowed to dwell in God's holy hill "despises a vile person but honors those who fear the Lord" (v. 4). In Psalm 101, the psalmist says that he wishes to "dwell with" the faithful (v. 6a), and those "whose walk is blameless" will serve in his house (v. 6b). The word "walk" here refers to a general orientation to life, a way that is set towards the righteousness. The psalmist also uses the word "walk" in verse 2: "I will walk with integrity of heart within my house" (ESV).

In this second section of the psalm, the psalmist sets a clear boundary between the "faithful in the land" and the "evildoer" (v. 8). The former will be his companion. The latter will not be allowed to be near him. One will know the evildoer by his actions and words, for he "practices deceit" and "speaks falsely" (v. 7). The psalmist concludes by declaring that he will actively make sure that the wicked are destroyed, cut off "from the city of the Lord" (v. 8).

---

8. Botha, "Psalm 101: A Supplication for the Restoration of Society in the Late Post-Exilic Age," 4.

# PSALM 102

Christians often use Philippians 2:14 to exhort one another not to complain: "Do everything without grumbling or arguing." We don't want to be like the Israelites in the desert, who complained and were punished. But are all complaints wrong? In the superscription, Psalm 102 is described as a "prayer" of an afflicted person who "pours out his complaint before the LORD" (superscription). Notice how the psalmist not only complains; he "pours out his complaint."[1]

This psalm helps us see that not all complaints are wrong, for complaints can also be offered as prayers. Hannah's words to Eli in 1 Samuel are similar to the superscription for Psalm 102: "I was pouring out my soul to the LORD" (1:15). The whole of Psalm 102 may be read as the psalmist's pouring out his heart to God. The final verse forms an inclusio with the superscription:

> Superscription: "before the LORD";
> Final verse: "before you" (v. 28).

Psalm 102 is an individual lament, containing the following elements: an invocation (v. 1), a petition (v. 2), a complaint (vv. 3–11), a declaration of trust (vv. 12–22), a complaint with a petition (vv. 23–24), and a concluding declaration of trust (vv. 25–28).

The dominance of complaint in Psalm 102 (nine verses!) is unique (see vv. 3–11) and makes the superscription appropriate. Another unique aspect to Psalm 102 is how the psalmist returns to lament (vv. 23–24) after making a declaration of trust (vv. 12–22). Even though the psalmist ends with an expression of trust (vv. 25–28), the sense of complaint dominates the psalm. The movement between complaint and expressions of trust resembles Lamentations 3, which begins with an individual lament (vv. 1–20) that is followed by a hymnic declaration of God's faithfulness (vv. 21–24), and then the last part of the song returns to lament – this time a communal lament (vv. 25–28).[2] In Psalm 102, the alternation between lament and hymn subverts the full expression of praise, and the hymn sections emphasize the element of lament. Thus the psalm is properly described as "a prayer of an afflicted person."

The overall structure of Psalm 102 may be outlined as follows:

> Lament (vv. 1–11),

---

[1]. In Filipino, *nagbuhos ng sama ng loob*.
[2]. For further discussion, see Villanueva, *The "Uncertainty of a Hearing"*, 213–247.

Hymn (vv. 12–22),
Lament (vv. 23–24),
Hymn (vv. 25–28).

### 102:1–11 LAMENT

The unique superscription for Psalm 102 deserves further discussion. Unlike most psalms with superscriptions, which contain a note of attribution (e.g. "Of David") and a description of the music ("a psalm"), here the psalm is described as "A prayer of an afflicted person who has grown weak and pours out a lament before the Lord." The word "afflicted person" can also be translated as "poor." Literally, the first part of the superscription may be translated, "a prayer of the poor when he is faint/when he fainted." Because the poor lack adequate support systems and resources, they are vulnerable and are the first ones to "faint." Thankfully, the poor person in Psalm 102 has someone to whom he can pour out his complaint. The Hebrew word for "complaint" (compare Ps 55:2) here is *siakh*, which can also be translated as "lament." Not all complaints are prayers, as some complaints are born out of disgruntled muttering. The difference between muttering and lamenting is that the former is borne out of unbelief (see the many complaints throughout the book of Numbers),[3] whereas the later is an expression of faith and intimacy with God (see comments for Psalm 73).

We normally do not express our negative emotions to people we don't know well, because it is like baring our soul. To pour out our complaints before the Lord, we have to be honest about our feelings and expose our deepest vulnerabilities. In verse 2, the psalmist feels that God is hiding from him, and so he prays, "Do not hide your face from me." The prophet Isaiah confirms that God hides his face from us, for he says, "your sins have hidden his face from you" (59:2). While sin separates us from God, it is not always the cause of God's "hiding." During times of extreme suffering or loneliness, we may feel as if God is hiding his face from us. In Psalm 102, the psalmist is desperate for immediate attention, and so he prays, "answer me quickly" (v. 2b).

While the psalm does not specifically describe the psalmist's situation of suffering, he renders his feelings vividly. His "days vanish like smoke" (v. 3), and he describes himself as "a desert owl" (v. 6) and "a bird alone on a roof" (v. 7).

---

3. E.g. Numbers 11:1–6; 12:1–2; 14:1–4; 16:41–42.

As I write, the world is in the midst of a pandemic caused by the coronavirus, and the Philippines has had one of the longest lockdowns in the world. Those who are sick with the COVID-19 virus have their days "vanish like smoke" (v. 3). Every day, we face the same loneliness, and if you have COVID-19, people treat you like a leper. The psalmist complains, "All day long my enemies taunt me" (v. 8a) and "use my name as a curse" (v. 8b).

The psalmist's suffering is physical (vv. 3b, 9), psychological (v. 4), emotional (vv. 6–7), social (v. 8), and spiritual (v. 2). In our modern era, the spiritual dimension is often ignored, but it is central for the psalmist. The psalmist feels that God is far away from him (v. 2), and he attributes his condition to God's "great wrath" (v. 10a). It seems as if God has lifted him up only to throw him down (v. 10b; compare Lam 2:1). In spite of all his suffering, he still cries out to God (v. 1), for he is desperate for his relationship with God to be restored (compare Lam 5:21).

## 102:12–22 HYMN

Though the word "but" at the beginning of verse 12 signals the transition to the declaration of trust, it also highlights the difference between the preceding lament and the present hymnic section. Note the contrast between "my days" (vv. 3, 11) and "forever" (v. 12; see vv. 23–24 below), where the "days" of the psalmist "vanish like smoke" (v. 3a) and are "like the evening shadow" (v. 11), but God sits "enthroned forever" (v. 12). Unlike "smoke" and "shadow," which are fleeting, the verb "sit" speaks of stability. Coupled with the word "forever," it depicts permanence. Thus the psalmist declares, "your renown endures through all generations" (v. 12).

The contrast between verses 11 and 12 is similar to Psalm 22, where the psalmist laments, "I cry out by day, but you do not answer" (v. 2), and yet God is "the one Israel praises" (v. 3). In this contrast, God is "enthroned" and therefore securely seated, while the psalmist is without rest (v. 2) because the Lord is not responding to his cries. In Psalm 22, the psalmist also contrasts his own experience with that of his ancestors. When his ancestors "cried out," they were "saved" (22:5), and yet the psalmist is "forsaken" and "far from deliverance" (v. 1). Moreover, the people mock him because God is not delivering him or rescuing him (vv. 7–8). Though God is "enthroned" (v. 3), the psalmist describes himself as "a worm and not a man" (v. 6).

Psalm 102 also contrasts the way that God treats the psalmist with the rest of the community (Zion). In verse 13, the psalmist declares that God "will arise and have compassion on Zion," which means he will punish the wicked on behalf of the poor (see Ps 12:5). And yet in the opening lament, God arises and lifts up the psalmist only to throw him down (102:10). Verses 14–22 express the psalmist's trust in God's faithfulness to Zion. God will show favor at the appointed time (v. 13) and will rebuild Zion (v. 16). Moreover, God will have mercy on those who are in anguish: he will respond to the prayer of the destitute" (v. 17) and "hear the groans of the prisoners" (v. 20). This language is similar to Lamentations 3, which also mentions the prisoners (v. 34). The words "look down" and "heaven" occur in both Psalm 102 and Lamentations 3:

> Lamentations 3:50: "until the LORD looks down from heaven and sees";
> Psalm 102:19: "The LORD looked down . . . from heaven he viewed the earth."

While the longings expressed in Lamentations 3 occur in Psalm 102, they will not transpire until the future (see v. 18), for they are not the present experience of the psalmist.

### 102:23–24 LAMENT

After the hymnic section (vv. 12–22), the psalm suddenly returns to lament (v. 23). One common interpretation is to read the hymnic section as the motivation for the psalmist's present situation, but if that were the case, a petition would have been more appropriate here. Instead, the psalmist pours out another even harsher complaint: "In the course of my life he broke my strength" (v. 23). This indicates that the preceding hymn is intended to support the lament. In Lamentations 3, the suffering of the community is expressed through the lament of the individual, whereas Psalm 102 expresses the hope of the community in contrast to the individual's lament. God will "rebuild Zion" (v. 16), but "he broke my strength" (v. 23). Notice how the psalmist distances himself from God by talking about him in the third person, which is similar to the experience of *tampo* ("hurt feelings"; see Psalm 73). The implicit contrast between "my days" (v. 11) and "you . . . abide forever" (v. 12) becomes more explicit in verse 24: "Do not take me away, my God, in the midst of my days" (v. 24a). This concluding line of the lament makes a clear and obvious distinction between "my days" (v. 11) and "your years" (v. 24).

## 102:25–28 HYMN

The repeated emphasis on "days" and "years" in Psalm 102 recalls Psalm 90, where the psalmist tells God, "A thousand years in your sight are like a day that has just gone by" (v. 4). Moreover, the psalmist declares that God was there "before the mountains were born" and remains "from everlasting to everlasting" (90:2). This is similar to the opening line of the second hymn in Psalm 102: "In the beginning you laid the foundations of the earth" (v. 25). In Psalm 90, people are described as "grass that is renewed in the morning; in the morning it flourishes and is renewed; in the evening it fades and withers" (vv. 5–6, ESV). The Hebrew word for "renew" (*chalaf*) that is repeated twice in these verses is repeated again in Psalm 102:26b: "like clothing you will change [*chalaf*] them and they will be discarded [*chalaf*]." In contrast to everything that will change, including the heavens, this hymnic section declares that God will "remain the same and your years will never end" (v. 27). The mention of "years" in this verse recalls the earlier petition in verse 24 ("you whose years endure").

The psalm begins with an emphasis on the psalmist's individual sense of isolation and loneliness (vv. 1–11), but then the community (Zion) helps the individual regain his bearings (vv. 12–22). The return to lament (vv. 23–24) suggests that the community is not enough. Ultimately, we need God, which is the emphasis at the end of the psalm. In the last verse, the psalmist declares: "The children of your servants will live in your presence . . . and be established before you" (v. 28).

# PSALM 103

The movement between Psalm 102 and Psalm 103 reveals the close relationship between praise and lament. In Psalm 102, a poor/afflicted person "pours out a lament before the Lord." In Psalm 103, we see how those who have learned to pour out their lament to God can praise the Lord with their "inmost being" (103:1). Much of the praise and worship in our church services today is shallow because we have not learned to plumb the depths of our lament.

The phrase, "all my inmost being" (103:1), is equivalent to the Filipino word *loob*, which is a core cultural term.[1] Literally, *loob* means "what is inside," which also refers to how we relate with others and to our outside world. Only those who are most intimate with us are invited to access our "inmost being," the joys, pains, praises, and complaints that are deep within us. As discussed previously, we do not experience feelings of hurt (*tampo*) with people who are not close to us.[2] Thus our ability to lament indicates intimacy with someone – or God. Praise arises after we encounter God within our "inmost being."

Psalm 103 is a hymn, though the call to worship is directed to one's soul rather than the congregation. While the community is important, it is easy to lose oneself within community-oriented cultures. Both the community and the voice of the individual are important in Psalm 103, which is held together by an inclusio (see repetition of "Praise the Lord, my soul," vv. 1–2, 20–22). Psalm 103 can be divided into three parts:

Praising God with one's inmost being (vv. 1–6),
Praising God with one's community (vv. 7–18),
Praising God with all of creation (vv. 19–22).

## 103:1–6 PRAISING GOD WITH ONE'S INMOST BEING

Long before modern psychology started talking about the importance of "self-talk," the psalmists were already engaging in it. The psalmist would ask himself, "Why, my soul, are you downcast?" (42:5). Or he would tell his soul, "return to your rest" (116:7). The word "soul" (*nephesh*) literally means "throat, gullet,"[3] but here it is used as a reference to the "self," with a particular focus on that

---

1. Albert E. Alejo, *Tao Po! Tuloy: Isang Landas Ng Pag-Unawa Sa Loob Ng Tao* (Quezon City, Philippines: Ateneo de Manila University Press, 1990).
2. For further discussion, see Villanueva, "Lament as *Pagtatampo sa Diyos*," *Psalms 1–72*, 137–138.
3. *TDOT*, 9:504.

which is within. Thus in the second part of Psalm 103:1, the psalmist enjoins "all my inmost being" to praise God's holy name (v. 1b). "Self-talk" implies an inward journey. As noted above, "all my inmost being" (v. 1b) is equivalent to the Filipino concept of *loob* (literally, "what is inside"). *Loob* is not just what is inside, but what is deep within (*kaibuturan ng puso*). One does not simply open one's *loob* to anyone, but only to those who are really close to us. It is those who are able to pour out their lament to God (see Psalm 102) who are able to say to their soul, "all my inmost being, praise his holy name" (103:1).

The word that is translated as "praise" (v. 1) literally means, "bless," and usually refers to someone superior honoring someone inferior (a priest blessing the congregation, a king blessing his people, a father blessing his children).[4] The word "bless" is rarely used by an inferior towards someone superior.[5] When "bless" is used towards God, the basic idea is gratitude. For example, in Genesis 24:48, the servant of Abraham says, "I bowed my head and worshiped the LORD and blessed the LORD . . . who had led me by the right way" (ESV). "Blessing the LORD" in this sense is a gesture of gratitude. In Psalm 103, the psalmist recalls the things that God has done and is moved to "bless" the Lord. In the context of worship, the word has come to mean "praise."

Praising God with one's "inmost being" implies an awareness of the manifold things that God has done for us. Thus the psalmist commands himself to "forget not all his benefits" (v. 2b). The word "benefits" (*gemul*) refers to God's "generous acts."[6] In the following verses, the psalmist reminds his soul of God's "purely deeds of loving-kindness."[7] The beautiful Filipino term, *kagandahang loob* (literally, "beautiful inside/heart"), captures this nicely. In this text, God's *kagandahang loob* is expressed using the Hebrew participles, which are verbal adjectives (both action words and adjectives). Thus the focus is not just on the action, but on the one who is doing the action. Hebrew participles also convey ongoing action, and so the actions express an ongoing characteristic of the subject.

In verses 3–6, the psalmist reminds his soul that the Lord is the one who:

"forgives all your sins" (v. 3a),
"heals all your diseases" (v. 3b),
"redeems your life from the pit" (v. 4a),

---

4. *TDOT*, 2:288–289.
5. *TDOT*, 2:291.
6. Robert Alter, *The Book of Psalms*, 258.
7. This is Delitzsch's translation of *gemul*. Keil and Delitzsch, *Keil and Delitzsch Commentary on the Old Testament*, 5:120.

"crowns you with love and compassion" (v. 4b),
"satisfies your desires with good things" (v. 5), and
"works righteousness and justice for all the oppressed" (v. 6).

The first "benefit" that the psalmist remembers is divine forgiveness, which will be the focus of verses 10–14. In verse 3, the Lord "who forgives" is also the one "who heals all your diseases." Forgiveness and healing are closely linked because of the general view in the Bible that sickness is caused by sin (e.g. Job; compare Jas 5:14–16). Sickness may also be associated with death. The word "pit" (Ps 103:4) is one biblical description of the realm of the dead (Ps 88:4–5). Thankfully, the psalmist can say to his soul that the Lord is also the one "who redeems your life from the pit" (v. 4). Not only is the psalmist delivered from the "pit," or death, but the Lord also "crowns" him with "love and compassion" (v. 4b). From the pit to the "crown"! But how are "love and compassion" related to the restoration of one who has been to the realm of the dead? The psalmist seems to be saying that these qualities are learned in the pit, for those who have been through the depths have more capacity for empathy and compassion.

Moreover, God is the one "who satisfies your desires with good things" (v. 5). Although this satisfaction has to do with things that renew one's "youth" (v. 5b), the meaning of verse 5a as well as the context of verse 6 both point beyond this. In the Hebrew, the word translated, "your desires" (v. 5), is literally, "your ornaments," but this does not make sense, so some follow the LXX, which has "desires." This is the reading reflected in the NIV. But a better alternative, which is followed by the majority of scholars, reads the Hebrew word *'od* ("length, endurance, age") as "your existence."[8] So the translation should be, "who satisfies you." The next word, which is translated, "with good things," is singular in the Hebrew and should simply be translated, "good." Thus the whole phrase reads, "who satisfies you with good" (see ESV). But what is the "good" here? In the context, it could refer to the things that give one satisfaction, "so that your youth is renewed like the eagle's" (v. 5b). But it could also refer to the last description in verse 6, "righteousness and justice for all the oppressed." This suggests that whatever "good things" (v. 5) the psalmist has received are not meant for him alone, but for the sake of others.

---

8. Leslie C. Allen, *Psalms 101–150* (Nashville: Thomas Nelson, 2002), 26. Zenger and Hossfeld cites Psalms 104:33; 146:2 as contextual support. Zenger and Hossfeld, *Psalms 3*, 31.

## 103:7–18 PRAISING GOD WITH ONE'S COMMUNITY

Towards the end of the first section, one notices a movement from the individual ("my soul") to his community. One does not worship alone, but with the community. The emphasis on the individual in the first section is important, as it teaches that worship or praise must be an individual experience. The words, "praise the Lord, my soul," at the end of the psalm form an inclusio that holds the whole psalm together. This emphasis on individual worship is important for Asian cultures in light of their communal emphasis, which sometimes neglects the individual. For example, in some cases, if the head of the family decides something, the whole family simply follows – including religious matters. But Psalm 103 underlines the importance of personal experience in worship. At the same time, the movement towards the community affirms the traditional communal focus in Asia. Our identity, including our success, is bound up with our community. As one of our Filipino proverbs says, "Those who do not know how to look back will not reach their destination."[9]

The psalmist looks back to that momentous event in their history, when God "made known his ways to Moses" (v. 7; see also Exod 33:13). The events in Exodus 32–34 lie in the background of Psalm 103:7–8. The Israelites disobeyed God's command by making an idol for themselves and worshiping it (Exodus 32). As a result, God told Moses, "I will not go with you" (Exod 33:3), and so Moses pleaded with God, who graciously allowed his glory to be revealed to Moses (Exod 33:17–23; 34:5–6). Thus Moses came to know the ways of God as declared in Exodus 34:6: "The Lord is compassionate and gracious, slow to anger, abounding in love . . ." These words are quoted in Psalm 103:8 to define the "ways" of the Lord (v. 7), which he revealed to Moses.

Verses 9–13 represent the psalmist's reflections on this passage from Exodus 34:6, which is quoted in verse 8. In verse 9, the psalmist uses a word from the court – "accuse." In the Exodus narrative, God had all the reasons to "accuse" his people. He had initiated a covenant with the people, which they had agreed to follow. Unfortunately, they did not fulfill their part of the bargain, and they rebelled against God's ways. Thus began a series of many "lawsuits" against Israel. There was no way the people could ever win this case, but the psalmist believes that God "will not always accuse" (v. 9), for he is a God "who forgives" (see v. 3). He does not treat his people in accordance with their sins (v. 10). The poet likens the greatness of God's love to the distance between heaven and earth (v. 11). Because of the greatness of God's love, he

---

9. *Ang hindi marunong tumanaw sa pinanggalingan, hindi makararating sa paroroonan.*

has removed their transgressions "as far as the east is from the west" (v. 12). God's love for his people is likened to a father's compassion for his children (v. 13). A compassionate father would know how feeble and vulnerable his children are, and so he deals with them accordingly. God "knows how we are formed . . . we are dust" (v. 14).

The statement, "we are dust," does not refer to moral weakness. It is not the same as our common Filipino saying, *sapagkat tayo ay tao lamang* ("because we are just human beings"), which is often used as an excuse for mistakes, including moral failures. Rather, the context points to humanity's mortal existence: "The life [literally, "days"] of mortals are like grass . . . the wind blows over it and it is gone" (vv. 15–16). The emphasis here is similar to Psalm 90, which also laments the brevity of human existence using the image of fading grass. But in Psalm 90, the psalmist contrasts the shortness of human life with the God who is "from everlasting to everlasting" (90:2), whereas in Psalm 103, the "days" of humans (v. 15) are contrasted with the "Lord's love," which is "from everlasting to everlasting" (v. 17). This everlasting love, however, is qualified by the words, "with those who fear him" (v. 17). This is the third time that the phrase, "those who fear him," occurs in the psalm (see vv. 11 and 13). Those who fear the Lord in Psalm 103 are those who are deeply aware of their own sinfulness in the face of God's mercy (vv. 9–14) and who gratefully respond in obedience (v. 18).

## 103:19–22 PRAISING GOD WITH ALL OF CREATION

Psalm 103 starts with a personal call to "praise the Lord, *my soul*" (v. 1), which is followed by a call to remember the nation of Israel's experience of God. The preceding section will be appreciated by those who are living in Asian countries that focus on nation-building and national identity. While Psalm 103 encourages the community of Israel to look back on the history of their people, it moves beyond the national by also looking towards the transcendent and universal. Because God "has established his throne in the heavens" (v. 19), the psalmist calls on the angels – the heavenly beings who minister to God – and all of the heavenly hosts to "praise the Lord" (vv. 20–21). Moreover, the psalmist calls upon "all his works everywhere in his dominion" to praise the Lord (v. 22). This means everything in the universe, because "his kingdom rules over all" (v. 19). The final line of the psalm, however, returns to the individual: "Praise the Lord, my soul" (v. 22). The praises of all creation, even of heavenly beings, will be meaningless to us unless we each choose to praise the Lord.

# PSALM 104

Psalm 104 is a meditation on creation, which has similarities with Psalm 19. In Psalm 19, the psalmist prays that the "meditation of my heart be pleasing in your sight" (19:1); in Psalm 104, he prays, "May my meditation be pleasing to him" (104:34). Psalm 104 is one of the main biblical texts on creation, with parallels to the famous creation account in Genesis 1.[1] One main difference between Genesis 1 and Psalm 104 is that the primary concern of the psalmist is not with the order of creation, but with the wonder of creation. As in Psalm 19, the psalmist sees in creation the glory of God, and his meditation on creation leads to praise.

Psalm 104 is a hymn, which is also similar to Psalm 103. Both psalms begin with a call to praise that is directed to "my soul," which is followed by a series of motivations for praise. These motivations for praise come in the form of Hebrew participles (see Psalm 103 above). In Psalm 103, the focus of the praise is on divine forgiveness, whereas in Psalm 104, the focus of the praise is on God's creation. Nevertheless, the importance of divine forgiveness is not overlooked in this hymn of praise for God's creation. At the end of Psalm 104, the psalmist mentions the "wicked" and "sinners" (v. 35), for only those who have received God's forgiveness can truly praise God's creation.

Structurally, Psalm 104 begins with a call to praise (v. 1). This call is repeated at the end of the psalm (v. 35), forming an inclusio. The main body of the psalm may be divided into six parts. The first section describes the "heavens" as a manifestation of God's greatness (vv. 2–4). The second section describes how God set the earth on its foundations and established boundaries so that the waters would not "cover the earth" (vv. 5–9). The third section is devoted to God's care for the earth and the sky and all the creatures that occupy these spaces (vv. 10–18). The fourth section describes how God established boundaries for the night and day (vv. 19–24). The fifth section is focused on God's care for the sea and all its creatures (vv. 25–30). The sixth section offers a concluding personal reflection and call to praise (vv. 31–35).

## 104:1–4 THE LORD WHO IS MY GOD

Psalm 104 begins with a call to worship that is addressed to oneself: "Praise the LORD, my soul" (v. 1; compare 103:1). Though the first person ("*my* soul") is

---

1. Levenson, *Creation and the Persistence of Evil*, 55–56.

oriented towards the personal, the call to worship is communal. All who share the sentiments expressed in the words of the psalm can participate in worship, but one has to experience the reality of God in one's own life first. Verse 1 mentions the covenant name of God, "Yahweh (Lord)," and adds "my God." Thus God is described in transcendent language as "very great" and "clothed with splendor and majesty," but he is also identified with personal, relational language as "my God" (v. 1).

Though God has "established his throne in heaven" (Ps 103:19) and his dwelling is "among the cherubim" (see Ps 80:1), he has also chosen to reveal himself to humanity. In Psalm 104, God makes himself and his ways known through the act of creation. The description, who "stretches out the heavens like a tent" (v. 2), may be understood as the creation of the heavens (Gen 1:1). Yet it is also "designed to identify and magnify Yahweh as the unique living God of the entire earth who is in the process of revealing his magnificence."[2]

The call to worship (v. 1) is followed by a series of Hebrew participles, which serve as the motivations for praise (compare Psalm 103). God is described as one who:

> "wraps himself in light" (v. 2a),
> "stretches out the heavens like a tent" (v. 2b),
> "makes the clouds his chariot" (v. 3),
> "rides on the wings of the wind" (v. 3), and
> "makes winds his messengers" (v. 4).

The image of God wrapped in light (v. 2) continues the theme of God's majesty (v. 1b), as he is now revealed in all his light and glory. Describing the clouds as God's chariot and depicting God as riding on the wind (vv. 3–4) are ways of saying that God has appeared (theophany) (compare Ps 18:9–13). Because God has chosen to reveal himself through his heavenly creation, he should be praised.

## 104:5–9 FROM THE HEAVENS TO THE EARTH

In this section, the focus shifts from the God who revealed himself through his heavenly creations (vv. 2–4; compare Ps 19:1) to the God who "set the earth on its foundations" (104:5). In Psalm 18, the psalmist testifies that when he cried out to God, the God who is in the heavens "reached down from on

---

2. Norman C. Habel, "He Who Stretches out the Heavens," *CBQ* 34, no. 4 (1972): 417.

high and took hold of me" (v. 16). In Psalm 104, we see a similar movement (see vv. 11–17 below).

The image of the earth "covered it with the watery depths" (v. 6) represents ultimate chaos, for in ancient times, the waters (seas, rivers) represented malevolent forces that were hostile to God. Verse 7 alludes to the divine conflict at sea,[3] where God defeated the powers of chaos: "at your rebuke the waters fled." The waters that covered even the mountains (v. 6) were made to flow into the valleys down below (v. 8). God "set a boundary they cannot cross" (v. 9), thereby holding the forces of chaos in check. These verses bring stability to the unpredictability that so often characterizes our human existence.

## 104:10–18 THE GOD WHO FEEDS HIS CREATURES

God not only provides stability, for he also provides water to drink and food to eat for all his creatures. In the hands of the loving God, the water representing chaos and disaster becomes a source of nourishment and life, for God causes the springs to flow "between the mountains" (v. 10) so that "all the beasts of the field" may drink from it (v. 11). Water was a rare commodity in the biblical land, and so the "blessed" life is described as a tree planted by streams of water (Psalm 1). In Psalm 104, one can even sense exultation and delight because of the abundance of water, for the birds sing by the rivers where they make their nests (v. 12). The birds are featured prominently in Psalm 104 (see v. 17), which reminds us of Psalm 84, where birds build their nests near God's sanctuary (v. 3). While we tend to focus first on big things, Psalm 104 prioritizes the smallest creatures in creation, for the psalmist mentions the small birds (v. 12) before describing how God "waters the mountains from his upper chambers" (v. 13a).

Verse 13b personifies the earth, saying that she is "satisfied with the fruit of your work" (ESV). In Hebrew, "earth" is feminine, which agrees with how we refer to "Mother Earth." The verb "satisfied" is repeated three times in Psalm 104 (see also vv. 16, 28). But what is "the fruit of your work"? The word "fruit" could be understood figuratively to refer to the things that God does – his acts of providing for his creatures. These actions satisfy the earth and make her happy. God even causes the grasses to grow, and their purpose is to feed the cattle (v. 14a).

In Psalm 104, humans do not receive a "special" place, as they do in Genesis 1, where they are presented as the apex of God's creation. Rather,

---

3. Day, *God's Conflict with the Dragon and the Sea*, 52.

humans are parallel with the cattle, for just as God made the grass grow for the cattle, so God made "plants for people to cultivate" (v. 14b). Humans are expected to work – not as a result of the curse, but as part of their responsibility. Yet God also wants humans to have "wine that gladdens" their hearts and "oil to make their faces shine" (v. 15).

Having satisfied the earth and its creatures, including humans, the psalmist describes the "trees of the Lord" as "well watered" (v. 16), a phrase that comes from the Hebrew verb *sabaʽ*, which also means "to satisfy." However, God "satisfies" the trees so that birds may "make their nests" and the "stork" can have "its home" (v. 17). This notion of purpose is supported by the use of the Hebrew preposition *le* ("for") in verse 18: "The high mountains are *for* the wild goats; the rocks are a refuge *for* the rock badgers" (ESV, emphasis mine). The psalmist declares that there is a purpose – a reason for being – for everything.

### 104:19–30 "ALL CREATURES LOOK TO YOU"

The creation of the heavenly lights in Genesis 1 has its counterpart in Psalm 104:19–23, where the moon and the sun mark the division between the night and the day. In Psalm 104, the emphasis is on divine action: "*You* bring darkness, it becomes night" (v. 20, emphasis mine). The psalm also identifies a function for night and the day: nightfall becomes an occasion for animals to look for their food (vv. 20–21). Yet even the strongest animals are dependent on God, for "the lions . . . seek their food from God" (v. 21). At the rising of the sun, the animals return to their places of shelter (v. 22), and it is time for humans to go out to "their work" (v. 23). Again, the psalmist emphasizes human labor.

At this point, one cannot help but join the psalmist in exclaiming, "How many are your works, Lord! In wisdom you made them all; the earth is full of your creatures" (v. 24). The word "creatures" come from a Hebrew word that means "wealth."[4] We are God's treasured possession (*tanging yaman*). The "sea," which represented forces of chaos in ancient times, is also identified as part of God's creation. That "vast and spacious" body of water, teeming with "creatures beyond number" (v. 25), is where the famous sea monster, the Leviathan, plays (v. 26). Like the lion, the Leviathan looks to God for food: "All creatures look to you to give them their food at the proper time" (v. 27).

During this time of the pandemic, when so many people are hungry, we need to embrace the theology of a God who gives food to the hungry. The

---

4. *TDOT*, 13:64.

psalmist's image of God's "open hand" beautifully describes our generous God: "when you open your hand, they are satisfied with good things" (v. 28). Yet there are also occasions when God hides his face (v. 29), and then his creatures are "terrified" (v. 29) and lament (Pss 102:2; 13:1). Verse 29b, "when you take away your breath, they die and return to the dust," could refer to death. Though all creatures are dependent on their Maker in Psalm 104, death does not have the final word. For God sends his Spirit, and "they are created" (v. 30). If the hiding of God's *face* brings about death, the sending of his Spirit brings about the renewal of the "*face* of the ground" (v. 30). The verb "send" (*shalach*) is repeated in verse 30 (see v. 10), emphasizing the life-giving and nourishing actions of God.

### 104:31–35 A REALISTIC VIEW OF CREATION

In Genesis 1, we are told that God saw his creation and said "it was good." In this final section of Psalm 104, the psalmist hopes that God will "rejoice in his works" (v. 31). Just as God has satisfied all his creatures with good things, the psalmist prays that God will also be satisfied with his works. The psalmist never loses the sense of awe and reverent fear for God, even in his exposition on God's graciousness and generosity to all of creation. God is *good*, but he is also dangerous. God "looks at the earth, and it trembles"; he "touches the mountains, and they smoke" (v. 32). God sends forth his hand to give, create, and sustain life, but he also hides his face and takes away breath (v. 29). Thus the psalmist vows to praise the Lord all his life (v. 33), and yet he is also careful to pray: "May my meditation be pleasing to him, as I rejoice in the Lord" (v. 34).

The psalm concludes with an unexpected glimpse of all of humanity into sin (Gen 1:34) after the creation. These concluding verses (vv. 34–35, esv) form the following structure:

"I rejoice" (v. 34b).
    *Imprecation:* "let sinners be consumed" (v. 35a).
"Bless the Lord, O my soul!" (v. 35b).

In the midst of the rejoicing over God's goodness to his creation, the psalmist cannot help but remember the presence of "sinners." Even in this hymn of praise, there is a hint of lament.

# PSALM 105

In the wonderful Filipino song, "*Dakilang Katapatan*" ("Great Faithfulness"), one line claims that God was there at the very beginning of our existence as Filipinos:

| You are great, O God | *Dakila ka, O Diyos* |
| You are faithful indeed | *Tapat ka ngang tunay* |
| From the very beginning of our race. | *magmula pa sa ugat ng aming lahi.* |

Psalm 105 is a hymn that recalls the history of Israel, beginning with the founding of their nation and the calling of Abraham. The people recount their history to remember how God has been with them from the very beginning. Even though the Israelites were few in number as they wandered from country to country as strangers and exiles, God accompanied them, protected them, and provided for their needs. Their life was not easy, but God always sent someone to prepare the way before them (e.g. Joseph, Moses). Written during the exilic/ postexilic time, this hymn was meant to encourage the people that God, who first worked in their fathers, was still present and "remembers his covenant forever" (Ps 105:8). Even through the most difficult situations, God has been fulfilling his promise.

Asian believers are not a direct part of the covenant of Abraham, but through our faith in Jesus Christ, we have become the children of God. The God of Abraham, Isaac, and Jacob has become our God. We can also say, as the Filipino chorus above expresses, that God has been there from the very beginning. Psalms 103 and 104 highlight that God is both great and mighty and also compassionate and good to his creation (103:13; 104:10–24). The Tagalogs in the Philippines believe in *Bathala*, the highest God, who is both transcendent and unreachable and also merciful, "said to be the sustainer, keeper, nourisher, and protector of mankind."[1] Perhaps even before the Spaniards came to the Philippines, God was revealing himself to our people. As we look back, we can see how God has already been at work in our lives and our people, even through our most difficult experiences.

---

1. F. Landa Jocano, "Notes on Philippine Divinities," *Asian Studies* 6, no. 2 (1968): 170.

## 105:1–6 CALL TO PRAISE

Psalm 105 begins with an extended call to worship (vv. 1–6). Sometimes, the call to praise is addressed to "my soul" (Ps 103:1). Other times, it is directed to "all the earth" (Ps 100:1). In Psalm 105, the "descendants of Abraham" (v. 6) are summoned to "give praise to the LORD" because of "what he has done" (v. 1). The description "wonderful acts" (*nifla'ot*) is repeated twice (vv. 2, 5).

As the people praise the Lord, they are also exhorted to "seek his presence continually" (v. 4b, ESV). In verse 4, the word "seek" is repeated twice, using two assonant Hebrew synonyms for "seek": *darash* and *baqash*. *Baqash* is used in verse 3 to describe "those who *seek* [*baqash*] the LORD." Thus praise has ethical implications. To seek God's "presence" (v. 4) in Hebrew is literally to seek God's "face." Psalm 104 teaches that God also hides his face (see v. 29) because of his anger over human sin, and this results in punishment (see Ps 106:40).

Verse 5 begins with the word "remember," which is a key term in Psalm 105 (see also Psalm 106). We can seek God continually by remembering his acts, where "remembering" is not about intellectual ascent, but rather a grateful response to what God has done. We remember God's works because God "remembers" his covenant forever (see v. 8).

## 105:7–11 GOD REMEMBERS HIS COVENANT

In the previous verses, the psalmist summons the people to praise God for his wondrous works, and the rest of the psalm is a historical recollection of God's marvelous deeds (vv. 12–45). Significantly, the recital of these deeds is framed by the people's relationship with God. The psalmist declares that the God whose wondrous deeds they are proclaiming is "the LORD our God" (v. 7). The word "LORD" is a translation of "Yahweh," the Hebrew name for God, which is the name by which God personally identified himself when he made a covenant with the people of Israel and their patriarchs – Abraham, Isaac, and Jacob (vv. 9–10). The psalmist does not emphasize the act of making a covenant, but rather God's act of remembering: God "remembers his covenant forever" (v. 8a). In verse 8b, the psalmist uses the word "thousand" to describe how God remembers his covenant "for a thousand generations" (v. 8b). In Psalm 90, the word "thousand" was used to contrast the awful brevity of human existence with the awesome breadth of God's years (v. 4). Here, it displays the people's persistent faith in the God who is faithful to his promise, which remained true even during the postexilic period and Israel's subsequent history – and continues into our present age.

# Psalm 105

## 105:12–22 God Prepares the Way to Egypt

Verse 12 marks the beginning of the historical review. Every historical review is made for one of three possible purposes. First, the psalmist may want to remind the people to keep God's covenant. Because God has fulfilled his promise to the people, they ought to respond properly through obedience to God's commandments. This purpose is implied in the earlier command to "remember the wonders he has done" (Ps 105:5). The people are to remember God's wonders because God remembers his covenant (v. 8). This purpose is renewed again at the end of the psalm (see v. 45).

Second, the psalmist may want to ask God to repeat what he did for his people in the past again in their time. For this purpose, the historical review serves as a petition. Although there is no explicit petition in Psalm 105, portions of this psalm were used in subsequent texts, along with an added petition. For example, Psalms 105 and 106 are quoted in 1 Chronicles 16, followed by a concluding petition: "Save us, God our Savior; gather us and deliver us from the nations, that we may give thanks to your holy name and glory in your praise" (1 Chr 16:35). Here, the purpose of the recollection and praise is to petition God for deliverance so that they will be able to praise the Lord.

Third, the psalmist may want to show the spectacular way in which God fulfilled his promise to Abraham and his descendants. We see this in Psalm 105:12–44. The psalmist begins the historical review by remembering the humble beginnings of the Israelites, who were "few in number" (v. 12). Deuteronomy 7 says that they were "the fewest of all peoples" (v. 7). This made them vulnerable to the powerful nations that surrounded them, but in spite of their small numbers, God protected them. Verses 13–14 recall the wanderings of Abraham and his descendants as described in Genesis, particularly how God protected Abraham and Sarah from Pharaoh (Gen 12:10–20; see also Genesis 20 and 26). The phrase, "Do not touch my anointed ones" (Ps 105:15), refers to God's protection of the patriarchs. Regarding God's protection of Abraham as a prophet, see Genesis 20:7.[2]

God not only provided spectacular protection for his people, but he also provided for them. Verses 16–22 recall the people's experience of famine (see Genesis 41). Abraham and his family also experienced famine and had to leave their land (Gen 12:10). Famine is one of the most difficult experiences as it

---

2. Some pastors use this statement to protect themselves from any accountability, but this is a wrong use of this biblical text. The verse is not a promise given to everyone, and it certainly does not shield anyone from accountability.

drives people away from their land and causes extreme suffering. Yet from the perspective of the composer of Psalm 105, God "called down famine on the land" (v. 16). The psalmist holds God responsible for the terrible experience of famine. At the same time, because God sent the famine, God also sent his servant, Joseph, to prepare the way for his people (v. 17).[3] For God sent Joseph to Egypt as a slave as a way of providing for his people during the famine. Then God worked through Joseph, and so the king made him a "ruler over all he possessed" (v. 21) and asked him to "teach his elders wisdom" (v. 22). The wisdom here was about how to manage the food crisis so that the land would survive the famine. Joseph's advice to the king was for him to look for a "wise man" to be in charge (Gen 41:33). After Joseph interpreted Pharaoh's dream, the latter told him, "there is no one so discerning and wise as you" (v. 39).

But sending Joseph into Egypt as a slave also entailed much suffering. The poet describes "his bruised feet with shackles" and how "his neck was put in irons" (v. 18). This description of Joseph's suffering goes into greater detail than the Genesis account and is reminiscent of the experience of exile. Imprisonment can be a metaphor for exile,[4] and the postexilic community saw their own suffering in Joseph's story – but through his suffering, God provided for their needs. Interestingly, the word used to describe how God frees Joseph in Psalm 105 is the same word used in Psalm 104 to describe how God opens his hand to feed his creatures:

> "the ruler of the peoples set him free [*patakh*]" (105:20b);
> "when you open [*patakh*] your hand, they are satisfied with good things" (104:28).

## 105:23–36 GOD WORKS MARVELOUSLY IN EGYPT

The previous section starts with the people's humble beginnings (v. 12). Although the people are now described as "very fruitful" (v. 24), according to God's promise to Abraham (Gen 17:6; compare Exod 1:7), they are living as foreigners in Egypt. A "foreigner" in the OT is on the same level as the widow and the orphan. Because foreigners do not belong, they are subject to abuse. This is the experience of some of our Overseas Filipino Workers (OFW), many of whom are forced to look for jobs outside the country in order to provide for their families. In Psalm 105, the people's experience of famine forced them to

---

3. The word "sent" recalls Psalm 104, which presents God as the one who sends his spirit (v. 30).
4. Daniel L. Smith, *The Religion of the Landless*, 49.

go to Egypt, but their suffering is interpreted as part of God's plan, for God "turned" the hearts of their enemies to "hate his people" (v. 25). Just as the famine in verse 16 is attributed to God, so the people's persecution by their enemies is attributed to God (v. 25). For again, just as God sent Joseph, here he has "sent Moses, his servant" along with Aaron (v. 26).

Verses 27–36 relate the signs and wonders that God displayed in Egypt through the plagues. The plague narrative can be found in three places in the biblical text: Exodus 7–12, Psalm 78, and Psalm 105. Lee rightly observes the similarities between Psalm 105 and the creation account in Genesis 1.[5] God's word of command, "And God said ['amar]," appears repeatedly in the creation account in Genesis 1. Psalm 105 shares a similar emphasis on God speaking and his word through the repetition of the same verb, 'amar ("to say, to speak"):

> "He spoke . . ." (v. 31);
> "He spoke . . ." (v. 34).

The Hebrew word *dabar* ("word") also occurs twice in Psalm 105 (vv. 27 and 28). Verse 27 literally reads, "the words of his signs," though the NIV merely translates it as "his signs." Though the inclusion of "words" sounds strange, the literal translation makes sense in light of the similarity between Psalm 105 and Genesis 1. One of the patterns in Genesis 1 is the "word-fulfillment style or word-event pattern."[6] God speaks, and something happens. God says, "Let there be light," and "there was light" (Gen 1:3). Similarly, in Psalm 105:[7]

> God sends darkness and there was darkness (v. 28);
> "He spoke, and there came swarms of flies" (v. 31);
> "He spoke, and the locusts came" (v. 34).

This word-fulfilment pattern is a powerful illustration of the God who keeps his promise to Abraham (v. 8).

One of the main differences between Psalm 105 and the plague narrative in Exodus is that the plague of darkness occurs ninth in Exodus, whereas it is mentioned first in Psalm 105. Following the comparison with Genesis 1, Psalm 105 follows a similar movement to the Genesis account. Anderson traces a movement in Genesis 1 from the creation of the luminaries (or heavens), to the separation of the waters and the filling of the waters with sea creatures, to the

---

5. Archie C. Lee, "Genesis 1 and the Plagues Tradition in Psalm 105," *VT* 40, no. 3 (1990): 257–263.
6. Lee, "Genesis 1 and the Plagues Tradition in Psalm 105," 261.
7. Lee, "Genesis 1 and the Plagues Tradition in Psalm 105," 261.

creation of land, vegetation, and humans.⁸ The order of the plagues in Psalm 105 may be likened to an undoing of creation, as the account begins with the sending of darkness (heaven, v. 28), which is followed by the turning of water into blood, which caused the fish to die (v. 29). The account then details the rest of the plagues – frogs, flies, gnats, the destruction of the vegetation, and the killing of the firstborn – which are all set in the land (vv. 30–36).

The sending of darkness is the fourth time that the verb "send" is used in Psalm 105:

> God "sent" Joseph (v. 16);
> The king "sent" for the release of Joseph (v. 20);
> God "sent" Moses (v. 26);
> God "sent" darkness (v. 28).⁹

Throughout the people's history God was superintending every event in their lives.

## 105:37–45 GOD SETS HIS PEOPLE FREE AND BRINGS THEM TO THE PROMISED LAND

The psalmist devotes a very short space to recount the exodus event (vv. 37–38, 43), the people's wilderness experience (vv. 39–41), and God's giving of the land to the people (v. 44). Compared to the time in Egypt, these later events do not seem to capture the poet's imagination, perhaps because the people's experience before and in Egypt resonates more with the postexilic reality. Because the people are living as exiles in a foreign land, they share affinities with the experiences of their forefathers, who also lived as strangers in a foreign land. But God's faithfulness binds together the people's experience, from their inception to their arrival in the Promised Land. God has worked in and through his servants to provide for his people, take care of them, and

---

8. Bernhard W. Anderson, "Stylistic Study of the Priestly Creation Story," in *Canon and Authority: Essays in Old Testament Religion and Theology*, ed. George W. Coats and Burke O. Long (Philadelphia: Fortress Press, 1977), 148–162.

9. The second part of verse 28 is problematic. The MT literally reads, "They did not rebel." The LXX does not have the negation. The question is, who is the subject of the verb? If we follow the MT, one view would be that Moses and Aaron were the subjects of the verb. They did not rebel, for they were obedient to the word (Exod 7:20). But if we follow the LXX, then the Egyptians could be the subject — meaning they rebelled. Their rebellion led to the sending of the other plagues. Another view is to read the verb as singular, with "darkness" as the subject. This would fit well with the first part of verse 28 and the pattern of word-fulfilment. Lee, "Genesis 1 and the Plagues Tradition in Psalm 105," 261.

liberate them, and so at the end of their time in Egypt, they can testify that "no one faltered" (v. 37). God guided them in the wilderness and "fed them well" (v. 40b). Literally, verse 40b reads, "he satisfied them with bread from heaven" (my translation).

With the growing hunger around the world due to the pandemic, one cannot ignore the space and importance given to the problem of hunger in this psalm. Earlier, it talks about famine, and here the setting is the desert, which is a place of scarcity, but in both places, God provided his people with food and water (vv. 16, 40–41). Immediately after saying that God gave the people bread and water, the psalmist says, "For he remembered his holy promise given to his servant Abraham" (v. 42). This recalls verse 8, thus embracing the whole historical review (vv. 12–41) in an inclusio (vv. 8–11, v. 42). It is significant that this statement about God remembering his promise is made right after the memory of God's provision of bread.

Verse 43 parallels verse 37, as both recall how God brought his people "out" of slavery. Whereas verse 37 says that God brought them "out with silver and gold," verse 43 adds an emotional element to God's deliverance, saying, "he brought out his people with rejoicing." The people are rejoicing because God "gave them the lands of the nations," and they became "heir to what others had toiled for" (v. 44). Thus their rejoicing meant lamenting for the nations whose lands and wealth were taken from them. Those of us who have experienced colonization find it very difficult to make sense of this verse.

To understand this verse, we must first remember that the Israelites were not like our colonizers. They were not in power. Second, God gave them the land so "that they might keep his precepts and observe his laws" (v. 45). Central to God's laws is his command to care for the most vulnerable, whose cries he will heed (e.g. Exod 22:22–27). Unfortunately, as the following psalm will recount, the people failed to keep God's covenant.

# PSALM 106

How can the people of God praise the Lord when they know they are under God's punishment? The people of Israel rebelled against God and did not keep the covenant. As a result, they were scattered among the nations (106:41). In response, the composer of Psalm 106 comes to God to intercede on behalf of his community. The psalmist gives two examples of individuals intervening between God and the people: Moses (v. 23) and Phinehas (v. 30). Both stood up before God, who was about to destroy his people, and the punishment was averted. The composer of Psalm 106 intends to do the same.

Psalm 106 is a prayer of confession, similar to the prayers of repentance that we find in Nehemiah 1 and 9 and Daniel 9. The term "confession" is an appropriate title for these texts, since the bulk of the prayer is an admission of the sins committed by the people. The usual way of confession is to ask for forgiveness. The petition, "forgive us" (*patawarin mo kami*), is the central element in our modern penitential prayer. Although asking for forgiveness is implied in the biblical prayers of penitence (including Psalm 106), it is not the main emphasis. Rather, as the title "confession" indicates, the emphasis is on admission. Indeed, the whole historical review in Psalm 106 is a recollection of eight sins or acts of rebellion committed by the people in different periods of their history and in various places. There is not even a petition for forgiveness in Psalm 106, but there is a prayer for restoration, which implies a petition for forgiveness.

Psalm 106 should be read along with Psalm 105, as the two psalms are closely connected in terms of the historical review, though the emphasis differs. Psalm 105 is a review of the many good things that God has done for the people, which should lead them to worship, but Psalm 106 shows how the people respond with utter disregard for God's "many kindnesses" (v. 7). In Filipino, we would describe the people with the expression, *walang utang na loob* ("no debt of gratitude"), which is one of the harshest words one can say about anyone. Psalm 106 demonstrates the people's unbelief, lack of trust, and disobedience despite God's goodness and kindness towards them.

The psalm may be outlined as follows:

    Introduction (vv. 1–3),
    Petition (vv. 4–5),
    Confession (vv. 6–46),
    Petition (v. 47),
    Doxology (v. 48).

# Psalm 106

## 106:1–3 INTRODUCTION

Psalm 106 begins with the famous Hallelujah, which is translated, "Praise the Lord" (v. 1). This is followed by a similar call to praise, "Give thanks to the Lord." Psalm 105, which is the "twin" of Psalm 106, begins in the same way (see 105:1). However, Psalm 105 is more elaborate, while Psalm 106 goes immediately into the typical motivation for praise in a hymn: "for he is good, his love endures forever" (106:1).

The question in verse 2 resembles the entrance liturgy used in other psalms, "Who can proclaim the mighty acts of the Lord?" (compare Pss 15:1 and 24:3). Psalm 106 also incorporates elements from other psalms, such as lament (see vv. 4–5). As in the entrance liturgy, the question is followed by a qualification. Responding to the question in verse 2, the psalmist declares, "Blessed are they who observe justice, who do righteousness at all times!" (v. 3, ESV; compare Pss 15:2–5; 24:4).

The employment of this element from the entrance liturgy reminds us of the importance of the ethical aspect in worship (see Psalm 95). In Psalm 103, God is described as one who "works righteousness and justice for all the oppressed" (v. 6). This famous pair, "justice and righteousness" (Pss 97:2; 89:14), is also used in Psalm 106 to refer to the worshiper (v. 3). Because the very "foundation" of God's throne is "righteousness and justice" (97:2b), those who worship God should conduct their affairs in accordance with God's character. Viewed from this perspective, one can appreciate the urgency and earnestness of the long confession (vv. 6–46). The final sin (see vv. 34–39) also relates to the issue of "justice and righteousness" (see comments below).

## 106:4–5 PETITION

As noted above, Psalm 106 is similar to the postexilic prayers of confession (see Neh 1:4–11; 9:6–37; Dan 9:4–19). In the prayers in Nehemiah 1 and Daniel 9, an individual prays on behalf of the community. The "I" speaks first, which is followed by "we" (Neh 1:4–5; Dan 9:4). In Psalm 106, we hear the voice of the individual: "Remember me, Lord" (v. 4).[1] As noted previously, the verb "remember" is not simply about mental ascent, but is tied up with action. When God remembers, he acts (Ps 105:8; compare Gen 8:1; 19:29). Here, the

---

[1]. The LXX has the first person plural for the verbs in verse 4, but the similar construction in the other prayers of confession supports the MT reading. The MT reading is also the harder reading compared to the LXX. Culturally, Filipinos also use the first person singular and plural interchangeably, even when the individual is speaking. This is especially true in prayers.

psalmist asks God to "come to my aid" (Ps 106:4b) so that he might be able to share in the "joy of your nation" (v. 5) by giving praise for God's deliverance.

## 106:6–46 CONFESSION

### 106:6–12 No "Debt of Gratitude" in Egypt

Because the prerequisite for God's deliverance is repentance, the speaker comes to God to confess the people's sins. Speaking on behalf of his people, the speaker admits: "We have sinned, even as our ancestors did; we have done wrong and acted wickedly" (v. 6). As with Nehemiah and Jeremiah, the speaker may not be directly responsible for the sins he is confessing, but the fact that the people are still in exile (see v. 47) implies that they are reaping the consequences of their forefathers' sins. Thus the psalmist identifies with the sins of his ancestors. After the initial identification ("we have sinned"), however, the prayer shifts to the sins of the ancestors (see "they" in v. 7).

The psalmist declares that "they," referring to the ancestors, "gave no thought to your miracles" (v. 7). Though God performed the miracles in Egypt right before their eyes, they did not gain any insight because they did not practice the psalmist's instruction in the previous psalm: "Remember the wonders he has done" (105:5). Moreover, "they did not remember your many kindnesses" (v. 7). This failure to remember in Psalm 106 mirrors the Filipino expression, *walang utang na loob* ("no debt of gratitude").

Because the people had the tendency to forget easily, "they rebelled by the sea" (v. 7). This recalls the event in Exodus 14:11–12, when the Egyptians pursued the Israelites after they left Egypt. Though they had not gone far from Egypt, they failed to trust God in the face of danger. According to the psalmist, God had to deliver the people "for his name's sake," that is, for his own glory (v. 8a). If God left his people to die at the hands of the Egyptians so quickly after leading them to freedom, what would they say about the Israelites and their God? This was the same argument that Moses used to persuade God not to destroy his people (Exod 32:11–14). Apparently, God is similar to traditional Asians, who are motivated by shame.

The psalmist describes the manner in which God delivered his people from the Egyptians spectacularly, with the sea drying up like a wasteland and the depths of the sea turning into a desert (v. 9). Because the people were amazed at these miracles, they "believed his promises" (v. 12a), and they broke into song and praise (v. 12b).

### 106:13–15 Testing God in the Wilderness

Yet once again, the people quickly forgot God's miracles (v. 13). In Hebrew, the first word in verse 13 is *mahar* ("hasten"). Just three days after the Red Sea experience, the people began to grumble when they could not find water (Exod 15:22–24). Even when God provided food to satisfy their cravings, they tested him (Ps 106:14; compare 78:29–30). So God became angry and "sent" them a "wasting disease" (v. 15). The verb "sent" is used in Psalm 105 as an expression of God's care for his people in the midst of their trouble (105:17, 20, 26) as well as punishment for their enemies (105:28). In Psalm 106, God "sends" his people judgment because of their rebellion.

### 106:16–18 Rebellion Against Leaders

Since the people were not afraid to put God to the test (v. 14), they disregarded their leaders' authority. While it is not wrong to complain against our leaders when they are doing something wrong, challenging their authority out of envy goes against the one who placed them there. Psalm 106 describes Aaron as "consecrated to the LORD" (v. 16b) and Moses as God's "chosen one" (v. 23). At the beginning of Book IV, the psalmist describes Moses as "the man of God" (Psalm 90, superscription). Nevertheless, two hundred and fifty people in the camp "rose up against Moses" and came against him and Aaron (Num 16:1–4). God defended his servants by having the earth swallow the rebels and a fire engulf their company (Ps 106:17–18).

### 106:19–23 Golden Calf and Moses's Intercession

Immediately, the psalm recounts another rebellion, when the people made an idol in the form of a golden calf (v. 19). The context of Psalm 106 is similar to Psalm 3. Though God "saved them" (106:21) by displaying his marvelous deeds in Egypt and delivering them at the Red Sea (v. 22), they exchanged "their glorious God" for an "image of a bull, which eats grass" (v. 20). In Hebrew, the phrase translated, "their glorious God," is simply "their glory." The context for Psalm 106 is similar to Psalm 3:3, which also uses this phrase. The translation, "their glorious God," most likely reflects a scribal correction (*tiqqune sopherim*) to the original reading in Hebrew, which was made out of reverence to God's dignity.[2] However, I think there is no problem with the literal translation, "their glory," since elsewhere the psalmist refers to God as "my glory," from whom salvation comes (Ps 3:3, 8). In Psalm 104, God

---

2. Zenger and Hossfeld, *Psalms 3*, 82. Compare the Jerusalem Bible translation: "exchanging the one who was their glory" (compare NEB).

is described as the one who "makes the grass grow for the cattle, and plants [*'esev*] for people to cultivate" (v. 14). All of creation depends on God for their sustenance (v. 27), and yet the people chose to worship an animal instead of God. The people worshiped the idol because they did not remember all of God's marvelous works and deeds (Ps 105:5).

In reaction to their idolatry, God became angry and wanted to destroy them. This recalls the incident in Exodus 32. Had it not been for Moses, who "stood in the breach," Israel would no longer be a nation (Ps 106:23). We learn two lessons from this incident. First, it teaches us that God is open to reasoning with his servants. In the Exodus account, Moses reasoned with God, arguing that if he destroyed his people, the Egyptians would question God's intention of liberating them. They would argue that he delivered his people only to destroy them (Exod 32:11–12). Amazingly, God "relented and did not bring on his people the disaster he had threatened" (Exod 32:14). Second, this incident teaches us the importance of human agency, especially for God's servants. In Psalm 106, Moses is referred to as "his chosen one" (v. 23).

## 106:24–27 Unbelief over God's Promised Land

The background for this confession is from Numbers 13–14, when the twelve spies return from surveying the Promised Land to give their report. Instead of seeing the goodness of the land that was promised to them by God, the people "despised" it (Ps 106:24). The psalmist, however, describes the land as "pleasant" (v. 24). In Hebrew, the word literally means "desirable." But even a "pleasant" gift becomes objectionable for someone who does not trust the giver. As verse 24b says, "they did not believe his promise." Having allowed their unbelief to color their vision, the people grumbled (v. 25) so loudly that they could no longer hear God, which led to disobedience. Thus God swore that they would perish in the wilderness (v. 26). God's judgment on their actions has consequences for their descendants as well. God will cause them to "fall among the nations," so they will be scattered (v. 27).[3]

This confession teaches that the sins of the forefathers have an effect on their descendants. However, even though God passed his judgment over the descendants in the desert, they were not left without hope. The composer of

---

3. It was common to correct *lehafitz* (to fall) into *lehappil* (to scatter), in view of the parallel text in Ezekiel 20:23. The former was used in the previous verse (106:26) and may have been transferred into verse 27 by mistake. We can't really know which was original. Nonetheless, the intent of judgment is not diminished even with the verb "to fall," which has the support of both the MT and the LXX.

Psalm 106 believes that he can do something about the people's situation. In the previous section, Moses "stood in the breach before him" (v. 23). In the following section, Phinehas "stood up and intervened" (v. 30). This section about God's judgment for the descendants falls between these two examples of God's faithful servants intervening to ask God to reconsider his divine judgment. In the present section, the judgment included the scattering of the people among the nations. The composer of Psalm 106 is one of these scattered peoples, and his prayer of confession may be understood as his attempt to "stand" in the gap, to intercede on behalf of his people so that God might give them restoration (see v. 47 below).

## 106:28–31 Idol Worship and Phinehas's Intervention

This confession recalls the incident in Numbers 25, where the people "yoked themselves to the Baal of Peor" (Ps 106:28; see Num 25:3) by having sexual relations with the Moabites and eating the sacrifice offered to their god. These actions provoked God to anger, and he sent a plague to destroy the people (Ps 106:29). They would have perished completely had it not been for Phinehas, who, like Moses, "stood up and intervened" (v. 30). According to Janowski, the word that is translated, "intervened," may be translated as "make intercession, enter a plea."[4] This supports the earlier point that the psalmist's intercession in Psalm 106 is similar to the pleas of Moses and Phinehas. Phinehas's intercession merited him favor in God's eyes that was comparable to Abraham (Gen 15:6).[5]

## 106:32–33 Rebellion Against the Spirit of God at Meribah

Several texts provide the background for this confession: Exodus 17 (vv. 1–7); Numbers 20; and Deuteronomy 32 (vv. 48–52). The people grumbled against Moses because there was no water, and so Moses went to God, who instructed him to "speak" to the rock and then the water would come out (Num 20:8). But instead of speaking to the rock, Moses "struck the rock twice with his staff" (Num 20:11). Psalm 106:33 places some of the blame on Moses: "rash words came from Moses' lips" (compare Num 20:10). Although the people angered Moses and rebelled against him, it was not right for him to become "bitter" and respond in the "rash" way that he did (v. 33).[6] Because Moses and Aaron

---

4. Bernd Janowski, "Psalm 106:28–31 *und die Interzession des Pinchas*," *VT* 33, no. 2 (1983): 243, quoted in Zenger and Hossfeld, *Psalms 3*, 90.
5. Zenger and Hossfeld, *Psalms 3*, 91.
6. The NIV translates verse 33a as "for they rebelled against the Spirit of God." But in Hebrew, it is simply, "for they rebelled against his spirit." It is not explicit who is the referent of the pronoun "his." The immediately preceding context supports reading Moses as the referent.

failed to trust the Lord (Num 20:12) and "broke faith" with him among the people of Israel (Deut 32:50–51), they were prohibited from entering the land that God promised to them.

## 106:34–39 Disobedience and Death of the Innocent

The last confession is for the people's disobedience to the Lord's command to "destroy the peoples, as the Lord commanded them" (v. 34). According to Deuteronomy 7, the destruction of the people was to be complete (vv. 1–5, 16). For this controversial command, Moberly provides an alternative reading that interprets the command for annihilation in Deuteronomy 7 as a "metaphor for unqualified allegiance to YHWH."[7] He argues that the emphasis is not on destroying the people but separating themselves so that they would not adopt their ways. We may compare this to the command of Jesus in Matthew 7 regarding temptation. Jesus says that if one's eye is causing him/her to "stumble," one has to "gouge it out" (Matt 5:29). If one's right hand is causing the same tendency, one has to be prepared to "cut it off" (v. 30). His point is that we have to be prepared to perform "drastic sacrifices" to keep God's command.[8] Interestingly, the Hebrew word for "snare" in Psalm 106:36 is translated in the LXX as *skandalon*, which is closely connected to the verb, "to cause to sin/stumble" (*skandalizo*) used in Matthew 5:29.

The above is one way of interpreting the complete destruction of the peoples (Ps 106:34). In any case, they failed to follow God's command and instead "mingled with the nations and adopted their customs" (v. 35). The nations had many customs, but the composer of Psalm 106 highlights child sacrifice. The people "sacrificed their sons and their daughters to the false gods" (v. 37), thereby shedding innocent blood (compare Jer 19:4–5). The word "blood" is repeated three times in Psalm 106:38, and this blood defiled the land (v. 38). Concluding with this confession of the people's violence emphasizes the seriousness of shedding blood, which we see throughout Scripture. One hears the cry of the murdered innocents at both the beginning and the end of the Bible, with the murder of Abel in Genesis 4 and the death of the martyrs in Revelation 6:9–10. It is not surprising, therefore, to find this emphasis on the blood of the innocent in the people's confession. The introduction for Psalm 106 contains a beatitude, "Blessed are those who act justly" (v. 3). To practice justice and righteousness involves caring for the rights of the most vulnerable.

---

7. R. W. L. Moberly, *Old Testament Theology: Reading the Hebrew Bible as Christian Scripture* (Grand Rapids: Baker, 2013), 62.
8. R. T. France, *The Gospel According to Matthew*, 127.

Israel failed to act justly and righteously by shedding the innocent blood of children. Jeremiah 7 makes a direct connection between shedding innocent blood (v. 6) and idolatry (vv. 18–19).

## 106:40–46 Summary: Deliverance, Rebellion, and God's Mercy

These verses summarize the period of the Judges (see Judg 2:14; 3:9; 2:18). As a consequence of the people's sins, God was not only "angry with his people" (v. 40a), but he even "abhorred" them (v. 40b). Thus he handed them over to the nations, who ruled over them (v. 41) and oppressed them (v. 42). This was completely opposite to their forefathers' experience, who "wandered from nation to nation," and yet God "allowed no one to oppress them" (105:13–14). Psalm 106:43 succinctly summarizes God's actions on behalf of his people: "Many times he delivered them." Though God was their savior "many times," the people proved themselves unworthy because "they were bent on rebellion" (v. 43).

Psalm 106 could have ended with this summary that justifies God's actions, but the composer of the psalm notes that God "looked upon their distress, when he heard their cry" (v. 44, ESV). The verbs, "looked" and "heard," recall Exodus 2:23–25 as well as the book of Judges. Exodus 2 narrates how the Israelites groaned because of their suffering in Egypt and how "God heard their groaning" (v. 24) and "looked on the Israelites and was concerned about them" (v. 25). The narrator interprets God's hearing and looking as a way of remembering his covenant with the patriarchs (v. 24). Remarkably, the composer of Psalm 106 is saying that in their current situation of exile, God is acting mercifully or graciously to them, just as he did for his people in Egypt. The composer also interprets God's merciful response as the result of God's remembering his covenant with his people (Ps 106:45).

### 106:47–48 PETITION AND DOXOLOGY

As noted above, one of the purposes of the historical review is to ask God to do what he did in the past in the people's present situation. Thus the psalmist concludes by asking God on behalf of his people, "Save us, Lord our God" (v. 47). Specifically, he is asking God to "gather us from the nations" (v. 47). This petition creates a tension with the previous verse, where God has already shown his mercy, but it is still awaiting completion. The petition also stands in tension with the beginning of the psalm, as the call to praise (v. 1) remains incomplete until the people are delivered. The motivation for the petition is so "that we may give thanks to your holy name" (v. 47).

The psalm ends with a renewed call to praise (v. 48), which serves as a doxology for Psalm 106 as well as Book IV.

# PSALM 107

Psalm 107 is the first psalm in Book V, the final "book" of the Psalter. Scholars have rightly observed that the Psalter contains an overall movement from lament to praise. Both Book I (Psalms 3–41) and Book II (Psalms 42–72) are mostly individual laments. Book III (Psalms 73–89) has ten communal laments out of sixteen psalms.[1] Book IV begins with a communal lament (Psalm 90), but there are more hymns than laments. In Book V, we begin with thanksgiving right away (Ps 107:1). Comparing the beginning of each book in the Psalter, we see the following:

| | | |
|---|---|---|
| Book I | Lament: | "Lord, how many are my foes!" (Ps 3:1). |
| Book II | Lament: | "Why, my soul, are you downcast?" (Ps 42:5, 11). |
| Book III | Lament: | "God is good . . . But as for me, my feet had almost slipped" (Ps 73:1–2). |
| Book IV | Lament: | "we finish our years with a moan" (Ps 90:9). |
| Book V | Thanksgiving: | "Give thanks to the Lord, for he is good" (Ps 107:1). |

Though Book V begins with thanksgiving, this does not mean that there is an end to lament. In fact, two of the harshest imprecatory psalms are found in Book V (Psalms 109 and 137). There are also laments towards the end of Book V (see Psalms 140–143). Moreover, Psalm 146, the first of the final group of Hallel psalms (Psalms 146–150), has some similarities with Psalm 107 in its recollection of situations of lament (see commentary on Psalm 146). Thus we should not think that once we move to praise, we leave the lament behind. In fact, the very things we thank God for often arise from situations of lament. Lament in the psalms, according to Gunkel, arises out of "*apparently life-threatening situations*, such as 'the distress,' 'danger,' and 'fear' which they [the psalmists] mention so often in these songs."[2] These are the situations we find in Psalm 107.[3] The psalm cites four narratives of "life-threatening

---

[1]. Psalms 74, 77, 79, 80, 82, 83, 85, 86, 88, and 89.
[2]. Hermann Gunkel and Joachim Begrich, *Introduction to Psalms: The Genres of the Religious Lyric of Israel*, Mercer Library of Biblical Studies (Macon, GA: Mercer University Press, 1998), 130, emphasis in the original.
[3]. As Zenger points out, "The designations of places and situations used in the psalm – desert, darkness, shadow of death, prison, gates of death, sea . . . signal 'the narrow and dangerous

situations," which represent the main body of the psalm: hunger (vv. 4–9), imprisonment (vv. 10–16), being "near the gates of death" (vv. 17–22), and facing dangers at sea (vv. 23–32).

The composer of Psalm 107 recalls these near-death situations as a form of teaching. At the end of the psalm, the psalmist gives an exhortation: "Let the one who is wise heed these things and ponder the loving deeds of the LORD" (v. 43). Psalm 107 continues the theme from Psalms 105 and 106, which both highlight the goodness of God despite the people's sinfulness (Psalm 105) and ungratefulness (Psalm 106). The people of Israel too easily forget the good things that God has done for them, and so the four narratives in Psalm 107 recall the people's "wickedness" (v. 34; see also vv. 11, 17), as a way of reminding them about how good and loving God has been to them. The psalm begins with this emphasis on God's goodness: "Give thanks to the LORD, for he is good" (v. 1), and each of the four narratives ends with a refrain of thanksgiving for God's love: "Let them give thanks to the LORD for his unfailing love" (vv. 8, 15, 21, 31). Giving thanks is one way to "ponder" the "loving deeds of the LORD" (v. 43). In the NT, after Jesus heals the ten lepers, he notices that only one comes back to give thanks, and so he says, "Were not all ten cleansed? Where are the other nine?" (Luke 17:17). This gospel narrative reinforces the importance of pondering on the good and "loving deeds of the LORD."

Psalm 107 combines elements of a hymn (v. 1), thanksgiving, and wisdom psalm. Yet it is not regarded as a thanksgiving psalm, since the speaker is not recalling his own experiences.[4] Rather, as noted above, it is an instruction in which thanksgiving plays an important role. Teaching and thanksgiving go together throughout the Psalter.[5]

## 107:1–3 INTRODUCTION

The first part of Psalm 107 is a hymn, as it begins with a call to praise and the motivation for praise (v. 1). Verses 2–3 identify the recipients of the call to praise – those who have been "redeemed" by the Lord. Only those who have

---

boundary between life and death.'" Zenger and Hossfeld, *Psalms 3*, 100.
4. Lee Roy Martin, "'Oh Give Thanks to the Lord for He Is Good': Affective Hermeneutics, Psalm 107, and Pentecostal Spirituality," *Pneuma* 36, no. 3 (2014): 370.
5. As McCann points out: "Although the Psalms may have originated primarily within the liturgical life of ancient Israel and Judah, they were nonetheless appropriated, preserved, and transmitted as instruction for the faithful." Clinton J. McCann, Jr. "The Psalms as Instruction," *Int* 46, no. 2 (1992): 117.

experienced God's goodness and love can give thanks to the Lord (v. 1b), and only those who have been "redeemed" can "tell their story" (v. 2). Without an experience of God's deliverance or restoration, there is nothing to declare.

This deliverance and redemption are both spiritual and physical. The Lord "gathered" them "from the east and west, from north and south" (v. 3). In Hebrew, the last direction – "south" – is literally "sea" (*yam*). Many modern translations follow the suggestion *yamin* ("south") to fit with the previous direction, "north."[6] However, the Hebrew original should be retained because there is no textual support for the alternative reading.[7] Moreover, the psalm gives particular prominence to the "sea." As Jarick observes, "the stanza concerning the sea is the longest and most descriptive of the four corner stanzas."[8] For non-seafaring folk, such as the Israelites, the sea presents a great threat. The sea is probably listed last in the four narratives because it is perceived as the most life-threatening situation.

## 107:4–9 HUNGER

The previous section ends with God gathering the people from all corners of the world (v. 3). Verse 4 helps us appreciate what that looks like. The people were wandering in the desert, which is an inhospitable landscape without any clear directional indicators, and so they could not find any place to dwell (v. 4b). In addition to being homeless, the people were also "hungry and thirsty" (v. 5). This first narrative of suffering is about hunger and thirst, which was a common experience of the Israelites in the desert. It remains a common experience of suffering today, especially in the midst of the pandemic, when so many people have lost their jobs. Many people are crying.

In verse 6, the first word in Hebrew, *tsa'aq* ("cry out"), reflects a critical situation. In Psalm 107, the people cry out to the Lord. In Hebrew, the word "Lord" is parallel to Yahweh, the name that was given to Israel in the midst of her slavery in Egypt. Just as Yahweh delivered the people in Egypt, so he "delivered" the people when they cried out to him in the desert (v. 6b). From their aimless wanderings, God "led them by a straight way" (v. 7a). Though they could not find a city to dwell in (v. 4), after they cried out to the Lord, he led them to an inhabited city where they could dwell (v. 7b).[9] In their

---

6. John Jarick, "The Four Corners of Psalm 107," *CBQ* 59, no. 2 (1997): 270.
7. Jarick, "The Four Corners of Psalm 107," 272.
8. Jarick, "The Four Corners of Psalm 107," 281.
9. The Hebrew word *moshab* ("dwelling") is repeated in verses 4 and 7.

experience of hunger and thirst, God provided them with satisfaction and fullness (v. 9). For all these reasons, the people are called upon to "Give thanks to the Lord" (v. 8).

## 107:10–16 IMPRISONMENT

In verse 2, those whom the Lord has "redeemed" are exhorted to give thanks to the Lord. In verse 10, we learn that those whom the Lord has redeemed are those "who sat in darkness" (v. 10).[10] Sitting in darkness here refers to imprisonment, literally, "prisoners in affliction and in irons" (v. 10b, ESV).[11] This fits with the understanding of exile as a form of imprisonment. Smith-Christopher demonstrates that "various forms of the Hebrew terms normally rendered 'imprisonment' turn up as metaphors for exile, along with the various use of terms of binding and fetters."[12]

The exile is associated with the people's rebellion (v. 11), for God "subjected them to bitter labor" (v. 12a) because of their sins. Yet the people cried out to God (v. 13) because "there was no one else to help" (v. 12b). Whereas the phrase "sat in darkness" (v. 10) depicts a downward movement, the word "cried" (v. 13) implies an upward movement, as you naturally get up and even raise up your hands when you are crying out for help. This act of rising up and raising hands and voices is a sign of hope, for God "brought them out of darkness, the utter darkness" (v. 14a). The repetition of the word "utter darkness" (*tsalmawet*, see vv. 10 and 14) links the condition of misery in verse 10 with God's response. For when the people cried out to the Lord from their situation of exile, God heard their prayer and "broke away their chains" (v. 14b). Verse 16 is even more explicit in connecting their situation to imprisonment, "for he breaks down gates of bronze and cuts through bars of iron."

---

10. Verse 10 begins with a Hebrew participle which is translated literally as "those who sit." The NIV simply translates it as "Some sat." But the Hebrew participle makes it clear the connection with the beginning of the psalm. The word, "redeemed" in "the redeemed of the Lord" (v. 2) is also a participle.
11. Thomas finds "prisoners in affliction" strange. Arguing on the basis of the Arabic verb for "became a captive," he proposes that the Hebrew word for "affliction" should be translated as captivity. David Winton Thomas, "Hebrew *'ny* 'Captivity,'" *JTS* 16, no. 2 (1965): 444–445.
12. Compare Daniel L. Smith-Christopher, *A Biblical Theology of Exile* (Minneapolis: Fortress Press, 2002), 72.

## 107:17–22 "NEAR THE GATES OF DEATH"

One can observe a growing emphasis on sin in the progression of the four life-threatening narratives. Though sin is not mentioned in the first narrative (vv. 4–9), it is implied by the desert (v. 4), which is associated with the rebellion of the people. The second narrative (vv. 10–16) mentions the people's rebellion as the cause of their suffering (v. 11). The third narrative begins by mentioning the people's "rebellious ways" (v. 17). A literal reading of the Hebrew seems to imply that their rebellion made them foolish: "Fools through their rebellion" (v. 17). However, "fools" are also those who act in rebellious ways. In either case, the psalmist makes it clear that rebellious ways lead to suffering (v. 17b), for the people are so severely sick that they "loathed all food" (v. 18). Earlier, those who are suffering in exile are hungry (v. 5). Here, there is food, but the people have no appetite. In other words, there is no longer a desire to continue living. As verse 18b says, they "drew near the gates of death." The word "utter darkness" (vv. 10, 14) comes from the Hebrew word, *tsalmawet*, which can be literally translated, "shadow of death." Here, the phrase is "gates of death," which later becomes the "grave" (v. 20).

But out of their situation of suffering, they cried out to the Lord, and he answered them (v. 19) by healing and rescuing them (v. 20). The summons to give thanks in this narrative is more elaborate than in the previous two narratives. In addition to the refrain, "Let them give thanks to the LORD for his unfailing love . . ." (v. 21), the psalmist adds an exhortation to "sacrifice thank offerings" (v. 22a). In Hebrew, this type of offering is called *todah* (see Psalm 100), which is a happy celebration, where the one who has been delivered or saved shares what the Lord has done. Thus verse 22b says, "tell of his works with songs of joy."

## 107:23–32 DANGERS AT SEA

The first word in verse 23 is the Hebrew verb *yarad*, which means "to go down" or "to embark."[13] The people here are "merchants on the mighty waters" (v. 23) who set out to the sea in ships to do business. The verb "to go down" (v. 23) signifies a downward movement parallel to the description "sat in darkness" (v. 10). The people "went down to the sea" (v. 23, ESV) and later "went down to the depths" (v. 26). But their tragic descent was preceded by an ascent, for "They mounted up to the heavens" (v. 26).

---

13. Allen, *Psalms 101–150*, 83.

The word "deep" (*mitsolah*) in verse 24 "exhibits obvious affinity with mythological notions" and is parallel to the word "depths" (from *tehom*, which means "primeval ocean") in verse 26.[14] This language recalls the ancient battle against the forces of chaos in the sea, for which the Israelites had the greatest dread. The desert, though a dangerous place, was familiar to the Israelites, but the sea was beyond their world of experience and therefore presented a greater threat. Thus the sea is mentioned last.

The presentation of this final experience of suffering, however, is cryptic, as one has to infer the meaning of some verses from the preceding context. The merchants were out in the sea to do business, where they saw the "works of the Lord" (v. 24). To understand the phrase "works of the Lord," see Psalm 104:24–26, which mentions some of the great sea creatures that were a marvel in ancient times. In Psalm 107:25, God sends a tempest, which causes trouble to the seafarers. Though the reason for the tempest is not clear, the preceding context implies some kind of sin. It could be that they became boastful because of their great achievements.[15] Finding themselves in trouble, they cried out to the one who sent the tempest (v. 28), and God heard their prayer and "stilled the storm to a whisper" (v. 29). The psalm emphasizes how God silenced the sea and how the people rejoiced "when it grew calm" (v. 30).

## 107:33–43 INSTRUCTION

In the previous section, the same God who causes the storm is able to silence it. Similarly, in this final section, the same God who turns "rivers into a desert" (v. 33) and "fruitful land into a salt waste" (v. 34) can also turn the "desert into pools of water" (v. 35). The mention of the desert recalls verse 4, but in verse 34, the association between the desert and the people's sinfulness becomes explicit, as God turns the "fruitful land into a salt waste *because* of the wickedness of those who lived there" (my emphasis). Any metaphorically "fruitful" land can become a "wasteland" because of wickedness.

But the good news is that the God who can turn a fruitful land into a desert (vv. 33–34) can also do the reverse. Earlier, the people are described as "hungry and thirsty" (v. 5). The "thirsty ground" in verse 33 echoes the word "thirsty" from verse 5, and verse 36 repeats the word "hungry" from verse 5. God turns the "parched ground into flowing springs" (v. 35b), where

---

14. *TDOT*, 8:516.
15. In Ezekiel 27, Tyre is spoken of in the metaphor of a merchant ship that is ruined at sea due to the city's pride in its economic commercialism.

"he brought the hungry to live" (v. 36). In verse 6, the people could not find a city to dwell in, but here the people establish a city where they can dwell (v. 36). With an established dwelling place, the people can now sow fields, plant vineyards, and reap a harvest (v. 37). But lest the people attribute all the productivity to their own strength, the psalmist says that they grew in numbers because God "blessed them" (v. 38). This is the reason why their livestock did not decrease or "diminish" (*ma'at*). In Hebrew, verse 38 ends with the word *ma'at* (to decrease or "to be small").

In verse 39, there is an unexpected contrast with the repetition of the Hebrew word *ma'at* ("to be small"). Though God did not cause the livestock to diminish (v. 38), they diminished because of "oppression, calamity and sorrow" (v. 39). This reminds us of the destructive impact of acts of oppression. Thankfully, the wonderful God of reversals not only brings down the nobles and makes them wander (v. 40), but he also "lifted the needy" (v. 41, ESV). The word "wander" (*taah*) in verse 40 is the same word used in verse 4 to describe how the people "wandered in desert wastelands." In verse 41, the word "needy" (*ebyon*) refers to those who are lowly and oppressed. God's lifting up of the lowly and oppressed is a powerful message which we need to ponder upon. The psalm ends with a call for discernment as the people "ponder the loving deeds of the LORD" (v. 43).

# PSALM 108

Psalm 108 shares compositional similarities with Psalm 40, which borrows its concluding section (vv. 13–17) from Psalm 70.[1] The composer of Psalm 108 also borrowed from other psalms, combining sections from two different psalms to form his composition. Psalm 108:1–5 is taken from Psalm 57:7–11; Psalm 108:6–13 is taken from Psalm 60:5–12. We no longer have access to the composer's original intention in bringing together these two psalms, but the combination does create a certain effect.

First, the composer of Psalm 108 combines an individual lament (Psalm 57) with a communal lament (Psalm 60), which brings together the individual and the community. Second, the composer borrows from the more positive parts of each psalm. Psalm 57 moves from lament (vv. 1–6) to an expression of trust (v. 7) and a vow of praise (vv. 8–11).[2] The composer of Psalm 108 excludes the lament (Ps 57:1–6) and begins with the expression of trust: "My heart, O God, is steadfast" (108:1; 57:7). The last part of Psalm 57 marks the height of the expression of praise, "Be exalted, O God, above the heavens; let your glory be over all the earth" (v. 11). The composer of Psalm 108 preserves this upward movement in verse 5. He does the same with Psalm 60. Psalm 60 consists of five parts: complaint (vv. 1–4), petition (v. 5), divine response (vv. 6–8), complaint with renewed petition (vv. 9–11), and declaration of trust (v. 12). Psalm 108 excludes the communal complaint (60:1–4) and begins with the petition and divine response (60:5–8).

These lines that the composer of Psalm 108 borrows from Psalms 57 and 60 all highlight trust and certainty. However, the joining together of the two psalms in their present arrangement in Psalm 108 creates an element of tension amidst the certainty. Just when Psalm 108 reaches its peak with the chorus, "Be exalted, O God . . ." (v. 5), it suddenly shifts to lament with the petition in the next verse: "Save us and help us" (v. 6). Moreover, the second part of Psalm 60 that Psalm 108 borrows contains a great disjuncture, for even after the divine response (108:7–9; 60:6–8), we find complaint (108:10–11; 60:9–10), which is followed by a petition (108:12; 60:11). While rejoicing and praise should follow the divine answer (108:7–9; 60:6–8), lament lingers. Moreover,

---

1. See Federico G. Villanueva, *The "Uncertainty of a Hearing,"* 124.
2. The first part contains a cry for mercy (vv. 1–2), complaint (v. 4), and petition (v. 5). Verse 5 contains the same refrain as in verse 11: "Be exalted, O God, above the heavens; let your glory be over all the earth" (v. 5). But the use of the refrain in verse 5 differs from verse 11. In verse 5, it is used in the context of petition. See Villanueva, *The "Uncertainty of a Hearing,"* 279.

the very last verse in both psalms is a declaration of trust that highlights the people's perseverance and faith rather than God's answer (108:13; 60:12). The resulting composition is similar to Psalm 12, where tension lingers (12:8) even after the divine oracle (12:5).[3] Although some may be disappointed with the overall effect of Psalm 108, it can bring encouragement to individuals and communities who are going through similar experiences.

## 108:1–5 PRAISE

Psalm 108 begins with a deep sense of serenity, certainty, and assurance: "My heart is steadfast," the psalmist tells God (v. 1). The word "steadfast" comes from the Hebrew word *kun*, which also means "established" or "sure."[4] One does not easily gain this composure. From Psalm 57 (from which the first half of Psalm 108 has been taken), we learn that before the psalmist reached this stage of confidence, he first cried out to God (57:2) and pleaded for mercy (57:1) and uttered his complaint (57:6).

Canonically, the four life-threatening situations described in Psalm 107 (vv. 4–5, 10–12, 17–18, 23–27) supply the situation of lament for the first part of Psalm 57 (vv. 1–6). Moreover, Psalm 107 contains testimonies about how people cried out to the Lord (see vv. 6a, 13a, 19a, 28a), and then God answered their prayer (see vv. 7b, 13b, 19b, 28b). Thus there is a sense of certainty and assurance when we enter Psalm 108.

However, in Psalm 57, the phrase, "my heart is steadfast," is repeated twice (v. 7), whereas it is only mentioned once in Psalm 108 (v. 1). In Psalm 57, the repetition of this phrase draws attention to the phrase, "have mercy on me," which is also repeated twice at the beginning of the psalm (v. 1). It is as if the psalmist is saying, "I can now say 'my heart is now steadfast' twice because I have cried 'have mercy on me' twice."[5] Kirkpatrick comments that "the poetical effect is much impaired by the abridgment" in Psalm 108,[6] but I think the abridgment is deliberate. By not repeating the line, "my heart is steadfast," the composer signals a return to lament in the second half of Psalm 108, indicating that even though there is confidence, it is not absolute.

In Psalm 108, the psalmist cries out to God for help once again in verse 6. There is a similar movement in Psalm 27, which also contains elements of

---

3. Villanueva, *Psalms 1–72*, 80–83.
4. *HALOT*, 2:464.
5. For further discussion, see Villanueva, *Psalms 1–72*, 279–280.
6. Kirkpatrick, *The Book of Psalms*, 647.

thanksgiving in the first part of the psalm. In fact, the first part of the psalm ends with a vow of thanksgiving (see 27:6). Yet in the very next verse, the psalmist returns to lament as he cries out for God to "hear my voice" (27:7).

Interestingly, this vow of thanksgiving, "I will sing and make music" (Ps 27:6), also appears in Psalm 108:1, where the psalmist expresses his resolve to give thanks to the Lord. One implication of the psalmist's repeated exhortations to give thanks to the Lord in Psalm 107 is that thanksgiving is not automatic; rather, we have to commit to give thanks. In Psalm 108, the psalmist actually "commands" the harp and the lyre to "awake" (v. 2). Whereas Psalm 108 repeats the verb "awake" twice (v. 2), Psalm 57 repeats it thrice (v. 8). Moreover, Psalm 57 says, "awake, my soul" (v. 8), whereas Psalm 108 says, "with all my soul" (v. 1). In both, the literal word for "my soul" is "my glory," which can be understood in the sense of "my best self."[7]

Thanksgiving is an act that is both personal and communal. When we experience answers to our prayers, deliverance, or healing, we want others in our church community to know. But in Psalm 108, the psalmist wants to praise the Lord "among the nations" and "among the peoples" (v. 3).[8] Verse 4 provides the motivation for the psalmist's thanksgiving: because God's love is "higher than the heavens" and his "faithfulness reaches to the skies." The final verse taken from Psalm 57 is the chorus, "Be exalted, O God" (57:5, 11; 108:5). This declaration of praise also expresses the longing that God's "glory be over all the earth" (57:5, 11; 108:5). In Psalm 108:1, the psalmist enjoins himself to praise the Lord, where the last part of this verse literally reads, "I will make music, indeed my glory." Thus the psalm traces a movement from "my glory" at the beginning to "your glory" at the end of the first section.

### 108:6-11 RETURN TO LAMENT

While the psalm could have ended on such a glorious note, the psalmist now quotes from the second half of Psalm 60, returning his composition to a petition: "Save us and help us with your right hand" (v. 6). This petition also has an element of lament, for in the Hebrew original, it is preceded by an end purpose: "that those you love may be delivered" (v. 6b). The NIV has reversed

---

7. Allen, *Psalms 101–150*, 93.
8. Literally, the Hebrew phrase, *bal-'amim*, means "not people." Zenger cites Tournay who argues that the phrase *bal-'amim* (compare also Pss 44:15b; 149:7b) is "'a derogatory way of writing,' which is meant to subtly deny the Gentiles their status as 'nations' as long as they have not yet acknowledged YHWH as their God." Zenger and Hossfeld, *Psalms 3*, 114.

the order of the verse, highlighting the petition instead of the purpose. But even in the original, the emphasis is on the petition, because the situation calls for divine action. Reading verse 6 with an emphasis on God's glory (from v. 5) makes it anticlimactic, because the hoped-for situation is not yet established.

The inherent tension between thanksgiving and lament in Psalm 108 is addressed by a word from God himself: "God has spoken from his sanctuary" (v. 7). One common scholarly theory is that in the process of lament, as an individual pours out his complaints to the Lord, a cultic prophet would come in and deliver a word from the Lord. This is most likely what we have in Psalm 108:7, when God speaks a word of assurance through his servant.

The divine word presents God as a victorious warrior, who returns from battle and "redistributes the territory of his empire and assigns particular positions and functions to individual regions within it."[9] The territories mentioned in Psalm 108:7–9 recall those in the Davidic kingdom. Read in the context of the exilic/postexilic period, this serves as an assurance that God remains in control, even over their enemies. The first two places, Shechem and Sukkoth (v. 7), are prominent because they were the first two areas where Jacob lived after being away from home (Gen 33:17–18). Both are in the region of Gilead. The next three places, Gilead, Manasseh, and Ephraim (v. 8a), represent the northern kingdom, while Judah (v. 8b) represents the southern kingdom. God claims ownership over all these. Ephraim and Judah occupy an honorable place, being God's "helmet" and "scepter," respectively (v. 8). In contrast, Moab, Edom, and Philistia – enemy countries in the western, eastern, and southern part of Judah – are belittled. Moab is the "washbasin," and Edom is the place where God will hurl his shoe (v. 9). The shoe here symbolizes a possession marker.[10] In Philistia, God will shout his victory (v. 9).

One would expect a hymn of praise or thanksgiving after this prophetic word, which ends with a shout of "triumph" (v. 9). The repetition of the chorus in verse 5 would be fitting, but instead, the psalmist asks a question: "Who will bring me to the fortified city?" (v. 10). Tate finds this verse an "enigma."[11] First, we do not know who the speaker is. Second, what is the purpose of going to the "fortified city"? This seems to be a reference to Edom (see v. 10b),

---

9. Zenger and Hossfeld, *Psalms 3*, 120.
10. "Land was surveyed in triangles, and a benchmark was constructed of fieldstones to serve as a boundary marker (Deut 19:14). Since they walked off the land in sandals, the sandals became the moveable title to that land." Walton, Chavalas, and Matthews, *IVP Bible Background Commentary: Old Testament*, 551.
11. Tate, *Psalms 51–100*, 107.

but is the psalmist asking about going to the "fortified city" (Edom) to seek refuge or to conquer it?

Since God is presented as a victorious warrior in the preceding divine oracle, it seems obvious that God will "bring" whoever is speaking in verse 10 to Edom, even if this means conquering it. But in verse 11, there seems to be doubt – even a sense of mocking unbelief – from the speaker's point of view: "Is it not you, God, you who have rejected us?" The God who speaks and gives the people assurance in verses 7–9 is also the God who seems to have rejected them in Psalm 60:1–4. Even though Psalm 108 does not include these verses from Psalm 60 (vv. 1–4), their sense is preserved in Psalm 108:11.

## 108:12-13 PERSISTENCE OF FAITH AMIDST UNCERTAINTIES

The people in Psalm 108 continue to come to God to ask for help (12a), even though they know that God caused their defeat by abandoning them. We see this same posture in Psalm 107 (see comments above on vv. 25–28). Despite the people's complaints and doubts, they acknowledge that there is no one else who can help them – not even themselves (108:12b) – and so they persist in their faith in God (v. 13).

# PSALM 109

Psalm 109 contains some of the most shocking prayers ever penned in sacred Scriptures:

"May his children be fatherless and his wife a widow" (v. 9);
"let his prayer be counted as sin!" (v. 7b, ESV).

Some would not even call this a prayer, but rather a "curse psalm."[1] Yet Psalm 109 remains part of our Bible and is considered to be part of God's word. As God's word, what can Psalm 109 possibly teach us? To answer this question, it is important to understand the perspective from which the psalm was written. Psalm 109 is a "prayer from below," as reflected in the word "needy," which is mentioned three times in significant places in the psalm (vv. 16, 22, 31). In verse 16, it provides the motivation for the imprecations (vv. 1–15). In verse 22, it provides the motivation for the psalmist's petition. In verse 31, it provides the motivation for the thanksgiving at the end of the psalm (vv. 30–31).

While it is easy to judge the imprecations in verses 1–15 as completely out of proportion, the psalmist is praying for these things because the wicked have been afflicting the weak and vulnerable. The wicked have "hounded" the poor and the needy "to death" (v. 16). God has made it clear in the Torah that those who mess with the poor and vulnerable will be punished horribly: "Do not take advantage of the widow or the fatherless. If you do and they cry out to me, I will certainly hear their cry. My anger will be aroused, and I will kill you with the sword; your wives will become widows and your children fatherless" (Exod 22:22–24).

The Hebrew word for "cry out" (*tsa'aq*) in Exodus 22:22 occurs several times in the canonical context of Psalm 109. In Psalm 107, "cry out" (*tsa'aq*) occurs four times at key points in the psalm as the people cry out to the Lord in the midst of their distress (vv. 6a, 13a, 19a, 28a). Each time, God answers them (vv. 6b, 13b, 19b, 28b). Although the word "cry out" does not occur in Psalm 109, one can hear the psalmist's cry as he pleads with God not to "remain silent" (v. 1) and as he prays, "Help me, LORD my God" (v. 26). The psalmist is confident that just as God answered his people when they cried out to him, God will do as he has promised for the widow and fatherless. Because God promised that he would punish those who afflict the vulnerable in Exodus 22, the psalmist prays: "May his children be fatherless [*yatom*] and his wife a widow

---

1. Erhard S. Gerstenberger, *Psalms Part 2 and Lamentations*, 257.

[*'almanah*]" (Ps 109:9). There is close correspondence between this petition and the words in Exodus 22: "your wives will become widows [*'almanah*] and your children fatherless [*yatom*]" (Exod 22:24).

Thus Psalm 109 has to be read theologically, from the perspective of God's righteousness and justice. The joint phrase, "righteousness and justice," refers to actions that are done for and on behalf of the most vulnerable (see comments in Psalm 82 above). God places great importance on the care and protection of the least and the weakest because his throne is founded on righteousness and justice (Ps 97:2). The foundations of the earth are shaken when there is injustice, and so God has to act to bring about righteousness and justice (see comments in Ps 82:5). In Psalm 82, even the gods suffer the punishment of death because they fail to uphold justice for the weak and fatherless (vv. 6–7).

## PSALM 109 AND THE FILIPINO CONCEPT OF *PAGSUSUMBONG*

Psalm 109 brings the importance of social justice among human beings to the fore. This prayer is not for the powerful, but some people today do need this prayer, especially those who are deprived of their rights. In the Philippine context, the poor are usually killed by the powerful in the so-called "war on drugs," leaving their children orphans and their wives widows.[1] To whom shall these poor people go for help when those who should be implementing the law are the ones who are violating them? In Filipino, we would say, *kanino sila magsusumbong*? (To whom shall they report?)

We may interpret Psalm 109 from the cultural concept of *pagsusumbong* (reporting).[2] First, there is the bully, who pursues his victims, hounding them to death (v. 16). Second, the victims are described as "poor and needy" (v. 16; compare v. 22). Third, the victims go to God, believing that he will punish the wicked according to their actions (v. 20) because of "the goodness of your love" (v. 21; compare v. 26).

---

1. Aileen May P. Mijares, "Rebuilding Lives Amid the Ruins of Duterte's War on Drugs," *Journal of Human Rights and Peace Studies* 6, no. 2 (2020): 255–292.
2. See Psalm 83 above for the concept of *sumbong*. See also, "The Imprecatory Psalms as *Pagsusumbong sa Diyos*," Villanueva, *Psalms 1–72*, 274–276.

# Psalm 109

Psalm 109 is an individual lament that is focused on the "enemy." According to Westermann, there are three related subjects in a lament: God, self (the one who laments), and the enemy.[2] Sometimes all three occur in one psalm (e.g. Psalm 13). Other times, one subject becomes the focus. In Psalm 22, God is the focus of the lament. In Psalm 109, the enemy is the focus of the lament. Because this lament is comprised of curses directed towards enemies, these psalms are also called imprecatory psalms.

This psalm may be outlined as follows:

Complaints against enemies (vv. 1–5):
    invocation (v. 1),
    petition (v. 1),
    motivation (v. 2),
    complaints (vv. 3–5).
Prayers against enemies (vv. 6–20):
    imprecations (vv. 6–15),
    motivation for the imprecations (v. 16),
    imprecations (vv. 17–19),
    summary (v. 20).
Petition and motivation (vv. 21–28):
    petition (v. 21a),
    motivations (vv. 21b–25),
    renewed call for help (v. 26),
    motivation (v. 27),
    final imprecation: may they be put to shame (vv. 28–29).
Concluding vow of praise (vv. 30–31).

## 109:1–5 COMPLAINTS AGAINST ENEMIES

At the beginning of Book V, Psalms 108–110 all contain "David" in their superscription. Though we do not really know if David composed Psalm 109, the editorial attribution is not without warrant. The cry for help amidst enemies bent on destruction characterizes the earlier lament psalms attributed to David (e.g. Psalms 3 and 12). The opening cry, "My God . . . do not remain silent" (Ps 109:1), exhibits the same sense of urgency as Psalm 12:1: "Help, Lord."

---

2. Claus Westermann, *Praise and Lament in the Psalms*, trans. Keith R. Crim and Richard N. Soulen (Atlanta, GA: John Knox Press, 1981), 169.

This petition, "Do not be silent," can be literally translated, "Do not be deaf" (109:1). Expressed positively, the psalmist is asking God to answer, to speak up.

Psalm 109 emphasizes speech. In verse 1, God is described as the God "whom I praise," and praise is associated with speech (see v. 30 below). In verse 2, the word "mouth" (*peh*) is repeated twice to refer to the "mouth of the wicked" and "mouth of the deceitful" (my own translation). Further, this verse also uses the verb "to speak" (*dbr*) along with the word "tongue" (*lashon*). Like "mouth," the "tongue" is described negatively as a "lying tongue," where both "mouth" and "tongue" are used as a synecdoche to represent the wicked. In the Psalms, the wicked are described in terms of how they speak. With their tongues, the wicked people make boasts (Ps 12:4) and threats (10:7; 73:8), and they hurl insults against heaven (73:9, 11). In Psalm 109, the psalmist complains that "words of hatred" surround him (v. 3). Moreover, there is a connection between the speech – "words of hatred" – and those uttering them – "they attack me without cause" (v. 3b). The enemies themselves appear in place of the "words of hatred."

Yet what is the specific situation for these attacking words of hatred? Verse 4 provides some hint. The word "accuse" comes from the Hebrew word *satan*, which generally refers to someone who opposes. In a legal context, it refers to the accuser or the trial opponent. The psalmist appears to be someone who has been falsely accused. Without any cause, his enemies have attacked him and accused him (v. 3; compare Ps 35:7). He laments that "In return for my friendship they accuse me" (v. 4). The meaning of verse 4b is cryptic. Literally, it reads, "and/but I prayer." To help us understand this verse, let us look at the structure of verses 4–5 (ESV):

> "In return for **my love** they accuse me" (v. 4a, emphasis added),
>   "but I give myself to prayer" (v. 4b).
> "So they reward me evil for good and hatred for **my love**"
>   (v. 5, emphasis added).

Notice that verses 4a and 5 repeat "my love" and express the same idea: the enemies have committed an unjust act. Sandwiched between these parallel lines is the statement, "and I prayer," which can also be translated, "I am prayer," though this hardly makes sense. In view of the above structure, the statement can be interpreted as saying that in response to the psalmist's accusers, he appeals to God, because there is no one else to turn to than the "God of justice."[3]

---

3. Zenger and Hossfeld, *Psalms 3*, 132.

We are not given the specific contents of his prayer. But the suceeding context points to the imprecatory prayer (vv. 6–19), which is a prayer for justice. In Psalm 109, the psalmist is like the orphan and the widow in Exodus 32 who cry out to God because they have no one else to turn to. Later, the psalmist expresses this same sense of dependence on God: "But you, Sovereign LORD, help me for your name's sake" (v. 21).

## 109:6–19 PRAYERS AGAINST ENEMIES

How would we react if we heard the following prayers uttered in our church?

"Let his prayer be counted as sin!" (v. 7b, ESV).
"May a creditor seize all he has" (v. 11).
"May strangers plunder the fruits of his labor" (v. 11).
"May his descendants be cut off" (v. 13).
"May the iniquity of his fathers be remembered before the
  LORD" (v. 14);
"May the sin of his mother never be blotted out" (v. 14).
"May their sins always remain before the LORD" (v. 15).

Some lectionaries have deleted Psalm 109, as these prayers have been deemed inappropriate for God's people, let alone the psalmist.

How should we interpret verses 6–19? These verses are shocking and harsh, to say the least. Why would the psalmist pray for God to "appoint someone evil to oppose my enemy" (v. 6)? Why does he wish that the children of his enemies would be "wandering beggars" (v. 10) or that no one would "take pity on his fatherless children" (v. 12b)? Some of the major commentators interpret these verses as a quotation from the enemies rather than part of the prayer of the psalmist.[4] In this interpretation, the biblical writer is not endorsing the views that they express.

Yet this view faces several difficulties. First, the Hebrew does not use a quotation mark. Although it is possible that this entire section (vv. 6–19) is a quotation, it is also possible that it is not. Second, the main argument for this being a quotation is the change from plural to singular in the presentation of the enemies. In verses 3–5, the enemies/accusers are presented as "they," whereas the imprecations in verses 6–19 are directed against a singular enemy. But this argument is rather weak, since the individual can represent

---

4. For a recent defense of this view, see Steffen Jenkins, "A Quotation in Psalm 109 as Defence Exhibit A," *TynBul* 71, no. 1 (2020): 115–135.

the group or community throughout the Psalter. We see this in some of the lament psalms, where the "I" can also represent the community. Conversely, the individual against whom the imprecations are directed could also be read as the representative of the collective ("they"/"them").[5] Third, in verse 20, the psalmist asks God to make what is mentioned in verses 6–19 the "payment to my accusers." The flow of the text favors the reading of verse 20 as a continuation of the preceding verses (see comment for v. 20 below).

The key to interpreting verses 6–19 lies in verse 16, which provides the reason or motivation for the subsequent series of petitions or imprecations: "For he . . . hounded to death the poor and the needy and the brokenhearted" (v. 16). The psalmist is asking God to do the terrible things in verses 7–19 because of the way that the wicked have treated the poor and the needy. As noted above, the treatment of the poor and needy is central to the Torah, and those who oppress them will suffer God's vengeance. As Exodus 22:22–24 says, "Do not take advantage of the widow or the fatherless . . . If you do and they cry out to me, I will certainly hear their cry . . ." While the content of their "cry" is not specified, those who have been abused, oppressed, illegally jailed, or unjustly killed know exactly how it feels, and those who have worked alongside the marginalized are familiar with this experience of being oppressed. The psalmist identifies himself as "poor and needy" (v. 22), and by praying the preceding imprecatory prayers, he is expressing the "cry" of those who have been oppressed.

In Psalm 109, the psalmist prays that God will destroy the wicked humans who hound the poor and needy to death. In verses 6–19, the psalmist asks God to destroy these wicked people who murder the poor. In the earlier verses (vv. 2–5), the wicked are described by their wicked speech, evil mouth, and "words of hatred." At the end of the present section, the psalmist says that the wicked "loved to pronounce a curse" (v. 17) and "wore cursing as his garment" (v. 18). Since this is the case, the psalmist asks God to let the wicked man's curse "come back on him" (v. 17).

---

5. In Filipino culture, it is not unusual to say "we" or "our," even when an individual is speaking alone, because of our emphasis on community. For example, even when a person is eating alone, she would pray, "Thank you for the food that you have given *us*." It would feel awkward to say, "me," for Filipinos are generally not used to eating alone.

# Psalm 109

## 109:20–29 PETITION AND MOTIVATION

Verse 20 carries forward the force of the previous section (vv. 6–19) as the psalmist asks God for retributive justice. Verse 20 can be literally translated, "This [is the] payment of my accusers from the Lord." The sense of the previous verses supports reading this as a jussive, a wish or petition: "May this be . . ." The word translated as "payment" comes from the Hebrew word *pe'ullah*, which means "reward" or "punishment."[6] This petition is consistent with verse 6, where the psalmist asks God to "let an accuser stand at his right hand." From the context of verse 16, we understand that the psalmist has asked this because the wicked did not show kindness to the poor and needy, but pursued them to death. Verses 17–19 show that the wicked love curses, and so the psalmist is asking God to recompense him in accordance to his works. This is an example of retributive justice, which is "from the Lord" (v. 20a, ESV).

Verse 20b strengthens the view that wicked speech represents wicked people, who are described as "those who speak evil of me." The description is in the participial form in Hebrew, which can be translated, "those who are speaking evil of me," which gives a sense of an ongoing experience. The danger remains imminent, ongoing. Thus resuming the earlier petition at the beginning of the psalm, "My God . . . do not remain silent" (v. 1), the psalmist pleads with God, "But you, Sovereign Lord, help me" (v. 21). In verse 4, he says, "but I give myself to prayer" (ESV), and here, he clings to God in the midst of his troubles, asking God to "deliver me" (v. 21), along with a number of reasons or motivations. First, God should deliver him "for your name's sake" (v. 21a). God has already revealed his name to Israel as Yahweh, the God who delivers the oppressed.

Second, God should deliver him "out of the goodness of your love" (v. 21b). The word "love" here comes from the Hebrew word *hesed*. Psalm 107, the first psalm in Book V, ends with an exhortation for those who are wise to "ponder the loving deeds of the Lord," and "loving deeds" is the translation of the plural form of *hesed* (107:43). Humans should be like their creator, Yahweh, for they should also practice *hesed* to their fellow humans. The failure of the wicked is that "he never thought of doing a kindness [*hesed*]" to the "needy" (v. 16).

In verse 22, the psalmist gives the third motivation, which is that "I am poor and needy." What the wicked failed to do for "the poor and needy" (v. 16), the psalmist is now asking God to do for him (v. 21). The third description

---

6. *HALOT*, 3:951.

after "poor and needy" in verse 16 is "brokenhearted," which comes from a Hebrew word that means "discouraged one, downcast one."[7] The poor and needy are already susceptible to discouragement because of their situation – and even more so when they are pursued, oppressed, and hounded to death. Verse 22b, "my heart is wounded within me," literally reads in the Hebrew as, "my heart is pierced within me." Verses 23–24 elaborate on this experience. Verse 23 recalls Psalm 102, which is described in the superscription as "a prayer of an afflicted person who has grown weak and pours out a lament before the Lord." The language of Psalm 109:23 is similar to Psalm 102:11, where the image of "a lengthening shadow" speaks of death (compare Ps 144:4; Job 8:9).[8]

In Psalm 109:24, the reference to "fasting," according to Walton, "occurs in the context of mourning."[9] It is not clear from the text whether the psalmist is suffering from some kind of sickness, but his appearance gives the impression that he is seriously ill. Moreover, he has become the "object of scorn" to his enemies, which is associated with the experience of shame. In ancient times as well as in traditional Asian cultures, a shameful situation is terrible. To "lose face" can be worse than death itself, and so shame is mentioned last. Immediately after this climax, the psalmist cries out to God, "Help me, Lord my God" (v. 26). He is desperate for God to act so that his accusers will know that God answers his prayers. The words, "has done [it]," in verse 27b and, "help me," in verse 21a, come from the same Hebrew word, *asah* ("to do"). Similarly, in Psalm 6, the psalmist is able to stand confidently against his enemies when he knows that God has heard his prayer (vv. 8–10).

Psalm 109:28 should be understood in connection with verse 17, which says that the wicked "loved to pronounce a curse." Here in verse 28, the psalmist says, "Let them curse" (ESV). Since cursing is what they love, let curses come to them. Specifically, he asks that they be put to shame, which is one of the most painful and difficult experiences. While the psalmist expects God to bless him (v. 28), he does not wish God's blessing for his accusers, but rather shame and disgrace (v. 29). Again, one has to interpret this prayer in light of what the accuser does to the weak and vulnerable.

---

7. *DCH*, 4:348.
8. Zenger and Hossfeld, *Psalms 3*, 24.
9. John Walton, Mark W. Chavalas, and Victor Harold Matthews, *IVP Bible Background Commentary: Old Testament*, 552.

# Psalm 109

## 109:30–31 VOW OF PRAISE

In the last two verses of Psalm 109, there is a change of mood as reflected in the vow of praise (v. 30). The psalm starts with an invocation to the God "whom I praise" (v. 1) and ends with this vow of praise, because "he [the Lord] stands at the right hand of the needy" (v. 31). The psalmist is grateful because he has Someone to whom he can "report" to (in Filipino, *merong mapagsusumbungan*) about his experience of being bullied to God. The "right hand" (v. 31) looks back to the petition in verse 6. The psalmist is confident because he knows that God is there to defend him. The verb "stands" signifies that God continues to actively take the side of the needy.

# PSALM 110

Psalm 110 has an especially important message for those of us who have had to live under foreign powers. One of the effects of colonization that has impacted many countries in Asia is how so many years of subjugation has resulted in low self-esteem among the native peoples.[1] Some Filipinos of my generation, for example, tend to view themselves as inferior to those in the West. We always say, "State side," whenever we receive products from the United States of America, which we see as superior to our own products. This includes books, and so we seldom read Bible commentaries written by Filipinos – only those written by Westerners. We tend not to believe in ourselves and to think we are small. Thus the need to strengthen our belief in our own capacity (*lakas ng loob*).[2]

In the current form that has come down to us in the Hebrew of the MT, Psalm 110 depicts a situation similar to the Philippines. The Psalter was finally put together after the people's experience of subjugation under the Babylonians. Though it may have originally been written during the preexilic period, those who put it together knew what it meant to live under oppressive rulers. Though they were living in the postexilic period, their situation was far from ideal, as they continued to live under foreign powers. Similarly, even though the Philippines gained its independence many years ago, we continue to experience colonization in subtle but oppressive ways. Thus we continue to have low self-esteem.

The rhetoric of Psalm 110 favors this reading, as there is an emphasis on encouragement and strengthening one's resolve. In Psalm 110, the speaker brings a message that is meant to encourage the recipient and strengthen him "in the work that lies before him."[3] He is invited to sit in a place of honor, assured that God will be fighting for him (v. 1). His "scepter" is described as "mighty," which would also bolster his confidence (v. 2). People who lack confidence, including leaders, often worry about whether people will support them. In verse 3, the speaker assures the leader that "your people will offer themselves freely." One of the most difficult textual problems in verse 3 is the word "dew," but this reference will make more sense when related to the story

---

1. Federico G. Villanueva, "The Transforming Power of Lament," in *The Gospel in Culture: Contextualization Issues through Asian Eyes*, ed. Melba Padilla Maggay (Manila: OMF Literature: Institute for Studies in Asian Church and Culture, 2013), 222–224.
2. José M. de Mesa, *Mabathalang Pag-Aaral*, Academica Filipina Digital (Manila: Vee Press and DLSU, 2010), 12.
3. Kirkpatrick, *The Book of Psalms*, 661.

of Gideon (see discussion of this verse below). The story of Gideon, of course, is also set within a context of foreign subjugation. Gideon views himself as insignificant, and so the text in Judges emphasizes that he is a "mighty warrior" (Judg 6:12). The Hebrew word for "mighty" (*khayil*) is also used in Psalm 110:2 to describe the "mighty scepter." For other correspondence between Psalm 110 and the Gideon narrative, see the discussion below.

The canonical context further supports the preceding interpretation. Canonically, Psalm 110 is related to the Psalms 108–109. Zenger describes Psalms 108–110 as the "Davidic trilogy."[4] While each of these psalms may have had a separate history of composition, the redactors brought them together at some point for their own purpose. Zenger argues that the redactional purpose was to respond to the lament in Psalm 89. However, I think the connection is closer to Psalm 109, as Psalms 109–110 are both attributed to David. Though Psalm 109 may have originally been a prayer of an individual who was falsely accused, redactional editing has made it a prayer of David. In Psalm 109, we hear the voice of someone who is being attacked and oppressed by the enemy, and so he is lamenting and crying out to God for justice. Thus Psalm 110 may be read as God's response to this lament. The very first word in Psalm 110 is the word "utterance" (*ne'um*), which refers to an oracle from the Lord as mediated through a prophet. The individual in Psalm 109 refers to himself as "poor and needy" (v. 22). Elsewhere, David also refers to himself in this way (see Pss 9:18; 40:17; 70:5; 86:1). The term "right hand" features prominently in Psalm 109 (vv. 6, 31), and it also occurs twice in Psalm 110 (vv. 1, 5). Both psalms also emphasize violence – the cursing and pursuit of the poor and needy in Psalm 109 and the crushing of enemy kings and rulers in Psalm 110.

## 110:1–3 THE WORD OF THE LORD TO "MY LORD"

As noted above, Psalm 110 is linked to the two previous psalms. Each of these three psalms (108–110) may have separate history of composition, but the redactors brought them together for a purpose. We do not have access to the "original" function of each psalm in the Davidic trilogy, but based on their present arrangement, genre, and content, we will be able to glimpse a possible purpose for the canonical shape.

As noted previously, Psalm 108 was composed by joining together parts of two lament psalms (Psalm 57 and Psalm 60). Psalm 109 is another lament

---

4. Zenger and Hossfeld, *Psalms 3*, 146.

psalm. Thus Psalm 110 is preceded by two lament psalms. If we follow the LXX tradition, Psalm 110 also shares an association with Psalm 2, thereby demonstrating a reversal of the movement between Book I and Book V. In Book I, laments (e.g. Psalms 3–14) follow the royal psalm (Psalm 2); in Book V, the royal psalm (Psalm 110) follows the laments (Psalms 108–109). The "Davidic trilogy" (Psalms 108–110) is subsequently followed by the Hallelujah psalms. This affirms the observation that in the latter part of the Psalter, there is a noticeable emphasis on praise.

At the same time, one does not throw away lament with this shift in emphasis to praise, since praise derives its significance from lament. Thus Psalm 110 should be read along with Psalms 108 and 109. One common theory, which has been popularized by Begrich, is that when an individual lamented in the temple, a cultic prophet would deliver a word from the Lord – an oracle of salvation. This tradition provides an explanation for the sudden change of mood from lament to renewed trust at the end of Psalm 109. One weakness of this view, however, is the lack of evidence that a cultic prophet actually came and gave an oracle within Psalm 109. This is where Psalm 110 features significantly, as it contains an oracle of the Lord that was delivered after the lament in Psalm 109. A weakness of the form-critical view is that it limits itself to the individual psalm rather than considering the surrounding psalms. In Psalm 109, there is a change of mood at the end, without an explanation about how this change occurred. But if we read Psalm 110 along with Psalm 109, we will see a possible explanation for this sudden change of mood. Psalm 109 is attributed to David, which makes the individual lament in this psalm "Davidic." Through the superscription, the redactors are drawing a link between these two psalms. By starting with the phrase, "The Lord says" (Ps 110:1), the canonical arrangement connects the words at the beginning of Psalm 110 to the lament in the previous psalm, thereby making Psalm 110 a response to the previous lament and providing an explanation for the change of mood.

The word "says" in the phrase, "The Lord says" (Ps 110:1), comes from the Hebrew word *ne'um*, which means "utterance" or "declaration."[5] This word is often used in prophetic literature to refer to the word from the Lord given through the prophet, and it is equivalent to the statement, "Thus says the Lord." This word ("says") is only used twice in the whole Psalter – here in Psalm 110 and in Psalm 36:1.[6] In response to the lament in Psalm 109, an

---

5. *BDB*, 610.
6. Psalm 36:1 is rather strange, since it says that "Transgression speaks to the wicked" (esv). Nonetheless, the sense of the word *ne'um* ("says") in the sense of speaking or saying is clear.

oracle is given through the speaker or bringer of the word, who could be a cultic prophet. The cultic prophet addresses the recipient of the divine word as "my lord," which is a common way of addressing a king in a royal court (e.g. 1 Sam 24:10; 2 Sam 15:21).

The actual word from the Lord is an invitation to the recipient to "sit at my right hand." This position at the "right hand of a king is the highest place of honour" (1 Kgs 2:19).[7] The original setting of the psalm could be the coronation of a king, and the tradition preserved in the LXX supports this view (see discussion of Ps 110:3 below). But in its present placement, the reference to the "right hand" has an added meaning, as the phrase, "right hand," occurs twice in Psalm 109 to connote a sense of defense and protection. As Walton observes, "A fully armed warrior would hold his weapon in his right hand and his shield in his left. The person to the right of a king would have the privilege of defending him. For a king to put someone there would be an affirmation of trust and therefore an honor."[8] The usage of the phrase in Psalm 110:1 differs slightly, but the second usage of the phrase in Psalm 110:5 is similar. God will be at the right hand of the king to serve as his defender. This makes the repetition of the phrase "right hand" in Psalm 110 significant, as it draws a deliberate connection to Psalm 109.

The assurance and promise given to the recipient is extraordinary, for the oracle not only promises honor but also complete submission by the king's enemies, who will be a "footstool for your feet" (v. 1), as well as domination, for the Lord will "extend" his rule (v. 2a). This does not imply that the king will no longer have to do anything, for the divine word looks to the future – "*until* I make your enemies a footstool" (v. 1). The divine action in verse 2a is balanced by human agency in verse 2b, as the king is commanded to "Rule in the midst of your enemies!" The king has to go right in the middle of enemy territory to implement this divine decree.

Taking such action would require a lot of courage, and so the ruler needs confidence and encouragement. Thus the main purpose of the oracle is to affirm the king. Verse 1 emphasizes the recipient's position of honor, and verse 2 describes the "scepter" of the king as "mighty." Then verse 3 alludes to the story of Gideon, reminding the ruler of his noble birth (see below). The primary purpose of the divine word seems to be to help the king remember the greatness and power of his rule.

---

7. Carl Friedrich Keil and Franz Delitzsch, *Keil and Delitzsch Commentary on the Old Testament*, 189.
8. Walton, Chavalas, and Matthews, *IVP Bible Background Commentary: Old Testament*, 552–553.

Verse 3 is "the most obscure verse in the whole Psalter,"[9] and there are alternative readings preserved in the various manuscripts. But even if we are not able to determine the original Hebrew reading, the line of interpretation proposed above is sustained in the Hebrew text and supported by the LXX. The statement, "Your troops will be willing on your day of battle" (v. 3), would encourage a newly installed king, as a common fear of new kings is whether they will be able to rally the people behind them. The word translated as "your troops" in the Hebrew means "your people." The word "willing" is translated from the Hebrew word *nedabot*, which literally means "freewill offerings." It is interpreted predicatively here with the plural to communicate intensification.[10] Just as the people are willing to offer sacrifices, so they are willing to fight for the king on the "day of battle." In Hebrew, this phrase literally means "on the day of your power." The NIV translation offers an interpretation, but it is not far-fetched, since a king's power is manifested in the time of his battle. It should be noted, however, that the LXX reflects a different translation. Instead of "your people" (*'ammeka*), the LXX has "with you." And where the MT has "on the day of your power," the LXX has "on the day of your birth" (*'immeka*). It is important to note that the reading in the LXX shares the same consonants with the MT. Thus when read with a different vocalization, the phrase, "on the day of your power,"[11] can also render the meaning, "on the day of your birth."[12] The reading at the end of the LXX has "I have begotten you,"[13] which connects with the idea of a noble birth, but the MT has "your youth."[14] Again, the consonants are the same, and so the only difference is the vocalization. There are many manuscripts supporting the LXX, which probably preserves the original reading. But the reading preserved in the MT is also important, for it was deliberately preserved for a purpose.[15]

Schenker argues that the MT text reflects an attempt to draw an analogy between Psalm 110 and the story of Gideon in the book of Judges.[16] This is

---

9. Allen, *Psalms 101–150*, 110.
10. Allen, *Psalms 101–150*, 109.
11. *beyom khelekha*.
12. *beyom khilekha*.
13. *yldtyk*.
14. *yaldutekha*.
15. Zenger concludes his detailed text-critical discussions with a note that the text as preserved in the MT should be "retained" since it serves a purpose within the "David trilogy of Psalms 108–110." Zenger and Hossfeld, *Psalms 3*, 143.
16. Adrian Schenker, "Textkritik und Textgeschichte von Ps 110 (109), 3: Initiativen der Septuaginta und der Protomasoretischen Edition," in *La Septante En Allemagne et En France: Textes de La Septante à Traduction Double Ou à Traduction Très Littérale*, ed. Wolfgang Kraus

a very interesting proposal, since the story of Gideon highlights the sense of inadequacy or incompetence of a leader who is chosen to rule (as discussed above). Gideon describes himself as the "least" among his family (Judg 6:15). The word translated as "least" comes from the Hebrew word *tsaʿir*, which also means "young," in the sense of small and insignificant.[17] In Psalm 110, the word "youth" occurs at the end of verse 3. The Hebrew word *yaldut* ("youth") means "childhood"[18] and "denotes early age in general . . . and is hardly a proper designation of 'young men.'"[19] This word only occurs in Psalm 110:3 and Ecclesiastes 11:10, and it is not a proper description for the "troops" of the king because it reflects weakness. But Psalm 110 also mentions the word "dew," as does the story of Gideon. Outside the Gideon narrative, Psalm 110 is the only instance where this word is used in the context of the investiture of a ruler.[20] In Gideon's story, "dew" is used to confirm God's calling. In Psalm 110, the NIV translates two Hebrew words, *leka tal* ("to you is the dew"), to refer to the young men as the king's troops: "your young men will come to you like dew" (v. 3). Yet these two words are absent in the LXX and represent the most challenging part of the difficult text of verse 3. In the MT, the text literally reads, "to you is the dew of your youth," which does not make sense. But the mention of "dew" could possibly be intended to link Psalm 110 with the story of Gideon. The smashing of the heads of kings in Psalm 110:5 recalls Gideon's victory over princes (Judg 7:25). Moreover, the difficult detail concerning drinking from the brook at the end of Psalm 110 (v. 7) would make sense if we recall Gideon and his three hundred men (Judg 8:4).[21]

Given the context of Psalm 110, along with the significant connections to Judges 5–8, it makes sense to read this psalm as an analogy to Gideon's story. Like Gideon, the ruler of Psalm 110 needs to be encouraged and empowered. He has to be shown that God is able to extend his territory, though he may see himself as a mere youth.

---

and Olivier Munnich (Fribourg, 2009), 185.
17. *HALOT*, 3:1041.
18. *NIDOTTE*, 2:458.
19. Thijs Booij, "Psalm 110: 'Rule in the Midst of Your Foes!,'" *VT* 41, no. 4 (October 1991): 397.
20. Schenker, "Textkritik und Textgeschichte von Ps 110 (109)," 184.
21. Schenker, "Textkritik und Textgeschichte von Ps 110 (109)," 185.

## 110:4–7 "THE LORD HAS SWORN"

Verse 4 parallels verse 1, as both contain a word from the Lord. At the same time, there is a noticeable elevation of the speech. In verse 1, an "utterance" is given, whereas in verse 4, "the Lord has sworn." Verse 4 also adds the emphasis that God "will not change his mind" (v. 4). To understand this verse, we have to make a connection with Psalm 89 and the context of the failure of the Davidic kingship.[22] The final verses of Psalm 89 contain a lament that asks God, "where is your former great love . . . which you swore to David?" (v. 49). Gideon asks a similar question to the angel of the Lord: "Where are all his wonders that our ancestors told us about . . .?" (Judg 6:13). In Psalm 110, these verses continue the emphasis we saw in the first section about the need for the king or ruler to receive encouragement and assurance.

Rather unexpectedly, the promise in verse 4 shifts to emphasize the priesthood – one that is described as "forever" and "in the order of Melchizedek" (v. 4b). The description of this everlasting priesthood recalls the promise given to David concerning his reign, which is also "forever" (2 Sam 7:13). But in light of the context of Psalm 89, this everlasting promise has been called into question. By highlighting the priestly office of the king and pulling it back to a time before the Davidic kingship, the divine word in Psalm 110 provides a new way of understanding the current situation. The failure of the Davidic kingship does not mean an end to everything that God has promised, for his promises stretch back even before David. The reference to Melchizedek (see Gen 14:18–20) also reminds the king that God's ways are not limited, for he works in mysterious ways that are outside the bounds of our familiarity.

The combination of king, priest, and violent military imagery presents an added difficulty to this psalm. How can the king be also a priest? How can the priest be associated with violent acts? As Purcell demonstrates in his study of ancient iconography, the "constellation of royal, priestly, and violent imagery in Psalm 110 is a pattern of literary imagery that accords with ancient Near Eastern . . . conceptions of kingship."[23] Thus we should be careful not to read modern, Western conceptions into the ancient text. The acts of the king can be described as "priestly" because they are done in the presence of God.[24] The more disturbing aspect of Psalm 110 is not the link between the king and the

---

22. Compare Zenger and Hossfeld, *Psalms 3*, 150.
23. Richard Anthony Purcell, "The King as Priest? Royal Imagery in Psalm 110 and Ancient Near Eastern Iconography," *JBL* 139, no. 2 (2020): 300.
24. Purcell, "The King as Priest? Royal Imagery in Psalm 110 and Ancient Near Eastern Iconography," 299.

priest, but the violence described in these verses. Verse 5 speaks of the "day of his wrath." The word "crush" is repeated twice: God will "crush kings" (v. 5), "crushing the rulers of the whole earth" (v. 6b). Even more disturbing, he will fill the nations with "corpses" (v. 6a, ESV).

The emphasis on violence associated with the king-priest alludes to Psalm 109, which also uses violent language. Based on this context, we can understand the language of Psalm 110 in light of the divine concept of justice. The name "Melchizedek" is not only a reference to the actual figure in Genesis 14, for it is also a combination of two Hebrew words – *malchi* ("king") and *tsedeq* ("righteousness" or "justice"). Within the context of Psalms 109 and 110, this name emphasizes the justice that God will eventually implement to all the nations. In Psalm 110:6, the psalmist declares that God will "judge the nations." The judgment of the nations occurs in Psalm 9 (a thanksgiving psalm) and Psalm 10 (a lament psalm), which both highlight the importance of justice. In Psalm 9, the psalmist declares that the Lord "judges the peoples with equity" (v. 8), and then he asks God to "let the nations be judged in your presence" (v. 19). The verb "judges" (*dyn*) in Psalm 9:8 and the word "nations" in Psalm 9:19 both occur in Psalm 110:6. Thus the justice that the people were longing for in Psalm 9 is promised in Psalm 110. God will finally arise and execute judgment on the nations. It is important that we do not lose sight of the theme of justice in Psalm 110, especially in the light of Psalm 109.

This promise for justice is particularly meaningful for those who are oppressed, lowly, and vulnerable, and it can provide much-needed encouragement for those who are on the brink of losing all hope. Moreover, the word *dyn* (judge) is also connected with Gideon, who was one of the judges in Israel. The difficult detail in Psalm 110:7 about drinking from a brook becomes intelligible when read alongside the Gideon story. The "divine protector . . . will not become exhausted in pursuing the enemies" but "will be like the heroic men with Gideon (Judg 7:4–6), who did not even kneel down to slake their thirst, but while still on their feet scooped water in their hands from a brook flowing by and drank."[25]

---

25. Zenger and Hossfeld, *Psalms 3*, 152.

# PSALM 111

To understand Psalm 111, one also has to consider Psalm 112 (see below), as these are considered to be "twin" psalms.[1] Both were composed using the Hebrew acrostic, where verse 1 begins with the first letter of the Hebrew alphabet, and the last verse begins with the last letter. A psalmist might compose a psalm using the acrostic form for the purpose of memorization or to convey a sense of completeness or wholeness. The opening verse of Psalm 111 expresses this sense of wholeness: "I will give thanks to the Lord with my *whole* heart" (v. 1, ESV, emphasis mine).

Psalm 111 is a psalm of praise, where the object of praise is all of God's "works." The psalm employs at least two Hebrew words for "work/s": *ma'aseh* and *poa'l*. The words "works/work" are repeated several times:

"works [*ma'aseh*] of the Lord" (v. 2),
"work [*poa'l*]" (v. 3),
"his works [*ma'aseh*]" (v. 6),
"works [*ma'aseh*] of his hands" (v. 7).

To praise God's works properly, one has to ponder them (v. 2). More importantly, one has to develop the "fear of the Lord," which is the beginning of wisdom (v. 10).

Psalm 111 combines elements of a hymn, thanksgiving, and wisdom psalm. The first line, "Praise the Lord," is a characteristic feature of a hymn, but here it takes the place of the superscription, and the psalm formally begins with the second line, where the Hebrew acrostic begins (see comments below). The call to praise (hymn) is immediately followed by a vow of thanksgiving, which is obviously a feature of the thanksgiving psalm. However, the psalm does not contain a personal account of God's deliverance, which is a core feature of the thanksgiving psalm. Instead, the thanksgiving is general and can be interpreted as referring both to past and present events. Moreover, the last part of the psalm incorporates a wisdom component (v. 10). Thus Psalm 111 combines various elements from all three of these forms – the hymn, thanksgiving, and wisdom psalms.

For interpretation, the canonical context of the psalm is more important. As noted above, Psalm 111 is closely connected to Psalm 112. Psalm 111 ends

---

1. G. T. M. Prinsloo, "Reading Psalm 112 as a 'Midrash' on Psalm 111," *OTE* 32, no. 2 (2019): 636–637.

with a note about the "fear of the Lord," and then Psalm 112 elaborates on what it means to "practice" this. Psalm 111 also has links with Psalm 104 in light of its emphasis on the "works" of the Lord (see Ps 104:13, 24). The word *teref* (food) is used in Psalm 111:5 to refer to human food, but its meaning is "prey," which is the word used in Psalm 104 to express God's generosity in giving (104:28) food to all the animals (104:21).

## 111:1 LESSONS IN THANKSGIVING

Instead of a superscription, Psalm 111 begins with the famous word, *hallelujah*, which combines the plural form of the verb *hll* ("praise") with *yah* (the abbreviation of the divine name, "Yahweh". Together, this is translated as a command to the congregation to "Praise the Lord," and it represents what we today refer to as a call to worship. In the Psalms, the call to worship is a characteristic feature of a hymn. Psalm 111, however, begins with the first acrostic line, "I will give thanks to the Lord with my whole heart" (v. 1b, ESV). In Hebrew, "I will give thanks" is one word and begins with the first letter of the Hebrew alphabet. So formally, the psalm begins with this vow of thanksgiving.[2] Psalm 9 also begins as an acrostic thanksgiving psalm, with a very slight variation: "I will give thanks to the Lord with *all* my heart" (v. 1).

We learn two important lessons about thanksgiving from Psalm 111:1. First, thanksgiving should be done with one's *whole* heart. As noted above, Psalm 111 was composed using the Hebrew acrostic, which conveys a sense of wholeness, and so this verse combines both the form and the message. Speech is a normal part of thanksgiving, as we praise the Lord with our lips and give thanks with our mouths, but unless our words of thanksgiving come from a heart that is wholly dedicated to the Lord, our praise will be vain and empty.

Second, our thanksgiving is meant to be shared with the community. The psalmist vows that he will give thanks to the Lord "in the council [*sod*] of the upright and in the assembly [*'edah*]" (v. 1c). Notice that the psalmist uses two words for the community – the council and the assembly. When we receive a blessing or encounter something wonderful, we want someone to be with us to share the experience. In the OT, the practice of offering a *todah* (thanksgiving offering) provides a venue for the community to express gratitude and offer thanksgiving as well as to celebrate together (see Psalm 116 below).

---

2. Prinsloo, "Reading Psalm 112 as a 'Midrash' on Psalm 111," 636.

## 111:2–3 PONDERING THE WORKS OF THE LORD

In most thanksgiving psalms, there is an individual testimony, but this is lacking in Psalm 111. Instead, the psalmist offers more general thanks for the "works of the Lord" (v. 2). These divine "works" (*ma'aseh* in Hebrew) are described as "great" (v. 2). In Psalm 104, the psalmist exclaims, "How many are your works, Lord!" (104:24), as he ponders the greatness of God's work of creation. Psalm 111 is cryptic in its formulation, due in part to the limitations imposed by the acrostic form, but this should not hinder us from reflecting on the words of the psalm in its surrounding context. As noted, Psalm 111 has affinities with Psalm 104. God's wonders in creation lead the composer of Psalm 104 to meditate on them. In Psalm 111, the psalmist points out that "all who delight" in the works of the Lord ponder them (111:2b). The word "pondered" comes from the Hebrew word *darash*, which means "to seek" or "to search." The ESV translates *darash* as "studied." In order to see the "works of the Lord," one has to approach them with an attitude of worship and thanksgiving (v. 1). The end of the psalm instructs us about the importance of the "fear of the Lord" (v. 10), which is the first requirement for the study of God's works.

But first, the psalmist expounds on the works of the Lord in verse 3, using another Hebrew word for "work" (*poa'l*), which means "deed, accomplishment."[3] Here, the Hebrew, *poa'l* is in the singular. This does not mean that the psalmist is referring to a single work of God; rather, it could be another way to express the entirety of God's work. More likely, however, the composer used the singular form to draw a connection with the word "righteousness" (*tsedaqah*), which occurs in the next line:

> "Full of splendor and majesty is his *work*,
> his *righteousness* endures forever" (v. 3, ESV).

Notice that "work" and "righteousness" are parallel. If Kugel is correct that the second line develops the thought expressed in the first line,[4] how might we interpret the development here? The Hebrew word *tsedaqah* is usually translated as "righteousness," but it can also mean justice[5] and acts of deliverance.[6]

---

3. *HALOT*, 3:951.
4. James L. Kugel, *The Idea of Biblical Poetry: Parallelism and Its History* (New Haven: Yale University Press, 1981), 23.
5. *HALOT*, 3:1006; B. Johnson, "צָדַק צֶדֶק צְדָקָה צַדִּיק," *TDOT*, 12:247.
6. Gerhard von Rad, *Old Testament Theology* (New York: Harper, 1962), 372–373. The term, "righteousness and justice," in Psalm 97:2 occurs within the context of a theophany (see v. 2a). Von Rad notes that a "special place where it was appropriate to speak of the righteousness of

It often occurs with the word "justice" (*mishpat*), and together these words refer to actions on behalf of the weak and the vulnerable.[7] The context of Psalm 111 supports this idea. In Psalm 112, the "twin" psalm of Psalm 111, the blessed are those "who conduct their affairs with justice" (112:5) and who give to the "poor" (v. 9a). This act of giving to the poor is described in verse 9b as "their righteousness." These verses establish a clear connection between actions taken for the needy and righteousness.

## 111:4–9 GOD'S WORKS AS MANIFESTATIONS OF HIS GRACE AND COMPASSION

In Psalm 111, the line about "righteousness" is followed by a statement about God's "wondrous works" (v. 4), which refers to the miracles that God performed in Egypt. One should not forget that these wondrous acts were done for slaves, and so, in the next line, the psalmist declares, "The LORD is gracious and compassionate" (v. 4b). The "wondrous works" (ESV) of God are his acts of mercy in response to the people's groaning and cries for help (Exod 2:23–25).

God's mercy is demonstrated through his generosity, specifically his provision of food. To those who are suffering hunger and thirst, the Lord provides satisfaction (107:9b). Even the lions depend on God for their food: "the lions roar for their prey [*teref*] and seek their food from God" (104:21). Psalm 111:5 uses this same Hebrew word for "prey": "He provides food [*teref*] for those who fear him." As *teref* is not the usual word for food, it may have been used for the purpose of the acrostic, or this rather unusual word might have been employed to draw a connection with Psalm 104.

God's generosity is also manifested in the giving of the "lands of other nations" to his people (Ps 111:6). The giving of the land is part of the covenant, which goes back to Abraham. Literally, the "lands" is the "*inheritance* of the nations" (v. 6). For non-Israelites, Gentiles, and especially those of us in Asia who have experienced foreign domination, this verse is not easy to accept. How could God give the lands of other nations to one nation? The next verses describe God's works, which are "faithful and just" (v. 7) and "enacted in

---

Jahweh was in the descriptions of theophanies" (von Rad, 373).
7. Moshe Weinfeld, "'Justice and Righteousness' Mshpt Wtsdqh the Expression and Its Meaning," 237. Dyer points out that justice in the prophets "closely connected to the care for the orphan, widow." Bryan R. Dyer, "Good News to the Poor: Social Upheaval, Strong Warnings, and Sincere Giving in Luke-Acts," in *The Bible and Social Justice*, ed. Cynthia Long Westfall and Bryan R. Dyer, McMaster New Testament Series (Eugene, Oregon: Pickwick Publications, 2016), 69.

faithfulness and uprightness" (v. 8). How can the giving of the lands of other nations to the nation of Israel be just and upright?

Theologically, this is a very difficult question. But if we read these verses contextually, from within the people's experience of slavery in Egypt as well as their experience of exile and colonization (111:9), God's actions are seen to be merciful and compassionate. God's "works" are not to be used as license for oppressing the weak, but as a means of redeeming them and judging their oppressors. As we will see in the next psalm, God expects his people to be "gracious and compassionate and righteous" (112:4) – in other words, just like him (111:4).

## 111:10 THE FEAR OF THE LORD

At the end of the psalm, the people are reminded that the "fear of the LORD is the beginning of wisdom" (v. 10; Prov 1:7). This biblical idea of the "fear of the LORD" is best captured in the story of the Hebrew midwives, Shiphrah and Puah, who were commanded by the king of Egypt to kill every newborn Israelite boy. But the text tells us that they did not obey the command of the king because "they feared God" (Exod 1:17). Murder is a sign of the absence of the fear of God.

The absence of the fear of God is due, in part, to a loss of wonder about God's works, and so it is important to ponder the works of the Lord (v. 2) because we come to know God through his works. But in order to "study" God's works, we also have to fear the Lord. We can develop a fear of the Lord through practice, for "all those who practice it [the fear of the LORD] have a good understanding" (v. 10b, ESV).[8] Psalm 112 provides further insights about what it means to "practice" the fear of God. It is important to note that the fear of the Lord is not the same as horror or dread, but a reverent awe in the presence of the creator God, who is gracious and compassionate. Thus Psalm 111 ends with a note of praise (v. 10c).

---

8. In the MT, the pronominal suffix of the verb "practice" is third person plural (them), but in the LXX it is singular ("it"). The antecedent is clearly the "fear of the LORD," thus, the LXX is here followed.

# PSALM 112

Psalm 112 and Psalm 1 both begin with phrase, "Blessed is the man" (1:1; 112:1, ESV),[1] and end with the word "perish" (1:6; 112:10). The word "blessed" (*'ashre*) begins with the first letter of the Hebrew alphabet, and the word "perish" (*to'bed*) begins with the last letter. Both psalms also emphasize the "law of the LORD" (1:2) and "his commandments" (112:1, ESV). By using the first and last letters of the Hebrew alphabet to form a psalm that focuses on the law, the psalmist is saying that one ought to obey the law from A to Z. This idea is further reinforced by the acrostic form in Psalm 112, for its twenty-two lines follow the twenty-two letters of the Hebrew alphabet. However, Psalm 112 differs from Psalm 1 in the way it integrates devotion to God with love of neighbor, especially the poor (see 112:9 below). Though love for the poor is not excluded as a characteristic of the righteous, it is not highlighted in Psalm 1, which emphasizes meditating on God's law and avoiding associations with the wicked.

As noted in the discussion on Psalm 111, scholars consider Psalm 112 to be a "twin" to Psalm 111. The two psalms follow the same "colon-alphabetic" pattern of the acrostic, which is distinct from "verse line" or "strophic-alphabetic" acrostics.[2] The content of the two psalms is not exactly the same, but some lines are repeated (see 111:3b and 112:3b, 9b; 111:4b and 112:4b). Yet these similarities are not as crucial as the sequence of the psalms. Psalm 112 follows Psalm 111 and seems to be a continuation of its themes. Though it is possible that both psalms were composed by the same hand, it is more likely that Psalm 112 was composed as an interpretation of Psalm 111. Psalm 111 ends with a note about the "fear of the LORD" (111:10), and Psalm 112 begins with a blessing for the "man who fears the LORD" (112:1, ESV). Psalm 111 focuses on the works of the Lord (see vv. 2, 3, 6, 7), and Psalm 112 continues that theme by focusing on the "righteous" human response to God's works and the blessings that flow from living in that way. The lines that are repeated in both psalms all pertain to certain godly attributes – either "righteousness" (111:3b; 112:3b) or being "gracious and compassionate" (111:4b; 112:4b). However, these attributes belong to God in Psalm 111, whereas they are

---

1. The minor difference is the definite article in Psalm 112:1 for "the man"; in Hebrew, it's simply "man."
2. Prinsloo, "Reading Psalm 112 as a 'Midrash' on Psalm 111," 669.

applied to humans in Psalm 112. The call for humans to imitate God's character is reflected in the sequence of these twin psalms.

Both psalms also have "Praise the LORD" in the superscription. This inclusion adds another dimension to the interpretation of Psalm 112. Zenger believes that this "Hallelujah" is part of the redactional composition.[3] Psalm 106 marks the first group of three Hallelujah psalms (Psalms 104–106), followed by the second group (Psalms 111–113), and then the third group (Psalms 115–117).[4] The Hallelujah in the superscription for Psalm 112 subsumes the whole psalm under the command or call to worship the Lord. Similar to Psalm 106, we may assume that the opening verse in Psalm 112 serves as a response to the God who is being worshiped. We are to be like the God we worship. In Psalm 103:6, God is praised as one who "works righteousness and justice for all the oppressed." In Psalm 106, after the psalmist asks, "Who can proclaim the mighty acts of the LORD?" (v. 2), there is the following response: "Blessed ['ashre] are those who act justly, who always do what is right" (v. 3). Just as God works righteousness and justice, so those who worship him ought to practice the same. In Psalm 112, this same sequence is implied through the Hallelujah and the opening verse, which begins with the phrase, "blessed is the man," and is followed by the question, "Who can proclaim the mighty acts of the LORD?" (v. 2). As noted above, the context of the twin psalms highlights the works of the Lord, and the response for both is similar: those who can worship the Lord are those who "fear the LORD" (111:10; 112:1). In this way, Psalm 112 creatively brings together the genre of the hymn with the wisdom psalm. Our worship and manner of living are bound together.

## 112:1–4 THE BLESSEDNESS OF THOSE WHO FEAR THE LORD

The word "blessed" can also be translated as "happy." We all have different ways of defining who is "happy." In today's world, some measure happiness in terms of how much money one has in the bank. Although Psalm 112 does include "wealth and riches" (v. 3), these are not the priority. Rather, happiness is measured by how one responds to God. The person who is "blessed" or "happy" is characterized by a "fear of the LORD" (112:1). To fear the Lord means

---

3. Zenger and Hossfeld, *Psalms 3*, 41.
4. This is followed by "a single psalm (135) framed by Hallelujahs as superscription and subscript, and finally they tie together the last five psalms (146–150) as a group, with each individual psalm framed by Hallelujahs, thus having ten Hallelujahs constituting an ongoing chain (concatenatio)." Zenger and Hossfeld, *Psalms 3*, 39.

obeying God rather than humans (see commentary on Ps 111:10; compare Acts 5:29). Moreover, the person who fears the Lord "greatly delights in his commandments" (112:1b, ESV). Notice that the verb "delight" (*khafetz*) is qualified by the word "greatly" (*me'od*). The noun form of the word "delight" also occurs in Psalm 1 to describe the blessed person: he is one "whose delight [*khefetz*] is in the law of the LORD" (v. 2).

Following the pattern in Psalm 1, Psalm 112 describes the blessedness of those who delight in God's commands – as well as the fate that awaits the wicked. In Psalm 112, however, those who delight in God's commands are given more space (vv. 2–9), and the consequence for the wicked is mentioned only at the end (v. 10). Clearly, the focus is on those who fear the Lord, for "the generation of the upright will be blessed" (v. 2b). In ancient times, having many children was considered to be a great blessing. Psalm 127:5 says, "Blessed is the man whose quiver is full of them,"[5] a verse that is referring to sons, because then there would be more men to defend the father. Psalm 112 says that "the children" of those who fear the Lord "will be mighty in the land" (v. 2).

Psalm 112 also refers to another blessing: "wealth and riches" (v. 3). In Genesis 12, God promises blessing to Abraham (vv. 2–3), and then in the next chapter, Abraham "had become very wealthy in livestock and in silver and gold" (13:2). Though material riches are a part of God's blessings, they are not the most important. Abraham was rich, but he did not allow his wealth to control his life or his heart. He freely gave up even the best part of the land for others (see Gen 13:5–13). In Psalm 112, "wealth and riches" (v. 3a) parallels the blessed person's "righteousness" (v. 3b).

Moreover, those who fear the Lord not only receive the blessings of children and material possessions, but they also serve as a "light" for others (v. 4a), for the light of "those who are gracious and compassionate and righteous" (112:4b) will dawn even in the darkness (v. 4a). The first two descriptions, "gracious and compassionate," were used in Psalm 111 to refer to God (v. 4b). Thus light dawns on those who imitate God. Note the additional description, "righteous," for humans (v. 4b).

---

5. The word *bayit* (house) is mentioned in verse 3 of Psalm 112. Compare Psalm 127:1 which also mentions *bayit*.

## 112:5–9 THOSE WHO FEAR THE LORD AS GRACIOUS AND JUST

Verse 5 begins with the word "good" in both English and Hebrew. This is another key word in the Psalms, which here refers to wellness. This verse continues the theme of light shining even in darkness, for "they will have no fear of bad news" (v. 7) because their hearts are secure (v. 8a), and they are assured of victory over their enemies (v. 8b). All these promises are "good" (v. 5). But the meaning of the word "good" in Psalm 73 is also helpful here, as the psalmist describes God as "good" (73:1). The implied meaning of "good" is similar to the descriptions in Psalm 112:7–8, but the psalmist in Psalm 73 did not experience these "good" things. Rather, as he confronted his struggles in the presence of God, he gained a deeper understanding of the word "good," for by the end of the psalm, he declares that what is good is "to be *near* God" (73:28, my emphasis).

In Psalm 112, it is good to be *like* God. Verse 5 may be translated literally as "Good/blessed is the man who is gracious and who lends [generously]." The word "gracious" (*khahun*) is the same word used in Psalm 111 to describe God ("the LORD is gracious [*khahun*] and compassionate," v. 4b). The blessed person exhibits his graciousness by generously helping those in need. In Psalm 15, one of the requirements for entering God's holy hill is that one "lends money to the poor without interest" (v. 5). Here in Psalm 112, the one who fears the Lord shows his generosity, especially to the most vulnerable. The poor are usually those who have to borrow money, and so they are often the victims of oppression. Yet the blessed person "conducts his affairs with justice" (v. 5b, ESV). Justice is primarily concerned with the poor and needy, and so the righteous person has "freely scattered" and given what he has to them (v. 9). Two verbs are used in verse 9 to describe the actions of the righteous: the usual word for "give" (*natan*) and the Hebrew word *pizzar*, which means "distribute," in the sense of "give abundantly."[6]

## 112:10 THE JUDGMENT OF THE WICKED

The last verse is devoted to the "wicked." This word occurs twice in verse 10, first in the singular and then the plural. Unlike the righteous person, the wicked receives nothing. Having no "good," no "light," nor any of the blessings mentioned above, the wicked can only watch ("The wicked will see,"

---

6. *TDOT*, 11:512.

v. 10a). And as the wicked see the righteous receiving blessings, success, and victory, they get angry, gnash their teeth, and waste away (v. 10b). Thus all of the wicked people's "longings" will "come to nothing" (v. 10c). The word "longing" (*ta'avah*) refers to the wicked's insatiable desires, which lead them to become greedy and to abuse the weak. Unlike the righteous person, who lends freely to the needy, the wicked "not only do not help the poor, but through their recklessness and violence they actually cause poverty; their wealth is the result of deliberate strategies of pauperization."[7] The word "longing" could also mean "plans and desires,"[8] but in any case, all of these "longings" (*ta'avah*) will "come to nothing" (*to'bed*) (v. 10c).[9]

---

7. Zenger and Hossfeld, *Psalms 3*, 175.
8. Zenger and Hossfeld, *Psalms 3*, 175.
9. The double use of the last letter of the Hebrew alphabet in verse 10 is an emphatic way to end an acrostic.

# PSALM 113

Psalm 113 is a hymn of praise, the first of the so-called "Great Hallel Psalms" (Psalms 113–118), which were sung or recited during the three central Jewish festivals (Passover, Pentecost, and Tabernacles), as well as the dedication of the Temple and the New Moon festivals. When Matthew 26:30 says that Jesus and his disciples "sung a hymn" during the Last Supper, it probably refers to these psalms.

The first part of Psalm 113 is an extended call to praise (vv. 1–3). The rest of the psalm provides the motivations for praise (vv. 4–9). For the psalmist, the main reason that God should be praised is not only because he is high and lifted up, but because he sets his eyes on those who are down below from where he is seated in the heavens. He is the God of reversals, raising the "poor from the dust" and lifting up "the needy from the ash heap" (v. 7).

Our motivations for praising God are often reflective of our own situations in life. Those who have experienced situations of poverty, oppression, or subjugation can identify personally with the words of this psalm. The oppressed are drawn to God by this contrast between the high and the lowly, for those who have power do not normally reach down to or look upon those who are down below.

Emphasizing that God is "up there" in the heavens is not a way to stress his distance, but rather a means of highlighting his mercy. Even though he is seated on high, he chooses to stoop down to reach those on earth. Just as God reaches down to the poor and needy, we ought to do the same. The canonical context of Psalms 111–113 supports this idea. Psalm 111 emphasizes the works of God, while Psalm 112 focuses on the human responses to God's work (vv. 5, 9). God is "blessed" because he "works righteousness and justice for all the oppressed" (Ps 103:6), and so those who worship him must imitate him by acting justly and doing "what is right" (Ps 106:3).

## 113:1–3 PRAISE THE LORD

The Hallelujah ("Praise the LORD") at the beginning of Psalm 113 serves as a superscription, connecting it with the preceding "twin" psalms (Psalms 111–112). Together, these three psalms are bound together through this common call to worship: Hallelujah. This canonical arrangement has implications for the interpretation of the psalm (see discussion below).

Those who are commanded to praise the Lord are addressed as "servants of the LORD" (v. 1, ESV).[1] The word "servants" here refers to the worshipers in the Temple, but it may also be interpreted as a reminder of the people's experience of being slaves, since the word "servant" (*'ebed*) can also mean "slave." This is the same word used for "'slaves' in the Exodus context."[2] The emphasis on the reversal of status in verses 7–9 alludes to the experience of slavery. God's action on behalf of the poor and needy (vv. 7–8) and the barren woman (v. 9) transforms the word "servant" so that the worshipers are no longer ashamed to call themselves "*servants* of the LORD."

The "name" of the Lord represents his character, which is manifested in how he treats his people, especially those who belong to the margins. The psalmist exhorts the worshipers to praise his "name . . . both now and forevermore" (v. 2). This is another way of saying, "always," but verse 3 has an even more elegant way of expressing it: "From the rising of the sun to the place where it sets," God is to be praised.

## 113:4–9 WHY THE LORD IS TO BE PRAISED

Like typical hymns, the call to worship is followed by a reason that the Lord should be praised. Verse 4 emphasizes God's exalted position – he is "exalted over *all* the nations" and "above the heavens." The word "exalted" comes from the Hebrew word *rum*, which means "to be high." According to verse 5, he is "seated on high" (ESV). But there is something very different about this God that causes the people to exclaim, "Who is like the LORD our God?" (v. 5a). For *this* God "stoops down to look" (v. 6a) upon those who are down below.

Though the Lord is enthroned in the heavens (Ps 103:19) and dwells among the cherubim (Ps 80:1), he hears "the groans of the prisoners" (Ps 102:20). Moreover, he not only hears and looks down, but he actually does something for those who are down below: he "raises the poor from the dust and lifts the needy from the ash heap" (Ps 113:7). The word "lifts" (v. 7b) comes from the same Hebrew word (*rum*), which is translated as "exalted" in verse 4. The "exalted" (*rum*) Lord raises (*rum*) the poor.

---

1. Literally, the Hebrew reads, "Praise the servants of the LORD." But this is obviously not what the text is saying, so translators render the "servants" as vocative, "O servants of the LORD, praise him."
2. Jeremy Schonfield, "Psalms 113–118: Qualified Praise," *European Judaism* 50, no. 2 (2017): 153.

Verse 7 uses two different words for "poor" – *dal* and *'ebyon*. *Dal* can mean "helpless,"³ whereas *'ebyon* is usually translated as "needy." Like many poor people today, the "helpless" and the "needy" not only lack material resources but also social status. They are without rights or influence and are always at the mercy of the powerful.⁴ Two of the five occurrences of the word *dal* in the Psalms pertain to experiences of injustice (Ps 82:3–4).⁵ According to Psalm 37:14, the "needy" (*ebyon*) often fall prey to killings. Moreover, they are exposed to hunger (Ps 132:15).⁶

In Psalm 113, the psalmist praises Yahweh because he restores human dignity to the poor and needy. In order to do so, verse 7 implies that God not only *looks* down from heaven, but he also *goes* down to the poor. In order to raise someone "from the dust" and lift him "from the ash heap," one has to stoop down, make oneself low. The Hebrew word for "stoops down" (v. 6) is *shafel*, which means "to be low, abased." Indeed, for Christians, this verse reminds us of what our Lord has done. As the Apostle Paul says, "though he was rich, yet for your sake he became poor, so that you through his poverty might become rich" (2 Cor 8:9).

Those who are in the dust and ash heap are far from situations of dignity and honor. In verse 5b, the psalmist says that God is "seated [*yashab*] on high." In verse 8, the psalmist declares that God "seats" (*yashab*) the poor and needy "with princes." As I write this, many poor Filipino drug users continue to be killed in Duterte's so-called "war on drugs," even in the midst of the pandemic. Yet the majority of our people find it hard to sympathize with the drug users, because the rich and powerful describe them as garbage (*salot sa lipunan*).⁷ This psalm reminds us of how God sees every human being. We are all created in the image of God. The word for "image" was used in ancient times to refer to kings, but "the OT has democratized this old idea. It affirms that not just the king, but every man and woman, bears God's image and is his representative on earth."⁸

---

3. *HALOT*, 1:221.
4. Alec Basson, "Two Instances of Mundus Inversus in Psalm 113," *Verbum et Ecclesia* 30, no. 1 (2009): 3.
5. The other occurrences are in Psalms 72:13; 113:7; 41:2 (*ADB* 5:406).
6. *ADB* 5:403
7. This is how someone described drug users: "We don't condone summary killings, but we want society to be cleansed of its scum. These people are garbage and, just like any garbage, you have to dispose of them." Nathan Gilbert Quimpo, "Duterte's 'War on Drugs': The Secularization of Illegal Drugs and the Return of National Boss Rule," in *The Duterte Reader: Critical Essays on Rodrigo Duterte's Early Presidency*, ed. Nicole Curato (Manila, Philippines: Bughaw, 2017), 155.
8. Gordon J. Wenham, *Genesis 1–15* (Waco, TX: Word Books, 1987), 30–31.

God not only restores the dignity of the poor and needy, but also the "childless woman" (v. 9). In ancient times, having children was an important sign of social status. "Childlessness . . . was a disgrace."[9] Being barren also has economic implications in agricultural societies that depend on human labor, where the birth of a child, especially males, enables more work to be done.[10] In such societies, barren women experience shame and uselessness, as we see in the story of Hannah (1 Samuel 1–2). Indeed, the composer of Psalm 113 most likely drew from the story of Hannah, as verses 6–8 are almost identical with lines from Hannah's prayer (1 Sam 2:7–8).

In verse 9, the word "sit" is repeated for the third time in Psalm 113. God, who is "seated" on high, not only "seats" the poor and needy with princes (v. 8), but he also "settles the childless woman in her home" (v. 9). The verb "settles" also comes from the verb *yashab* ("to sit"); literally, this verse can be translated, "God causes the childless woman to sit in her home." Thus the final "Hallelujah" at the end of this psalm is most appropriate!

---

9. Artur Weiser, *The Psalms. A Commentary*, trans. Herbert Hartwell (SCM Press: London, 1962), 708.
10. Basson, "Two Instances of Mundus Inversus in Psalm 113," 4.

# PSALM 114

The opening verse of Psalm 114 reminds us of our experience of colonization in the Philippines: "When Israel came out of Egypt, Jacob from a people of foreign tongue" (v. 1). Like the Israelites, Filipinos were under the Spaniards for a long time – more than three hundred years (1521–1898).[1] We, too, were exposed to a "foreign tongue" (Spanish). Some scholars find it strange that the psalm mentions "foreign tongue" instead of "slavery," which is the primary association for the Israelites' life in Egypt. But those of us who have lived under foreign rulers know how the "foreign tongue" has been a means of subjugation. Zenger points out that "the use of foreign tongues by political enemies intensifies their enmity and life-threatening character, not only because it excludes mutual understanding but also because political enemies and especially military occupiers usually threaten and taunt in their foreign language."[2] In our case, the Spaniards made sure that their language remained "foreign" to us as a means of controlling and dehumanizing us. They thought that if we learned Spanish, we would be able to argue with them – and since they thought we were lower in intelligence and incapable of learning anyway, they didn't bother to teach us in the first place. Let us remain *indios*, which was what they called us – a word that is very close to "idiot."

Psalm 114 is relevant to our situation. As we discussed previously, one of the main themes of Psalm 113 is the God of reversals, who "raises the poor from the dust and lifts the needy from the ash heap" and then "seats them with princes" (vv. 7–8). Psalm 114 continues this theme, declaring that God "turned the rock into a pool, the hard rock into springs of water" (v. 8).

The majority of scholars consider Psalm 114 to be a hymn, though the only characteristic of this genre is the closing description of God as one "who turned the rock into a pool . . ." (v. 8). This declaration is similar to the series of participles in Psalm 103, but Psalm 114 does not open with a call to worship. Though the exhortation in verse 7 that invokes the "earth" to "tremble at the presence of the Lord" implies a call to worship, the only explicit connection to the hymn genre is the psalm's canonical context. As noted above, Psalm 114 is usually read, along with Psalm 113, as the second of the so-called

---

1. There were some debates as to how long exactly were the Israelites in Egypt. This question "has been the subject of considerable interpretation," Durham, *Exodus*, 172. What we do know was that their life there was one of great suffering.
2. Zenger and Hossfeld, *Psalms 3*, 194.

"Great Hallel Psalms" (Psalms 113–118). In this light, we may consider the "Hallelujah" and subsequent call to worship at the beginning of Psalm 113 as being carried into Psalm 114.

## 114:1–2 "WHEN ISRAEL CAME OUT OF EGYPT"

Psalm 114 relates the Exodus event, which is why it is also known as the Egyptian Hallel. Verse 1 begins with the Exodus event: "When Israel came out of Egypt." However, there are two differences between this event as it is related in Psalm 114 and the Exodus narrative itself. First, God is not mentioned in verse 1. In fact, the title "God" only appears in verse 7. In verse 2, the Hebrew does not say "God's sanctuary," but simply, "his sanctuary." This does not mean, of course, that God was not actively involved in the whole process of the Israelites being delivered from Egypt and settled in the Promised Land. The context of the preceding psalm also makes it clear that, for the original readers, God is clearly present. But the literary construction of Psalm 114 creates space for the agency of the people – though God brought them out of Egypt, *they* "*came* out of Egypt" (v. 1).

Second, Israel's experience in Egypt is normally associated with slavery, but this is not mentioned in verse 1. Instead, as discussed above, there is the phrase, "foreign tongue," which only occurs here in the Hebrew Bible. What does this phrase imply about the people's experience? As we noted above, "foreign language" signifies subjugation, and so one of the reasons that the Spaniards did not teach Filipinos Spanish was to maintain control over us. It also reflected their view that we were less capable of engaging at their intellectual level. In the OT, being with people who speak a different language is part of God's judgment upon his people (see Deut 28:49; Isa 28:11; Isa 33 [esp. v. 19]; Jer 5:15). As Bosman observes, "It seems to be a frequent characteristic of judgments against Israel and Judah that it entails being confronted by a strange language they did not comprehend. The reference to being exposed to such a strange and incomprehensible language forms part of a stereotypical depiction of an oppressive and threatening foreign nation."[3]

The word "foreign language" also highlights the people's sense of homelessness. For many generations, the people were without a home that they could call their own as they lived in a foreign land under taskmasters who oppressed them. But now, after Israel "went out" of Egypt, they became "his sanctuary"

---

3. H. L. Bosman, "Psalm 114 as Reinterpretation of the Exodus During and After the Exile," *OTE* 26, no. 3 (2013): 577.

(v. 2). The word "sanctuary" is literally used to refer to the Jerusalem temple, God's sanctuary (Pss 63:2; 74:3), but here, the text is referring to "Judah." For after coming out of Egypt, "Judah became God's sanctuary" (114:2). By identifying the community of Israel as the sanctuary of God, the psalm conveys that the homeless people have themselves become a home. In our case, the arrival of Christianity in the Philippines through colonization has made us homeless in our own land, but many Filipinos have welcomed Christ – and so, for many Filipinos, the symbol of the cross reminds us that Jesus is one with our suffering under our colonizers. Thus Christ is our home amidst our ravaged cities and broken homes.

God's plan is not only for Israel to be his sanctuary, but also "his dominion" (114:2, ESV). Israel as a nation is to become the place from which God's rule will flow throughout the earth. The word "dominion" has political connotations, with a focus on the manner in which a ruler reigns.[4] To be ruled by a God who is like Yahweh is a great blessing (Ps 33:12) and a matter for praise (compare 113:5).

### 114:3–4 "THE SEA LOOKED AND FLED"

We may say that verses 1–2 provide a summary of the journey from Egypt (v. 1) to the ideal situation in the Promised Land (v. 2),[5] and then verses 3–4 describe how they got there, using language that borrows from ancient myths about creation and the subjugation of the sea.[6] Coming out of Egypt, the people encountered the sea, which in ancient mythology represented the forces of chaos. In the Babylonian epic, Marduk must defeat Tiamat, the sea monster, before he can create the world. For the people of Israel, subjugation did not stop once they were out of Egypt, as they had to defeat another monster – and to overcome it, they needed a power beyond their own, just as they did in Egypt. Another noticeable feature of verses 3–4 is the way they personify the creation: "The sea looked and fled, the Jordan turned back. The mountains leaped like rams, the hills like lambs." Though the text does not explicitly mention what or who the sea and the Jordan saw that made them flee, the internal reader knows that they saw the One who claimed Judah for himself

---

4. Zenger combines "sanctuary" and "dominion,"–"sanctuary of his dominion," with the sanctuary understood as the place "from which the God-king exercises his dominion." Zenger and Hossfeld, *Psalms 3*, 195.
5. Archibald van Wieringen, "Two Reading Options in Psalm 114: A Communication-Oriented Exegesis," *RB* 122, no. 1 (2015): 51.
6. Gerstenberger, *Psalms Part 2 and Lamentations*, 282.

as his sanctuary and dominion. In verse 4, after the sea gives way for Israel to pass, the mountains and the hills yield to the will of the great deliverer.[7] Both these verses are set in the past tense.[8]

### 114:5–6 "WHY WAS IT, SEA, THAT YOU FLED?"

In verses 5–6, these same elements of creation (sea, Jordan, mountains, and hills) are interrogated by the poet: "Why was it, sea, that you fled?" (v. 5a). All four characters in the previous verses are addressed directly. Obviously, the poet is not seeking information by asking these rhetorical questions. Wieringen explains that the questions "can best be read as refreshing the knowledge that the text-internal reader already has."[9] But the tone of the verses is closer to lament than a simple reminder. Thus the psalm could be read from a situation of trouble, as the people are confronted once again with a similar struggle to the one they encountered when they came out of Egypt. By asking these questions, the poet is confronting this troublesome situation, asserting his confidence in God's deliverance based on the community of Israel's previous experience. Note that the verb "looked" (*ra'ah*, "to see"), which is used in verses 3–4, is missing in verses 5–6. Something that the elements *saw* caused them to flee: and the obvious implication is that they saw the Lord.

### 114:7–8 "TREMBLE, EARTH, AT THE PRESENCE OF THE LORD"

Thus the psalmist can confidently say to the "earth," which represents all of creation – including the sea, river, hills, and mountains that are mentioned in the previous verses – "tremble . . . at the presence of the LORD" (v. 7). The word "presence" is repeated twice in verse 7. Because the sea and the Jordan saw the "presence" of the Lord, they fled.

The psalm does not mention the people's troubling situation, but they have confidence that they will be able to endure because the God of reversals, who delivered them from Egypt and sits the poor with princes, is the same God who turns "the rock into a pool, the hard rock into springs of water" (v. 8). This verse is not merely an allusion to the incident in Exodus 17, when God instructs Moses to strike the rock at Horeb, and he will make water come out

---

7. For the translation of the verb *raqad* ("leaped") into "yield," see Wieringen, "Two Reading Options in Psalm 114: A Communication-Oriented Exegesis," 52, n. 22.
8. See the *qatal* and the *wayyiqtol* in verse 3.
9. Wieringen, "Two Reading Options in Psalm 114: A Communication-Oriented Exegesis," 54.

of it so that the people can quench their thirst (v. 6); nor to the incident in Numbers 20, when God instructs Moses to command the rock at Meribah to yield water (vv. 8–11). Rather, in Psalm 114, God is turning the rock into a pool – and his "presence" is performing this miracle, not Moses.[10] What gives us hope in the midst of our continuing struggles for freedom, justice, and *shalom* is the confident conviction that the presence of this same God of reversals continues to be with us.

---

10. Wieringen, "Two Reading Options in Psalm 114: A Communication-Oriented Exegesis," 56.

# PSALM 115

Psalm 115 is one of the so-called, "Great Hallel Psalms" (Psalms 113–118). Praise arises out of the depths and Psalm 115 reflects the struggles of the community to maintain their faith in God amidst the many tragedies that beset them. The people around them taunt them by asking, "Where is their God?" (v. 2). Scholars associate this psalm with a "crisis of belief," and so it has been described as a psalm for a "perilous situation."[1] Allen believes that the psalm was originally a liturgical communal lament, with the accent shifting to praise when it was incorporated into the Psalter. Though it is no longer easy to classify in terms of genre, Psalm 115 contains some of the elements of a communal lament, including the petition (v. 1), the complaint (v. 2), and the declaration of trust (vv. 3, 17–18).

As with some other lament psalms (e.g. Psalms 77, 108), the community persists in faith amidst many challenges and temptations. In this way, the psalm testifies to the people's robust faith as they seek to make sense of Yahweh's apparent absence. Their belief in the God who continues to "remember" them carries them through their desert experience. The emphasis on blessing (vv. 12–15) highlights their continuing faith in the God who is powerful and able to help them in their trouble.

## 115:1–3 LAMENT OF THE COMMUNITY

The opening words of the psalm in the NIV – "Not to us, LORD . . . but to your name be the glory" (v. 1) – suggests that the text is saying that glory should be given to God, not the people. The Hebrew, however, contains a different nuance. Literally, it says, "*give* glory to your name." Unfortunately, the verb "give" was lost in translation. Moreover, the preposition that is translated "to" can also mean "for" in the Hebrew. Thus verse 1 can be translated, "Not for us, LORD, not for us, but for your name, give glory." Like the petition, "hallowed be your name," in the Lord's Prayer, the people are pleading with God to work in their midst[2] – not for their own sake, but for the sake of God's glory: "for the sake of your steadfast love and your faithfulness" (v. 1b, ESV).

---

1. Reuven Hammer, "Two Liturgical Psalms: Salvation and Thanksgiving," *Judaism* 40, no. 4 (1991): 485.
2. Hammer, "Two Liturgical Psalms: Salvation and Thanksgiving," 485.

The psalm does not tell us about the difficult situation that the people are facing, but from verse 2, we can glean that other people are trying to shame them by taunting, "Where is their God?" As noted previously, shame was a huge concern among ancient people – and this is still true among Asian cultures today. The prayer of Moses in Exodus 32 envisages a similar situation. After God decides to destroy the people, Moses expresses his concern, arguing that if God destroys his people after saving them, it will diminish God's own glory, because the surrounding nations will think that God only delivered the people from Egypt to "kill them in the mountains and to wipe them off the face of the earth" (Exod 32:12a). So Moses pleads with God to "relent" and "not bring disaster" on the people (v. 12b). In Psalm 115, however, there is no explicit response from God. Instead, there is an assertion of faith: "*But our God is in heaven*" (Ps 115:3, my translation). The majority of modern English translations (e.g. NIV, ESV) do not include the conjunction *waw*, which can be translated as "and" or "but." Even some of the major commentaries don't mention it.[3] However, I think this conjunction is important and has an adversative sense, "but."

Scholars believe that Psalm 115 arose during the time of the exilic/postexilic period. If this is true, then the nations around them would have naturally ridiculed them by saying, "where is their God?" The people might have doubted as well, wondering whether God was still at work in their midst.[4] In response to the taunting of the nations as well as the temptation to doubt, the people in Psalm 115 assert, "*But* our God is in heaven" (v. 3a, my translation). The second part of verse 3 emphasizes the God who takes action: "he does whatever pleases him" (v. 3b). The words, "he does," come from the Hebrew word *'asah*, which means "to make, to do." The emphasis is not only on God's action, but on the freedom God has to do anything that he wills. The statement, "He does whatever pleases him" (v. 3b), "denotes the unlimited power of the supreme authority,"[5] which opens up the possibility that God's apparent inaction in the present does not mean that God is absent. God is still doing something, even when the nations – and the people themselves – may not see any evidence of God's action.

---

3. E.g. Allen, *Psalms 101–150*.
4. Zenger and Hossfeld note that scholars associate the psalm with the "crisis of belief" brought about by the exile/postexilic. Zenger and Hossfeld, *Psalms 3*, 203.
5. Avi Hurvitz, "The History of a Legal Formula: Kōl 'ašer-Hāpēs 'āśāh (Psalm 115:3; 135:6)," *VT* 32, no. 3 (1982): 257.

# Psalm 115

## 115:4–8 THE LIVING GOD AND THE IDOLS

These verses convey that the God of the Israelites is unlike the idols of the other nations. The idols are "made [*'asah*] by human hands" (v. 4). The verb "made" here is the same word that is translated as "he does" (*'asah*) in the previous verse. Whereas God "makes," the idols are "made." The idols cannot speak, though they have mouths (v. 5a). Speech is very important for worshipers, since they needed to hear what their deity is saying. Moreover, the idols have "eyes, but cannot see" (v. 5b), and they have "ears, but cannot hear" (v. 6a). The deity's ability to see and to hear are particularly important in times of crisis. In the midst of the people's lament, they had one desire: for God to look down from heaven (Lam 3:50). And when they cried out to the Lord, they testified that he "heard their groaning" and "saw" them (Exod 2:23–25). In verse 6b, the deity's inability to smell is linked to the sacrifice of burnt offerings. After the flood, Noah sacrificed a burnt offering to God, and "the Lord smelled the pleasing aroma" (Gen 8:20–21). But if an idol cannot smell the sacrifices made by the people of other nations, then how can the deity be pleased?

The idols do not have the different senses of a living being, as they cannot speak, hear, smell, nor feel. For as verse 7a says, "They have hands, but cannot feel" (v. 7a). Moreover, though they have feet, they are unable to walk (v. 7b). Finally, they cannot "utter a sound with their throat" (v. 7c), which could mean that they can't breathe. In short, there is no life in them. By comparing those who make these idols to the idols themselves, the psalmist is saying that the makers are "lifeless" or dead, as well (v. 8). At the end of the psalm, the psalmist contrasts these "dead" worshipers ("it is not the dead . . .") with the people of Israel, ". . . who praise the Lord" (v. 17).

## 115:9–16 EXHORTATION TO TRUST AND PETITION FOR BLESSING

In light of this emphasis on God as the one who "makes" or "acts" in contrast to the idols, who are incapable of action, the psalmist exhorts the people to "trust in the Lord" (vv. 9–11). This exhortation to trust in Yahweh implies that the people might be asking where their God is, just as the nations have been taunting (see Isa 63:11, 15).

Yet the psalmist encourages the people by saying that "the Lord remembers us" (v. 12). God's remembrance often occurs amidst situations of trouble (see Gen 8:1; 18:29), and to "remember" means to act. Thus after God remembered Noah and all the wild animals in Genesis 8, the flood waters started to recede (vv. 1–3). In Psalm 115, the promise of blessing follows God's remembering (v. 12). The word "bless" is repeated four times in verses 12–13.[6] Verse 13 says that God "will bless those who fear the Lord – small and great alike." The hope in verse 14 for the Lord to "give you increase" (ESV) conveys the people's identification with those who are "small." To be "blessed" is to experience increase, abundance, prosperity, and so the people pray: "May you be blessed by the Lord, the Maker of heaven and earth" (v. 15a). The word "Maker" comes from the same Hebrew verb for "to do, to make" (*'asah*) used earlier in (vv. 3–4). Verse 16 elaborates on the heaven and the earth that God made. Earlier, the psalmist declares that "God is in heaven" (v. 3), but here the psalmist declares that because God made the heavens and the earth, both belong to him (v. 16). For "the highest heavens belong to the Lord" (v. 16a),[7] and the earth is his as well and so he can give it to humankind (v. 16b). This verse conveys God's great generosity (see also Ps 104:27), reminding us how wonderful it is to be alive – and to be generous at the same time!

## 115:17–18 WORSHIPERS OF THE LIVING GOD

The last two verses recall the opening verse of the psalm through the repetition of the particle of negation, "not." In Hebrew, the first word in verses 1 and 17 is "not," which is repeated twice in both verses. These closing verses reveal that in verse 1, the petitioners were asking God to give or sustain their life. The statement, "It is not the dead who praise the Lord," is an implicit petition, asking God to bring life to their existence, for only those who are alive can worship the Lord (see Ps 88:10–12). Thus in the following psalm, the "death" of God's servants is "precious" (see comments in Ps 116:15). In the final verse of Psalm 115, the people declare that they will "bless the Lord" (v. 18), affirming their trust that the God whom they worship is alive, powerful, and gracious.

---

6. For a psalm with a similar emphasis on bless/blessing, see Psalm 67.
7. Literally, the MT reads, "The heaven is heaven to Yahweh." The LXX has the reading, "the heaven of heaven belongs to the Lord."

# PSALM 116

The previous psalm asserts that "it is not the dead who praise the LORD" (115:17), but those who are alive. In Psalm 116, the psalmist feels overwhelmed by the goodness of God for delivering him from death. The word "death" is mentioned three times in Psalm 116 (vv. 3, 8, 15). Because of the poetic nature of the language in this psalm, we cannot infer much about the psalmist's particular situation, but it is clear that he has faced death and experienced God's gracious deliverance. For this, the psalmist offers thanks.

Though the psalm is an individual thanksgiving psalm, Allen points out that it also contains elements of lament.[1] Rather than moving from lament to thanksgiving, however, Psalm 116 alternates between the two. Whereas some individual lament psalms alternate between lament and thanksgiving (e.g. Psalms 27, 31, 35),[2] Psalm 116 alternates between thanksgiving and lament:

Thanksgiving (vv. 1–6),
Recollection of past distress (vv. 7–11),
Thanksgiving (vv. 12–14),
Situation of lament (vv. 15–16b),
Answer and vow of thanksgiving (v. 16c–19).

This rather untidy movement has led some scholars to regard the psalm as having "no order,"[3] but this form-critical perspective is confined to a one-sided understanding, where thanksgiving is completely separate from lament. We encounter the same problem with the form-critical understanding of lament, which only allows for a one-way movement from lament to praise/thanksgiving as the determining factor for this genre. Thus, for example, when Gunkel sees a thanksgiving psalm moving to lament (e.g. Psalms 9–10), he resorts to exegetical surgery.[4]

One interpretive framework that can help us make sense of the non-linear structure of Psalm 116 is to acknowledge the presence of both thanksgiving and lament in the psalm. Whereas the thanksgiving highlights divine agency, the situation of lament brings out the important role of human agency. Prinsloo rightly observes the prominence of the name of Yahweh as well as

---

1. Allen identifies the following verses as the situation of lament to which the psalmist looks back: verses 3, 10, 11, 16a. Allen, *Psalms 101–150*, 152.
2. Villanueva, *The "Uncertainty of a Hearing,"* 163–185.
3. Hermann Gunkel, *Die Psalmen* (Göttingen: Vandenhoeck & Ruprecht, 1926), 500.
4. Villanueva, "From Thanksgiving to Lament: The Shape of Psalm 120," 482.

the "dominant occurrence of the first person singular" in Psalm 116,[5] which identifies Yahweh and the petitioner as "the two most important actants in the psalm."[6] Building on this point, I argue that the use of the personal pronoun highlights the importance of human agency. In thanksgiving psalms, there can be a tendency to focus on the work of Yahweh alone. As will be seen below, the petitioner plays a crucial role as well.

## 116:1–6 THANKSGIVING

"I love," is the first in a series of first-person subject-predicate clauses in Psalm 116. Indeed, one feature of this psalm is "the dominant occurrence of the first person singular,"[7] which highlights human agency. We encounter the next first-person clause in verse 2b, "I will call." While we tend to think of thanksgiving as focused on God as the object of the thanksgiving, Psalm 116 highlights the important role of the individual who is formulating the thanksgiving. We see this in the chiastic structure of verses 1–2, as outlined below:

"I love the LORD,[8] (A)
   for he heard my cry . . ." (v. 1). (B)
   "Because he turned his ear to me, (B')
I will call on him as long as I live" (v. 2). (A')

In this structure, we see the interplay between divine action ("he heard" and "he turned his ear") and human response ("I love" and "I will call"). Even in the testimony part of the thanksgiving (vv. 3–4), the role of the individual is advanced.

Verses 3–4 represent the core feature of the thanksgiving psalm, which is the testimony of the psalmist[9] – the danger he endured and how the Lord delivered him. Jonah 2:3 is a classic example: "In my distress I called on the LORD, and he answered me" (see also Psalm 120 below). Psalm 116 is unique in that the psalmist supplies us with the content of his prayer: "LORD, save

---

5. The name Yahweh appears "no less than 15 times" (vv. 1, 4 [2x], 5, 6, 7, 9, 12, 13, 14, 15, 16a, 17, 18, 19; יָהּ [Yah] in 19b). The personal pronoun, "I" occurs "in pairs" in verses 10, 11 and v. 16a and v. 16b. Willem S. Prinsloo, "Psalm 116: Disconnected Text or Symmetrical Whole?," *Bib* 74, no. 1 (1993): 74.
6. Prinsloo, "Psalm 116: Disconnected Text or Symmetrical Whole?," 74.
7. Prinsloo, "Psalm 116: Disconnected Text or Symmetrical Whole?," 74.
8. Here I follow the translation of the NIV, but please note that in the original "the LORD" is only implied (see above).
9. Westermann, *Praise and Lament in the Psalms*, 106–108.

me!" (v. 4b). He not only wants his audience to know that he "called on the name of the Lord" (v. 4a), but he also wants them to hear his cry for help! This prayer inserts the human agent into the narrative about God's action. We know from the history of Israel that the people always cried out to God before they experienced his deliverance (see Ps 107:6, 13, 19; Exod 2:23–25).

Yet not everyone who cries out to God receives a response, and so laments cry out, "how long?" (e.g. Psalm 13) and "why?" (e.g. Ps 22:1). When God's deliverance finally comes, the person who has been crying out to God is filled with an overwhelming sense of divine compassion. We can sense this in the words of the psalmist as he declares, "The Lord is gracious . . . our God is full of compassion" (116:5).

Between the psalmist's declaration about God's nature in verse 5, however, and his cry for help in verse 4, there is a "gap" that needs to be filled, for nothing has been mentioned about God answering his prayer. Of course, we know from the preceding context (vv. 1–2) that the Lord has "heard," and so we can fill in the "gap" created by this sudden transition from the cry in verse 4 to the confession in verse 5. Those who have experienced God's salvation breaking through the darkness of the night know how it feels to utter the words of relief and gratitude in verse 5: "The Lord is gracious . . ." Sometimes, our prayers of gratitude are accompanied by tears of joy, especially as we remember the painful situation of suffering into which God has intervened.

In verse 6a, the psalmist describes himself as "simple" (ESV), which comes from the Hebrew word *peti* ("simple," "naïve," or "unwary," as in the NIV). We know that the psalmist is referring to himself, as he recalls in verse 6b that "when I was brought low, he saved me." The phrase "brought low" is a metaphor for his previous experience of distress.[10] Earlier, the psalmist describes his experience using the words "death" and "grave" (Sheol) as he laments, "I was overcome by distress and sorrow" (v. 3).

## 116:7–11 RECOLLECTION OF PAST DISTRESS

Having experienced God's gracious and compassionate response, the psalmist feels overwhelmed. While suffering can be extremely stressful, experiences of healing and deliverance can also bring their own stressors. Thus even after the Lord hears his prayer, the psalmist has to remind his soul to "Return to your rest" (v. 7a). This verse confirms the active role that a recipient of divine grace

---

10. *BDB*, 195.

has to play. After exhorting himself to rest (v. 7a), the psalmist assures himself that "the LORD has dealt bountifully with you" (v. 7b, ESV). In verse 8, the psalmist addresses God directly, as if reminding himself (as well as God) about what God has done for him: "For you, LORD, have delivered me from death, my eyes from tears, my feet from stumbling." In this statement, the psalmist affirms that Yahweh is the one who heard him and delivered him when he cried for help (see v. 4b).

Verse 9 further confirms the active role of the recipient of divine grace with another first-person declaration. While the Lord delivered "my feet from stumbling" (v. 8), the psalmist declares, "I will walk before the LORD" (v. 9a, ESV; compare vv. 1a, 2b). This act of walking is the counterpart to God's deliverance. Walking before the Lord means being "in the land of the living," or simply, staying alive (v. 9b). But the LXX adds an ethical dimension, for the Greek translation has, "I will be pleasing before the LORD."

After making several first-person declarations in the previous verses – "I love" (v. 1), "I will call" (v. 2), "I will walk" (v. 9) – the psalmist now says, "I believed" (v. 10, ESV). The Hebrew verb can also be translated in the present tense as, "I believe."[11] Recalling his past experience of lament, the psalmist continues to "believe, even when I spoke: 'I am greatly afflicted'" (v. 10, ESV). The word "even" (*ki*) can also be translated as, "because," "though," "even," or "for." The preceding context supports the concessive reading of the particle, "even," for in spite of his situation, he continues to trust in the Lord. Verse 11 continues this meaning for the particle *ki* ("even though"), as he continues to believe *even* when he felt that "Everyone is a liar" (v. 11).

## 116:12–14 THANKSGIVING

There is another sudden transition from verse 11 to verse 12 (see also vv. 4–5 above). Verse 11 ends with a bitter realization, "Everyone is a liar," which is followed by an exclamation of gratitude: "What shall I return to the LORD for all his goodness to me?" (v. 12). The word "return" recalls verse 7, where the psalmist enjoins himself to "return to your rest." We now sense that the psalmist has "returned," and so he can reflect on how he can "return" to the Lord because of all that God has done for him (v. 12). In Filipino, we would describe this verse using the term *utang na loob* (literally, "debt of inside"), which the recipient incurs after receiving something that makes him or her feel grateful.

---

11. Zenger and Hossfeld, *Psalms 3*, 213.

In response to this sense of *utang na loob*, the recipient will give something to the giver in return for what he or she has given. In the Old Testament, this *utang na loob* can come in the form of a thanksgiving offering (*todah*) (v. 14).

By comparing verse 4 with verse 13, we can see how the order of the psalmist's cry to the Lord for salvation is reversed:

"I called on the name of the Lord" (v. 4a):
"'Lord, save me!'" (v. 4b).
". . . cup of salvation" (v. 13a),
"[I will] call on the name of the Lord" (v. 13b).

The cup of salvation (v. 13a) refers to the deliverance that the psalmist experienced after he "called on the name of the Lord" (v. 4b). The sentence, "I called/call on the name of the Lord" (vv. 4 and 13) is exactly the same in Hebrew, but their respective contexts suggest that their meanings are different. The first is a cry for help (v. 4a), and so the second should be some kind of a praiseful thanksgiving (v. 13b). Yet it could also be an expression of the psalmist's continuing commitment to "call on the Lord," similar to his earlier promise to "call on him as long as I live" (v. 2b). Receiving the answer to our prayer is not the end of our calling on the Lord (compare Ps 28:9, where the psalmist's reception of an answer leads to another petition).

## 116:15–16B SITUATION OF LAMENT

Verse 14 is repeated again in verse 18, which is part of the final section (vv. 16c–19). If the psalm had proceeded directly to this section, it would have formed a great climax. Instead, the psalmist mentions "death" again in verse 15. Barré considers this to be "one of the strangest passages in the Psalter,"[12] because a literal translation of the verse would be, "that Yahweh wants his saints to die, that their death brings him pleasure – which is, of course, preposterous."[13] One problem with preserving the word "death" is that the psalmist never views death as something positive (see v. 3). Psalm 115 is very clear that "It is not the dead who praise the Lord" (v. 17; compare Ps 88:10–12). Thus Barré advances the proposal that the word we have in Psalm 115 is not the Hebrew word for "death," but the word "faith/trust."[14] But his argument is problematic, for as Prinsloo points out, it is based on "extratextual

---

12. Michael L. Barré, "Psalm 116: Its Structure and Its Enigmas," *JBL* 109, no. 1 (1990): 61.
13. Barré, "Psalm 116: Its Structure and Its Enigmas," 71.
14. Barré, "Psalm 116: Its Structure and Its Enigmas," 72.

evidence," and the word "death" is a key word in this psalm (see vv. 3, 8).[15] Instead, Prinsloo maintains the word "death," but suggests reading the word *yaqar* as "a serious matter" rather than "precious," as is commonly understood. This is in line with Emerton's proposal, which reads *yaqar* as "grievous."[16]

I think this interpretation is supported by the context. Specifically, this reading would make the petition in the following verse more sensible: "O LORD, I am your servant" (v. 16a, my translation). As Gunkel rightly observes, verse 16a is similar to the petition in verse 4b. In Hebrew, both begin with the word *'annah*, which is a particle of entreaty – "ah now! I (we) beseech thee!"[17] Or, "oh, please."[18] This particle is used a number of times in the context of prayer (see 2 Kgs 20:3; Isa 38:3; Jonah 1:14; 4:2; Ps 118:25; Neh 1:5). After telling God that "the death of his faithful servants" are grievous in his sight (v. 15), the psalmist cries out, "O LORD, I am your servant; I am your servant, the son of your maidservant" (v. 16ab, ESV). The Hebrew reading in the MT communicates a logical connection between verses 15 and 16 by using the preposition "for" (*ki*). Literally, verse 16a reads, "Oh, please, LORD! For I am your servant." Similar to the "gap" between verses 4–5, there is a "gap" that needs to be filled between the words "LORD" and "For" in verse 16a. Verse 15 helps to fill this gap: since the death of God's servants is "grievous" to God, the implied petition is that God would not allow the psalmist to die, because he, too, is God's servant.

## 116:16C–19 ANSWER AND VOW OF THANKSGIVING

Verse 16c testifies to the psalmist's experience of a direct response from God: "you have freed me from my chains." This verse marks the third sudden change of mood in the psalm. The first comes in verse 5, after the psalmist's cry for help in verse 4b; the second comes in verse 12, after the psalmist's bitter lament in verse 11 ("Everyone is a liar"). In both of these shifts, there is no explicit response from God, just the implied outcome of his response in light of the psalmist's subsequent hymn (v. 5) and expression of thanksgiving (v. 12). In

---

15. Prinsloo, "Psalm 116: Disconnected Text or Symmetrical Whole?," 81.
16. Prinsloo, "Psalm 116: Disconnected Text or Symmetrical Whole?," 81. John A. Emerton, "How Does the Lord Regard the Death of His Saints in Psalm 116:15," *JTS* 34, no. 1 (1983): 155.
17. *BDB*, 58. Its alternate form is *'nna.'*
18. William Lee Holladay and Ludwig Köhler, *A Concise Hebrew and Aramaic Lexicon of the Old Testament, Based upon the Lexical Work of Ludwig Koehler and Walter Baumgartner* (Grand Rapids, MI: Eerdmans, 1971), 22.

this third mood shift, however, there is a clear response from God, and this facilitates a smooth transition into the thanksgiving within the final section (vv. 16c–19).

As mentioned above, verse 18 repeats verse 14 verbatim. Here, however, the psalm ends with thanksgiving, as the psalmist mentions "the courts of the house of the Lord" (v. 19), where he will fulfill his vows (v. 18). With this note, the redactors add a final call to "Praise the Lord" (v. 19c).

# PSALM 117

Psalm 117 is the shortest psalm in Psalter. In spite of its brevity, it is a classic representation of the hymn genre. Psalm 117 is to hymns what Psalm 13 is to laments. Gunkel considers Psalm 13 to be the representative model of the lament genre, and we might consider Psalm 117 to be the model hymn. In the span of only two verses, all three elements of a hymn are present:

> Call to praise: "Praise the LORD" (v. 1);
> Motivations for praise: "For great is his love . . ." (v. 2);
> Renewed call to praise: "Praise the LORD" (v. 2).

Because Psalm 117 is very short, it is "either regarded as part of Psalm 116 or as part of Psalm 118."[1] But there are strong reasons for maintaining the independent status of this psalm. Both the Hebrew text and the Greek translations respect the independence of Psalm 117. Moreover, its overall theme and emphasis are unique. As Jones demonstrates, the use of the familiar terms, "love" (*hesed*) and "faithfulness," in Psalm 117 differ from those in the other psalms (see discussion below).[2]

In spite of its uniqueness, its particular place among the Great Hallel psalms (Psalms 113–118) is significant. Sandwiched between two longer psalms (Psalms 116 and 118), Psalm 117 serves as a useful transition into the final Hallel psalm (Psalm 118). In its present arrangement, the thanksgiving of an individual (Psalm 116) flows into a communal hymn of praise (Psalm 117), which prepares us for a combined individual and communal thanksgiving (Psalm118). Together, these three psalms form a chiastic structure:

> Individual thanksgiving (Psalm 116),
>    Hymn of the community (Psalm 117),
>    Thanksgiving of the community (Ps 118:1–4),
> Individual thanksgiving (Ps 118:5–28).

As this structure reveals, Psalm 117 contains a hymn of the community. As will be elaborated below, the praise of the community in turn embraces the whole of humanity. One of the important contributions of the Psalms is its comprehensive and expansive presentation of worship, which contrasts sharply with the individualistic tendencies in modern day worship, as reflected

---

1. Fanie Snyman, "Reading Psalm 117 against an Exilic Context," *VT* 61, no. 1 (2011): 112.
2. Ethan Jones, "Zeit, Raum und Völker: חסד ואמת in Ps 117," *Biblische Notizen* 178 (2018): 106.

in many of the English worship songs we sing. I often wonder why we keep on singing Western songs when our own Tagalog songs are more communal. In contrast to the overuse of "I" in English worship songs, we have many Tagalog songs that employ the first person plural, *kami* ("us") and *atin* ("our"). One classic example is the song, *Dakilang Katapatan* ("Great Faithfulness"), which begins with the line, *Sadyang kaybuti ng ating Panginoon* ("Our [*ating*] Lord is indeed good").

## 117:1 CALL TO PRAISE

While our Filipino culture may be more "communal" than other cultures, it is not broad enough, as the scope of our reach (*sakop*) can be limited to our close family or relatives. Thus it is important to capture the vision from the biblical text that will help enlarge our reach (*sakop*). The call to praise in Psalm 117 is not only addressed to the Temple community or the congregation gathered in the Temple, but to all the "nations": "Praise the Lord, all you nations" (v. 1a). In the next line, the psalmist calls "all the peoples" to "extol" him (v. 1b). The words "nations" and "peoples" clearly convey the extensive breadth of the psalmist's vision. Notice also that the word "all" is mentioned twice. The popular saying among Filipino young people, *sana all* ("hope everyone's included"), conveys this expansive sense of "all." The use of the word "nations" could be a reflection of the exilic/postexilic setting of Psalm 117, since Israel would have been exposed to the other nations during that time. If this is true, then it is remarkable that those who had been slaves and were living in exile had the audacity to call on the other nations – including their colonizers and masters – to praise their God! How did this come to be? Verse 2 provides the answer.

## 117:2 MOTIVATION FOR PRAISE

The people call "all" to praise God because they have experienced God's blessings, and they know that God's blessings are for everyone rather than for the community of Israel alone. This understanding goes back to the story of God calling Abraham to become a blessing to the nations. The Israelites were blessed so that they could become a blessing to others. As they pray for blessing, they extend this blessing to all the nations. Thus they pray in Psalm 67:4, "May the nations be glad and sing for joy, for you rule the peoples with equity."

The psalmist calls the nations to praise the Lord because "great is his love toward us" (v. 2a). The word "us" here does not only refer to the congregation, as the context of the preceding verse incorporates "all the nations" and "all the peoples" into the "us." The personal experience of the psalmist in Psalm 116 is no longer confined to the individual, for Psalm 117 incorporates the experience of all people, including those who are outside the community. Just as God moved in the life of the individual with overwhelming grace and compassion (see comments on Ps 116:5 above), the people in Psalm 117 are overwhelmed by "his love," which is "great." Unfortunately, the NIV translates the Hebrew word, *gabar*, as "great," though it is actually a verb that means "to be superior"[3] or "to be strong."[4] It is important to reflect the verbal sense of the word in the translation, for as Jeremias notes, "Compared to the hymns of the great nations in Mesopotamia and Egypt, biblical Israel was rather hesitant to use adjectives for God in hymns. Rather, the people would tell of what they had experienced of God."[5] Following the LXX, verse 2a may thus be translated, "For his steadfast love became strong toward us."[6] Alter translates it, "For His kindness overwhelms us."[7]

---

3. *HALOT*, 1:175.
4. *TDOT*, 2:368.
5. Jörg Jeremias, "Worship and Theology in the Psalms," in *Psalms and Liturgy*, ed. Dirk J. Human and C. J. A. Vos (London: Clark, 2004), 91, 89–101.
6. John R. Kohlenberger III, ed., *The Comparative Psalter: Hebrew-Greek-English*, 211.
7. Robert Alter, *The Book of Psalms*, 414. This is similar to the feeling expressed in Psalm 116:5.

# PSALM 118

One of the unique features of Psalm 118 is its combination of individual and communal elements. It begins with a communal hymn or a thanksgiving (vv. 1–4), which is followed by an individual thanksgiving (vv. 5–29). The combination of both individual and communal perspectives reflects the communal element of our individual experiences. Even when we have an individual experience, we are not meant to keep that to ourselves, but to share it with the community. As Psalm 34:3 says, "Glorify the Lord with me." When an individual experiences something "good" from the Lord, it is natural to share it with others. It's hard to celebrate alone! Thus at the end of the thanksgiving in Psalm 116, the psalmist declares that he will "sacrifice a thank offering . . . in the presence of all his people" (vv. 17–18). Psalm 118 highlights the response of the community to an individual's thanksgiving. The joy and victory of an individual is also the joy and victory of the community. Together, the entire community bursts forth with a call to "Give thanks to the Lord" (v. 1).

The interplay between the individual and the community is supported by the canonical context. As noted in the structural analysis of Psalm 117 (above), Psalms 116–118 form a chiastic structure, beginning with an individual thanksgiving (Psalm 116), followed by a hymn of the community (Psalm 117), followed by a thanksgiving of the community (Ps 118:1–4), and concluding with an individual thanksgiving (Ps 118:5–28). The close link between the individual and the community is further confirmed by the inclusio in Psalm 118 (vv. 1, 29), which has the effect of embracing the individual thanksgiving within the communal hymn.[1]

Psalm 118 may be outlined as follows:

> Thanksgiving of the community (vv. 1–4),
> Thanksgiving of the individual (vv. 5–18),
> Thanksgiving liturgy (vv. 19–28),
> Concluding communal thanksgiving (v. 29).

---

1. The hymn and the thanksgiving of the community, according to Booij, seem to come from "a common background"; i.e., "in the life of the community." Thijs Booij, "Psalm 118 and Form Criticism," *Bib* 96, no. 3 (2015): 372.

## 118:1–4 THANKSGIVING OF THE COMMUNITY

One of the challenges for interpreting Psalm 118 is the inclusion of both individual and communal elements of a thanksgiving hymn. But this challenge produces one of the most important insights in the study of the thanksgiving psalm in general, for it shows how the individual and the community are closely linked in the activity of thanksgiving. In Psalm 118, we see how the community rejoices in thanksgiving because of an individual's experience of deliverance.

In verses 1–4, we may envision a worship leader standing in front of the community, exhorting the people to "give thanks to the LORD" (v. 1). The worship leader calls on three groups of people to give thanks: "Israel" (v. 2), "the house of Aaron" (v. 3), and "those who fear the LORD" (v. 4). The first refers to the people of Israel in general. The "house of Aaron" (v. 3) points to the community's religious leaders. Some scholars understand "those who fear the LORD" (v. 4) as a reference to the nations or peoples outside Israel who now worship Yahweh.[2] Others view the title as a "comprehensive designation for the religious community."[3] Both are possible, but the latter is more immediate to the context of Psalm 118. We see some glimpses of the liturgical structure preserved here. After the call to give thanks, we hear the response of the gathered community: "his love endures forever" (vv. 1b, 2b, 3b, 4b). This response is repeated four times in the first four verses (compare Psalm 136).

This four-fold response from the community is followed by an individual thanksgiving, highlighting the close connection between the experience of the individual and the community. Nothing that transpires in one person's life is confined to that individual person, for the entire community is affected. In our laments, the community is with us (see the canonical arrangement of Psalms 42–44, where the individual laments in Psalms 42–43 are followed by a communal lament in Psalm 44). And in our thanksgiving, the community praises the Lord with us. Our experience of deliverance or blessing is meant to be shared with our community so that, together with the community, we can give thanks to the Lord. The shape of Psalm 118 also challenges the community to embrace the experience of one of its members as its own. A victory or deliverance of one of its members is also the deliverance of the community.

---

2. Zenger and Hossfeld hold that the title "applies to the people from among the world's nations who no longer trust in their gods but only in YAHWEH (compare Pss 115:11; 118:8–9) and worship him as the only God (compare Ps 118:28)." Zenger and Hossfeld, *Psalms 3*, 237.
3. Allen, *Psalms 101–150*, 166.

## 118:5–18 THANKSGIVING OF THE INDIVIDUAL

Verse 5 contains the core elements of a thanksgiving psalm: an account of the individual's experience of distress, his cry for help to the Lord, and his deliverance (compare Ps 116:3–4; Jonah 2:2). The most important part of this testimony is the fact that God "answered" his cry for help. The Hebrew in verse 5b literally reads, "The LORD *answered* me in a broad place" (my emphasis). The verb "answered" assumes the meaning of "to set" ("he set me in a broad place"), thereby suggesting that the divine "answer" is defined by the act of bringing the psalmist to a "broad place."

---

### GOD'S DELIVERANCE AS *KAGINHAWAAN* (WELL-BEING)

In Filipino, the word for "well-being" is *kaginhawaan*, which is close to the word for "breathing" (*hininga*). The psalmist describes his experience as being "hard pressed," (v. 5a), which comes from the Hebrew word *tsar*, meaning "narrowness."[1] The feeling is like being strangled. But then the Lord sets him in a broad place, where he can breathe freely.

---

1. *TDOT*, 12:456.

---

The experience of receiving this divine "answer" gives the individual a strong confidence to face the distressing situation that is before him. Similarly, in Psalm 6, after the psalmist cries out to the Lord and weeps through the night, the Lord "answers" him, and this gives him the boldness to confront his enemies. He tells them: "Away from me, all you who do evil, for the LORD has heard my weeping" (6:8). In Psalm 118, the individual is no longer afraid of "those who hate me" (v. 7, ESV). Because he has received a divine "answer," he can now look at them "in triumph" (v. 7).

God's response to the psalmist's prayer not only brings him confidence, for it also helps him realize that "it is better to take refuge in the LORD than to trust in humans" (v. 9). The canonical context, along with the context of the following verses, both indicate that this process of realization has not been easy. In Psalm 116, the individual who is offering a thanksgiving recalls a painful experience, during which he believed, "Everyone is a liar" (v. 11).

We can sense a similar sentiment in Psalm 118, as the psalmist reflects that it is better to take refuge in the Lord than in humans. One cannot even trust in princes (v. 9). The language in verses 10–12 portrays an isolated individual, who is suffering alone while the rest of the world conspires against him. The phrase, "they surrounded me," is repeated three times in these verses. This situation is similar to Psalm 62, where the psalmist cries out, "How long will you assault me? Would all of you throw me down?" (v. 3). The sense of "all of you" against "me" is overwhelming. In Psalm 118, the memory of how "all the nations surrounded me" recalls an image of swarming bees, which is used elsewhere to describe the surrounding enemy nations (Isa 7:18; Deut 1:44).

But because the individual trusts in the Lord, he is able to stand against his enemies. In verses 10–12, the phrase, "but in the name of the Lord I cut them down," is also repeated three times. In the context of the preceding verses, the words, "in the name of the Lord," mean trusting in the Lord. Note that the word "trust" is repeated twice in verses 8–9.

In verse 13, there is a sudden shift to second person direct address. While the NIV translates the verb in this verse passively, "I was pushed back" (compare ESV), the Hebrew literally reads, "You pushed me." The first person passive is attractive, because it does not make sense to have God be the one who caused the psalmist's suffering, since he declares that "the Lord helped me" in the parallel line of verse 13b. How can God both inflict suffering and give relief? Later in verse 18, the psalmist says, "The Lord has chastened me severely, but he has not given me over to death." This reminds me of a prayer by a little girl when the waters of Typhoon Yolanda were sweeping through their building: *Jesus, tama na po* ("Jesus, please enough"). In this short prayer, the girl expresses a similar view to the psalmist, for she sees God as the one who is causing the Typhoon, but at the same time, God is also the one who is able to deliver her. God is both the "punisher" and the "deliverer."[4]

The construction of verses 13a and 18a are similar, as both consist of an absolute participle and a finite verb. Verse 13a literally reads, "You have pushed me hard," while verse 18a reads, "The Lord has chastened me severely." Verse 13, however, abruptly shifts to second person direct address. It is also possible that this verse is an address to the psalmist's enemies or a representative of the psalmist's enemies. I think that this is the primary reference here. The

---

4. Federico G. Villanueva, "My God, Why?: Natural Disasters and Lament in the Philippine Context," in *Why, O God?: Disaster, Resiliency, and the People of God*, ed. Athena E. Gorospe, Charles Ringma, and Karen Hollenbeck-Wuest (Manila, Philippines: OMF Literature and Asian Theological Seminary, 2017), 87–90.

psalmist does not specify the enemy, but whoever he or they may be, his/their actions are interpreted as part of the "chastening" of the Lord (v. 18). What is important for the psalmist is that this "chastening" did not lead to death. He has been delivered. Yahweh has become his salvation (v. 14).

As mentioned earlier, the psalmist attributes his deliverance to the workings of the Lord (see "name of the Lord" in vv. 10–12). The word "right hand" is repeated three times in verses 15–16. "Right hand" is a metaphor for God's power and might, conveying the psalmist's confidence that he "will not die but live," so that he may "proclaim what the Lord has done" (v. 17). One can already hear the rejoicing and shouting of the people as a result of this individual's victory (v. 15). Here again, we see how the experience of the individual is shared by the community. The language of the psalm has led some scholars to identify the individual who is speaking here as the king or someone with great influence. This is possible, but the language could also be the thanksgiving offering of an ordinary believer.

## 118:19–29 THANKSGIVING LITURGY

This section includes elements of the entrance liturgy (see Psalm 15 and Psalm 24). One of the important theologies in the entrance liturgy is its emphasis on the character of the worshiper. Those who are about to enter the holy hill of the Lord are expected to bear the marks of righteousness (see Ps 15:2–4). Here in Psalm 118, those who rejoice with the individual are those who belong to the "tents of the righteous" (v. 15). Moreover, the gates of the Temple are described as "gates of the righteous" (v. 19), and it is "the gate of the Lord through which the righteous may enter" (v. 20). This theological emphasis highlights the importance of living a life that is worthy of the Lord for those who enter into his presence. We often enter a church without thinking about how we are living our lives.

> **JOSE RIZAL'S CRITIQUE OF FILIPINOS' PRACTICE OF WORSHIP**
>
> Our National hero, Jose Rizal, observes how Filipinos go to church to hear mass and say prayers without giving any thought to how they live each day. He writes:
>
> > you can rob the orphan and the widow, or take away the honor of a man who has no other patrimony; you can call him the most injurious and basest names; you can make him pay with bitter tears his sad fate and your enviable situation; in short, even maltreat him, slap him, and kill his mortal life. You can do all this and even more, and no one will say that you are a bad Christian so long as you hear mass, you confess, you take communion, and attend all processions, praying all day and fasting on fast days marked on the calendar.[1]
>
> ---
>
> 1. Rizal, "The Religiosity of the Filipino People" translated by Dr. Encarnación Alzona. https://www.thefilipinomind.com/2005/10/religiosity-of-filipino-people-dr.html; accessed on July 6, 2020.

In Psalm 118, the psalmist has been pushed hard and is about to fall. He might have been maltreated by the worshipers themselves or a member of one of the groups of worshipers, or he might have been regarded as a nobody and been trampled upon by them. The psalmist describes himself as "the stone the builders rejected" (v. 22a). Yet something totally unexpected transpires before the community's eyes, for the stone that was rejected "has become the cornerstone" (v. 22b). The psalmist can only attribute this to the Lord's intervention (v. 23). Because of the "name of the Lord" (vv. 10–12) and his "right hand" (vv. 15–16), the psalmist can declare: "This is the day that the Lord has made; let us rejoice and be glad in it" (v. 24, ESV). Many evangelicals and Pentecostals know this as a famous song, which we often sing on all occasions. But we should remember that this song was sung on a day of thanksgiving, when someone experienced deliverance. There are days when we cannot and should not sing this song, such as during times of disorientation. During these times, we need songs and prayers of lament. A common mistake among Christians is to sing one type of song for every occasion. As one song says, "Blessed be Your name/ On the road marked with suffering/ Though there's pain in the offering/ Blessed be Your name." Yet many times this response does not fit our experience, and therefore we cannot sing these words with authenticity.

Curiously, the declaration of praise, "This is the day . . ." is followed by a petition: "Lord, save us! Lord, grant us success!" (v. 25). How are we to interpret this? First, an individual's experience of God's salvation and deliverance should extend to others so that the person who experienced an answer to prayer can invite God to do the same for the entire community. Just as the psalmist says, "I will give you thanks, for you answered *me*" (v. 21), he also prays, "Lord, save *us*!" (v. 25). It is important to remember that even if God has answered our prayers, many others have not yet experienced God's deliverance. And so, whenever we share what the Lord has done in our lives, we should also express our longing for God to do the same for others. Through our testimony, we hope that the faith of others in our community will be strengthened.

Verse 26 brings us back to the entrance liturgy, which blesses the one "who comes in the name of the Lord." From the context, this could refer to the person giving thanks. Having asked the community to open the gates of righteousness (v. 19), the psalmist can now enter, and the community gives him its blessing. The description, "in the name of the Lord," may be interpreted as a reference to the one who trusts in the Lord, who does not come in his own might, but by God's right hand and power. In the second half of verse 26, the singular becomes plural as the community declares, "We bless you [plural] from 'the house of the Lord'" (v. 26b). The sudden shift to the plural reminds us that the individual who is offering thanksgiving is not alone. He comes with his community, with those who belong to "the tents of the righteous" (v. 15).

Having welcomed the individual back into the community of the righteous, the people affirm that the Lord has "made his light shine on us" (v. 27), language that recalls the Aaronic blessing (Num 6:24–26; compare Psalm 67). The second part of verse 27 could refer either to "the sacrificial animal to be slaughtered (compare "the horns of the altar" in v. 27c) or as the festal activities."[5] Corresponding to the people's affirmation of Yahweh as God, the psalmist declares, "You are my God, and I will praise you . . ." (v. 28). This individual declaration is then encapsulated by the concluding communal thanksgiving in verse 29 to "give thanks to the Lord." As noted previously, verse 29 is a repetition of the communal thanksgiving in verse 1. Together, these verses form an inclusio, thereby embracing the individual thanksgiving within the community.

---

5. Zenger and Hossfeld, *Psalms 3*, 230.

# PSALM 119

Psalm 119 is the longest psalm in the Psalter and the longest chapter in the whole Bible. It consists of 176 verses, which are divided into sections (or strophes) of eight verses, with each section corresponding to the twenty-two letters of the Hebrew alphabet (the name for each letter is given in the title for each section below). The composer of this extensive acrostic did not identify himself/herself, and the redactors did not attribute the poem to anyone. We find a close parallel to Psalm 119 in Lamentations 3, which devotes three verses to each letter of the Hebrew alphabet.[1]

Because of the length and formal acrostic structure of Psalm 119, some scholars find it repetitious and wearisome. Weiser describes the psalm as "a many-coloured mosaic of thoughts which are often repeated in a wearisome fashion."[2] He points his readers to a German hymn for a summary of Psalm 119 and devotes less than two pages of commentary to the entire psalm. Yet the acrostic is part of the message of the psalm, which reflects completeness in both its form and content. The diligent attempts that the psalmist has lovingly exerted to compose a psalm of this length reflect his longing to fulfill the commands of the Lord. Though Weiser can summarize his comments for Psalm 119 in less than two pages, the purpose of the psalm is not simply to follow the "logic" of the argument of each verse or strophe to distill the main principles. Psalm 119 is also intended to be a prayer. As Soll asserts, "Beyond the structural matrix of alphabetic acrostic and Torah words . . . it is the psalm's character as prayer that gives it coherence as a literary unity."[3] Bonhoeffer observed this long ago, writing that "in this entire psalm God is addressed." We do not encounter "an 'it,' an idea, but a 'thou meets us in the commandments.'"[4]

Psalm 119 is written as a conversation between the psalmist and God, which is founded on the psalmist's relationship with God. God never speaks directly, but is present in every line that the psalmist directs to God. In order to enter this conversation, the reader or interpreter has to consider the main

---

1. The following are alphabetic acrostics in the Bible: Psalms 25, 34, 37, 111, 112, 119, and 145; Lamentations 1, 2, 3, 4, and Proverbs 31:10–31. William Michael Soll, *Psalm 119: Matrix, Form, and Setting* (Washington, DC: Catholic Biblical Association of America, 1991), 11.
2. Weiser, *The Psalms. A Commentary*, 739.
3. Soll, *Psalm 119*, 59.
4. Dietrich Bonhoeffer, *Meditating on the Word*, trans. David McI. Gracie (Cambridge, MA: Cowley, 1986), 116.

referent in the conversation, which is God. If the psalm is not read as a prayer, it becomes monotonous, boring, almost meaningless. But when read as a dialogue held in relationship, the psalm becomes a delight! Those who share in the sentiments of the psalm will find it particularly insightful. Rather than falling into the trap of simply filling in the eight verses of each section with sentences beginning with that particular Hebrew letter, the psalmist uses the acrostic form as a way to deepen intimacy with God. One of the proverbs in Filipino may be of help in appreciating what the psalmist is doing in Psalm 119. It says: "Those who are honest about what they really feel bring the relationship to closer intimacy" (*Ang nagsasabi ng tapat nagsasama ng maluwat*). In Psalm 119, the psalmist expresses his heart to God, sharing his desires, longings, actions, plans, as well as his laments and questions.

## 119:1–8 ALEPH

*Aleph*, the first strophe (vv. 1–8), recalls the very first psalm in the Psalter, as the opening beatitude ("blessed"), the word "way," and the centrality of the Torah (law) are all present in Psalm 119:1 as well as Psalm 1:1–2, though there are four differences. First, while Psalm 1 refers to the blessedness of "the man" (Ps 1:1, ESV), Psalm 119 emphasizes the community by identifying the "blessed" as "*those* whose ways are blameless" (v. 1).

Second, Psalm 1 begins with a negative emphasis by outlining three parallel descriptions of what the blessed person does *not* do: he does *not* walk, stand, sit with the wicked (v. 1). This is followed by what he *does* do – or where his delight is ("in the law of the LORD," v. 2). Psalm 119 starts by identifying four parallel characteristics of those who are "blessed." The first three characteristics are positive: those "who walk according to the law of the LORD" (v. 1); "those who keep his statutes" (v. 2a); and those "who seek him with all their heart" (v. 2b). The fourth characteristic is negative – "they do no wrong" (v. 3a) – but it is balanced by another positive statement – "but walk in his ways" (v. 3b, ESV).

Third, God is never addressed directly in Psalm 1, but in Psalm 119:4, the psalm becomes a prayer, a meditation in the very presence of the Lord. Rather than talking about God in the third person, the psalmist addresses God directly, saying, "You have laid down precepts that are to be fully obeyed" (119:4). This relational connection establishes the very foundation of the law, the ultimate reason that it should be "fully obeyed," which is that it comes directly from God.

Fourth, Psalm 1 clearly contrasts the righteous with the wicked, where the righteous are always successful (v. 3). Throughout Psalm 119, however, the psalmist struggles to attain the righteous ideal or standard that he describes in verses 1–3. In verse 5, he exclaims, "Oh, that my ways were steadfast . . .," conveying his longing to be the kind of person who is "blessed." At the same time, he is aware of the gap or distance between himself and his ideal. As Soll says, "At the heart of the strophe is a tension between ideal and reality."[5]

But the psalmist never gives up. Throughout Psalm 119, the psalmist displays his determination to "learn your righteous laws" (v. 7). Yet the last verse of *Aleph* also introduces the importance of divine agency. After pledging to keep God's decrees (v. 8a), the psalmist prays, "do not utterly forsake me" (v. 8b). This first petition in the psalm is intriguing, as it seems to imply that God has abandoned him. Thus the psalmist pleads with God *not* to forsake him any longer (compare Isa 49:14; 54:7).[6] This negative petition contrasts with the earlier positive emphasis. If the psalmist keeps all of God's commands, then he is asking God to refrain from abandoning him.

### 119:9–16 BETH

The opening beatitude in the preceding strophe, *Aleph*, reveals what the psalmist considers to be of prime value: a blameless life, conducted according to the law of the Lord. The opening question in *Beth* – "how can a young person stay on the path of purity?" (v. 9a) – builds on the "Aleph" strophe, expressing the psalmist's sincere desire to be counted among those "whose ways are blameless" (v. 1). Though verse 9b is usually translated as an answer to the question in 9a, it can also be read as a continuation of the question. For instance, Soll suggests translating verse 9 as, "How can a youth purify his way to keep it according to your word?"[7] The usage of the preposition "how" along with the infinitive of the verb "to keep" occurs earlier in verse 5, highlighting the psalmist's continuing struggle with the gap between the ideal and his situation. Yet we also see his determination to maintain a blameless life. With the exception of two half lines (vv. 10b and 12b, which are actions attributed to God in the form of a prayer), the rest of *Beth* focuses on human actions.

In response to the question, "how can a young person stay on the path of purity?" the psalmist asserts his own agency, declaring, "I seek you with all

---

5. William Michael Soll, "The Question of Psalm 119:9," *JBL* 106, no. 4 (1987): 688.
6. Kirkpatrick, *The Book of Psalms*, 706.
7. Soll, "The Question of Psalm 119:9," 687.

my heart" (v. 10a). The words "seek" and "all heart" occur earlier (v. 2) as one of the marks of a blessed person. By repeating these words here, the psalmist is making a commitment to do whatever he can to live a blameless life. Yet he admits that he cannot do this alone and so needs help from God. Curiously, his petition for divine action is described in the negative: "do not let me stray from your commands" (v. 10b). This pattern is similar to verse 8, which also contains a positive action by the psalmist followed by a prayer for God *not* to "utterly forsake me" (see above).

The petition, "do not let me stray," is followed by another verse that highlights human agency: "I have hidden your word in my heart" (v. 11a). The second part of this verse – "that I might not sin against you" (v. 11b) – corresponds to the negative petition in verse 10b ("do not let me stray"). In verse 12a, there is a shift to praise, which is followed by another petition, suggesting that praise is made for the purpose of asking God to "teach me your decrees" (v. 12b).

The rest of the verses resume the emphasis on human agency as the psalmist proclaims the things he does: declares God's laws (v. 13), rejoices in God's statutes (v. 14), meditates on God's precepts (v. 15), and delights in God's decrees (v. 16a). *Beth* ends with the assertion, "I will *not* forget your word" (v. 16b, ESV), which contrasts with the end of the first strophe, "do *not* utterly forsake me" (v. 8b). While the psalmist may be wondering if God will abandon him, the psalmist vows that he will "not forget" (v. 16b).

The stress on human agency is an important reminder because of our tendency to overemphasize "salvation by grace alone" and "dependence" on God. Filipino Christians often say, *ipasa-Diyos mo na lang* ("Just leave everything to God"). More than three centuries of colonialism and continuing economic subjugation have resulted in a culture that tends to be overly dependent on others, including God. Filipinos are very religious and depend on God for everything. This is reflected in a common expression among elderly people, *kung may awa ang Diyos* ("If God's mercy will permit"). While trusting in God is an important virtue that is taught in Scripture, it can hamper the need for human action and render all our attempts to be inadequate. As one famous Filipino saying puts it, *Nasa Diyos ang awa, nasa tao ang gawa* ("Mercy belongs to God, but actions belong to humans").

### 119:17–24 GIMEL

The third strophe, *Gimel*, picks up on the main theme of the preceding strophe, which is expressed in the question, "How can a young man keep his way pure?" (v. 9a). The psalmist mentions two ways to maintain purity at the beginning and end of the *Beth*: "guarding it according to your word" (v. 9b, ESV) and "delighting in God's decrees" (v. 16). The words "guarding" (*shamar*) and "delighting" (*shaʿaʿ*) also occur at the beginning and end of *Gimel*: "that I may . . . keep [*shamar*] your word" (v. 17); "Your statutes are my delight" [*shaʿaʿ*] (v. 24).

The psalmist maintains his commitment to keep and delight in God's word, but as hinted earlier, he also acknowledges his need for God's help (see vv. 1b, 10b). While the *Beth* strophe emphasizes human agency, *Gimel* emphasizes the psalmist's dependence on God through four petitions (vv. 17, 18, 19b, 22).

The first petition is a prayer for God to "be good to your servant" (v. 17). The phrase "be good" comes from the Hebrew word *gamal*, which also means "deal bountifully." In Psalm 116, the psalmist says to himself, "Return, O my soul, to your rest; for the LORD has dealt bountifully with you" (v. 7, ESV). Here, the psalmist asks God to be good to his servant so "that I may live" (119:17).[8] The words, "that I may live," signify a situation that is far from ideal. A closer look at the context indicates that the psalmist is going through a very difficult situation. In verse 19, he says, "I am a stranger on earth." To be a "stranger" or foreigner is a very vulnerable situation, as neither is given the usual rights of a resident. The psalmist talks about his experience of "scorn and contempt" (v. 22) and complains that "rulers sit together and slander me" (v. 23). Despite all these struggles, he maintains his commitment to keep God's commands. He wants to live so "that I may obey your word" (v. 17). While some people would do anything just to obtain the life they want, the psalmist is expressing that his purpose for living is to keep God's commands.

The second petition is a prayer for God to open the psalmist's eyes so that he may "see wonderful things in your law" (v. 18). He is consumed with "longing for your laws at all times" (v. 20), and he tells the Lord, "Your statutes are my delight" (v. 24). We normally do not associate a book, or even the Bible, with "longing" and "delight." These emotions are typically associated with beauty or the wonders of an intimate relationship.

The third petition offers some illumination about the psalmist's longing for God's "law," "decrees," and "statutes." After lamenting that he is "a stranger on earth," he pleads with God, "do not hide your commands from me" (v. 19b).

---

8. The NIV's translation, "while I live," tries to make sense of the ambiguous construction, since the Hebrew simply says, "I live." But some manuscripts place the *waw* before the verb, allowing for the translation, "that I may live," which I think is better.

The negative petition, "do not hide," often occurs in lament psalms, with "your face" as its object. For example, Psalm 69:17 says, "Do not hide your face from your servant" (see also Pss 27:9; 44:24; 84:14). By substituting the words "your commands" instead of "your face," the psalmist is revealing that the commands, words, and laws of the Lord are not just written words, but the very presence of the Lord himself, who is one with his word. Similarly, when Jesus asks his disciples whether they are leaving him, too, Peter replies, "Lord, to whom shall we go? You have the words of eternal life" (John 6:68).

The fourth and last petition in *Gimel* further underlines the difficulty confronting the psalmist, for he prays for God to "remove from me their scorn and contempt" (v. 22). Many Asians who live in more communal contexts can identify with the psalmist's feeling, as the experience of being shamed or scorned can feel worse than death. Some would rather die than be put to shame. No wonder the psalmist begins his prayer with the petition, "Deal bountifully with your servant, *that I may live*" (v. 17).

### 119:25–32 DALETH

The opening verse of the fourth strophe, *Daleth*, develops this theme of life. Earlier, the psalmist expresses his longing to live (v. 17a), but here he becomes even more direct: "give me life" (v. 25b, ESV). He employs the language of lament, complaining that his "soul clings to the dust" (v. 25a; compare Ps 44:26). Indeed, the whole *Daleth* strophe consists of elements that are typical of the lament: a complaint (vv. 25a, 28a), followed by a series of petitions (v. 25b, 26b, 28b, 29b, 31b), ending with an expression of certainty or assurance of trust (v. 32).

The change of mood at the end of *Daleth* is not due to an oracle of salvation, which is often proposed to explain the "certainty of a hearing," as there is no indication in the text of an external, objective phenomenon that could explain the shift of mood. What is clear, however, is the psalmist's persistence and devotion, which is expressed in the repetition of the verb "cling" (*dabaq*). Even though the psalmist's soul "clings [*dabaq*] to the dust" (v. 25, ESV), he continues to "cling" to the statutes of the Lord (v. 31) because he has "chosen the way of faithfulness" (v. 30).

### 119:33–40 HE

Each of the eight verses in the fifth strophe, *He*, contains a petition. The first two petitions – "teach me, LORD" (v. 33) and "give me understanding" (v. 34)

– remind us that knowing God's word is a gift from God. Though many are knowledgeable and clever of other things, one needs divine understanding to know "the way of your decrees" (v. 33). At the same time, this prayer demands commitment from the one who prays, who has to be prepared to "follow it to the end" (v. 33b). It's often easy to begin, but to finish well, one has to love the whole process. Thus one has to be committed to keeping God's law "with all my heart" (v. 34; compare v. 2).

Next the psalmist asks God to lead him in the "path of your commands" (v. 35), because this path is not only difficult, but also full of danger and the temptation for "selfish gain" (v. 36b). The Hebrew word for "gain" (*betsa'*) "always refers to dishonest (Exod 18:21), extorted gain (Isa 33:15b), which as such resembles bloodguilt (Ezek 22:12–13)."[9] To overcome this serious temptation, one has to turn *to* God and turn away *from* evil. The next two prayers, "incline my heart to your testimonies" (v. 36a, ESV) and "Turn my eyes away from worthless things" (v. 37a), correspond to these actions of turning *to* and turning *away*. The second prayer in this pair of petitions recalls the first temptation in the Bible, which concerns the eyes, for "when the woman saw that the fruit of the tree was good for food and pleasing to the eye" (Gen 3:6), she took of the fruit and ate it. This eventually led to death. The psalmist describes the temptation for "unjust gain" as "worthless" (v. 37a), because there is no life in it. Thus the psalmist prays, "give me life in your ways" (v. 37b, ESV). The psalmist repeats this petition to "give me life" at the end of the *He* strophe (v. 40).

Having declared his commitment to obey God's commands and keep them "to the end" (v. 33b), the psalmist asks God to "fulfill your promise" (v. 38a), and his motivation for this prayer is "so that you may be feared" (v. 38b). The context of the subsequent verses provides some hint about the nature of God's promise. In verse 39, the psalmist speaks about "the disgrace I dread." We might imagine a situation in which "arrogant" people are taunting him (compare vv. 42, 51), and so the promise may be interpreted as an act of deliverance. Deliverance in verse 40b is equivalent to the preservation of life. Because the psalmist keeps God's word (v. 34), an act of deliverance from God would lead people to fear God (v. 38b).

---

9. *TDOT*, 14:456.

# Psalm 119

### 119:41–48 WAW

As noted earlier, verses 9–16 (the second strophe, *Beth*) highlight the importance of human agency. The sixth strophe, *Waw*, continues the emphasis on human responsibility, but also acknowledges that human action is dependent on God's action. The opening verse in *Waw* is a prayer that God's "unfailing love come to me" (v. 41). There is another petition in this strophe, which asks God to "never take your word of truth from my mouth" (v. 43), but the rest of the verses describe actions performed by the psalmist himself.

In the third strophe (*Gimel*), the psalmist asks God to be good to him "so that I may obey your word" (v. 17), but here he promises to "obey your law, *forever and ever*" (v. 44, emphasis mine). In the previous strophe, *He*, the psalmist pleads with God to "take away the disgrace I dread" (v. 39), but here, he is prepared to "answer anyone who taunts me" (v. 42). In fact, he "will speak" even "before kings" and "will not be ashamed" (v. 46, NEB). The experience of shame no longer presents a threat for him. He loves God's commands more than anything else and is willing to take a risk. Twice, the psalmist repeats the words, "I love," to refer to God's commands (vv. 47–48). At the end of *Waw*, the psalmist declares, "I will lift up my hands toward your commandments" (v. 48, ESV). This expression is similar to Psalm 134:2: "Lift up your hands to the holy place" (ESV). One possible meaning of the lifting up of hands here is that the object (e.g. the sanctuary, God's commandments) to which the lifted hands are directed is the focus of the psalmist's religious affection and commitment (see v. 72 in *Teth* below).

### 119:49–56 ZAYIN

The first word in the seventh strophe, *Zayin*, is "remember": "remember your word to your servant" (v. 49). The word "remember" is prominent in this strophe (see also vv. 49, 52, 55). In verse 49, "word" refers to a promise made by God to his servant, and upon this "word," the psalmist places his hope. In times of suffering, it is this promise that gives him life (v. 50).

The situation envisaged in verse 50 is far from easy, for the psalmist speaks of "arrogant" people "mocking me unmercifully" (v. 51). In verse 53, he refers to these people as "the wicked," those "who have forsaken your law." Thinking of these people solicits "indignation" from the psalmist (v. 53). He refers to "the house of my sojourning" (v. 54, ESV), which reflects a lack of stability and rootedness, the common lot of strangers living in exile (compare v. 19).

In verse 55, he also mentions the "night," which points to the suffering he mentions in verse 50.

Yet amidst all his distress, the psalmist continues to hope in God's promise: "Your promise preserves my life" (v. 50b). As he asks God to "remember" his promise (v. 49), he does not give up (v. 51b) because he "remembers" God's laws (v. 52). Even when darkness falls, he declares, "I will remember your name" (v. 55).

In the concluding verse of *Zayin*, the reference to the word "this" is not clear. Literally, the first part of the verse reads, "This was/has been to me" (v. 56a). The NIV connects the word "this" to the second part of the verse: "This has been my practice: I obey your precepts." But this translation misses the rich sentiment expressed in the previous verses, which is that the psalmist is able to continue despite all his difficulties, suffering, and indignation over those who do not keep God's law, "because I have kept your precepts" (v. 56b, my translation).

## 119:57–64 HETH

In the eighth strophe, *Heth*, the psalmist begins by declaring that the Lord is his "portion" (v. 57a), which is a way of saying, "the LORD is all that I need." The author of Psalm 73 says something similar: "Whom have I in heaven but you? And earth has nothing I desire besides you" (73:25). He also calls God, "my portion" (73:26). In Psalm 119, because God is his "portion" (v. 57a), the psalmist can promise "to obey your words" (v. 57b). The words "to obey" (literally, "to keep") occur twice in this strophe (vv. 57, 60; see also v. 17 in *Gimel* and v. 44 in *Waw*). Obeying God means pleasing him. As Jesus tells his disciples, "My food is to do the will of him who sent me" (John 4:34). Doing God's will involves entreating his favor (v. 58) and considering (v. 59) our ways to see if we are still living in accordance with God's word/will. After the psalmist "considers" his ways (v. 59), he turns his steps to God's statutes. As soon as he discovers what God desires, he does not wait until tomorrow to do what needs to be done. Like Abraham, who woke up very early after God commanded him to offer his son, the psalmist hastens and does not delay in obeying God's commands (v. 60). Yet this is not easy, for the wicked are trying to "ensnare" the psalmist (v. 61a, ESV). Even still, he does not "forget your law" (v. 61b).

In fact, he wakes up in the middle of the night to give thanks to the Lord for his "righteous laws" (v. 62). Moreover, his love for God's word spills over into the social dimension, for because he loves God's commands (see vv. 47–48), he is drawn to people who fear the Lord and obey his precepts. He is a "friend" to them (v. 63).

The last verse in *Heth* declares: "The earth, O LORD, is full of your steadfast love" (v. 64, ESV). How can the earth be "full" of the Lord's "steadfast love" when there are wicked people all around (v. 61; see also vv. 69–70)? For the psalmist, as long as there are those who long for God's precepts (see v. 40 in *He*) and commit themselves to obeying God's commands despite the challenges and difficulties of life (vv. 60–61), the Lord is present. For those whose "portion" (v. 57a) is the Lord, the whole earth "is full of your steadfast love" (v. 64).

### 119:65–72 TETH

The word "good" occurs six times in *Teth*, the ninth strophe, which follows the Hebrew acrostic (in Hebrew, the word "good" is *tob*, which begins with the letter *teth*). The psalmist asks God to "do *good* to your servant" (v. 65) because God is *good* in his person and *good* in his actions (v. 68). Thus the psalmist wants to learn "*good* judgment" (v. 66). The word "teach/learn" (*lmd*) occurs three times in this strophe (vv. 66, 68, 71). There is never a time when we will no longer need to learn, for even after the psalmist experiences the goodness of the Lord (v. 65), he continues to pray, "teach me" (v. 66).

In the fifth usage of *tob* ("good"), the psalmist acknowledges that "it was *good* for me to be afflicted" (v. 71), because he learned through these experiences. However, this is not so for the wicked, because "their hearts are callous" (v. 70). The word "callous" comes from the Hebrew word *tapash*, which also means "insensitive."[10] Even when the wicked experience afflictions or other forms of chastisement, their hearts remain hardened (compare Rev 9:20–21). Psalm 119 teaches us about the importance of our capacity to feel. The wicked are described as "unfeeling" (v. 70), but the psalmist feels affliction and knows how to "delight" in God's law (v. 24). The final occurrence of the word "good" is devoted to the law, which is "more precious [literally, 'good' (*tob*)] to me than thousands of pieces of silver and gold" (v. 72).

### 119:73–80 YODH

*Yodh*, the tenth strophe, continues the theme of learning in spite of affliction, but it broadens the concept of affliction by adding the actions of the arrogant

---

10. *HALOT*, 2:379.

(v. 78). Both the Lord and the wicked afflict/wrong the psalmist (see vv. 75 and 78, respectively), but there is a difference. The Lord's affliction is done in "faithfulness" (v. 75), because the affliction comes from the same hands that made and formed the psalmist (v. 73; compare Psalm 139). The wicked's affliction, on the other hand, is done in "falsehood" (v. 78, ESV). There is a contrast between the Hebrew words *'emunah* ("faithfulness," v. 75) and *sheqer* ("falsehood," v. 78).

The difficulty, however, is in discerning which affliction is from the Lord and which is from the wicked. Sometimes the Lord uses the wicked to discipline his people, as in the case of the Babylonians (see Habakkuk 1). However, even though God may use the wicked, he will still punish them. Thus in verse 78, the psalmist prays, "May the arrogant be put to shame." The social dimension of the psalmist's faith is also important, for the psalmist hopes that those "who fear you rejoice when they see me" (v. 74, see also v. 79). Fellow followers of the Word can help discern God's voice in times of affliction.

## 119:81–88 KAPH

The eleventh strophe, *Kaph*, is similar to *Daleth*, as both contain elements of lament. But *Daleth* follows a form-critical view of a typical lament, as it shifts to certainty at the end, whereas *Kaph* is predominantly a complaint/lament (vv. 81, 82, 83, 85, 86, 87). The three subjects of lament – self, God, enemy – are all present. Westermann helpfully shows how the lament reflects all three of these relationships with oneself, others/enemies, and God.[11]

Regarding the relationship with self, the psalmist complains that his "soul faints with longing for your salvation" (v. 81). In the following verse, he continues, "My eyes fail, looking for your promise" (v. 82a). From this focus on "self," the psalmist turns to his relationship with God in the next line: "When will you comfort me?" (v. 82b). He feels that God has forgotten him, which is probably the meaning of the simile, "like a wineskin in the smoke" (v. 83).[12] Thus he laments, "How long must your servant wait?" (v. 84). He has been waiting for justice to be served. In verse 84, the psalmist turns to his relationship with his enemy when he asks God to "do justice" against his persecutors.

---

[11]. Westermann, *Praise and Lament in the Psalms*, 169.
[12]. Zenger and Hossfeld comments: "Perhaps it simply means that the skin is hung up above the fireplace until it is needed again (for example, at the next grape harvest). That is how the petitioner feels." Zenger and Hossfeld, *Psalms 3*, 275.

He complains that his enemies "dig pits to trap me," an act that the psalmist describes as "contrary to your law" (v. 85). The word "law" here has the sense of God's will. Thus the actions of the wicked are not in accordance to the will of God. In the *Yodh* strophe, the psalmist draws a contrast between the actions of God, which are done in "faithfulness" (*'emunah*, v. 75), and those of the wicked, which are from "falsehood" (*sheqer*, v. 78). The psalmist repeats these two words in *Kaph*: "All your commandments are sure [*'emunah*]; they persecute me with falsehood [*sheqer*]" (v. 86).

The complaints against all three subjects in this lament create a strong sense of contradiction. Even though the psalmist makes two petitions at the end ("help me," v. 86; "spare my life," v. 88), there is no resolution (compare Psalm 13).

## 119:89–96 LAMEDH

Continuing the previous lament from *Kaph*, the first three verses of *Lamedh*, the twelfth strophe, offer an expression of trust, declaring the enduring stability of God's word (v. 89) and God's faithfulness to all generations (v. 90), which both remain "to this day" (v. 91). These verses are the OT counterpart to Matthew 24:35: "Heaven and earth will pass away, but my words will never pass away." Psalm 119 also mentions "heaven" (v. 89) and the "earth" (v. 90).

Throughout *Lamedh*, the psalmist testifies to the dependability of God's word. He declares, "If your law had not been my delight, I would have perished in my affliction" (v. 92) because the "wicked are waiting to destroy me" (v. 95). The words "perished" (v. 92) and "destroy" (v. 95) both come from the same Hebrew word, *'abad*. But the psalmist trusts that God can deliver him, because "all things serve you" (v. 91b). In Hebrew, there is a wordplay between "perish" (*'abad*, v. 92) and "serve" (*'abad*, v. 91). Because everything is at God's disposal, he can easily deliver the psalmist. While even perfection has a limit, "your commands are boundless" (v. 96).

The word "eternal," which the psalmist uses earlier to describe God's character (v. 89), is repeated in verse 93: "I will never [*le'olam*] forget your precepts." Thus the psalmist asserts his enduring commitment to God's word by comparing it to God's "eternal" (*le'olam*) character. In *Heth*, the psalmist calls God, "my portion" (v. 57), but here he declares, "I am yours . . . for I have sought your precepts" (v. 94, ESV). Thus he can plead with God to "save me" (v. 94a).

## 119:97–104 MEM

There is an emphasis on learning throughout Psalm 119 (e.g. vv. 66, 68, 71). *Mem*, the thirteenth strophe, continues this emphasis by focusing on the importance of "meditation," which is mentioned twice in this psalm (vv. 97, 99, ESV). Meditation does not simply mean thoughtful contemplation. In Psalm 1, the act of meditating on God's law is contrasted with not walking in the way of the wicked (vv. 1–2). In Psalm 119, the one who meditates on God's word:

- keeps his "feet from every evil path" (v. 101),
- does "not depart from your laws" (v. 102), and
- "hates every wrong path" (v. 104b).

Note the verb "hates" in the last line. The verses underline the importance of saying "no" to temptations (v. 101; compare 2 Tim 2:22). In many churches, Christian formation is usually focused on the intellect, neglecting the emotions, but saying "no" to evil means "hating" that which is wrong (v. 104; compare Rom 12:9). Moreover, meditating on God's word is more than memorization, for it means loving God's law: "Oh, how I love your law" (v. 97). For the one who loves God's words, they are "sweeter than honey to my taste" (v. 103). For a similar emphasis on the emotions, see the *Sin* and *Shin* strophe (vv. 161–168) below.

Next the psalmist compares himself with his enemies, teachers, and the elders (vv. 98–100). Compared with all these, the psalmist claims that he is "wiser" (v. 98), has "more insight" (v. 99), and "more understanding" (v. 100). How should we understand this? It is easy to see how the psalmist could be wiser than his enemies. As discussed above, knowledge and learning is moral, not merely intellectual. Thus the psalmist could be right that he is wiser than his enemies, who may be good in other aspects, but lacking in righteousness. But it is much harder for the psalmist to prove the statements, "I have more insight than *all* my teachers" and elders. Maybe the psalmist has his own reasons for being so confident about his obedience to God's laws. These verses could be read as hyperbolic to emphasize the value of meditating on God's word. If so, then we should not take these statements literally.

## 119:105–112 NUN

In the fourteenth strophe, *Nun*, the psalmist employs the metaphor of light to describe "your word" (v. 105). This metaphor highlights the illuminating role of God's word, which makes the psalmist wiser than his enemies and more insightful than his teachers (see *Mem*, vv. 98–99). But wisdom and insight are not merely intellectual, for they are primarily moral. Because God's word is a "lamp for my feet," it provides guidance and wisdom so that a person may lead a blameless life (see *Aleph*, v. 1). Because the "path" on which the psalmist walks is slippery and dark, he needs the word of God to serve as a light (v. 105b).

But in order to have the word of God as one's lamp/light, one has to make a commitment "to follow your righteous laws" (v. 106) by walking "according to the law of the LORD" (see *Aleph*, v. 1). Moreover, one has to keep this commitment "to the very end" (v. 112). In the experience of the psalmist, this does not come easily, for he learned to trust in God's word through his affliction (see *Teth*, v. 71). Thus he confesses, "I have suffered much" (v. 107a). In verses 109–110, the psalmist describes the dangers he's been through: the wicked people "have set a snare for me" (v. 110), and he has had to take "my life in my hands" (v. 109), which refers to "the readiness to put one's life in danger of one's own accord."[13] Yet his sufferings have led him to cry out, "preserve my life, LORD, according to your word" (v. 107b). Because God has preserved his life through his precepts (see *Lamedh*, v. 93), the psalmist offers "freewill offerings of praise" to the Lord (v. 108). This offering could refer to the "recitation of the Torah (or our Torah psalm!) as a sacrificial gift."[14]

## 119:113–120 SAMEKH

The previous strophe, *Nun*, stresses the importance of having the commitment to follow God's word until the end, even in the midst of life's difficulties (see *Nun*, vv. 105, 112). In *Samekh*, the fifteenth strophe, the psalmist expresses his contempt for "double-minded people" who fail to follow God's law (v. 113). His "hate" towards them is similar to God's, for he rejects "all who stray from your decrees" (v. 118). The act of "straying from" is a characteristic of double-minded people, who cannot keep heading one direction for long, especially when the road gets bumpy and hard. Unlike the psalmist, who fears God, these double-minded people do not regard God, and so God considers them to be "like dross," which he discards (v. 119).

---

13. Hans Walter Wolff, *Anthropology of the Old Testament*, 1996, 20, quoted in Allen, *Psalms 101–150*, 190.
14. Zenger and Hossfeld, *Psalms 3*, 278.

The psalmist, on the other hand, has chosen the narrow path, which is full of difficulties. One of these difficulties is that he has gained enemies (see *Mem*, v. 98): the wicked people who hate what is right. In verse 115, he orders all these enemies to "go away from me, you evildoers!" His prayers to "sustain me" (v. 116) and "uphold me" (v. 117) indicate that he is going through distressful times.

But thankfully, amidst the persecution and taunting of these insolent enemies, the psalmist has found a "hiding place" (v. 114, ESV) in the Lord.

## 119:121–128 AYIN

Throughout Psalm 119, the psalmist declares that he will keep God's laws/decrees (see for example *Beth*, vv. 9, 16). In *Ayin*, the sixteenth strophe, we have an example of what it means to follow God's commands (v. 121). Because the laws reflect the character of God, they represent what is important to God. From other psalms, we know that "righteousness and justice are the foundation of his throne" (Pss 97:2b; 89:14) and that justice for the poor and the oppressed is of the utmost important to the Most High (Psalm 82). In the OT, the term, "righteousness and justice," is used in connection with the laws concerning the proper treatment of the vulnerable (Exod 22:22–27). When the psalmist declares at the beginning of *Ayin* that he has done "what is righteous and just" (119:121a), this includes actions taken to uplift the weak and the oppressed and doing what is right. The strophe begins with an emphasis on doing what is right (v. 121) and ends with the psalmist hating "every wrong path" (v. 128). When we hate "every wrong path" and defend the cause of the poor, we will find ourselves in trouble, because the poor are usually the victims of injustice, and so their oppressors will turn against us. After doing what is right and just, the psalmist pleads with God, "do not leave me to my oppressors" (v. 121b; see also v. 122).

Yet God's answer does not seem to be forthcoming, for the psalmist says, "My eyes fail, looking for your salvation" (v. 123). Because it is "time" for the Lord "to act" (v. 126), the psalmist cries out, "Deal with your servant according to your love" (v. 124). This desperate situation leads the psalmist to proclaim other motivations about why God should act now:

- "I am your servant" (v. 125);
- "I love your commands more than gold . . ." (v. 127);
- "I consider all your precepts right" (v. 128).

## Psalm 119

### 119:129–136 PE

The word "wonderful" is the first Hebrew word at the beginning of *Pe*, the seventeenth strophe. This word comes from Hebrew word *pele'*, which appears in its plural form in verse 129. In its plural form, "wonderful" generally refers to "God's mighty acts on behalf of all Israel, through which it was delivered from afflictions in the past and preserved as a people."[15] Thus the words "marvelous" and "spectacular" are also apt translations of the word. When the psalmist says that God's statutes are "wonderful," he is saying that God's word is "more precious than thousands of pieces of silver and gold" (see v. 72 in *Teth*; compare v. 127 in *Ayin*). Like the parable of the hidden treasure, it would be wise to sell everything one has to have that treasure (Matt 13:44). Because God's "statutes are wonderful," the psalmist resolves that he will "obey them" (119:129).

God's "wonderful" word "gives understanding to the simple" (v. 130). The word "simple" (*petî*) refers to the "simple and inexperienced"[16] and "clearly expresses a lack of experience and maturity and the attendant incapacity and helplessness."[17] When the "simple" open themselves to the "unfolding" of God's word, they receive understanding. The word "unfolding" (v. 130) comes from the Hebrew word *petakh*, whose verbal meaning includes "to open." To receive from God's word, one has to be open. Thus "opening" his mouth, the psalmist will "pant, longing for your commands" (v. 131). These gestures signify a posture of openness and may be read as a prelude to the petitions that follow, which express the psalmist's need for help and understanding. The psalmist admits that he is "simple" and therefore asks God for the following:

- mercy: "Turn to me and have mercy on me" (v. 132);
- direction: "Direct my footsteps according to your word" (v. 133);
- redemption: "Redeem me from human oppression" (v. 134);
- divine favor: "Make your face shine on your servant" (v. 135).

These petitions reflect a posture of humility and openness. Unfortunately, not all who are "simple and inexperienced" are open to God's prompting and learning, for many choose to stray from the paths of righteousness. Thus the psalmist laments: "Streams of tears flow from my eyes for your law is not obeyed" (v. 136). Again, we see here the importance of emotions as a mark of

---

15. *TDOT*, 11:540.
16. *TDOT*, 12:168.
17. *TDOT*, 12:167.

spiritual maturity. Those who love the word of God weep when it is violated. When we do not grieve in the face of wickedness, something is seriously wrong with our obedience.

### 119:137–144 TSADHE

The laws reflect the nature of the one who establishes them. The first word in *Tsadhe*, the eighteenth strophe, is "righteous": "Righteous are you, O Lord" (v. 137), who "laid down" these statutes (v. 138). Because the Lord "laid down" the commands (see also *Aleph*, v. 4), they are "right" (v. 137). The Hebrew word for right/righteous (*tsdq*) is repeated four times in this strophe (vv. 137, 138, 142, 144). The "statutes" of the Lord are described as both "righteous" and "fully trustworthy" (v. 138b). The promises of the Lord are "thoroughly tested" (v. 140), like metals which have been fully refined (compare Ps 12:6).

Thus the psalmist is greatly affected when enemies "ignore your words" (v. 139; compare *Pe*, v. 136). His reaction – "My zeal consumes me" (v. 139, ESV) – is similar to Jesus's response when the Temple was turned into a den of robbers (Mark 11:15–17). Interestingly, the LXX has "zeal for your house" in verse 139. Earlier, the psalmist is flooding with tears because God's "law is not obeyed" (v. 136). The "trouble and distress" that the psalmist describes in verse 143 might be connected to his deep concern for God's law. He also describes himself as "lowly and despised" (v. 141). The word "lowly" comes from the Hebrew word *tsaʿir*, which is parallel to *dal* ("low" or "insignificant").[18] In spite of his lowly situation, he does "not forget" God's precepts (v. 141) and continues to ask God to give him "understanding" so that he might "live" (v. 144).

### 119:145–152 QOPH

*Qoph*, the nineteenth strophe, is full of expressions that are common in the lament psalms:

- "I call . . . answer me" (v. 145);
- "I call out to you" (v. 146);
- "I cry for help" (v. 147);
- "hear my voice" (v. 149).

The text does not provide details about the psalmist's situation, which is true for most laments, but it does convey a sense of urgency. The psalmist says,

---

18. *TDOT*, 12:426.

"I rise before dawn and cry for help" (v. 147a). We may think that lament is a sign that hope is lacking, but lament can actually be an indication of hope. As Christians, we can lament in the same way that the psalmist does, who cries out for help because "I have put my hope in your word" (v. 147b). In Lamentations, crying and weeping are signs of persistent faith, as the speaker insists, "My eyes will flow unceasingly, without relief, until the Lord looks down from heaven and sees" (Lam 3:49–50). In Psalm 119, the psalmist's "eyes stay open through the watches of the night" (v. 148a), pleading with God to "preserve my life" (v. 149) while meditating on God's promises (v. 148b). The psalmist complains that those who are "far from your law" are "near" (v. 150), and yet he immediately declares that the Lord is "near" (v. 151). Notice the alternation between the words "far" and "near." God's nearness is shown in the way that the psalmist is crying out to the Lord, who "laid down" (vv. 4, 138) statutes that have been "established" to last "forever" (v. 152).

## 119:153–160 RESH

Lament continues in the next strophe, *Resh*. The previous strophe, *Qoph*, begins with the common lament expressions: "I call" (vv. 145–146) and "I cry" (v. 147). The *Resh* strophe also employs several common lament petitions. First, the petition, "preserve my life," is repeated three times (vv. 154, 156, 159). The Hebrew word for "preserve my life" (*khaya*) can also mean "let live," "give life," or "revive."[19] Second, the psalmist asks God to "look on my suffering and deliver me" (v. 153). Third, the psalmist prays that God will "defend my cause" (v. 154; compare 35:1; 43:1).

The psalmist is plagued by "many" persecutors (v. 157), and so he appeals to the Lord's "great" compassion (v. 156). The words "great" and "many" in these verses share the same Hebrew word, *rab*. Though the psalmist has many enemies, he has an advantage because he senses God's nearness (v. 151). He can always cry out to God and give a report about whatever is troubling him. By contrast, "salvation is far from the wicked" (v. 155a) because "they do not seek your decrees" (v. 155b). For the psalmist, what's really important is whether one seeks God's decrees and obeys God's word. For the one who does not obey God's word, the psalmist's reaction is one of "loathing" (v. 158). Before God, he wants to be known as someone who "loves your precepts" (v. 159).

---

19. *BDB*, 311.

### 119:161–168 SIN/SHIN

In *Resh*, the previous strophe, the psalmist complains about his many persecutors (v. 157). In the twenty-first strophe, *Sin/Shin*, we learn that "rulers" are among those who persecute him (v. 161). Though this situation might cause some to tremble and fear, the psalmist is not afraid of the rulers, for his heart only trembles before God's word (v. 161b). He is not afraid of what powerful people say, for the fear of God reigns in his heart. This fear, this "trembling at your word" (v. 161), leads the psalmist to "rejoice" (v. 162). The same "word" that causes "trembling" also brings about rejoicing because of the "promise" that God made for "those who love your law" (v. 165). To love God's law means to "hate and detest falsehood" (v. 163). In these few verses, the psalmist exhibits extremely varied emotions: fear, joy, hate, and love.

The great promise that awaits those who love God's word is that they will have "great peace" and "nothing can make them stumble" (v. 165). The word "peace" here comes from the word "shalom," which means well-being, prosperity, a blessed life. Moreover, the promise is not just for *shalom* but "great" *shalom*! No wonder the psalmist declares, "I love your law" (v. 163). And later, he proclaims this even more strongly, saying, "I love them greatly" (v. 167). The "great" *shalom* has found a "great" lover.

### 119:169–176 TAW

Psalm 119 consists of several laments, but unlike the typical lament, which ends on a note of confidence or praise, the final strophe does not follow the common pattern by ending in praise. The opening lines of any strophe often convey the "priority" or main idea in the strophe. If this is true, then *Taw*, the twenty-second strophe, emphasizes the element of the petition in a lament. Just as the psalmist declares earlier that the Lord is near (see *Qoph*, v. 151), now he prays, "May my cry come near before you" (v. 169, my translation). The very first word in verse 169 is the Hebrew word *tiqrab*, which means "to be near." The parallel petition in verse 170 is similar, but the psalmist appeals to "your promise," recalling the "great" promise in the previous strophe (*Shin*, v. 165).

Although the psalmist wants to offer praise to the Lord (vv. 171–172, 175), he remains in a situation of lament as he waits for the "salvation" that he trusts will come from the Lord (v. 174). The psalmist admits that he has "strayed like a lost sheep," and yet he also pleads, "seek your servant, for I have not forgotten your commands" (v. 176). This brings out the sense of contradiction reflected throughout the psalm. As von Rad observes:

> The theological peculiarity of Ps. cxix is that it has entwined the two ["extreme form" of righteousness and "extreme suffering of abandonment"] indissolubly, for the same man who takes his delight in the revelation of the will of Jahweh, so as to set it above all earthly possessions, and whose heart is consumed with longing for it, is nevertheless put to shame (v. 22), threatened by princes (v. 23), his soul cleaves to the dust (v. 25), he is ensnared by the cords of the wicked (v. 61), slandered (v. 69), oppressed (v. 78), persecuted (v. 84), etc.[20]

The very last verse of Psalm 119 puts into question the declaration at the very beginning of the psalm. Psalm 119 opens with a declaration about the blessedness of those "who walk according to the law of the LORD" (*Aleph*, v. 1), but it concludes with one who likens himself to a "lost sheep" even though he has not forgotten God's commands (v. 176). The word "lost" comes from the Hebrew word *'abad*, which literally means, "perished" or "destroyed." The contradiction at the end of Psalm 119 is not a simple one.

---

20. Gerhard von Rad, *Old Testament Theology*, vol. 1 (Edinburgh and London: Oliver and Boyd, 1962), 400.

# PSALM 120

Psalm 120 is the first of the fifteen so-called "Songs of Ascents" (Psalms 120–134). One explanation for this name is that these psalms were sung/recited by pilgrims as they went up to the Temple in Jerusalem. Another theory is that the songs arose out of the context of the return from exile. Both theories reflect a direction or movement towards the Temple, which in turn brings out the people's longing for a return.

The upward movement reflected in the word "ascent" signifies a positive movement, which in turn contrasts with the downward movement we see in Psalm 120. "To 'ascend' is to be close to Yahweh, to experience life. To 'descend' is to sink down into the Deep, the realm of death."[1] Psalm 120 is expected to provide an enthusiastic beginning to the journey up to the Temple. But Psalm 120 could be a quite disappointing psalm, and according to Cox, "It does not seem appropriate for the occasion."[2]

Psalm 120 is a lament psalm,[3] but unlike the usual lament psalm, which contains a resolution at the end, Psalm 120 moves from thanksgiving to lament. I describe this pattern as a "tragic lament." Although this form is not common, the "tragic lament" can be found elsewhere (see Psalms 9–10; 40; 89). But why would someone compose a tragic lament psalm? We always want a happy ending, as we so often see in Korean dramas. One function of a "tragic lament" is to provide space for the contradictions and tensions that are inherent in the life of faith.

Tragic laments are those that do not have a resolution at the end. This is important, as Christians often emphasize victory only. Indeed, for a long time, Christianity has promoted triumphalism. Like the upward movement in the Songs of Ascent, there is an expectation that when you go to church, you should be okay. But as I write (amidst the coronavirus pandemic), this overly optimistic attitude does not reflect where most people are today. Many of our Overseas Filipino Workers (OFW) have lost their jobs and can no longer send

---

1. G. T. M. Prinsloo, "The Role of Space in the ŠYRY HM'LWT (Psalms 120–134)," *Bib* 86, no. 4 (2005): 461.
2. Samuel Cox, *The Pilgrim Psalms: An Exposition of the Songs of Degrees* (London: R. D. Dickinson, 1885), 14. For Cox, Psalm 121 would have made a good psalm for the beginning of the "Songs of Ascents." Cox took pains in explaining why Psalm 120 should be included among the "Songs of Ascent." But when it came to Psalm 121, he simply endorsed it. Cox, *The Pilgrim Psalms: An Exposition of the Songs of Degrees*, 24.
3. For a more focused discussion on Psalm 120, see Villanueva, "From Thanksgiving to Lament: The Shape of Psalm 120."

money to their families back home. The uncertainties and feelings of loneliness and abandonment of this time make Psalm 120 a much-needed companion.

Psalm 120 was deliberately placed to follow the longest psalm (Psalm 119) and composed as the beginning of the "Songs of Ascent." Though Psalm 120 can easily fall under the long shadow cast by Psalm 119, Zenger argues that Psalm 120 is a "*literary* composition" that "was deliberately created . . . for the collection made up of Psalms 120–134."[4] Unfortunately, Zenger misses the important element of tension and the tragic sensibility in Psalm 120.[5] For him, verse 1 contains a "programmatic allusion to Zion/the Temple as the place from whence Yahweh hears and saves."[6] This interpretation places the emphasis on the certainty and assurance that awaits those who call on Yahweh. However, as I will demonstrate in the commentary below, Psalm 120 is full of tension and contradiction, picking up exactly where Psalm 119 ends.

Psalm 120 may be outlined as follows:

Thanksgiving (v. 1),
Petition (v. 2),
Certainty of a hearing (vv. 3–4),
Complaint (vv. 5–7).

## 120:1–2 FROM THANKSGIVING TO LAMENT

By itself, verse 1 can easily be considered a thanksgiving. Though short, it has the main element of a thanksgiving – an account of the psalmist's experience of deliverance or answer to prayer. According to Westermann, this account, which usually consists of "one sentence," is the core on which the thanksgiving psalm is developed. (He cites Pss 116:1 and 138:3 as examples.)[7] In Psalm 120:1, we have the core of the thanksgiving as the psalmist recalls how in his "distress," he "called to the Lord," and the Lord "answered me" (v. 1, ESV).

However, instead of following the pattern of a thanksgiving psalm, Psalm 120 turns into a lament. Immediately after the thanksgiving, just after the words of the testimony, the psalmist cries out, "Save me, Lord" (v. 2). Though the psalmist has just testified about how God answered his prayer, now he is

---

4. Zenger and Hossfeld, *Psalms 3*, 305.
5. Nonetheless, I agree with Zenger about the purposeful and deliberate composition and placement of this psalm.
6. Zenger and Hossfeld, *Psalms 3*, 305.
7. Westermann, *Praise and Lament in the Psalms*, 106. Gunkel acknowledges that verse 1 is the beginning of a thanksgiving. Gunkel, *Die Psalmen*, 538.

asking God to deliver him again. The situation in verse 2 is difficult, as the psalmist pleads for deliverance from "lying lips" (120:2; compare Ps 12:2). Throughout the Psalter, the wicked are known by their speech:[8] "those who tell lies" (Ps 5:6, 9–10) and are "full of . . . threats" (Ps 10:7). The presence of these people is extremely serious, for if "everyone lies to their neighbor" (Ps 12:2), we are in big trouble! Thus the psalmist cries, "help!" (Ps 12:1).

Form-critically, the shift from thanksgiving to lament is unexpected. Petition should lead to an expression of trust or a vow of praise, which then forms the beginning of the thanksgiving. As Westermann declares, "The petition that has been heard leads to declarative praise."[9] Thus Gunkel finds Psalm 120 "rather odd,"[10] and so he repoints the verb *'nh* ("answer") in verse 1 to read, "I call *so that he may answer me*." In this instance, we see the limitations of the Gunkel style of form criticism, where if the text does not fit in with the typical movement of a lament, he adjusts the text to fit the general structure.[11] Yet in verse 1, the verb refers to a past narrative.[12] Thus the psalmist is recounting a past experience, not a present one.

What other scholars may find "rather odd" here yields important pastoral and theological insights. The unexpected turn from thanksgiving to lament is a needed corrective to an overly secure and certainty-focused life of faith. Psalm 120 reminds us that even when we have moved into a season of new orientation, we sometimes find ourselves suddenly back in a season of disorientation. The life of faith is complicated, and our seasons of life will change in unexpected ways. The only unchanging reality is Yahweh. In Hebrew, the first words in verse 1 are, "To Yahweh," which I think is deliberate. The psalmist could have started with, "I called" (compare Ps 138:3; Jonah 3:2), but he starts with the name "Yahweh" to connect it with the petition that follows, which also begins with the name "Yahweh" (Ps 120:2). What binds the thanksgiving and the lament together is the name of the Lord. We are able to weather the unpredictable seasons of life because the Lord of thanksgiving is also the Lord in times of lament.

---

8. Gordon J. Wenham, *Psalms as Torah: Reading Biblical Song Ethically* (Grand Rapids, MI: Baker Academic, 2012), 107–109.
9. Westermann, *Praise and Lament in the Psalms*, 102.
10. Gunkel, *Die Psalmen*, 537.
11. Gunkel, *Die Psalmen*, 538.
12. John A. Cook, *Time and the Biblical Hebrew Verb: The Expression of Tense, Aspect, and Modality in Biblical Hebrew* (2016), 298–300.

# Psalm 120

## 120:3–7 FROM CERTAINTY TO COMPLAINT

This short psalm of only seven verses is characterized by sudden shifts. In verse 1, the narrator talks about Yahweh, whereas in verse 2, the narrator addresses Yahweh directly in the form of a prayer. In verse 3, there is another shift as the psalmist addresses the "deceitful tongue." Allen rightly observes that the point of view in this difficult verse is similar to Psalm 6, which directly addresses "you workers of evil" (v. 8).[13] Psalm 120:4 could be read as the psalmist's confident answer to the question he raises in verse 3. The NIV makes it explicit that the "warrior's sharp arrows, with burning coals" are the Lord's punishment on the wicked. If this view is correct, then verse 4 marks another transition to a "certainty of a hearing," for the psalmist is assured that Yahweh will deliver him.

Yet in the next verse, the psalmist cries out in a lament once again: "Woe to me" (v. 5). The cry "woe!" and the Hebrew word for motivation, *ki* ("that"), both belong to the form of the lament (see Lam 5:15; Jer 10:19; 15:10).[14] Thus verse 5 makes a second reverse movement in this psalm, from the certainty of a hearing back to lament (the first reverse movement occurs between the thanksgiving in v. 1 and the psalmist's petition to "Save me, LORD" in v. 2). These shifts effectively shatter the form-critical view.

The psalmist cries "woe" because he dwells in "Meshek," "among the tents of Kedar" (v. 5). The location of "Meshek" and "Kedar" is not given, but these places may be interpreted figuratively as "equivalent to 'barbarians' or 'heathens'" and may "denote any hostile and unreasonable enemies."[15] Thus "the psalmist may have lived in the Diaspora"[16] This reminds me of the experience of many of our OFWs who have been abused in foreign lands. The psalmist is complaining because he has been living "among people who hate peace" (v. 6), but he is "for peace" (v. 7). By "speaking" for peace in verse 7, he is implying that he is a person of peace. As we noted in verse 2, the wicked are known by their speech, which is destructive. The text brings out a sense of isolation. The psalmist is presented as an "I," someone speaking for peace alone in the midst of many who are speaking for war. This situation would be torturous, and the

---

13. Allen, *Psalms 101–150*, 147. The main question is who/what is the subject of the verb "do" (literally "give") and to whom/what is the "you" referring to in this verse? In the first view, the subject of the verbs in verse 3 is Yahweh, and "you" refers to the "deceitful tongue," or the wicked. The second view takes "deceitful tongue" as the subject of the verb, with Yahweh as the one being addressed. In the second case, the petition in verse 2 turns into a bitter lament in verse 3. The difficulty with this view, however, is verse 4, which fits more with the first view.
14. Gunkel, *Die Psalmen*, 538.
15. Arnold Albert Anderson, *The Book of Psalms*, vol. 2 (Grand Rapids: Eerdmans, 1992), 850.
16. Anderson, *The Book of Psalms*, 850.

psalmist has tragically been in this situation for "too long" (v. 6). In Filipino, we would say, *sobra na, tama na*! ("It's too much, enough!"). When we reach this point, where do we go? Where do we find hope? Psalm 121 points us to the source of our true help.

# PSALM 121

Psalm 121 is the second psalm in the "Songs of Ascent" (see the superscription). It is similar to Psalm 120 in that the opening verse differs from the rest of the psalm. Psalm 120 begins with a thanksgiving (v. 1), which is followed by a tragic lament (vv. 2–7).[1] Psalm 121 begins with a lament (vv. 1–2), which is followed by words of assurance (vv. 3–8).

This psalm is "commonly . . . interpreted as a dialogue between a pilgrim and a priest," where the first two verses represent the words of the pilgrim, and the rest are "words of assurance" from the cult officials.[2] This is a helpful background for interpreting this psalm, which begins with an individual asking, "where does my help come from?" (v. 1b). It is important not to miss the important element of lament and the sense of tension in this opening verse by rushing quickly to the "answer" in verse 2. In order to appreciate that answer, we have to linger with the psalmist's question, from which the psalmist's answer emerges (v. 2), along with the "priestly" words of encouragement through the rest of the psalm (vv. 3–8).

Psalm 121 is similar to Psalm 91, as both are considered to be psalms of confidence and assurance in times of uncertainties. Yet these psalms can be abused if they are used to raise people's hopes falsely, for not everyone experiences protection, and even the faithful slip and fall (see v. 3). Moreover, those who are going through times of uncertainty and perplexity do not need words of assurance as much as presence. Rather than stretching the words of this psalm to make promises to someone who is struggling, it would be more helpful to think about how we can use the psalm as a creative means of being present. Psalm 119 teaches us that divine words are also a way to be present (see comments on Ps 119:19 above).

## 121:1–2 LAMENT AND EXPRESSION OF TRUST

One question concerning verse 1 is whether it is making a statement of trust or expressing a sense of anxiety and uncertainty.[3] The phrase, "I lift up my eyes," expresses a sense of desperation and vulnerability rather than confidence

---

1. By "tragic" lament, I mean a lament without resolution.
2. Gerstenberger, *Psalms Part 2 and Lamentations*, 324.
3. Zenger takes the former view. For him, the phrase, "I lift up my eyes" "signals longing and trust." Zenger and Hossfeld, *Psalms 3*, 322. Influenced by his own interpretation of the whole psalm, Zenger translates the second part of the verse as a statement–"from where my help

and trust. The same phrase is also used in Psalm 123, which conveys a sense of utter helplessness. Those who are lifting their eyes liken themselves to "slaves" who are completely dependent on their master's response (123:2). They are crying out in lament, pleading for mercy, because their suffering is too much to bear (123:3). The context of Psalm 121:1 indicates a similar situation. The psalmist is lifting up his eyes because he needs help, and so he asks, "where does my help come from?" Throughout the Psalms, God is the helper of the poor (Ps 72:12), the fatherless (Ps 10:14), and those in despair (Ps 86:17). All three of these texts employ the same Hebrew word for "help" (*'ezer*).

The opening verse of Psalm 121 is similar to the traditional cries of lament: "how long?" "when?" "why?" (e.g. Pss 13:1–2; 22:1–2).[4] Whereas the opening verse of Psalm 120 embodies the thanksgiving psalm (v. 1), the opening verse of Psalm 121 embodies the lament psalm (v.1). In one verse, each of these psalms represent either the thanksgiving or the lament. This accounts for the brevity of the psalms in the "Songs of Ascents," which each have an average of only six verses.[5]

Immediately after the lament, "where does my help come from?" the psalmist answers his own question: "My help comes from the LORD" (v. 2). Confronted by dangers, troubles, and perils symbolized by "the mountains" (v. 1a), the psalmist declares that his help comes from "the Maker of heaven and earth" (v. 2b).[6]

## 121:3–8 WORDS OF ASSURANCE

The psalmist's response to his own question/lament is similar to a declaration of trust at the end of a lament (e.g. Ps 13:5). Yet this first person declaration of trust is followed by a series of promises. In verse 3, there is a shift to second

---

comes from," transforming the whole of verse 1 as a statement of confidence and trust. But as Zenger himself admits, the Hebrew word *m'yn* (literally, "from where") "as a rule introduces a question." Zenger and Hossfeld, *Psalms 3*, 316.
4. Gerstenberger, *Psalms Part 2 and Lamentations*, 322.
5. Loren D. Crow, *The Songs of Ascents (Psalms 120–134): Their Place in Israelite History and Religion*, SBL Dissertation Series (Atlanta: Scholars Press, 1996), 129.
6. In the midrash on the "Binding of Isaac," we get a glimpse of what it feels for someone so desperate to utter the first verse of Psalm 121. As Abraham reaches of the knife, "his mouth fell wide open with weeping as a great cry of anguish erupted from him. Then, his eyes blinking frantically, he looked up to the Presence and pleaded in a rising voice, 'I lift mine eyes to the mountains; whence will my help come?'" Though answer eventually came, it arrived only after the "venting of his [Abraham's] anguish, the protest of the angels, and the deliberation of God." Karl A. Plank, "Ascent to Darker Hills: Psalm 121 and Its Poetic Revision," *Literature and Theology* 11, no. 2 (1997): 155.

person direct address. Is the speaker the same in the previous two verses? Or is there another speaker (a cultic priest or the entire community) now addressing the psalmist? Both are possible. In the first view, the psalmist shares with others what he has experienced. Having gone through this perilous journey, he is equipped to offer encouragement to those who are about to embark on a similar journey. The second view highlights the importance of the community. We all need someone to encourage us through our times of uncertainty.

The sheer number of encouraging verses betray the psalmist's need for continuing assurance. As Plank observes, "Assurance means little where no anxiety can exist."[7] Notice the following negative statements:

- "He will *not* let your foot slip" (v. 3a).
- "He who watches over you will *not* slumber" (v. 3b).
- "Behold, he who watches over Israel will *not* slumber and will *not* sleep" (v. 4, my translation).

Though the psalmist expresses some certainty in verse 2, he needs to be reminded again of the truth that God will not abandon him. The fourfold "not" statements remind the psalmist of the mountains before him (121:1). The "mountains" have been interpreted either as symbolizing the place where God dwells (Zion) or the "perils of a journey through a mountain-range, with its steep paths, ravines and gorges, the hiding-places of wild beasts and robbers."[8] If the latter, then the statements in verses 3–4 are meant to assuage his feelings of fear. The psalmist could be having doubts about whether he will be able to navigate the dangers ahead of him in his journey. The threefold repetition of the verb for sleeping ("slumber," which is repeated twice in vv. 3–4, and "sleep" in v. 4) probably betrays the feeling that God seems to be doing nothing. In Filipino, we have a popular song entitled, *Natutulog ba ang Diyos?* ("Is God Sleeping?"). Perhaps the psalmist is asking a similar question in Psalm 121?

If so, then the psalmist is reminded that the Lord "watches over you" (v. 5). The word "watch" occurs six times in the psalm and comes from the Hebrew word, *shamar*, which means "to keep." In Psalm 119, the psalmist repeatedly expresses his longing to keep the Torah (e.g. vv. 5, 9, 17). Yahweh expects humans to care for the Torah,[9] and the promise in Psalm 121 is the divine counterpart for that expectation. The divine promise is for constant

---
7. Plank, "Ascent to Darker Hills: Psalm 121 and Its Poetic Revision," 163.
8. Weiser, *The Psalms. A Commentary*, 746.
9. Bob Becking, "God-Talk for a Disillusioned Pilgrim in Psalm 121," *The Journal of Hebrew Scriptures* 9 (2009): 8.

protection, both day and night. Verse 6 recalls the protection and guidance that the Israelites experienced in the desert (the cloud by day and the pillar of fire by night; see Exod 13:21). The divine protection is not only constant, but also comprehensive, for "The LORD will keep you from *all* harm" (Ps 121:7). The last verse applies this protection to the psalmist's "coming" and "going" (v. 8), which is an apt description for a "song of ascent." As the pilgrim sets out to go up to the hill of the Lord, he is assured that divine guidance and protection will accompany him every step of the way – all the way to his destination and back home again.

# PSALM 122

Psalm 122 is the third psalm in the "Songs of Ascent." According to Cox, this is the song that the pilgrims sing when they arrive in the Holy City.[1] He considers the psalm to be the most emphatic pilgrim psalm among the collection.[2] Unlike Psalm 120, there is a clear upward movement in Psalm 122. Whereas Psalm 120 places us at the bottom of a looming mountain, and Psalm 121 casts a vision for the setting out on the journey, Psalm 122 brings us to our destination: "Our feet are standing in your gates, Jerusalem" (v. 2).

The psalm begins with an invitation, "Let us go to the house of the LORD" (v. 1b), for which the psalmist is "glad" (v. 1a). This scenario is different from today, when many church members struggle to get out of bed every Sunday to gather as a congregation. While many people today are not excited about going to church, the psalmist rejoices about going to the Temple. There are three reasons for his gladness. First, the Temple is a place of rejoicing (v. 1). Second, the tribes go there to "praise the name of the LORD" (v. 4). Third, the Temple is the place of prayer for the community (v. 6). Moreover, the threefold repetition of "Jerusalem" is woven into the structure of the psalm as the people rejoice in Jerusalem (vv. 1–2), praise God in Jerusalem (vv. 3–5), and pray for Jerusalem (vv. 6–9).

## 122:1–2 REJOICING IN JERUSALEM

While some people today do not get excited when they are invited to church, the psalmist rejoices when his neighbors tell him, "Let us go to the house of the LORD" (v. 1). The phrase, "house of the LORD," is repeated at the end of the psalm (v. 9), holding the whole psalm together in an inclusio. Even the most vulnerable creatures – tiny birds – find their home in the house of the Lord (Ps 84:3). And even outsiders are welcome in the Temple, which is called the "house of prayer for all nations" in the book of Isaiah (Isa 56:7). Peace is a central theme in Psalm 122 (see vv. 6–9 below). Thus it is a joy to go to the Temple.

Reading this psalm together with Psalm 121, we can observe a progression. In Psalm 121, the psalmist begins his journey with some anxiety about how he will navigate the perilous paths before him (v. 1: "where does my help come

---

1. Cox, *The Pilgrim Psalms*, 48.
2. Cox, *The Pilgrim Psalms*, 48.

from?"). After receiving encouraging promises, he is strengthened to make that journey. Having made that journey successfully, he now finds himself standing within the gates of Jerusalem (122:2). He can rejoice and be glad, for the Lord has not let his "foot slip," but has watched over him as promised (121:3).

### 122:3–5 PRAISING IN JERUSALEM

From rejoicing, the second section moves to statements that highly praise Jerusalem, similar to those we find in other Zion psalms (Psalms 46; 48). Jerusalem is described as being "built like a city" (122:3). Though the subject of the passive verb "built" is not specified, we may infer from Psalm 127 that the Lord is the one who built it (127:1). The words "house," "build," and "city" occur in both Psalms 122 and 127. Psalm 127 emphasizes that "Unless the LORD build the house, the builders labor in vain" (127:1). In Psalm 127, the word "house" (v. 1) is parallel to the word "city" (v. 2), and in Psalm 122, the city of Jerusalem is closely identified with the house of the Lord. The city is where all the "tribes of the LORD" go up "to praise the name of the LORD" (v. 4). It is also the place where justice is administered. The phrase, "thrones for judgment" (v. 5), refers to "the legal institutions, seats of justice" that were instituted by the Davidic monarchy.[3]

In verse 5, the word "judgment" (*mishpat*) is mentioned right after "praise." One purpose of going to the Temple is to worship the Lord, but without a concern for justice, our worship is useless (Amos 5:21–24) because God's throne is founded on "righteousness and justice" (Pss 97:2; 89:14). The psalmist declares, "The King . . . loves justice" (99:4), and the prophets have made it clear that justice should be administered in the city (Mic 3:9–12; Isa 1:21–23).[4]

### 122:6–9 PRAYING FOR JERUSALEM

Psalm 122:6, "Pray for the peace of Jerusalem," is often used by Christians to defend the modern state of Israel, and they see it as their responsibility to pray for "the peace of Jerusalem." In Hebrew, the words for "pray" (*sha'al*, literally, "ask"), "peace" (*shalom*), "security" (*shalwah*), and the name "Jerusalem" (*yerushalaim*) all share similar sounds. The psalmist wishes that the city of Jerusalem will live up to its name as a city of peace and security (v. 7), a place where justice is administered (see v. 5).

---

3. Mays, *Psalms*, 393.
4. Mays, *Psalms*, 393.

But if "Jerusalem" no longer lives up to her name, then we are not obligated to pray for it. As the Lord commanded Jeremiah: "So do not pray for this people nor offer any plea or petition for them . . . for I will not listen to you" (Jer 7:16). God will not listen because the people of Jerusalem are oppressing the foreigners, fatherless, and widows (Jer 7:6). The instruction to pray for the prosperity of the city (Ps 122:6) is "for the sake of the house of God" (v. 9a). The Temple is a house of prayer for all the nations to pray to the King whose throne is founded on justice and righteousness. Thus Jesus protests when he goes into the Temple and sees it being used as a "den of robbers" (Mark 11:15–17).[5]

---

5. According to N. T. Wright from the perspective of the "poorer classes," the Temple symbolized "the oppression they suffered at the hands of the elite." N. T. Wright, *Jesus and the Victory of God*,(London: SPCK, 1996), 412.

# PSALM 123

Psalm 123 expresses the people's suffering in words that capture the experience of those who have experienced foreign domination: "As the eyes of slaves look to the hand of their master" (v. 2). During the colonization period, Filipinos lived as slaves in our own land. To some extent, this continues to be true even today, as the effects of colonization are still very present.

The genre of Psalm 123 reflects the tragic experience of the people. In verse 1, an individual speaks, but then this "I" shifts to "we" through the rest of the psalm (vv. 2–4). Thus Gunkel sees the psalm as a mixture "between the individual and communal complaint song."[1] Allen, however, sees it as a "communal lament."[2] I think this psalm clearly reveals the limits of these categories of "individual" and "communal" lament, for in Psalm 123, the experience of the individual is closely connected with the community, and so the psalmist can speak in the collective voice ("we"). From this perspective, the psalm can be viewed as an individual lament.

However, it does not follow the typical form of an individual lament, for as Zenger observes, there is no certainty of a hearing at the end.[3] Moreover, the psalm moves from a "confession of trust" (vv. 1–2) to "an emphatic petition" (vv. 3–4),[4] which reverses the order of the typical individual lament. Zenger calls the psalm an "open conclusion,"[5] as there is no resolution even at the end of the psalm. This shares a parallel with Psalm 120, which is another lament that also has no resolution at the end. The language of Psalm 120 also has some similarities with Psalm 123 (see discussion of 123:4 below).

The "openness" of the psalm in terms of its absence of resolution or the presence of the certainty of a hearing at the end reflects the situation depicted in the psalm. Moreover, the shape of Psalm 123 may be deliberate in order to convey the sense of the tragic.

## 123:1–2 EXPRESSION OF TRUST AND COMPLAINT

Psalm 123 opens similarly to Psalm 121, as the first verse of both psalms uses the words, "I lift up my eyes," though there are two main differences. First,

---

1. Gunkel and Begrich, *Introduction to Psalms*, 347.
2. Allen, *Psalms 101–150*, 216.
3. Zenger and Hossfeld, *Psalms 3*, 346.
4. Zenger and Hossfeld, *Psalms 3*, 345.
5. Zenger and Hossfeld, *Psalms 3*, 346.

in Psalm 121, the speaker looks up "to the mountains" (121:1), whereas in Psalm 123, the individual looks "to you" (123:1). Second, in Psalm 123, the Hebrew phrase, "to you," stands at the very beginning of verse 1. There is no ambiguity here, whereas the "mountains" in Psalm 121 could either symbolize the perils of the journey that await the pilgrim or God's presence in Mount Zion. In Psalm 123, however, the parallel line in verse 1 explicitly identifies the "you" to whom the psalmist is lifting his eyes: "you who sit enthroned in heaven" (v. 1b).

Despite these differences, the two psalms agree that there is always someone to whom the people can turn in times of trouble. Confronted by unknown dangers and troubles, the psalmist acknowledges God as his helper (121:2). No matter how hard the situation may be, the people can always come to God to ask for mercy (123:2). The situation envisaged in Psalm 123 is very difficult, which is reflected in the shift between verses 1–2:

"*I* lift up my eyes" (v. 1);
". . . *our* eyes look to the LORD *our* God" (v. 2).

In Psalm 121, the individual receives words of assurance from others, but in Psalm 123, there are no such words of encouragement from others because everyone is suffering. The individual and his community are "all in the same boat."

The entire community in Psalm 123 is in an extremely difficult situation, which is suggested by the comparison of the community to slaves. Those who live under foreign powers exist as slaves. I write this commentary on the five-hundredth year anniversary of the arrival of our Spanish colonizers in the Philippine islands. The Philippines lived under their rule for more than three hundred years. The lament in Psalm 13, "How long?" captures the cry of our people. To suffer under foreign powers is hard enough, but to suffer for such a long time is indescribable torture. According to Botha, one of the "striking features" of Psalm 123 is the "delayed identification" of the collective "our" at the end of verse 2. This delay is "probably done to emphasize the prolonged suffering of Yahweh's people."[6]

---

6. Phil J. Botha, "Social Values and the Interpretation of Psalm 123," *OTE* 14, no. 2 (2001): 191. Compare Wilfred G. E. Watson, *Classical Hebrew Poetry: A Guide to Its Techniques* (Sheffield: Sheffield Academic Press, 2001), 368: "Note that the delaying function of the tricolon in 2bcd was deliberately chosen to express the feeling of waiting and suspense it portrays."

The image of slaves looking to the hand of their master speaks of utter dependence.[7] There is nothing in the slave's power or capacity to change the course of their life's condition. Change is only possible if the master intervenes. The psalmist describes the desired action or intervention from God as "mercy."

> ## THE FILIPINO WORD FOR "MERCY" AND PSALM 123
>
> In Filipino, the word "mercy" is translated as *awa*, which conjures the most pitiable condition imaginable. Whatever intervention God may choose to perform will be viewed as *awa* because of their pitiable condition of prolonged suffering.

### 123:3–4 PLEA FOR MERCY

The twice repeated petition, "have mercy on us" (v. 3), indicates a sense of urgency.[8] We find a similar construction in Psalm 57:1, though Psalm 57 turns to exaltation and praise towards the end, while Psalm 123 remains a lament. The people describe their suffering in terms of the core characteristics of their shame- and honor-based society. The people have experienced "contempt" (v. 3) and "ridicule" (v. 4). Our Spanish colonizers would call us *indios*, and our American colonizers considered us to be children or "little brown brothers." We were never considered to be equals, but always inferior. When a Filipino met a Spanish on the road, he had to turn to the side, or he would be caned. To be treated like this in your own land is even more unbearable than ridicule and contempt. The people in Psalm 123 ask for mercy twice because "we have had more than enough of contempt" (v. 3b, ESV). As we say in Filipino, *sobra na, tama na!* ("enough is enough!").

Verse 4 repeats the words, "we have had more than enough," but instead of using the word, "we," the text changes to "our soul." In Hebrew, the construction is very similar to Psalm 120:6. As the people look at themselves, they feel within their innermost being all the pain and suffering that has been

---

7. Botha, "Social Values and the Interpretation of Psalm 123," 196.
8. Gerstenberger, *Psalms Part 2 and Lamentations*, 331.

brought about by the people whom they describe as "those who are at ease" (123:4, ESV). This word may also be translated as "undisturbed."[9] They are undisturbed, because no matter what they do, they continue to succeed. Thus they not only become "undisturbed," but also "proud" (v. 4). The situation is similar to the lament in Psalm 73 (see comments above), but unlike Psalm 73, there is no resolution in Psalm 123. The psalm ends with a desperate plea for mercy.

---

9. Botha, "Social Values and the Interpretation of Psalm 123," 193.

# PSALM 124

Psalm 124 resembles some of the testimonies we hear in Christian gatherings, when individuals share about how the Lord has intervened in their lives. They might say, "Had it not been for the Lord, I would not have survived," or, "things would have been much worse." After this testimony, those listening might express praise by calling out, "Praise be to the Lord" (see v. 6). In Psalm 124, however, the entire community is testifying about the Lord's intervention. As Prinsloo observes, the use of the pronoun "us" is "the most prominent feature of the poem."[1]

Scholars debate about whether this is an individual thanksgiving or a communal thanksgiving psalm. Some even doubt if there is a "communal thanksgiving" genre. But the central element to the thanksgiving psalm is the testimony about how the Lord intervened, and so Psalm 124 can actually be read as a testimony about how the Lord intervened in the life of the community. With an elaborate testimony that is presented in a dramatic manner, the psalm expresses the thanksgiving of the entire community. At the same time, we also hear the voice of an individual who is exhorting the community to give praise to the Lord (see v. 1). Thus it is not always easy to distinguish between an individual and communal thanksgiving (see comments regarding Psalm 118 above). In Filipino culture, which is traditionally very communal, an individual often speaks in terms of "we," even if he/she is the only one speaking, as a way of representing the consciousness of the group.

Psalm 124 may be read as a continuation of Psalm 123, as Psalm 124 provides the answer that the community is seeking in Psalm 123. Where Psalm 123 ends without any resolution as the people plead with the Lord to "have mercy on us" (v. 3), in Psalm 124 we can see their plea for "mercy" being granted through their freedom from bondage (see v. 7).

The psalm may be divided into two main sections as follows:

"If the Lord had not been on our side" (vv. 1–5);
"Our help is in the name of the Lord" (vv. 6–8).

Within this structure, the emphasis falls on the last verse, linking this psalm to Psalm 121, which describes the Lord with the exact same title: "the Maker of heaven and earth" (121:2b; 124:8b). Both psalms also employ the word

---

1. Prinsloo, "Historical Reality and Mythological Metaphor in Psalm 124," *OTE* 18, no. 3 (2005): 3.

"help," though there is a shift from the personal in Psalm 121 ("my help," v. 1a) to the communal in Psalm 124 ("our help," v. 8a).

## 124:1–5 "IF THE LORD HAD NOT BEEN ON OUR SIDE"

The phrase, "If the LORD had not been on our side," is repeated twice in the opening verses (v. 1a, 2a), forming the following structure:

"If the LORD had not been on our side" (v. 1a),
    "let Israel say" (v. 1b);
"If the LORD had not been on our side" (v. 2a).

The language in these lines resembles a liturgy, where the worship leader calls on the congregation to respond. We see another example of this in Psalm 118:2: "Let Israel say, 'His love endures forever'" (see also vv. 3–4). In Psalm 124, the content of the response is formulated by describing what might have been if the Lord had *not* been on our side. For Moses, the accompanying presence of the Lord is the distinguishing mark of the people of Israel (Exod 33:16). God's presence is so important for Moses that he told the Lord, "If your Presence does not go with us, do not send us up from here" (Exod 33:15). Though not everyone in the community of Israel might acknowledge the importance of God's presence, the author of Psalm 124 is very concerned that the people of Israel recognize the presence of God as a defining aspect of their identity.

The second half of verse 2 introduces what would have happened if the Lord had *not* been with them "when people attacked us" (v. 2b). The Hebrew word for "people" here is *'adam*, which could either mean an individual or people in a collective sense, though the context supports the collective. Those who attacked the people are described using the third person plural, conveying that the enemy is not an individual, but a "multitude of hostile forces."[2]

The element of hostility becomes more evident in the descriptions of the opponents of the people in verses 3–5, where the poet employs the language of ancient Near Eastern mythology. "Floods" and "rivers" (v. 4) belong to the mythology of Canaan and Babylon, and the sea monster, Leviathan, is known for swallowing the living whole. If the Lord had not been for us, the people testify, then "they would have swallowed us alive" (v. 3). In Hebrew, verse 3b literally speaks of the opponents' anger "burning up against us." This

---

[2]. Gert T. M. Prinsloo, "Historical Reality and Mythological Metaphor in Psalm 124," 3. Compare Alastair G. Hunter, *Psalms*, Old Testament Readings (London: Routledge, 1999), 201.

heightens the earlier description in verse 2b, which literally reads, "when they rose up against us."

Verses 4–5 (ESV) form the following chiastic structure:

"then the flood [*hammayim*] would have swept us away,
    the torrent would have gone over [*'abar*] us [*nafshenu*];
    then over [*'abar*] us [*nafshenu*] would have gone
the raging waters [*hammayim*]."

At the center of the structure is the word "us," or literally, "our soul" (*nafshenu*). The "flood" and "raging waters" (both from the Hebrew word *hammayim*) represent the chaotic forces that are at work against "us." The verb "gone over" (*abar*), which is repeated twice, literally speaks of drowning. Verse 5 suspends the subject of the verb, "gone over," to highlight the destructive nature of the forces of chaos. In verse 4, the Hebrew is simply *hammayim* ("flood"), but in verse 5b, the waters are described as "raging." The Hebrew word for "raging" occurs only here in the OT. The context supports the idea of "rising." In verse 2, their hostile enemies "rose up against" them (ESV), and the waters are presented as "over us" in verse 4. The people would have been swept up by the flood and drowned under the rising water.

## 124:6–8 "PRAISE BE TO THE LORD"

But the people praise the Lord, because he has "not let us be torn by their teeth" (v. 6). The language further highlights the hostility of the enemies. The emphasis on the negative recalls the words of assurance expressed in the series of negative statements in Psalm 121 (see vv. 3–6) as well as the pitiable condition of the people at the end of Psalm 123, where the people cry out to God for mercy (v. 3).

God's intervening act of mercy in Psalm 124 is described using the language of freedom. The people liken themselves to a bird who has "escaped" (v. 7). The image of an escaped bird conveys vulnerability and weakness and reminds me of our Filipino lament song, *Bayan Ko* ("My Country"), which likens our people to a weak, feeble, and vulnerable bird who is longing to be free. Like a bird trapped in a cage, we have been imprisoned in our own land by our colonizers for a very long time, and we long for freedom, so we often sing this song during times of national revolution. Psalm 124 speaks of the "snare" being "broken" and declares that the people "have escaped" (v. 7). Unfortunately, this longed-for freedom remains elusive for so many of us. Though our colonizers have long gone, the structures of colonization remain, and our own people have become our colonizers. In spite of this, some Christians can still proclaim that the Lord is "our help" (v. 8). The God whom our colonizers introduced to us has become our God, and if it were not for this God of mercy, we would not have survived. During the time of the Spanish colonization, Filipinos saw Jesus as a companion in their suffering. The story of Jesus's suffering became a powerful symbol of comfort and hope and a means of empowering our people to overcome our colonizers.[3]

---

3. Reynaldo Clemeña Ileto, *Pasyon and Revolution: Popular Movements in the Philippines, 1840–1910* (Quezon City, Metro Manila: Ateneo de Manila University Press, 1979).

# PSALM 125

Psalm 125 is the sixth of the fifteen Songs of Ascents (Psalms 120–134) and contains one of the most extensive descriptions of the characteristics of those who follow God. In only five verses, the psalmist identifies six descriptions of the people of God:

"those who trust God" (v. 1),
"his people" (v. 2),
"righteous" (v. 3, mentioned twice),
"those who are good" (v. 4a), and
"those who are upright in heart" (v. 4b).

These verses highlight the close connection between faith and doing good, trusting in God and righteousness. It should also be noted that in the Hebrew, the descriptions are all in the plural. Faith grows in community, as we allow others to participate in our struggles (Psalm 121), and as we share in the sufferings of our people (Psalm 123). The community that experiences God as their help (Ps 124:8) learns to put their trust in God (Ps 125:1).

But trusting in God is an ongoing process, for the life of faith in community is characterized by the tension between our affirmations of faith and our present reality. The former is expressed in verses 1 and 2, which speak of the stability and security of the people of God, respectively. The latter is implied in verses 3–5. Psalm 125 is not easy to categorize in terms of one genre, as verses 1–2 contain elements of songs of confidence,[1] whereas verses 3–5 contain elements of complaint (implied in v. 3, see below, and petition in vv. 4–5). A number of scholars also view the psalm as a lament of the community.[2] I think the latter is a better description of the psalm, as communal laments tend to embrace the elements of struggle and tension, since a number of these laments do not contain the certainty of a hearing at the conclusion of the psalm (e.g. Psalms 120 and 123). The overall movement of the psalm from a declaration of trust to a petition conveys this sense of tension or contradiction.

---

1. Gerstenberger, *Psalms Part 2 and Lamentations*, 338.
2. Philip Johnston and David G. Firth, eds. *Interpreting the Psalms: Issues and Approaches.* Downers Grove; Leicester, England: InterVarsity Press; Apollos, 2005, 399.

# Psalm 125

## 125:1–2 CONFESSION OF TRUST

As noted above, Psalm 125 emphasizes the characteristics of God's people. The psalmist stresses the blessedness of "those who trust in the Lord," who are "like Mount Zion, which cannot be shaken" (v. 1), and who are assured of God's guidance and protection (v. 2). These verses recall the so-called Zion psalms, which speak of the stability of the mountain where God is present (see Ps 46:5; 48:1–3).

Verse 2 forms a chiastic structure with verse 1:

"Those who trust in the Lord
 are like Mount Zion, which cannot be shaken" (v. 1).
"As the mountains surround Jerusalem,
 so the Lord surrounds his people" (v. 2).

Verse 1a speaks about stability, and verse 2a highlights the sense of protection and security, of being surrounded, kept safe. This recalls the story of the prophet Elisha, whose servant was afraid because an army had surrounded (*sbb*) the city; but after the prophet prayed for the Lord to open his eyes, the servant saw that the mountain was surrounded (*sabib*) by horses and chariots of fire (2 Kgs 6:17). The same Hebrew word for "surround" (*sbb*) that is used in 2 Kings is also used in Psalm 125:2. These first two verses of Psalm 125 also present the nature of the people's covenantal relationship with God. In verse 1, the people are described as "those who trust in the Lord"; in verse 2, they are described as "his people."

## 125:3–5 TENSION AND PETITION

At the beginning of this section, the subject changes suddenly from "those who trust" (v. 1) and Yahweh's protection (v. 2) to the "scepter of the wicked" (v. 3). This unexpected shift raises questions about the previous focus on stability and security. Yet this turn to the "scepter of the wicked" is not accidental, for it marks a deliberate "unsetting of the comfortable picture in the first two verses."[3] Verses 1–2 provide the background for the statement in verse 3, which repeats the word "righteous" twice to disclose the link between the earlier affirmations and the present situation of the people. The expectation is that those who are "righteous" will have stability and protection, but verse 3 indicates that the righteous "might use their hands to do evil" (v. 3b) if the

---

3. Hunter, *Psalms*, 206.

current situation continues. As Weiser argues, "These words of the psalmist are likewise dictated by his fear that his fellow believers might lose their trust in God."[4] If God continues to tolerate evil, even his righteous people might lose their faith and become like the wicked. The scenario is similar to the experience of the author of Psalm 73, who confesses that when he saw the prosperity of the wicked, his feet almost slipped.

Verse 4 turns to a petition, one of the elements of lament. The psalmist asks God to "do good to those who are good." This petition flows from the previous verse, for "if God is truly God . . . then for his own sake he cannot tolerate any wickedness which arrogates to itself rights that belong to God alone."[5] God needs to do something for the righteous; he cannot allow the wicked to "remain on the land allotted to the righteous" (v. 3, ESV).

The presence of this petition after the assertions of trust in verses 1–2 further develops the element of tension in the psalm. The final verse describes the wicked as "those who turn to crooked ways" (v. 5). This establishes a contrast between the righteous and the wicked, which we also find in Psalm 1. While Psalm 1 describes the righteous person by using the image of the tree planted by streams of water, Psalm 125 employs the strong image of Mount Zion to describe how Yahweh himself is surrounding his people. But in spite of this marvelous affirmation, the psalm acknowledges that the situation is not as stable as Psalm 1. Like the laments that follow Psalm 1, we see that the upright in heart still find themselves in situations where the wicked continue to rule, and so the righteous are tempted to give up. Thus the psalmist ends with a prayer: "may the LORD destroy them, as he destroys all evildoers" (v. 5, NEB).[6]

---

4. Weiser, *The Psalms. A Commentary*, 758.
5. Weiser, *The Psalms. A Commentary*, 758.
6. The NIV and ESV translate verse 5 as statement of affirmation. But the context of the petition in verse 4 as well as the tension reflected in the overall structure of the psalm favors the translation in the NEB. The word "destroy" comes from the Hebrew word *halak* ("to lead away"). See Allen, *Psalms 101–150*, 224.

# PSALM 126

"Already but not yet," is an apt description for Psalm 126. For God has *already* "restored the fortunes of Zion" (v. 1), and *yet* the people are still asking the Lord to "restore our fortunes" (v. 4). This poses a challenge to identifying the genre of the psalm. The first section of the psalm (vv. 1–3) resembles a thanksgiving psalm, with its focus on God's restoration and the people's praise. But the second section of the psalm (vv. 4–6) resembles the lament, as it contains a petition (v. 4) and an expression of confidence (vv. 5–6). The overall movement of the psalm is similar to a communal lament, which moves from praise to lament (e.g. Psalms 44 and 89). Both Psalms 44 and 89 recall Yahweh's past acts of deliverance before moving to lament and petition. Although Psalm 126 ends with a positive note (vv. 5–6), the overall structure, especially with the presence of the petition in the middle (v. 4), leaves a sense of uncertainty. The continuing uncertainty reminds us that restoration is a process. "Those who go out weeping *will* return with songs of joy" (v. 6) – but not yet.

The people acknowledge that to be able to sustain the process of restoration, they need the Lord. As the following psalm says, "Unless the Lord builds the house, the builders labor in vain" (127:1). Psalms 126 and 127 are similar in their grammatical construction. Psalm 126 begins with an infinitive construction, where "when" (in the sense of "if") is followed by "then" (126:1–2). Psalm 127 begins with two conditional "if" statements, with each followed by a statement of apodosis (127:1–2). The canonical context of Psalm 126 highlights the element of condition: *When* Yahweh restores . . . there is rejoicing. This has been their experience in the past. And so now, in the present, they ask God to restore them so that "those who sow with tears will reap with songs of joy" (126:5). The weight of the hoped-for future falls on God's response to the petition in verse 4:

Past experience: "when the Lord restored . . ." (v. 1);
    People's reaction: "songs of joy" (v. 2).
Petition: "restore us" (v. 4);
    People's hope/trust: "songs of joy" (v. 5–6).

The psalm highlights two closely related themes – restoration and rejoicing. The Hebrew word *shub* ("restore") occurs at the beginning of each section (vv. 1, 4). The Hebrew word *rinnah* ("songs of joy") also occurs within both sections (vv. 2, 5, 6).

## 126:1–3 "WHEN THE LORD RESTORED THE FORTUNES OF ZION"

In the previous psalm, "those who trust in the LORD" are likened to "Mount Zion" – a mountain "which cannot be shaken but endures forever" (125:1). Thus it was a great shock when the Babylonians captured Jerusalem and destroyed the Temple. However, that was not the end of the story. Once again, God intervened and "restored the fortunes of Zion" (126:1). The first part of the psalm (vv. 1–3) relates the reactions of the people when they recalled what God had done.

The people compared their reaction to "those who dreamed" (v. 2). Today, when we say, "it was a dream," we mean that it is not real. We thought it was real, and we wished it were true, but it was just a dream. But in the OT, dreams are often used as God's means of communicating reality to his people. In their view, "dreams were part of reality."[1] Thus, when the people compare themselves to people who dreamed, they are not hoping that something is true or wishing that something will happen. Rather, they are conveying a sense of overwhelming surprise that something unexpected has transpired. Thus in the next verse, they are overjoyed. Their mouths are filled with "laughter," their tongues "with songs of joy" (v. 2).

Verse 2 begins with the word "then," which marks a progression in the narration from the opening word, "when," in verse 1. The word "then" is repeated twice in verse 2, though the NIV does not translate the first one. The second occurrence of the word "then" marks the high point of the narration: "Then it was said among the nations" (v. 2b). After the people's defeat and exile, they experienced painful suffering because of the shame, loss of honor, and ongoing taunting of the people around them. Thus when they hear other people say, "The LORD has done great things for them" (v. 2), they receive back the honor and dignity that was painfully taken from them. Verse 1 simply mentions the restoration of the fortunes of Zion, without specifying what that means. Verse 2 makes it clear that the restoration has such a wide-ranging effect that the surrounding nations have become aware of it – which could include the return of the people to their land and the rebuilding of the Temple.

The restoration is an overwhelmingly great event, and so the psalmist repeats the word "great" twice (vv. 2b, 3a). In Hebrew, the word "great" is not an adjective, as it appears in the translation, "*great* things." Rather, it is a verb (*higdil* from *gadal*), which means to "'prove oneself great' (not simply 'do

---

1. Zenger and Hossfeld, *Psalms 3*, 342.

great things')."² While the restoration is an overwhelming, marvelous act, the people rejoice because of their great God, who has chosen to do the act of restoration "for us" (v. 3a). Thus they declare, "we were filled with joy" (v. 3b).³

## 126:4–6 "RESTORE OUR FORTUNES"

The second section has a clear connection with the preceding one. Verse 4 begins with the same Hebrew word (*shub*) as verse 1, which means "to return." But there is also a change. Verse 1 employs the infinitive construct as a form of narration ("When the LORD restored"), while verse 4 uses the imperative form ("Restore our fortunes"). Earlier, the people are full of rejoicing "when the LORD restored the fortunes of Zion" (v. 1), but here they are asking the Lord to "restore our fortunes" (v. 4). We are reminded that restoration is not a one-time event but an ongoing process.

Though the Hebrew word for the object of God's restoration ("fortunes") in verses 1 and 4 is the same,⁴ there is a slight difference. In verse 1, the text says, "the fortunes of Zion," whereas in verse 4, the text says, "our fortunes." Though the life and existence of the people of Israel is entwined with the fate of Zion, the two are different. This is also true in our time, when we know that what happens on a national level may not be true at the local or individual level. Though Zion's glory may have been restored at the international level, that reality may not have been reflected in the life of ordinary people. Verses 5–6 pertain to the life of peasants and farmers. The analogy applies to the most mundane aspects of their daily existence – sowing and reaping – rather than what is being said "among the nations" (v. 2).

The people ask for this restoration to be "like streams in the Negev" (v. 4b). The imagery of water is important. They need water when they sow, but when the land lacks water, the sowing is done in "tears." Verse 5 could be translated as a wish, a continuation of the petition in verse 4. As Hunter translates it, "May those who sow in tears reap with shouts of joy."⁵ Some translations shift from the plural to the singular, from "Those who sow in tears" (v. 5) to "He

---

2. Zenger and Hossfeld, *Psalm 3*, 371.
3. Zenger and Hossfeld, *Psalm 3*, 369. The NIV translates verse 3b as present. But the verse is parallel to verse 1b.
4. See LXX which has the same word for "restoration." The word *shibat* could be a mistake for *shevut/shevit* which we find in verse 4. See Alter, *The Book of Psalms*, 447.
5. Hunter, *Psalms*, 206.

who goes out weeping" (v. 6, ESV).⁶ While other translations use the plural in both verses, I appreciate the shift, as we zoom from the "nations," to "us," and finally to this one individual person who is weeping as he goes out to sow. Psalm 126 and Psalm 6 are the only two psalms that mention crying in two verses.⁷ The emphasis on tears and weeping in the second part of Psalm 126 reminds us of the painful process of restoration. While the first part of the psalm emphasizes that restoration is a great time for rejoicing, the second part indicates that there is "weeping" before the "songs of joy." The emphasis is on the joy, but those who have yet to experience what it means to be "restored" will identify with the individual who is walking along, weeping, as he carries his seeds for sowing.

---

6. The LXX has the plural form in both verses. But I think the MT should be preserved, since the LXX has the smoother reading.
7. David A. Bosworth, "Weeping in the Psalms," *VT* 63, no. 1 (2013): 39.

# PSALM 127

The main message or theme of Psalm 127 is expressed in its opening refrain, "Unless the Lord . . ." (v. 1). For without the help of our God, all our labors are in vain. The psalm applies this principle to two aspects of human existence: work (vv. 1–2) and family life (vv. 3–5). Dependence on God is a common theme among the Songs of Ascent, to which Psalm 127 belongs (see below). In Psalm 121, the psalmist acknowledges that our help comes from the Lord (v. 2). In Psalm 123, the people compare themselves to slaves looking at the hands of their masters, waiting for mercy (v. 2).

Canonically, Psalm 127 is closely connected to the preceding psalm. As I have demonstrated above, Psalms 126 and 127 are similar in their grammatical construction. They also complement each other. Whereas Psalm 127 helps us understand the connection between a psalmist's petition and the expression of trust that follows, Psalm 126 provides a picture of what it feels like when the Lord's action (restoring, building, watching) is absent. In Hebrew construction, the words, "builders" (127:1) and "those who sow" (126:5), are both plural participles. Likewise, the words, "the one who carries" and "watchman," are singular participles. Just as there is a movement from plural to singular in Psalm 126:5–6, there is a parallel movement in Psalm 127:1–2. In Psalm 126, "Those who sow" do so "in tears," and "the one who carries seed to sow" goes out "weeping" (vv. 5–6). These images from Psalm 126 describe what it feels like when our building, watching, and working seems to be "in vain." The words "in vain" are repeated three times in Psalm 127, highlighting this experience of having one's unsuccessful plans lead to "tears" and "weeping."

The main theme or message of the psalm also fits its genre. Psalm 127 is a wisdom psalm, and so its purpose is to teach and instruct, though this does not mean that it is not also for the purpose of worship. As part of the Songs of Ascent (Psalms 120–134), the psalm is written to be recited or sung by the pilgrims on their way to Jerusalem, where they will offer worship to God. Thus the instruction happens in the context of worship.[1] The orientation towards worship, which is made concrete by the upwards journey to the Temple, reinforces the importance of depending on God. We go to church (or to the Temple) as a way of acknowledging that apart from God, we can do nothing.

---

1. J. Clinton McCann, "The Psalms as Instruction," *Int* 46, no. 2 (1992): 117.

## 127:1–2 "UNLESS THE LORD"

In the first section, the poet employs significant repetition and parallelism to communicate his message effectively. Verse 1 consists of two lines that correspond with each other. Both begin with the word "unless" (literally, "if," from the Hebrew *'im*), and both mention the name "Yahweh." Moreover, the verbs, "build" and "watch," and the nouns, "house" and "city," correspond to each other. Finally, as noted above, the phrase "in vain" is repeated three times – twice in verse 1 and once in verse 2, which connects these two verses.

Some scholars debate about the reference to "house" in verse 1, as the Hebrew (*bayit*) can refer to the Temple, the palace, a house, or even a household. Earlier, Jerusalem was described as a place built (*banah*) "like a city" (122:3). The same verb for "build" (*bayit*) and the noun "city" occur in Psalm 127. The previous psalm talks about the restoration of Zion (126:1), and so "house" could be referring to the Temple (127:1). Yet the second part of Psalm 127 emphasizes the household and family, and so this could be referring to the house where a family builds a home (see discussion of v. 3 below). I don't think it's important to know exactly what the psalmist is referring to in building the house. The main point of the verse is that without the Lord, all efforts will be in vain.

The word "vain" is used here with an adverbial function, with the sense of "unsuccessful, without result, ineffective."[2] The image of sowing in the previous psalm captures the meaning of the verse here. We sow, but the Lord makes the seed grow. Unless the Lord causes the seed we have sown to sprout and grow, we will return with tears and weeping (compare Ps 126:5–6).

The first word in verse 2 is "in vain" (*shawe*), which is important for two reasons. First, it develops the main idea expressed in verse 1. Second, by placing "in vain" at the beginning of verse 2, the psalmist reverses the order in the structure of verse 1. Instead of beginning with the protasis ("if"), the sentence begins with the apodosis ("in vain"), thereby highlighting the outcome or result. Though we may "rise early and stay up late," verse 2 says that without the Lord, all our efforts are in vain. The "bread" in verse 2, which is a product of one's labor, is described as "anxious toil" (ESV). By reversing the structure of verse 1, the psalmist has space to introduce an additional idea: "for he grants sleep to those he loves" (v. 2b). The flow of the verse favors the LXX reading, which reflects the Hebrew word *ki* ("for") instead of the Hebrew *ken* ("thus," or "so"). The word "sleep" (v. 2b) contrasts with "anxious toil" (v. 2a). The text is not promoting laziness. Yet when our toil lacks meaning, we can

---

2. Zenger and Hossfeld, *Psalms 3*, 386.

become restless.³ It is possible for those who go out reaping to remain empty, even when the harvest is plenty. The text reminds us that a fruitful harvest is a gift from the Lord.

## 127:3–5 "CHILDREN ARE A HERITAGE FROM THE LORD"

In the second section, the psalmist applies the same principle of dependence on the Lord to the family setting. There is a wordplay between the Hebrew word *banah* ("to build") and *banim* ("children"). Just as sleep and success are gifts from the Lord, children are an "inheritance from the LORD" (v. 3). The word "inheritance" (*nakhalah*) is equivalent to the Filipino word *mana*, which describes something that is passed on to children from their parents – including land. In the OT, *nakhalah* is often used in connection to the land.

The stress on "inheritance" highlights the giver's generosity rather than the recipient's efforts, but the verse does not diminish the value of human efforts. In the second half of verse 2, the children are described as a "reward" (*sakhar*). The Hebrew word *sakhar* means "wages" (for work) or "payment."⁴ Though children are given by God, this does not deny the important role that parents play. Children are compared to "arrows *in the hands* of a warrior" (v. 4). How parents "handle" their children will determine whether or not the children will be a "reward." As Estes explains, "The sons of youth are those whom the father has had ample opportunity to influence and mold. Just as the warrior would not choose his arrows indiscriminately, so the father fills his quiver with sons who are prepared for long-range effect."⁵

The last verse is not suggesting that one ought to have more children since the man who has more children is "blessed" (v. 5). We need to remember that our situation today is different from ancient times. A "quiver" full of arrows refers to a house full of children, and so the man who has more children is "blessed" because, in ancient times, social support mainly came from one's own family or clan. Verse 5 mentions "the gate," which refers to the place where the court decisions are made. If an enemy challenges a court's decision, the man who has more children has a greater likelihood of being able to defend himself. Verse 5 conveys that it is a great blessing to receive a heritage from the Lord, and children are, indeed, "a heritage" from the Lord (v. 3). Anything we have that gives us an advantage (or blesses us) is a gift from the Lord.

---

3. Compare Daniel J. Estes, "Like Arrows in the Hand of a Warrior (Psalm 127)," *VT* 41, no. 3 (1991). He sees Psalm 127:1–2 to be about "the problem of human significance" (310).
4. *HALOT*, 3:1331.
5. Estes, "Like Arrows in the Hand of a Warrior (Psalm 127)," 308.

# PSALM 128

Psalm 128 is "generally classified as a wisdom psalm."[1] One of the key themes of the wisdom genre is the fear of the Lord. The parallel description, "those who fear the LORD" or "the one who fears the LORD," occurs twice in the psalm. Psalm 128 gives us a picture of what it looks like to fear the Lord (v. 1b) and the blessings that are promised to those who do so (vv. 2–6).

Canonically, Psalm 128 is linked to Psalm 127, and scholars consider them to be "twin" psalms.[2] Psalm 128 develops the theme of dependence on the Lord from Psalm 127. Whereas Psalm 127 only mentions the father and his children, Psalm 128 focuses on the wife (v. 3) and the home setting.

Structurally, the psalm may be divided into two parts:

> Blessings on the one who fears the LORD (vv. 1–4) and
> Blessing from Zion (vv. 5–6).

The repetition of the phrase, "who fears the LORD" (vv. 1, 4), marks an inclusio for the first part of the psalm. In the second part of the psalm, the focus shifts from the house (vv. 2–3) to Zion/Jerusalem (vv. 4–5).

## 128:1–4 BLESSINGS ON THE ONE WHO FEARS THE LORD

The wisdom literature emphasizes that "the fear of the LORD is the beginning of wisdom" (Prov 9:10). What does it mean to "fear the LORD"? The previous psalm teaches us that when we fear the Lord, we acknowledge that without God, all our efforts will be in vain (127:1–2). This does not mean that human efforts are not important, for as Psalm 128:2 says, "you will eat the fruit of your labor." If we do not sow, we will not reap. Even the Apostle Paul says, "the one who is unwilling to work shall not eat" (2 Thess 3:10). But at the same time, we recognize that God is the one who gives us both strength and success for all our endeavors.

In Psalm 128, being successful, fortunate, and happy is connected to fearing the Lord, for those who fear the Lord are regarded as "blessed" (v. 1). The Hebrew word for "blessed" is *'ashre*, which means "happiness" or "fortunateness." In Filipino, we would say, *masuwerte* ("fortunate"). Some Christians feel uncomfortable about being "fortunate" (*masuwerte*), which they regard

---

1. Allen, *Psalms 101–150*, 242.
2. For similarities between the two psalms, see Dirk J. Human, "'From Exile to Zion': Ethical Perspectives from the Twin Psalms 127 and 128," *OTE* 22, no. 1 (2009): 75, n. 19.

as "too secular," and would rather use the more spiritual term, "blessed" (*mapalad*). But for the psalmist, these two concepts are related: happiness or fortunateness (*'ashre*) is the outcome of being blessed (*barakh*).³ The word *barakh* is mentioned in verse 4, forming the following structure:

"Happy [*'ashre*] is everyone who fears the LORD" (v. 1);
    a list of the blessings of those who fear the LORD
        (vv. 2–3);
"Thus shall the man be blessed [*barakh*] who fears the LORD"
    (v. 4, NRSV).

As mentioned above, the words, "happy" (v. 1) and "blessed" (v. 4), along with the phrase, "who fear the LORD" (vv. 1, 4), form an inclusio with the center verses (vv. 2–3).

"The one who fears the LORD" (v. 1a) is described in the parallel line as "one who walks in his ways" (v. 1b), which highlights the importance of individual accountability. As Christians, we believe that each one of us will give an account for how we live our life. The image of walking (Ps 128:1b) is a metaphor for how we live our life (compare Eph 5:15–17). In the highly communal culture of many Asian countries, there is a tendency to go with the crowd and become who the community wants us to be, to believe what the community believes, to act as the community wants us to act. But the one who fears the Lord is "the *one* who walks in his ways" (128:1b).

The individual (singular) who is blessed "will eat the fruit of your labor" (v. 2). As outlined in the structure above, verses 2–3 refer to the blessings of those who fear the Lord. To eat the fruit of one's labor could refer broadly to benefiting from one's work or, in the language of Psalm 126, it could mean reaping what one has sown (126:5–6). The Israelites knew what it meant to have others take the fruits of their labor. For example, during the time of Gideon, their harvest was taken by their enemies (Judges 6). During their time in exile, they could not even plant their own vineyards. Thus the person who is able to eat the fruits of his/her labor is described as "happy" (v. 2, NRSV). The word "happy" is also mentioned at the beginning of verse 1, and its repetition in verse 2b forms an inclusio with verse 1. This makes Psalm 128 one of the most compact psalms in its usage of the beatitude form.⁴

The language of a beatitude reveals our values, and Psalm 128 considers the following to be blessings. First, those who have the capacity to "eat" the

---

3. Villanueva, *Psalms 1–72*, 21.
4. In addition to the beatitude, verse 2b adds, "it is good to you" (v. 2b, my translation).

fruits of their labor are blessed. Though this can be understood broadly to refer to any fruit, the word "eat" refers to food. Moreover, in verse 3b, the children are likened to "olive shoots around your *table*" (compare Ps 23:5). Having food on the table is considered to be a great blessing, especially by those who know what it means to be hungry. In Psalm 107, one of the first things that the Israelites remember as they give thanks to the Lord is how "hungry and thirsty" they used to be, how "their lives ebbed away" (v. 5). As I write this, our government has again placed our city under lockdown due to the rise of COVID-19 cases. Unfortunately, this means more people will go hungry. How I wish we would all experience the blessing referred to in Psalm 128!

Second, anyone whose wife is flourishing within the house is blessed. As noted above, the previous psalm focuses on the children (127:3) and the father ("the man," v. 5), but does not mention the wife. But in Psalm 128, the wife is likened to a "fruitful vine within your house" (v. 3). Wives in ancient times were confined to the four corners of the house. The Hebrew word for "within" in verse 3 literally means, "distant part, innermost part,"[5] the place where one can hardly be seen or noticed. The combination of a vine flourishing within the innermost part of the house does "not portray a natural environment," as Gillmayr-Bucher observes.[6] But this image is probably deliberate to emphasize that those who fear the Lord will flourish, even in places where one might not expect it – and all who dwell within the house of those who fear the Lord will also flourish.

Third, the children form the second part of the parallel line of verse 3, developing the concept in the first line. Thus one sign of a "fruitful" wife is her children, who are described as "olive shoots *around* your table" (v. 3b). Again, olive shoots are supposed to be outside, but here they are inside the house, around the table. The table is where mealtimes transpire, and the psalm evokes an image of a happy family seated together around a table filled with laughter and stories as they share a meal.

Together, these images form a picture of a blessed life. As verse 4 puts it, "Yes, this will be the blessing for the man who fears the LORD." The word "yes" comes from the Hebrew word, *hinneh*, which literally means, "behold."

---

5. *DCH*, 4:299.
6. Susanne Gillmayr-Bucher, "'Like Olive Shoots around Your Table': Images of Space in the Psalms of Ascent," in *The Composition of the Book of Psalms*, ed. Erich Zenger (Leuven: Uitgeverij Peeters, 2010), 493.

## 128:5–6 BLESSING FROM ZION

The last two verses are a prayer that the individual who fears the Lord will, indeed, experience all the blessings in the previous verses. The psalmist prays that "the LORD will bless you from Zion" (v. 5). This verse further recognizes that all help comes from the Lord (compare Ps 121:1–2), for any individual who experiences these blessings will know that they have come "from Zion." And all those who fear the Lord know that everything depends on him (see v. 1 above; compare Ps 127:1–2).

The shift to "Zion" in verse 5 marks the final movement in Psalm 128, which starts with the general ("all who fear the LORD," v. 1), then moves to the particular – the small space of a house/home and family (vv. 2–4) – and then shifts to Zion and Jerusalem (vv. 5–6). This shift "from the house to Jerusalem, from a man to Israel"[7] is an important reminder of the link between the individual house and the wider community – how the individual home affects the broader society and vice versa. Thus within each home, the fear of the Lord should be evident, but we should not confine ourselves to small, personal, inner spaces.

> **BROADENING OUR *SAKOP* (SCOPE OF OUR REACH)**
>
> Many Filipinos tend to be regionally oriented, confined to our own family or relatives – what we call *sakop* ("scope"). But Psalm 128 challenges us to broaden our *sakop* to include our fellow countrymen, for the psalmist prays that the individual will not only see the prosperity of his home, but "the prosperity of Jerusalem" (v. 5). Moreover, the psalm ends with a wish for "peace on Israel," and in our ever-growing global village, we can apply this blessing not only to our respective countrymen, but to all human beings.

---

7. Gillmayr-Bucher, "'Like Olive Shoots around Your Table': Images of Space in the Psalms of Ascent," 493.

# PSALM 129

Psalm 129 is similar to Psalms 120 and 123 in that it laments the continuing pitiful condition of the people of Israel. Psalm 120 ends by saying, "Too long have I lived among those who hate peace" (v. 6), and Psalm 123 concludes with, "we have had more than enough of contempt" (v. 4, ESV). Psalm 129 picks up where these two psalms end: "Too long have they afflicted me from my youth" (v. 1, my translation).[1]

The words, "too long" and "more than enough," come from the same Hebrew word (*rab*). Psalm 129 reflects an even worse situation than Psalms 120 and 123, which both include a direct petition to God (120:2; 123:3). In Psalm 129, the people cannot even utter a direct petition, but can only offer a wish: "May all who hate Zion be turned back to shame" (v. 5). Perhaps they are already too weak to pray directly to God.

Nevertheless, the poet remembers and gives voice to the suffering of his people, saying, "let Israel say" (v. 1). The phrase, "let Israel say," also occurs in Psalm 124 in the context of praise, when Israel is exhorted to speak about how the Lord has saved them (v. 1). Christians tend to be eager to share stories about answered prayers, victory, deliverance, but not to voice lament. It is not easy to share experiences of lament. As O'Connor observes, "Intense physical pain silences speech; overwhelming suffering is language-destroying."[2] But Psalm 129 teaches us about the importance of voicing (note the word "*say*" in v. 1) our experiences of suffering, defeat, shame, and extreme physical pain (see v. 3 below).

While people often talk about needing to move on during times of suffering, we can't move on if we do not first remember and mourn, which are both important to the healing process (see comments in Psalm 79 above). Psalm 129 continues to remember the people's suffering in the context of their faith in Yahweh. Structurally, the psalm may be outlined as follows:

"Let Israel say" (v. 1):
    Name affliction (vv. 1–3).
        Declaration: "The LORD is righteous" (v. 4).
        Petition: "May all who hate Zion be turned back in shame" (v. 5).
    Name affliction (vv. 6–7).
"Those who pass by do not say" (v. 8).

---

1. Here I translated the Hebrew word, *rab*, as "too long" in light of the context of v. 1b (see below).
2. O'Connor, *Lamentation and the Tears of the World*, (Maryknoll: Orbis, 2002), 101.

# Psalm 129

The whole psalm forms an inclusio with the repetition of the word "say" (vv. 1, 8) and may be divided into three sections. The first (vv. 1–3) and third (vv. 6–8) sections recount the people's experience of suffering. In the middle section (vv. 4–5), the psalmist makes an expression of trust. Psalm 129 is a lament, which I would classify as a "tragic lament" because it ends with a sense of tension rather than resolution (see discussion below).

## 129:1–3 ISRAEL'S LONG EXPERIENCE OF SUFFERING

This section recalls the people's experience of affliction and torment in the hands of their enemies, which has gone on for a long time. The Hebrew word *rab*, which is translated as "greatly" in the NIV (vv. 1a, 2a), is better rendered as "often" or "too long." The words, "from my youth," support this (v. 1). The complaint in this verse is similar to Psalm 120:6: "too long [*rab*] have I lived among those who hate peace." The psalmist uses the first person ("from *my* youth") to express the people's experience on a personal level. This is similar to the depiction in Lamentations 1:2, where the city and its inhabitants are personified as an individual (Lady Zion, who weeps bitterly in the night).

The people's suffering not only goes on for a long time, but it is also extremely cruel. The image in verse 3 depicts torment, for instead of plowing a field, the psalmist says, "plowmen plowed my back." As a child, I remember going to the field with my family to watch a farmer plow his field. With the help of his carabao, the farmer would make long furrows as he plowed. But in Psalm 129, the farmer is pulled down from his carabao and made to lie down with his face on the ground so that plowmen could plow his back. The imagery evokes torment and cruelty, which leads to a sense of "powerlessness." Assis elaborates:

> The image of the people, likened to a person lying prostrated, face down, while the plow turns his back, bespeaks the powerlessness of the people in the exile. A person lying in this face down position is utterly passive and can offer no resistance . . . This motif of helplessness is particularly difficult for the sufferer to bear; he does not struggle and he offers no opposition. Beyond the immense pain is the loss of the ability to counter it.[3]

But contrary to Assis's point above, Israel does not remain "utterly passive." She does not lose her "ability to counter" her opponents, for the composer of

---
3. Elie Assis, "The Structure, Genre, and Meaning of Psalm 129," *SJOT* 31, no. 1 (2017): 150.

Psalm 129 has the courage to confront their painful past and articulate their ongoing struggle. It is to Israel's advantage that she has poets who continue to remember: "'They have greatly oppressed me from my youth' – let Israel say" (v. 1).

Countries that have suffered under foreign colonizers, such as the Philippines, tend to forget or deny our past. As I write this commentary, our country is commemorating the five-hundredth year of Spanish colonization (1521). Unfortunately, some of our people no longer care about what happened in the past – let alone want to remember or commemorate it. They may be too burdened with the current pandemic and so no longer have the strength to look back. One of the great tragedies in our nation is that we have not lamented as a people for the affliction and torment we suffered under our colonizers. It's easier to focus on the positive "contributions" that our colonizers brought to our country. But if we do not confront our painful past, we will have a hard time moving forward.

## 129:4–5 TENSION BETWEEN PAST AND FUTURE DELIVERANCE

The psalmist is able to confront Israel's past and urge his people to do the same because of his faith in Yahweh, which is characterized by his capacity to hold things in tension. In verses 4–5, he declares that "the LORD is righteous" (v. 4b). The word "righteous" not only has a moral connotation, but is also used in connection to acts of deliverance. Because the Lord is righteous, "he has cut me free from the cords of the wicked" (v. 4b). However, the situation of suffering is not yet resolved, for even though the action of the Lord is described in the past ("he has cut me free," v. 4), the enemies are yet to be subdued: "May all who hate Zion be turned back in shame" (v. 5). God's past act of deliverance and the psalmist's longing for their enemies to be put to shame are juxtaposed, creating a tension. This ability to live through eyes of faith in the face of a complete absence of resolution sustained the faith of the OT Israelites and continues to sustain Christians today.

## 129:6–8 CONTINUING SUFFERING

Verse 5 is an imprecatory prayer, similar to others in the Psalms (e.g. 83:13–15). Most scholars interpret verses 6–8 as a continuation of the imprecatory prayer. The people wish that "all who hate Zion" will not only be put to shame, but will also wither "like grass" (v. 6) and struggle with a meager harvest (v. 7).

Moreover, they pray that "those who pass by" will "not say to them, 'The blessing of the Lord be on you'" (v. 8).

However, I think we should also consider the alternative view offered by Assis,[4] who proposes that the subject of verses 6–8 is not the enemies of Israel, but Israel herself. He argues that it is not uncommon to switch subjects in poetry,[5] and so in verses 6–8, the psalmist is resuming his theme of what Israel should continue to "say" or talk about, so as not to forget her suffering. In my structural analysis above, I demonstrate that verses 6–8 are parallel to verses 1–3, as both sections talk about the suffering of Israel. Verse 7 mentions the "reaper," which recalls Psalm 126:5–6, where Israel sows in tears but later reaps with songs of joy. Yet Psalm 129:6–8 is describing the condition of the people in exile. As Assis argues, verse 6 depicts "the transience of Jewish existence in the exile. The Jews' lot in exile is one of impermanence and insecurity, like the grass that quickly withers, before it is reaped."[6] In the same way, verse 7 also "employs agricultural imagery, this time to underscore the people's dwindled state in exile."[7]

As noted above, verse 8 forms an inclusio with verse 1 through its repetition of the verb "to say":

"let Israel say" (v. 1);
"Those who pass by did not say" (v. 8, my translation).

The NIV translates the beginning of verse 8 as, "May those who pass by not say to them," which continues its translation of having the enemies as the subject of the verb. However, it is rather unnatural to apply the blessings to enemies. An Israelite would never say to a foreign enemy, "we bless you," and such a blessing would be far from the psalmist's mind. In light of the context of the preceding verses, it is better to interpret the blessing in terms of the common experience of reapers as they return home. In Ruth 2:4, the reapers would be greeted by others with blessing. But in Psalm 129, the psalmist insists that a blessing would be inappropriate for their experience of extreme suffering. Verse 8 employs an ellipsis, carrying the subject of verse 8a into verse 8b: "those who pass by did not say . . . 'we bless you in the name of the Lord.'" With such a tragic ending, the opening line in the following Psalm is just right: "Out of the depths . . ." (Ps 130:1).

---

4. Assis, "The Structure, Genre, and Meaning of Psalm 129."
5. Assis, "The Structure, Genre, and Meaning of Psalm 129," 148.
6. Assis, "The Structure, Genre, and Meaning of Psalm 129," 148.
7. Assis, "The Structure, Genre, and Meaning of Psalm 129," 148.

# PSALM 130

Psalm 130 is known by its opening line, "Out of the depths" (*De Profundis*). The word "depths" is a rich metaphor that can mean several things, including depression.[1] Because of the pandemic, many people feel that they are in the depths economically, emotionally, mentally, psychologically, and spiritually. One of the lessons we can learn from Psalm 130 is its admission of these depths. When the psalmist cries, "Out of the depths," he is actually saying, "I'm way down here, in the depths!" This admission is crucial, because the first step towards restoration and healing is to admit that one is sick or has a problem. One of the problems with the particular brand of Christianity that we have inherited from the West is its tendency towards triumphalism. Because we have victory in Christ, it is difficult for some people to admit that they are in the depths. As a result, many Christians remain in the depths – and thus sink even further into the depths. The more we deny our issues, the worse they become.

The OT believers were able to survive their many calamities because they knew how to confront their darkness (e.g. see communal laments, such as Psalms 44, 89). The people's experience expressed in Psalm 129 is of the "depths." Being under foreign powers, prostrate with your face on the ground while the wicked "plow" your back (Ps 129:3), plummets to unspeakable "depths." Yet the people can face their darkness because there is someone to whom they can cry out from these depths.

Though some scholars have a hard time determining the genre of Psalm 130,[2] it has all the elements of a lament psalm: an invocation (v. 1), a description of distress ("darkness," v. 1), a petition (v. 2), a declaration of trust (v. 3), and an implied "certainty of a hearing" (v. 7). Zenger, however, describes Psalm 130 as a "prayer of petition"[3] because the description of the psalmist's distress or complaint is only conveyed in the word "depths." Yet the experience of distress is also reflected in the psalmist's petition, which is a cry from the depths, pleading with the Lord to "hear my voice" (v. 2a) and to incline his ear towards the psalmist's voice (v. 2). This voice comes from someone who is in trouble, who is pleading for "mercy," hoping he'll be heard (v. 2b). In Filipino, the word for pleading and complaining come from the same word

---

1. William Styron, *Darkness Visible: A Memoir of Madness* (New York: Random House, 1990).
2. Allen writes: "It is by no means clear to which genre this psalm should be assigned." Allen, *Psalms 101–150*. Some read the verbs in verses 1 and 5 as referring to the past, thus the Psalm is considered as a Thanksgiving psalm.
3. Zenger and Hossfeld, *Psalms 3*, 426.

(*daing*). One problem with the form-critical view is that it creates a dichotomy between complaint and petition, when they are closely related.

## 130:1–2 CRY FROM THE DEPTHS

Commentators do not usually provide an explanation for the superscription in Psalm 130, let alone its relationship to the opening verse. Instead, they refer readers to an earlier discussion of the title.[4] It is not necessary to explain the superscription/title for every single psalm in the collection, particularly since at this point we are near the end of the Songs of Ascent (Psalms 120–134). However, I think that further elaboration is relevant for Psalm 130, because the title, "A Song of Ascents," is in tension with the opening line, "out of the depths." The title creates an expectation of a positive movement ("Ascents"), but the "depths" moves in the opposite direction.[5] It's like going up a staircase and suddenly falling down. One of the most difficult experiences is when our sadness or negative experiences just don't make sense. Some Christians believe that they should be happy all the time. As one of the most famous songs in Filipino says, *Ang buhay ng Kristiyano ay laging masayang tunay* ("The life of a Christian is truly happy all the time"). This lyric is equivalent to the popular saying, "God is good all the time."

The term "out of the depths" (*maʿamaqim*) occurs four times in the OT, usually in connection with the sea or "deep waters" (Isa 51:10; Exod 27:34; Ps 69:2, 14).[6] Of these three texts, Psalm 69 is also a lament. Because Psalm 130:3 mentions "sins," it is tempting to associate the "depths" with an experience of despair caused by one's sins.[7] Along with Psalms 6, 32, 38, 51, 102, 143, Psalm 130 is considered to be one of the Seven Penitential psalms, which makes this

---

4. For example, Zenger and Hossfeld point their readers to an excursus on "The Composition of the So-Called Pilgrim Psalter, Psalms 120–134." Mitchell J. Dahood talks about the title at the beginning of his comments in Psalm 120 (194–195), but not in Psalm 130 (234). Mitchell J. Dahood, *Psalms III: 101–150*, AB (Garden City: Doubleday, 1970).
5. Linda M. McMullen and John B. Conway, "Conventional Metaphors for Depression," in *The Verbal Communication of Emotions: Interdisciplinary Perspectives*, ed. Susan R. Fussell (Mahwah, NJ: L. Erlbaum Associates, 2002), 167–181. This article argues that the conceptual metaphors of up and down, particularly in western society, have contributed to the idea that up is good/happy and down is bad/low, not ideal. It can provide explanation for the tendency in western society to read "ascents" as positive, thus, ignoring the more dynamic meaning of language.
6. Rick R. Marrs, "A Cry from the Depths (Ps 130)," *ZAW* 100, no. 1 (1988): 83.
7. Patrick D. Miller argues: "The verses that follow indicate that in this case the fearful depths from which the cry goes up to God are not the threat of external or hostile forces but the mental, emotional, and spiritual dark night of the soul that finds itself plunged into sin and guilt." Patrick D. Miller, "Psalm 130," *Int* 33, no. 2 (1979): 177.

connection even easier. However, even though the word "sins" is mentioned twice (vv. 3, 8), there is no explicit admission of guilt or confession. We should not limit the sense of the word "depths" to sin, as the "depths" can refer to any form of extreme mental, physical, or social suffering – including depression.[8]

One of the problems and potential dangers of depression is the growing sense of isolation, when we think, "There is nobody else, it's just me." Psalm 130 is very helpful because it declares that we are not alone, but can cry out to someone: "Out of the depths I cry to you, LORD" (v. 1). The direct address emphasizes that there is a *"you."* The OT believers knew from their experience that when they cried out to the Lord in their distress, he heard them (see Exod 2:23–25). Thus the psalmist cries out to the Lord for help in the midst of a deep, dark pit (Ps 130:2). Verse 2 could be a direct quotation of his prayer from the depths (compare Ps 116:4), which consists of three lines pleading for a hearing:

> "O LORD, hear my voice!
> Let your ears be attentive
> to the voice of my pleas for mercy!" (130:2, ESV)

## 130:3–4 A VIEW FROM THE DEPTHS

One of the worst things that suffering people hear from others is that they are in the depths because of their sins. In Filipino culture, tragedy is often associated with sin. When we get sick or when tragedy strikes, we think it's because we did something wrong. The sense of guilt becomes even stronger when it is reinforced by other people.

Psalm 130 can be a gracious companion for those who are suffering. Even though the Israelite culture is similar to Filipino culture in its association of sin and tragedy, the psalmist's emphasis is not on sin but on *mercy*. Instead of blaming himself, the psalmist says, "If you, LORD, kept a record of sins, LORD, who could stand" (v. 3). The psalmist is aware that "the wicked will not stand in the judgment" (Ps 1:5), and yet he declares, "But with you there is forgiveness" (130:4). Compassion and mercy are learned in the depths. It's easy for those who are outside the pit to miss what can be learned down in the dark depths, since those who have been there for some time have gotten used to the absence of light, and so they can see better.

---

8. I have tried to apply Psalm 130 to my own experience of depression. See Federico G. Villanueva, *Lord, I'm Depressed*, 2020.

# Psalm 130

## 130:5–6 WAITING IN THE DEPTHS

In the depths, we not only have the opportunity to learn how to be compassionate, but also how to wait. The word, "wait," is repeated twice in verse 5: "I wait for the Lord, my whole being waits." In this section, there is a shift from addressing the Lord directly ("you," vv. 1–4) to talking about the Lord in the third person (vv. 5–6). This shift implies a sense of absence, through which the psalmist realizes his longing for God's presence.[9] The Hebrew of verse 6 does not mention the word, "wait," but literally reads, "My soul to the Lord." But the verb "wait" is implied, and so the NIV correctly inserts the word in the translation: "I wait for the Lord." However, the ellipsis created by dropping the verb is important, because it focuses our attention on the word, "Lord."[10] The Lord becomes the focus of our waiting. Whatever the psalmist is waiting for is second to seeking the Lord, for all his hope is anchored on the Lord.

His hope is also persistent, for the psalmist compares his waiting with "watchmen who wait for the morning" (v. 6), a phrase that is repeated twice for emphasis. The "watchmen" could refer to those who guard the city gates at night, who wish that the light of the morning would come so that the dangers of the night can be contained more easily. Those in the depths need a double portion of patience. The psalmist's emphasis on waiting reminds us that healing and restoration is a process.

Unfortunately, we do not like going through a "process," because we have gotten used to getting what we want quickly, immediately. We push a button and a huge gate opens, and so we wish that there was a button we could push to evaporate all our darkness. Sadly, some people can't wait and think it's better just to end it all. They waited and waited and no answer came.

## 130:7–8 HOPE FROM THE DEPTHS

Interestingly, there is nothing in Psalm 130 about receiving an answer to prayer. The psalmist does not testify about getting healed, forgiven, or restored. In verse 6, he is still waiting. Yet suddenly in verse 7, the perspective shifts again

---

9. Luis Alonso Schökel comments, "The manner of God's presence is awareness of his absence. Absence which is not noticed nor deeply felt is a simple absence which causes no grief. But absence which is felt is a means of being present in the consciousness, bringing anxiety and grief." Luis Alonso Schökel, "The Poetic Structure of Psalm 42–43," *JSOT*, no. 1 (January 1, 1976): 8.
10. Alter explains that in ellipsis, "what is accomplished . . . is a freeing of space in the second verse . . . which can then be used to elaborate or sharpen the meaning." Alter, *The Art of Biblical Poetry*, 24.

from third person to second person address directed to the people of Israel. In these closing verses, the psalmist turns his attention from prayer (vv. 1–4) and reflection (vv. 5–6) to exhortation (vv. 7–8).

Through his waiting and praying, the psalmist has gained a new perspective. Though he may not be totally delivered from the depths yet, he can already speak words of hope to his community: "Israel, put your hope in the LORD" (v. 7a). The word "unfailing love" (v. 7b) comes from the Hebrew word *hesed*, which can also be translated as "grace." The same grace that the psalmist experiences in the depths is the same grace that will sustain his community. Despite the people's sins (v. 8), there is hope, because God is a forgiving God (v. 4).

In this shift, the psalmist moves from waiting on God to ministering to others, which shows us that we do not need to be completely healed to serve others. Our attempts to serve others, even within our own darkness, can become a part of our healing process.

# PSALM 131

Psalm 131 is the second shortest psalm (after Psalm 117), but it contains a powerful image of a believer's relationship with God: that of a mother with her child. Though some scholars debate whether an actual mother composed this psalm, it is clearly written from the perspective of a mother. It is comparable to a similar image of God comparing his love with a mother's love for her child in the book of Isaiah (49:15). Using images that are close to our own experience is one of the most effective means of speaking about things that are intimate to us, including our relationship with God.

Psalm 131 is one of the Songs of Ascent (Psalms 120–134), which were sung/prayed by pilgrims as they went up to Jerusalem for worship. Everyday family life experiences are common in this collection (see Psalms 127, 128). Psalm 131 reminds us that the ordinary experiences of our daily life form the core content of our journey towards the center (Jerusalem/the Temple). As Grohmann points out, in "the movement of walking up to the temple, Psalm 131 describes a counter-movement of looking down to small issues."[1] Yet I must say that the relationship between a mother and her child is not a "small issue." It is tempting to think that what happens inside the church has prime importance, whereas what happens in the home is not that important. But some of our most ordinary experiences are the very best means of knowing God and growing in intimacy with him. In our worship of God, we encounter a king and a father – and certainly one who is also a mother to us. Because God is like a mother to us, we can confidently face life's challenges.

Canonically, Psalm 131 can be considered as a "twin" with Psalm 130. Both psalms begin with an individual's experience (130:1; 131:1), and both broaden towards the experience of Israel at the end (130:7; 131:3). Both also contain an overall movement from prayer (131:1–2; 130:1–5) to an exhortation to Israel (131:3; 130:7–8). The exact phrase, "Israel, put your hope in the Lord," is also found in both psalms (131:3; 130:7). Thus in interpreting Psalm 131, we need to consider Psalm 130 as well. For example, Psalm 130 can help us understand how the psalmist in Psalm 131 can say that he is not proud (see below).

---

1. Marriane Grohmann, "The imagery of the 'weaned child' in Psalm 131," in *The Composition of the Book of Psalms*, ed. Erich Zenger (Leuven: Uitgeverij Peeters, 2010), 519.

In terms of genre, Psalm 131 is considered to be a psalm of confidence, comparable to Psalms 16, 23, 62.[2] The language is closest to Psalm 62, where the words, "quieted myself" (Ps 131:2), are also used (Ps 62:5).[3] Structurally, Psalm 131 forms an inclusio with the word, "Lord" (Yahweh), which appears at the beginning (v. 1) as well as the end (v. 3), when Israel is called upon to put their hope "in the Lord." The psalm consists of two main sections: meditative prayer (vv. 1–2) and an exhortation (v. 3).

## 131:1–2 MEDITATIVE PRAYER

The superscription indicates that this song belongs to the collection of Songs of Ascent (Psalms 120–134). Moreover, it links the psalm to David with the words, "Of David." The portrayal in 2 Samuel 7:18–29 could have led those who put together the collection to attribute the psalm to David, as David is pictured as one who has been "humbled before YHWH," one who "attributes his great success not to himself, but to YHWH alone."[4] The emphasis in Psalm 131 on not being proud or haughty fits this image from 2 Samuel. In verse 1, the word "not" is repeated three times:

> "My heart is *not* proud,
> My eyes are *not* haughty
> I do *not* concern myself with . . . things too wonderful for me."

What is inside the heart is reflected outside through the eyes. Thus a heart that is not proud is revealed in one's eyes.

More traditional Asian cultures might find these assertions rather strong, as we do not usually say that we are not proud, which is another way of saying that we are humble. Instead, we just keep quiet – especially when praying to the Lord! But the psalmist is not ashamed to tell the Lord that he is not proud. The very first word in Hebrew in verse 1 is "Yahweh," which clearly identifies verses 1–2 as a prayer. However, this prayer is more meditative than the prayers in other psalms. Though the psalmist is addressing Yahweh, there is no petition or praise directed to him. Instead, the psalmist reflects upon his own "heart" (v. 1a). Among other senses, the word "heart" in Hebrew refers to

---

2. Grohmann, "The imagery of the 'weaned child' in Psalm 131," 513.
3. Zenger and Hossfeld, *Psalms 3*, 449. See Psalm 62 as "related in concept to Psalm 131."
4. Zenger and Hossfeld, *Psalms 3*, 449.

"one's inner self," the "seat of feeling and emotions."[5] In verse 2, the psalmist refers to his "soul."

Being open or honest to God about the state of our heart or soul is important, but we should also consider why we are feeling that way. In this psalm, we might ask why the psalmist regards himself as not proud? The canonical context can provide guidance, as Psalms 131 and 130 are considered "twin psalms."[6] Psalm 130 speaks about the psalmist's experience of the "depths," which means he is at his lowest point. As discussed in the comments for Psalm 130, those who experience the "depths" are often more humble because they know that some things are beyond their control. When the psalmist says that he is crying to God "out of the depths" (130:1), he is admitting that he is *in* the depths, which is a place of humility and vulnerability. Waiting in the depths (130:5–6) has made the psalmist more patient and also more humble.

In Psalm 131, when the psalmist says that he is not proud, he is revealing his self-knowledge. Because he is aware of his limitations, he says, "I do not concern myself with great matters or things too wonderful for me" (v. 1b). The psalmist is not saying that it's wrong to think of great things, but that one should be aware of one's own limitations. In Hebrew, verse 1b literally reads, "I do not walk in great things, and in things more wonderful than me." The emphasis is on things that are "*more* wonderful than me" or "things too wonderful for me" (compare Ps 139:6). The psalmist's experience of the depths (Psalm 130) has made him more sober about how he understands the things around him.

The experience of the depths has also made him more rested. Psalm 130 manifests the psalmist's capacity for waiting (see vv. 5–6 above). Though there is a time for crying out, lamenting, and pouring out of our hearts before the Lord, this is not the end. Our lament must flow into quietness and trust. But how can we move towards this place of quietness and trust? Verse 2 highlights the importance of human agency in arriving at this place of rest. First, we need to admit our depths (130:1). Second, we must go through the process of lament (130:2). Third, we wait upon the Lord (130:5–6). Fourth, we walk humbly rather than with haughty eyes (131:1a). Fifth, we seek to learn more about ourselves so that we can accept our limitations (131:1b). Finally, we seek to remain calm and to quiet our souls before the Lord (131:2).

---

5. *HALOT*, 2:514.
6. Grohmann, "The imagery of the 'weaned child' in Psalm 131," 518–519.

The phrase, "I have calmed myself" (v. 2), comes from the Hebrew verb *shawah*, which means "to settle" or "to soothe."[7] This posture is the opposite of being disturbed or agitated, like a baby who is crying out for its mother. We can soothe our soul by being quiet. In the parallel line, the psalmist says that he has "quieted" his soul. In Hebrew, the word for "quieted" is *damam*, which is the same word used in Psalm 62, where the psalmist admonishes his soul to "wait in silence" on God alone (v. 5, ESV). Silence is a much-needed discipline today, especially in our very noisy world. We need to recapture the art of both external and internal silence, for it is possible to be in a quiet place and yet to have our hearts agitated and disturbed. Conversely, it is not easy to be quiet when we are surrounded by noise from our surroundings (advertisements, screens, social media, etc).

Calming and quieting oneself is a process that takes both time and effort. In biblical times, "children were nursed a long time and weaned at the age of three years."[8] The psalmist compares himself to a "weaned child." There is a lot of discussion about how to read the preposition translated as "with" in verse 2b ("I am like a weaned child *with* its mother"). This translation is based on the Hebrew preposition "upon" (*'ale*), which could be a poetic rendering of the more common form "on me" (*'alay*). Some propose a repointing of *'ale* to *'alay*.[9] For example, Knowles translates verse 2b as follows:

"Like a weaned child *on me* [*'alay*] its mother,
Like the weaned child *on me* [*'alay*] is my soul."[10]

If this reading is the original, then we can better understand what it means to quiet or calm one's soul. If "the literary speaker of the psalm is a mother,"[11] then she would know how to calm her child. With much patience and waiting she has learned how to wean her child. So now, as she reflects on her own relationship with the Lord, her experience with her child can assist her. The

---

7. *HALOT*, 4:1437.
8. Grohmann, "The imagery of the 'weaned child' in Psalm 131," 516. She cites 2 Maccabees 7:28 as support.
9. Melody D. Knowles argues: "This repointing not only makes logical sense in the line, it also renders parallel the two appearance of the *'ly* in v. 2b." Melody D. Knowles, "A Woman at Prayer: A Critical Note on Psalm 131:2b," *JBL* 125, no. 2 (2006): 387.
10. Brent A. Strawn affirms the conclusion of Knowles and adds his own contribution. He repoints the first *gamal* (weaned child) with the definite article in parallel to the second occurrence of the word which has the definite article. Brent A. Strawn, "A Woman at Prayer (Psalm 131, 2b) and Arguments 'from Parallelism,'" *ZAW* 124, no. 3 (2012): 421–426.
11. Grohmann, "The imagery of the 'weaned child' in Psalm 131," 521.

composure reflected in the weaned child is one way to nurture a restful and humble spirit.

## 131:3 EXHORTATION

From the opening meditative prayer, the psalm concludes with an exhortation to Israel, the psalmist's community of faith. This shift instructs us about the importance of the community. Every experience of healing or restoration that leads to our healing ought to be communicated to others, for any gift that is received through the depths is not for us to keep, but is meant to be shared with the broader community. Whether the community accepts what we offer, or not, we should always try to help others if we have received help. The Filipino phrase *utang na loob* (literally, "debt of the heart") expresses this sense of doing something as a grateful response for what we have received.

In Psalm 131, the psalmist offers his community "hope" (v. 3) in the Lord, even in the depths. Though we may not be able to see the light, others who have seen it can share it with us, which can help us continue to hope in the Lord, from whom our help comes (Psalm 121). In Hebrew, the word "hope" (*yakhel*) also means "wait." Thus hope does not mean that our problem has been solved, but as long as we have hope in the Lord, we can continue to wait.

# PSALM 132

Psalm 132 is the longest hymn in the collection known as the Songs of Ascent (Psalms 120–134), and it follows the shortest hymn in the collection (Psalm 131). Thematically, there are connections between Psalms 131 and 132, as the latter psalm continues the themes of humility, rest, and hope that are expressed in the former. First, in Psalm 131, the psalmist confesses to the Lord that his heart is not proud (v. 1), and then in Psalm 132, he emphasizes David's "extreme self-denial" (v. 1, JPS) by making a vow that he will not rest (vv. 3–5) until he finds a "resting place" for the Lord (vv. 8, 14). David's vow in Psalm 132 (vv. 3–5) creates a dynamic interaction with the psalmist's act of calming and quieting his soul in Psalm 131 (v. 2). Second, at the end of Psalm 131, the psalmist exhorts the community of Israel to hope in the Lord, which provides the motivation for the psalmist's prayer in Psalm 132.

The act of prayer is an expression of hope. We can only come to the Lord and present our petitions to him when we continue to believe in him and hope that he will intercede and act. When read from its final redaction in the post-exilic context, where the situation was far from ideal, Psalm 132 expresses the people's longing for restoration in continuity with the Davidic line and the well-being of Zion.[1]

Psalm 132 is a prayer[2] that contains two strategically placed parallel petitions (vv. 1, 10) that are formulated positively and negatively as follows:

> Petition 1: "LORD, *remember* David" (v. 1);
> Petition 2: "For the sake of your servant David, *do not reject* your anointed one" (v. 10).

Moreover, the prayer in Psalm 132 is dominated by a parallel motivation, which immediately follows the parallel petition:

> Motivation 1: David "swore" (*nishbaʿ*) an oath to the LORD (vv. 2–5);
> Motivation 2: The LORD "swore" (*nishbaʿ*) an oath to David (vv. 11–12).

---

[1]. According to Thijs Booij, Psalm 132 is first about the well-being of Yahweh's dwelling, second of the priests and faithful, and third of David's house. Thijs Booij, "Psalm 132: Zion's Well-Being," *Bib* 90, no. 1 (2009): 78.

[2]. Though there are debates on the genre of the psalm, we cannot deny the fact that Psalm 132 is a prayer. It is also close to the lament in that it contains two of the elements found in the lament—petition and motivation.

Both motivations use the verb "swore" (*nishba'*), and both correspond to one another by showing a progression. Just as David swore to the Lord, so the Lord also swore to David. Though the Lord's oath is an affirmation of David's oath, it goes beyond it, for human oaths may falter, but God's oath will never fail. Thus the psalmist says that it is a "sure oath" (v. 11).

Based on the petitions and motivations outlined above, the psalm has two main sections (vv. 1–9; vv. 10–18) that each have a petition and a motivation. While the fulfillment of the oath is present in the first section, it is absent in the second section. Regarding the first section, we know that David's vow to the Lord was fulfilled, for the people have "heard" (v. 6) others saying, "Let us go to his dwelling place" (v. 7). Though the second section contains an extended promise from the Lord to David (vv. 11–12) about how the needy and faithful will dwell in Zion (vv. 13–18), there is no explicit fulfillment of this promise. Thus the psalm ends without closure. Verses 11–18 may be read as a motivation for the second petition, asking God to fulfill what he promised "for the sake of David" (v. 10).

Together, the petitions and motivations reflect the difficult situation of the people of Israel. Allen notes that the petitions are "dominating the whole psalm, the rest being a series of arguments motivating Yahweh to answer the prayers."[3] However, I think that the motivating arguments dominate the psalm. When we are desperate, we will use whatever motivations we can muster to try to secure the help we are seeking. At the same time, our motivations reflect our values and our theology.

As mentioned above, there are two motivations in Psalm 132. The first highlights the importance of taking initiative and self-sacrifice. David was willing to forgo his own comfort (need for rest) until he had found a resting place for the Lord. The second demonstrates the importance of God's word or promises. Throughout the OT, it is common for people to use God's word when asking God for something. For example, Moses quotes God's promise to the patriarchs in Exodus 32 when he pleads with God not to destroy the people for worshiping the golden calf (see v. 13). This further supports the view that the promise recounted in the second section of Psalm 132 (vv. 11–18) is a motivation for the petition (v. 10).

The first motivation is particularly relevant for our Filipino context, where there is a tendency to entrust everything to God. We often hear people say, *ipasa-Diyos na lang* ("just leave everything to God"). Yet the prayer in Psalm

---

3. Allen, *Psalms 101–150*, 65.

132 teaches us that God values our initiative, our expressions of love, self-sacrifice, and dedication to him.

## 132:1–9 "LORD REMEMBER DAVID AND ALL HIS SELF-DENIAL"

There is a similarity between Psalm 132:1 and Lamentations 5:1, which both begin with a petition for the Lord to "remember" (*zekor*) the difficulties of David or the people: "*remember* what has happened to us" (Lam 5:1); "*remember* all the hardships he endured (Ps 132:1, ESV).

Lamentations 5:1 recalls the destruction of Jerusalem and the people's subsequent exile. Psalm 132:1 refers to the sacrifices David made to fulfill his vow to the Lord. The word translated as "hardships" ("self-denial" in NIV) comes from the Hebrew word, *'anah*, which means "to afflict" or "to oppress" (*'nh*). Verse 2 begins with the Hebrew relative particle *'asher* ("which" or "who"), which connects the vow of David to his hardship.

His vow pertains to finding and building a physical place for the Lord's dwelling (v. 5). The planning, organizing, and building involves his mind and his whole heart, as he will not rest until he accomplishes his oath. Moreover, the endeavor is an expression of his relationship with the Lord, and so he is willing to sacrifice his comfort and convenience. From the perspective of the psalmist, God should be moved by David's dedication and commitment, which he describes as "self-denial" (v. 1).

Though it is easy to make a vow, it is hard to fulfill it. But the psalmist asserts that David accomplished his vow, for he testifies that "we have heard it in Ephrathah" (v. 6). Ephrathah is "identified in several passages as the home territory of David (Ruth 4:11; Mic 5:2)."[4] What they heard was people saying, "Let us go to his dwelling place" (v. 7). Moreover, they "found it in the fields of Jaar" (v. 6b). The word "found" corresponds to David's vow that he will not rest "until I find" a place for the Lord (v. 5). The "fields of Jaar" could be "Kiriath Jearim, where the ark stayed for twenty years."[5]

Prior to the building of the Temple, the ark stayed in a tent. Verses 7–8 could be understood as part of an "ark procession to the Davidic tent sanctuary."[6] The shout, "Arise, LORD," was originally associated with a war cry (see Num 10:35) and was also used in the procession. In the psalm, however, it

---

4. Walton, Chavalas, and Matthews, *IVP Bible Background Commentary: Old Testament*, 555.
5. Walton, Chavalas, and Matthews, *IVP Bible Background Commentary: Old Testament*, 555.
6. Allen, *Psalms 101–150*, 272.

is possible that this shout is being used as part of the motivation.[7] Not only have the people "heard" about and "found" the ark of God in his dwelling, but they have actually held a procession there. As part of the motivation, this processional shout becomes a means of asking God to act in their midst just as he has acted previously. Because the people find themselves in a very difficult situation, they cry out to God, "Arise, Lord" (v. 8). There has been some debate about how to translate the Hebrew preposition *le* ("to, for") in verse 8. Some argue that it should be translated as "from," but this suggests that God is already in their midst and is being asked to arise *from* his "resting place" (v. 8). Yet the usual meaning of the preposition *le*, along with the following context (see v. 10 below), supports the translation, "to," as in: "Arise, Lord, come *to* your resting place" (v. 8).

## 132:10–18 "DO NOT REJECT YOUR ANOINTED ONE"

The implication of the petition for God to "arise" and "come *to*" his "resting place" (v. 8) is that the Lord has left his people. There is an interplay between the petitions, "arise" (v. 8) and "do not turn away the face of your anointed one" (v. 10b, ESV). The second main petition (v. 10b) parallels the petition in verse 1, and David features prominently in both. Whereas David's self-giving action forms the basis for petition in verse 1, the petition in verse 10a is based on David's own person ("for the sake of your servant David"). This focus on David becomes clear in verse 10b, for he is "your anointed one." The people are asking the Lord not to "turn away" from their king, which is also a way of saying, "do not abandon us," since the lives of the people are intertwined with the life of their king.

The petition is followed by the psalmist's motivation, which combines the royal tradition (vv. 11–12) with the Zion tradition (vv. 13–18). Indeed, this is the most extensive motivation for a petition within the Songs of Ascent.[8] In the first section, the psalmist appeals to David's oath (vv. 3–5), but in the second section, he appeals to the Lord's oath to David (vv. 11–12), a motivation that is connected with the royal theology of Psalm 89. God himself "swore an

---

[7]. David B. Schreiner posits that Psalm 132 shows signs of a "postexilic expansion of a preexilic psalm," noting that "many of the data often cited as evidence for an early date of composition appear in vv. 1–12." David B. Schreiner, "Double Entendre, Disguised Verbal Resistance, and the Composition of Psalm 132," *BBR* 28, no. 1 (2018): 20.

[8]. According to Human, Psalm 132 is the "densest reflective theological text" among the Songs of Ascent. Dirk J. Human, "Psalm 132 and Its Compositional Context(s)," *Scriptura* 116, no. 2 (2017): 75.

oath to David" that there would always be someone from his line who would sit on his throne (Ps 132:11), but this oath had a condition (see "if," v. 12), which was that David's descendants must "keep my covenant" (v. 12). So how can the people claim this promise, since they have been exiled, which means that they did not keep the covenant? The text does not answer this question, which creates a tension between Yahweh's oath and the people's implied failure.

Thus the psalmist adds another motivation from the Zion tradition: the Lord has "chosen Zion" (v. 13). Similar to the motivation in verses 11–12, the psalmist includes a direct speech from the Lord in verses 14–18. As noted earlier, quotations from the Lord are often used in prayer as a motivation. In verse 14, the Lord declares that Zion is the place where his "resting place will be for ever and ever" (v. 14a). While having someone sit on David's throne is dependent on his descendant's faithfulness to the covenant, Yahweh has promised that "here [in Zion] I will sit enthroned, for I have desired it" (v. 14b).

God's priority for the poor is demonstrated in verse 15, for he has also promised that he will bless Zion with "abundant provisions" (*tsayid*). In this context, the Hebrew word *tsayid* means "food,"[9] which is one of the most basic needs. It is mentioned here because the poor need food. The Hebrew word for "poor" used here is *'ebyon*, which also means "needy." Even in the midst of the pandemic due to COVID-19, I hear poor people say that they would rather die of COVID than hunger. In Psalm 132, the Lord promises that he will "satisfy" the poor "with food" (v. 15).

After the psalm talks about satisfying the needy with food, it talks about clothing Zion's priests (v. 16). Verse 16 is parallel to verse 9:

"Let your priests be clothed with righteousness" (v. 9, ESV);
"Her priests I will clothe with salvation" (v. 16, ESV).

"Righteousness" (v. 9) means "well-being."[10] "Salvation" refers to "help" or "deliverance" that comes from God.[11] Thus the vision of the psalm is holistic, not confined to the "spiritual," as some Christians understand this word. "Salvation" also involves the political realm.

The last two verses return to the royal theme. Verse 17 repeats the word "anointed" from verse 10, making an explicit reference to the petition for which the divine words serve as the motivation. The original language begins with the word, "there," which refers to Zion, the place that God has chosen

---

9. *HALOT*, 3:1021.
10. *HALOT*, 3:1005.
11. *HALOT*, 2:449.

to be his dwelling. The Lord promised that he will "make a horn grow" and "set up a lamp for my anointed one" (v. 17). "Horn" is a symbol for power. "Lamp" speaks of "permanence of the dynasty."[12] For this to transpire, the enemies have to be defeated. The emphasis on the defeat of the enemy and the exaltation of the anointed king further confirms that "salvation" refers to the people's deliverance (v. 18). Verses 17–18 can also be read as a response to the prayers or petitions above, but structurally, they function more as motivations for the petitions.

---

12. Allen, *Psalms 101–150*, 275.

# PSALM 133

The main theme of Psalm 133 is expressed in its opening verse: "brothers" dwelling "in unity" (v. 1, ESV). Though the original language only mentions "brothers" (v. 1), the scope is much broader (see discussion below). The psalm speaks of the goodness, beauty, and blessing of being united, which is something we long for in our families, tribes, *barangays* (villages or districts), and countries.[1]

The psalm does not provide explicit information about how to achieve unity. Instead, it celebrates it and calls attention to its "goodness." The word "good" is repeated twice (vv. 1, 2). The Hebrew word for "good" (*tob*) is translated as "precious" in verse 2. The psalm also employs two images to describe the goodness of dwelling together in unity: oil and dew. These images provide some hints about how such unity can come about. The oil on Aaron's beard most likely refers to his consecration, signaling the spiritual and religious dimension of unity's origin. Some scholars disagree with the introduction of Aaron's consecration, since it disturbs what would have been a secular activity.[2] But in many traditional Asian cultures, there is no separation between the secular and the sacred. For example, in the Philippines, religion occupies a central role in public life. Similarly, in Psalm 133, the act of consecrating Aaron, which is symbolized by oil running over his beard onto the collar of his robe (v. 2), links the blessing of unity to God's blessing. When we experience this unity, it is like being Aaron as he receives the blessing of the anointing. The spiritual dimension is further supported by the fact that Psalm 133 is part of the Songs of Ascent, which the people would sing or recite on their way to Jerusalem to worship. Thus we should not separate the secular from the spiritual. Family life and the most ordinary events of daily life are all immersed in the "oil" of consecration.

The threefold repetition of the word "running down"/"falling on" (*yored*) in verses 2–3 indicates the direction from which the "blessing" of unity comes. As the people go *up* to Jerusalem to worship, so the blessing of unity comes *down* from Zion. The word "there" in verse 3b is emphatic: "There [in Zion] the LORD bestows his blessing." The emphasis is clearly on the divine or spiritual dimension from which the blessing of unity arises. But, of course, this

---

1. I wish to see this in my own country, the Philippines, which consists of about seven thousand islands and over a hundred different languages, not to mention religious diversities.
2. Zenger and Hossfeld cite some of these scholars. Zenger and Hossfeld, *Psalms 3*, 472.

psalm does not discount human agency. We each need to do our part to live together as brothers and sisters in unity.

> ## PSALM 133 AND THE CONCEPT OF *KAPWA* (FELLOW HUMAN BEINGS)
>
> A helpful Filipino cultural concept, *kapwa* ("fellow human being"), is rooted in the concept of being equal (*magkapantay*). Enriquez "emphasized that we should treat both *ibang tao* (other people) and *hindi ibang tao* (not others) as our *kapwa*."[1]
>
> ---
>
> 1. Cited in Jose Antonio et al., "Revisiting the Kapwa Theory: Applying Alternative Methodologies and Gaining New Insights," *Philippine Journal of Psychology* 41, no. 2 (2008): 2.

The genre of Psalm 133 is not straightforward. Some consider it to be a wisdom psalm. For example, Allen notes that most commentators since Gunkel have categorized it as a "noncultic wisdom poem."[3] And though Zenger does not directly discuss the genre of Psalm 133, he writes that the message of the psalm falls "within the perspectives of wisdom theology."[4] Others, such as Berlin, consider the psalm to be "an ode to Zion with a religious and nationalistic message" rather than a wisdom psalm.[5] And Gerstenberger calls the psalm an "Announcement of Blessing."[6]

Structurally, the psalm may be outlined as follows:

Goodness of unity (v. 1),
Metaphors of oil and snow (or "dew") (vv. 2–3a),
Blessing from Zion (v. 3b).

### 133:1 "HOW GOOD AND PLEASANT IT IS!"

The first word in the original language is *hinneh*, which means "behold!" or "look!" and is used to draw attention to something. Here, the speaker is calling

---

3. Allen, *Psalms 101–150*, 277.
4. Zenger and Hossfeld, *Psalms 3*, 483.
5. Adele Berlin, "On the Interpretation of Psalm 133," in *Directions in Biblical Hebrew Poetry* (Sheffield: England, 1987), 146.
6. Gerstenberger, *Psalms Part 2 and Lamentations*, 372.

our attention to something good or wonderful that he sees before him, which is "brothers" dwelling together in unity. The exact nature of the unity in verse 1 is not clear. Is it unity among "God's people," as reflected in the NIV translation? Or does it refer to the "undivided kingdom"?[7] Or is it simply speaking about good relationships in a family (between brothers, children, parents, etc.)? Though we no longer have access to the original meaning, we can use relevant biblical texts as well as our own experiences to help us in our interpretation.

The story of Abraham and his nephew Lot is a helpful text, for they journeyed together through many places over a long period of time, and our psalmist might have said of them, "Behold, how good and pleasant it is when brothers dwell in unity!" (v. 1, ESV). And perhaps they could have stayed that way if greed had not crept in. Ironically, the conflict between them did not arise until "Abram was very rich in livestock, in silver, and in gold" (Gen 13:2), and Lot "had flocks and herds and tents" (v. 5). The text says that the land could no longer support both of them because "their possessions were so great that they could not live together" (v. 6). Moreover, there was strife between the herders of their respective flocks (v. 7). Thus they separated from one another (vv. 10–11), which later resulted in the destruction of Lot's family (Genesis 19). Unfortunately, this sort of strife is common even today. In my own context, family members disown each other and fight with one another over land ownership.

## 133:2–3A METAPHORS OF OIL AND SNOW

We have a famous Filipino love song entitled *Tubig at Langis* ("water and oil"), which shows the difficulty, if not the impossibility, of those belonging to entirely different social groups becoming joined together in love. But in Psalm 133, these two images share a common movement, for both oil and snow (or "dew"), which turns to water, flow down from above. The oil that is poured on Aaron's head runs "down" to his "beard, down on the collar of his robe" (v. 2). The "dew of Hermon" falls down on Mount Zion (v. 3a). This downward movement points "above," from where the oil and dew flow. When we acknowledge that everything we have is from above, we can learn to share it with others.

The precious oil, which is poured in abundance over Aaron's head (compare Ps 23:5), trickles down into his beard and benefits it as well. And Aaron's

---

7. Berlin, "On the Interpretation of Psalm 133," 142.

beard, which the poet ingeniously repeats, flows down in waves to the collar of his robes (Exod 28:32; 29:33), so that they, too, receive adornment and anointing. Similarly, high-rising Hermon, which is surrounded by clouds and blessed with rich dew, does not retain all that moisture, but rather pours it onto the lower heights through a network of brooks.[8]

The answer to the problem of division and conflict between brothers and sisters can be found in the generosity and extravagance of the oil and snow flowing down from above. Yet this is a rare sight and is certainly not easy to achieve. The animosity between Christians and Muslims in the southern part of the Philippines has been going on for hundreds of years and remains to this day. The downward flowing movement in this psalm also highlights the importance of divine agency. To live in unity, we need help from above!

### 133:3 BLESSING FROM ZION

The word "there" links this psalm with Psalm 132, where the same word is used in a similar sense (132:17). Zion is the place of divine activity, and it is "there" that Yahweh "has commanded the blessing" (133:3b, ESV). This blessing is "life forevermore" (v. 3b). Read within the context of verse 1, the dwelling together of families, communities, tribes, and countries are considered to be "blessing" and "life."

---

8. Gunkel, *Die Psalmen*, 571; cited in Zenger and Hossfeld, *Psalms 3*, 473–474.

# PSALM 134

In his instructions on worship, the Apostle Paul exhorts Timothy: "Therefore I want the men everywhere to pray, lifting up holy hands without anger or disputing" (1 Tim 2:8). The previous psalm celebrates the blessing of unity (Ps 133:1). Here, in Psalm 134, the worshipers are exhorted to "lift up your hands in the sanctuary" (v. 2). The close connection between Psalm 133 and Psalm 134 teaches us that how we relate to one another is part of our worship.

Psalm 134 is the last psalm among the Songs of Ascent (Psalms 120–134) and has many links with Psalm 133. First, both psalms begin with the word *hinneh* (literally, "behold" or "look," 133:1; 134:1). Second, both feature Zion as the place from where the blessing comes (133:3; 134:3). Third, Psalm 133 ends with the "blessing" (*berakhah*) that the Lord bestows (v. 3), while Psalm 134 begins with an exhortation to "Come (*hinneh*) and bless (*barakh*) the LORD" (v. 1, ESV).

The word "bless" has the same sense as "praise," which can be seen in the similar formulation in Psalm 135:1, where "praise" is used instead of "bless." Psalm 134 not only serves as the conclusion to the Songs of Ascent collection, but it also provides a smooth transition into the subsequent psalms. We praise the Lord because we have experienced his blessing. Thus our worship is a response to what God has done. At the same time, those who worship ought to exemplify a life that reflects holiness. In Psalm 134, the servants of the Lord are enjoined to "Lift up your hands to the holy place" (v. 2, ESV). Psalm 133 reminds us that holiness is closely associated with living together in unity (v. 1). We cannot lift our hands in worship or in prayer if we are arguing or disputing. The Apostle Paul, in one of his instructions for worship, exhorts "the men everywhere to pray, lifting up holy hands without anger or disputing" (1 Tim 2:8).

The "brothers" dwelling in unity from Psalm 133 (v. 1) become the "servants of the LORD" in Psalm 134 (v. 1). Some debate the identity of these "servants of the LORD." Because this term is weighty and cannot be applied to anyone, the most natural identification would be the priests who serve in the Temple. Moreover, Psalm 135:1 also mentions the "servants of the LORD," and the subsequent verses make it clear that the term refers to those who are serving in the Temple (v. 2). However, by extension, we might also say that the term can be applied to the worshipers themselves, who recite or sing these songs as pilgrims.

# Psalm 134

In terms of genre, the psalm consists of a "hymnic call to praise" (vv. 1–2) and a "priestly benediction."[1] Structurally, the psalm may be outlined as follows:

Exhortation to praise (vv. 1–2) and
Blessing or benediction (v. 3).

## 134:1–2 EXHORTATION TO PRAISE

As noted above, Psalm 134 begins with the Hebrew word *hinneh* ("behold"). Unfortunately, the NIV does not reflect this word in its translation, but begins instead with "Praise," which is the second word in the Hebrew of verse 1. The word *hinneh* is immediately followed by the imperative, "praise," which is unique. This points to a possibility that the word "behold" (*hinneh*) has been added to draw a connection with the previous psalm, where the word "behold" (*hinneh*) also occurs as the opening word. This further establishes a connection with Psalm 133, which can help us understand Psalm 134.

The exhortation to praise is addressed to "all the servants of the LORD" (v. 1). These servants are described as those "who minister by night in the house of the LORD" (v. 1b). This verse has led to a number of theories about night liturgies or services in the Temple. Accordingly, the servants of the Lord were the priests on guard duty. Walton explains that the "temple was guarded twenty-four hours a day so that neither its sanctity would be violated nor its valuables stolen."[2] In this sense, the message of the psalm reflects a view of worship that incorporates the "mundane." Even guarding the Temple is incorporated into worship. Yet "servants" here should not be confined to those who are guarding/ministering by night, since we do not really know whether night liturgies actually existed.[3] Moreover, as noted above, this term can be applied to the priests serving in the Temple. Finally, the "servants of the LORD" can also be applied to the pilgrims themselves, the worshipers who go up to Jerusalem. As noted above, since Psalm 134 is part of the Songs of Ascent, there is room for this appropriation.

The exhortation to "lift up your hands to the holy place" (v. 2, ESV) applies more to the pilgrims who are approaching the Temple rather than the priests who are already in the Temple. The NIV's rendering, "lift up your hands *in*

---

1. Allen, *Psalms 101–150*, 281–282.
2. Walton, Chavalas, and Matthews, *IVP Bible Background Commentary: Old Testament*, 556.
3. Zenger and Hossfeld, *Psalms 3*, 486.

the sanctuary," is less likely because of the accusative use of the word.[4] The upward movement signified by the title, "A Song of Ascent," is reinforced by the lifting of the hands, which is still a posture of worship in our churches today. In Psalm 134, the people are instructed to lift up their hands because Jerusalem is on elevated ground and the one who is being worshiped is "the Maker of heaven and earth" (v. 3).

## 134:3 BLESSING

The psalm starts with a call to "bless" the Lord (v. 1) and ends with a blessing: "May the LORD bless you from Zion" (v. 3). This order is instructive, as it emphasizes human actions before divine action. Twice, the worshipers are exhorted to "praise the LORD" (vv. 1, 2b), and between these, they are commanded to "lift up your hands" (v. 2a). After the people participate in these three actions, the psalmist invokes the blessing from the Lord in the last verse. While worship flows out of our encounter with the God who blesses us, we should not forget the importance of human initiative. In Psalm 132, the psalmist esteems David's initiative in finding a place for the Lord. All that we do for the Lord is an important part of our worship.

---

4. Allen translates it as "toward." Allen, 281; compare Zenger and Hossfeld, *Psalms 3*, 484.

# PSALM 135

There are different reasons for praising the Lord and calling others to praise him. In Psalm 135, the psalmist calls people to praise God because he has defeated their enemies and fulfilled his promise by giving them the lands of their enemies. The psalm briefly reviews God's salvific acts in Egypt and his defeat of the kings of many nations before leading his people into the Promised Land. Thus God has proven that he is "greater than all gods" (v. 5) and "does whatever pleases him" (v. 6).

But what about the defeated nations whose land has been destroyed to fulfill this promise? Is it right to praise the Lord for his goodness to us at the expense of others?[1] The psalmist not only remembers what happened, but also composes a hymn of praise for what happened. Unfortunately, Western commentators seldom tackle this issue because they do not see a problem. Mays affirms that the "LORD's election of Israel is the demonstration that all the gods are idols."[2] Commenting on verse 12, which contains a direct reference for God's actions in Egypt and the giving of the land to Israel, Allen writes: "So tremendous is this work of grace that it deserves unending praise to echo back to Yahweh through the corridors of time."[3] Zenger is one of the few scholars who addresses the acts of violence in Psalm 135,[4] explaining that this was the way things were done in the ancient Near East, but that the violent actions of God were meant to end all violence. This text should never be used to legitimize violence, but those of us who have experienced life under foreign powers continue to question why God chose Israel at the expense of others. It is painful to join Israel in praising God for taking the land of others. As Christians, even though the Scriptures say that God loves all people, "Those not elected cannot be expected not to be hurt by not being of the seed of Abraham, whom God loves above all others."[5] I try to deal

---

1. This reminds me of the testimony of a man in the Philippines, whose house was spared when the flash floods changed its course, but what about the houses and families that were destroyed as a result of this shifting of the flash flood?
2. Mays, *Psalms*, 417.
3. Allen, *Psalms 101–150*, 291.
4. Zenger and Hossfeld, *Psalms 3*, 501. Weiser and Kirkpatrick do not address this question. Weiser, *Psalms*, 788–790; Kirkpatrick, *The Book of Psalms*, 773–776.
5. Michael Wyschogrod, *The Body of Faith: God and the People Israel* (Lanham, MD: Rowan and Littlefield, 1996), 64. Wyschogrod goes on to say God is a father to "all peoples, elect and nonelect" (65).

with this issue in my comments below, though briefly due to the limitations of the commentary.

Psalm 135 is a hymn of praise, and all the elements of a hymn are present. The psalm begins with a hymnic exhortation to praise (vv. 1–3), which is followed by motivations for praise (vv. 3–4), and concludes with a call for praise (vv. 19–21). After the long Psalm 119 and the Songs of Ascent (Psalms 120–134), Psalm 135 resumes the pattern of Psalms 111–118, which either begin or end with the word, *hallelujah* (a combination of the plural form of the verb *hll*, "praise," with *yah*, an abbreviation for "Yahweh"). This word is translated as a command for the people to "Praise the LORD." Psalm 135 also shows close links with the final two Songs of Ascent (Psalms 133–134) as well as Psalm 115.[6]

## 135:1–4, 19–21 HYMNIC CALL TO PRAISE

Psalm 135 begins and ends with a call to praise (vv. 1–4, 19–21). Verse 1 is very similar to Psalm 134:1, with minor variations. Instead of the imperative, "bless," Psalm 135 has "praise," but the two are used in the same way: to give honor and praise to the Lord. The repetition of the description of the servants as those "who stand" in the house of the Lord (v. 2) shows a deliberate attempt to link this psalm with Psalm 134, which is the last Song of Ascent (Psalms 120–134). Whereas Psalm 134 mentions the "house of the LORD" (v. 1), Psalm 135 develops the theme of the people of Israel worshiping in God's house, citing the "courts of the house" and including the worshipers in the description of the "courts of the house of *our* God" (v. 2; compare vv. 19–21).

Verse 3 provides an important element of a hymn: the motivation for praising God ("for the LORD is good"). This anticipates Psalm 136, which begins with this same motivation for praising God (v. 1). At the same time, the description of God's name as "pleasant" (135:3b) recalls Psalm 133:1. This confirms that Psalms 133 and 135 are connected, for when God's people live together in unity, praising the Lord, this is pleasant, indeed!

The motivation for praise is usually introduced in Hebrew by the preposition *ki* ("for"). Verse 4 begins with this preposition, linking it to the exhortation to praise at the beginning of verse 3. At the same time, verse 4 specifies what the psalmist means when he says that the Lord is "good" (v. 3). The Lord is "good" (v. 3) because he has "chosen Jacob to be his own" (v. 4a). Verse 4

---

[6]. See Judith Krawelitzki, "God the Almighty?: Observations in the Psalms," *VT* 64, no. 3 (2014): 435.

contains two parallel statements. In verse 4b, "Israel" corresponds to Jacob, where Israel is a "treasured possession" and Jacob is "his own."

## 135:5–18 "OUR LORD IS GREATER THAN ALL GODS"

The Lord is not just "good" (v. 3), for next the psalmist asserts,[7] "I know that the LORD is great" (v. 5). This combination of "goodness" and "greatness" draws the community of believers to praise the Lord. Even though God is highly exalted – "greater than all gods" (v. 5b) – he has chosen to reveal himself to his people (v. 4). In verses 6–18, the people recall some of the events in their history that have manifested the greatness of God.

Verse 6 is parallel to verses 15–18, which offer an extended polemic against the gods of the other nations. (For a discussion of verses 15–18, see comments in Ps 115:4–8.) Unlike the other gods, who are not able to do anything, "the LORD does whatever pleases him" (135:6a; 115:3b). God's scope of action is boundless, for he works "in the heavens and on the earth," including the waters and the depths (v. 6b). Verse 7 briefly demonstrates God's power in the "heavens," but the psalmist focuses on what God does "on the earth," specifically on behalf of Israel, his chosen people. Verses 7–12 summarize God's actions in Egypt (vv. 7–9) until he gives the land to the people (vv. 10–12).

God is presented as "the God who strikes" (vv. 8, 10).[8] What he did to the "firstborn of Egypt" (v. 8), he did to "many nations" (v. 10). To fulfill his promise to Israel, he "killed mighty kings" (v. 10b). As Zenger and Hossfeld observe, "Verses 10–12 recapitulate the gift of the land to Israel. This begins with the conquest of the kingdoms east of the Jordan, the realms of Sihon and Og, as described in Numbers 21, and then continues and concludes with the conquest of the cities and kingdoms west of the Jordan, depicted in the book of Joshua."[9]

Unfortunately, the story of conquest, as narrated in the book of Joshua and praised in Psalm 135, has been used to support violence against weaker nations, which was also true in the Philippines. As Templer (who mentions the Philippines) notes:

> the conquest of Canaan's biblical narrative . . . has provided the prime political-theological rationalization via scriptural narrative (the sacralization of politics) for the project of western imperial

---

7. An individual speaks in verse 5.
8. Zenger and Hossfeld, *Psalms 3*, 493.
9. Zenger and Hossfeld, *Psalms 3*, 498.

and racist expansion, since 1500, into the peripheries and the divinely sanctioned subjugation and extermination of native peoples across the globe. Its ideology constitutes the dark ethnocentric underbelly of genocide in the foundation myths of the US Republic, the Spanish conquest of the Americas and Philippines.[10]

For those who have suffered under foreign powers, Psalm 135 is disturbing and shocking. It is hard to understand how God can be "good" to one people by driving other people out of their lands. The psalmist praises Yahweh for giving "their land as an inheritance . . . to his people Israel" (v. 12). Zenger explains this action by saying that this land is God's anyway. "Because, as verse 4 says, he has chosen Israel for his 'special possession' or 'crown jewel' (this concept also echoes metaphors of kingship), he gave them 'the land,' which in fact is his possession, as their inheritance."[11] Though theologically, it is true that all lands are God's, the land is also "*their* land" (v. 12). Note that Zenger writes "the land" instead of "their land."

## HOW CAN WE PRAISE A GOD WHO GIVES THE LANDS OF OTHERS TO ONE NATION?

What should Christians who live in countries that were former colonies of more powerful Christian countries do with a text like Psalm 135? Rather than ironing out any tension in the text, I think we need to confront this head-on and seek to interpret the text in the light of the wider witness of Scripture. Scripture emphasizes that the God of the Bible allows himself to be questioned and makes space for people to lament against issues of injustice (e.g. Psalm 10; Gen 18:23–25; Hab 1:2–4). Rather than stifling our questions, we need to bring them into the open. Some Christians are not willing to confront their painful past and refuse to lament the ways that the cross has been used to control and colonize us. But like Jesus, our Lord, we can also ask God, "why?"

---

10. Templer, "The Political Sacralization of Imperial Genocide," 380; quoted in Hélène Dallaire, "Taking the Land by Force: Divine Violence in Joshua," in *Wrestling with the Violence of God: Soundings in the Old Testament*, ed. Daniel R. Carroll and J. Blair Wilgus, Bulletin for Biblical Research Supplements 10 (Winona Lake, IN: Eisenbrauns, 2015), 56.
11. Zenger and Hossfeld, *Psalms 3*, 499.

# Psalm 135

Questioning God is much better than burying our questions about the past. As we lament and pour out our pain in the presence of the Lord, we will encounter the God of the colonized and the weak, who has always been with slaves, for the Israelites themselves were slaves. Contrary to other accounts, "the Israelites were far from being a band of relentless barbarians who were marching forward confidently aiming to destroy everyone and everything on their path under the leadership of their God."[1] Instead, they were "a semi-organized group of people who were feared by the inhabitants of the land, not because of who they were but because their God was mightier than the gods of the surrounding nations (Josh 2:9)."[2] Psalm 136 provides another perspective about how God works from "our low estate" (v. 23).

---

1. Dallaire, "Taking the Land by Force: Divine Violence in Joshua," 72.
2. Dallaire, "Taking the Land by Force: Divine Violence in Joshua," 72.

# PSALM 136

Psalm 136 is identified as a "twin" to Psalm 135, as both psalms share the following:

> An emphasis on God's incomparable greatness
> (135:5–6; 136:4),
> A motivation for praising God because he is "good"
> (135:3; 136:1),
> A selection of events that recall God's greatness:
> > Israel's deliverance from Egypt (135:8–9; 136:10–16),
> > the giving of the Promised Land to Israel (135:10–12; 136:17–22).

But Psalm 136 also has unique elements. Foremost, the chorus, "His love endures forever," is repeated twenty-six times, and this refrain gives the psalm its "unique compositional and artistic character."[1] Psalm 136 is known in Jewish tradition as "the great Hallel [praise]."[2] The threefold call to thanksgiving (vv. 1–3) and the concluding exhortation identify the psalm as a "Hodu psalm" (along with Psalms 105–107; 118; 136). *Hodu* is the Hebrew word for "Give thanks." Psalm 136 also shares similarities with the Egyptian Hallel psalms (Psalms 113–118) and the final Hallel psalms (Psalms 146–150).[3] Though some of the events recalled in Psalm 136 are the same as those recollected in Psalm 135, the element of praise becomes more explicit because of the refrain. The refrain "functions like an illuminated, revolving diamond, that gradually radiates the multifaceted image of Yahweh's acts and attributes from different angles."[4]

Though both Psalms 135 and 136 highlight the greatness of God, the perspective is different. Contrary to Zenger, the "selection of YHWH's deeds listed" in Psalm 136 is not the same "as in Psalm 135." While Zenger argues that Psalm 135 is "shaped by the perspective of YHWH's omnipotence,"[5] I think that Psalm 136 is "shaped" by the people's perspective of themselves and their experience. As the people declare in verse 23, "He remembered us

---

1. Dirk J. Human, "Psalm 136: A Liturgy with Reference to Creation and History," in *Psalms and Liturgy*, ed. Dirk J. Human and C. J. A. Vos (London: Clark, 2004), 74.
2. Schonfield, "Psalms 113–118: Qualified Praise," 148.
3. Human, "Psalm 136," 74.
4. Human, "Psalm 136," 74.
5. Zenger and Hossfeld, *Psalms 3*, 504.

in our low estate." We can appreciate God's greatness even more in our weakness, which makes the recitation of God's mighty acts in Psalm 136 more real and meaningful.

Moreover, the perspective in Psalm 136 is broader than Psalm 135. Instead of highlighting the election of Israel (135:4), Psalm 136 highlights the creation (vv. 5–9). Though the giving of the land remains a high point, the psalm goes far beyond this to include "every creature" (v. 25). The psalm does not end with a praise to the God of Israel, nor to the God of the earth, but "to the God of heaven" (v. 26). Though Israel is prominent, it is one with the rest of creation, who all share in the experience of divine generosity. This reminds us of the Abrahamic blessing, for God did not choose Israel for itself, but so that, through the children of Abraham, "all peoples on earth will be blessed" (Gen 12:3).

Structurally the psalm shows a threefold division:

Threefold exhortation to praise (vv. 1–3),
Motivations for praise (vv. 4–25),
Concluding call to praise (v. 26).

## 136:1–3 EXHORTATIONS TO PRAISE

As a hymn, Psalm 136 begins with a call to praise. The exhortation, "give thanks," is repeated four times in the psalm, with three at the beginning (vv. 1–3) and one at the very end (v. 26). The psalm abounds in listing motivations for praise, but the first reason is "for he is good" (v. 1; compare 135:3). The whole psalm then expounds on why the people believe that God is good. As an antiphonal hymn, the first part of each verse is recited by the Temple personnel, and the second part (the chorus) is recited by the congregation, who declare twenty-six times (in twenty-six verses) that "His love endures forever." The word translated as "love" comes from the Hebrew word *hesed*,[6] which denotes "faithfulness, goodness, graciousness." *Hesed* is active, describing "an act that preserves or promotes life . . . [an] intervention on behalf of someone suffering misfortune or distress . . . [a] demonstration of friendship or piety."[7] *Hesed* endures.[8] Thus the word is commonly translated as "loyal," "steadfast," and "faithful love." A famous Filipino song captures the meaning

---

6. *HALOT*, 1:337.
7. *TDOT*, 5:51.
8. *TDOT*, 5:51.

very well: *Dakilang Katapatan* ("Great Faithfulness").⁹ Because of God's great faithfulness, the people believe that God is *good*.

> ## GOD AND GODS IN THE FILIPINO CONTEXT
>
> After the psalmist praises the Lord "for he is good" (v. 1), he declares the Lord's greatness. He is the "God of gods" (v. 2) and the "Lord of lords" (v. 3). Prior to the introduction of Christianity, Filipinos believed that there were many gods who were ruled by a chief God, who was known by different names among different people groups. Among the Tagalogs, he is known as *Bathala*,[1] who is the creator of all things – the sky, the earth, and all the vegetation. As Jocano notes, "He dwelt in the highest realm of the eternal space called *kawalhatian* or sky."[2] Interestingly, like Yahweh, he is also good, "just and merciful."[3] While he is kind and good to those who obey his laws, he is exacting towards sinners. Could it be that God was already revealing himself to Filipinos long before the Spaniards introduced Christianity to us?
>
> ---
>
> 1. Jocano, "Notes on Philippine Divinities," 169.
> 2. Jocano, "Notes on Philippine Divinities," 170.
> 3. Jocano, "Notes on Philippine Divinities," 170.

### 136:4–22 MOTIVATIONS FOR PRAISE

The call to praise (vv. 1–3) governs verses 4–22, which describe who God is or what he has done and serve as further motivations for giving thanks. Verse 4 is a general description of the uniqueness of God and is similar to the statement in Psalm 135 that proclaims God's greatness above all Gods (v. 5) and his capacity to do whatever pleases him (v. 6). The word "alone" (136:4) is important.

Verses 5–9 recite God's acts of creation, following Genesis 1. Zenger and Hossfeld note that the sequence is "evidently inspired by Genesis 1."¹⁰ But Psalm 136 explicitly incorporates the element of praise. God's creation of the

---

9. Composed by Arnel de Pano. As a child, I remember singing this song with tears in my eyes during one of the most difficult times in our family life.
10. Zenger and Hossfeld, *Psalms 3*, 507.

heavens (v. 5) and the earth (v. 6), together with the creation of the "great lights" (vv. 7–9), are all expressions of his enduring love.

Verses 10–22 recall what God did in Egypt and as the peopled journeyed to the Promised Land. God is described as one "who struck down the firstborn of Egypt" (v. 10). The phrase, "who struck down," is repeated in verse 17, where God is the God "who strikes down great kings" and also "killed mighty kings" (v. 18). These acts of violence are difficult to explain with respect to God. We wish that there would no longer be violence, but we know that sometimes the deliverance of the weak involves violence. The Israelites were slaves in Egypt, and they were oppressed and treated ruthlessly by their masters. They could not liberate themselves but needed a much greater force. As they journeyed to the Promised Land, they were confronted by powerful enemies that could have crushed and annihilated them if it had not been for the "God who strikes down" (vv. 10, 17). In the Psalms, those who pray to God are confronted and oppressed by powerful enemies (Pss 18:17; 142:6). The Israelites were not powerful like our colonizers, but were powerless.

## 136:23–26 "IN OUR LOW ESTATE"

Verse 23 shifts from a third-person description about God's actions to a first person plural application. The verse begins emphatically with the words, "who in our low estate remembered us" (my translation). Note that the words, "low estate," precede the word, "remember." As the people "remember" their God – the great God who created the heavens and the earth, the great and powerful deliverer – they are amazed that this powerful and highly exalted God has chosen to remember them in their "low estate" (v. 23).

Though God reveals himself as the one who is in the heavens, he also reaches down to those who are below: "That God dwells on high but looks far down . . . is a fundamental element of his engagement on behalf of the poor and needy (Ps 113:4–9)."[11] The emphasis on God as the "God of Gods," "Lord of lords" (vv. 2–3), creator (vv. 5–9), great deliverer, miracle worker (vv. 10–22), and "God of heaven" (v. 26) highlights God's concern and care for the least and vulnerable. Because verse 24 "addresses rescue from foes, the 'low estate' here [v. 23] can be interpreted as political oppression."[12] In the turbulent political situation of the postexilic period, Psalm 136 is a praise that empowers the weak.

---

11. *TDOT*, 15:446.
12. *TDOT*, 15:446.

# PSALM 137

We are often exhorted in our Christian communities to praise the Lord, no matter what the situation may be. Praise is usually accompanied by music, and one of the favorite songs in Asian churches is, "God is good, all the time!" In the midst of the pandemic, a well-known pastor led his congregation in singing this song on social media. As I write, the daily new cases of COVID-19 in India have reached more than 300,000, the highest in the world. Many well-known pastors have died, one of my Indian friends told me.

How can we sing praises to the Lord in the midst of so much suffering? This is the question that Psalm 137 is asking: "How can we sing the songs of the LORD?" (v. 4a) when their Temple, city, families, and everything they had were destroyed. Now they are suffering in a foreign land. We have no way of knowing whether the psalm was written in Babylon or Jerusalem, but they are clearly "there" rather than "here," where they ought to be. This psalm insists that "in the wake of the destruction," all singing and discourses about God "must change from praise to lament."[1]

Scholars, such as Westermann, often only emphasize the movement from lament to praise in the Psalms.[2] Similarly, the Christian message is often only communicated in terms of a victorious ending. But the poet who composed Psalm 137 disagrees, and the redactors who put the Psalms together support his perspective. There is a strong contrast between Psalm 137 and its surrounding context, as Psalms 135–136 and 138 are all praise/thanksgiving psalms:

> "Praise the LORD" (Ps 135:1);
> "Give thanks to the LORD, for he is good" (Ps 136:1);
> "I will praise you, LORD" (Ps 138:1).

Moreover, the second half of each of the twenty-six verses in Psalm 136 ends with the declaration, "His love endures forever."

So Ahn asks, "why would Psalm 137, accentuated by laments and curses, be placed in the midst of these thanksgiving and praise psalms?"[3] Unfortunately, he classifies Psalm 137 as a thanksgiving psalm, saying that "Psalms 135–137 are, then, a small cluster of praise and thanksgiving psalms."[4] But Psalm 137

---

1. Adele Berlin, "Psalms and the Literature of Exile: Psalms 137, 44, 69 and 78," in *The Book of Psalms: Composition and Reception*, ed. Peter W. Flint, et al. (Leiden; Boston: Brill, 2005), 71.
2. Westermann, *Praise and Lament in the Psalms*, 74–75.
3. John J. Ahn, "Psalm 137: Complex Communal Laments," *JBL* 127, no. 2 (2008): 275.
4. Ahn, "Psalm 137: Complex Communal Laments," 275.

is not a thanksgiving or praise psalm. Though its specific genre is debated, most scholars consider it to contain elements of lament. Ahn's answer to his own question diminishes the lament in Psalm 137, making it a mere vehicle for thanksgiving: "This is a bold but unconventional editorial move that proposes to give thanks and praise *through* laments laden with honest feelings of enmity."[5] When he argues – "Thanksgiving and praise arise not only from positive elements in life. Rather, the true mark of these practices is finding the courage and strength *to praise and give thanks when there is nothing worthwhile or praise-worthy*"[6] – he is contradicting the exact point of Psalm 137:4, which is a protest *against* praising and giving thanks "when there is nothing worthwhile or praise-worthy."

The contrast between Psalm 137 and its surrounding context is further demonstrated through its main theme, which is concerned with "remembering." The verb "remember" is mentioned three times (vv. 1, 6, 7). In between, we find two negative expressions of this verb – not remembering (v. 6) or forgetting (v. 5). These verses form the following structure:

"when we remembered" (v. 1);
    "If I forget you" (v. 5);
    "If I do not remember" (v. 6);
"Remember, Lord" (v. 7).

Though the word "remember" is mentioned only once in Psalm 136, it occurs at the climactic point in the psalm, when the people express their deep gratitude to God because "he remembered us in our low estate" (v. 23). Together, Psalms 135 and 136 recount how God remembered the people in their times of difficulty. But in Psalm 137, as they sit "by the rivers of Babylon," they can only weep "when we remembered Zion" (v. 1).

Moreover, in Psalm 135, the Lord is blessed "from Zion" (v. 21). According to Zenger, this verse is "surprising," since the "historical recollections extend only from exodus to the occupation of the land."[7] Thus he argues that Zion is referenced to draw a connection between Psalm 135 and Psalms 134 and 133. But from the perspective of Psalm 137, this reference to the end of Psalm 135 creates tension, for the people are away from Zion, whether literally or figuratively. Though Psalm 133:3 says, "For there [Zion] the Lord bestows his blessing," the people in Psalm 137 are not in Zion, but "there" in Babylon (v. 1).

---

5. Ahn, "Psalm 137: Complex Communal Laments," 275, emphasis mine.
6. Ahn, "Psalm 137: Complex Communal Laments," 275–276, emphasis mine.
7. Zenger and Hossfeld, *Psalms 3*, 521.

The word "there" (*sham*) is repeated twice (vv. 1, 3), underlining the "'otherness' of this location."[8]

Structurally, Psalm 137 may be divided into three sections:

Indirect protest (vv. 1–4),
Implied complaint (vv. 5–6),
Petition and imprecation (vv. 7–9).

## 137:1–4 INDIRECT PROTEST

The first verses of Psalm 137 may be compared with Rachel's cry in Jeremiah (Jer 31:15). Like Rachel, who refuses to be comforted, so the people in Psalm 137 refuse to sing "songs of joy" (v. 2), for "How can we sing the songs of the Lord while in a foreign land?" (v. 4). The foreign land that they are "in" is "by the rivers of Babylon" (v. 1). The psalm begins with the "emblematic" feature of Babylonia: its canals,[9] for Babylonia "was characteristically a land of streams."[10] This is similar to the Philippines, which is surrounded by water. One of the major people groups are called *Tagalog,* which comes from the words, *Taga* ("dwellers") and *ilog* ("river"), meaning dwellers by the river. When the text says, "by the rivers of Babylon," it's referring to the places where "the Judean exiles resided."[11] But wherever they lived, they "sat and wept" (v. 1b). The word "sat" expresses a downward movement that is characteristic in mourning and denotes an absence of action. The people could not do anything but weep, so they hung up their harps on poplars (v. 2). This verse continues the sense of ceasing. Both "sat" and "hung" have the subject "we," indicating deliberate actions. In light of the failure, destruction, and calamities of the people of Israel at that point in their history, they could not continue as usual.

The taunting of enemies is common in the lament psalms (e.g. Pss 22:7–8; 42:9–10). In Psalm 137, "our captors asked us for songs, our tormentors demanded songs of joy" (v. 3), but they refused and cried a lament in protest: "How can we sing the songs of the Lord while in a foreign land?" (v. 4). The word "how" comes from the Hebrew word *'eyk*, which is also used "in mourning" (2 Sam 1:19; Isa 14:4, 12; Ezek 26:17).[12] Mourning is also a form of protest, but who is the primary audience in Psalm 137?

---

8. Berlin, "Psalms and the Literature of Exile," 67.
9. Berlin, "Psalms and the Literature of Exile," 67.
10. Kirkpatrick, *The Book of Psalms,* 781.
11. Berlin, "Psalms and the Literature of Exile," 67.
12. *HALOT,* 1:39.

## Psalm 137

The tormentors are never addressed directly, and even though Jerusalem is addressed directly in verses 5–6, she is being personified. The only direct address is to the Lord (see v. 7), and so the people's lamentation and refusal to sing could be read as an indirect protest to God. The people could have taken up their harps and protested to their enemies' faces by singing the "songs of Zion" (v. 3) in a foreign land. These "songs of the Lord" (v. 4) proclaim God's greatness because he promised to protect the city and its people from external attacks. As Psalm 46 declares, "though the earth give way and the mountains fall into the heart of the sea, though its waters roar and foam . . . There is a river whose streams make glad the city of God, the holy place where the Most High dwells" (vv. 2–4). Yet the city and the Temple were destroyed, and the people were uprooted from their land and exiled to Babylon. Contextually, the people were no longer in Zion, but were "there" by the rivers of Babylon (137:1). Thus they could only weep as they remembered Zion.[13]

### 137:5–6 IMPLIED COMPLAINT

In verse 5, there is an implied contrast between God, who seems to have forgotten Zion, and the people, who refuse to "forget" Jerusalem even though they are living in a foreign land. Although God has "remembered" his people in the past (Ps 136:23), here the people have to petition him to "remember" what their enemies have done to them (137:7). The absence of divine remembering is contrasted with the people's remembering, even as they wept (v. 1). The poet's decision *not* to sing may be perceived as forgetting Zion, and so he vows, "If I forget you, Jerusalem, may my right hand forget its skill" (v. 5). In the next verse, he asserts, "If I do not remember you, may my tongue cling to the roof of my mouth" (v. 6). These statements highlight human agency in the absence of divine action. In Psalm 77, which laments the absence of God's "unfailing love" (v. 8), the psalmist asks, "Has God forgotten to be merciful?" (77:9). Nevertheless, the psalmist declares, "I will remember the deeds of the Lord; yes, I will remember your miracles of long ago" (77:11).

Zion is also the place where God's action takes place (132:17) and blessings flow (134:3), but the experience of exile has obliterated all these blessings. God has forgotten Zion. The psalmist does not say, "If I forget the Lord," but instead vows not to forget Jerusalem (which is synonymous to Zion here). By describing Jerusalem as "my highest joy" (v. 6), the psalmist comes close to

---

13. This is similar to what we find in Lamentations, where God complained against an indirect manner, often referred to in the third person (see for example, Lam 1:11–12, 18; 2:1–8).

referring to God, for elsewhere he describes God as "my exceeding joy" as he takes up his "lyre" (*kinnor*) in praise of God (43:4, ESV). Both Psalm 43 and Psalm 137 mention the lyre (*kinnor*). In Psalm 43, the psalmist vows that he will play the lyre to praise the Lord (v. 4), but in Psalm 137, the people refuse to play the lyre to sing God's praise (v. 2).

### 137:7–9 PETITION AND IMPRECATION

Though the psalmist pours out a protest and complaint to God, he never forgets God and continues to cling on to God.[14] The psalmist has no one else to go to, and so he pleads with God to "Remember" (v. 7). The text is cryptic: "Remember, O LORD, against the Edomites the day of Jerusalem" (v. 7a, ESV). The poet may have had the events mentioned in Obadiah 9–11 in mind, when God humbles the Edomites. The NIV smoothens the reading by adding further detail: "Remember, LORD, what the Edomites did on the day Jerusalem fell" (v. 7). The petition is for retributive justice, asking God to do to the sons of Edom what they did to Israel.

In verses 8–9, the psalmist applies this to Babylon. There are other imprecatory prayers in the Psalms (e.g. Psalms 83, 109), but Psalm 137 goes even further by describing those who will seize and dash Babylonian infants against the rock as "blessed" (v. 9, ESV).[15] This verse takes the Psalter to one of its lowest points, for it is no longer the one who meditates on the law of the Lord who is "blessed" (Psalm 1), but the one who executes violent acts against babies. The comments of C. S. Lewis about imprecatory prayers apply here: "It is monstrously simple-minded to read the cursing in the Psalms with no feeling except one of horror at the uncharity of the poets."[16]

At the same time, we need to consider the people's situational context so that we can read Psalm 137 from the perspective of those who are praying. Psalm 137 is written from a situation of extreme suffering, which the people indicate by speaking of "our captors" and "our tormentors" (v. 3). The

---

14. Claus Westermann, "The Complaint against God," in *God in the Fray: A Tribute to Walter Brueggemann*, ed. Tod Linafelt (Minneapolis, MN: Fortress Press, 1998), 239.
15. Some scholars argue that the subject of the word "happy" in verses 8–9 is God even though the word is used in the Psalms with human actors. Hossfeld and Zenger, *Psalms 3*, 520; Ahn, "Psalm 137: Complex Communal Laments," 288. This is because of the context of verse 7. But the shift from a second person direct address from verse 7 to verses 8–9 weakens this argument. There is no need to attribute the subject of the word "happy" to God, for in a way God is also involved through the human agent. This also has the support of the usual use of the word "happy" in the Psalter.
16. C. S. Lewis, *Reflection on the Psalms* (London: Fount, 1958), 22.

## Psalm 137

destruction of Jerusalem and the experience of exile were traumatic experiences. Lamentations was written in response to the exile, and the poet laments that even "compassionate women have cooked their own children, who became their food when my people were destroyed" (Lam 4:10). Earlier, Lady Zion confronted God, saying, "Look, Lord, and consider: Whom have you ever treated like this? Should women eat their offspring, the children they have cared for?" (Lam 2:20). The Hebrew word for "children" (*'olal*) used in Lamentations 2:20 is the same word used in Psalm 137:9. In the psalm, as the people recall what was done to their own children, they respond with hatred and the longing for retribution. As C. S. Lewis rightly notes, the people's "hatreds are the reaction to something. Such hatreds are the kind of thing that cruelty and injustice . . . produce."[17]

This deep sense of hatred over cruelty and injustice is articulated in verse 9: "Blessed shall he be who takes your little ones and dashes them against the rock." But this verse should not be taken at face value, for it is not endorsing this attitude. The "blessed" individual in Psalm 1 is experiencing life "as it should be," whereas the "blessed" person in Psalm 137 is experiencing life when everything went awry. Verses 8–9 follow the explicit petition in verse 7 and may be understood as a continuation of the people's prayer to God. But unlike many Christians today, whose prayers tend to be nice, pious, and "safe," the prayer in Psalm 137 is frank, honest, and open. Instead of remaining silent and suppressing their feelings about the suffering they have experienced, the people pour out their bitter complaint to God. They can no longer take the violence and injustice, and so they become caught up in the same hatred and violence that formulated their prayers. C. S. Lewis thinks that the psalmists committed sin in these prayers, but they also knew that God has "implacable hostility . . . for the sin of those enemies" who committed injustice.[18] In Psalm 139, the psalmist tells God that he is angry with bloodthirsty people (v. 19) and has "nothing but hatred for them" (v. 22). Yet in the end, he prays, "Search me, O God" (v. 23). Psalm 137 needs to be read alongside Psalm 139, as together these psalms teach us about the importance of honesty towards God along with a deep concern for justice. The psalmists took the risk of being honest and vulnerable to God – and in the process grew in intimacy with God (see discussion of Psalm 139 below).

---

17. Lewis, *Reflection on the Psalms*, 22. His comment is not directly on Psalm 137, but it can be applied to it.
18. Lewis, *Reflections on the Psalms*, 27.

# PSALM 138

Psalm 138 begins the final series of Davidic psalms in the Psalter (Psalms 138–145). This is rather unexpected in light of the note at the end of Book 2, which says, "This concludes the prayers of David son of Jesse" (Ps 72:20). One characteristic of the Davidic psalms is that they are mostly laments (see Psalms 3–41). As the Psalter moves towards the end, the laments fall to the side and are taken over by praise. Indeed, praise does take over in the final Hallelujahs (Psalms 145–150). But before those final psalms of praise, there is a resurgence of the lament in the Davidic psalms (Psalms 138–145). Of these eight Davidic psalms, four are widely recognized as laments (Psalms 140–143). These laments follow the supposed "answer" (Book 4) to the lament at the end of Book 3 (Psalm 89). Thus lament persists despite the supposed "answer." I find the resurgence of lament in the Psalter more realistic than some scholars, as the long process of healing requires us to return again and again to the same issues, particularly in cases of trauma. Even when we have moved to thanksgiving, we will need to return to lament.

Scholars consider Psalm 138 to be a Thanksgiving song of an individual. The majority of the psalm follows the usual pattern of a thanksgiving, which consists of a declaration of thanksgiving (vv. 1–2) and a testimony (v. 3). Yet many scholars are surprised to find a petition at the end of this psalm (v. 8b). Zenger writes: "The third colon surprises us with its final petition. Apparently, the uncertain state of the petitioner between distress and confidence is ongoing."[1] It could be that this surprise about the transition from thanksgiving to petition is due to the influence of a form-critical view of the psalms, which tends to see a one-sided movement from lament to praise. According to this view, it is not impossible for a psalm to return to petition after a vow of thanksgiving (see Ps 27:6–7). But Psalm 138 reminds us that the life of faith and human existence is untidy and unpredictable. Even towards the end of the Psalter, when one might anticipate less lament and tension, Psalm 138 catches us off guard, reminding us of the tragic element in all life.

The psalm may be outlined as follows:

> Declaration of thanksgiving and testimony (vv. 1–3),
> Call to praise and motivation (vv. 4–6),
> Expression of confidence and petition (vv. 7–8).

---

1. Hossfeld and Zenger, *Psalms 3*, 531.

# Psalm 138

## 138:1–3 DECLARATION OF THANKSGIVING AND TESTIMONY

Like a typical thanksgiving song, Psalm 138 begins with the declaration of intent to give thanks to the Lord. This thanksgiving is offered "with all my heart" (v. 1a), a description that expresses wholehearted devotion to God. One can only thank God if one's heart is fully devoted to him. This expression takes on additional force in verse 1b, as the thanksgiving to Yahweh comes "before the gods" (v. 1b). This verse transports us to the world of the ancient Near East (see Psalm 82), which is similar to the Asian worldview, where the universe is inhabited and ruled by many gods rather than one God. Yet the psalmist declares that he is offering his thanksgiving to "you" (v. 1), which clearly refers to Yahweh. Though the psalmist does not mention the name of Yahweh in verse 1, he refers to "your name" twice in verse 2 (ESV): "I . . . give thanks to *your name* . . . for you have exalted above all things *your name* . . ." Later verses mention the name of Yahweh six times (once in v. 4, twice in v. 5, once in v. 6, twice in v. 8).

Thus the psalmist declares his devotion to Yahweh in the presence of other gods. To Yahweh alone, he bows down in worship "for your unfailing love and your faithfulness" (v. 2). The psalmist declares his intention to give thanks to God because he is faithful and gracious. This is not a general statement about God, but something the psalmist has experienced. Continuing the direct address from verses 1–2, the psalmist directs his testimony *to the Lord* (v. 3). Yet in the testimony portion of most thanksgiving songs, the psalmist recounts *to the congregation* all the dangers he went through, how he cried out to the Lord, and how the Lord answered him and saved him (compare Pss 116:3–5; 118:5). Moreover, in Psalm 138:3, the psalmist does not describe his "trouble" (*tsarah*) in his testimony (see Pss 116:3; 120:1; Jonah 2:3; compare 118:5). One probable reason for these differences is that the psalmist's testimony is not yet complete, because he is still in the midst of the "trouble." In verse 7, the psalmist finally employs the word "trouble" (*tsarah*) to describe his present situation. Viewed from the end of Psalm 138, the testimony and the thanksgiving as a whole function as the basis for the psalmist's petition (see v. 7 below).

## 138:4–6 CALL TO PRAISE AND MOTIVATION

The psalmist not only wishes to give thanks to Yahweh "before" other "gods" (v. 1), but he also calls on "all the kings of the earth" to give thanks to the Lord (v. 4). The psalmist provides two motivations for why the kings should all give thanks. First, "they have heard the words of your mouth" (v. 4b, ESV). Second, they will "sing the ways of the Lord" (v. 5a).

The "words" and "ways" are related to one another. In verse 6, the psalmist summarizes how God's ways are revealed in his relationship with others: "For though the Lord is high, he regards the lowly" (v. 6a). Some scholars translate the second line of verse 6a as a continuation of the description of God's greatness. For example, Zenger's translation says, "and high is he, yet he sees from afar."[2] Similarly, the NIV says: "though lofty, he sees them from afar." But I think it is better to read verse 6b in a way that reflects the parallelism of verse 6a, as reflected in the ESV: "but the haughty he knows from afar."[3]

In verse 6, the psalmist depicts what he finds remarkable about God. Yahweh is "exalted" above all "gods" and "kings." Amidst the company of the greatest and the most powerful, the most powerful and greatest of all "regards the lowly" (v. 6a). The word "regards" comes from a Hebrew word (*ra'ah*), which literally means "to see." Often, the higher people go, the less they can see those who are down below. But the highest God of all *sees* the "lowly." This recalls Psalm 136:23: "He remembered us in our low estate." The Hebrew word for "low" (*shfl*) is used as a noun in Psalm 136:23 ("low estate") and as an adjective in Psalm 138:6 ("lowly"). God, who is on high, prioritizes the orphans, the weak, and the poor (see Pss 82:3–4; 113:7–9).

We are naturally drawn to those who have the power. As the saying goes, "it's not what you know, but who you know." If you have connections in high places, you are secure, and things get easier. Yet in the Psalms, those who have power, the rich, are also "haughty" (Pss 10:4–5; 73:6–9). Unlike us, God doesn't even want to be close to them, for "he knows them from afar" (138:6b). Instead, God chooses to be close to the lowly. He knows their ways and watches over them (1:6). This is the sense of Psalm 138:6. Thus Zenger's translation (which is also reflected in the NIV) is contradictory, for God does not see the lowly from afar. Rather, he is close to them and sees the wicked from afar.

This is the "way" of the Lord that the psalmist wants "all the kings of the earth" to praise in song. This longing is similar to the Lord's Prayer: "Let your kingdom come on earth, as it is in heaven" (Matt 6:9). Jesus longs for the entire earth to experience the kingdom of God, just as the psalmist longs for "all the kings" to envision and represent the rule of God's justice on earth.

---

2. Zenger and Hossfeld, *Psalms 3*, 526.
3. The LXX also supports this reading. Compare Allen, *Psalms 101–150*, 311; Alter, *The Book of Psalms*, 477.

# Psalm 138

## 138:7–8 CONFIDENCE AND PETITION

Yet the psalmist is also aware that this vision of God's justice remains a future reality. Though he is confident that the Lord is with him (v. 7b), he is also aware that he is walking "in the midst of trouble" (v. 7a). There is an interplay between the earlier testimony (v. 3) and the present situation (v. 7), as the missing "trouble" in the testimony now appears in the psalmist's petition. While verse 3 addresses God directly, verse 6 talks about God in the third person (the usual form of a testimony). This places the focus on verse 7, which represents his present situation.

Having started with a thanksgiving and a hymnic call to praise, the psalm concludes with a petition. Many scholars find this "surprising," perhaps because the form-critical view emphasizes the different genres, where the form of a thanksgiving is distinct from a petition. In this view, lament always moves to certainty. But there are expressions of certainty in verse 7, which are similar to the declarations of certainty in a lament. In Psalm 138, the expression of certainty is followed by a declaration of trust (v. 8ab). The psalm could have ended with verse 8b: "your love, Lord, endures forever." But instead, the psalm concludes with a petition: "do not abandon the works of your hands" (v. 8c). By placing this petition at the end – rather than before the expression of certainty – the psalmist creates a sense of tension between the vision he longs for and his present reality.

# PSALM 139

One of the central messages of Psalm 139 is that God knows us, and so we might as well be honest before him. The psalmist is brutally honest about his hateful feelings against wicked, bloodthirsty men – unlike many of our familiar prayers. He wants these wicked people dead, and so he wishes that God would just kill them. The psalm contains one of the harshest imprecations in the Psalter (next to Psalm 109 and Psalm 137). But as the psalmist becomes honest with God about his feelings, thoughts, and wishes, his heart is exposed, and he comes to realize that he could also be guilty – and so he asks God to search and know his heart and anxious thoughts.

Genre-wise, Psalm 139 is one of the most difficult to categorize, and so some consider it to be a mixed genre. The first part could be a thanksgiving or praise, as the psalmist bursts into praise and wonder in the midst of his meditation. But then, without any transition, he suddenly shifts to an imprecation, which is an element of the lament:

"I praise you . . . How precious also are your thoughts to
 me . . ." (vv. 14–18);
"If only you would slay the wicked!" (v. 19).

How can one praise the Lord one moment and then curse others the next? While this may seem strange or even blasphemous, Psalm 139 shows us how such brutal honesty can lead us along the pathway of transformation. For at the end of the psalm, there is a distinct shift from cursing to humble praying.

Canonically, Psalm 139 shows connections with Psalm 138 in its similar overall movement from praise to petition. Just as Psalm 139 moves from praise (v. 14) to petition (vv. 23–24), Psalm 138 begins with thanksgiving (v. 1) and ends with petition (v. 8). Moreover, Psalm 138 begins with the exact same word as Psalm 139: "I praise you ['*odekha*]" (138:1; 139:14a). While Psalm 138 ends with the petition, "do not abandon the *works of your hands*" (138:8), Psalm 139 takes the phrase, "works of your hands," and turns it to an object for praise: "your works are wonderful" (139:14b).

The overall structure of Psalm 139 may be outlined as follows:

God knows me (vv. 1–6);
"Where can I go?" (vv. 7–12);
God cares for me (vv. 13–18);
"Search me, O God" (vv. 19–24).

# Psalm 139

## 139:1–6 GOD KNOWS ME

After the superscription, the very first Hebrew word in Psalm 139 is *Yahweh* ("Lord"), which explicitly frames the psalm as a prayer that is addressed to the Lord. Verse 1 expresses the main theme for the first three sections of the psalm (vv. 1–18): "You have searched me and you know me." The word "search" is used to refer to a "substantial," thorough activity.[1] When applied to God, the search becomes more complete, perfect. The only other use of this verb in Psalm 44:22 has the meaning of "discover" or "find." God does not need to search, because his searching is equivalent to finding. So when the psalmist says to the Lord, "you have searched me" (v. 1), he is saying, you know me indeed!

The verb, "to know," is repeated three times within the first section (vv. 1, 2, 4). Verse 1 ends with this verb, and verse 2 begins with it, adding "you" to make it emphatic: literally, "You, you know." The psalm employs merisms[2] quite extensively to reinforce how completely God knows the psalmist. As Ross puts it, "God knows every move he makes."[3] The first two merisms in the opening lines of verses 2–3 form a chiastic structure:

> sitting (v. 2a),
>   rising (v. 2a),
>     going out (v. 3a),
> lying down (v. 3a).

The parallel lines of verses 2–3 highlight the intimate nature of God's knowing: "you perceive my thoughts from afar" (v. 2b), and "you are familiar with all my ways" (v. 3b). Note the words "from afar" (v. 2b) and "all" (v. 3b). The word "thoughts" in Hebrew could refer to one's desires or what one intends to do,[4] and the psalmist is saying that God already knows all of this far in advance. Because God already knows the intentions of the psalmist's heart, the Lord knows what he is going to think or say even "before a word is on my tongue" (v. 4). Again, the word "all" is repeated: "you know it altogether" (v. 4b, ESV). This idea is preceded by the Hebrew word *hinneh*, which means "behold" or "indeed."

---

1. David G. Firth, "Psalm 139: A Study in Ambiguity," *OTE* 32, no. 2 (2019): 499.
2. A merism is a poetical device in which two words are used to represent everything in between both ends of a scale. In Psalm 139:2–3, the psalmist is saying that God knows everything, from his lying down at night to his rising in the morning, from his going out into the day until he returns to bed at night.
3. Allen P. Ross, *A Commentary on the Psalms Volume 3 (90–150)* (Grand Rapids: Kregel, 2016), 820.
4. *HALOT*, 3:1256.

So far, God's knowledge appears to be positive, but in verse 5, a negative sense begins to surface, similar to how we feel today about the extensive intrusion of the Internet, CCTV, and hidden cameras in our private lives. As a parody of Psalm 139 describes it:

> O Google, O Facebook,
> you have searched me and known me.
> You know when I sit down and when I rise up;
> you discern my thoughts from far away.
> O Amazon, you search out my path and my lying down,
> and are acquainted with all my ways.
> Even before a word is on my tongue,
> O Cyber Lords, you know it completely.[5]

Verse 5 employs another merism concerning spaces: "behind and before." God not only knows all our movements, but he is also actively involved in making sure that we are surrounded on all sides. The verb translated as "hem" can have the positive sense of being protected, but it can also have a negative connotation of being restricted or controlled. In Hebrew, the verb can also mean to "besiege."[6] This sense is supported by verse 5b, where God's hand (more specifically, the "palm" of his hand) is "upon me." God is not just behind and before the psalmist, but he is also hovering above him. The psalmist has nowhere to go where God is not present, a point that will be elaborated in the next section. The psalmist finds this knowledge not only constricting, but also overwhelming (v. 6).[7]

### 139:7–12 "WHERE CAN I GO?"

The psalmist repeats the question, "where?" twice in verse 7. In Psalm 55, the psalmist wishes that he could flee far away: "Oh, that I had the wings of a dove! I would fly away . . ." (v. 6). Similarly, in Psalm 139, the psalmist asks, "Where can I flee from your presence?" (v. 7b). The word "presence" comes from the Hebrew word, *panim*, which literally means, "face." Why does the psalmist want to flee from God's "face"? At the end of Psalm 39, the psalmist asks God to "Look away from me, that I may enjoy life again before I depart

---

5. Thomas G. Long, "Psalm 139 and the Eye of God," *Journal for Preachers* 43, no. 4 (2020): 41.
6. *BDB*, 848; *DCH*, 7:106.
7. The LXX has "your knowledge." BHS notes suggest adding the definite article–"the knowledge." In either case, it is clear that the reference is to God's knowledge of the psalmist reported in the previous verses.

# Psalm 139

and am no more" (v. 13). Perhaps in Psalm 139, the psalmist is feeling similarly restricted and wants to be free. Yet the ambiguity of the psalm prevents us from making a clear-cut decision.[8] Even if we read these verses negatively, they can be employed for positive purposes (see comments to vv. 19–22 below).

In verse 8, the psalmist imagines where he could flee from God – moving upward to heaven and then descending to Sheol. This recalls the upward and downward movement in verse 2: "when I sit and when I rise" (v. 2). Whereas the psalmist imagines going up to the heavens, he speaks of making his bed in the depths. Verse 9 traces a similar development, where the psalmist imagines himself rising "on the wings of the dawn" and then settling down "on the far side of the sea." As in Psalm 55, the psalmist wants to escape, to "fly away and be at rest" (v. 6). The phrase, "be at rest," comes from the same Hebrew word used in Psalm 139:9: "I will settle" (*shakan*). Both psalmists may be imagining the same thing.[9]

The references to Sheol and the sea both represent hostile forces in the ancient Near East worldview. Though it is unimaginable for God to be in Sheol (Ps 88:3, 10–12), the psalmist could see God being there (139:8). And though the sea represents chaos and cosmic hostility,[10] the psalmist imagines God leading him and holding him with his right hand (v. 10). Thus the psalmist's viewpoint of God shifts from being negative to positive. The key to this transformation is the psalmist's probing reflection and his honest articulation of his feelings. We'll witness this transformation again in the final section of the psalm (vv. 19–24).

The word "darkness" dominates verses 11–12, which may be connected to the references to Sheol and the sea (vv. 8, 10). The psalmist is confident that even in the darkness, he will experience God's light. Yet the darkness may also allude to the psalmist's longing to flee, as darkness serves as the best cover for those who want to hide ("Surely the darkness will hide me," v. 11a).[11] If this is the case, then the psalmist's longing to escape God is frustrated. In verses 11 and 12, the psalmist stresses that darkness cannot hide anyone from God, because "darkness is as light to you" (v. 12b).

---

8. Firth, "Psalm 139: A Study in Ambiguity."
9. Psalms 139 and 55 are both attributed to David.
10. E.g. see commentary above on Psalms 89, 93–95, 104, 107, 114, 124.
11. The word "hide" in the MT comes from a difficult and unusual word (*shuf*), whose etymology is "most uncertain." Most commentators amend the reading to the Hebrew word for "to cover" (*sakakh*). Allen, *Psalms 101–150*, 318–319.

## 139:13-18 GOD CARES FOR ME

Verse 13 begins with the word "for," which supplies the explanation for the preceding two sections (especially vv. 1–6). God "knows" (v. 1) the psalmist, because God "created" his "inmost being" (v. 13). The word translated as "create" comes from the Hebrew verb, *qanah*, which generally means to "acquire, buy, purchase."[12] But its usage here means to "create, make, form."[13] The second line develops this idea by highlighting the process of God's forming or creating: "you knit me together in my mother's womb" (v. 13b). God was already at work, even before the psalmist was born (see also Ps 22:9–10). The Septuagint reads, "you supported me from my mother's womb."[14]

Thus the psalmist praises God because "your works are wonderful" (v. 14). The word "wonderful" is repeated twice in verse 14.[15] Since God's works are wonderful, the creator himself is wonderful, and his creation knows it: "I [literally, "my soul"] know full well" (v. 14c). The keyword, "know," is repeated here and applied for the first time to the speaker. The psalmist's knowledge is not the same as God's knowledge, which is perfect and comprehensive. Rather, the verb is simply conveying that the creation itself knows that she is wonderful, just like her maker. While the emphasis is on the creation, the praise ultimately goes back to the creator, who knit us together and formed us. As the prophet Isaiah writes, "we are all the work of your hand" (Isa 64:8).

The use of the word "hidden" in verse 15a recalls the meditation in the previous section (vv. 7–12). For there is no place – not even the lowest depth (Sheol) or the farthest side of the sea (vv. 8–9) – where the psalmist can hide. The descriptions, "secret place" and "depths of the earth" (v. 15b), refer to the mother's womb (v. 13b). In the ancient Near East, "the womb would have been as remote to the human eye and knowledge as any region in the netherworld."[16] Just as God is present in the remotest and farthest regions of the earth, he is at work in the mother's womb. In Hebrew, the noun "woven"

---

12. *DCH*, 7:267.
13. *DCH*, 7:268. For an alternative meaning, see *TDOT*, 13:61, which argues that the word does not mean to create but beget.
14. Kohlenberger III, *The Comparative Psalter: Hebrew-Greek-English*, 249.
15. The first occurrence is contested. The MT has the first person form of the verb (I am wonderful), while other ancient texts (e.g. LXX) has the second person (you are wonderful). The former is followed by the majority of English translations, such as we find in the NIV: "I am fearfully and wonderfully made." Allen's translation is an example of the second reading: "you are awesomely wonderful." Allen, *Psalms 101–150*, 317. But even if we adopt the first option, the second is not sacrificed, since the manner of creation–fearfully and wonderfully–reflects the creator himself.
16. Ross, *A Commentary on the Psalms Volume 3 (90–150)*, 828.

(*roqem*) refers to an "embroiderer," a "weaver of coloured fabric," an "embroiderer of coloured thread."[17]

Verse 16 expresses positively the negative expression in verse 15, for God's "eyes saw my unformed body" (v. 16a).[18] God's all-seeing omnipresence here is similar to a parent who carefully watches every movement and development in her child, recording the first syllable or word uttered, taking photos of the first bath, first birthday, and so on. The psalmist notes that "every one of" these moments "were written in your book" (v. 16, ESV). The NIV translation, "all the days ordained for me were written in your book before one of them came to be," is theologically loaded, as it implies that everything is preordained. But the Hebrew literally reads, "days were formed and not one in them" (v. 16c). The word "days" refers to the time before the psalmist's birth ("my unformed body," v. 16a), and so the text could be saying that God already saw all the psalmist's days as God was forming his body and took note of everything, not missing even one detail. The verb "form" (*yatsar*) is the same word used in the Genesis narrative to describe the creation of man (Gen 2:7).

Psalm 139:17 parallels the thanksgiving in verse 14. Reflecting on the wondrous works of the Lord in creating his unformed body, the psalmist exclaims, "How precious to me are your thoughts, God!" (v. 17a). The word, "thoughts" (*rea'*), occurs earlier, referring to the psalmist's thoughts. These two occurrences interact with each other, for while God perceives the psalmist's thoughts from afar (v. 2), the psalmist describes God's thoughts about him as "precious" (v. 18a). The word "precious" has a positive sense, but can also be translated as "costly."[19] The previous context (vv. 6–12) supports the more negative sense of the word. God keeps a record of all the psalmist's days (even those in the womb) in his book. There is a wordplay between the "book" (*sefer*) and "count" (v. 18). God's knowledge is beyond the psalmist's ability

---

17. *DCH*, 7:553. This is the sense of the word when its participial form is used as a noun.
18. The Hebrew of verse 16 is challenging. The verse in the BHS has seven textual notes! The first part is straightforward – "You saw my unformed body" (in Rabbinic tradition, the word for "unformed body" has come to mean "embryo" or something that is still formless). The next part literally reads, "and on your book all of them were written." What is the antecedent of "them" – is it referring to "unformed bodies"? The next colon speaks of "days" – "days were formed." So the "them" could be referring forward to the "days." This could be behind the NIV's decision to translate the earlier line as "all the days ordained for me were written in your book." Going back to the "days are formed," the ESV's addition of "for me" is one way to make sense of the reading. But the last three words in Hebrew are the most challenging – "not one in them." The LXX, has the literal reading, "no one is among them."
19. Firth, "Psalm 139: A Study in Ambiguity," 506.

and comprehension. If the psalmist were to count God's thoughts, they would "outnumber the grains of the sand" (v. 18).

The second part of verse 18 presents a challenge, as the connection with the preceding line is not clear. What does the impossibility of "counting God's thoughts" (v. 18a) have to do with "when I awake, I am still with you" (v. 18b)? Instead of reading these two lines together, we can read verse 18b as a transition into verse 19 and the final section of the psalm. The psalmist's reference to waking does not suggest that the psalmist has been dreaming or in a trance, but that his meditation on God's wonderful nature was the last things he thought about before going to sleep. And then when he wakes up, he still has a sense of God's wonderful presence. Upon waking in the morning, his meditation continues, but now it takes the form of a prayer.

## 139:19–24 "SEARCH ME, O GOD"

The previous section ends with the psalmist waking up. Canonically, the alternation between morning and evening prayer in Psalms 3–5 is helpful here. We might imagine morning prayer to be full of praise and thanksgiving, but the morning prayer in Psalm 5 begins with the psalmist pleading and crying as he asserts that God is "not a God who is pleased with wickedness" (v. 4). "You hate all who do wrong" (v. 5b), the psalmist declares, and then he utters an imprecatory prayer: "Declare them guilty, O God! Banish them for their many sins!" (v. 10). An emphasis on "hate" is also present in Psalm 139, which repeats the word "hate/hatred" four times (vv. 21–22). Moreover, the psalmist asks God to "slay the wicked" (v. 19), which echoes the imprecatory prayer in Psalm 5 ("banish them," v. 10).

How can someone praise the Lord for his wonderful works (v. 14) and then utter a prayer asking God to kill another person? Isn't every person "fearfully and wonderfully made" (v. 14)? As the story of creation reminds us, God's precious creation can become violent (see Gen 4:8). In the final verse of Psalm 104, which goes into great detail praising the greatness of God's creation (vv. 1–34), we find a similar prayer: "But may sinners vanish from the earth and the wicked no more" (v. 35). In Psalm 139, the "wicked" are described as "bloodthirsty" (v. 19), and they have no fear of God and take God's name in vain (v. 20).

In spite of the wickedness of these people who do not fear God, some Christians are shocked by this prayer that asks God to kill someone. Yet we need to interpret all imprecatory prayers in the Psalter in light of God's justice, which considers both the situation of the psalmist as well as the wicked whom the psalmist is asking God to kill (e.g. see Psalms 140; 83; 109). Though we may not agree with the psalmist's prayer, we can admire his honesty before God. He admits that he has "nothing but hatred for them" (v. 22). The Hebrew literally reads, "I hate them with complete hatred" (reflected in the ESV). The Hebrew here means "completeness of hatred, extreme form of hatred."[20] The psalmist can only be this honest because he believes that God already knows him completely anyway. Nothing can be hidden from God, for even "before a word is on my tongue you, LORD, know it completely" (v. 4). The text also indicates that the psalmist is being confronted by these bloodthirsty, wicked people. His life is in danger, and he has nowhere to go, and so he cries out to the Lord.

Even more, the most important contribution of Psalm 139 to our understanding of imprecatory psalms lies in the psalmist's humility. In the closing verses, the psalmist repeats the exact same words from the beginning of the psalm: "search" and "know" (vv. 1, 23). At the beginning, the psalmist declares that God has "searched me . . . and you know me" (v. 1). At the end, he asks God to "search me . . . and know my heart" (v. 23). If God has already searched and known the psalmist, why does he ask God to do it again? I think that the first verse is directed to God, whereas the psalmist utters the closing petition for his own sake. Having been honest and open with God, he becomes more sensitive to the condition of his own heart, and he realizes that he, too, might be sinning like the wicked. And so he concludes with a prayer that God will "see if there is any offensive way in me" (v. 24). The word translated as "offensive" comes from a Hebrew word that means "pain" (specifically, it is connected to "toil") or "hurt." Thus, a literal reading of verse 24 is, "way of hurt" (i.e., a "way that hurts"). Verse 24 describes two different "ways": the "way of hurt" (v. 24a) and the "way everlasting" (v. 24c).

The first way can be understood in the context of verse 19, which refers to the wicked as "bloodthirsty." The psalmist wants to make sure that he does not follow the way of the wicked, which is the way that hurts. Rather, he prays that he will follow the "way everlasting." In Psalm 86, the psalmist prays for the Lord to "teach me your way" (v. 11), which leads him to praise "your name forever" (v. 12).

---

20. *HALOT*, 4:1732.

# PSALM 140

Psalm 140 is a typical individual lament, as it contains an invocation, a series of petitions, complaints or motivations, and concludes with a declaration of trust. The psalm contains three main petitions (vv. 1, 4, 8). The first two petitions are followed by complaints (vv. 2–3, 4c–5), and the third petition is preceded by a motivation (vv. 6–7), which marks a transition. Though the psalm ends with a declaration of trust (vv. 12–13), it is preceded by a series of imprecations (vv. 9–11).

The imprecations take up the psalmist's cry from the previous psalm: "If only you, God, would slay the wicked! Away from me, you who are bloodthirsty!" (139:19). In Psalm 140, the description, "bloodthirsty" (literally, "men of blood"), is similar to "the violent," which literally means, "man of blood" (vv. 1, 4). After asking God for deliverance and protection from "violent" people, the psalmist prays that "burning coals fall on them" and that they "may be thrown into the fire" (v. 10). Even at this late stage in the Psalter, the imprecatory prayer remains fierce.

This may be shocking for some Christians, since Jesus taught us to love our enemies. But before dismissing imprecatory prayers completely, we should first remember that the wicked people against whom the psalmist is praying are "bloodthirsty" (see comments in Psalms 83 and 137). Second, the victims of these violent people are weak and powerless, the "poor" and "needy" (Ps 140:12). They have no one to run to, and so they come to God and beg for justice. Third, the imprecatory prayers in the Psalter are prayers for justice. Though God loves all people, he is a God of justice.

Psalm 140 is similar to Psalms 9–10, which also contain an imprecatory prayer (see 10:15). The words "justice" (*mishpat*) and "judgment" (*din*) also occur in both psalms (9:4; 140:12). Psalm 140 talks about the "desires" of the wicked (v. 8), while in Psalm 10, "the wicked boasts of the desires of his soul" (v. 3, ESV). Thus the psalmist asks God to "break the arm of the wicked man . . . so that mere earthly mortals will never again strike terror" (vv. 15, 18). In Psalm 140, the psalmist asks God *not* to let the plans of the wicked succeed so that they will *not* be able to exalt themselves (see commentary on v. 8 below).

# Psalm 140

## 140:1–5 PETITIONS AND COMPLAINTS

The first section of the psalm contains two parallel petitions (vv. 1, 4) followed by two parallel complaints (vv. 2–3, 4c–5). The word "violent" (literally, "man of blood," in Hebrew) appears in both petitions:

"Rescue me . . . from the violent" (v. 1);
"Keep me safe . . . from the violent" (v. 4).

The complaints that follow these petitions are also similar. Both employ the word "devise" (*khashab*) to describe the wicked and violent people:

"who devise evil plans in their hearts" (v. 2);
"who devise ways to trip my feet" (v. 4).

The previous psalm emphasizes that God knows us through and through (139:1–5): God knows our "thoughts from afar" (139:2b) and searches our hearts (v. 23). In Psalm 140, the psalmist asks God for deliverance and protection against violent people because God knows the "evil plans" they "devise in their hearts" (v. 2). The psalmist complains that wicked people can hide: "The arrogant have hidden a snare for me" (v. 5a). Moreover, they scheme evil plans "every day" (v. 2). Verse 2 describes the scheming of the wicked generally, but the focus of their attacks becomes more directed in verses 4–5: "keep *me* . . . preserve *me* . . ." (v. 4); "they have set traps *for me*" (v. 5b, emphasis mine).

As in other psalms, the nature of the danger is not specified. Psalm 140 mentions war (v. 2), but instead of wielding weapons of war, the wicked "make their tongues as sharp as a serpent's" (v. 3). This synecdoche depicts the wicked through their speech. In verse 5, the wicked are described as "arrogant," which is also connected with their speech (compare Ps 12:4). In the Psalms, the wicked are often characterized by their tongues, and sinful speech is the most prominent "of all the sins forbidden in the Decalogue."[1] Sinful speech is also connected to violence (140:2–3; see also 5:6; 10:7; 27:12).

## 140:6–8 MOTIVATION AND PETITION

The second section of the psalm begins with the motivation for the psalmist's petitions. This reverses the pattern from the previous section, which begins with a petition that is followed by a complaint (which is a form of the motivation). The psalmist's motivation in verses 6–7 is more explicit than the previous complaints: "You are my God" (v. 6). This declaration is addressed

---

1. Wenham, *Psalms as Torah*, 107.

to Yahweh: "I say to the LORD [*Yahweh*]" (v. 6). By confessing that Yahweh is "my God," the psalmist is expressing his trust in him (see Ps 22:9–10) and acknowledging that God has been there from the very beginning and cares for every detail of his life (see Ps 139:1–5).

The declaration, "you are my God," also intimates the expectation that God will protect and deliver the psalmist from harm. Because the Lord is "my God," Yahweh will not allow the wicked to succeed. The initial petitions in the first section are both formulated positively (vv. 1, 4), but the third petition is formulated negatively, which signals an intensification: "do *not* grant the wicked their desires" (v. 8, emphasis mine). The "desires" of the wicked refer to the evil things that they are devising against the psalmist (vv. 2, 4–5), and so the psalmist asks God *not* to "let their plans succeed" (v. 8b). Otherwise, they will exalt themselves (v. 8b).[2]

## 140:9–11 IMPRECATORY PRAYERS

The psalmist asks God to intervene so that the wicked cannot exalt themselves. In Hebrew, the verb form of the adjective "arrogant" (*ga'ah*) means "to be high" (see v. 5). To make sure that the wicked will not exalt himself, the psalmist prays, "may the mischief of their lips engulf them" (v. 9). The Hebrew word used for "engulf" literally means "to cover," which implies a downward movement. Thus the psalmist is asking God to prevent the wicked person from lifting up himself.

Verse 10 continues this emphasis on a downward movement as the psalmist prays for:

burning coals to "fall" on the wicked (v. 10a),
the wicked to be "cast" down into the "miry pits" (v. 10b).

These images convey total destruction. The "burning coals" allude to the destruction of Sodom and Gomorrah (Gen 19:24), and the "miry pits" recall the events of Numbers 16, when Korah and his followers and all their families were swallowed up by the earth after they rebelled against Moses (Numbers 16). Psalm 140:10 ends with the phrase, "never to rise," which is a reversal of the final words in verse 8 ("they will be exalted," ESV).

---

2. The translation of verse 8 is difficult. The NIV does not include the last word in its translation (the Hebrew word *rum*, which means to be high/exalted). Instead, it transfers the word *rum* to the verse 9, disregarding the *Selah* that divides these two verses. In any case, the main idea is still preserved. The point is that if the wicked's plans are not thwarted, they will become more boastful: "Those who surround me proudly rear their heads" (v. 9).

Verse 11 also expresses a negative wish: "May slanderers *not* be established in the land" (emphasis mine). The word "slanderers" in Hebrew literally means, "man of tongue." This verse reiterates the close link between an evil tongue and violence. And so the psalmist prays, "may disaster hunt down the violent" (v. 11).

## 140:12–13 DECLARATION OF TRUST

There is a sudden change of mood in the last section, which contains what form-critics refer to as the "certainty of a hearing." From crying out prayers against the wicked, the psalmist is suddenly confident: "I know" that "the LORD secures justice for the poor" (v. 12). We do not have access to what happened in the psalmist's situation to cause this change of mood. Contrary to the Oracle of Salvation theory promoted by Begrich,[3] there is nothing in the text to indicate the entry of a cultic prophet/priest who delivered a word from the Lord, thereby creating this sense of confidence (see commentary on Psalm 110). It is better to interpret this shift as part of the prayer process. As the psalmist honestly pours out his heartfelt lament to God, he experiences a sense of liberation and relief when he encounters the God who cares about the poor and the needy.[4]

The emphasis on justice for the poor and needy provides an important interpretative lens through which we can understand the imprecatory prayers in the Psalms. In addition to the value of being honest with God (see Psalm 139), imprecatory prayers affirm the firm belief in God's justice for those who are poor, marginalized, and oppressed – and so have no one else to act on their behalf.

The psalm ends without a clear answer to the psalmist's petition, but there is the assurance that "the upright will live in your presence" (v. 13). The last verse in the previous section ends with a prayer that the wicked will not be "established in the land" (v. 11). This concluding section could have ended with a promise that "the upright will live in the land," but that may still be a future hope. Nevertheless, the righteous will live in God's "presence," which is the distinguishing mark of the people of Israel (Exod 33:16; see also commentary on Psalm 124).

---

3. Gunkel and Begrich, *Introduction to Psalms*, 130.
4. Compare Friedrich Heiler, *Prayer: A Study in the History and Psychology of Religion* (London; New York: Oxford University Press, 1932), 260.

# PSALM 141

By praying against the wicked and their violent acts, the psalmists guard themselves from the temptation to be influenced by the "way of hurt" (Ps 104:24). Psalm 141 may be interpreted through the following story by Elie Wiesel: "A righteous man came to Sodom and pleaded with the people to change their ways. No one listened. Finally, he sat in the middle of the city and simply screamed. Someone asked him, 'Do you think that will change anyone?' 'No,' said the righteous man. 'But at least, they will not change me.'"[1]

In Psalm 141, the psalmist declares that his "prayer is continually against their evil deeds" (v. 5). This psalm continues the series of imprecatory prayers from the preceding psalms (Psalms 139–141; see discussion below). The psalm speaks of judges being "thrown down" on cliffs (v. 6) and the wicked falling "into their own nets" (v. 10). The psalmist, who is exposed and vulnerable in the face of evildoers, has no one to save him but God, and so he urgently pours out his prayer.

The genre of the psalm is an individual lament, consisting of the usual elements:

>   invocation (v. 1),
>   petition (vv. 1–4),
>   complaint (v. 7),
>   declaration of trust (v. 8),
>   petition (vv. 9–10).

Unlike a typical lament, however, Psalm 141 ends with a petition (vv. 9–10), which goes against the expectation of form critics, who always look for resolution or a "certainty of a hearing" at the end of a lament psalm. This "certainty of a hearing" is a divine word delivered through a cultic prophet, which indicates that a prayer has been answered. The absence of resolution at the end of Psalm 141 reflects the grave situation of the psalmist and highlights one of the main functions of the imprecatory prayers (see discussion below).

---

1. Jeffrey K. Salkin, *Va-Yera' (Genesis 18:1–22:24) and Haftarah (2 Kings 4:1–37): The JPS B'nai Mitzvah Torah Commentary* (Philadelphia: The Jewish Publication Society, 2018), 6.

# Psalm 141

## 141:1–2 "May My Prayer Be Set Before You Like Incense"

The psalm begins with an invocation, "O Lord" (v. 1, ESV), which identifies it clearly as a prayer. The psalmist is praying with a sense of urgency: "come quickly to me" (v. 1). He repeats the word, "I call," at both the beginning and end of the verse. The language is typical of individual laments, but Psalm 141 is unique in that the psalmist prays that his "prayer be set before you like incense" (v. 2). The word "set" comes from the Hebrew word *kun* ("to establish"), which recalls Psalm 140, where the psalmist prays that the wicked will "not be established [*kun*] in the land" (v. 11). Later in Psalm 141, we will hear a similar imprecatory prayer (see v. 10). Moreover, the word "prayer" (*tefillah*) in verse 2 is repeated in verse 5 in connection to praying "against the deeds of evildoers."

The canonical context for Psalms 140 and 141 suggests that the prayer referenced in Psalm 141:2 includes the imprecatory prayers from Psalm 139 (vv. 19–22) and Psalm 140 (vv. 8–11). While some Christians may readily reject these imprecatory prayers, the psalmist asks for his prayer to be "like incense" and the lifting up of his hands to be like the "evening sacrifice" (141:2). The psalmist is not asking for his prayer to take the place of these rituals, but rather that his prayer will be acceptable to God. Ideally, these rituals would have functioned as pleasing sacrifices to God, which implies that imprecatory prayers could also be pleasing to God. As noted above, the psalmists offer these prayers to guard themselves from being influenced by the wicked.

## 141:3–7 "Set a Guard Over My Mouth"

Thus the psalmist prays, "Set a guard over my mouth" (v. 3). This petition highlights the importance of one's words. As mentioned previously, the wicked are known by their tongues (140:3, 11; see also 109:3–4). One's words are connected to one's heart, for it is from the heart that different kinds of evil come (see Mark 7:21–23). Thus the psalmist prays, "Do not let my heart be drawn to what is evil" (Ps 141:4). But evil is not only internal, for it also involves the social aspect. As the Apostle Paul warns, "Bad company corrupts good character" (1 Cor 15:33). Thus the psalmist asks God not to let him "take part in wicked deeds along with those who are evildoers" (Ps 141:4). We see this same emphasis in Psalm 1 (v. 1).

Yet wicked deeds are tempting, and so the psalmist likens them to "delicacies" (v. 4b). As noted above, people's deeds are connected with their speech or words. One characteristic of the speech of the wicked is that it is "smooth" (*khalaqot*). The "lips" of the wicked are also described as "smooth" in Psalm 12:2 (in Hebrew, the literal translation of the word for "smooth" is "flattering lips"). In Psalm 141, the psalmist prays that God "keep watch over the door of my lips" (141:3b), because it is tempting to say only nice, polite, and politically correct things.

But the psalmist would rather hear the painful rebuke of a righteous person than the "flattering" words of a wicked person, for he insists: "Let a righteous man strike me – that is kindness" (v. 5). In fact, the psalmist prefers these bitter words of correction to the "delicacies" of the wicked (v. 4). Moreover, his prayers are "against" evildoers (v. 5b). Though prayers today are mostly a private matter, prayers in the Psalms were public and meant to be heard – even by enemies against whom the prayers are directed.[2]

We do not know the exact contents of the psalmist's prayer, but we have some idea from verse 6a, where the psalmist envisions the day when "their judges are thrown over the cliff" (v. 6a).[3] This image depicts a painful and brutal death and echoes the imprecatory prayer in Psalm 58: "Break the teeth in their mouths, O God; tear out the fangs of those lions!" (v. 6).

When the wicked experience calamity or judgment, people realize the value of any rebuke or warning delivered against them: "then they shall hear my words, for they are pleasant" (141:6b). The subject of the pronoun ("they") is not explicit, but it does not refer to the wicked, since they were thrown over the cliff and must be presumed dead. More likely, it refers to those belonging to the company of the wicked, who survived and now realize the importance of the psalmist's words. The description, "pleasant," is the same word used in Psalm 133 to speak about the unity of brothers and sisters. When words of rebuke are true and just, they can be pleasant – even though they are painful.

Verse 7 is challenging, as it contains a "remarkable complexity,"[4] but I think we can discern a reasonable progression in the text. The immediate context of verse 6 links the rulers who are being "thrown down" to the evildoers in verse 5. Verse 7 also talks about destruction, but here it describes the

---

2. Gerald T. Sheppard, "'Enemies' and the Politics of Prayer in the Book of Psalms," in *The Bible and the Politics of Exegesis: Essays in Honor of Norman K. Gottwald on His Sixty-Fifth Birthday*, ed. David Jobling, Peggy L. Day, and Gerald T. Sheppard (Cleveland, OH: Pilgrim Press, 1991), 69.
3. The Hebrew of verse 6a is difficult. The first word could mean, "thrown down." The problem is that it occurs in a verse that is "probably a corrupt text" (*HALOT*, 4:1558). The MT literally reads: "Their judges were thrown down on the hands of the rock." The LXX, on the other hand, reads: "Their judges were swallowed up close to a rock." But the basic idea is clear enough–throwing down into a rock.
4. Thijs Booij, "Psalm 141: A Prayer for Discipline and Protection," *Bib* 86, no. 1 (2005): 102.

condition of the psalmist and his people. Their scattered bones "symbolize the people's lamentable condition (compare Ps 53:6; Ezek 37:1–2, 11)."[5] In the light of this pitiable situation of oppression and destruction, the psalmist pleads with God for salvation.

## 141:8–10 "LET THE WICKED FALL INTO THEIR OWN NETS"

The emphasis in verse 8 is on vulnerability: the "eyes" of the psalmist "are fixed" on the Lord. This language echoes Psalm 123, where the "eyes" of the slaves are focused on the hand of their master (v. 2). The psalmist has no one to turn to for help. Even the "judges" side with the wicked (this is implied in Ps 141:6). Thus the psalmist pleads with God: "do not give me over to death" (v. 8b). The verb here comes from a Hebrew word (*ʿrh*), which means "to expose."[6] The sentence literally reads, "do not expose my throat/soul/neck."

Verse 9 further exposes the vulnerability of the psalmist, as the evildoers have set traps before him. These "snares" are as innumerable as the evildoers who hid them. By contrast, the psalmist is all alone (note the repetition of "me" in v. 9). The psalm ends with the psalmist's prayer for the wicked to "fall into their own nets, while I pass by in safety" (v. 10). The lament ends with an open petition rather than explicit resolution.

---

5. Booij, "Psalm 141: A Prayer for Discipline and Protection," 102.
6. *HALOT*, 2:882.

# PSALM 142

Some Asian cultures today look down on crying out loud,[1] especially among men. Yet it is very important for us to learn how to cry out our pain. Psalm 142 is characterized by the phrase, "cry out," which appears twice (vv. 1, 5) and serves as a key structural marker in the psalm.

Attributed to David, this psalm is said to be a "prayer" from "when he was in the cave" (see superscription). Psalm 142 is one of the thirteen psalms that offer a brief historical account from the life of David. Its superscription is similar to the situation envisaged in Psalm 57, which mentions that David "fled from Saul into the cave." David is often presented in the historical superscriptions as being in trouble. Yet the most difficult thing that David recounts in Psalm 142 is that "no one cares for my life" (v. 4). Though his spirit is faint (v. 3), he is not giving up because "you know my way" (v. 3, ESV). In spite of David's trouble, this psalm declares that he is not alone: there is someone to whom he can cry out for help from the darkness of his "cave."

Psalm 142 is an individual lament, consisting of the following elements:

> introductory cry for help (vv. 1–2),
> declaration of trust (v. 3a),
> complaint (vv. 3b–4),
> cry for help (v. 5a),
> declaration of trust (v. 5b),
> petition (vv. 6–7a),
> motivation for petition (v. 7b).

As noted above, the word "cry out" is a key structural marker that divides the psalm into two main parts: the initial cry for help, declaration of trust, and complaint (vv. 1–4), and the second cry for help, declaration of trust, petition, and motivation (vv. 5–7). The verb "cry out" also traces a progression from the first descriptive part (v. 1), where the psalmist cries out to the Lord in the third person, to the second part, where the psalmist addresses his cry is directly to the Lord (v. 5). Contrary to some scholars, the last part of the psalm does not contain a "vow of praise" or an "Assurance of being heard."[2] Rather, the phrase, "that I may praise your name" (v. 7b), is better understood

---

1. James MacLynn Wilce, *Crying Shame Metaculture, Modernity, and the Exaggerated Death of Lament* (Malden, MA; Oxford: Wiley-Blackwell, 2009), 3.
2. Westermann, *Praise and Lament in the Psalms*, 66–67.

as a motivation for the preceding petition (v. 6–7a). From this perspective, the psalmist is arguing that God should "set me free from my prison" so "that I may praise . . ." Moreover, the final line in verse 7 should also be read as an elaboration of the previous motivation for praise, as it describes what transpires in occasions of thanksgiving. Yet this will only be a reality when the Lord finally deals bountifully with the psalmist (see discussion of v. 7 below).

## 142:1–4 "I CRY ALOUD TO THE LORD"

The superscription describes this psalm as "a prayer." Though individual prayers can be offered quietly to God, there are times to cry out loud. In Psalm 142, the psalmist cries out with a loud voice. In Hebrew, the word "my voice" (*qoli*) appears at the very beginning of verse 1 and is repeated again in the parallel line (v. 1b). The emphasis on "my voice" is supported by the repetition of the verb, "cry aloud," in verses 1 and 5.

Sometimes prayers must be cried out loud, and yet crying aloud is becoming more unacceptable in our modern times.[3] We rarely hear anyone crying out loud in church, and it can be difficult to find any place to cry aloud in the Philippines, as most houses are joined together (*dikit-dikit*). If someone cries aloud, a neighbor (*kapitbahay*) will hear, and so we have to be creative if we are going to find spaces where we can cry aloud. One church member shared with me that he would cry aloud when it was raining heavily and thundering so that he wouldn't be heard by his neighbors.

Psalm 142 traces an upward-downward movement as the psalmist cries out to the Lord with his voice in verse 1 (upward) and then pours out his heart (downward) in verse 2. Verse 3 marks another downward movement as the psalmist admits that his "spirit grows faint within me," which suggests that he is feeling really down. Those who are going through a downward spiral must be able to unload the burdens that are dragging them down, and so the psalmist declares, "I pour out before him my complaint" (v. 2; see also superscription in Psalm 102). As Christians, we are often taught not to complain, but throughout the Psalter, the psalmists complain. The preservations of these complaints over time reveals that our God is compassionate and understands all that we have to endure.

The psalmist declares, "When my spirit faints within me, you know my way!" (v. 3). Because God knows the "path where I walk" (v. 3b) and cares for

---

[3]. Wilce, *Crying Shame Metaculture, Modernity, and the Exaggerated Death of Lament*, 3, 90.

each of us (see Ps 139:3),[4] the psalmist is not afraid to come "before him" and "tell my trouble" (142:2b). In Hebrew, the phrase, "before him," literally means, "in his face" or "in his presence." When we are in trouble, we can always cry out to the Lord and ask for help.

The psalmist tells the Lord his trouble,[5] which is that "people have hidden a snare for me" (v. 3b). His complaint is that there are "people" against "me." The psalmist looks to his right, where the defender or helper is usually found, and there is no one there (v. 4). The situation is similar to the experience of the psalmist in Psalm 121, who asks, "where does my help come from?" (v. 1). The most difficult situation is when we are in trouble and have no one to help us. This is especially the case in community-centered cultures like in Asia. As Basson observes, "in a society where individual identity was embedded in the community, any form of isolation was tantamount to social death."[6] The words, "no one," are repeated twice in Psalm 142:4:

"no one is concerned for me" (v. 4a);
"no one cares for my life" (v. 4c).

In between these two unfortunate statements, the psalmist laments that he has "no refuge" (v. 4b). The first section ends with no hope of escape, a situation that would have been tragic, but then the psalmist cries out to the Lord again.

## 142:5–7 "I CRY TO YOU, LORD"

In verse 5, the psalmist cries aloud to the Lord again (compare v. 1). Crying is sometimes viewed as a sign of weakness or losing one's hope. In the previous section, we observed a downward movement as the psalmist went from crying out to the Lord (v. 1) to pouring out his complaint to the Lord (v. 2). Though he concludes that section by saying, "I have no refuge," here he declares, "You are my refuge" (v. 5).[7] Even though the psalmist no longer has anyone to help him, God remains his strength and his refuge.[8] At the end of verse 4,

---

4. The word "path" (*'orakh*) occurs in both Psalms 142:3 and 139:3.
5. Or, as we say in Filipino, *nagsumbong siya kay Lord* (he told the Lord).
6. Alec Basson, "Image Schemata of Containment and Path as Underlying Structures for Core Metaphors in Psalm 142," *OTE* 21, no. 2 (2008): 265.
7. In Hebrew, the word used for "refuge" in verses 4 and 5 is different (*manos* and *makhseh*, respectively), but they are used interchangeably here.
8. I remember when my three-year-old son was lost in a big mall. Realizing that there was no way I could find him, I cried out to the Lord, "Lord, I have no one who can help me. But you know everything. Please help me find my son!" Afterwards, we saw our son being accompanied by two security guards.

the psalmist laments that there is no one who "cares for my life." But at the end of verse 5, he declares that God is "my portion in the land of the living." Thus for the psalmist, the act of crying out becomes an expression of hope and a mark of resilience.

His faith in the Lord enables him to persist in prayer. Rather than being a matter for discouragement, the psalmist's unfortunate experience becomes the means for his perseverance. Verse 6 contains the motivation for his prayer: "I am brought very low" (ESV). Next he describes "those who pursue" him as "too strong for me" (v. 6b). The psalmist can find "no one who cares for him (v. 4), and there are many persecutors who are seeking to destroy him (v. 6b). Thus the psalmist cries out to God to rescue him (v. 6b).

Verse 7 betrays the psalmist's feeling that his pursuers have already caught him and have placed him in a "prison." The word "prison" may not refer to an actual imprisonment, but it certainly describes his "desperate condition in the light of adversity and isolation."[9] The image of "prison" further highlights the sense of isolation and loneliness he expresses in verse 4. Our current experience of the pandemic, which has resulted in numerous extended lockdowns, has caused so many people to feel this sense of isolation and loneliness. How we long for the day when we will be able to get out of this prison!

The psalm ends with a petition to be set free so "that I may praise your name" (v. 7a). Praising is often accompanied by sacrifice and is offered within the community. The psalmist is looking forward to the day when the righteous will be gathered around him as he offers a public thanksgiving and offering to the Lord. Though the NIV translates the last line, "because you have been good to me" (v. 7), the overall tone of the psalm supports the translation reflected in the LXX: "*when* you deal bountifully with me."[10] As with the previous psalm, there is no clear resolution at the end of Psalm 142, which concludes with an open petition. The psalmist hopes that one day he will offer thanksgiving to the Lord, but that will only take place when the Lord finally answers his prayer.

---

9. Basson, "Image Schemata of Containment and Path as Underlying Structures for Core Metaphors in Psalm 142," 270.
10. Compare Basson, "Image Schemata of Containment and Path as Underlying Structures for Core Metaphors in Psalm 142," 264.

# PSALM 143

Psalm 143 emphasizes the importance of our identity when we pray. At both the beginning and the end of the psalm, the psalmist refers to himself as "your servant" (vv. 2, 12). The prayer contains quite a few motivations or reasons about why God should answer the psalmist's prayer (see vv. 8–12 below), but the psalmist's identity as a servant serves as the climax and most important motivation. Indeed, the concluding line of the psalm is, "for I am your servant" (v. 12).

This psalm highlights the importance of self-knowledge, which balances the emphasis in the previous psalms on God's knowledge of us. For example, in Psalm 139, the psalmist confesses to God, "you know me" (v. 1), and in Psalm 142, he asserts, "you know my way" (v. 3, ESV). But believing that God knows us is incomplete if we do not have knowledge of ourselves. As Calvin writes, "The knowledge of God and that of ourselves are connected."[1] He goes on to assert, "Without knowledge of self, there is no knowledge of God."[2]

The emphasis on knowing God and knowing oneself mirrors the nature of God, for as Zimmerli points out, "God himself can be recognized" in the responses of his people.[3] Prayer is one of the ways we respond to God, and the prayer of the psalmist in Psalm 143 reveals that God values relationship. Jesus made this clear when he warned his disciples that in the last days, many will say to him, "Lord, Lord," but he will tell them, "I never knew you" (Matt 7:22–23). Relationship entails knowing, which leads to intimacy.

Psalm 143 is a prayer of individual lament, consisting of the following elements:

> invocation (v. 1),
> petition (vv. 1–2, 7–12),
> declaration of trust (v. 5–6a),
> complaint (vv. 3–4, 6b),

---

[1]. John Calvin, *Calvin: Institutes of the Christian Religion*, ed. John T. McNeill, trans. Ford Lewis Battles, vol. 1 (Louisville, KY: Westminster John Knox Press, 2006), 35.
[2]. Calvin, *Calvin: Institutes of the Christian Religion*, 37.
[3]. Walther Zimmerli, *Old Testament Theology in Outline* (Edinburgh: T & T Clark, 1978), 141. Zimmerli does not specifically discuss the complaints against God. For Zimmerli the responses come in the form of actions of obedience, thanksgiving or petition (141–155). This is true in our human relationship as well. For example, if the children are always afraid whenever their father arrives home, then that tells us about the kind of father he is. Or if a leader gets mad every time he hears complaints, this betrays his character as a dictator.

motivations (vv. 7–12).

Unlike the typical form-critical view of an individual lament, Psalm 143 does not end on a positive note. As we saw at the end of Psalms 140–142, the last verses are petitions that do not have any clear resolution. Thus the psalm can be categorized as a lament ending with an open petition.[4]

The psalm yields a two-part structure, with verses 1–6 comprising the first section and verses 7–12 comprising the second section. The use of the *Selah* at the end of verse 6, along with the noticeable intensification of verses 7–12, support this structure. The opening and closing verses of the psalm also form an inclusio:

Beginning:
    "in your righteousness" (v. 1)
    "your servant" (v. 2).
End:
    "in your righteousness" (v. 11)
    "your servant" (v. 12).

## 143:1–6 "LORD, ANSWER ME"

Psalm 143 begins with the psalmist pleading with God to hear his prayer, which is a common motif in the individual lament. The difference here is the emphasis on the word "righteousness." The first usage of this word is implied, as it is used as an adjective at the end of the previous psalm to refer to the "righteous" who surround the psalmist (142:7). Second, it is used as a noun to refer to God's "righteousness" (143:1). Third, it is used as an adjective to convey that "[no one] is righteous" (v. 2). The word "righteousness" (*tsedaqah*) is a central concept in the OT, and it is so common that its meaning can easily be missed. There is a difference between the English word, "righteousness," and the Hebrew word, *tsedaqah*. The English usage connotes righteousness as a norm or standard according to which actions are measured or judged. This is also the case with the German word, *gerechtigkeit*. There is a tendency to transfer this English and German meaning of the word "righteousness" to the Hebrew, but von Rad argues that this is based on "the presuppositions of the

---

4. Contra Zenger and Hossfeld who consider verses 10b–12 as a "promise of rescue" (571), which "announces his confidence in divine rescue from his trouble." Zenger and Hossfeld, *Psalms 3*, 575.

West."⁵ The OT concept of righteousness is more relational and situational, which is closer to the Filipino concept of what is "right" (*katwiran*) where actions are determined by contextual and relational factors rather than adherence to a written rule or law. Thus it is not easy to judge someone, because one has to consider numerous factors.

The complexity of the word "righteous" is demonstrated in the way it is used in Psalm 143. At the end of the psalm, the psalmist uses his identity as the servant of God as a basis for his petition (see v. 12 below). Yet at the same time, the psalmist knows that if he is judged on the basis of his righteousness, he will not pass, for "no one living is righteous before you" (v. 2b). Thus he asks the Lord to "not bring your servant into judgment" (v. 2a). Instead, he asks the Lord to deal with him "in your righteousness" (v. 1). In the OT, "righteousness" also commonly refers to God's actions, and so Deborah sings of "Yahweh's righteous acts" (Judg 5:11),⁶ and the psalmist remembers "all your works" and "what your hands have done" (143:5). Thus the psalmist is hoping that the Lord will once again perform his righteous acts.

Though we can't know the particulars of the psalmist's situation, he complains of his enemy (v. 3). As in most individual laments, the psalm does not provide details about the enemy, but rather focuses on the effect of the enemy's actions on the psalmist. The enemy pursues him, "crushes" him "to the ground," and "makes" him "dwell in the darkness like those long dead" (v. 3). The language is metaphorical, but whatever the enemy did, it certainly damaged the psalmist's spirit, for he says, "my spirit grows faint within me, my heart within me is dismayed" (v. 4).

In the midst of all these persecutions, the psalmist tries to "remember" what God has done in the past (v. 5). This language is similar to the lament in Psalm 77. The words "remember," "long ago" (*miqqedem*), "meditate" (*hagah*), and "consider" (*sykh*), along with the phrase, "I meditate on all your works," all occur in both psalms (77:11–12; 143:5). But in Psalm 77, the psalmist's remembering leads him to enumerate God's marvelous deeds, whereas in Psalm 143, the remembering of "the days of long ago" is followed by a lament. The psalmist stretches out his hands to God (v. 6a), a gesture that seems to signify giving up in light of the psalmist's utter exhaustion. Verse 6b literally reads, "my soul is like a weary ['*ayep*] land to you" (translation mine). The word "land" comes from the same word that is translated as "ground" in verse 3, where the

---

5. Gerhard von Rad, *Old Testament Theology*, 370.
6. von Rad, *Old Testament Theology*, vol. 1: 272.

psalmist says that he has been crushed by his enemy to the ground. In verse 6, the psalmist "becomes" the ground – weary, worn-out, with nothing left to offer. David, to whom this psalm is attributed, is always in danger, running for his life. The word "weary" in Psalms 63:1 and 143:6 recalls the story in 2 Samuel 16, which describes David and his men as "exhausted" (*'ayef*) after they fled from Absalom (v. 14).[7]

## 143:7–12 "ANSWER ME QUICKLY, LORD"

At the beginning of the second section, verse 7 repeats the petition from verse 1 – "answer me" (ESV) – but with greater urgency: "Answer me quickly." In verse 4, the psalmist's "spirit grows faint," but now his "spirit fails" (v. 7). The pattern of the petition is similar to verses 1–2 (moving from a positive to a negative petition). After praying, "answer me quickly," he continues, "do *not* hide your face from me." He is afraid that if the Lord does not answer him, he "will be like those who go down to the pit" (v. 7b), which is a metaphor for death.

Verses 8–10a all begin with a petition that is followed by a motivation:

| Verse | Petition | Motivation |
|---|---|---|
| 8a | "Let me hear of your steadfast love" (ESV) | "for in you I trust" |
| 8b | "Make me know the way I should go" (ESV) | "for to you I entrust my life" |
| 9 | "Rescue me from my enemies" | "for I hide myself in you" |
| 10a | "Teach me to do your will" | "for you are my God" |

There is a tension between the psalmist's desire for something tangible and his posture of trusting in God. On the one hand, he wants to "hear" (v. 8a) and to "know the way" (v. 8b), and he asks for practical deliverance from his enemies (v. 9). On the other hand, he acknowledges that God is his only refuge (vv. 9–10). A common denominator of the psalmist's motivation is his trust

---

7. Firth argues that the use of the word "weary" in Psalms 63 and 143, "may recall this story as the word is not used elsewhere in the Psalter or the Davidic narratives in the Books of Samuel, Kings or Chronicles. Gillian C. Firth writes: "The evocation of this scene with Absalom links also to the heading of Psalm 3 which places David in his flight from Absalom, reminding us that David was in danger throughout his career, not only fleeing from Saul before he was crowned, but also from Absalom in his mature kingship." Gillian C. Firth, "The Re-Presentation of David in Psalms 140–143," 256.

in God. The final petition differs from the previous ones, as the psalmist asks God to "teach" him to "do your will" (v. 10a).

We know from the NT that the Holy Spirit guides us into all truth. Psalm 143:10 gives us an early glimpse of this, for right after the petition for God to "teach me to do your will" (v. 10a), the psalmist continues, "may your good Spirit lead me on level ground" (v. 10b). The word "spirit" is mentioned twice earlier in the psalm to speak of the human spirit (vv. 4, 7), which is diminishing, failing. The psalmist's soul is being crushed to the ground (v. 3) and is likened to a weary land (v. 6). But the psalmist believes that God's "good Spirit"[8] can bring him to "level ground" (v. 10b), which suggests a "place of safety, comfort, and prosperity."[9]

In verse 11, the psalmist reverses the pattern of his prayer, placing the motivation before the petition:

| Verse | Motivation | Petition |
| --- | --- | --- |
| 11a | "For your name's sake" | "preserve my life" |
| 11b | "in your righteousness" | "bring me out of trouble" |

This shift is deliberate, as the psalmist repeats the word "righteousness" (compare v. 1), signaling the end of his prayer.

The final verse returns to the subject of the "enemies," offering an imprecatory prayer that they will be silenced and destroyed. The psalm concludes with a final motivation, "for I am your servant" (v. 12), which highlights the importance of our identity before the Lord. While there are a lot of possible reasons that we may think God should answer our prayers (see vv. 8–11), we should never forget who we are before the Lord. As with the previous psalms (Psalms 140–142), Psalm 143 ends without resolution. Even though everything seems to have failed, the psalmist is sustained by his identity as God's servant (vv. 2, 12).

---

8. The doctrine of the Holy Spirit is an NT development. The words, "holy spirit," only appear in Psalm 51:11 and Isaiah 63:10, whereas Psalm 143 simply has "spirit," which is described by the adjective, "good." This verse refers to God himself, rather than the separate person in the Trinity.
9. *BDB*, 449.

# PSALM 144

Psalm 144 reveals the God "who stoops down," looking back to Psalm 18, which declares that God "reached down from on high and took hold of me" (v. 16), and also anticipating Psalm 146, which declares that "the Maker of heaven and earth . . . lifts up those who are bowed down" (vv. 6, 8). As Christians, we know the reality of this theological truth, because Jesus came down to bring the good news to the poor.

The psalmist wonders, "Lord, what are human beings that you care for them?" (144:3). This famous question is also asked in Psalm 8, when the psalmist looks at "your heavens" (v. 3) and wonders, "what is mankind that you are mindful of them?" (v. 4). The phrase, "your heaven," occurs again in Psalm 144. The knowledge of the God who reaches down to the lowly gives courage to the psalmist, who dares to ask, "Part your heavens, Lord, and come down" (v. 5).

This petition conveys a sense of urgency and is preceded by the famous line ("What is mankind?"), which follows the opening verses of praise:

> Praise (vv. 1–2),
> > "What are human beings?" (vv. 3–4),
> Petitions (vv. 5–7).

The movement from praise (vv. 1–2) to petition (vv. 5–7) reflects a sense of contradiction, but the psalmist is not giving up (see discussion of vv. 8–11 below).

Psalm 144 consists of two main sections: verses 1–11 and verses 12–15. The first section begins with praise (vv. 1–2), which is followed by a meditation (vv. 3–4) that echoes Psalm 8 (see above). The meditation is followed by petitions (vv. 5–7), which echo the words in Psalm 18:9, 14. However, these words form the declarations in Psalm 18, whereas they are petitions in Psalm 144. The petitions are followed by a motivation (v. 8), which is repeated again in verse 11. In between these repeated motivations, there is a vow of thanksgiving (vv. 9–10) and another petition (v. 11a).

The second section (vv. 12–15) seems to be unconnected to the first, as the two sections do not seem to relate to one another.[1] This juxtaposition creates a gap, which needs to be filled. Most English translations follow the Hebrew of the MT, reading verses 12–15 as the anticipated outcome when God answers

---

1. Holtz argues for the unity of the psalm. Shalom E. Holtz, "The Thematic Unity of Psalm CXLIV in Light of Mesopotamian Royal Ideology," *VT* 58, no. 3 (2008): 367–380.

the prayer of the psalmist. These verses speak about the blessedness of the people – "our sons," "our daughters" (v. 12), "our barns," "our sheep" (v. 13), "our oxen" (v. 14) – and look forward to a time when there will be "no cry of distress in our streets" (v. 14). But the translation in the LXX presents an alternative reading, which reflects the continuing struggle of the people (see discussion below).

## 144:1–11 PRAISE AND PETITIONS

The opening praise (vv. 1–2) resembles Psalm 18:

"Blessed be the LORD, my rock" (144:1a, ESV);
"The LORD lives, blessed be my rock" (18:46, ESV).

Note that the parallel phrase, "blessed be my rock," is preceded by the word "life" (*hay*) in Psalm 18:46, where it is used as a verb ("[he] lives"). The last line of Psalm 144:2 is also similar to Psalm 18:47b, as both refer to the subjugation of peoples "under me."[2] However, the "Blessed be . . ." statement occurs near the end of Psalm 18 (v. 46), after the psalmist has recounted how the Lord delivered him from his enemies, whereas in Psalm 144, it forms the opening praise (v. 1a).

Immediately after the opening praise, the psalmist asks, "LORD, what are human beings that you care for them?" (v. 3). As noted above, this verse echoes Psalm 8:4, but that psalm begins and ends with praise, whereas the question in Psalm 144:3 is preceded by praise (vv. 1–2) and then followed by petitions (vv. 5–7). Moreover, unlike Psalm 8, the question in Psalm 144 highlights human frailty (v. 4). How are we to understand Psalm 144:3–4 in light of the surrounding context?

One way to understand these verses is to see them as a reflection of our awe that a God who is so high and great has chosen to stoop down to work with mere mortals. The psalmist praises God because he "trains my hands for war, my fingers for battle" (v. 1). The word "fingers" (*'etsba'*) also occurs in Psalm 8, where the heavens are described as "the work of your fingers" (v. 3). The same "fingers" who formed the skies also train the psalmist's fingers for battle. Thus the psalmist cannot help but wonder, "what are human beings that you care for them?" (v. 3). David asks the same question after the Lord makes a

---

2. Psalm 144:2b has "my people" while 18:47b has "peoples." The latter should be the preferred reading in Psalm 144 in view of the "violence" of the verb "subdue." Allen, *Psalms 101–150*, 359.

covenant with him: "Who am I, Sovereign Lord, and what is my family, that you have brought me this far?" (2 Sam 7:18).

Because the God who created the heavens cares for "mere mortals," the psalmist dares to ask, "Part your heavens, Lord, and come down" (v. 5). The petitions in verses 5 and 6 are similar to the affirmations in Psalm 18 (see vv. 9, 14, 16, 44–45). For instance, in Hebrew, the petitions, "part your heavens" and "come down" (144:5), are also used in Psalm 18:9 to describe what God has done ("He parted the heavens and came down"). However, they are expressions of praise in Psalm 18, whereas they are petitions in Psalm 144. The opening petition (144:5) reflects both the urgency and the intensity of the psalmist's trouble. Thus what is resolved in Psalm 18 becomes the problem in Psalm 144. As McCann observes, "It is particularly noticeable that the 'aliens' . . . whom God had dealt with on the king's behalf in Ps 18:44–45 are precisely the problem in Psalm 144."[3]

This problem with the foreigners surfaces in verses 7 and 11. Literally, the word "foreigners" come from the Hebrew, *bene nekar*, which literally means, "sons of foreigners." We will discuss the significance of this term, particularly the word "sons," below. The foreigners are described as those "whose mouths are full of lies" (vv. 8, 11), which is the psalmist's characteristic way of describing the wicked (e.g. Pss 10:6–7; 73:8–9; 140:1–3). Words and violence are intertwined, posing a serious danger to the people, and so the psalmist pleads with the Lord to deliver him from the "hands of foreigners" (v. 11).

Verses 5–11 form the following structure:

Petitions and motivation (vv. 5–8),
    Vow of thanksgiving (vv. 9–10),
Petitions and motivation (v. 11).

In between the description of the foreigners, "whose mouths are full of lies" (vv. 8, 11a), the psalmist vows that he will "sing a new song" to God (v. 9). Verse 9 is very similar to Psalm 33:2b–3a. The singing of a "new song" occurs in six psalms (33:3; 40:3; 96:1; 98:1; 144:9; 149:1). The structure of Psalm 144:5–11 is similar to Psalm 57, where the psalmist sings his song of thanksgiving, "Be exalted, O God, above the heavens . . ." (v. 5), in between two motivations for his prayer for mercy: he is lying down "among ravenous beasts" whose "teeth are spears and arrows" (v. 4), and they have hidden a snare for him (v. 6). The psalmist wants to be able to glorify God in the midst

---

3. McCann, "Psalms," 1254–1255.

of his troubling situation. In Psalm 144:9–10, the psalmist utters a vow of thanksgiving in the midst of his petitions and motivation to ask God to deliver him and his people, just as he did with David (v. 10).

### 144:12–15 BLESSINGS FOR WHOM?

In the NIV, verse 12 begins with the word, "Then," but in Hebrew, the first word is *'asher*, which is a relative pronoun ("whose") that usually introduces a series of relative clauses. The word *'asher* functions as a relative pronoun twice in the preceding section (vv. 8, 11). In verse 12, the LXX translates the Hebrew word *'asher* as a relative pronoun, forming a parallel with the two earlier uses of the word:

"whose [*'asher*] mouths are full of lies" (v. 8),
"whose [*'asher*] mouths are full of lies" (v. 11),
"whose [*'asher*] sons are like young plants" (v. 12,
　　following the LXX).

By translating the Hebrew as a relative pronoun, the LXX provides a smoother transition from the first section. However, doing so also introduces a radical transformation of the meaning of verses 12–14, because the antecedent of the relative pronoun, "whose," is the wicked. According to the LXX translation, the blessings described in verses 12–14 no longer apply to the psalmist's community and their children, but to the "sons of the foreigners" (v. 7). Indeed, there is a deliberate attempt in the LXX to convey this shift, for instead of the first-person plural ("our") in "our daughters" (v. 12), "our barns," "our sheep" (v. 13), the LXX has the third person plural ("their"), "their daughters" (v. 12), "their barns," "their sheep" (v. 13). In the LXX reading, the sons of the foreigners are likened to "well-nurtured plants," who are "in their youth" (v. 12).[4] This robust condition contrasts sharply with the community of Israel that is described in Psalm 129, which portrays the continuing struggle of the people as they live in a foreign land (see discussion of Psalm 129 above).

Yet the LXX reading results in a rather awkward ending: "They counted happy the people to whom these things fall; happy are people whose God is the LORD" (v. 15).[5] Nevertheless, it provides an alternative explanation for the gap

---

4. Dahood argues that the preposition "in" (*be*) has the meaning, "from," referring to Lamentation 3:27 and Job 31:18 as support. Dahood, *Psalms III: 101–150*, 332.
5. Translation from the LXX by Kohlenberger III, *The Comparative Psalter: Hebrew-Greek-English*, 257.

## Psalm 144

created by the juxtaposition of the two sections of Psalm 144. Its tragic sense also fits with the first part of the psalm, which moves from praise (vv. 1–2) to a series of petitions (vv. 5–7) without any clear resolution. Verse 11 ends with a petition for God to "rescue me from the hands of foreigners." The reading in the LXX also helps us appreciate the petition in verse 5: "Part your heavens, Lord, and come down." We don't utter such prayers unless we are in a really terrible situation (compare Isa 64:1).

# PSALM 145

Psalm 145 is an acrostic psalm that was structured around the Hebrew alphabet. One of the functions of an acrostic psalm is to convey a sense of comprehensiveness. Psalm 145 is an acrostic hymn that seeks to praise the Lord, as it were, from **A** to **Z**. The word "all" is repeated seventeen times in the psalm, which reinforces the sense of comprehensive praise:

| Occurrence | Verse | Use of "All" |
| --- | --- | --- |
| 1 | v. 2 | "all day" |
| 2 | v. 9 | "good to all" |
| 3 | v. 9 | "all he has made" |
| 4 | v. 10 | "all your works" |
| 5 | v. 13 | "all times" (everlasting) |
| 6 | v. 13 | "all generations" |
| 7 | v. 14 | "all who fall" |
| 8 | v. 14 | "all who are bowed down" |
| 9 | v. 15 | "the eyes of all" |
| 10 | v. 16 | "all living thing" |
| 11 | v. 17 | "all his ways" |
| 12 | v. 17 | "all he does" |
| 13 | v. 18 | "all who call on him" |
| 14 | v. 18 | "all who call on him in truth" |
| 15 | v. 20 | "all who love him" |
| 16 | v. 20 | "all the wicked" |
| 17 | v. 21 | "all flesh" |

Although the acrostic form aims towards completeness, it restricts the composer to follow the order of the Hebrew alphabet, and so the poet has to think of a word that begins with a particular letter for each line. At the same time, the composer has to find a word that conveys his message. In this way, the acrostic reveals what is most important for the psalmist. For example, for the letter *tsade* (*ts*) in verse 17, the composer writes *tsadiq* (the word for "righteous") to produce the line, "The LORD is righteous." Or in verse 1, the acrostic form structures so that the emphasis falls on the worshiper's initiative: "*I* will exalt you." In Hebrew, the phrase, "I will exalt you" (*'aromimkha*), begins with the letter *alef*, which is the equivalent of the English letter "a." In English, of course, the acrostic of verse 1 is difficult to capture, but in Filipino, the word "I" is "*ako*," which corresponds nicely to the Hebrew acrostic.

Though praise is our response to God and his actions towards us, it should always come from a willing heart. Thus the act of praise highlights human agency. Though Psalm 145 highlights the word "all," "all" do not worship God or acknowledge him as Lord. Even though God is "good to all" (v. 9), "all" do not respond with reverence and gratitude, for some are "wicked" (v. 20).

One of the most powerful messages of Psalm 145 is that the great king, whom King David praises, cares for those who are bowed down (compare Ps 136:22). There is a beautiful interplay between the center of the psalm (vv. 11–13) and the subsequent verses. In Hebrew, verses 11–13 begin with the letters k, l, and m, respectively. Read in reverse, these letters form the root word for king in Hebrew: *mlk* (*melekh*).[1] These verses speak of the king's "everlasting kingdom" and his "dominion," which "endures through all generations" (v. 13). There is no greater king than this! And yet, this great king "upholds all who fall and lifts up all who are bowed down" (v. 14).

## 145:1–9 THE KING WORSHIPS "MY GOD THE KING"

Psalm 145 is attributed to David (see superscription) and is the very final "Davidic psalm" in the four collections of Davidic psalms in the Psalter. The Davidic psalms in this fourth collection are mostly laments (Psalms 140–143), but Psalm 145 is a psalm of praise that anticipates the final hallelujah psalms in the Psalter (Psalms 146–150).

David is presented as a first-person speaker throughout the psalm, which begins with him praising "my God the King" (v. 1) and ends with a vow of praise: "my mouth will speak in praise of the Lord" (v. 21b). As the highest person in his own kingdom, David's exaltation and praise of God as the great king is a powerful reminder that there is never a time when God does not rule above us. Worship is important, because it puts us in our proper place before God.

In verse 1, the king declares, "I will exalt you." The word "exalt" comes from the Hebrew root, *rum*, which means "to be high" (*rum*). In addition to the verb, "exalt," the psalm uses two other related words: "bless" (vv. 1b, 2a) and "praise" (*hll*, v. 3). The famous Hallelujah is derived from verse 3.

---

1. Nancy L. deClaissé-Walford, "Psalm 145: All Flesh Will Bless God's Holy Name," *CBQ* 74, no. 1 (2012): 58.

The king describes the Lord as the one "most worthy of praise" (v. 3a) for the following reasons:

> because of his works (vv. 4, 9),
> because of the glorious splendor of his majesty (v. 5, compare v. 12b), and
> because of his goodness (vv. 6–8).

The psalm mentions the word "works" four times (vv. 4a, 9b, 10a, 17b), always referring to God's works. More specifically, "works" refers to humans and creation in general (vv. 9b, 10a) as well as the things that God does or has done (vv. 4a, 17b). Humans, as God's "works," praise the Lord (v. 10a), and the object of their praise is God's "works," which one generation "commends" to another (v. 4). All of God's works reveal that God is "most worthy of praise" (v. 3a).

But what makes God "most worthy of praise" (v. 3a) is that he is both glorious and majestic and also "abundant" in "goodness" (v. 7). Verse 5 extols the "glorious splendor of your majesty." The word "splendor" (*hodh*) is associated with the Hebrew words for "greatness" (*gedhullah*), "power" (*gebhurah*), "glory" (*tifereth*), and "victory" (*netsach*).[2] Yet this God is also "good" (*tob*), a word that is repeated twice (vv. 7, 9). Although God's works are great (v. 6b), God is most remembered for his "abundant goodness" (v. 7). In verse 7, the first Hebrew word, *zekher*, means "remembrance" or "fame." This word is parallel to the reference to "your name" in verses 1–2.[3] But what makes God famous is his goodness, for the famous line in verse 8 that is quoted directly from Exodus 34:6 is surrounded by the word "good":

> "They celebrate your abundant **goodness**" (v. 7).
>     "The LORD is gracious and compassionate" (v. 8;
>         Exod 34:6).
> "The Lord is **good** to all" (v. 9).

---

2. *TDOT*, 3:352–353.
3. Many politicians in the Philippines put their names on government cars, offices, and properties, to make themselves known. The Lord does not need to "write" his name anywhere, for his own works reflect his goodness as well as his greatness.

# Psalm 145

## 145:10–21 ALL GOD'S WORKS PRAISE THE KING, WHO IS LIKE NO OTHER

The second section of the psalm continues to praise God for his greatness and goodness. In verse 10, the king declares that "all your works praise you, Lord," because God's kingdom is "an everlasting kingdom" (v. 13a). Though kingdoms and dynasties rise and fall, God's "dominion endures through all generations" (v. 13). Even though God is greater than any other king, the "Lord upholds all who fall and lifts up all who are bowed down" (v. 14). The common expression in Filipino, *hindi na ma-reach* ("can no longer be reached"), conveys how the higher one goes, the harder it is to reach those who are down below. But this is not the case for our God, who dwells in the highest place, and yet stoops down to help those who fall. The word translated, "upholds," comes from the Hebrew word *somekh*, which means "to support." In order to "support" someone who is falling (see v. 14a), we have to get underneath the person. In order to lift up those who are bowed down, we have to reach down, sometimes even kneel. What a humble position for our great God! The incarnation testifies to how Jesus came down and became one with those "who fall" and "are bowed down" (v. 14).

Those "who fall" and "are bowed down" (v. 14) could refer to those whose "spirit grows faint" within them (142:3) or who have no one to care for them (142:4). In Psalm 145, they are those who are desperate and hungry. The expression, "the eyes of all look to you" (v. 15), expresses utter dependence and recalls Psalm 104:27. These desperate people have nowhere to turn, no one whom they can depend on but God, and so they abandon themselves to his care (compare Ps 10:14). In his goodness, God responds to the cry of those who fall, for the psalmist declares that "You give them their food at the proper time" (145:15b; compare 104:27). The word "food" indicates that these people are literally hungry, and when you are starving, you fall down.

According to the Gospel of Mark, when Jesus saw that the people around him had "nothing to eat," he "called his disciples to him and said, 'I have compassion for these people; they have already been with me three days and have nothing to eat. If I send them home hungry, they will collapse on the way, because some of them have come a long distance'" (Mark 8:1–3). Jesus understood hunger, because he experienced it himself when he fasted in the desert (Matt 4:2). Because Jesus identified with the poor,[4] he was sensitive to

---

4. Wolfgang Stegeman writes: "On the basis of a large number of data in the gospels and in other texts, we concluded that there was an economic and political crisis in Jewish Palestine

those who were hungry. More people today are becoming hungry, both for literal food and other things, such as purpose in life, or basic creaturely desires (145:16b). The image of God's open hand (v. 16a) depicts God as generous.

Even though God is good to all, he expects people to respond in faithfulness and truth. In verse 10, there is a shift from "all your works" giving thanks (v. 10a) to "your faithful people" blessing God (v. 10b). Though all of creation declares God's praise, not all people "tell of the glory of your kingdom" (v. 11). Rather, only God's faithful people can properly praise the Lord, for even though the Lord is close to "all who call on him" (v. 18a), the second line qualifies that God is only close to those who "call on him in truth" (v. 18b).[5] Moreover, only "those who fear him" (v. 19a) will receive a hearing from the Lord (v. 19b), and God will only watch over those who "love him" (v. 20a). The psalm makes a clear distinction between those who fear and love the Lord and the wicked, who will be destroyed (v. 20b).

Worship not only puts us in our proper place before God, but also challenges us to put our trust in the Lord rather than trusting in ourselves or strong and powerful leaders. We cannot worship "my God the king" (v. 1) and praise him with our lips (v. 21) if our heart is far from him.

---

in the time of Jesus, and we described the Jesus movement as a 'poverty movement' by and for poor Jewish men and women." Wolfgang Stegeman, "Background III: The Social and Political Climate in Which Jesus of Nazareth Preached," in *Handbook for the Study of the Historical Jesus*, ed. Stanley E. Porter and Tom Holmén (Leiden: Brill, 2011), 2313.
5. Allen translates "in truth" as "sincerely." Allen, *Psalms 101–150*, 367.

# PSALM 146

Psalm 146 is the first of the final five Hallel psalms. The famous "Hallelujah" is derived from the word *hallel* ("praise"). There are three main Hallel collections in the Psalter: the Egyptian Hallel (Psalms 113–118), the Great Hallel (Psalm 136 or Psalms 135–136), and the Concluding Hallel (Psalms 146–150). Our praise of God reflects our knowledge of God, and Psalm 146 praises God because he "made heaven and earth" (v. 6, ESV) and "reigns forever" (v. 10). But in between these descriptions of God as the creator (v. 6) and the reigning king (v. 10), he is also praised for caring for the weak and vulnerable (vv. 7–9). Psalm 146 places those who do not have a place in society at the very center of who God is. In Hebrew, the descriptions of God as the creator and upholder of the weak are set in participial form, which establishes them as parallel:

> "who made heaven and earth" (v. 6, ESV),
> "who executes justice for the oppressed" (v. 7a, ESV),
> "who gives food to the hungry" (v. 7b, ESV).

The surrounding psalms contain a similar parallel emphasis (see Pss 145:1, 14; 147:4–6). As acknowledged throughout this commentary, our theology influences our ethical living, and Psalm 145 offers a powerful teaching about how we ought to live our lives for others in light of the God whom we profess to worship and adore. Jesus himself modeled the theology of worship and praise that is reflected in this psalm throughout his own ministry (see Luke 4:18–19).

The psalm follows the typical hymn, which begins with a call to praise (vv. 1–2) that is directed to the community as well as to oneself (v. 1). The presence of the community becomes more explicit in the exhortation (vv. 3–4) and the address to Zion at the end of the psalm (v. 10). The psalm also outlines the psalmist's motivations for praise – the second component of the hymn (vv. 6–10a). These elements of the hymn provide the overall structure for the psalm, which can be divided into two parts:

> Call to praise and exhortation (vv. 1–4),
> Motivations for praise (vv. 5–10).

## 146:1–4 CALL TO PRAISE AND EXHORTATION

The opening call to worship in Psalm 146 is similar to Psalm 103:

> "Praise the LORD, my soul" (146:1);
> "Bless the LORD, my soul" (103:1).

Though Psalm 146 uses the verb "praise" (*hll*), and Psalm 103 uses the verb for "bless" (*barakh*), these two verbs can be used synonymously (see Ps 145:1–2). After the psalmist enjoins his "soul" to praise the Lord, he declares, "I will praise the LORD all my life" (v. 2a). This declaration intensifies in the parallel line, as the psalmist vows to praise the Lord "as long as I live" (v. 2b). A more literal translation of the phrase, "as long as I live," would be, "as long as I am."[1] The psalmist is aware of the transient nature of human existence, for he acknowledges that "when their spirit departs, they return to the ground" (v. 4a). The word "ground" (*'adama*) is the same word used in Genesis 2, where God formed the man from the dust of the ground (*'adama*). Then God "breathed into his nostrils the breath of life," and "the man became a living being" (Gen 2:7). But just as humans came from the ground, they will also return to the ground, and then "their plans come to nothing" (Ps 146:4b).

Thus the psalmist warns the people not to put their trust in princes (v. 3). The word "princes" comes from the Hebrew word *nedibah*, which "denotes a noble, a leader among the people." As a social group, princes "embody the highest human power in tribe and state."[2] They are the elite, the untouchables of our time. Yet the psalmist reminds the people that even princes are "human beings, who cannot save" (v. 3b), for they also return to the ground.

The movement from praise (vv. 1–2) to exhortation (vv. 3–4) highlights an important value of worship, as it trains us to put our trust in God alone rather than ourselves and those who are powerful. Trusting in God does not mean that we don't believe in ourselves, for we need to have confidence in our abilities. Yet we also need to be aware of our limitations. Psalm 146 is written from the perspective of those who are living in the lowest levels of society, such as foreigners, orphans, and widows (see vv. 7–9 below). Though those who are vulnerable can be easily swayed by human promises of salvation and help, the psalmist reminds them that true help comes from the Lord alone.

### 146:5–10 REASONS FOR PRAISE

The psalmist identifies those whose "help" and "hope" is in "the God of Jacob" as "blessed" (v. 5). The word "blessed" comes from the Hebrew word *ashre*, which is also used in Psalm 1:1 to describe the righteous person who meditates on the Law of the Lord. The phrase, "the way of the wicked," at the end of verse 9 provides a further connection to Psalm 1:1. However, Psalm 146 emphasizes

---

1. *HALOT*, 2:796.
2. *TDOT*, 9:224.

divine agency (God is the subject of all the verbs in vv. 6–9), whereas Psalm 1 stresses human agency.

The vulnerability of the following groups of people highlights the need for divine agency:

> "oppressed" (v. 7a),
> "hungry" (v. 7b),
> "prisoners" (v. 7c),
> "blind" (v. 8a),
> "bowed down" (v. 8b; compare 145:14),
> "foreigner," "fatherless," and "widow" (v. 9).

The three groups named in verse 9 are a famous trio (see Exod 22:20–22; Jer 7:6) and were deliberately placed at the end of the list, since the experiences described in the preceding verses often apply to them. Foreigners do not belong and do not have any rights, and so they are prone to oppression. In a male-dominated society, widows are in an unfortunate situation. Both widows and orphans often experience hunger and do not have anyone to defend them. Like the foreigner, they can easily be put in jail and have their rights violated. All three groups are often "bowed down" because of their situation and unable to help themselves.

But the creator God himself,[3] "who made heaven and earth, the sea, and all that is in them" (v. 6, ESV; compare Gen 2:4), "upholds the cause of the oppressed" (v. 7a). God is different from the gods of the surrounding nations because humans are extremely valuable to him. In the Babylonian creation epic, *Enuma Elish*, the creation of humans came almost as an afterthought, so that the gods would have someone to help them. But God created humans according to his own image (Gen 1:26–27). Thus all humans deserve to be treated fairly.

Although the above groups of people share similar needs, their situations are unique, and yet the creator God meets each of their individual needs, for he alone:

> "executes justice for the oppressed" (v. 7a, ESV),
> "gives food to the hungry" (v. 7b),
> "sets prisoners free" (v. 7c),

---

3. Verses 6–9 outline the reasons why God should be praised and why the people who trust in God are "blessed." As in Psalm 103, Psalm 146 contains descriptions of who God is, which are also formulated in the participial form (compare Pss 146:6–9; 103:3–6). The first description in Psalm 146:6 resumes the connection to the creation account (see vv. 3–4 above).

"gives sight to the blind" (v. 8a),
"lifts up those who are bowed down" (v. 8b),
"watches over the foreigner" (v. 9a), and
"sustains the fatherless and the widow" (v. 9b).

God responds to each of these groups of oppressed people according to their need and situation. Though he created the vast universe, he knows and cares for each individual person's need.

Sadly, some people do not treat their fellow humans (*kapwa*) in this way. Psalm 104 praises God for the wonders of his creation, and then suddenly mentions sinners at the end in an anticlimactic manner. Although the psalmist praises the God of creation, he is also aware of the presence of the wicked. Psalm 147 also mentions the "way of the wicked" (v. 9c, ESV), which is the way of destruction, oppression, and the negation of everything that is good. Thus God not only helps the poor and the oppressed, but he also brings ruin to the wicked (v. 9c, ESV). For the creator God is also the king (v. 10),[4] and injustice and oppression cannot exist in his kingdom (Psalm 82), so the wicked must depart.

The last line returns to a didactic exhortation as the psalmist proclaims, "your God, O Zion," will reign "for all generations" (v. 10b). The psalmist wants the people to know that this is the God whom they are praising. Worship teaches us to trust in the Lord rather than ourselves or other humans and also challenges us to become more like God. Thus our hymnody must be based on sound theology, because it shapes how we understand and respond to our world.

---

4. See John Day for the link between kingship and creation. John Day, *God's Conflict with the Dragon and the Sea*, 23–24.

# PSALM 147

Psalm 147 continues to praise the creator God, who brings about the work of restoration and healing. God not only has power over all creation – calling each star by name (v. 4), causing the sky to rain (v. 4), covering the land with snow and turning it into water (vv. 15–18) – but also "heals the brokenhearted and binds up their wounds" (v. 3). In Psalm 146, the creator God cares for the oppressed, hungry, prisoner, blind, those who are bowed down, the foreigner, the fatherless, and the widow (vv. 7–9). The people of Israel experienced all these forms of suffering during their time in exile, which can be described as a prison experience.[1] Many of the Israelites became fatherless or widows, and all became foreigners. As they look back on their time of exile, they can now declare that God "builds" them up (v. 2a), "gathers" them (v. 2b), and "heals" their brokenness (v. 3).

In light of all this, the first line of Psalm 147 is very appropriate: "Praise the Lord! For it is good to sing praises to our God" (v. 1, ESV). The psalm consists of three calls to worship, which serve as structural markers that divide the psalm into three sections:

"Praise the Lord!" (v. 1),
"Sing to the Lord with grateful praise" (v. 7),
"Extol the Lord, Jerusalem" (v. 12).

The verses that follow each of these calls to worship contain the psalmist's motivations for praise (vv. 2–6, 8–11, 13–20).

## 147:1–6 "PRAISE THE LORD!"

The title of this psalm, along with the other final Hallel psalms (Psalms 146–150), is derived from the word, "Hallelujah," which is an imperative verb in Hebrew (a command). After the call to praise the Lord, the next line begins with the Hebrew preposition *ki* ("for" or "because"), thereby signaling the motivation for the call to praise: "for [*ki*] it is good to sing praises to our God" (v. 1, ESV). The word "good" recalls the emphasis on God's goodness in Psalm 145. Because of the Lord's "abundant goodness" (145:7), it is "good" to praise him (147:1). Because God, the creator and king, cares for the least, it is not only "good" to praise him, but also "pleasant and fitting to praise him" (v. 1b).

---

1. Smith-Christopher, *A Biblical Theology of Exile*, 72.

The terms "good" and "pleasant" are only used together here and in Psalm 133. In Psalm 133, it is good and pleasant for people to live together in unity (v. 1); in Psalm 147, it is good and pleasant when the community gathers to "sing praises to our God" (v. 1).

Both Psalm 146 and Psalm 147 share the sentiment concerning God's kindness to the marginalized (see 146:7–9). Even though God is the creator and king, he cares for the least and most vulnerable, and both psalmists have experienced this. The image of "building up" (147:2a) implies that something has fallen apart or broken. God upholds those who fall down (145:14), which includes cities and their inhabitants, for "he gathers up the exiles of Israel" (147:2b). The experience of the exile has broken the people's spirits. Many of them have lost their loved ones and become widows and orphans. Yet they are praising God because he "heals the brokenhearted" and "binds up their wounds" (v. 3).

Even though their God is so great and strong (v. 5), he cares for the poor (v. 6). Though "he determines the numbers of the stars" (v. 4a), "he calls each of them by name" (v. 4b). This powerful and awesome creator God (146:6) "sustains the humble" (147:6a). The verb "sustains" (*'wd*) is used previously in Psalm 146:9 to describe God's support for the "fatherless and the widow," two groups who experience the greatest material need and are vulnerable to abuse because they do not have any support. The word translated as "humble" can also mean "poor," and its contrast with the "wicked" in Psalm 147:6 suggests that "poor" is the primary meaning. Gerstenberger finds it "anticlimactic" for the hymn to revert to the topic of the poor, since the psalm has already "reached out far beyond the human sphere."[2] But this misses an important emphasis in the psalm, which is that the God of the universe, who determines the number of the stars and knows each one by name, also cares for the poor, who are brokenhearted and wounded. The one who "gathers [*kns*] the exiles of Israel" (v. 2b) is also the one who "gathers [*kns*] the waters of the sea into jars" (33:7).

## 147:7–11 "SING TO THE LORD WITH GRATEFUL PRAISE"

There is a similar emphasis in the second section, where the call to praise (v. 7) is followed by a description of God, "who covers the heavens with clouds" (v. 8a, ESV). The word "heavens" in verse 7 shifts our focus upwards to God's greatness after verse 6, which ends with God casting "the wicked to

---

2. Gerstenberger, *Psalms Part 2 and Lamentations*, 443.

the ground." Yet once again, God's greatness is praised to highlight his care for the least and vulnerable. God covers the "heavens with clouds" to care for the earth, for he "supplies the earth with rain and makes grass grow on the hills" (v. 8). God cares for the tiniest things that often escape our notice, such as the grass and the ground. He also cares for animals and even "young ravens" (v. 9; see also Ps 84:3). For in the midst of "the sounds of musical productions in the temple (vv. 1, 7) and wind, rain, and hail in the countryside (vv. 8; 17–18)," God hears "the sound of the desperate crying of a nestful of hungry young ravens" (v. 9).[3] Ravens have been known as those who abandon their young, and yet God will not neglect them. Jesus also mentions the ravens in one of his teachings (Luke 12:24).[4]

There is a beautiful interplay between the "young ravens" (v. 9), who depict vulnerability and weakness, and the "strength of the horse" (v. 10a). One would expect God, who is "great" and "mighty in power" (v. 5), to be pleased with the "strength of the horse" and the strong "legs of the warrior" (v. 10), but instead, he is pleased with "those who fear him" (v. 11a). This phrase could refer broadly to those who have decided to place their trust in the Lord rather than human power, but contextually, it refers primarily to those who do not have access to power – the poor (v. 6; 146:7–9). Though not everyone who is poor fears the Lord, the poor are vulnerable and often have no one to put their trust in except the Lord. The phrase, "those who fear the Lord," also refers to those outside of Israel who decide to serve the Lord (see discussion below).

### 147:12–20 "Extol the Lord, Jerusalem"

The last section identifies Jerusalem/Zion as the audience to whom the call to praise is addressed. Jerusalem represents both the city and the people. Though God has started the process of rebuilding the city in verse 2, now he is strengthening the bars of its gates (v. 13a). The gates are an important part of the city – the place where the courts are held and important decisions are made. By focusing on the "bars" of Jerusalem, the psalm conveys an image of protection, which connects with the next verse: "he grants peace to your borders" (v. 14a). In the first section, the psalmist praises God for starting the process of binding the people's wounds and healing the brokenhearted (v. 3). Here, in the third

---

3. James Limburg, "Quoth the Raven: Psalm 147 and the Environment," in *A God so Near: Essays on Old Testament Theology in Honor of Patrick D. Miller*, ed. Brent A. Strawn and Nancy R. Bowen (Winona Lake, IN: Eisenbrauns, 2003), 111.
4. James Limburg, "Quoth the Raven: Psalm 147 and the Environment," 105.

section, he describes how God has blessed "your children within you" (v. 13b, ESV). This blessing becomes concrete in the next verse when God satisfies them with "the finest of wheat" (v. 14). In many Asian countries, the finest rice would be the equivalent to "finest wheat." For Filipinos, no matter how delicious the dish may be, if there is no rice – and if the rice is not properly cooked – satisfaction will never be complete.

Verses 14–18 illustrate the effectiveness of God's word. Perhaps people are wondering how the process of healing, binding of wounds, blessing, and granting *shalom* will come about. The psalm assures the people by saying that when God "sends his command to the earth," its fulfillment comes "swiftly" (v. 15). The psalmist employs two related phenomena to illustrate this point: snow and water. Earlier, the psalmist describes how God "supplies the earth with rain" (v. 8), and here he declares that God gives snow (v. 16a). He likens the snow to "wool," both to highlight its whiteness and also to emphasize the abundant manner in which it covers the earth. The parallel line confirms the latter view: he "scatters the frost like ashes" (v. 16b). Moreover, God hurls down "hail" (v. 17a),[5] an image that conveys a negative experience. Those who live in cold places know the fierceness of the cold, especially when the wind is strong. Thus the psalmist asks, "Who can withstand his icy blast?" (v. 17b). Yet the God who gives the snow and scatters it like ashes is also the God who can turn it into water by the power of his "word," for "He sends his word and melts them" (v. 18a), and "he makes his wind blow and the waters flow" (v. 18b, ESV).

In verse 19, the psalmist applies these illustrations to the people of Israel, repeating the phrase, "his word," for the third time:

> "his word runs swiftly" (v. 15b);
> "He sends his word" (v. 18a);
> "He has revealed his word to Jacob" (v. 19a).

The word that God revealed to Jacob is sure and will accomplish the purpose for which it was sent (compare Isa 55:10–11). But will the people obey the word that has been revealed to them?

The psalmist recalls how the people of Israel are privileged, because God has not revealed his "laws and decrees" (v. 19) to any other nation (v. 20). There is a tension in the psalm between the concerns of the people of God (Israel) and "those who fear the LORD" (v. 11). While the first and third sections are

---

5. In Hebrew, the word is "ice," which probably refers to hail.

addressed to Israel, the second section focuses on "those who fear the LORD" (v. 11). According to Schwartz, this refers to foreigners who are not the chosen people of God and yet chose to follow the God of Israel. The absence of any mention of Jerusalem or the people of Israel in the second section supports this, and there seems to be a deliberate attempt on the part of the composer to create a disjuncture. As Schwartz observes, "the second stanza omits the element of rebuilding Jerusalem, creating a blatant asymmetry in the psalm."[6] She argues that the "alternation between national and universal in the psalm indicates a delicate balance between a national and universal perception."[7] While she does not see a tension between the two, I think that juxtaposing the stanzas does create tension between the two perspectives. As an Asian Christian (non-Israelite) interpreter, I sense a disjunction in the final verses of Psalm 147 that emphasize the national view. For isn't God the God of all people?

At the same time, God's presence in history is "a presence to particular men in particular situations."[8] We can only encounter the reality of God's revelation in the particular and specific historical events of our experiences. While we should not deny our particularity, those who receive the privilege of encountering God also have a responsibility to bear witness about that revelation ("his laws and decrees to Israel," v. 19) to others. As Fackenheim writes, "To be sure, unless it were that of a mere tribal deity, such a presence must have universal implications. These implications, however, are manifest only in the particular; and they make of the men to whom they are manifest . . . witnesses, in, through, and because of their particularity to the nations."[9] Israel will not be a good witness if she overemphasizes her privileged position, for Psalm 146 presents God as caring for the weak and vulnerable. Coupled with the people's own experience during the exile, this presentation of God should remind Israel that she, also, must reflect this same attitude to those outside of Zion. At the end of Psalm 146, the psalmist declares that this is "your God, O Zion, for all generations" (v. 10). As discussed in the commentary for Psalm 146, this God is also the God of the foreigner and the marginalized.

---

6. Sarah Schwartz, "Bridge over Troubled Waters: Psalm 147," *JSOT* 42, no. 3 (2018): 321.
7. Schwartz, "Bridge over Troubled Waters," 339.
8. Emil L. Fackenheim, *God's Presence in History: Jewish Affirmations and Philosophical Reflections* (Northvale, NJ: J. Aronson, 1970), 8.
9. Fackenheim, *God's Presence in History*, 8.

# PSALM 148

Psalm 148 is the third of the final five Hallel psalms in the Psalter (Psalms 146–150) and occupies the central place in this group. Atkins remarks that "Psalm 148 is perhaps the best example of the entire creation being called together to offer a hymn to God."[1] Like the other Hallel psalms, Psalm 148 contains elements of the hymn. One of the elements of the hymn is the call to praise. The following comparative analysis of the calls to praise in each of the five Hallel psalms demonstrates the central place of Psalm 148 in this collection:

| Psalm | Call to Praise | Addressee |
|---|---|---|
| 146 | "Praise the Lord, my soul" (v. 1). | my soul |
| 147 | "Extol the Lord, Jerusalem; Praise your God, Zion" (v. 12). | Jerusalem/Zion |
| **148** | "Praise the Lord from the heavens" (v. 1). Praise the Lord from the earth" (v. 7). | heaven and earth |
| 149 | "Let Israel . . . Zion . . . praise his name . . ." (vv. 2–3). | Israel/Zion |
| 150 | "Let everything that has breath praise the Lord" (v. 6). | everything that has breath |

As can be seen above, Psalm 148 is the most extensive in terms of its addressees. While the surrounding psalms (Psalm 147 and Psalm 149) call on the people of Israel/Zion to praise the Lord, Psalm 148 broadens the call to include everything in heaven and earth, thereby anticipating the call in Psalm 150 for everything that has breath to praise the Lord (v. 6). "Everything that has breath" includes the psalmist, and so the invocation to "my soul" in Psalm 146 also looks forward to this final exclamation of praise. All of these exclamations find their expression in Psalm 148, which envisions everything in heaven and on earth praising the Lord. The word "all" is repeated ten times in the psalm (vv. 2 [2x], 3, 7, 9 [2x], 10, 11 [2x], 14). The overall structure of Psalm 148 shares the vision reflected in the Lord's Prayer, which asks the Father for God's kingdom to come and his will to be done on earth as it is in heaven.

The two calls to worship serve as structural markers that divide the psalm into two main sections (vv. 1–6 and 7–14):

---

1. Peter Joshua Atkins, "Praise by Animals in the Hebrew Bible," *JSOT* 44, no. 3 (2020): 506.

# Psalm 148

Call to worship "from the heaven" (v. 1),
Call to worship "from the earth" (v. 7).

## 148:1–6 "PRAISE THE LORD FROM THE HEAVENS"

The psalm begins with a call to worship that is directed to those "from the heavens" (v. 1a). This opening verse ends with the phrase, "in the heights above" (*bammeromim*), which forms a parallel with the word "heavens" in the first line. The word "heavens" is repeated five times in the psalm, four times in the first section (vv. 1, 4 [3x]) and once in the second section (v. 13). Verse 4a literally reads, "Praise him, *heavens* of *heavens*," which is understood in a superlative sense to mean, "the entire enormous expanse of heaven."[2]

The phrase, "from the heavens," refers, first of all, to those belonging to the heavenly realm: "angels" and "heavenly hosts" (v. 2). We are more familiar with "angels,"[3] but what are the "heavenly hosts"? Yahweh is known as the "Lord of hosts" (Pss 24:10; 46:7), and the OT mentions cherubim and seraphim. According to Psalm 80, God dwells among the cherubim (v. 1), and Isaiah 6 sees seraphim above the throne of the Lord (Isa 6:1–2). Obviously, there are so many things we do not know about the heavenly realm, but the psalmist calls on "all" of these hosts to praise the Lord. Note that the word "all" is repeated twice in verse 2.

Second, the phrase, "from the heavens," refers to the "sun and moon" (v. 3a) and the "stars" (v. 3b). In Genesis 1, the sun and moon are called the "two great lights" (Gen 1:16). In the surrounding cultures of Israel and even Israel itself, the sun, moon, and stars were considered to be gods (2 Kgs 23:5). In our own Filipino context, the sun is traditionally considered to be a "mighty god."[4] But in the Bible, these three lights are created by God. In Genesis 1, the stars are mentioned as an afterthought (Gen 1:16). But in Psalm 148, all three are called upon to praise the Lord (v. 3).

Third, the phrase, "from the heavens," refers to the "waters above the skies" (v. 4b). The fact that the psalmist mentions this last is intriguing, for the "waters" were viewed as a threat in ancient cosmology. The subsequent motivation for praise (vv. 5b–6), which stresses God's control over the created

---

2. *TDOT*, 15:205.
3. Though, of course, this does not mean we really know them. There are so many things we don't know about the heavenly realm.
4. See "The Origin of the Stars." Damiana L. Eugenio, *Philippine Folk Literature the Myths* (Diliman, Quezon City: University of the Philippines Press, 2001), 116.

order, supports this view. In the classic ancient cosmology, which originated from Mesopotamia, "heaven is a solid vault (Ps 19:2[1]), which keeps the waters of chaos above and beside it from invading the cosmos (Gen 1:6–8; Ps 148:4). To it are attached as lights the sun, moon, and stars (Gen 1:14–17)."[5] The mention of the waters in this verse further supports the overall perspective of the psalm, which is "from the earth."

The next call to praise moves "from the heavens" (v. 1) to the "highest heavens" (v. 4a). This refers to the "container" for everything that is mentioned in the previous list. Unlike Genesis 1, which mentions the heavens (created on the second day) before the luminaries (created on day 4), Psalm 148 mentions the lights before identifying the "highest heavens," where the angels and hosts of heaven dwell and the three lights are contained. By combining the "contents" with the "container," the psalmist is invoking all that is in heaven – including heaven itself – to praise the Lord.

## 148:7–14 "PRAISE THE LORD FROM THE EARTH"

The second section calls everything on earth to praise the Lord. The list of those being invoked to praise the Lord on earth is twice as long as the list for those "from the heavens," as shown in the following table.

| "From the heaven" (vv. 1–6) | "From the earth" (vv. 7–13) |
|---|---|
| angels | great sea creatures |
| heavenly hosts | ocean depths |
| sun and moon | lighting |
| stars | hail |
| highest heavens | snow |
| waters above the skies | clouds |
|  | stormy winds |
|  | mountains and hills |
|  | fruit trees and cedars |
|  | wild animals and cattle |
|  | small creatures and flying birds |
|  | humans |

---

5. *TDOT*, 15:211. See Exodus 20:4 (Deut 5:8) for a summary of this worldview.

The psalmist emphasizes the earth in the second section because he is "from the earth" rather than "from the heavens." He knows very little about the "heavens," which explains why there are fewer items on the first list. Nevertheless, he calls on those "from the heavens" to praise the Lord because the Lord dwells in the heavens (Ps 80:1). Furthermore, he begins by calling on those in the heavens to praise the Lord because this is where the worship of God is fully realized. While the psalms declare that "God reigns over the nations" (47:8), they also acknowledge the continuing presence of sinners (104:35) and wicked people (146:9b; 147:6). In heaven, "Yahweh's lordship is not polluted, and in essence not even contested," but on "earth, Yahweh and his creation are contested by the humans."[6] By enjoining those "from the earth" to praise the Lord, Psalm 148 reflects the vision that one day "everything that has breath" will praise the Lord (see Ps 150:6).

As in the first part, those "from the earth" and all the places on the earth are called to praise the Lord. The first to be named are the "great sea creatures" (v. 7). In Hebrew, the sea creature is called *tannin*, which means "sea-monster, sea-dragon."[7] By mentioning the sea creature, the psalmist is including the sea as "from the earth." In the ancient Hebrew worldview, the world consisted of three tiers: heavens, earth and sea.[8] The sea represented the forces of chaos, and so *tanin* ("sea dragon") and the "depths" (*tehom*) in verse 7 represent the forces associated with destruction and chaos.[9] By placing these forces first in the list "from the earth," the psalmist forms a chiasm with "the waters" (v. 4), which is the last item in the above list "from the heavens." The "ocean depths" (*tehom*) refer to the "deep waters" or simply the "depths."[10] Just as the "highest heavens" are personified above, the "depths" (*tehom*) are personified here.

In the next verses, there is an upward movement from the "depths" to those on the ground. First, the psalmist mentions various natural phenomena – lightning, hail, snow, and mist. The word for "lightning" (v. 8) is literally "fire," though in the context, it refers to lightning. The lightning, snow, hail, and

---

6. Rolf Knierim, "Cosmos and History in Israel's Theology," *HBT* 3 (1981): 79.
7. *HALOT*, 4:1764.
8. Kyle Greenwood, *Scripture and Cosmology: Reading the Bible Between the Ancient World and Modern Science* (Downers Grove: IVP Academic, 2015), 71.
9. "Hebrew *tᵉhôm* is a vigorous and often grim word, which never entirely renounced its mythical past. A primordial strength pervades *tᵉhôm* throughout. It stands for: a) the primeval ocean; b) the waters round the earth after creation, which continually threaten the cosmos; c) these waters as a source of blessing for the earth." Nicholas J. Tromp, *Primitive Conceptions of Death and the Nether World in the Old Testament*, Bib et Orientalia 21 (Rome: Pontificio Inst Biblico, 1969), 59.
10. *DCH*, 8:593.

mist are all personified and called upon to praise the Lord. Next, the psalmist mentions "mountains and hills" (v. 9a), which have a similar function to the "highest heaven" and the "ocean depths," as they represent the places on the earth that serve as a "container" for the trees (v. 9b), animals, small creatures, birds (v. 10), and humans (vv. 11–12). As in the previous section, even the "container" is called upon to praise the Lord.

Humans occupy a special place in the psalm, which devotes two verses to elaborate on the social aspect of human life, mentioning kings and peoples, princes and rulers (v. 11). The psalmist even includes aspects of gender and age – "young men and women" and "old men and children" (v. 12). As in Genesis 1, humans are mentioned last, but in Psalm 148, this does not imply that humans are most important. The first section of the psalm mentions the "waters above the skies" (v. 4) last, and angels and heavenly hosts first (v. 2). In the second section, humans are mentioned at the end of the list of many other creatures and things of the earth – sea creatures, trees, snow, cedars, and so on. Humans are identified as one with the rest of creation, and together, all who are "from the earth" are exhorted to "praise the name of the LORD" (v. 13a).

Verse 13b provides two grounds for praise: first, God's name alone is exalted; second, God's "splendor is above the earth and the heavens." The second motivation builds on the first. God is not only exalted, for he is also "above" everything. His splendor is not only "above the earth," but also "above the heavens," a phrase that deliberately lifts the Lord to the highest place. Interestingly, instead of the typical phrase, "heaven and earth," verse 13b reverses the order to say, "the earth and the heavens."[11] This could emphasize the fact that the psalmist is writing from the perspective from earth (see above). But no matter how high God is, he cares for those on earth, both humans (see Ps 146:6–9) and the rest of creation.

To give a concrete example of God's care, the psalmist concludes with a reference to his community's experience, for God has "raised up for his people a horn" (v. 14). In verse 1, the word "heights above [*rum*]" comes from the same root as the verb "raised [*rum*]," which is used in verse 14. The horn is a symbol of strength and power, and so the psalmist is saying that the people are strengthened by God. In the next line, "his people" become "his faithful servants" (*khasid*). In Psalm 145, the "faithful servants" (*khasid*) are described as those "who fall" and are "bowed down" (see vv. 10, 14). In Psalm 148, the psalmist says that God has strengthened them. We may assume that this is

---

11. This order occurs only here and in Genesis 2:4b. McCann, "Psalms," 1271.

the result of the people coming near to God to give him praise, for the psalm concludes by describing the people of Israel as those "who are near to him" (v. 14c, ESV). Psalm 145 also affirms that "the Lord is near to all who call on him" (v. 18). Thus the people praise the Lord for what he has done for them. This is the sense of the difficult phrase, "praise for all his saints" (148:14b).

# PSALM 149

In 1521, Christianity came to the Philippines with the cross in one hand and with a sword on the other. The image in Psalm 149 is similar: "the praise of God in their mouths" and "a double-edged sword in their hands" (v. 6). This controversial verse can be interpreted as a justification for world domination in the name of God (holy war). To interpret this psalm, we need to consider the text very closely as well as its canonical context, as it should be read along with Psalms 94 and 146 (see discussion below). The psalm does not support conquerors or colonizers, for the human agents are described as "poor/oppressed" (see comments regarding v. 4b below). Rather, the psalm conveys a message of empowerment for the weak – not a license for the powerful to keep dominating others.

The psalm may be divided into two sections (vv. 1–5 and vv. 6–9). The first section resembles a typical hymn, beginning with a series of calls to praise (vv. 1–3), followed by the motivation to praise (v. 4). Verse 5 resumes the call to praise, though its purpose is to encourage the worshipers, who are "bowed down" (Ps 146:8b) after their long period of exile (see discussion below). Verse 6 could be viewed as a hinge,[1] but it provides more of a foundation for the verses that follow, as verses 7–9 all begin with infinitive verbs, which presumably flow from the actions in verse 6.

## 149:1–5 "SING HIS PRAISE IN THE ASSEMBLY OF HIS FAITHFUL PEOPLE"

Like the typical hymn, Psalm 149 begins with a call to praise: "Sing to the LORD a new song" (v. 1a). This "new song" is defined in the parallel line: "his praise in the assembly of his faithful people" (v. 1b). The "new song" corresponds to "his praise" (v. 1b), which declares who God is and what God has done. God is "their Maker" and "their King" (v. 2). While this theology is not "new," the people have experienced the reality of these declarations anew,[2] for God "adorns the humble with salvation" (v. 4b, ESV) and "takes delight in his people" (v. 4a). Notice the continuing action of the verbs "adorns" and "takes

---

1. Willem S. Prinsloo, "Psalm 149: Praise Yahweh with Tambourine and Two-Edged Sword," *ZAW* 109, no. 3 (1997): 406.
2. For further discussion on the meaning of "new song," see Villanueva, *Psalms 1–72*, 186; Patterson, "Singing the New Song," 432.

delight." Because of the present situation of the people and God's continuing acts of salvation, the people sing "a new song" to the Lord (v. 1a).

The people are exhorted to sing this "new song" (v. 1a) "in the assembly of his faithful people" (v. 1b), which highlights the importance of the gathered community.[3] Although praise can be done privately, in hymns and thanksgiving psalms, it usually takes place in the midst of the community of God's people (see Ps 116:18–19 for an example of congregational thanksgiving). It's not easy – if not impossible – to celebrate alone. The "assembly of his faithful people" is further described as "Israel"/"Zion" (v. 2). The phrase, "faithful people," is repeated three times in the psalm (vv. 1, 5, 9) and comes from the Hebrew word, *hasidim*, which means "pious ones." The *hasidim* (plural in Hebrew) refers to those "who were faithful, devoted to God's service."[4] This phrase reminds us that worship is not for everyone. There are qualifications for entering God's holy place (see Psalms 15 and 24). Though everyone is commanded to worship the Lord, the people have to be faithful to God in order to worship properly. Not everyone in Israel/Zion is "faithful."

The worshipers are also described as "his people" (v. 4a) and as "humble" (v. 4b). The word "humble" (v. 4b) comes from the Hebrew word *'anawim*, which means "poor, weak and afflicted."[5] The canonical context of Psalm 149 confirms this meaning. As noted above, verse 2 declares that God is "their Maker" and "their King," and we see this same description of God in Psalm 146:5, 10 (see figure below). By describing God as "their Maker" and "their King," the composer of Psalm 149 is alluding to Psalm 146.

| Psalm 146 | Psalm 149 |
| --- | --- |
| "Maker of heaven and earth" (v. 5) | "their Maker" (v. 2a) |
| "The LORD reigns [*malakh*] forever" (v. 10) | "their King [*melekh*]" (v. 2b) |

It should be clarified, however, that *'anawim* does not refer to all who are poor, nor the poor alone. Some poor people are not faithful to the Lord. In Psalm 147:11, the psalmist declares that "the LORD delights [*rotse*] in those who fear him." The same exact word for "delight/take delight in" is used in Psalm 149:4: "the LORD takes delight [*rotse*] in his people."

---

3. The ellipsis (in v. 1b) creates a space to introduce the "assembly."
4. *BDB*, 339.
5. *BDB*, 776. Zenger and Hossfeld translate *'anawim* as "oppressed/poor." Zenger and Hossfeld, *Psalm 3*, 641. Compare Alter's translation–"lowly" and the Jerusalem Bible's "weak." Alter, *The Book of Psalms*, 512.

Zenger also sees Psalm 149 as showing a "picture similar to that in Psalm 146," but he does not include the description of God from Psalm 146:5 in his discussion.[6] Yet I think this description is relevant to Psalm 149, as saying that God is the "Maker of heaven and earth" (146:5) declares that he is the creator of everything and everyone. In Psalm 146, the emphasis on God as creator and king highlights his actions on behalf of the poor and weak, for in between the declarations about God being creator (146:5) and king (v. 10), there is a list of the weak and vulnerable (vv. 6–9), including the trio of "foreigner," "fatherless," and "widow" (v. 9). Similarly, the composer of Psalm 149 describes the recipients of God's salvation as "poor" (*'anawim*, v. 4b), which provides an important hermeneutical key to the difficult verse 6 (see discussion below).

The first part of Psalm 149 ends with another exhortation (v. 5), but it is not an explicit call to praise the Lord. Rather, the purpose of the call is to encourage the worshipers. Verse 5a literally reads, "Let the faithful people exult in glory" (translation mine). It is not clear what the phrase "in glory" means, but the preceding context (v. 4) provides a clue. Verse 4b describes God's salvific acts as God's way of adorning the "poor" (*'anawim*). Thus the phrase, "in glory," is connected to God's action on behalf of the poor. Because the poor are often oppressed, they are "bowed down" (Ps 146:8b). This was also true for those living in the exilic/postexilic community. Because of their long period of subjugation and oppression, they would have struggled to rejoice or exult "in glory" (149:5) and would have been used to feeling shame. Thus they had to be encouraged. Because God "takes delight" in his people and "adorns" them with salvation (v. 4), they can exult "in glory" (v. 5), which signifies standing up straight with heads held high. The psalmist wants the faithful people to appropriate this confident exultation in the way that they praise and live, but what about those who might still find it hard to "exult in glory"? The psalm does not push them to demonstrate their exultation outwardly, but gives them space to do it privately. This is one possible meaning of the enigmatic phrase, "on their beds" (v. 5b).[7]

---

6. Zenger and Hossfeld, *Psalms 3*, 647.
7. Prinsloo, "Psalm 149: Praise Yahweh with Tambourine and Two-Edged Sword," 402–403.

## 149:6–9 "PRAISE OF GOD IN THEIR MOUTHS AND DOUBLE-EDGED SWORD IN THEIR HANDS"

The second half of the psalm reflects a sense of the "already but not yet." The first part of the psalm calls on the people to sing praises to the Lord and to revel in God, their maker and king. Yet in verse 5, we also see that the worshipers need some encouraging. Because God's actions are described in the ongoing present tense rather than the past tense, we can perceive that the war has not yet been won (or as we say in Filipino, *hindi pa tapos ang laban*). Thus the *hassidim* ("faithful people") must have "the praise of God . . . in their mouths" and "a double-edged sword in their hands" (v. 6).

Verse 6 is one of the most controversial verses in the Psalms because of its violence and the combination of warfare and praise. The line, "praise of God in their mouths," looks back to the emphasis on singing and praising in the previous section, but the parallel line, "double-edged sword in their hands," can be problematic. Some have interpreted the word "sword" as "words" or a reference to the psalm itself,[8] which is possible, since the psalm uses poetic language. But in the context, there is a clear interplay between the "praise" that is in their "mouths" and the "sword" that is in their "hands." The praise clearly refers to words, and the "sword" conveys taking action. As noted above, the series of Hebrew infinitives in verses 7–9 refer to actions connected to verse 6, particularly the second line. Thus the purpose of the "double-edged sword in their hands" (v. 6b) is:

> "to inflict vengeance" (v. 7),
> "to bind their kings" (v. 8),
> "to carry out the sentence" (v. 9).

Moreover, the term "double-edged sword" is associated with killing someone with a sword (Deut 20:13; Judg 6:16–21). This expression occurs only three times in the OT (Ps 149:6; Judg 3:16; Prov 5:4), but the related term, "edge [mouth] of the sword," occurs about thirty-three times in Joshua and Judges alone, when the Israelites wield their swords against their enemies.[9]

Though Psalm 149 may seem to be promoting the idea of a "holy war," the psalm is describing an act of "vengeance on the nations" (v. 7). The verbal root of the word vengeance (*neqama*) expresses "the notion of revenge."[10] The

---

8. Hossfeld and Zenger, *Psalms 3*, 651–652.
9. Anthony R. Ceresko, "Psalm 149: Poetry, Themes (Exodus and Conquest), and Social Function," *Bib* 67, no. 2 (1986): 189.
10. *TDOT*, 1.

notion of vengeance recalls the declaration in Psalm 94, which describes God as "a God who avenges" (v. 1). But Psalm 94 makes it clear that this vengeance is only made on behalf of the "widow," the "foreigner," and the "fatherless" (v. 6) – the very same trio mentioned in Psalm 146:9. Thus Psalm 149 is not a biblical text that supports conquerors or colonizers, because the human agents who are possible participants in the execution of "vengeance on the nations" (v. 7) are identified as the poor (*'anawim*, v. 4). In Psalm 94, God is also referred to as the "Judge of the earth" (v. 2), and so he is expected to execute his judgment justly. The description, "written" judgment (v. 9), implies the psalmist's certainty that the execution of this judgment will be just.

Though the text seems ambiguous about the agents of these acts of vengeance, the third person pronoun, "their," in the phrase, "sword in *their* hands" (v. 6), refers to the *hassidim* ("faithful," v. 5), who are also described as the *'anawim* ("poor," v. 4). By describing the faithful poor as having a "sword in their hands," the poet adorns them with honor, as the poor are often viewed as passive agents who are weak and without resources. Today, many development projects that are "planned" supposedly to benefit the poor are implemented without even consulting them.[11] But Psalm 149 restores the dignity of the poor by giving them a part in God's salvific acts. They are not mere spectators, simply standing by while the action is taking place, for they are enjoined to be part of the action. As Psalm 149:9b says, "this is honor" (ESV) for all "his faithful people [*hassidim*]."

---

11. In the Philippines, we see this in rehabilitation projects in the aftermath of the destruction caused by Typhoon Yolanda as well as in the case of Marawi, after the war.

# PSALM 150

In Psalm 150, we come to the conclusion of the entire Psalter as well as the last of the final five Hallel psalms (Psalms 146–150). As such, it represents the climax to the preceding psalms. Psalm 150 brings the Psalter to its grand finale through a series of calls to praise. The psalm is enveloped by the famous Hallelujah – literally an exhortation: "You (plural) praise Yahweh" (vv. 1, 6b). The Hallelujah forms an inclusio, which holds the whole psalm together. This is a common feature among all final five Hallel psalms (see Psalms 146–150).

Yet Psalm 150 differs from the previous four Hallel psalms in its tenfold repetition of the call to praise (vv. 1b–6a), which may be an allusion to the Ten Commandments (Exod 20:1–17). The Psalter begins with an emphasis on the "law of the LORD" (Psalm 1), and the longest psalm (Psalm 119) is devoted to a meditation on the law of the Lord. Another possible symbolic meaning for the tenfold repetition is its expression of "completeness."[1] Similarly, Psalm 148 calls on "all" those "from the heavens" and "from the earth" to praise the Lord, repeating the word "all" ten times (see comments on Psalm 148). The Hebrew word for "all" (*kol*) in Psalm 148 is the same word for "everything" at the end of Psalm 150: "Let everything [*kol*] that has breath praise the LORD" (v. 6).

The call to praise is a key characteristic of the hymn. In comparison to other hymns, Psalm 150 is unique because it does not contain any motivations for praise. Thus some scholars doubt if Psalm 150 is a proper hymn. According to Zenger, it is "'only' a hymnic exhortation."[2] Others see the psalm as "an introduction to a hymn," but not a proper hymn.[3] Yet perhaps there are no motivations for praise because there is no longer any need for them. Psalm 150 is a literary composition, which was deliberately designed by the redactors to serve as the conclusion for the final collection.[4] The composer/s no longer need to persuade anyone about the need to praise the Lord, because all of the reasons for praise were provided in the final Hallel hymns (Psalms 146–149), along with many of the preceding psalms. Psalm 150 has nothing more to add than to exhort others to praise God's "surpassing greatness" (v. 2). Having journeyed with the psalmists through all their struggles and laments,

---

1. Dirk J. Human, "'Praise beyond Words': Psalm 150 as Grand Finale of the Crescendo in the Psalter," *Hervormde Teologiese Studies* 67, no. 1 (2011): 5.
2. Zenger and Hossfeld, *Psalms 3*, 656.
3. Human cites Seidel. Human, "'Praise beyond Words': Psalm 150 as Grand Finale of the Crescendo in the Psalter," 3.
4. Zenger and Hossfeld, *Psalms 3*, 657.

from their being bowed down to their being lifted up, one cannot help but shout, "Hallelujah!"

The Psalter as a whole provides many possible reasons for praise. Each interpreter should listen to one's own particular context in deciding which reasons should receive special emphasis.[5] From my own context, there are two particular reasons for praise that come to mind. First, the Lord should be praised because of his concern for the underprivileged:

> He hears the cries of the foreigner, the orphan, and the widow (Ps 94:3, 6).
> He cares for the weak and most vulnerable (Ps 82).
> Although he is high and lifted up, he "remembered us in our low estate" (Ps 136:22).
> He gives food to the hungry (Ps 107:9).

Second, the space given to laments in the Psalter reveals the nature of God. Though he is the creator and king, he reaches down to us from on high and allows us, as sinful people, to express to him our doubts, questions, and *tampo* (feelings of hurt, see Psalm 73). Unlike leaders who cannot be questioned, God is humble enough to be questioned. The many laments, which pour out questions of "why?" and "how long?" create a sense of awe and wonder. Who is this God, whom all the angels and gods praise, and yet who stoops down to hear the silent cry of a prisoner, to feel the aching stomach of the hungry, and to see the struggle of the stumbling blind? (Ps 107). Moreover, this humble God is also compassionate, for he "gives food to the hungry . . . sets prisoners free . . . gives sight to the blind" (146:7-8), as well as empowering, for he "lifts up those who are bowed down" (146:8).

The praise at the end of the Psalter does not erase the laments or cancel the struggles, doubts, failures, resentment, anger, and loneliness expressed in the previous psalms, for praise has no meaning and depth apart from our honesty and vulnerability. In Psalm 107, the first psalm in Book V, the psalmist opens with a call to "give thanks to the LORD" for his goodness (v. 1) and then exhorts the people to "give thanks to the LORD for his unfailing love" four times (vv. 8, 15, 21, 31). Each of these exhortations to give thanks is preceded by a narrative of suffering – hunger, imprisonment, death, chaos (vv. 4-6, 10-12, 17-18, 23-27). As the last psalm in the final Halell and the final psalm in

---

5. Compare Saphir F. Athyal, "Toward an Asian Christian Theology," in *What Asian Christians Are Thinking: A Theological Source Book*, ed. Douglas J. Elwood (Quezon City: New Day Publishers, 1976), 73.

the Psalter, Psalm 150 holds all the motivations for praise from the previous psalms in its memory.

### 150:1–2 "PRAISE GOD"

The opening line in Psalm 150, "Praise the LORD" (v. 1a), is repeated at the end of the psalm (v. 6b), and together these lines serve as bookends that hold the whole psalm together. These bookends further reinforce the tenfold repetition of the call to praise (vv. 1b–6a). *Everything* should praise the Lord.

The word used for God in the first line is "LORD," which is *Yahweh* in Hebrew. This form of the divine name is used in the inclusio (vv. 1a, 6b), but the first word in the tenfold calls to praise is "God" (*'El*) rather than "LORD" (*Yahweh*). Verse 1b literally reads, "Praise God [*'El*]." One possible reason for this change is that Psalm 150 reflects an attempt to pattern the psalm according to the alphabetic psalms. Ceresko argues that Psalm 150 is patterned after the acrostic psalms.[6] Although not as fully developed as the other acrostic psalms, Psalm 150 shows traces of the acrostic pattern, comparable to Psalm 1. The first word in Psalm 1, "blessed" (*'ashre* in Hebrew), begins with the first letter in the Hebrew alphabet (*alef*). The last word, "perish" (*to'bed*), begins with the final letter of the alphabet (*taw*). In Psalm 150, the word "God" (*'El*) in the line, "Praise God in his sanctuary" (v. 1b), also begins with the first letter in the Hebrew alphabet (*alef*). The jussive form of the verb "praise" (*tehallel*) in the tenth call to praise, "let everything that has breath *praise* the LORD," begins with the last letter of the Hebrew alphabet (*taw*).

| Psalm | Beginning | Ending |
|---|---|---|
| Psalm 1 | *'ashre* (אַשְׁרֵי) | *to'bed* (תֹּאבֵד) |
| Psalm 150 | *halelu-'el* (הַלְלוּ־אֵל) | *tehallel* (תְּהַלֵּל) |

The use of the acrostic further emphasizes the completeness reflected in the tenfold imperative. The two spheres mentioned in verse 1, "sanctuary" and "mighty heavens," represent the comprehensive nature of the call to praise. The "sanctuary" is the earthly representation of the dwelling of God in heaven. The "mighty heavens" represent the heavenly realm. In Hebrew, the word for "heaven" in verse 1 is "firmament" (*raqia'*), which represents the heavenly

---

6. Anthony R. Ceresko, "Endings and Beginnings: Alphabetic Thinking and the Shaping of Psalms 106 and 150," *CBQ* 68, no. 1 (2006): 42–44.

realm and holds the waters above the earth in Hebrew cosmology. Together, the words "sanctuary" and "firmament" represent a merism, which is a way of saying everything (compare, "Praise the Lord from the heavens" and "from the earth," Ps 148:1, 7). This opening verse anticipates the final call to praise at the end of the psalm (v. 6a).

The description "mighty" in "mighty heavens" (v. 1b) emphasizes the power of God, who "established" the heavens "forever" (148:6). God's "acts of power" and "his surpassing greatness" (150:2) are not only evident on earth, for his glory is also above the heavens. Thus it is not only the community of God's people on earth ("in his sanctuary," v. 1) who are exhorted to praise the Lord. The heavenly hosts "in his mighty heavens" are also enjoined to praise the Lord (v. 1).

## 150:3–5 PRAISE THE LORD WITH MUSIC

In ancient times, as well as in some of today's churches, worship is accompanied by instruments, sometimes even a whole orchestra. Psalm 150 has the most comprehensive list of instruments in the Psalter: "(33:2–3; 43:4; 47:5; 49:4; 57:8; 68:25; 71:22; 81:3; 92:3; 98:5–6; 108:2; 137:2; 144:9; 147:7; and 149:3."[7] The list begins with the "trumpet" (*shofar*) (v. 3a), which has both cultic and military connotations. The *shofar* was blown to signal an alarm, attack, or warning of danger, to call warriors together, to signal a theophany during temple worship, or to indicate when people should bow down, shout, or praise. The *shofar* also announced festive occasions such as the New Moon, Full Moon, and New Year festivals, or when the Ark was transported to Jerusalem (2 Sam 6:15).[8]

The harp and lyre (v. 3b) are stringed instruments used to accompany singing, which are comparable to our guitar today (Pss 33:2; 57:8). The mood of Psalm 150 is festive, as indicated by "dancing" and the "tambourine" (v. 4a). Psalm 149 also exhorts the people to "praise his name with dancing," and with the "tambourine and lyre" (v. 3, ESV). In Miriam's song of celebration, "Miriam . . . took a tambourine in her hand, and all the women went out after her with tambourines and dancing" (Exod 15:20, ESV). Then she breaks into song, which "resounds with hymnic praise to Yahweh, the liberating

---

7. Human, "'Praise beyond Words': Psalm 150 as Grand Finale of the Crescendo in the Psalter," 5.
8. Human, "'Praise beyond Words': Psalm 150 as Grand Finale of the Crescendo in the Psalter," 5, n. 29.

God."⁹ The celebration of God's praise in Psalm 149 also arises out of the vision of the people being liberated from their oppressors (vv. 7–8). There is great celebration because the "God [*'el*] of vengeance" (94:1, ESV) has crowned "the humble with victory" (149:4). This supports the motivation for praise discussed in the introduction.

We do not know the exact nature of the "strings and the pipe" that are mentioned in Psalm 150:4b. The "pipe" is usually understood as a "flute" or "lute," but it is also linked with the *kinnor* (lyre) (see Job 30:31).¹⁰ Verse 5 mentions "cymbals" twice, though we are not sure if it is referring to two different kinds of cymbals. The literal translation of the Hebrew for these instruments is "cymbals of hearing/sound" (v. 5a) and "cymbals of loud blast/clashing" (v. 5b). There is a progression from the "sounding cymbals" to the "crashing cymbals"¹¹ as the psalm reaches its crescendo, with the cymbals being the loudest. All the instruments join together to make the sound of praise be heard.

## 150:6 "LET EVERYTHING THAT HAS BREATH PRAISE THE LORD"

Psalm 145 ends with the call, "Let every creature [literally, "flesh"] praise his holy name" (v. 21). Psalm 150 broadens this call to include "everything that has breath" (v. 6). The Hebrew word for "breath" (*nishamah*) is used in Genesis 2:7 to refer to the "breath of life," which God breathed into the man so that he could become a living creature. Birds and animals are also said to have "breath" (*nishamah*, Gen 7:22). Some argue that Psalm 150 only refers to humans, while others include animals, but not inanimate objects, such as rocks or places. Still others believe that Psalm 150 includes all of these things.¹² Psalm 148 calls on the "highest heavens" (v. 4) as well as "all ocean depths" (v. 7), which supports the idea that the call to praise in Psalm 150 includes "everything."

Praise the LORD!

---

9. Bernhard W. Anderson, "The Song of Miriam: Poetically and Theologically Considered," in *Directions in Biblical Hebrew Poetry*, ed. Elaine R. Follis (Sheffield, England: JSOT Press, 1987), 291.
10. Human, "'Praise beyond Words': Psalm 150 as Grand Finale of the Crescendo in the Psalter," 7.
11. This is the translation of Alter, *The Book of Psalms*, 516.
12. Atkins, "Praise by Animals in the Hebrew Bible," 511.

# SELECTED BIBLIOGRAPHY

Note: This Bibliography represents only a partial list of the references used. The majority of the references, mostly journal articles, are not included here but are found in the footnotes.

Adu-Gyamfi, Yaw. "Psalm 82 and Injustice: Implications for African Church Leaders." *Ogbomoso Journal of Theology* 19, no. 1 (2014): 15–40.
Ahn, John J. "Psalm 137: Complex Communal Laments." *JBL* 127, no. 2 (2008): 267–289.
Allen, Leslie C. *Psalms 101–150*. Nashville: Thomas Nelson, 2002.
Alter, Robert. *The Book of Psalms: A Translation with Commentary*. New York: W.W. Norton, 2007.
Amzallag, Gérard Nissim. "The Meaning of Todah in the Title of Psalm 100." *ZAW* 126, no. 4 (2014): 535–545.
Anderson, Arnold Albert. *The Book of Psalms*. Vol. 2. Grand Rapids: Eerdmans, 1992.
Assis, Elie. "The Structure, Genre, and Meaning of Psalm 129." *SJOT* 31, no. 1 (2017): 142–154.
Atkins, Peter Joshua. "Praise by Animals in the Hebrew Bible." *JSOT* 44, no. 3 (2020): 500–513.
Barré, Michael L. "Psalm 116: Its Structure and Its Enigmas." *JBL* 109, no. 1 (1990): 61–78.
Basson, Alec. "Image Schemata of Containment and Path as Underlying Structures for Core Metaphors in Psalm 142." *OTE* 21, no. 2 (2008): 261–272.
———. "Two Instances of Mundus Inversus in Psalm 113." *Verbum et Ecclesia* 30, no. 1 (2009): 1–14.
Becking, Bob. "God-Talk for a Disillusioned Pilgrim in Psalm 121." *The Journal of Hebrew Scriptures* 9 (2009): 2–10.
Berlin, Adele. "On the Interpretation of Psalm 133." In *Directions in Biblical Hebrew Poetry*, 141–147. Sheffield: Sheffield Academic Press, 1987.
———. "Psalms and the Literature of Exile: Psalms 137, 44, 69 and 78." In *The Book of Psalms: Composition and Reception*, edited by Peter W. Flint, Patrick D. Miller, Aaron Brunell, and Ryan Roberts, 65–86. Leiden; Boston: Brill, 2005.
Bonhoeffer, Dietrich. *Meditating on the Word*. Translated by David McI. Gracie. Cambridge, MA: Cowley, 1986.
Booij, Thijs. "Psalm 110: 'Rule in the Midst of Your Foes!'" *VT* 41, no. 4 (1991): 396–407.
———. "Psalm 141: A Prayer for Discipline and Protection." *Bib* 86, no. 1 (2005): 97–106.

———. "Some Observations on Psalm 87." *VT* 37, no. 1 (1987): 16–25.
Bosman, H. L. "Psalm 114 as Reinterpretation of the Exodus During and After the Exile." *OTE* 26, no. 3 (2013): 559–582.
Botha, Phil J. "Psalm 101: A Supplication for the Restoration of Society in the Late Post-Exilic Age." *Hervormde Teologiese Studies* 72, no. 4 (2016): 1–8.
———. "Social Values and the Interpretation of Psalm 123." *OTE* 14, no. 2 (2001): 189–198.
Bratcher, Robert Galveston, and William D. Reyburn. *A Translator's Handbook on the Book of Psalms*. Helps for Translators. New York: United Bible Society, 1991.
Buber, Martin. "The Heart Determines: Psalm 73." In *Theodicy in the World of the Bible*, ed. James L. Crenshaw. Philadelphia: Fortress Press, 1983.
Calvin, John. *Calvin's Commentaries (Complete)*. Translated by John King. Accordance electronic ed. Edinburgh: Calvin Translation Society, 1847.
Ceresko, Anthony R. "Endings and Beginnings: Alphabetic Thinking and the Shaping of Psalms 106 and 150." *CBQ* 68, no. 1 (2006): 32–46.
Coetzee, Johan H. "Psalm 85: Yearning for the Restoration of the Whole Body." *OTE* 22, no. 3 (2009): 554–563.
Cox, Samuel. *The Pilgrim Psalms: An Exposition of the Songs of Degrees*. London: R. D. Dickinson, 1885.
Craigie, Peter C. *Psalms. 1–50*. Waco, Texas: Word Books, 1983.
Daffern, Megan I. J. "The Semantic Field of 'Remembering' in the Psalms." *JSOT* 41, no. 1 (2016): 79–97.
Dahood, Mitchell J. *Psalms III: 101–150*. Anchor Bible. Garden City: Doubleday, 1970.
Day, John. *God's Conflict with the Dragon and the Sea*. Cambridge University Press, 1985.
DeClaissé-Walford, Nancy L. "Psalm 44: O God, Why Do You Hide Your Face?" In *My Words Are Lovely: Studies in the Rhetoric of the Psalms*, edited by Robert L. Foster and David M. Howard, 121–131. New York: T & T Clark, 2008.
———. "Psalm 145: All Flesh Will Bless God's Holy Name." *CBQ* 74, no. 1 (2012): 55–66.
Eder, Sigrid. "Do Justice and Peace Really Kiss Each Other? Personifications in the Psalter and an Exemplary Analysis of Ps 85:11." *VT* 67, no. 3 (2017): 387–402.
Eichler, Raanan. "The Meaning of יֹשֵׁב הַכְּרֻבִים." *ZAW* 126, no. 3 (2014): 358–371.
Emerton, John A. "How Does the Lord Regard the Death of His Saints in Psalm 116:15." *JTS* 34, no. 1 (1983): 146–156.
———. "Neglected Solution of a Problem in Psalm 76:11." *VT* 24, no. 2 (1974): 136–146.

# Selected Bibliography

Estes, Daniel J. "Like Arrows in the Hand of a Warrior (Psalm 127)." *VT* 41, no. 3 (1991): 304–311.

Firth, David G. "Psalm 139: A Study in Ambiguity." *OTE* 32, no. 2 (2019): 491–510.

Firth, Gillian C. "The Re-Presentation of David in Psalms 140–143." Ph.D. thesis, Ridley College, 2016.

Gerstenberger, Erhard S. *Psalms Part 2 and Lamentations*. Grand Rapids, MI: Eerdmans, 2001.

Gillmayr-Bucher, Susanne. "'The Rivers Have Lifted up Their Voice': Imagining the Mighty Waters in Psalm 93." *OTE* 32, no. 2 (2019): 378–397.

Greene, Nathaniel E. "Creation, Destruction, and a Psalmist's Plea: Rethinking the Poetic Structure of Psalm 74." *JBL* 136, no. 1 (2017): 85–101.

Grohmann, Marriane. "The imagery of the 'weaned child' in Psalm 131." In *The Composition of the Book of Psalms*, edited by Erich Zenger, 513–522. Leuven: Uitgeverij Peeters, 2010.

Gunkel, Hermann. *Die Psalmen*. Göttingen: Vandenhoeck & Ruprecht, 1926.

———. *The Psalms: A Form-Critical Introduction*. Philadelphia: Fortress Press, 1967.

Gunkel, Hermann, and Joachim Begrich. *Introduction to Psalms: The Genres of the Religious Lyric of Israel*. Mercer Library of Biblical Studies. Macon, GA: Mercer University Press, 1998.

Habel, Norman C. "He Who Stretches out the Heavens." *CBQ* 34, no. 4 (1972): 417–430.

Hammer, Reuven. "Two Liturgical Psalms: Salvation and Thanksgiving." *Judaism* 40, no. 4 (1991): 484–497.

Hays, Rebecca Whitten Poe. "Trauma, Remembrance, and Healing: The Meeting of Wisdom and History in Psalm 78." *JSOT* 41, no. 2 (2016): 183–204.

Hossfeld, Frank-Lothar, and Erich Zenger. *Psalms 2: A Commentary on Psalms 51–100*. Edited by Klaus Baltzer. Translated by Linda M. Maloney. Minneapolis, MN: Fortress Press, 2005.

Human, Dirk J. "'From Exile to Zion': Ethical Perspectives from the Twin Psalms 127 and 128." *OTE* 22, no. 1 (2009): 63–87.

———. "'Praise beyond Words': Psalm 150 as Grand Finale of the Crescendo in the Psalter." *Hervormde Teologiese Studies* 67, no. 1 (2011).

———. "Psalm 132 and Its Compositional Context(S)." *Scriptura* 116, no. 2 (2017): 75–92.

———. "Psalm 136: A Liturgy with Reference to Creation and History." In *Psalms and Liturgy*. Edited by Dirk J. Human and C. J. A. Vos, 73–88. London: Clark, 2004.

Jenkins, Philip. "The Travels of Psalm 91." *The Christian Century* 135, no. 2 (2018): 36–37.

Jenkins, Steffen. "A Quotation in Psalm 109 as Defence Exhibit A." *Tyndale Bulletin* 71, no. 1 (2020): 115–135.

Jenni, Ernst, and Claus Westermann, eds. *Theological Lexicon of the Old Testament*. Translated by Mark E. Biddle. Peabody, MA: Hendrickson Publishers, 1997.

Johnston, Philip, and David G. Firth, eds. *Interpreting the Psalms: Issues and Approaches*. Downers Grove; Leicester, England: InterVarsity Press; Apollos, 2005.

Keil, Carl Friedrich, and Franz Delitzsch. *Keil and Delitzch Commentary on the Old Testament*. Translated by Francis Bolton. Vol. 5. Grand Rapids, MI: Eerdmans, 1989.

Kirkpatrick, A. F. *The Book of Psalms*. Cambridge, England: University Press, 1895.

Knierim, Rolf. "Cosmos and History in Israel's Theology." *HBT* 3 (1981): 59–123.

Knowles, Melody D. "A Woman at Prayer: A Critical Note on Psalm 131:2b." *JBL* 125, no. 2 (2006): 385–389.

Kohlenberger III, John R., ed. *The Comparative Psalter: Hebrew-Greek-English*. Oxford: Oxford University Press, 2007.

Kraus, Hans-Joachim. *Psalms 60–150: A Commentary*. Minneapolis: Fortress Press, 1993.

Kselman, John S. "Sinai and Zion in Psalm 93." In *David and Zion: Biblical Studies in Honor of J. J. M. Roberts*, 69–76. Winona Lake, IN: Eisenbrauns, 2004.

Lemos, T. M. "Shame and Mutilation of Enemies in the Hebrew Bible." *JBL* 125, no. 2 (2006): 225–241.

Levenson, Jon Douglas. *Creation and the Persistence of Evil: The Jewish Drama of Divine Omnipotence*. Princeton, NJ: Princeton University Press, 1994.

Lewis, C. S. *Reflection on the Psalms*. London: Fount, 1958.

Longman, Tremper III. "Psalm 98: A Divine Warrior Victory Song." *JETS* 27, no. 3 (1984): 267–274.

Marrs, Rick R. "A Cry from the Depths (Ps 130)." *ZAW* 100, no. 1 (1988): 81–90.

Mays, James Luther. *Psalms*. Louisville: John Knox Press, 1994.

McCann, J. Clinton. "Psalms." In *NIB*, Vol. 4. Nashville: Abingdon Press, 1996.

McCann, J. Clinton Jr. "The Psalms as Instruction." *Int* 46, no. 2 (1992): 117–128.

McClellan, Daniel O. "The Gods-Complaint: Psalm 82 as a Psalm of Complaint." *JBL* 137, no. 4 (2018): 833–851.

Miller, Patrick D. "Cosmology and World Order in the Old Testament: The Divine Council as Cosmic-Political Symbol." *HBT* 9, no. 2 (December 1987): 53–78.

———. "Psalm 130." *Int* 33, no. 2 (1979): 176–181.

Mowinckel, Sigmund. *The Psalms in Israel's Worship*. Translated by Dafydd Rhys Ap-Thomas. 2 vols. Grand Rapids, MI; Dearborn, MI: Eerdmans; Dove Publishers, 2004.

Obiorah, Mary Jerome. *"How Lovely Is Your Dwelling Place": The Desire for God's House in Psalm 84*. St. Ottilien: Eos, 2004.

# Selected Bibliography

Ortlund, Eric. "An Intertextual Reading of the Theophany of Psalm 97." *SJOT* 20, no. 2 (2006): 273–285.

Patterson, Richard Duane. "Singing the New Song: An Examination of Psalms 33, 96, 98, and 149." *Bibliotheca Sacra* 164, no. 656 (2007): 416–434.

Pleins, J. David. *The Psalms: Songs of Tragedy, Hope, and Justice*. Maryknoll, NY: Orbis Books, 1993.

Prinsloo, G. T. M. "Historical Reality and Mythological Metaphor in Psalm 124." *OTE* 18, no. 3 (2005): 790–810.

———. "Reading Psalm 112 as a 'Midrash' on Psalm 111." *OTE* 32, no. 2 (2019): 336–668.

———. "The Role of Space in the ŠYRY HMʻLWT (Psalms 120–134)." *Bib* 86, no. 4 (2005): 457–477.

Prinsloo, Willem S. "Psalm 116: Disconnected Text or Symmetrical Whole?" *Bib* 74, no. 1 (1993): 71–82.

———. "Psalm 149: Praise Yahweh with Tambourine and Two-Edged Sword." *ZAW* 109, no. 3 (1997): 395–407.

Purcell, Richard Anthony. "The King as Priest? Royal Imagery in Psalm 110 and Ancient Near Eastern Iconography." *JBL* 139, no. 2 (2020): 275–300.

Rad, Gerhard von. *Old Testament Theology*. Vol. 1. New York: Harper, 1962.

Roberts, J. J. M. "The Enthronement of Yhwh and David: The Abiding Theological Significance of the Kingship Language of the Psalms." *CBQ* 64, no. 4 (October 2002): 675–686.

Ross, Allen P. *A Commentary on the Psalms Volume 3 (90–150)*. Grand Rapids, MI: Kregel, 2016.

Savran, George W. "The Contrasting Voices of Psalm 95." *RB* 110, no. 1 (2003): 17–32.

Schonfield, Jeremy. "Psalms 113–118: Qualified Praise." *European Judaism* 50, no. 2 (2017): 147–157.

Schreiner, David B. "Double Entendre, Disguised Verbal Resistance, and the Composition of Psalm 132." *BBR* 28, no. 1 (2018): 20–33.

Schwartz, Sarah. "Bridge over Troubled Waters: Psalm 147." *JSOT* 42, no. 3 (2018): 317–339.

Smith, Stephen J. "The Shape and Message of Psalms 73–78." *CBQ* 83, no. 1 (2021): 18–37.

Smyth, Damian Barry. "Psalm 95: The 'today' Clause." *The Downside Review* 128, no. 453 (2010): 284–294.

Soll, William Michael. *Psalm 119: Matrix, Form, and Setting*. Washington, DC: Catholic Biblical Association of America, 1991.

Strawn, Brent A. "A Woman at Prayer (Psalm 131,2b) and Arguments 'from Parallelism.'" *ZAW* 124, no. 3 (2012): 421–426.

Tate, Marvin E. *Psalms 51–100*. Dallas: Word Books, 1990.

Tournay, Raymond J. *Seeing and Hearing God with the Psalms: The Prophetic Liturgy of the Second Temple in Jerusalem*. Translated by J. Edward Crowley. Sheffield: Sheffield Academic Press, 1991.

Van Leeuwen, Raymond C. "Why Do the Trees of the Forest Sing a New Song? (Psalms 96 and 98)." *The Covenant Quarterly* 62, no. 3 (2004): 22–34.

Villanueva, Federico G. "From Thanksgiving to Lament: The Shape of Psalm 120." *VT* 70, no. 3 (2020): 479–497.

———. *Lamentations: A Pastoral and Contextual Commentary*. Carlisle, UK: Langham Global Library, 2016.

———. *Lord, I'm Depressed: The Lament Psalms and Depression*. Manila, Philippines: OMF Literature, 2020.

———. *Psalms 1–72. A Pastoral and Contextual Commentary*. Carlisle, UK: Langham Global Library, 2016.

———. *The "Uncertainty of a Hearing": A Study of the Sudden Change of Mood in the Psalms of Lament*. VTSup. Leiden: Brill, 2008.

Waldman, Nahum M. "The Breaking of the Bow." *The Jewish Quarterly Review* 69, no. 2 (October 1978): 82–88.

Walton, John, Mark W. Chavalas, and Victor Harold Matthews. *IVP Bible Background Commentary: Old Testament*. Leicester: Inter-Varsity, 2000.

Weiser, Artur. *The Psalms. A Commentary*. Translated by Herbert Hartwell. SCM Press: London, 1962.

Westermann, Claus. *Praise and Lament in the Psalms*. Translated by Keith R. Crim and Richard N. Soulen. Atlanta, GA: John Knox Press, 1981.

Wieringen, Archibald van. "Two Reading Options in Psalm 114: A Communication-Oriented Exegesis." *RB* 122, no. 1 (2015): 46–57.

Zenger, Erich, and Frank-Lothar Hossfeld. *Psalms 3: A Commentary on Psalms 101–150*. Edited by Klaus Baltzer. Translated by Linda M. Maloney. Minneapolis: Fortress Press, 2011.

## Asia Theological Association
54 Scout Madriñan St. Quezon City 1103, Philippines
Email: ataasia@gmail.com  Telefax: (632) 410 0312

## OUR MISSION

The Asia Theological Association (ATA) is a body of theological institutions, committed to evangelical faith and scholarship, networking together to serve the Church in equipping the people of God for the mission of the Lord Jesus Christ.

## OUR COMMITMENT

The ATA is committed to serving its members in the development of evangelical, biblical theology by strengthening interaction, enhancing scholarship, promoting academic excellence, fostering spiritual and ministerial formation and mobilizing resources to fulfill God's global mission within diverse Asian cultures.

## OUR TASK

Affirming our mission and commitment, ATA seeks to:

- **Strengthen** interaction through inter-institutional fellowship and programs, regional and continental activities, faculty and student exchange programs.
- **Enhance** scholarship through consultations, workshops, seminars, publications, and research fellowships.
- **Promote** academic excellence through accreditation standards, faculty and curriculum development.
- **Foster** spiritual and ministerial formation by providing mentor models, encouraging the development of ministerial skills and a Christian ethos.
- **Mobilize** resources through library development, information technology and infra-structural development.

To learn more about ATA, visit www.ataasia.com or facebook.com/AsiaTheologicalAssociation

Langham Literature, along with its publishing work, is a ministry of Langham Partnership.

Langham Partnership is a global fellowship working in pursuit of the vision God entrusted to its founder John Stott –

> *to facilitate the growth of the church in maturity and Christ-likeness through raising the standards of biblical preaching and teaching.*

**Our vision** is to see churches in the Majority World equipped for mission and growing to maturity in Christ through the ministry of pastors and leaders who believe, teach and live by the word of God.

**Our mission** is to strengthen the ministry of the word of God through:
- nurturing national movements for biblical preaching
- fostering the creation and distribution of evangelical literature
- enhancing evangelical theological education

especially in countries where churches are under-resourced.

**Our ministry**

*Langham Preaching* partners with national leaders to nurture indigenous biblical preaching movements for pastors and lay preachers all around the world. With the support of a team of trainers from many countries, a multi-level programme of seminars provides practical training, and is followed by a programme for training local facilitators. Local preachers' groups and national and regional networks ensure continuity and ongoing development, seeking to build vigorous movements committed to Bible exposition.

*Langham Literature* provides Majority World preachers, scholars and seminary libraries with evangelical books and electronic resources through publishing and distribution, grants and discounts. The programme also fosters the creation of indigenous evangelical books in many languages, through writer's grants, strengthening local evangelical publishing houses, and investment in major regional literature projects, such as one volume Bible commentaries like the *Africa Bible Commentary* and the *South Asia Bible Commentary*.

*Langham Scholars* provides financial support for evangelical doctoral students from the Majority World so that, when they return home, they may train pastors and other Christian leaders with sound, biblical and theological teaching. This programme equips those who equip others. Langham Scholars also works in partnership with Majority World seminaries in strengthening evangelical theological education. A growing number of Langham Scholars study in high quality doctoral programmes in the Majority World itself. As well as teaching the next generation of pastors, graduated Langham Scholars exercise significant influence through their writing and leadership.

To learn more about Langham Partnership and the work we do visit **langham.org**

www.ingramcontent.com/pod-product-compliance
Lightning Source LLC
Chambersburg PA
CBHW050133240426
43673CB00043B/1654